INTRODUCTION TO
COMPUTER PROGRAMMING
WITH
Visual Basic® 6

A Problem-Solving Approach

Alka R. Harriger
Susan K. Lisack
John K. Gotwals
Kyle D. Lutes

D0202315

201 West 103rd Street • Indianapolis, IN 46290

INTRODUCTION TO COMPUTER PROGRAMMING WITH VISUAL BASIC 6: A PROBLEM-SOLVING APPROACH

Library of Congress Catalog Number: 98-88876

ISBN: 1-58076-241-7

02 01 00   4 3

Interpretation of the printing code: the rightmost double-digit number is the year of the book's printing; the rightmost single-digit number, the number of the book's printing. For example, a printing code of 99-1 shows that the first printing of the book occurred in 1999.

Composed in *AGaramond* and *MCPdigital* by Que Education and Training

Trademark Acknowledgments

PUBLISHER:
Robert Linsky

EXECUTIVE EDITOR:
Randy Haubner

DIRECTOR OF PRODUCT MARKETING:
Susan L. Kindel

OPERATIONS MANAGER:
Christine Moos

SENIOR DEVELOPMENT EDITOR:
Lena Buonanno

SENIOR PROJECT EDITOR:
Karen A. Walsh

PROJECT EDITOR:
Tim Tate

COPY EDITOR:
Keith Cline

SOFTWARE COORDINATOR:
Angie Denny

COVER DESIGNER:
Ruth Lewis

BOOK DESIGNER:
Louisa Klucznik

INDEXER:
Kevin Fulcher

PROOFREADER:
Mary Ellen Stephenson

PRODUCTION TEAM:
Steve Balle-Gifford
Darin Crone
Laura Robbins

CONTENTS AT A GLANCE

TABLE OF CONTENTS

Preface

To the Student

Welcome to the exciting and challenging world of programming! With new software development environments such as Visual Basic, you can create attractive, sophisticated Windows programs in a short time. Remember, however, that the look of the program is only a small part of the total package. For the program to be useful, it must *do* something. That is the point of programming—developing the logic for the program to make it do something useful. Because Visual Basic is event driven, it is also important to think about *when* something should happen, such as when the user clicks a button or types a value. This book teaches you basic programming concepts that include problem analysis, interface development, logic organization and design, and program development and testing. Learning the entire thought process behind writing programs will equip you with a solid foundation in programming. This foundation will prepare you to learn other computer languages or more advanced features of Visual Basic on your own.

To the Teacher

Computers continue to make amazing progress in speed and capabilities. Ideally, we as teachers want our students to use state-of-the-art software as they learn fundamental programming concepts. Visual Basic is a popular application development tool with useful features for designing professional-looking screens and coding and testing programs. With this tool, the programmer has easy access to all the buttons, boxes, pictures, and menus that you commonly see in shrink-wrapped software today. Although it is fun to try using each of these objects in a program, the students can learn much of this on their own after understanding basic concepts about adding an object to a form, setting its properties, and using its methods and events in code. The continuing challenge is to *develop logical thinking skills* to be able to translate a problem description into appropriate logic structures and coding statements. The event-driven nature of Visual Basic further requires that students learn how to organize their code into appropriate events related to GUI objects.

Introduction to Computer Programming with Visual Basic 6: A Problem-Solving Approach will furnish students with a problem-solving framework for developing event-driven programs. Through repeated illustrations of this framework in end-of-chapter case studies, students can see how to identify the major input, processing, and output needs of a program. From this list, they learn how to sketch an interface that serves all the needs identified during problem analysis. Next, they develop and document the macro-level logic by using an Object-Event Diagram (OED). The OED is a transitional tool that shows students how to use the interface they just designed to begin organizing their program into events that relate to specific objects. After the events have been identified, traditional program development tools are used to depict design logic, develop adequate test plans, translate logic designs into Visual Basic code, test and debug as necessary, and finalize the documentation of the package.

To further emphasize our focus on problem solving, chapter discussions and case studies use just three Visual Basic controls: text boxes, labels, and command buttons. For instructors who want to present additional controls, we include a comprehensive list of User Interface Objects in Appendix A. Having this information in a separate section gives the instructor total control of the amount and sequence of GUI coverage for a particular course. Related objects are grouped together in this section, and short examples are provided to illustrate their application. End-of-chapter problems also provide opportunities for instructors to cover additional controls, as needed or desired.

Approach

When event-driven tools such as Visual Basic were first introduced in the classroom, classroom coverage of the new GUI features made application development fun and exciting. Unfortunately, too much focus on GUI topics took important time away from teaching fundamental programming concepts. Students could develop intricate interfaces, but had difficulty organizing and developing the code underneath the GUI to make it *do* something. Our teaching philosophy for an introductory programming course is to equip students with the essential skills needed to develop computer applications using any language. This philosophy requires that students gain a framework for creating programs, not just memorize the syntax rules of a particular language.

Introduction to Computer Programming with Visual Basic 6: A Problem-Solving Approach was written in response to the need for a textbook that focuses on teaching programming. To accomplish this objective, we identified three goals for this book. First, we want to teach a disciplined process for developing a computer program that includes logic design before the coding step and sufficient testing after. Second, we want to teach universal programming concepts so that our students have the tools to transition to other programming languages. Third, we want the students to follow standards as they write their code, including naming and indentation conventions.

The disciplined process we recommend is introduced early in Chapter 1 and reinforced with a complete case study at the end of each chapter. To help students understand the relationship of GUI objects and their events, we developed a tool called the Object-Event Diagram (OED). As students transition from interface design to logic development, the OED helps them organize major processing steps using the event-driven paradigm. Because each event procedure is like a mini-program, there is still a need for logic design in the individual event procedures. Hence, both flowcharts and pseudocode are used in most of the chapters to illustrate major logic structures. Teachers can choose the one they like better. Pseudocode is easier to type and takes less space, but for the majority of students who tend to learn visually, seeing a graphical design tool increases their understanding.

To achieve the goal of teaching universal programming concepts, this book concentrates on the various logic structures and types of programming statements used in most programming languages, instead of teaching all the "bells and whistles" of

Visual Basic. In chapter discussions and the majority of case studies, we have purposely elected to design GUIs that generally use only three controls: labels, text boxes, and command buttons. This does not mean, however, that the students must be limited to these controls. The fundamental concepts of properties, methods, and events apply to all GUI objects, so students should be able to transfer their understanding of these concepts when using "new" controls. In fact, the students should be encouraged to demonstrate their understanding of the general nature of screen objects by incorporating a new control in several programming exercises. Several exercises suggest modifying the chapter examples to incorporate new controls, or writing a new program to try a different control. Using Appendix A, "Visual Basic User Interface Objects," as a handy reference, the instructor has the added flexibility to use different controls in different semesters, or to introduce them in a different order.

Our final goal was the most challenging to achieve because each of us practiced slightly different standards. Our situation is not unlike what students will experience when they begin each new job. Students need to recognize that different languages and/or different companies are likely to have their own standards conventions. Therefore, to function effectively within the organization or with the new tool, they must learn the convention and then use it consistently to allow others to quickly read and understand the code. In selecting our standards for the text, we spent considerable time debating the advantages and disadvantages of each. In each case, our final decision was based on the pedagogical value of the specific standard in teaching a programming course.

We follow the widely accepted prefix notation standards for naming GUI objects, for example, but opted for a somewhat unique scope prefix. When using Visual Basic, students may notice that the word *module* has multiple definitions, depending on context. Traditional programming had yet another meaning for *module* to refer to blocks of code such as procedures and functions. Rather than add to the students' confusion by using the "m" prefix for "module" scope, we use the "f" prefix for "form" or "file" scope. This standard helps students remember that the placement of the declaration helps determine the variable's scope. Additionally, because one of our conventions is to explicitly declare the types of all variables, we elected not to include type prefixes on variable names. Because it is just as easy to press Shift+F2 on a variable to quickly look up its type, we thought that there was no added benefit to requiring type prefixes.

Assumptions About the Student

Introduction to Computer Programming with Visual Basic 6: A Problem-Solving Approach is aimed primarily at the undergraduate introductory programming course. Because this course is typically offered in the freshman or sophomore year, this book could be used by a variety of two- or four-year institutions. Students from a wide variety of disciplines, both computing-related and not, could benefit from a programming course like this to gain essential programming skills and improve their logical thinking.

Visual Basic is a Windows application with the typical File, Edit, and Help menus. Programmers must use the computer as a tool to type and edit their programs, which are then saved in files. Hence, this book assumes that readers have some basic computer literacy as well as mouse and keyboarding skills. It is helpful to have experience using at least one common Windows application such as a word processor or a spreadsheet, where you have used typical editing (cut, copy, and paste) and file manipulation (opening, saving) features. Additionally, because each Visual Basic program consists of multiple files, it is important to know how to create folders and how to copy, move, rename, or delete files.

Only basic math and algebra skills are assumed for this book, such as calculating a percentage, taking a percentage of another number (for example, sales tax), or converting units (for example, centimeters to inches). When more difficult math is required, the equation is provided. This means that students should be able to read an algebraic equation and recognize the mathematical operations required (multiplication, division, exponentiation, and so on) and their correct order of operations.

Key Features

The content and features of this book were designed to support our goal of teaching students how to program using any language. They are also a result of extensive class testing by all the authors.

Back to the Basics: Programming Fundamentals

This book concentrates on presenting a disciplined program development process, using fundamental logic control structures and teaching the concepts and statements of a programming language. Chapter 1, "Introductory Programming Concepts and the Visual Basic Environment," lays the foundation for the beginning programmer by introducing the six steps of program development. The remaining chapters follow through with illustrative case studies. Using a limited number of Visual Basic controls throughout the text gives the instructor more time to teach programming fundamentals and makes it possible for the student to concentrate on learning these fundamentals.

Case Studies

End-of-chapter case studies are used to illustrate and continually reinforce the six steps of the program development process. In each case study, a programming problem is presented and solved by following the steps from problem analysis through interface and logic design, coding, and testing. Complete documentation of the process is included in the case study section of each chapter. These examples also provide the instructor with complete problems that can be used for illustration purposes in lecture, developed together during lab, or studied by the students at home. Often at the end of the chapter, programming exercises ask the students to make modifications to the case study problem.

Appendix of Visual Basic User Interface Objects

Students learn the basic concepts of setting properties for GUI objects and putting code in an event procedure early in the book. Appendix A, "Visual Basic User Interface Objects," serves as a handy reference that groups related objects together and describes their primary uses, key properties, events, and methods. Many illustrative code examples are included. Students should be able to incorporate other GUI features on their forms. By moving the majority of the GUI discussion to the appendix, the main text can focus on algorithms and logic structures. An added benefit of this separate appendix is the increased flexibility for the instructor to cover specific GUI elements as appropriate and to cover different controls from semester to semester.

Appendix on Program Design and Translation to VB Code

Although the entire text uses a problem-solving approach, some instructors may find it useful to have a more thorough coverage of logic design in a separate section. Appendix B, "Program Design and Translation to VB Code," serves as a more complete reference for logic design concepts that employ flowcharts for visual illustrations. Furthermore, it includes a set of translation rules to convert design logic into corresponding Visual Basic code. For students who have already taken a problem-solving course, this appendix serves as a reference for the design standards used in this text. In other situations where an instructor wants to teach the logic design structures before doing any coding, or after learning a few basic coding statements, this appendix can be used as a teaching aid at the appropriate time of the semester, just like any other chapter. Finally, for students who follow the suggested process of design prior to coding, the list of translation rules can serve as a reference guide when they convert their program logic into Visual Basic code.

Object-Event Diagrams (OEDs)

Because Visual Basic is event-driven, *where* the code is written is as important as the code itself. Because this is not always obvious, particularly for people who do have experience with a traditional, structured programming language, the OED tool will help students think about the importance of the events, as well as document how their programs' procedures are organized. When following the recommended six-step program development process, this tool provides students with a natural transition from user-interface development to macro-level logic design. The first level identifies the project, and the second level identifies GUI objects, all of which can be gleaned from the just-developed interface. The third level identifies the events that will respond to certain actions related to specific GUI objects. By considering the interface from the user's perspective, the student must think about what user actions will result in some immediate processing by the program. Each object may have zero, one, or many events that could result in some action by the program. For any event that seems to be fairly complex, traditional functional decomposition can be employed to subdivide an event into sub procedures and functions. The OED serves as a visual table of contents to the overall organization of code blocks and their relationship to GUI objects. Instructors can take advantage of this tool to document specific modularity requirements by providing students with the OED(s) for an assigned program. Using OEDs, students will realize which events must be coded and how to decompose them further, if necessary.

Reusable Code Module

Designing reusable code is a goal of many professional programmers, yet it takes good planning to be able to show students how to accomplish this in an introductory programming course. In this textbook, several procedures designed and coded in earlier chapters are used again in later chapters. The student is instructed to place these routines in a separate code module to make later reuse easier. Using these examples for ideas, instructors can add to this module or encourage students to add to this module when they write other general-purpose routines that may be useful in other programs.

Common Case Study for File, Database, and Object-Oriented Programming Chapters

Most of the illustrative examples and all the program case studies in Chapters 9–12 use the same or similar problems to illustrate the chapter's new concepts. This feature helps students recognize the value of each approach as well as the differences in implementation.

One Chapter on Files and Two Chapters on Database Programming

Visual Basic is a very popular tool used to develop business applications, and most business applications store data in some form of a relational database. Nonetheless, fundamental knowledge of sequential files is very important because it is still commonly used in industry to share data between applications and operating systems. Chapter 9, "Sequential Files," teaches the still common sequential file concepts.

Because the predominant types of business applications use databases rather than files, this textbook includes two chapters on database programming. Many textbooks teach students database programming using only the data control and bound controls. Although these techniques allow applications to be developed without much coding, their use is limited to simple examples. Chapter 10, "Introductory Database Programming," teaches fundamental database concepts using the data control and bound controls. Chapter 11, "Database Programming with Data Objects and SQL," introduces more advanced database programming using Data Access Objects (DAO) and SQL statements. Including this second chapter allows the instructor to teach more complex database programming topics and provides better preparation for programming database applications for industry.

Visual Basic 6.0 now includes Microsoft's latest database access technology: ActiveX Data Objects (ADO). ADO requires ODBC drivers and has been designed to allow access to many types of data, both in relational databases as well as nondatabase information such as your computer's folder and file structure. Although ADO might be the standard technique for data access in the *future* due to Microsoft's recommendation, it is still rather new and likely not as robust as DAO. DAO has been available since version 3.0 of Visual Basic, making it the most mature of the data object methods of database access in Visual Basic. It is a reliable choice for working with native Jet databases, such as any of the Access databases illustrated in the textbook. Furthermore, the intrinsic data control also still uses DAO and is still likely the most efficient method for connecting directly to Jet (MS Access, .MDB) databases. Because this book focuses on programming fundamentals, and because DAO is still the easiest database access technique to use, we elected to use DAO. Our decision is further supported in the article "VS 6.0 Benchmarks: New Features Don't Impact Speed," by Ash Rofail and Yasser Shohoud (*Visual Basic Programmer's Journal*, Vol. 8, No. 14, [December 1998]).

Object-Oriented Programming Chapter

Chapter 12, "Object-Oriented Programming," is devoted to fundamental object-oriented programming concepts and techniques for developing object-oriented programs using Visual Basic. This is important because object-oriented programming is becoming an almost standard method for developing software. Although Visual Basic does not support true inheritance, it does support most object-oriented program development concepts. This chapter covers these concepts and techniques in more depth than other books targeted for introductory Visual Basic programming courses.

End-of-Chapter Evaluation and Test Material

The end-of-chapter materials include a "Key Terms" section that lists all the new terms introduced in the chapter, general "Test Your Understanding" questions that reinforce the reading material of the chapter, and "Programming Exercises." After Chapter 3, "Arithmetic Operators and Scope," every chapter also includes larger "Programming Projects." For adopting instructors, solutions to problems will be made available. These solutions can be used as grading keys or for classroom illustration. Students should try to define each key term and answer the "Test Your Understanding" questions. This quickly shows how well students have picked up each chapter's concepts. The exercises and projects provide activities that can be completed to improve programming skills and to learn the material better.

Program Standards and Style

Programming standards and style rules are introduced early, and consistently illustrated in the examples. These include the following:

- Prefixes on all objects
- Required variable declarations by inclusion of Option Explicit
- Scope prefixes on variables and constants
- Header blocks and comments in the code
- Consistent indentation to allow quick identification of procedures and all logic structures

By developing good habits from the start, students should continue to develop programs that are easier to understand and maintain. Instructors benefit by having illustrative programs that follow good programming practice.

Another programming standard advocated by other authors and Visual Basic Help is the use of type prefixes on variable declarations; however, it is far from being standard practice. Browsing through a copy of any industry periodical (such as the *Visual Basic Programmer's Journal*) or the sample applications that are included with Visual Basic illustrates this point. The use of type prefixes is still just a personal preference and its merits, particularly for local variable declarations, are questionable. We elected to use explicit type declarations with shorter names instead of adding another standards naming rule. Too many data types abound (you can even create your own data types). If you need to find an object's data type, just click it and press Shift+F2; Visual Basic jumps to the declaration statement.

Concerted Effort to Avoid Including Bad GUI Design and Coding Techniques

Students are not taught bad practices that will later have to be corrected if they pursue careers as software developers in industry. Many books teach students to use the *End* statement to terminate program execution. Although the *End* statement does immediately end the application, it does not allow important events such as *Form_Unload* and *Class_Terminate* to be executed. As documented in Visual Basic help, the correct way to end a VB application is to unload all forms from memory. This type of termination will allow all end-of-application processing to be completed.

In addition, user interfaces throughout the book are designed using simple controls with standard sizes. Students are encouraged to follow common Windows user-interface guidelines and are discouraged from creating ostentatious or inefficient user-interface designs. For example, we avoid using the picture box control because most of the examples can be designed with less system-intensive controls. Some instructors may wonder why we don't cover more of the controls that come with Visual Basic. ActiveX controls have the potential to increase programmer productivity. However, reckless use of ActiveX controls can cause severe application distribution problems. Our book does explain how to use some ActiveX controls, but also warns about their pitfalls.

Use of Online Aids Encouraged

Most software packages today come with online help facilities that may even duplicate the material found in any printed manuals that may be available. Students can become better programmers if they learn how to use these available tools to find answers to questions instead of first going to the instructor. The use of Visual Basic Help is illustrated in Chapter 2, "Data Types, Variables, and Assignment Statements," and reinforced with several exercises. Also introduced in Chapter 2 are some of the important debugging features of Visual Basic. Because the rudimentary instructions on using the built-in debugging aids are described in the text, the instructor can assign the reading and focus on other elements in the class. As each new logic structure is introduced, the instructor can then use the debugging features to trace the logic's execution. Students can refer to the instructions anytime to review how to trace through their programs.

Pedagogy

Every chapter contains a list of learning objectives immediately following the introduction. Throughout the chapter, students see small logic and program examples that they can implement as they read. Tips and Notes are highlighted in sidebars. All the key points of the chapter are brought together in a complete case study at the end of each chapter. Besides illustrating the main points of the chapter, the case study also reinforces the program development process, by discussing each step and showing the transition from one step to the next. Each case study starts with an analysis of the problem, which includes assessing its input, processing, and output needs. From this, a user interface is designed. Program design follows with a determination of key events for each control (diagrammed in one or more OEDs) and development of detailed logic for each event in the form of flowcharts and pseudocode. A test plan is also created at this stage using a table format containing a variety of data input and the expected results. The design is then translated into code, with suggestions for coding and testing in small segments. Selected output from the test data are shown to illustrate the expected results of the test data input by the programmer.

Each chapter ends with a summary of important concepts and a list of key terms. These are followed by a series of "Test Your Understanding" questions that require written responses based on the chapter reading. A number of "Programming Exercises" are provided to allow students to practice key concepts on the computer, and "Programming Projects" provide larger-scale problems the students can use to practice the complete program development process.

Organization

Because many concepts of programming are interrelated and build on one another, this book was written under the basic assumption that students would start with Chapter 1 and cover each chapter in sequence. We selected the order of topics with the goal of presenting the more complex topics as early as possible to provide more opportunities for continued illustrations and reinforcement. For instructors who prefer some flexibility on the order of topics, the later section titled "Suggestions for Using This Text" highlights three alternatives for covering the material in a different order.

The chapter titles and a brief description are as follows:

Chapter 1: Introductory Programming Concepts and the Visual Basic Environment

This chapter introduces some programming terminology, presents the steps in program development, and familiarizes the student with the Visual Basic development environment. The student is encouraged to follow along to create, save, and run a short computer program. A simple case study is provided to discuss how the program development steps will be applied in future chapters. Flowcharting symbols are introduced so that both flowcharts and pseudocode can be presented in upcoming chapters.

Chapter 2: Data Types, Variables, and Assignment Statements

In this chapter, the student starts to learn how to program. Topics include deciding whether a value is string or numeric, whether to use a literal value or a variable, and how to assign values to object properties or variables. Comments, concatenation, and multiple forms are also included. Multiple forms are introduced to illustrate the use of a method (*Show*). Introducing multiple forms early sets the stage for the variable scope discussion in the next chapter.

Chapter 3: Arithmetic Operators and Scope

The primary goal of this chapter is to show how to perform calculations in Visual Basic. The arithmetic operators and their precedence are presented. The use of conversion functions to explicitly convert values between string and numeric types (for calculation and then for display) is encouraged. Different levels of variable scope are also discussed in detail. The remaining chapters can then illustrate all three levels of scope, as appropriate.

Chapter 4: Simplifying Programming Through Modularity

At this early stage, it is already possible to build programs that duplicate several statements. For example, a form with many text boxes may need to clear them, lock them, or unlock them from several parts of a program. Hence, the concept of creating additional program modules, similar to the way Visual Basic creates event procedures, is introduced in this chapter so that students can use this tool to simplify their program logic. Also, defining and calling procedures and functions is a difficult concept for many students. By introducing it early, there are many more opportunities throughout the semester to create and use functions and procedures so that students will become comfortable using them. A number of the functions and procedures provided in Visual Basic are also presented.

Chapter 5: Decisions and Data Validation

The various forms of the *If-Then-Else* statement are presented in this chapter, along with various types of data validation. The *MsgBox* and *InputBox* functions are introduced as possible tools to report bad data situations to the user. The nesting of *If* statements for more complex problems is also discussed.

Chapter 6: The Case Structure and Error Handling

This chapter covers several alternatives to the standard *If-Then-Else* statement, including use of *ElseIf* and *Select Case*. Because any problem using *ElseIf* or *Select Case* could be coded using regular *If-Then-Else* statements, the topics from this chapter could be skipped to provide more time to cover later topics. Chapter 6 also presents another alternative to *If-Then-Else* statements for data validation—trapping for errors using the *On Error GoTo* and *Resume* statements. Finally, the use of random numbers can be useful in certain program situations related to decisions, so a discussion is also presented in this chapter.

Chapter 7: Repetitive Structures

Students are presented with a loop design process to follow after they have determined that repetition is necessary. Pre-test, post-test and counting loops are covered. The counting loop is presented as a special case of the pre-test loop. The discussion about loops with early exit illustrates two versions of a program. In one version, the loop uses a normal exit; in the other version, the loop contains an early exit.

Chapter 8: Arrays, Searching, and Sorting

The concept of arrays is presented, followed by their use in a number of algorithms. Loops are used heavily to process array values, display array values, search for values, and sort the arrays. Both the sequential and binary search are discussed. Only the selection sort is discussed, which gives students a chance to see nested loops. Static and dynamic dimensioning of arrays is included. Several examples of where arrays are built in to Visual Basic, such as control arrays, combo boxes, and list boxes, are mentioned. Finally, user-defined types (UDTs) are presented as a means for storing together all related information of different types. UDTs are then applied to arrays in the chapter case study.

Chapter 9: Sequential Files

Four types of sequential files, along with sample programs for each type, are covered in this chapter. A file containing records with comma-separated values (CSV) is presented as an example of a file with variable record-length records. Display-formatted records are described and a sample program is developed for this type of file. Two types of files with fixed-length records are also discussed in depth. The case study program at the end of the chapter designs and develops a program that reads two files, accepts user input, and produces an output file. Variations of this program are also developed in the two database chapters, Chapters 10 and 11.

Chapter 10: Introductory Database Programming

This chapter shows the student how to use the data control to access data in a database. Techniques for retrieving and modifying database data are presented, as well as the Visual Basic statements used to work with these databases. Steps to create an application that navigates a database by setting specific properties of the data control and data bound controls without writing any code are illustrated. Steps for writing code to customize the database access to search, add, delete, and modify information in the database are also presented. The case study processes the same data from Chapter 9, but uses databases for storage and retrieval. By covering both chapters, the student can see the differences in implementation when using files rather than databases.

Chapter 11: Database Programming with Data Objects and SQL

When creating more complex applications (multiple-user or client/server), developers use Visual Basic's database objects rather than the data control and write their own code using structured query language (SQL) to do much of the processing that is handled by bound controls. Chapter 11 illustrates many of these techniques using the Data Access Objects (DAO) model. The same data from Chapters 9 and 10 is used for comparison purposes.

Chapter 12: Object-Oriented Programming

In this chapter, the principles of Object-Oriented Programming (OOP) are discussed as well as how you apply them in Visual Basic. The chapter discusses how to create your own objects by using classes and property procedures. Additionally, the Visual Basic Collection is introduced as a way of making working with lists of objects a bit easier. The same data from Chapters 9–11 is used for comparison purposes.

Appendix A: Visual Basic User Interface Objects

The purpose of Appendix A is to list commonly used Graphical User Interface (GUI) objects and their commonly used properties, events, and methods. Forms, intrinsic controls, menus, and ActiveX controls are all discussed. Brief coding examples are included to illustrate how these objects are typically used. The complete code for all examples at the end of each section is included.

Appendix B: Program Design and Translation to VB Code

Graphical flowcharts are one type of tool used by program designers to visually document their program's logic. Appendix B defines standardized, graphical flowcharting notation for depicting the logic for program solutions. It also provides a set of translation rules to convert these graphical flowchart solutions into equivalent Visual Basic code.

Appendix C: Useful Functions, Procedures, and Statements

Visual Basic has numerous intrinsic functions, procedures, and assorted statements to make programming easier. Appendix C lists a subset of the ones we think will be the most useful. The student is encouraged to use this appendix to get a general idea of what is available, and to then use the Visual Basic Help file for complete descriptions and syntax. Some of these keywords are listed in previous chapters and are repeated here for completeness.

Tear Card

A flexible and easy-to-use tear card appears in the front of the book. Two important items are included on this card: (1) "Suggested Prefixes for Visual Basic Controls" lists the recommended three-character prefixes for most of the commonly used objects; and (2) "Table of ASCII Values" provides the numeric ASCII code and corresponding character of each of the 256 possible character values. When comparing strings, it is useful to know these values to determine which characters are "less than" or "greater than" other characters. Visual Basic also contains functions and events (for example, *Asc, Chr, KeyPress*) that require knowledge of each character's ASCII value.

Suggestions for Using This Text

In a typical 15-week semester, we can usually cover 75 percent of this text. During class testing in the Fall 1998 semester, our course for majors covered Appendix B and Chapters 1–9. Students were referred to Appendix A only after fundamental programming concepts had been covered. Even then, they used it as a reference to learn how to include option buttons, check boxes, frames, and two or three other controls in their program exercises or projects. During the same time, the non-majors course covered Chapters 1–9. In prior semesters in the non-majors course, material equivalent to Chapters 1–10, Appendix B, and half of Appendix A was covered. Sometimes Appendix B has been used in its entirety before presenting any Visual Basic specifics, to concentrate only on logic structures. Other times, the logic was presented in the chapters along with the corresponding coding statements as needed.

Added Flexibility with Controls Appendix

Grouping the Visual Basic controls discussions in Appendix A provides a great deal of flexibility to instructors. Instructors who want to concentrate on developing logic design and coding skills can just follow the regular chapters and tell students to read the appendix on their own to learn about using other controls. Instructors who like to vary the assignments from one semester to another are free to use different controls each semester. Also, because the controls are not tied to a particular chapter, they can be learned in any order. Instructors who want to teach more specifically about the Visual Basic environment can pick one or two controls to teach along with each chapter.

Suggested Lesson Plans for 15-Week Semesters

The following alternatives are included to give instructors ideas on how to control the sequence and amount of coverage of the topics presented in this textbook. Plan A uses the approach that students first need a foundation in logic design before they should be given any programming tasks. It also integrates controls throughout the semester, as appropriate. Plan B integrates logic design throughout the semester based wholly on chapter discussions. By focusing on the three elementary controls, coverage of all chapters is possible. Plan C introduces essential Visual Basic concepts to generate student interest in programming at the start. Then logic design is covered right before starting decisions. Appropriate controls are then introduced as needed along the way. If programming is presented in a two-course sequence, a final alternative is to cover Chapters 1–8 in the first course and Chapters 9–12 and Appendix A in the second course.

Weeks	Plan A	Plan B	Plan C
1–2	Appendix B	Chapters 1–3	Chapters 1–2
3–6	Chapters 1–4 Appendix A (frames and lines)	Chapters 4–6	Chapters 3–4
7–9	Chapters 5–6 Appendix A (option buttons and check boxes)	Chapters 7–8	Appendix B Chapter 5 Appendix A (option buttons and check boxes)
10–12	Chapter 7 Appendix A (list boxes and combo boxes) Chapter 8	Chapters 9–10	Chapters 6–7 Appendix A (list boxes and combo boxes)
13–15	Chapter 9 Appendix A (menus and common dialog box)	Chapters 11–12	Chapters 8–9

The Teaching Package: Print and Technology Resources

We have developed a comprehensive print and technology teaching and learning resources package that is coordinated with the main text and designed to maximize teaching flexibility and convenience. An accompanying CD-ROM contains student project files. Visual Basic 6.0 can be used in conjunction with this book. An *Instructor's Resource Manual and Test Bank* includes the following:

- Guidance on how to integrate Appendix A controls throughout the book

- Solutions to all end-of-chapter questions, exercises, and projects

- Test bank of questions, including multiple-choice questions

- Solutions disc

A supporting Web site at **www.queet.com** includes additional teaching resources.

Acknowledgments

This textbook would not have been possible without the assistance of several individuals whom we would like to recognize here. Our department head, Jeff Whitten, has supported us by giving teaching assignments that allowed us to work together productively as a team. Our editorial staff at Que Education and Training have also been very supportive of this project from the beginning. In particular, Executive Editor Randy Haubner was instrumental in showing us that Que Education and Training could produce and market the book. Developmental Editor Lena Buonanno has served as the conduit between the author team and the production team to ensure a quality product. Project Editor Tim Tate has been very cooperative and helpful throughout the entire production process.

In addition to the Que Education and Training staff, we want to recognize all the reviewers who critiqued the manuscript and provided useful recommendations:

Chittibabu Govindarajulu, Southwest Missouri State University

David Grebner, Lansing Community College

Jeffrey Griffin, Purdue University

Marvin Harris, Lansing Community College

Bhushan Kapoor, California State University at Fullerton

Akhil Kumar, University of Colorado at Boulder

J. Douglas Robertson, Bentley College

Jack Van Deventer, Washington State University

Melinda White, Santa Fe Community College

Reviewer comments, along with the invaluable feedback from our colleague, Guity Ravai, who graciously helped class-test the manuscript in the non-majors course, helped improve the final quality of the textbook. Another group that helped improve the quality of the final book includes the students enrolled in CPT 250 and CPT 175 who used the manuscript as their primary textbook. Their feedback helped us to see their perspective and resulted in several improvements added to the current edition. Another group of students who gave critical support in preparation for the production process also deserves special acknowledgment. The long nights and entire weekends that Christie Archer, John Ulmer, and Gwen Sarault dedicated to our book enabled us to meet our production deadlines. These same students—along with Mike McGuire, Jon Helms, Chris Geer, Jason Piteo, Vicki Hecht, Fred Davis, Rick Moore, and R.J. Lewis—helped by developing solutions that followed our standards for the end-of-chapter problems and some also suggested ideas for possible problems.

Finally, we thank our families for their support and understanding throughout this project. Alka Harriger thanks her husband, Brad, and their three children, Josh,

Logan, and Amber, for showing their continued love and support even when this project took away precious family time. Susan Lisack especially thanks her husband, J.P., for putting up with the many fast-food meals and weekends alone. John Gotwals thanks his wife, Yixia, and his children, Clayton and Lucy, for their support during this authoring project. Kyle Lutes would like to thank his wonderful wife, Sally, and his remarkable new son, Kameron, for being so accepting of the long hours and peculiar work schedule that his career has required.

About the Authors

Alka R. Harriger is a Professor in the Computer Information Systems and Technology Department at Purdue University. Since joining the department in 1982, Professor Harriger has taught a variety of courses to majors and non-majors, including courses on introductory programming using Visual Basic. Additionally, she has authored/co-authored a number of papers, many of which were presented at national/international conferences. Professor Harriger's other activities have included serving as the Editor for the *Journal of Information Systems Education* for its first six years. Alka has a master of science degree in Computer Science from Purdue University, as well as a bachelor of science degree in Math and Computer Science and a bachelor of arts in Mathematics, both from California University of Pennsylvania.

Susan K. Lisack is an Assistant Professor in the Computer Information Systems and Technology Department at Purdue University. Professor Lisack received her bachelor of science degree in Mathematics and her master of science degree in Computer Science from Purdue University, and has taught a wide variety of programming courses since joining the department in 1980. Currently, she is teaching an advanced Visual Basic programming course that focuses on programming with data structures and databases. Professor Lisack has authored a number of papers that have been presented at recent academic conferences.

John K. Gotwals is an Associate Professor in the Computer Information Systems and Technology Department at Purdue University. Professor Gotwals received his Ph.D. from Purdue University and has taught a wide variety of programming courses. Currently, he is teaching an Object-Oriented Programming course using Java and a programming course using Visual Basic. Professor Gotwals has co-authored two refereed journal articles that relate to this textbook.

Kyle D. Lutes is an Assistant Professor in the Computer Information Systems and Technology Department at Purdue University. He joined Purdue in January 1998 and holds both a bachelor of science degree and a master of science degree in Computer and Information Science. Professor Lutes is a Microsoft Certified Professional and has more than 15 years' experience as a professional software developer. He has worked on large software development projects for a variety of industries. The technologies he has used include Visual Basic, C++, ActiveX, client/server, SQL, relational database management systems, object-oriented database management systems, VMS, REXX, MVS, COBOL, CICS, and VSAM. Kyle has authored a number of papers that have been presented at academic conferences and published in industry journals.

CHAPTER 1

INTRODUCTORY PROGRAMMING CONCEPTS AND THE VISUAL BASIC ENVIRONMENT

Introduction

This book is about computer programming. Before you begin to program, however, you should have experience using the computer, know how to work with files, and understand some basic computer terminology. It is our assumption that you have used computers in the past, whether for word processing, email, games, or spreadsheets, and know how to use the mouse, select items from menus, edit text (cut, copy, and paste), and manipulate files in the Windows environment.

Visual Basic is an application development tool that enables you to create computer programs that solve specific problems or serve specific purposes. Your programs will generally consist of Graphical User Interfaces (GUIs) and Visual Basic code statements. The GUI provides a way for users to interact with the programs to provide input, trigger processing, and view displayed results. The Visual Basic code tells the computer what to do when the user or system triggers the processing.

When you first learn how to write computer programs, you must develop several sets of skills at the same time:

- You have to learn how to use the computer, including its menus, buttons, and various windows, and how to write and run your programs.

- You have to develop your logical thinking to break a problem down into the steps a computer must execute.

- You have to learn the statements and structures of the particular programming language with which you are working.

The primary purpose of this chapter is the first item: to familiarize you with the computer environment you will be working in, including all windows and tools you will use regularly to create programs. Visual Basic includes an **Integrated Development Environment** (often referred to as **IDE**) that provides the programmer with many different tools that all work together to help create a program that eventually works correctly. The Visual Basic IDE includes capabilities to design interactive forms in the Windows environment, enter and edit Visual Basic program code, compile and run the programs, and use a variety of debugging tools.

A secondary purpose of this chapter is to introduce you to some terminology and the problem-solving process for program development. We define several terms such as structured programming, event-driven programming, Object-Oriented Programming, and visual programming. The programming example at the end of the chapter illustrates both how to use the development environment to create a program as well as how to apply the program development life cycle steps to a programming task. In case you are tempted to create some wild and colorful screens for your programs, several principles for designing user interfaces are also presented.

To get the most out of this chapter, you should have access to a computer that has Visual Basic installed on it so that you can find the items on the screen as they are being discussed and try out the steps listed. If you spend time now practicing these steps, when you start writing programs in Chapter 2, "Data Types, Variables, and Assignment Statements," you can immediately type in the programs and get them running.

Objectives

After working through this chapter, you should be able to:

- Explain how a program file is converted from source code to an executable program.

- Define event-driven programming, events, event procedures, and methods.

- Define visual programming.

- Define structured programming.

- List and describe the steps in program development.

- Name at least five guidelines for good user interface design.

- Get in and out of the Visual Basic environment.

- Select controls and place them on a form.

- Modify the properties of the controls that are on the form.

- Type in Visual Basic code for an event procedure.

- Save the files of a project.

@ Run a program.

@ Get printed copies of code files and screen snapshots.

@ Recognize how the program development process is applied to a simple problem.

Application Development Terminology

Even the fastest computer hardware with gigabytes of storage is useless until it is told what to do. The computer must be given sets of instructions that it can understand. A series of instructions that the computer can follow to solve a certain kind of problem is called a **program**. All the various programs used to support a computer are collectively called **software**. From the user's point of view, a computer program contains the instructions necessary to convert some input into the desired output (see Figure 1.1).

Figure 1.1   *User's top-level view of a computer program.*

Application Development Tools: Software to Help Build Programs

Application development tools provide programs that help you write and test programs. They generally provide several different facilities, including an editor, file-management features, a compiler, the capability to build an executable file, debugging tools, online help, and version control. They may also include facilities to aid you in designing the user interface, such as in Visual Basic. If these facilities are all available under one program, we say the tool is **integrated**.

Application development tools are used to write application software. This book shows you how to write application software for yourself and for others.

Compiling, Building, and Running Programs

The programming language statements that you type into a computer program file are called **source code**. This source code must be translated into machine code, or **object code**, before the computer can execute it. A **compiler** usually performs this translation. The compiler uses the source-code file as input, and produces an object-code file as output. Often this object-code file must be combined with other object-code files and library routines to create an **executable file**. This step may be called **linking** or **building**. An **interpreter** is like a compiler, but it translates the source code into object code one line at a time rather than the entire program simultaneously. This approach leads to slower execution, but enhances the programmer's ability to write and debug a program. Since its inception, Basic has traditionally been an interpretive language, although current versions of Visual Basic also give the programmer several compile options.

After an executable file (sometimes referred to as an .EXE file because that is the usual file extension) has been created, it can be executed multiple times without further compiling or building, so long as no change is made to the program's source code. If the executable is a *standalone* file, you can run it on another computer as long as that computer has a compatible operating system. The compiler, libraries, or application development environment used to create the program are not required. Sometimes the executable file is not standalone, and it is necessary to have a file of *dynamic link library (DLL)* routines along with the executable file to be able to run the program on another computer. Such is the case with Visual Basic programs. Through a utility program provided with Visual Basic, however, you can create a distribution system on a set of setup disks that includes the program's executable code and all required files, including DLL files. You can then use these setup disks to install the program on any compatible computer system.

Event-Driven Programming

Programs written in Visual Basic are called **event-driven programs**. The interface for a Visual Basic program consists of one or more windows (called forms), containing one or more controls, or screen objects. Each control has a number of events that it can respond to. An **event** is something that happens that the computer can detect. An event is triggered through some user action or system action. Typical events include the following:

- Clicking a mouse button
- Typing a character on the keyboard
- A tick of the computer's internal clock (passage of time)
- Moving the mouse
- Deleting or changing a value
- A control receiving the focus
- A control losing the focus

Event-driven programs give the user a lot of control over the actions of the application. This is in contrast to conventional or procedural programs where the program controls the sequence of actions and occasionally asks the user to answer a question. In an event-driven environment, the program is constantly waiting for an event to occur. When an event occurs, such as the click of a particular button, the program will execute the programming statements associated with that event, called an **event procedure**. When that event procedure completes execution, control returns to the application to wait for another event to occur, unless the event procedure terminated the application.

Most Visual Basic books (including this textbook) use the term *event* to refer to both the event (trigger) and its associated *event procedure* (related processing). If you see the term *click event*, for example, it could refer to either the click of a mouse button in a particular area on the screen or the processing steps executed as a result of clicking on that button. You can determine whether the term refers to the event or to its event procedure by the surrounding context. Because each control or screen object can have multiple events, we refer to the specific event by the name of the screen object as well as the name of the specific event (for example, the "Calculate button click" event or a "text box lost focus" event).

Controls, Objects, and Object-Oriented Programming

Much of Visual Basic's popularity results from the ease with which user interfaces can be created using predefined objects. In **Object-Oriented Analysis and Design (OOAD)**, the designer identifies key object types (things, concepts) that are a part of the problem, and how they interact with each other. The general characteristics or attributes of these objects that are important to the application are identified. The operations that the objects must perform are also identified. In **Object-Oriented Programming (OOP)**, the programmer takes these real-world concepts and tries to define **classes** in the computing language to represent the object types. The attributes that describe the object become the properties or fields of the class, and the operations that can be performed on the class are called methods. Both the properties and methods are **encapsulated**, or packaged together. This leads to **information hiding**, where the user of the class doesn't need to know how the methods are coded, but just needs to know what data to send to a method so that it can do its job. Other characteristics of Object-Oriented Programming are the capability to create hierarchies of classes that *inherit* data and methods from classes higher up in the hierarchy, and *polymorphism* (which you would learn about in an OOP course).

Components

Components are self-contained units that can be the building blocks of an application. Having components is like having a library of prebuilt objects sitting on a shelf waiting for you to use them. Each component represents one type of user-interface object (like a button) or a database or a system function. The programmer can select the desired components and connect them together to build an application.

When you design a screen (or form) in Visual Basic, you use predefined screen objects called **controls** *or* components, each of which are self-contained units that include many customizable attributes, called **properties**, and predefined processing steps called **methods**. You can also use a Class Builder Utility to create class hierarchies. Unfortunately, Visual Basic does not yet support true inheritance. Therefore, it is considered an object-based programming language and not a true Object-Oriented Programming language.

Visual Programming

The term **visual programming** is often applied to application development environments like Visual Basic, but some people would argue that these are not visual programming packages at all. Others define two different contexts for the term *visual*; one type of system is said to be a "visual environment," and the other has a language with a "visual syntax."

Visual Environment

When the application development system contains graphics tools to help the programmer create and manipulate a program that is written in a textual language, this is a visual environment. The visual portion of Visual Basic programming is in the development of the form or user interface design. As you will see later in this chapter, Visual Basic has a toolbox of controls that provides an easy point-and-click interface to select and place controls on the form. The programmer can then move, resize, and align controls until the user interface has the desired effect.

Visual Syntax

Purists would say that true visual programming means that the grammar or syntax of the language is expressed in a graphical manner via pictures or diagrams, instead of being typed in as text by the programmer. These diagrams could show containment or relationships between elements of the program. As you type program statements using the Visual Basic editor, you will see some context-sensitive boxes of options pop up to assist you with constructing the Visual Basic statement, but most of what you type is textual. Therefore, purists would disagree with a statement that Visual Basic employs visual programming.

Structured Programming

Structured programming, which gained popularity during the 1970s, offered one of the first disciplined approaches for developing the logic of a program, with the goal of making programs easier to understand and therefore easier to develop, test, and modify. The basis of structured programming is the idea that all logic can be expressed using only combinations of three restricted control structures, where each structure has a single entry point and a single exit point. **Modularization** is also encouraged, in which a larger problem is divided into simpler sections (called modules) that are easier to understand and maintain. The three restricted control structures are as follows:

- Sequential structure

- Conditional structure (selection structure)

- Repetitive structure (iterative structure)

In a **sequential structure**, the steps are each executed once, in the order they are listed, from top to bottom. The other two structures involve making a decision. In the **selection structure**, also called a **conditional structure**, a decision marks a two-way branch point where either one set of steps or another set of steps will be processed. With the **iterative structure**, or **repetitive structure**, a decision marks the beginning point or ending point of a series of steps, processed repeatedly.

Modular programming helps encourage reuse of blocks of code and facilitates the development and verification of complex programs and systems. One way to identify the modules is to use a top-down decomposition of the problem. The program designer starts with a general statement of the program, divides it into its main tasks, and then continues by dividing each task into increasingly detailed sets of routines. Once the top-down design is done, program implementation can be done in a top-down, bottom-up, or combined fashion. With top-down implementation, the high-level modules can be coded and tested first. Later, the lower-level detail can be added and tested. With bottom-up implementation, the more detailed modules are coded and tested individually. When related modules are done, their higher-level module is coded and tested. This process is repeated until the whole program is finished.

Steps in Program Development

Computer programs have to be typed, edited, and saved into files on the computer. When you are writing very short programs to help learn a computer language, there is not much need for a formal process to design and write a program. As soon as the programs begin to involve several events and to contain modules longer than half a page, however, it is easy to accidentally leave out statements or use the wrong name for something. At that stage, having a systematic process for developing a program will save time in the long run. The general **steps in program development** are listed here and shown in Figure 1.2. They are also illustrated by an example in each chapter's case study.

> Step 1: Analyze the problem to make sure you understand the requirements and can identify the input, processing, and output needs of the program.
>
> Step 2: Design or create the user interface.
>
> Step 3: Design the logic for the problem, including the macro-level view to identify events, the micro-level view to identify the detailed program logic, and the test plan with sample input and anticipated results.
>
> Step 4: Code the program by translating the logic design into corresponding Visual Basic statements.
>
> Step 5: Test and debug the program using the test plan created in step 3.
>
> Step 6: Assemble the final documentation.

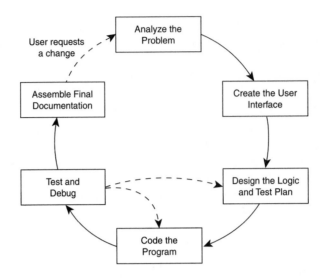

Figure 1.2 *Program development life cycle.*

Analyzing the problem requires a thorough reading of the problem statement. It is helpful to create a table that lists the inputs to be provided by the user, the outputs of computed results from the program, and the major processing steps to transform the inputs into the outputs. After the list is complete, the intended user should review it to ensure that your interpretation of the program matches the user's intent.

Designing the interface involves creating a set of windows or forms that contain screen objects to serve each of the functions listed in the analysis phase. The goal here is to make sure that each input, output, and processing need has a screen object (control) on the form to receive inputs, show results, or to trigger some processing. Appendix A, "Visual Basic User Interface Objects," describes many of the common controls available for Visual Basic, along with a discussion of the purpose of that control (input, processing, or output). Showing the form to the user can be a useful communication tool to make sure the program will meet the user's needs.

Designing the logic involves three distinct steps. The programmer must perform the following:

- Identify the events.

- Develop the detailed program logic.

- Devise a thorough test plan.

After the form has been designed, we will use an **Object-Event Diagram (OED)**, which is a graphical tool, to help us document the events associated with specific controls on the form. For each event depicted in the diagram, we will use program flowcharts, outlines, or pseudocode to depict the detailed program logic that defines the particulars of the event. During this step, we also construct a table of sample input data and anticipated results.

Coding a program means to translate the logic into statements of a particular programming language (like Pascal or C or BASIC) and enter them into the computer. Using the logic design from the preceding step, you can follow a set of translation rules to convert your design into Visual Basic code. Appendix B, "Program Design and Translation to VB Code" describes translation rules for a variety of logic constructs that you can use to convert your design into a working Visual Basic program. If you follow the program development process as recommended, this should be the easiest and most straightforward part of programming. Nonetheless, many people skip over the earlier steps or prefer not to follow a systematic process. This approach leads to *accidental programming*—developing programs without a plan, and then continually debugging during the time allotted with the expectation that the program will eventually produce the desired results. Generally, these "accidental programmers" will spend more time debugging their program than if they had followed a well-defined process.

Testing and debugging a program means to find and remove errors from that program. If you carefully completed the previous steps and translated the design correctly, you should not find errors. Even the best programmers introduce errors during translation, however, particularly typographical errors. Visual Basic will help you correct many of these typographical errors if they violate Visual Basic syntax. After you have corrected all the syntax errors, the best way for you to have confidence that your program works is to use the test plan you created during the design stage. Run the program, enter the input data from your test plan, and compare the program's results to the results you anticipated in your test plan. If they do not match, you will need to debug the program further. Otherwise, as long as the test plan was thorough, you can be fairly confident that the program works!

Now that the program works, you must *assemble program documentation* before delivering the program to your user. Much of the documentation has been created already by virtue of following this systematic program development process. However, your user may require additional documentation such as a user's manual, a set of **snapshots** (screen captures) to document how the screens look during program execution, or a setup disk to facilitate program installation.

Through this discussion, you should see how each step naturally follows the preceding step. In each stage of program development, it is possible to overlook an important detail or introduce some other error. By following a systematic process, however, you are more likely to uncover these problems sooner in the process, resulting in improved success in your initial programming as well as in future maintenance activities.

■ TIP

Follow a systematic program development process for improved programming success.

The steps in program development are frequently referred to as the *program development life cycle*. Users will think of other things that the program could do to help them. Business rules and processes are constantly changing. Often, these ideas and changes will result in a request for an update to existing software. The "cycle" occurs when the change is requested and you repeat these same steps to make the modification. Some people list this as another complete step of the process:

Step 7: Maintain or update the program (that is, repeat steps 1 to 6).

Smaller cycles can also occur within these program development steps, as shown with dotted lines in Figure 1.2. For large programs, it will be easier to code and test (or perhaps design, code, and test) a small portion of the program, and then design, code, and test an expanded or different section of the program. This process is repeated until the entire program is completed.

Designing User Interfaces to Make Programs Easy to Use

As the name implies, the *user interface* is what the user sees and interacts with when a program is running. Depending on the design process, the user interface may be given to you as part of the programming specifications, or you may be asked to design a user interface that provides the functionality of the specifications. Visual Basic provides all the tools needed to include a variety of buttons, text boxes, menus, pictures, check boxes, and so forth on the user interface of your program, in a wide variety of colors, fonts, and sizes. It is beyond the scope of this book to present comprehensive guidelines for designing user interfaces; entire books have been written about this. If you continue to program, you may want to reference one of these.

The following list presents a few common-sense guidelines for creating a user interface:

- *Arrange the screen in a logical manner*—Typically this means left to right, top to bottom, with the most important item in the upper-left corner of the screen. Support this ordering by making sure the user can tab through the controls in that order. Visually group related controls, either by spacing or by placing the controls inside a box of some kind.

- *Help the user*—Provide keyboard as well as mouse access wherever possible. If you know what the user is likely to do next, have the program set the focus there automatically. Disable elements so that the user doesn't waste time selecting something that cannot be done at the time. Write clearly worded error messages that are free of technical terms and excess words. Provide a help system for users. This book won't take time to teach help design, but there are many examples that you can use as a framework to develop help systems for your own programs. A well-indexed and interconnected help system is very important in today's Windows software and is even replacing written documentation.

- *Be consistent*—If you have more than one button, make them all the same size. Maintain consistent margins and spacing. If a program has multiple screens, make sure common elements look the same and appear in the same location on all screens. Align multiple controls, generally on the left.

- *Use color sparingly*—One use of color is to highlight the current selection. In general, don't use too many different colors on one screen. Soft, muted colors that complement one another usually work better than bright colors.

- *Limit the number of fonts*—Italic and serif fonts may be hard to read onscreen. Not all computers have the same fonts available.

If you want to design commercial applications that run under Microsoft Windows, you need to follow the guidelines documented by Microsoft. There you will find more specific guidelines on spacing and capitalization. Buttons, for example, should use book title capitalization rules; labels, on the other hand, use sentence-style capitalization. Also, if multiple buttons appear on a form, they should be aligned on the upper-right of the screen or in a row across the bottom. Fortunately, many of the other guidelines have been built into the Visual Basic controls.

What Is Visual Basic?

Visual Basic is an integrated application development environment that provides a multitude of tools to assist programmers in creating Windows programs. As a Rapid Application Development (RAD) tool, it facilitates prototyping a system with its easy point-and-click method to design the screens for a program. Visual Basic's toolbox provides most of the common controls a programmer might want to include in a Windows program. The properties of any control placed on a form are readily accessible via a **Properties window**. A **Code window** enables the programmer to enter, review, and edit any of the program's code. File-management commands, compile and execute commands, and debugging tools are also easily accessible in the Visual Basic environment. We are now ready to begin exploring the different elements of the Visual Basic environment.

Elements of the Development Environment

When you start Visual Basic, several elements of the Visual Basic IDE are generally visible (see Figure 1.3). The elements that you typically use each time you write a Visual Basic program are the **Form window**, Code window, Properties window, **Project Explorer window**, toolbox, **toolbar**, and the **menu bar**. Some of these elements are separate windows that can be rearranged and/or resized to suit your needs and preferences. Our discussion will assume that you have not changed the default locations of these windows. Let's take a brief look at each of these elements.

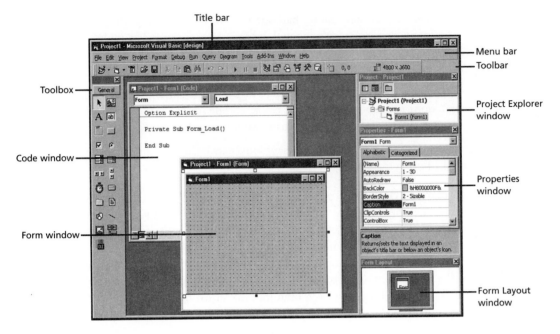

Figure 1.3 *Elements of the Visual Basic environment.*

Title Bar

As you can see in Figure 1.3, the title bar appears as a shaded bar at the top of a window. A descriptive name for the application is listed in this shaded bar. Visual Basic's title bar (see Figure 1.4) lists the name of your program (Project1 is the default), the name of the application being used to create the application (Microsoft Visual Basic), and the current mode [design]. The title bar also includes the application's control menu on the extreme left, and the minimize, maximize, and close buttons on the extreme right. All Windows applications, including ones you will create using Visual Basic, have a similar title bar. For a classroom setting, it is a good idea for you to include your name after the application name in the title bar.

Figure 1.4 *Visual Basic title bar and menu bar.*

Menu Bar

Many Windows applications have a menu bar that appears immediately below the title bar. In Visual Basic, as with most Windows applications, the leftmost menu is the File menu, which enables you open, save, or close files, and exit from Visual Basic. Next to it is the Edit menu, which contains the cut, copy, and paste commands. The View, Project, and Run menus also contain options that we will use later.

If you look closely at the menu titles, you should notice that each title has a unique, single letter underlined. The underlined letter is called the **access key** for the corresponding menu option. This feature gives the user two ways to activate the menu: press Alt plus the access key letter of the desired menu title, or click on the desired menu title with the mouse. (Access keys are easy to implement in Visual Basic by typing an ampersand (&) in front of the letter that should be underlined.) After a menu title is activated, its corresponding submenu will appear. Each of these items may also have their own submenus or may trigger processing immediately. As you develop more advanced user interfaces, you will want to include menus in the programs you write.

Toolbar

Figure 1.5 illustrates the **toolbar**, which is located immediately beneath the menu bar. Some of the most common menu selections are available here as buttons. This gives you one-click mouse access to things that might require several clicks through the menus.

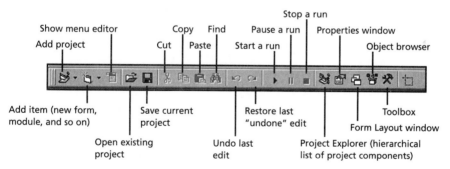

Figure 1.5   *Visual Basic toolbar.*

When you are ready to save a program, for example, you can click on the disk icon. If it is a new program, the Save File dialog box appears enabling you to specify the drive, path, and filename for each file that must be saved. If it is a previously saved program to which you made changes, all files with changes will be automatically updated. Because a Visual Basic program consists of multiple files, beginning programmers are cautioned against saving via the menus. Activating the File menu and selecting the Save As option will only save the currently selected file in the Project Explorer window. Therefore, using the toolbar button is not only fewer clicks, but in the case of saving changes, it ensures that all files get saved. If you are unsure of the function of a particular button, you can point your mouse at the button, and a hint appears that tells you what its function is. Try clicking the toolbar button for Project Explorer two or three times. This button acts as a toggle switch to specify whether this window should be in view.

Toolbox

In the extreme left side of the screen is a tall, thin window containing several icons. This window is called the **toolbox**. The toolbox is a collection of tools or controls used to build the desired user interface. Each control is represented as a button with an icon on top. Figure 1.6 shows the standard controls (also called *intrinsic controls*); however, you can add many other controls to the toolbox. If none of the controls provided with Visual Basic suit your needs, you can purchase additional customized controls from third-party vendors.

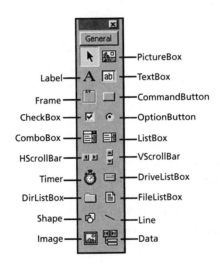

Figure 1.6 *Visual Basic toolbox.*

Most of the controls we use in this book are already in the toolbox, such as a label, a command button, and a text box. If you hold your mouse point over one of these, a ToolTip or hint appears with the name of the control. Positioning the mouse cursor over the button that has a capital *A* on it will show a pop-up ToolTip with the word Label. By clicking on the control in the toolbox, and then clicking on the form, you can easily place controls on your form.

Project Explorer Window

On the right side of the screen, you should see three windows, arranged vertically. The topmost of these is called the Project Explorer window (see Figure 1.7). The source code for each program in Visual Basic is called a **project**, and consists of all the files associated with the program. The Project Explorer window contains a hierarchical view of these files. Initially, we have two files: a project file that keeps track of all the files and objects in your program, and a form file that contains both the programming code and user interface. As our programs become more complex, we will add additional forms as well as a standard code module. Figure 1.7, for example, shows that the sample program consists of one project file (ExQuadEqn.vbp) with three forms (ExQuadAbout.frm, ExQuadMain.frm, and ExQuadSummary.frm), and one standard module (ExGlobalVars.bas).

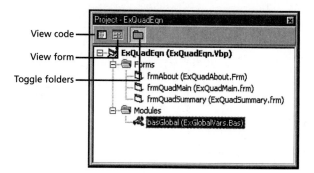

Figure 1.7 *Project Explorer window.*

Three buttons with icons appear above the hierarchical list. Visual Basic's ToolTips will show you that they are used to view the code, view the object, or toggle the view of the object folders. The buttons in this window can help you accomplish several activities, including identifying the files to be saved, switching from one file to the next, and switching between the form and the code. You save the module file by selecting it in this window by clicking on it with the mouse, and then selecting the Save As option on the File menu. By clicking on the icons below the title bar, you can switch between the Code window and the Form Design window of the current file. By double-clicking on another file in the hierarchical list, you can switch to that file.

Form Window

The **Form window** is the large rectangle in the center of the screen that contains a grid of black dots (see Figure 1.8). You use it to design the interface that the user will see when the program runs. It is a separate, sizable, movable window. This means you can drag it to a new location on your screen or drag the edges to make your form wider or narrower, taller, or shorter, as needed for your application. The grid dots are provided to help you in aligning controls on the form. To get even more freedom in moving this form around the screen, you can go to Options under the Tools menu, select the Advanced tab, and check *SDI Development Environment.*

Figure 1.8   *Form window.*

Properties Window

The user interfaces that you create will consist of one (or multiple) forms, containing one or more controls. Each control and each form is a predefined object with a number of attributes or properties. The Properties window (see Figure 1.9) displays the names of these properties and their current values. As the programmer, you can customize each of the screen objects by assigning different values to appropriate properties. Because the form and various controls each has its own set of properties, only properties and values for the currently selected control display in the Properties window. You can select the form or another control already on the form by clicking it. Alternatively, as soon as you place a control from the toolbox on the form, that control becomes the currently selected control.

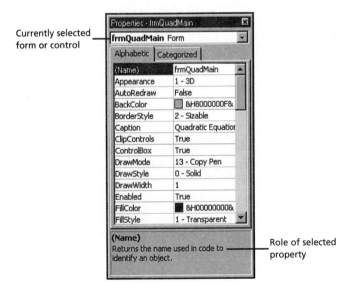

Currently selected form or control

Role of selected property

Figure 1.9   *Properties window.*

The default location for the Properties window is immediately below the Project Explorer window. The name of the control whose properties are being displayed is listed in the drop-down list box at the top of the Properties window. Below this is an organized list of attributes. By clicking on the alphabetic or categorized tabs, you can view this list alphabetically or by category of controls, respectively. The attributes are displayed in a two-column table. The words down the left side are the *property names*; the characters on the right side are the *property values* of the corresponding properties. The Value column is where you can type in new values to change the starting values of the properties.

Figure 1.9, for example, shows that the currently selected object is the form. From the properties in view, you can verify that its name is frmQuadMain, its appearance is three dimensional, it will not be automatically redrawn, it has a specific background color, its border style makes it sizable, and so on. If there are many properties, you can use the vertical scrollbar to move through the list of properties and their values. Immediately below the list of properties is a description of the role of the currently selected property.

Form Layout Window

The Form Layout window helps the programmer easily define the initial placement of the user interface form when the program is executed (see Figure 1.10). Previous versions of Visual Basic required the programmer to include special program code to control the starting position of the form. The Form Layout window contains an image of a computer screen and a blank form. The relative placement of the form on the user's screen is depicted by the placement of the blank form on the computer screen image in the Form Layout window. The startup position can be changed to suit the user's or programmer's preferences by manually dragging it on the screen using the mouse. A better alternative is to assign a specific value to a special property (Startup Position) in the Properties window for the Form object. Therefore, in practice, we recommend that you close this window to allow more space to enlarge the remaining windows on the right side and view more of their details simultaneously.

Figure 1.10   *Form Layout window.*

The last form property we will change is the default font style for the form. To accomplish this, highlight the Font property. In the Value column, you will notice a button containing three dots. By pressing this Settings button, you will bring up the Font dialog box, which you may have seen in other Windows applications. In this dialog box, select the Times Roman font style, 12-point size, and Bold, and then click OK. Now any other controls that you add to this form will use these font styles. If you wish to change the font style for an individual control later, you can do that by selecting that control and changing its Font property using the same process.

General user interface guidelines recommend against changing form colors and font styles from their defaults. Therefore, you should avoid these changes unless there is a user-specified need for doing so.

Add a Text Box to the Practice Form

Now it is time to add the individual controls to the form and change a few properties for each control. Position the mouse over the different buttons on the toolbox to see how the ToolTips pop up to remind you of the names of the controls.

➢ Select the TextBox control by clicking on it in the toolbox, and then place it in the upper-left corner of the Form window.

With the text box selected, change the Name property of the text box to txtName. Then scroll down in the Properties window to locate the Text property and type your name. You should see your name appear inside the text box on the form. To change the color of the letters, select the ForeColor property, click on the Palette tab, and click on the desired color. The color of your name in the text box should appear in the selected color. Suppose you decide that the text box should have your teacher's name rather than your name. To make this change, just select the Text property again, highlight the current value next to the Text property, and type the new value on top of the old value. Again, the new value should appear immediately on the form. To erase the contents of the text box so that it appears empty on the form, select the Text property, highlight the value, and press the Delete key. Did you notice that the contents inside the text box on the form just got erased?

Add a Label to the Practice Form

➢ Next, place a label on the form so that it occupies the middle third of the form.

Change the label's Name property to lblMessage. If you want the form's color to show through the label, you can change the label's BackStyle property to transparent. To accomplish this, select the BackStyle property and Click on the arrow in the Value column to view the available choices. Select the Transparent option. Currently, this label displays Label1 on the form, but we want it to show Hello World. Change the value of the label's Caption property to Hello World. The last change for the label is the color of its letters. Change the ForeColor property to a dark blue.

Add a Command Button to the Practice Form

➤ Finally, place a command button on the form.

Change its Name property to cmdShowMessage and its Caption property to &Show Message. Again, what you enter for the caption will immediately appear on the form inside the button. The ampersand (&) at the beginning of the caption causes the letter *S* to be underlined on the button. By placing the ampersand elsewhere in the caption, a different letter would be underlined. (If you actually want the ampersand character to appear on the control, type two ampersands in a row.) By underlining a letter on a caption in this way, you provide the user with greater flexibility in using this program through access keys. Instead of being limited to clicking on the button with the mouse, the user could alternatively press Alt+S to accomplish the same result.

If you followed the preceding instructions, your form should now look similar to that in Figure 1.14. You changed the property values of several objects (the form, a label, a text box, and a command button) to customize the appearance of the user interface of your program.

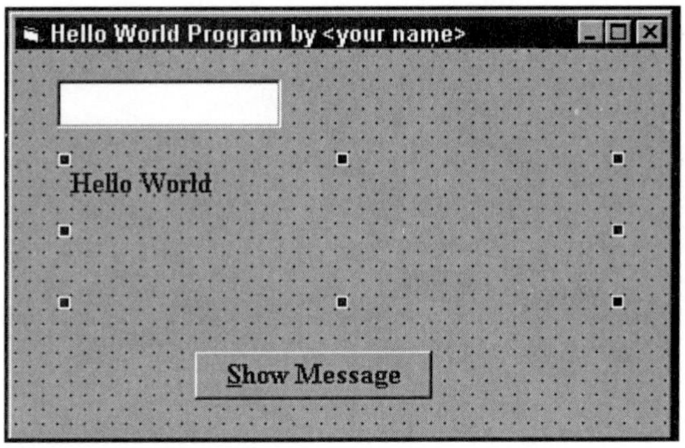

Figure 1.14 *Practice activity final form.*

Writing Code for Events

In addition to properties that mostly affect how a control looks onscreen, a control also has events that it can respond to. The events for a particular control can be viewed in the Code window. If you click on the View Code button in the Project Explorer window (refer to Figure 1.7), the Code window appears. The top of the window contains two drop-down lists. The left drop-down list is the Object list box and contains the names of all objects on the current form. You can see the list by pressing on the down arrow and scrolling through the alphabetic list of object names that you assigned to the Name property when you designed the form. After an object is selected from the left drop-down list, the right drop-down list, called the Procedure list box, contains all built-in event procedure names for the selected object.

Each type of control has a default event procedure. When the object is selected from the Object list box, the default event procedure is assumed, and a skeletal procedure is created for it in the Code window. Any Visual Basic program statements between the lines that begin and end the procedure will be processed when the associated event is triggered at Run Time.

The form's default event procedure is *Load*, for example. Therefore, double-clicking on the form will create a skeletal *Form_Load* event procedure in the Code window, as illustrated in Figure 1.15. If you type in Visual Basic statements that will center the form, these statements will be executed when the *Form_Load* event is triggered (when the program is first loaded). As a result, the user will see the form centered on the screen at the start of program execution.

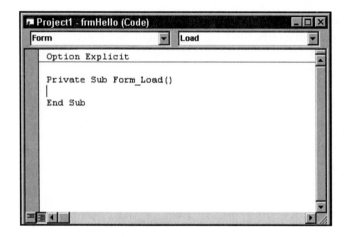

Figure 1.15   *Code window with skeletal procedure.*

The command button's default is the *Click* event.

➢ In the current example, select the command button *cmdShowMessage* from the object list.

The procedure list will automatically default to *Click*, and the *cmdShowMessage_Click* skeletal event procedure will be created. Type the line:

```
lblMessage.Caption = "Welcome to my world, " & txtName.Text
```

between the Private Sub and End Sub lines, as shown in Figure 1.16.

Figure 1.16 *Code window with skeletal procedure and finished procedure.*

Now, when the user clicks on the *Show Message* command button, the line you typed will be executed, causing the welcome message to appear in the message label.

Saving the Project

At this point, we have created a form with a few controls as well as written some program code. It is a good idea to now save the project. In Visual Basic, a project consists of more than one file. This gives the programmer more flexibility, but it takes time for beginning programmers to become accustomed to this. Minimally, there is a main project file, and a form file that contains both the interface descriptions and program code. As we create more complex programs, other files can be added to the project. We discuss these additional files when we add them to our projects; for now, however, we focus on the project file and single form file.

Saving to Program Folders

During your learning process, you will write many small programs. You should develop the habit of storing all files related to a specific program in a separate folder with a descriptive name. If you are going to work on different computer systems (the school's computing lab, your office, your home, and so forth), you will often need to copy your programs. You should always copy the entire project folder with its contents, rather than the individual files in the folder, to the new location. If you copy the individual files rather than the folder, important information in the project file can get lost, causing Visual Basic to display an error message that suggests that a form could not be located. By copying the folder, you can open up the project in the same way as when you initially created it and do so without problems. You can either create the folder in Windows Explorer before saving the project, or you can create the folder through Visual Basic when you identify the first project file to be saved.

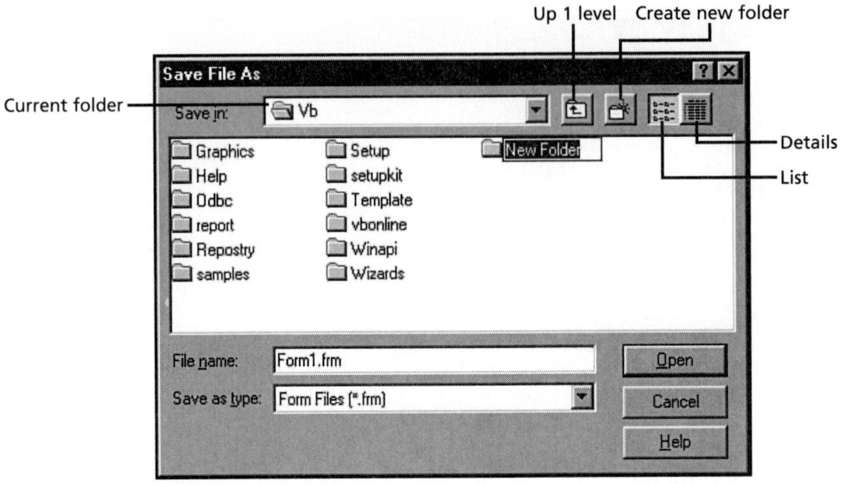

Up 1 level   Create new folder

Current folder

Details
List

Figure 1.17 *Save File As dialog box.*

The easiest and fastest way to save your program is to click on the disk icon on the toolbar. This action causes Visual Basic to load the Save File As dialog box for each file that must be saved (see Figure 1.17). When the initial dialog box comes up, you should first select the folder where the file should be saved (for example, Hello World), and then enter the name of the form file descriptively (for example, Hello World Form). If the folder has not yet been created, you can create the folder by clicking on the Create New Folder icon and typing over the default name New Folder (highlighted in Figure 1.17). Once renamed, you will need to select this folder by double-clicking on it. This will show the newly created folder name in the drop-down *Save in* list box. The final step in saving a project for the first time is to save the main project file. When the next dialog box comes up, make sure that the project file will be stored in the correct folder, and pick a meaningful name (for example, Hello World Project).

TIP
Store each project in a new folder.

After saving all files that comprise the program, subsequent changes are saved more quickly by pressing the disk icon again. Visual Basic will assume that the same folder and filenames should be used. The file dialog boxes will not appear unless a new program file is added. As you do the practice activity, after you have saved the form and project files for the first time, it is a good idea to click on the disk icon after completing several additional steps.

Running Visual Basic Programs

When you were creating the user interface, as well as writing the code using the code editor, your program was in Design Time mode. After you type in the Visual Basic code for a section of a program, you need to determine whether it works correctly. To do this you run, or execute, the program. You can either click on the Start toolbar button, or you can select the Start command from the Run menu. (If you use the Run menu, you will also see that you can use the F5 function key to start execution.) When you run the program created in the previous sections, the form will appear, without the grid dots, and wait for your action.

A Visual Basic program usually consists of a number of event procedures triggered by the system or a user action. The example program only contains code for one event that occurs when the command button named *cmdShowMessage* is pressed, or clicked. If you never click on the command button, the program will not execute this code. The moment you click the button, this event is triggered and the statement you typed is processed. This statement causes the label named *lblMessage* to show a message that includes whatever the user typed in the text box. As the user, you can change what is inside the text box as much as you like, but the label changes only after you click the command button.

When the form is shown, enter your name in the text box, and then click the *Show Message* command button. The message label should immediately change from nothing to the message, which includes your name. Practice changing the contents of the text box and clicking on the command button to get a better idea of when the code you wrote is processed.

There are several ways to tell that your program is in Run Time mode rather than Design Time mode. These include the following:

- The word [run] appears in the Visual Basic window title bar.

- The Properties window disappears.

- The grid dots on the form go away.

- The program name appears in the taskbar at the bottom of the Windows screen.

Return to Design Time Mode

After you finish running your program, you need to get out of Run Time mode and return to the development (or Design Time mode) environment that you started in. To return to Design Time mode, you can perform one of the following actions:

- Click the Close button in the far right of the title bar of the executing program window (Don't close the wrong window!).

- Click the Control menu in the far left of the title bar of the executing window and select Close.

- ■ Double-click the Control menu in the far left of the title bar of the executing window.

- ■ Click the End button on the Visual Basic toolbar.

When you are back in Design Time mode, you can continue to work on the project by changing the form design or by typing in more code.

Making Changes to the Current Project

In creating the preceding example, you could see how Visual Basic simplifies the task of designing a user interface as well as writing program code. You should always keep in mind that just because you can do something easily in Visual Basic, however, that doesn't make it a good choice. For example, return to the Code window and select the command button from the left drop-down list. Select the *MouseDown* event procedure in the right drop-down list. Inside the skeletal procedure, type a line with the code frmHello.Left = 0 on it. Now when you run the program, enter a name in the text box and click on the command button. The form jumps to the left edge of the screen because of the *MouseDown* action. When you click on the command button, the program displays the message as before. The last change created a second event procedure for the button. We could repeat this process for each of the events listed for the command button, and the resulting program could do many different things, depending on which event the user triggers. Likewise, we could write events for each of the other objects—the label, the text box, and the form—and test them in a similar manner. Unfortunately, a program like this would become user unfriendly because of its confusing design.

Close the Project

You can close a Visual Basic project in a few different ways, depending on whether you want to work on another project or want to quit working in Visual Basic altogether. Each of the following procedures closes the current project:

- ■ From the File menu, select Remove Project.

- ■ From the File menu, select Open Project or New Project and open or start another project. (Because only one project can be open at a time, Visual Basic automatically closes any open projects before opening a new project.)

- ■ From the File menu, select Exit. (Visual Basic automatically closes any open projects before exiting.)

When closing a project, if anything needs to be saved, Visual Basic will ask you whether to save it. It is not a good idea to rely on Visual Basic to remind you to save your programs, because you may be in a hurry to log off the computer. That's when mistakes can be made. Get in the habit of saving every time you make changes to a project and before running it. Visual Basic's check should just act as a safety net in case you forget.

Creating a New Project

If you have been working on a project in Visual Basic and want to start a new project, you should choose New Project from the File menu. The screen should look like it did when you first started Visual Basic. Repeat the steps of the previous sections to set up the form and write the code for your new project. Don't forget to save the project files after typing in a number of code lines and before running the program.

Opening an Existing Project

After you have written a few Visual Basic programs, you will find various reasons for wanting to access them again. Maybe you ran out of time and now want to type in the rest of the code, or you might have errors to correct. Maybe you are starting a new assignment, and think you can use parts of a previous project to solve the new problem. Whatever the reason, to open a previously saved project, follow these steps:

1. Select Open Project from the Visual Basic File menu.

2. Select the desired drive and folder, (only *.VBP, *.MAK, and *.VBG files will be shown in the list).

3. Select the *main project file* (the **.VBP file**) and click the Open command button.

The last step is very important. When you select the main project file, Visual Basic automatically opens the **.FRM file**(s) for you and display the main form of the project. If you select the .FRM file to open rather than the main project file, you will be creating a new project that will use *only* the selected form.

Saving Changes to an Existing Project

After you have saved the project files one time, you often make changes or additions to the form or code and want to save these changes into the same file. To do this, you can do either of the following:

 ■ Click the disk icon on the toolbar. Visual Basic will automatically save any file that has changed.

■ Select Save Project from the File menu. Visual Basic will automatically save any file that has changed.

Printing the Forms, Code Files, or Output Samples

At some point, you will want printouts of your forms and code. Printouts of the forms can be useful as you plan out the logic and code of a project, or to get reactions from a potential user of the program. Printouts of the code itself can be used to show others the progress you have made, to aid you in stepping through your code to find errors, and as final documentation of a completed project.

Visual Basic has a Print option under its File menu that will print the form image, form text (descriptions of the screen objects and customized properties), and code for all or part of a project. Figure 1.18 shows the Print dialog box. The *Range* options enable you to print information for a single file module, for all files in the project, or only selected code. The *Print What* check boxes enable you to print the form image as it looks at design time, the code, and/or the form text that lists all screen objects and describes their customized properties.

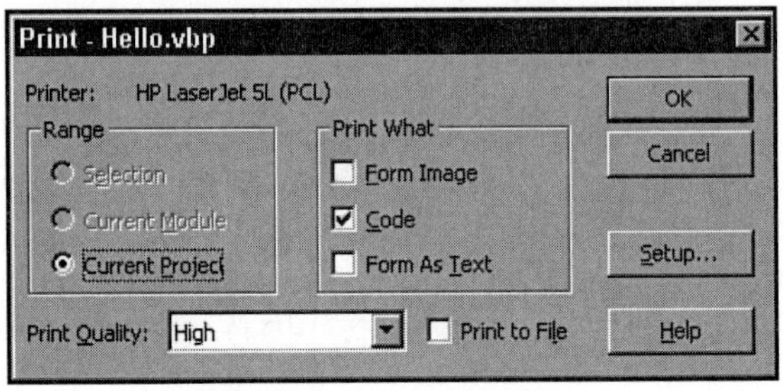

Figure 1.18 *Visual Basic's Print dialog box.*

You can print all the components in one step by selecting *Current Project* for *Range* and checking all three *Print What* check boxes. You may experience some printer problems using this shortcut in a networked environment with a shared printer, however. If your program consists of multiple forms, and you print everything in one step, you may notice that some pages do not print correctly. In this case, you can always print each file one at a time and collate the pages manually.

Another type of printout that you may want from time to time is a set of *output screens*. These screen shots (also called *snapshots* or *screen captures*) can be useful for creating user instructions, proving to your instructor that your program produces correct output, or for a presentation or paper about the capabilities of the program when you can't demonstrate it. To capture the contents of an output screen, you will be working simultaneously with Visual Basic and a word processor like Microsoft Word. To make the most efficient use of space, one suggestion is to place a table in the word processing document with two columns and enough rows to print six or eight screens per page. After this has been set up, follow these steps:

1. Run the program until the desired screen output is showing.

2. Press Alt+Print Screen to capture only that output window in the Clipboard. (Note that using the Alt key with the Print Screen key causes only the active window to be captured to the Clipboard. If you just press the Print Screen key, everything showing on your screen will be captured to the Clipboard.)

3. Switch to a word processor like Microsoft Word (open the word processor if necessary).

4. Type a descriptive statement in the next table cell and press Enter.

5. Paste the captured output into the word processor at the current table cell (Edit, Paste Special or Ctrl+V).

6. Switch back to the program and repeat from step 2 for additional screen captures desired.

Hello Program Case Study

This section walks you through the steps a programmer would normally go through when analyzing, designing, writing, and testing a program. Practice these steps as you read about them. After you have created this program, you will need to make sure that all files that make up your project have been saved correctly. This requires that you become familiar with the various types of files created by Visual Basic at different stages of the programming process so that you can properly manage them when saving, copying, or deleting. Let's get started!

Thus far, we have only described the environment you will be using when you create Visual Basic programs. The focus of this text, however, is on teaching important programming concepts that can be applied to any visual, event-driven programming language, including Visual Basic. Therefore, your first programming example will illustrate not only how you should use different controls of the Visual Basic environment to create your program's interface, but more importantly, how to apply the program development process to a specific programming task.

As you learned earlier in this chapter, the program development life cycle (PDLC) consists of six steps with natural transitions that begin with analyzing the problem and conclude with a fully documented program that can be delivered to the user. Visual Basic is used during certain stages of program development to design the user interface, code the program, run and test the program, save the files into a folder, and print the program information. Because Visual Basic is a Rapid Application Development (RAD) tool, *iterative program development* can be employed by creating a small subset of the actual program and repeating the PDLC steps as necessary until all elements of the program have been added and the entire project works correctly.

We have already created a subset of this project during our practice activity. If we start with that program, add a new element, test it to make sure it works, and repeat the process for each new enhancement, we will be developing the program iteratively. The benefit of the iterative approach is that each version of the program will produce immediate results, providing important feedback to determine the accuracy of the current iteration of the program. Because our first "real" project is relatively short, we will not use the preceding program, but instead start over as if this were a new project. The primary goal of this project is to illustrate how to apply the PDLC to a programming task. After we have followed the PDLC once through, we will consider the final program as our first iteration of the project. In the programming exercises at the end of this chapter, you may add enhancements to this project to create the next iteration(s).

4. Create a new project in Visual Basic by following these steps:

   a. Start a new project in Visual Basic.

   b. Practice placing controls on a form.

   c. Delete some controls from the form.

   d. End up with just one command button and one label on the form.

   e. Set the caption of the form to be Chapter 1, Problem 4 - <your name>.

   f. Set the caption of the command button to Make Visible.

   g. Set the caption of the label to Hi <your name>!!.

   h. Set the visible property of the label to false.

   i. Change the name of the form to frmCh1Try4, the name of the command button to cmdMakeVis, the name of the label to lblGreet.

   j. Double-click on the command button. You should now be in the code window in the *cmdMakeVis_Click* event procedure.

   k. Between the *Private Sub* and *End Sub* statements, type in the Visual Basic statement:

      lblGreet.Visible = True

   l. Save your form file under the name Ch1Try4form and your project file under the name Ch1Try4proj, both in a folder called Chap1 Hello 4.

   m. Run your program. When your program is running, you should be able to click on the *Make Visible* command button and the label that says Hi <your name>!! should appear.

5. Update the program created in exercise 4 by adding a command button called cmdHide with the caption Hide. Write the program code to change the Visible property of the label lblGreet to False. Run the program and alternate between pressing the *Make Visible* and *Hide* buttons. Describe the impact of this iteration of the program.

6. Create a new Visual Basic program that will display the contact information for your teacher or two of your friends when the corresponding button is pressed. In addition, the program will terminate when the *Exit* button is pressed. A sample form design is shown here. The only controls used are four command buttons and six labels (three with a fixed description and three that will change depending on whether the *Teacher* button, *Friend1* button, or *Friend2* button is pressed).

CHAPTER **2**

DATA TYPES, VARIABLES, AND ASSIGNMENT STATEMENTS

Introduction

The programming portion of the Visual Basic application development tool is based on the BASIC programming language, which has matured over the years into a full-featured, structured programming language. Visual Basic adds other features to the BASIC language to facilitate writing modern applications that use a wide variety of components and respond to events in a Windows environment. With this chapter, we start to write small programs to get a feel for the syntax of the Visual Basic language. A computer language, much like English or any other language, has certain rules for constructing statements. Syntax has to do with the structure of a statement, such as its grammar rules and punctuation rules. With English and other human communication languages, you can usually figure out what someone means, even if the grammar or punctuation rules are broken. With computer languages, on the other hand, the computer cannot understand your program unless you follow the strict syntax rules of the programming language.

One of the early concepts a programmer learns is to identify the various types of information that the program will be using. Your programs might use the price of a dozen oranges (in dollars and cents), an employee's name (a group of characters), or the number of payments needed to pay back a loan (a whole number), for example. It is considered good programming practice to identify the type of each value at the beginning of a program or block of code so that the computer can detect errors when erroneous data values are used. Unlike some languages such as Pascal and C, Visual Basic does not require this identification. In this book, however, we will explicitly declare all our data types to indicate our understanding of the data. Specifying the type of each item might seem like extra work, but the payoff for you is that the compiler can then perform additional error checking on your program.

51

When you develop your computer program, you will also have to distinguish between data that may change and those data items that will rarely, if ever, change. The number of hours a part-time employee works during each pay period may often change and is classified as a *variable*. If an hourly worker works more than 40 hours, however, the hourly rate must be multiplied by a factor of 1.5. These two numbers, 40 and 1.5, will rarely change and are classified as *constants*.

Objectives

After completing this chapter, you should be able to

@ Explain the difference between string and numeric literals and give examples in Visual Basic.

@ List several reasons why naming conventions in computer programs are desirable.

@ Identify the assignment operator in Visual Basic and construct statements to assign new values to component properties while the program is running.

@ Explain what is meant by string concatenation and give examples in Visual Basic.

@ Define what a comment is, and include comments in a Visual Basic program.

@ Categorize data items into appropriate data types.

@ Define the term variable.

@ Declare and use variables in an event procedure.

@ Declare and use symbolic constants.

@ List three important debugging tools available in Visual Basic and demonstrate how to use them.

@ Write and run small Visual Basic programs containing multiple controls and simple event procedures.

Programs and Program Statements

In general, a program is a set or sets of instructions (called *code*) for the computer to follow to complete a specific task. The overall structure of a Visual Basic program is greatly influenced by the design of the user interface. Each control placed on a form can respond to a variety of events. A text box, for example, can recognize when it gets the focus, when its contents change, when the user clicks in it, when the user double-clicks in it, and so on. If the program is supposed to do something in response to a particular event, the programmer must write a set of instructions, or Visual Basic statements, and put them in an event procedure.

Therefore, a Visual Basic program generally consists of one or more sections of code, called **event procedures**, each containing a set of Visual Basic program statements. When the program begins executing a section of code, the statements are generally executed in sequence, starting with the first statement and continuing until the end of the block of code.

As discussed in Chapter 1, "Introductory Programming Concepts and the Visual Basic Environment," you get into the code block for an event by double-clicking the control on the form or by clicking the View Code button in the Project Explorer window. In the Code window, you should notice two drop-down lists at the top of the window, labeled Object and Procedure. The Object list gives you access to the form and to each control, whereas the Procedure list gives you access to the corresponding events of the selected object. When you double-click the control or select an object from the Object list, Visual Basic automatically selects the object's default event and creates a skeletal event procedure in the Code window with the *Private Sub* line and *End Sub* line for that event procedure. It then puts the cursor between the two statements, because this is where you write the Visual Basic program statements telling the computer what to do when that event is triggered. Once in the Code window, if you want to write code for a different event of the same object, you can scroll through the Procedure list and select the desired event. Again, Visual Basic will create the skeletal procedure, and position the cursor so that you can type the program code.

As with most text editors, you can add as well as remove text in Visual Basic's Code window. To remove an empty skeletal procedure, for example, you can highlight it and press the Delete key. You can use the usual cut, copy, and paste editing to facilitate code writing. If you want to, you can also type the entire event procedure, including the Private Sub and End Sub lines, directly in the Code window. We recommend that you use one of the previously discussed methods that automatically create skeletal procedures, however.

After you type a program statement and move to another line, Visual Basic may adjust the appearance of the statement by adding or removing spaces as well as possibly changing the case of some words in the statement. Visual Basic is not case sensitive, which means you can use uppercase or lowercase letters in any combination for any predefined word or programmer-defined name, but Visual Basic automatically adjusts the capitalization for a particular name so that it is uniform throughout the program. You don't have to use any special punctuation to end a statement, as in some other languages. For better readability, each Visual Basic statement should be on its own line in the program.

Every Visual Basic statement contains some combination of the following:

- Keywords or reserved words
- Literals or symbolic constants
- Variables
- Operators or special symbols

Keywords

Keywords, also called **reserved words**, are words or symbols that Visual Basic recognizes as having some predefined meaning as part of the Visual Basic programming language. You have already seen several of these words, such as *Private*, *Sub*, and *End*. We will learn more of these words as we progress through the book. Many other words are used as property names of a form or of controls on the form. You should make a point of becoming familiar with these names as you write Visual Basic programs, by regularly reviewing the contents of the Properties window.

String Data Versus Numeric Data

Two major categories of values that a programmer works with are strings and numbers. A **string** is just a sequence of contiguous characters treated as a single data item, such as a name or an address. The string can even include numeric digits, because they are characters on the keyboard. String values are generally stored and later displayed again. Numbers, or **numeric** values, are frequently used in mathematical calculations, and are stored in a different format from strings to facilitate these computations. Identification codes that are entirely numeric, but will not be used in mathematical computations, would be considered string data rather than numeric data.

■ TIP

Use string data types when the data item will *not* be used in mathematical computations.

Literals or Constants

At some point, we might want to tell the user to "Click the button to continue." This phrase (sequence of characters) is called a **string literal**. If we want to multiply a price by the 5 percent tax rate, the number 0.05 is a **numeric literal**. **Literals** are specific values that we want to use in a program, often to set an initial value of something. Literals are sometimes referred to as **constants**, or literal constants. As just discussed, literals can be classified into two types: string and numeric. String literals are any sequence of characters surrounded by quotation marks. (The quotation marks are not actually part of the value of the string literal, but are necessary to indicate that the characters are being used as a string literal.) Examples of string literals include the following:

```
"(333) 444-5555"
"xxx-xx-xxxx"
"Enter your name"
"123"
"" ←  A zero-length string, an empty string
```

Notice that it is possible to have a zero-length string that contains no characters, not even a space.

What happens when your string of characters contains a quotation mark, like *Just say "No"*? Can you make it into a string literal? It turns out that you can. Just type two quotation marks in a row at the point where you want the quotation mark. Hence, the following string literal would include the quotation marks at the desired location:

`"Just say ""No"""` ←   *Use two quotation marks in a row to get one quotation mark in the string literal.*

Note the three quotation marks in a row at the end of the preceding example. The first two quotation marks will cause the quotation mark (") to display after the word *No*. The last quotation mark is the closing quotation mark for the string literal.

Numeric literals are used when you are working with numbers, especially if they are to be used to perform arithmetic calculations. Numeric literals contain some combination of the digits 0 to 9, and may contain one decimal point and/or a sign (+ or –) at the beginning. If the number is positive, the plus (+) sign is generally omitted. A numeric literal may not begin with a decimal point. Figure 2.1 illustrates some numbers that are valid numeric literals and also some that are not valid.

Valid	Not Valid	Reason Not Valid
21	(765)432-1111	Contains parentheses and dash
–308	492–	Negative sign at end
3.14159	2.11.13	Two decimal points
0.125	.06	Starts with decimal point
700000	$10,456.00	Contains $ and comma
700000.125	"424"	Contains quotation marks

Figure 2.1   *Examples of valid and invalid numeric literals.*

Naming Conventions

Most Visual Basic programs will contain a form, so you will place some or all of the program's controls or screen objects on the form (see Chapter 1) before writing the Visual Basic code. The form and each control make up the Graphical User Interface (GUI) with which the user interacts. Each GUI object has a Name property listed in the Properties window. The value of this Name property will be used in the Visual Basic code to identify which object is being used in that statement. Visual Basic assigns default names such as Text1, Text2, Text3, Command1, Command2, and so forth to each control as you place it on the form. Because these names aren't very descriptive, it becomes difficult to remember whether Text1 is for a person's last name, first name or a product ID, and whether the purpose of Command1 is to calculate, update, or clear something. Because of this, most programmers and computing departments develop naming standards to give meaningful names to various elements in a program.

Filename Conventions

The first naming convention that you should establish is for the filenames and form names. One suggestion is to decide on a name for the program (for example, Color Demo or Lab2 Prob3), and create a folder on your disk with this name. Also, put this name in the title bar of the project's main form, and use it as the form's name (minus spaces) in the Properties window, prefixed with *frm*. Some people like to include the word *Main* in the main form name in case there will be more than one form. Hence, the form's Name property could be *frmColorDemoMain*. Next, use a similar name as the filename for the main form file and project file (for example, when you save the form and project, name the files *ColorDemoMain*).

Control Name Conventions

Another important naming convention is for the control names or GUI objects on your form(s). In this book, we will start each control name with a three-letter abbreviation to indicate the type of the control, followed by a meaningful name to indicate its purpose. When you use a standard prefix on control names, it has the added advantage of causing the names for all controls of the same type to be together in the alphabetic listing of form controls in the drop-down list at the top of the Code window. It also prevents the control names from conflicting with other property names, variable names, or reserved words. Figure 2.2 contains a list of the four fundamental controls we use in this text and their recommended three-letter prefixes. The tear card at the front of this book contains a more complete list of standard prefixes for other commonly used controls. Using these prefixes, you might name two command buttons *cmdCalculate* and *cmdClear*, two labels *lblName* and *lblStreet*, and some text boxes *txtUserID*, *txtFirstName*, and *txtLastName*. Notice that the letters in the control names are all lowercase except for the first letter of each new word used in the name.

VB Control Type	Three-Letter Prefix
Command button	cmd
Form	frm
Label	lbl
Text box	txt

Figure 2.2 *Some Visual Basic controls and suggested naming prefixes.*

The "Dot" Notation

After you have assigned a name to a control, you can use this name whenever you want to refer to that control in your program. Instead of referring to the *whole* control, however, you almost always want to refer to *one particular property* of that control. The syntax to refer to a property is this:

```
controlname.propertyname
```

To refer to the Text property of a text box named *txtLastName*, for example, you would use *txtLastName.Text* in your program. Similarly, to refer to the Caption property of the label *lblAnswer*, you would use *lblAnswer.*Caption in your Visual Basic code. Because this notation represents a value of a particular property and not an action, you would only see this notation as part of a longer statement and not on a line by itself.

Besides properties, controls also have methods. **Methods** are predefined processes that the control knows how to perform. The same "dot" notation applies to methods:

```
controlname.methodname
```

Because a method denotes an action, it would appear on a line by itself, preceded by the optional word *Call.* When the computer reaches a statement of this form while running the program, the *method* would be executed. Later in this chapter, we will use the *Show* method of a form.

Assigning Property Values in Code

We learned in Chapter 1 how to set initial property values of the form or its controls using the Properties window. This works fine until we want the property value to change during program execution. In this case, we must type into our program a statement that *assigns* a new value to the property. We will use the **assignment statement** for this purpose. The assignment operator in Visual Basic is the equal sign (=). Think of the equal sign as meaning "gets assigned" or "receives." The general format of this kind of assignment statement is as follows:

```
controlname.propertyname = newvalue
```

You must substitute an actual *control name, property name*, and *new value*. The *new value* could be either a string or numeric literal, depending on the type of value expected by the property. Also *new value* could be another compatible property value, a variable (see the section titled "Variables" later in this chapter), or an expression that performs a calculation (see Chapter 3, "Arithmetic Operators and Scope"). The most important thing to remember is that the assignment goes from right to left. You could think of the equal sign as being a left-pointing arrow. During program execution, whatever is on the right of the assignment operator is evaluated to get its value, and that value is assigned to the item on the left. Or, stated another way, whatever is named to the left of the equal sign receives a new value.

Some examples of assignment statements include the following:

```
txtTitle.Text = "Mr." ←   "Text" is a string property.
txtName.Text = "" ←   Clears the text box by assigning an empty string.
frmMain.Left = 50 ←   "Left" is a numeric property.
lblName.Caption = txtName.Text
```

Now you can write a variety of simple programs using the assignment statement. Let's create a program that will enable the user to change the background color of a label.

A Practice Program

➤ Start a new project in Visual Basic.

➤ Save the new form and project files by clicking the disk icon on the toolbar. Create a Chapter 2 folder. Create a Traffic subfolder. Give the form file the name AssignDemo and the project file the name AssignDemo.

➤ Add two labels and three command buttons to the form as shown in Figure 2.3.

➤ Use the Properties window to do the following:

1. Set the name property of the form to frmAssignDemo, the labels to lblTitle and lblColor, and the buttons to cmdStop, cmdSlow, and cmdGo.

2. Change the caption of the form to Assignment Demo — by *<your name>*. Set the StartUpPosition property to 2-Center Screen.

3. Change the caption of the buttons to S&top, &Slow, and &Go, respectively.

4. Delete the caption of the top label (*lblTitle*) so that nothing shows on the form. (We will add code to place the words Traffic Color: on the form.)

5. Delete the caption of the large, square label (*lblColor*) so that nothing shows on the form. (We will add code to place the words TRAFFIC INSTRUCTION on the form.) Change this label's Alignment property to 2-Center and its Font to Bold, Size 12. Set the BorderStyle property of label *lblColors* to 1-Fixed Single.

➤ Create a *Form_Load* event for the form by double-clicking on the form. Type in the following assignment statements:

```
lblTitle.Caption = "Traffic Color:"
lblColor.Caption = "TRAFFIC INSTRUCTION"
```

When the preceding Visual Basic statements are executed, the words Traffic Color: will appear in the top label and the words TRAFFIC INSTRUC-TION will appear in the large, square label.

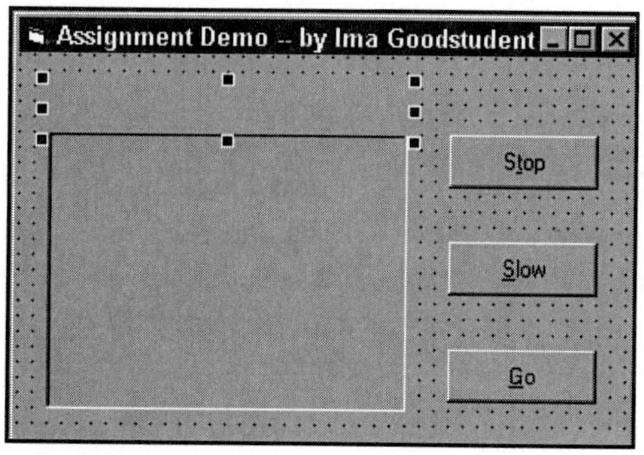

Figure 2.3   *Form layout for* Assignment Demo *program.*

➤ Create a *Click* event for *cmdStop* and type in the following assignment statements:

```
lblColor.BackColor = vbRed
lblColor.Caption = "STOP"
```

➤ Create a *Click* event for *cmdSlow* and type in the following assignment statements:

```
lblColor.BackColor = vbYellow
lblColor.Caption = "SLOW"
```

➤ Create a *Click* event for *cmdGo* and type in the following assignment statements:

```
lblColor.BackColor = vbGreen
lblColor.Caption = "GO"
```

➤ Save the changes to the project by clicking on the Save Project Toolbar button. Your Visual Basic code file should now look like that in Figure 2.4.

```
Option Explicit

Private Sub cmdGo_Click()
    lblColor.BackColor = vbGreen
    lblColor.Caption = "GO"
End Sub

Private Sub cmdSlow_Click()
    lblColor.BackColor = vbYellow
    lblColor.Caption = "SLOW"
End Sub

Private Sub cmdStop_Click()
    lblColor.BackColor = vbRed
    lblColor.Caption = "STOP"
End Sub

Private Sub Form_Load()
    lblTitle.Caption = "Traffic Color:"
    lblColor.Caption = "TRAFFIC INSTRUCTION"
End Sub
```

Figure 2.4   *Visual Basic code for* Assignment Demo *program.*

> Run the application by clicking the Run arrow on the toolbar. When the application's form appears, click the Stop button.

This causes the event procedure *cmdStop_Click* to begin executing (see Figure 2.5). The first assignment statement stores the value *vbRed* in the BackColor property of the label *lblColor*, changing the background color of the label to red. (The name "vbRed" is built in to Visual Basic to provide easy access to the numeric value of the red color). The second assignment statement makes the word STOP appear in the same label.

Can you predict what will happen if one of the other two buttons is clicked? Try it to see the actual results.

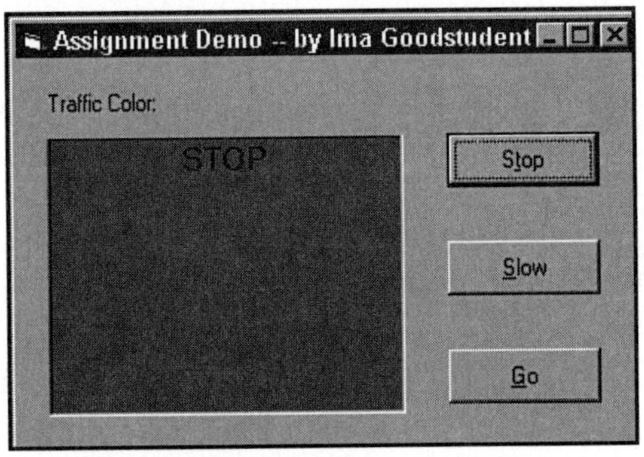

Figure 2.5   *Output after clicking the* Stop *button.*

String Concatenation

Concatenate means to link together in a series or chain. In a programming context, it means to join or connect two or more character strings into a single, longer, character string. Concatenation in Visual Basic is indicated by the "&" operator. For example "Jerry" & "Smith" would result in the string literal "JerrySmith". In this case, that is probably not the desired result. We would have to go back to the code and add a space after the *y* or before the *S* or add a separate string literal to get a space between the two names, as shown in the following three examples:

```
"Jerry " & "Smith"
"Jerry" & " Smith"
"Jerry" & " " & "Smith"
```

We could use string concatenation in the program example of the previous section to move the words in the large square label several lines down from the top.

> Modify your code for the *Stop* button with this statement:

```
lblColor.Caption = vbCrLf & vbCrLf & "STOP"
```

Each occurrence of *vbCrLf* represents a carriage return and line feed (equivalent to pressing the Return key on a typewriter). Two *vbCrLfs* concatenated together create two blank lines, which cause the word STOP to appear on the third line of the label. Run the program and click the *Stop* button to observe the effect of this concatenation.

➤ Make the same change to the code in the *Slow* and *Go* event procedures and test your changes. Don't forget to save these changes.

Concatenation is not restricted to string *literals*. Any strings can be combined together. You can concatenate a string literal and a string control property or two control properties that are strings. If there is a text box used for entering a person's last name (named *txtLast*), and a label named *lblGreet*, for example, a program might contain a statement such as this:

```
lblGreet.Caption = "Dear Mr. or Ms. " & txtLast.Text & ":"
```

We will use this statement in the next practice problem. The preceding statement could also be split into three statements that produce the same result:

```
lblGreet.Caption = "Dear Mr. or Ms. "
lblGreet.Caption = lblGreet.Caption & txtLast.Text
lblGreet.Caption = lblGreet.Caption & ":"
```

If you examine the second and third statements, you might wonder how a label could equal itself concatenated with additional characters. This goes back to our discussion of the assignment operator. You must remember that the equal sign does not mean "equality" in these statements. It stands for the process of getting the value on the right side of the equal sign and assigning it to the item on the left side.

You should be aware that early versions of Visual Basic used the plus sign (+) for concatenation of strings, and therefore the plus sign can still be used. We do not use it in this book, however, because the plus sign is also used to indicate addition of numbers. By using the ampersand (&), it is always clear that the intent is to concatenate strings.

Continuing Long Lines

If you are concatenating two or more lengthy string literals or property value names, the code statement may not fit on one line so that it can all be seen on the screen. You can continue a long statement to two or more lines by using the space and underscore (_) characters at the end of each line that will continue. A message to the winner of a new car might be coded like this, for example:

```
lblMessage.Caption = "Congratulations, " & txtFirstName.Text & _
                     ". You have just won a NEW CAR !!"
```

It is important that when you combine line continuation and string concatenation in the same statement, you close a partial string literal with a quotation mark or complete the name of an object before using the line continuation symbol. You cannot continue a line in the middle of a name or literal value.

Another Practice Program

➢ Start up a new project in Visual Basic and put a text box, two labels, and a button on the form. Name the form frmConcatDemo, the top label lblLastName, the text box txtLastName, the button cmdGreet, and the bottom label lblGreet.

➢ In the Properties window, set the captions of the form, the two labels, and the button, as shown in Figure 2.6. Clear the Text property of the text box. Change the Border Style of the bottom label to 1-Fixed Single and set the BackColor to gray. You could also change the Alignment or Font properties of the bottom label.

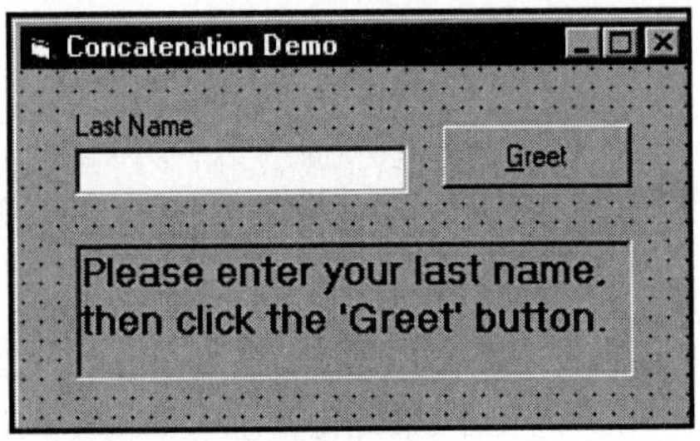

Figure 2.6 Concatenation Demo *form.*

➢ Create a *Click* event for the *Greet* button that changes the caption of the label to Dear Mr. or Ms. followed by the name that the user typed in the text box, as shown in Figure 2.7. This is the same line of code developed earlier in this section:

```
Option Explicit

Private Sub cmdGreet_Click()
    lblGreet.Caption = "Dear Mr. or Ms. " & txtLastName.Text & ":"
End Sub
```

Figure 2.7 *Contents of code window for* Concatenation Demo *program.*

➢ Save and run the program. Type in a last name and click the *Greet* button. Your screen should look like that of Figure 2.8. Type in a different last name and click the *Greet* button again. Then delete the contents of the text box and click the *Greet* button a third time.

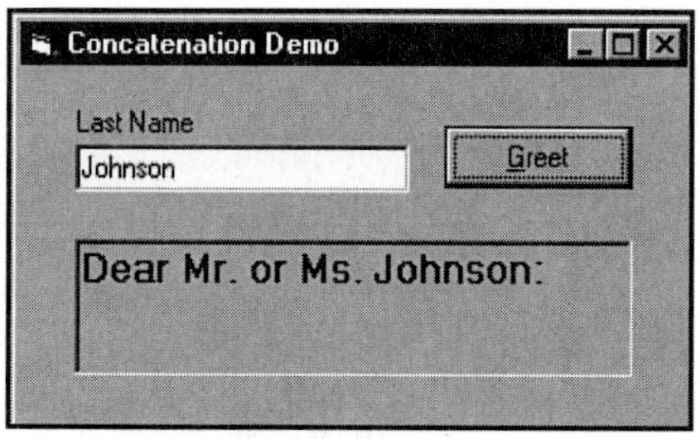

Figure 2.8 *Output after clicking the* Greet *button.*

Comments

Most of the program statements we discuss in this book are processed by the computer during program execution. Strange as it may seem, however, a programmer often wants to add lines to a program that the computer should ignore. **Comments**, or remarks, are words of explanation within a program that provide information for other programmers who need to use or update the program in the future. These comments frequently document the purpose of the program, give the name of the person who wrote or revised it, and say when it was written. A comment may also be used to clarify the purpose of a block of code within a larger program.

Various special characters, or **delimiters**, are used to indicate comment statements. In Visual Basic, comments begin with the apostrophe ('). Any characters to the right of an apostrophe will be interpreted as part of a comment, and will be ignored by the computer (unless the apostrophe is inside a string literal). Hence, the following could be comments in a Visual Basic program:

```
' Clear screen
```

or

```
' PURPOSE:     When the user clicks the Clear button, all text
              boxes and answer labels are erased
```

or

```
' PROGRAM:     Employee Registration Program
' PURPOSE:     This program will collect employee demographic data,
'              store it in employee files, and clear the screen
'              between employees.
' PROGRAMMER:  Ima Goodstudent
' DATE:        November 15, 1998
```

Comments can be placed almost anywhere within the code. We will commonly place comments at the top of the code file and before each event procedure (see Figure 2.9). The comment can also be on the same line as an executable statement, to clarify its purpose, as in the following line of code:

```
frmAssignDemo.BackColor = vbBlue      ' Set the form color to blue
```

■ TIP

Document each event procedure in your program with a comment statement indicating its purpose.

One helpful feature of the Visual Basic environment is its capability to display different types of statements in different colors or different font styles. When you type in a comment, for example, all the characters of the comment are likely to be green, the keywords may be blue, and the normal text black. If you watch carefully for the syntax highlighting, it can help you correct mistakes. Therefore, if you start a block of comment lines but forget to put the apostrophe at the beginning of one line, the letters won't turn green. If you think you are typing a keyword and it never turns blue, you know to check the spelling more carefully. You can change the font colors or styles used for syntax highlighting by selecting Options from the Tools menu, selecting the Editor Format tab, and selecting the colors and font desired for different types of code lines.

➤ Add a comment block to the beginning of the *Concatenation Demo* code file, and before the Private Sub line. Figure 2.9 shows one format for these comments. Your instructor or employer may develop his or her own standards that you should follow.

```
' Program:    Chapter 2: Concatenation Demo
' Form:       frmConcatDemo
' Programmer: John Miller
' Purpose:    Create a greeting that includes the provided name

Option Explicit

' Purpose:  When the Greet button is clicked, a greeting
'           including the name in the text box is concatenated
'           and displayed in the lower label.
Private Sub cmdGreet_Click()
    lblGreet.Caption = "Dear Mr. or Ms. " & txtLastName.Text & ":"
End Sub
```

Figure 2.9   *Contents of code window for* Concatenation Demo *program with comments added.*

Variables

Sometimes a program needs to remember a piece of information that will not be the same from one use of the program to another, or that changes while the program is running. If this is not a value that is being displayed on the form, the program can store it in memory. To help the programmer remember where the value is stored in memory, the programmer can designate a name for that memory location. This location in the computer's memory that has a programmer-given name is called a **variable**. Stored in that memory location is the value the program needs to remember. The programmer must decide on the name and also indicate what type of data will be stored in that memory location. The **data type** that the programmer selects affects how much memory is allocated for the variable and exactly how the value is represented in memory. Let's take a look at the fundamental types that are available.

Types of Data

The item entry form shown in Figure 2.10 could be used to input data for a parts order from an electronics distributor. The customer enters the part number and verifies that the description is correct and the unit price is competitive. After the quantity is entered, the program calculates the total price and displays it onscreen.

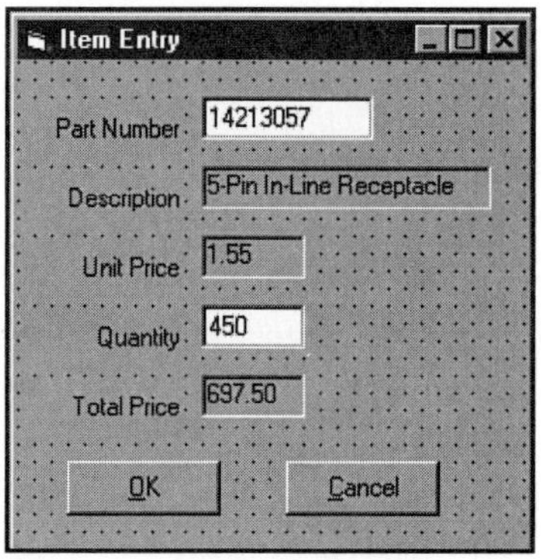

Figure 2.10   Item Entry *form containing different types of values.*

Three different types of data are represented on this form. The Description field can contain characters such as letters, spaces, dashes, and numbers and is classified as a string. The Unit Price and Quantity fields can only contain numeric characters and are likely to be used in arithmetic calculations, so they are classified as numeric. There is, however, one important distinction between the unit price and quantity data items: Quantity will never contain a decimal point. Another way of stating the same thing is to classify quantity as **integer** and total price as **real** or **floating point**. Figure 2.11 displays the basic classification scheme for data item types.

As shown in Figure 2.11, the final level of classification is whether the data item is a constant or a variable. If the value of a data item is known at design time, and the value will not change while the program is executing, this item is a constant. If the value of a data item changes as the program runs, or the value is not known until after the program begins execution, the data item is classified as a variable. To get some practice in classifying data items, you should examine carefully the examples in Figure 2.12.

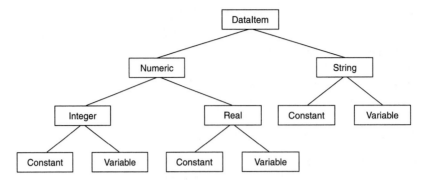

Figure 2.11 *Classification scheme for data items.*

Description	Sample Value	Integer	Real	String	Constant	Variable
Weight in kilograms	6.47		X			X
Social Security number	181–27–5446			X		X
Employee ID	111223456			X		X
Name of a month	July			X		X
Number of products sold	2500	X				X
Number of days in a week	7	X			X	
Name of first month of year	January			X	X	
Avogadro's number	6.023×10^{23}		X		X	
Pi	3.14159		X		X	

Figure 2.12 *Examples of classifying values.*

As you look at Figure 2.12, you may wonder why Employee ID is classified as type string. Remember the rule about using strings whenever a data item will not be used in a mathematical operation? In the case of Employee ID, it is unlikely that any arithmetic operations will be performed, and possible that string manipulations may be performed. If Employee ID is the person's Social Security number, for example, two hyphens or slashes are frequently inserted when the number is displayed. If it is stored as a string, this is easy to do. If it is stored as a number, it will first have to be converted to a string. Consequently, always use string when you know that you will not use a value in a mathematical computation.

Although Visual Basic has a number of different data types, in this textbook we will work primarily with four types of data—Long, Double, Currency, and String—that go along with the main classification types of Figure 2.11 (integer, real [non-monetary], real [monetary], and string).

Long

In Visual Basic, a Long type can store a *signed integer* in the range –2,147,483,648 to 2,147,483,647, where *signed* means that the number can be positive or negative. If you are wondering where this particular range of numbers comes from, it is derived from the fact that 1 bit of a 32-bit number is used to store the plus or minus sign along with the other 31 bits used to store the magnitude. Because the computer is still based on binary arithmetic, 2^{31} gives the maximum value of 2,147,483,648, but we must subtract one to allow for storing the zero value. A variable of type Long occupies 4 bytes of storage.

Double

Visual Basic has several different kinds of real data types, but we will use the Double type. A Double has a range of $\pm 4.9 \times 10^{-324}$ to $\pm 1.8 \times 10^{308}$, can contain 15–16 significant digits, is stored in 8 bytes of memory, and is generally used to store a numeric data item that has a fractional value. We will use a Double for any numeric item that can't be stored in a Long as well as for calculations with decimals. Note that a 10-digit figure representing the world's population or the annual income of a large corporation cannot be stored in a Long, but could be stored in a Double.

Round-Off Errors

Although the Double can be used to store very large and very small numbers, the use of a Double can introduce an element of imprecision or error into your calculations. This error is often referred to as **round-off error**. The error arises from the fact that a computer does arithmetic with binary numbers, so many decimal (base 10) numbers cannot be stored *exactly* in a Double data item. Storing a number as simple as 0.1 into a type Double variable introduces a small amount of error. Even though the error is small, if the variable is used repeatedly to perform a calculation, the error can propagate and become large enough to affect the calculation's result. The result shown in Figure 2.13 is from adding 0.125 to itself 10,000 times, and adding 0.100 to itself 10,000 times. Because 0.125 can be stored in a type Double exactly, the result of that calculation is exact, while a very small amount of error is apparent in the other calculation. If you use type Double when working with monetary calculations, you will sometimes have to take special precautions so that the results of your calculations are accurate to the nearest cent. Visual Basic has another type, Currency, that minimizes these problems.

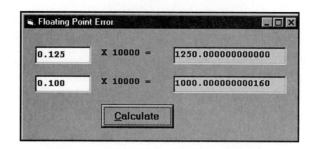

Figure 2.13 *Example of round-off error in a floating-point number.*

String

Visual Basic's String data type can be used to store any data value. The number of characters contained in a string is called its *length* and can be up to 2 billion characters long. Because both the length of a string and the characters that make up the string are stored, it is very easy for your program to determine the length of even a very long string.

In most programming languages, including Visual Basic, the program can perform operations on strings such as comparing strings to determine alphabetic order, joining strings (string concatenation), splitting strings, changing a string's case, and searching for the position of one string contained within another string. In some cases, due to Visual Basic's automatic type conversion, you can even perform arithmetic directly on strings; the programs we write, however, will first convert a number stored in a string to a number of type Long, Double, or Currency, and vice versa.

Figure 2.14 summarizes the characteristics of these fundamental data types used throughout the textbook. The values in the Range column describe the largest and smallest numbers that can be saved in a variable of that type.

Data Type	Range	Number Bytes	Comments
Long	−2,147,483,648 to 2,147,483,647	4	Cannot process fractional values
Double	$\pm 4.9 \times 10^{-324}$ to $\pm 1.8 \times 10^{308}$	8	15–16 significant digits
Currency	A scaled integer between −922,337, 203,685,477.5808 and 922,337, 203,685,477.5807	8	15 significant digits to the left of the decimal point and 4 digits to the right of the decimal (designed to minimize round-off errors with monetary data)

Data Type	Range	Number Bytes	Comments
String	Approximately 2 billion characters	1 per character	Additional overhead of 10 bytes per string

Figure 2.14 *Characteristics of four Visual Basic data types.*

Declaring and Using Variables

Remember that variables refer to a location in memory. Before a variable may be used, the program must declare a variable by specifying a name and a data type. Specifying the data type tells the computer how much space the variable needs. Specifying a descriptive name makes it easier to write and read the program because we don't have to know the numeric memory address. Because the useful lifetime of a program may be quite long, anything you can do to make your programs easier to understand is an important and worthwhile goal. In particular, the selection of variable names greatly affects your program's readability.

■■■ TIP
Always use meaningful names for variables and controls.

Choosing Names for Variables

Refer again to the item entry form of Figure 2.10 and assume that a variable is needed for each value displayed on the form. The labels on the form suggest a descriptive name for each variable. In addition, we must select names that fulfill Visual Basic's naming requirements (Figure 2.15) and follow standard naming guidelines (Figure 2.16).

Variable Names

1. Must not exceed 255 characters

2. Must begin with a letter

3. Cannot contain an embedded period, space, or type-declaration character

4. Must be unique

5. Are not case sensitive

6. Cannot be the same as a keyword

Figure 2.15 *Visual Basic rules for naming variables.*

Most of the naming rules are straightforward, but rules 3 and 5 need further discussion. Rule 3 refers to "type-declaration characters." These are special characters used in older versions of Visual Basic to indicate variable types. For example, #, $, %, &, @, and !.

Rule 5 says VB variable names "are *not* case sensitive." This means it doesn't matter whether you type a variable in capital letters, lowercase letters, or a mixture of upper- and lowercase. As long as it is spelled the same, it will be interpreted as the same variable name. Actually, it doesn't matter how you type it in after the first occurrence, because Visual Basic adjusts the capitalization in variable names to match the initial declaration.

Variable Names Should

1. Be meaningful and descriptive

2. Use consistent abbreviations for the same word

3. Use entire words or initial syllables

4. Use mixed case, with a capital letter at the start of each new word

---

Figure 2.16 *Standard guidelines for naming variables.*

Following these guidelines, we select PartNumber, Description, UnitPrice, Quantity, and TotalPrice as the variable names to go with our *Item Entry* example.

Choosing Data Types for Variables

Now we must assign a data type to each variable. Refer to Figures 2.11 and 2.14 to review the classification scheme and data types we are using in this textbook. To assign a data type, you should apply the rules listed in Figure 2.17.

- If the data item is not used in arithmetic operations, it is assigned type String.

- If the data item represents a monetary value, it is type Currency.

- If the data item has a fractional value, it is assigned type Double.

- If the data item is an integer that is in the range –2,147,483,648 to 2,147,483,647, it is assigned type Long.

- If the data item is an integer, but outside of the range –2,147,483,648 to 2,147,483,647, it is assigned type Double.

Figure 2.17 *Rules for selecting the data type for a variable.*

By applying these rules, we can decide on the names and data types for each of these data items. Figure 2.18 displays the results of our name and data type selections.

Variable Name	Type	Sample Value
PartNumber	String	14A213057
Description	String	5-Pin In-Line Receptacle
UnitPrice	Currency	1.55
Quantity	Long	450
TotalPrice	Currency	697.50

Figure 2.18   Item Entry *variable names and data types.*

Declaring Variables

Now that we know how to choose names and data types for variables, we must specify this information in the program by writing a set of instructions called **variable declarations**. The compiler will use this information to reserve storage for our variables and to check our program for errors in the code that uses these variables. Variable declarations are typically grouped together at the beginning of an event procedure, in statements that start with the keyword **Dim**, followed by the variable name, the keyword **As**, and a data type. The general format is this:

```
Dim VariableName As Type
```

The variable declarations for a particular procedure are inserted between the name of the procedure and the first executable statement. See Figure 2.19 for an example of how to declare the five variables listed in Figure 2.18.

```
Option Explicit

Private Sub cmdOK_Click()
    Dim PartNumber   As String
    Dim Description  As String
    Dim UnitPrice    As Currency
    Dim Quantity     As Long
    Dim TotalPrice   As Currency

End Sub
```

Figure 2.19   *Declaring variables for an event procedure.*

Adding Option Explicit

When we include *Option Explicit* in our programs, all variables *must* be declared before they can be used. This is beneficial, because if you misspell a variable name, the compiler will inform you if the misspelled name doesn't appear in a *Dim* statement.

If you want Visual Basic to automatically include this statement at the beginning of every program, select Options in the Tools menu and check *Require Variable Declaration* on the Editor page (see Figure 2.20). From now on, Visual Basic will automatically put the *Option Explicit* statement at the beginning of every new program file.

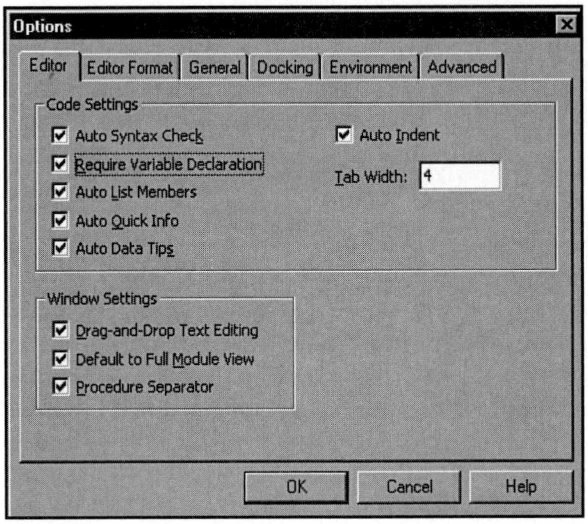

Figure 2.20 *Automatic insertion of* Option Explicit *in new Visual Basic program files.*

Using Variables in Assignment Statements

Variables are often used in assignment statements along with control properties and literals. If the program needs to assign a value to a variable, the variable will appear on the left side of the assignment statement:

```
variable = new value
```

The first time a variable is used it should always appear on the left side of an assignment statement to *receive* its initial value. Later it can also appear on the right side of an assignment statement, if the program needs to *use* its value. Let's add a variable to the *Assignment Demo* program of Figures 2.3 and 2.4.

Adding a Variable to Our Practice Program

➢ Using Windows Explorer, make a new folder named Traffic v2 and copy the Traffic folder contents into it.

➢ View the contents of the Traffic v2 folder and double-click on the *AssignDemo* project file. (This will load Visual Basic and open the *AssignDemo* program in the new folder.)

➤ Change the code in the three command button click event procedures to declare a variable and use it in assignment statements, as shown in Figure 2.21.

➤ Add comments to the beginning of the file and before each event procedure.

```
' Program:    Chapter 2: Assignment Demo -- Version 2
' Form:       frmAssignDemo
' Programmer: Ima Goodstudent
' Purpose:    Show the colors used in a traffic light.
Option Explicit

' Purpose: When the Go button is clicked, the color of the large
'          label is set to green, and the word GO is assigned to it
Private Sub cmdGo_Click()
    Dim LightColor As Long    ' Color of traffic light

    LightColor = vbGreen
    lblColor.BackColor = LightColor
    lblColor.Caption = vbCrLf & vbCrLf & "GO"
End Sub

' Purpose: When the Slow button is clicked, the color of the large
'          label is set to yellow, and the word SLOW is assigned to it
Private Sub cmdSlow_Click()
    Dim LightColor As Long    ' Color of traffic light

    LightColor = vbYellow
    lblColor.BackColor = LightColor
    lblColor.Caption = vbCrLf & vbCrLf & "SLOW"
End Sub

' Purpose: When the Stop button is clicked, the color of the large
'          label is set to red, and the word STOP is assigned to it
Private Sub cmdStop_Click()
    Dim LightColor As Long    ' Color of traffic light

    LightColor = vbRed
    lblColor.BackColor = LightColor
    lblColor.Caption = vbCrLf & vbCrLf & "STOP"
End Sub

' Purpose: When the program first begins the initial words are
'          assigned to the labels
Private Sub Form_Load()
    lblTitle.Caption = "Traffic Color:"
    lblColor.Caption = vbCrLf & vbCrLf & "TRAFFIC INSTRUCTION"
End Sub
```

Variable declarations

Figure 2.21   *Using a variable in the* Go, Slow, *and* Stop *click procedures.*

➤ Run the application by clicking the Run arrow.

When the form appears, click the button labeled *Stop*. The *cmdStop_Click* event procedure shown in Figure 2.21 begins execution. The first assignment statement stores the value *vbRed* in the variable *LightColor*. The second statement changes the background color of the label *lblColor* to red by copying the value stored in *LightColor* to the BackColor property of the label, and the third assignment statement makes the word *Stop* appear in the same label. Adding a variable to this program makes absolutely no difference in how this program works from the user's point of view.

A variable such as *LightColor* that is declared inside a procedure does not exist until the procedure begins execution, and no longer exists after the procedure has finished execution. We happened to use the same variable name in the other click event procedures, but in each case, we are likely using a different memory location that is assigned when the procedure begins executing and is freed up when the procedure terminates. We will discuss this topic in greater detail when we discuss scope in Chapter 3. When the memory location is initially allocated, a numeric variable has the value zero, and a string variable contains an empty string. Not all languages guarantee initial values of variables like this, so it is a good practice to include statements in your program to set the initial value of variables. Note in Figure 2.21 that variable *LightColor* appears on the left side of the assignment operator before it appears on the right side.

The expression on the right side of the assignment operator can only be assigned to the variable on the left if the data types are compatible. You can't assign a string of characters to a numeric variable, and you can't assign numeric expressions to string variables. Therefore, it would neither make sense nor be valid to have the statement

```
LightColor = "Blue"
```

because "Blue" is type String and *LightColor* is type Long. Another example is somewhat subtle. What happens if you try to assign a floating-point number to a type Long variable? Consider the following code fragment:

```
Dim Result As Long
Result = 4.23
```

If you try to run a program that contains these statements, it will end up with the value 4 in the *Result* variable. Try this with other values like 5.8, 3.5, and 8.5 to see what happens. You should avoid assigning real numbers to a variable with an integer data type (Integer or Long) so that you don't get unexpected rounding or truncating of numbers.

Swapping Values

One task that occurs from time to time in computer programs is the need to exchange two values. Suppose we have two text boxes (*txtName1* and *txtName2*) on a form, and the program needs to exchange the values in the two boxes when the *Exchange* button is clicked (see Figure 2.22).

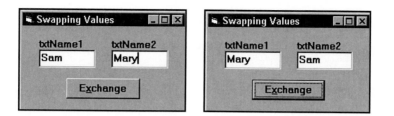

Figure 2.22 Swap Names *program, before and after clicking the* Exchange *button.*

In our initial attempt to code this, we might come up with the following:

```
Option Explicit

Private Sub cmdSwap_Click()
    txtName2.Text = txtName1.Text        ' First statement
    txtName1.Text = txtName2.Text        ' Second statement
End Sub
```

Figure 2.23 shows what results from running this version of the program. Notice that the same name ends up in both boxes. Can you explain why it doesn't work correctly?

Figure 2.23 *Erroneous* Swap *program, before and after clicking the* Exchange *button.*

The explanation lies in considering each statement separately, but in the given sequence. The first statement

```
txtName2.Text = txtName1.Text
```

takes the current contents of txtName1 (Sam) and assigns it to txtName2.Text. At this point, txtName1 has not been changed, so both txtName1 and txtName2 contain the same name (Sam). The second statement

```
txtName1.Text = txtName2.Text
```

takes the current contents of txtName2, which is now Sam, and assigns it to txtName1, so again, both text boxes still have the same name (Sam) in them. The original value in txtName2 was lost as a result of the first assignment statement.

The solution is to define a temporary variable to remember the original value of txtName2. After declaring a string variable called TempName and using it in the program, our code now looks like this:

```
Option Explicit

Private Sub cmdSwap_Click()
    Dim TempName As String

    TempName = txtName2.Text        ' First statement
    txtName2.Text = txtName1.Text   ' Second statement
    txtName1.Text = TempName        ' Third statement
End Sub
```

Figure 2.24 tracks the value of each variable or property value as the event procedure executes.

VB Statement	TempName	txtName1	txtName2
At start of procedure		Sam	Mary
TempName = txtName2.Text	**Mary**	Sam	Mary
TxtName2.Text = txtName1.Text	Mary	Sam	**Sam**
TxtName1.Text = TempName	Mary	**Mary**	Sam

Figure 2.24 Swap *program with temporary variable, results after executing each statement.*

Other Data Types

With the fundamental data types previously discussed, you can write a wide variety of programs of increasing complexity. At some point, you will want to incorporate additional data types that serve specific purposes or conserve memory. The table in Figure 2.25 lists most of the data types available in Visual Basic, and compares the memory requirements and types of values they can store. The Boolean data type will be discussed in Chapter 5, "Decisions and Data Validation," and Date will be used as needed in particular program examples and exercises.

Data Type	Storage Requirements	Range/Precision
Boolean	2 bytes	True or False
Byte	1 byte	0 to 255
Integer	2 bytes	–32,768 to 32,767
Long	4 bytes	–2 billion to +2 billion
Single	4 bytes	Wide range of floating-point numbers, 7 digits precision

Data Type	Storage Requirements	Range/Precision
Double	8 bytes	Wide range of floating-point numbers, 15 digits precision
Currency	8 bytes	Accuracy to 15 digits left of decimal and 4 digits right of decimal
Date	8 bytes	Stores dates and times
String	10 bytes +	Up to 2 billion characters string length
Variant	At least 16 bytes, varies	Can contain any kind of data

Figure 2.25 *Common data types in Visual Basic.*

Symbolic Constants

A **symbolic constant**, or **named constant**, is a name that can be used in place of a literal value. Although constants do not change during the execution of a program, occasionally some constants may need to be changed because of changes in company procedures or changes in tax laws. The name of a department and the overtime multiplier of 1.5 are both examples of items that are constant during the execution of a program, but might have to be changed at some time in the future. Unfortunately, it is quite a chore, and it is easy to make errors when existing programs are searched on a line-by-line basis for all occurrences of a particular literal value. If a labor union negotiated a change in the overtime multiplier from 1.5 to 1.75, for example, all programs that might possibly contain the overtime multiplier would have to be searched. It might seem that all that is needed is to use an editor, perform a global search for 1.5, and replace each value of 1.5 with 1.75. But this method is not safe and error free—certain programs may use 1.5 in equations that have no connection with the overtime multiplier 1.5 and should not be changed to 1.75.

Many programming languages, including Visual Basic, enable the programmer to associate (declare) a name with a constant expression similar to the way you associate a name with a variable. By using this feature, you could assign the name *OvertimeFactor* to the constant 1.5. Then, instead of "hard-coding" 1.5 in every program statement that uses the overtime factor, you would use the name *OvertimeFactor*. If you need to change the *OvertimeFactor* from 1.5 to 1.75, you would only have to make the change at the one place where *OvertimeFactor* is defined, and all the computations would then use the updated value of 1.75. Even if the value is unlikely to change, symbolic constants also provide meaningful names for literal values so that the program's code is self-documenting. We have already seen several examples that are provided by Visual Basic, including *vbRed*, *vbGreen*, *vbLf*, and *vbCrLf*.

Like variables, symbolic constants must be declared. Constant declarations follow the reserved word **Const**, and the general format of the declaration is as follows:

```
Const name As type = value
```

You must substitute a meaningful *name*, an appropriate *type*, and a *value* into the constant declaration. (The "As *type*" clause is optional, but we will always include it in this text to help remind us what data types we are using.)

Many programmers adopt a standard to precede constant names with the letter *c* to remind them that the name is for a constant value, and not a variable. Generally all the constant declarations are kept together at the top of the Code window to facilitate making changes in the future. Figure 2.26 shows two constants declared at the top of the Code window. You should compare Figure 2.21 with Figure 2.26. The procedures are equivalent, except the one in Figure 2.26 uses two constants.

➤ Make a Traffic v3 folder and copy the Traffic v2 folder into it.

➤ Open the project file in this new folder and make the changes in your program, as shown in Figure 2.26.

➤ Run the program to confirm that the two programs do indeed act alike.

You should note that the two constants, *cStartTitle* and *cStartInstr*, in Figure 2.26 are not variables, and the compiler will issue an error message if you insert the statement

```
cStartInstr = "STOP"
```

in the *cmdStop_Click* procedure.

In large projects where the same constants might be used in several different files, it is customary to group these "system-wide" constants together into a separate code file.

```
' Program:    Chapter 2: Assignment Demo — Version 3
' Form:       frmAssignDemo
' Programmer: Ima Goodstudent
' Purpose:    Show the colors used in a traffic light
Option Explicit                                    ┌─────────────────────┐
                                                   │ Constant declarations │
Const cStartTitle As String = "Traffic Colors:" ◄──┘
Const cStartInstr As String = vbCrLf & vbCrLf & "TRAFFIC INSTRUCTIONS"

' Purpose: When the Go button is clicked, the color of the large
'          label is set to green, and the word GO is assigned to it
Private Sub cmdGo_Click()
    Dim LightColor As Long    ' Color of traffic light

    LightColor = vbGreen
    lblColor.BackColor = LightColor
    lblColor.Caption = vbCrLf & vbCrLf & "GO"
End Sub

' Purpose: When the Slow button is clicked, the color of the large
'          label is set to yellow, and the word SLOW is assigned to it
Private Sub cmdSlow_Click()
    Dim LightColor As Long    ' Color of traffic light

    LightColor = vbYellow
    lblColor.BackColor = LightColor
    lblColor.Caption = vbCrLf & vbCrLf & "SLOW"
End Sub

' Purpose: When the Stop button is clicked, the color of the large
'          label is set to red, and the word STOP is assigned to it
Private Sub cmdStop_Click()
    Dim LightColor As Long    ' Color of traffic light

    LightColor = vbRed
    lblColor.BackColor = LightColor
    lblColor.Caption = vbCrLf & vbCrLf & "STOP"
End Sub

' Purpose: When the program first begins the initial words are
'          assigned to the labels
Private Sub Form_Load()                        ┌──────────────────────┐
    lblTitle.Caption = cStartTitle             │ Constants used in code │
    lblColor.Caption = cStartInstr ◄───────────┘
End Sub
```

Figure 2.26   *Using symbolic constants in* AssignDemo *program.*

Ending a Program—When the User Wants to Quit

Think about other Windows applications that you have used. How do you typically stop the program from executing? Your response might include the following:

- Click the Close button in the upper-right corner of the window.
- Select Close from the System menu.
- Select Exit from the File menu.
- Click an Exit or Quit button.

As you have started to work with Visual Basic, you have seen that the Close button and the System menu are built in to the Visual Basic form, so the user can end any Visual Basic program that you write using these two features. Most likely, you will also want to provide an Exit button (or menu option). That means you must write some code for the click event of the button that will end the program. What events are triggered when the user clicks the Close button? Let's try the Help in Visual Basic.

➤ Choose Index from the Help menu (the Index tab should be selected), and type in close. Look up some of the selections. None of them apply to our question. Sometimes you have to try more than one word before you find what you are looking for.

➤ Type closing, select closing forms, and click the Display button.

You should see the information shown in Figure 2.27. This information mentions a *QueryUnload* event and an **Unload** event that both occur when a form closes.

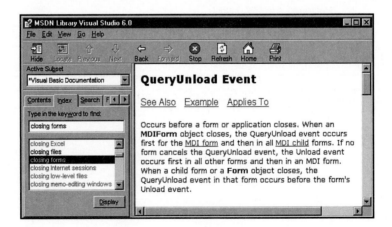

Figure 2.27   *Looking up "closing forms" in VB Help.*

➤ Click on the word Example in this Help screen.

One of the statements in the example uses the word *Unload* in an exit click event with a comment that this exits the application. That's what we're looking for!

➤ Replace closing forms in the keyword text box with the word unload. Notice that there is an *Unload* event and an *Unload* statement. Look at the Help information for both of these.

The Help file tells us that the *Unload* event can be triggered by the *Unload* statement. Hence the code for our *Exit* or *Quit* button click events will consist of one statement:

```
Unload formname
```

Of course, you must substitute the actual name of the form for *formname*.

Debugging Tools and Techniques

As you continue to write more complex programs, you will inevitably make mistakes in the code you write. **Debugging** is the process of finding and correcting these program defects. The errors in a program can be classified as follows:

- Syntax errors
- Run Time errors
- Logic errors

Incorrectly constructed code statements cause **syntax errors**. These statements may contain grammar errors, punctuation errors, or misused reserved words. The compiler is designed to locate syntax errors and display error messages. The messages try to inform you of the type and location of the error, with varying degrees of success. Do not rely on the compiler to find all your typing errors, because sometimes the compiler finds a way to interpret an erroneous statement in a manner totally different from what you intended.

Run Time errors occur in statements that are legally constructed, but that try to perform an illegal operation during program execution. A common example is an arithmetic equation that tries to divide by zero. Most Run Time errors are actually a form of logic errors.

Logic errors cause a program to produce incorrect results or fail to perform in the manner intended. The computer cannot read the programmer's mind; therefore if a program says to make a label blue when it should be green, the computer will go ahead and make it blue. In this case, it will be a very easy mistake to notice, because the user will see the bad color when the program is running. Someone will still need to determine which statement is wrong and correct it, however. This may be a quick process if the program consists of only a few event procedures that each contain one or two lines of code. In longer programs, however, you might never locate the problem by just looking at the code. It is even more frustrating when the program doesn't produce *any* output, and gives no error message.

Two traditional approaches to debugging are to perform a **code review** and to insert additional statements in the code. In addition, Visual Basic offers a number of powerful debugging tools to assist you in the process of tracking down the location of errors. These debugging tools are integrated into Visual Basic, enabling you to debug a program without leaving the development environment.

You should learn to use the following six debugging skills:

- Performing code reviews
- Displaying intermediate results
- Setting breakpoints
- Watching variables
- Viewing data tips
- Executing a single line at a time

Perform Code Reviews

Often the best place to start when your program has an error is with a newly printed copy of your code and a copy of the logic design or problem statement. Go through the code line by line, comparing it with the logic design or problem statement to make sure you have not left any statements out, or put them in the wrong order. If you are unsure of the logic, use actual values and pretend you are the computer. Perform each statement in the proper order to see whether you would get the correct answer. Next check that you have declared all variables in the proper place and of the correct type. As we learn more statements, other items can be added to this checklist. Code reviews are sometimes called **code walkthroughs**.

Display Intermediate Results

If you are writing a lot of new code, or your program gives no useful output, it can be extremely helpful to insert extra statements that display a short message, display the new value of a variable, or display the result of an intermediate calculation. Visual Basic gives you more than one way to do this. You could add an extra label to the form, or use the *MsgBox* function to display a message. Let's create a simple program to practice using an extra label and the *MsgBox* function for this purpose. The form in Figure 2.28 has three buttons (*cmdCalc*, *cmdClear*, and *cmdExit*) and two text boxes (*txtInput1* and *txtInput2*) for the program's intended processing. It also has one extra label (*lblStatus*) for intermediate status messages.

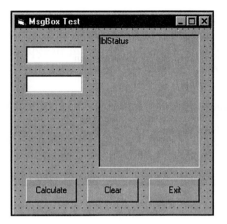

Figure 2.28 *Test form for displaying intermediate messages.*

In preparation for possible problems when coding and debugging this program, the programmer has used the *MsgBox* function at the start of the *Click* event procedure of each button and in the *GotFocus* event procedure of each text box. (The *GotFocus* event is triggered each time the focus is put on that control, either by tabbing to it or clicking on it.) Another statement at the end of each procedure adds a message to the large label. For now, we won't worry about inserting the code for the actual processing of the program. The code for each event procedure is given in Figure 2.29. The *vbLf* constant causes the linefeed character to be concatenated onto the label so that each entry in the label goes to a new line. Run the program, click on each text box and button, and watch the sequence of messages from the *MsgBox* function and in the status label.

```
Option Explicit

Private Sub cmdCalc_Click()
    Call MsgBox("Just started Calculate click")
    ' actual code goes here
    lblStatus.Caption = lblStatus.Caption & "End of cmdCalc_Click " _
        & vbLf
End Sub

Private Sub cmdClear_Click()
    Call MsgBox("Just started Clear click")
    ' actual code goes here
    lblStatus.Caption = lblStatus.Caption & "End of cmdClear_Click " _
        & vbLf
End Sub

Private Sub cmdExit_Click()
    Call MsgBox("Just started Exit click")
    ' actual code goes here
    lblStatus.Caption = lblStatus.Caption & "End of cmdExit_Click " _
        & vbLf
End Sub
```

continues

Watch Variables

When your program pauses at a breakpoint, you may want to check whether certain variables contain the correct value at that moment in execution. Visual Basic enables you to put variables and other values in a **Watch window**, which shows each variable name selected, and its current value (Figure 2.33). To add variables to the Watch window, follow these steps:

1. Click somewhere within the variable name.

2. Click the right mouse button.

3. Select Add Watch.

4. Click the OK button.

Watches			
Expression	Value	Type	Context
👓 LightColor	<Out of context>	Empty	frmAssignDemo.cmdGo_Click

Figure 2.33   *A Watch window with the variable* LightColor *from* cmdGo_Click.

You can add variables to the Watch window before or during program execution. Because variables declared within a procedure do not exist in memory until the procedure is executing, those variables will have an <Out of context> message next to them until the procedure where they are defined is executing. If you want to see the values of the variables in the Watch window during program execution, you will need to put a breakpoint in the procedure where the variable is defined. In Figure 2.34, we put a breakpoint in the *cmdGo_Click* event procedure. In the Watch window, you can see that the numeric value stored in variable *LightColor* for the color green is 65280.

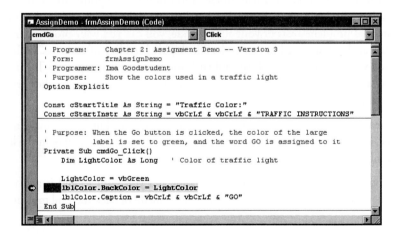

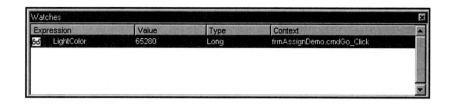

Figure 2.34 *Program stops at breakpoint. New value of* LightColor *in Watch window.*

Viewing Data Tips

When the computer is in Break mode, you can take advantage of a handy, built-in debugging aid that requires no more work than positioning the mouse over specific code. When you pause while your cursor is over a variable, a small Data Tips window appears displaying the current value of the variable. In Figure 2.35, the cursor is positioned over the variable *LightColor*.

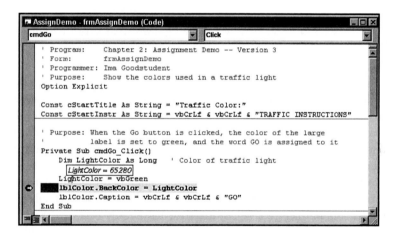

Figure 2.35 *Viewing a data tip.*

Execute a Single Line at a Time

When you reach a section of code that might contain an error, it is often useful to single-step through the code. **Single-stepping** means that you successively ask the computer to execute one line of code. After executing that one line of code, the next line is highlighted, but execution pauses so that you can check variable values. If all is okay, you can then cause another line of code to execute. Visual Basic calls this the *Step Into* command, which you access by pressing F8 or by selecting Step Into from the Debug menu. In Figure 2.36, the user clicked the Go button, the program stopped at the breakpoint, and the user pressed F8 twice. The line of code with the arrow to its left will be executed next.

When the user wants to close the Benefits form so that the screen isn't so cluttered, the *Unload* statement discussed earlier can be used:

```
Unload frmBenefits
```

Let's try this in a very simple example.

➢ Start a new project in Visual Basic.

➢ Put a label and a button on the form.

➢ In the Properties window, follow these steps:

1. Name the form frmMain and the button cmdShowSecond.

2. Set the caption of the form to Two Forms Demo -- Main Form.

3. Set the caption of the label to MAIN FORM, the Alignment to 2-Center, and the color to Yellow.

4. Set the caption of the button to Display Second Form.

➢ Add a second form to the project (click the Add Form button on the toolbar).

➢ Add a label and a button to this new form.

1. Name this form frmSecond and the button cmdCloseSecond.

2. Set the caption of the form to Two Forms Demo -- Second Form.

3. Set the caption of the button to Close Second Form.

Figure 2.37 *Forms for the* Two Forms Demo *program.*

➢ Click the Save Project button on the toolbar, select the desired disk drive and directory, and then type in SecondForm for the filename (you are naming the second form's file) and click OK. Next type in MainForm for the filename (you are naming the file for the first form) and click OK. Finally, type in TwoFormDemo as the filename of the project.

➢ On the main form (frmMain), add the Show statement to the *cmdShowSecond_Click* event, as shown in Figure 2.38:

```
Private Sub cmdShowSecond_Click()
    Call frmSecond.Show
End Sub
```

Figure 2.38   *Code for main form of the* Two Forms Demo *program.*

➤ On the second form (frmSecond), add the Unload statement to the *cmdCloseSecond_Click* event, as shown in Figure 2.39:

```
Private Sub cmdCloseSecond_Click()
    Unload frmSecond
End Sub
```

Figure 2.39   *Code for second form of the* Two Forms Demo *program.*

➤ Save the project, run the application, and click the buttons.

Notice that if both forms are showing, and you close the main form, you still must close the second form. Usually when you close the main form of a project, it should take care of all the details of exiting from the project. Therefore, we will unload the second form when the main form closes.

➤ Add a *Form_Unload* event procedure to the main form, containing an *Unload* statement. Add comments to each file and procedure. The finished result should look similar to Figures 2.40 and 2.41.

```
' Program:   Chapter 2: Two Forms Demo
' Form:      frmMain
' Programmer: Ima Goodstudent
' Purpose:   This program lets the user switch to the 2nd form
Option Explicit

' Purpose: When the Display Second Form button is clicked,
'          the second form becomes visible.
Private Sub cmdShowSecond_Click()
    Call frmSecond.Show
End Sub

' Purpose:  When the user closes this form, the second form is also
'           unloaded from memory, thus ending the application
Private Sub Form_Unload(Cancel As Integer)
    Unload frmSecond
End Sub
```

Figure 2.40   *Finished code for main form of the* Two Forms Demo *program.*

```
' Program:    Chapter 2: Two Forms Demo
' Form:       frmSecond
' Purpose:    This form lets the user switch back to the main
'             form or end the program
Option Explicit

' Purpose:  When the Close Second Form button is clicked, the second
'           form is unloaded from memory.
Private Sub cmdCloseSecond_Click()
    Unload frmSecond
End Sub
```

Figure 2.41 *Finished code for second form of the* Two Forms Demo *program.*

Modal Dialog Boxes

A second form is often used when the user has requested an action that requires additional input to complete the task. This is called a **dialog box**, which is generally *modal* in nature. A form is *modal* when the user must close it before being able to perform any other action within that same application. In Visual Basic, for example, when you go to the File menu and select Print, a Print dialog box appears and you must close that dialog box before you can do anything else in Visual Basic. When a modal form is shown, the other forms are usually not hidden.

To show a modal form in Visual Basic, use the *Show* method with the *vbModal* option, as follows:

```
Call frmOptions.Show(vbModal)
```

The dialog box form should then be unloaded when the user has finished interacting with it.

Identifying Events

We have now learned about several of the fundamental concepts and statements in programming. The programmer must learn to recognize when and where these statements should be used in a program. We have previously stated that Visual Basic is an *event-driven* language. When the program runs, the user sees a form that most likely contains several controls. The user makes the decisions whether to type in a text box or click on a button, and in which order to do this. So the user's actions will control, to a large extent, what happens next in the program. After that action has been completed, control returns back to the form. Therefore, your program is continually waiting for the next user action. When an action (or event) occurs, such as clicking on a button, the program executes any code for that event. Hence, a Visual Basic program consists of many separate blocks of code, called *event procedures*, that execute when a particular event occurs. Each control has multiple events it *can* respond to, but the programmer decides which events it *will* respond to based on the desired behavior of the program. The programmer needs to visualize how the user will interact with the program, and then identify appropriate events for which to write code.

The form itself has a number of common events, such as *Load, Unload,* and *Activate.* The *Activate* event occurs when the form becomes the active window. The default event of the form is the *Load* event. It occurs when the form is loaded into memory. Often the form is loaded into memory once, early in the program's execution, but it may become visible or active multiple times. Hence, actions that should be performed only once would be placed under the *Load* event, but actions that should occur every time the form is active would be placed under the *Activate* event. Some methods, such as *SetFocus,* can't be called while the form is loading, but can be called during the *Activate* event. The *Unload* event occurs when the form is being removed from memory, which often occurs at the end of the program. Hence, this event may contain statements that are to execute as the program ends. Many programs have more than one way that they can be ended. They may have an Exit button, for example, an Exit item on a menu, and even the System menu's *Close* command. Because all these will unload the form, any additional "wrap-up" code can be written one time in the form's *Unload* event, but it will be executed no matter which way the user ends the program.

Each control on the form has multiple events defined. Text boxes, for example, can respond to more than 20 events. The default event of a text box is the *Change* event. This occurs when the value in the text box changes. Deleting the contents of the box or typing an additional character can cause the change. The change can be as the result of a user action or an assignment statement in the program. One problem with the *Change* event is that it is triggered for each character changed. If the user is typing in a 20-character name, the *Change* event is triggered 20 times. A text box also has a *GotFocus* event that occurs when the text box first receives the focus, and a *LostFocus* event that occurs when the focus leaves the text box and moves to another control.

With all these events available, the programmer must take time to think about the purpose and consequences of each event, and select the best ones for the project at hand.

Customized Letter Case Study

In this chapter, we have discussed the basic structure of Visual Basic coding statements, and learned how to declare variables, assign values to variables and to properties of controls, concatenate string values, execute methods of a control, and include multiple forms in a project. We will now apply many of these new concepts in an exercise to input information about a potential client and send that client an advertising letter.

The XYZ Corporation manages marketing campaigns for a number of companies. They frequently get names and addresses of potential clients, and mail customized letters to these people. Now they would like a program that enables them to input a client's name and address, and then use this information to personalize a letter to that person. The letter should first appear on the screen so that the user can verify the name and address and decide whether to print the letter. Because untrained employees will likely use this program, it should also have a Help screen with instructions. The first campaign is for a travel company. The letter that they envision sending would look like this:

```
                            XYZ Corp.
                      1234 Buena Vista Blvd.
                      Good City, FL  56789

          Ms. Jolene Jurss
          555 Rolling Hills Ln.
          Sylva, NC  80808

          Dear Ms. Jurss,

          Congratulations!  I have just drawn the name
          Jolene Jurss as the WINNER OF A CRUISE.
          To claim your prize, call 1-800-777-9999 now.

          Jolene, I await your call.


          Fred Jippum
          Manager
```

Step 1: Analyze the Problem

The final product of this program is a personalized letter. It must be properly formatted with the company's name and address at the top, followed by the client's name and address, a greeting using the client's name, and the letter body containing the client's name in two places. This letter needs to appear on both the screen and the printer. Because the client's name will change from one letter to the next, the program needs a way to input the person's title, first name, last name, street, city, state, and zip code. The program needs to know when the user finishes typing the inputs and is ready for the letter to be assembled. The user also needs a way to indicate whether to print the letter, whether to start a new client, or whether to exit the program. It may be helpful to list this information in an organized manner, as shown in Figure 2.42.

Input Needs	Processing Needs	Output Needs
Client's name	Create the letter	Customized letter on
■ Title	■ Copy name to letter	screen, containing
■ First name	■ Copy address to	■ Client's name
■ Last name	letter	■ Client's address
Client's address	■ Combine name with	Printed letter
■ Street	letter body	Instructions on
■ City	Print the letter	screen
■ State	Start a new client	
■ Zip code	Display instructions	
	Exit program	

Figure 2.42 *Analysis Table of problem inputs, processing, and outputs.*

Step 2: Design and Create the User Interface

This program could be viewed as having three major tasks: displaying instructions, inputting the client data, and displaying the letter. Our initial design decision is to put the instructions on a separate form. We have previously discussed three Visual Basic controls that can handle the input (text box), processing (command button), and output (label) needs of a simple program. Using these controls, let's complete the Analysis Table by matching an appropriate control with each need (see Figure 2.43).

	Input Needs	Processing Needs	Output Needs
Main Form	Text box and descriptive label for each of the following: ■ Client's title ■ First name ■ Last name ■ Street ■ City ■ State ■ Zip code	Five command buttons to ■ Create the letter ■ Print the letter ■ Clear the screen ■ Display instructions ■ Exit the program	Large label to contain the letter
Help Form		One command button to hide the Help form	One or more labels to contain the instructions

Figure 2.43 *Analysis Table containing controls required for* Marketing Letter *program.*

We now place the controls on the forms in a neatly organized layout and show it to the user for approval (see Figures 2.44 and 2.45). As you do this, be sure to give each control a meaningful name, following the naming standards discussed previously.

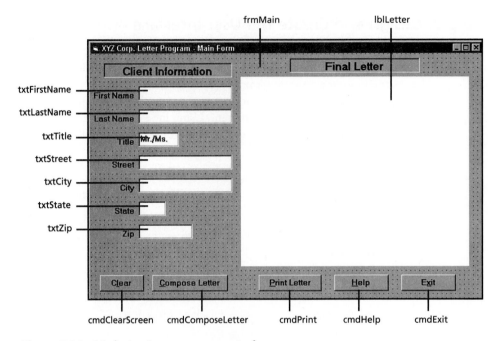

Figure 2.44 Marketing Letter *program, main form.*

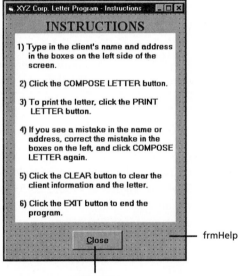

Figure 2.45 Marketing Letter *program, Help form.*

Step 3: Design the Logic for the Program

Now we need to start identifying the events that will trigger some processing in this program. Because the purpose of putting a command button on a form is for the user to click on it, and there are six buttons on the forms of this program, we can expect to have six button click event procedures. But controls have multiple events they can respond to, so we must identify whether the program will react to any other events. This program has both an Exit button and the System menu on the main form, for example, so we must remember that the user has two ways to end the program.

Step 3a: Design the Macro View (Object-Event Diagrams)

Because each event is associated with a particular control on the forms, we could start by listing all the controls and deciding whether there is an associated event. This can be done in a list format, table format (see Figure 2.46), or in an Object-Event Diagram (see Figure 2.47). For now, we will keep the program simple and only have click events for each button and the *Form_Unload* event.

Control	Event
MAIN FORM	Form_Unload
Labels	None
Text boxes	None
Clear button	Click
Compose Letter button	Click
Print Letter button	Click
Help button	Click
Exit button	Click
HELP FORM	
Large label	None
Close button	Click

Figure 2.46   *Event-planning table.*

continues

97

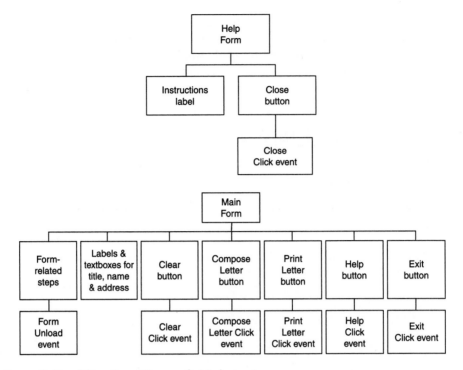

Figure 2.47   *Object-Event Diagrams for* Marketing Letter *program.*

Step 3b: Design the Micro-Level View (Flowcharts or Pseudocode)

Now we must plan what processing is to take place when each event occurs. We identified seven separate events, so we must plan the logic for each of these. This can be depicted with either a flowchart or pseudocode for each event. Figure 2.48 shows both for your comparison. The main form has six events. The *Form_Unload* event occurs when the user clicks on the *Close* button or selects Close from the System menu. This will cause the main form to close automatically, but if the Help form was previously viewed by the user, it will still be loaded into memory even though it is invisible. Therefore, this event procedure unloads the Help form from memory.

The *Clear* click event occurs when the user clicks on the *Clear* button. This procedure clears all the text boxes and the letter label (the title defaults to Mr./Ms.). The goal of the *Compose Letter* click event is to assemble the entire letter in a correct format. It includes the company's name and address, the client's name and address, and the body of the letter. The client's name and address is obtained from the text boxes and concatenated in the appropriate places with the other words.

The main purpose of the *Print Letter* click event is to print the letter. As you work with Visual Basic, it is often a good idea to find out the capabilities of the controls you are using. In this case, it is the label that contains the letter. Looking up the label in Help does not yield any applicable methods, but the label is on the form.

If we look at the methods of the Form object in Help, we find one called *PrintForm* that sends the form image to the printer. So here is one easy way for us to get something printed in Visual Basic. Applying a little additional ingenuity, we can make the other controls on the form invisible so that they won't print. This is left as an exercise.

The only action of the *Help* click event is to display the Help form. (The main form stays visible.) The *Exit* click event ends the program, which means both forms may need to be unloaded from memory. The only event on the Help form is the *Close* button click event, which hides the Help form but leaves it in memory, in case the user wants to view it again.

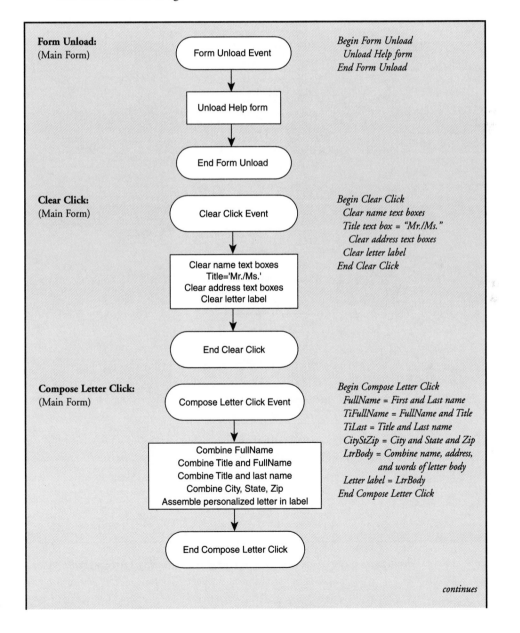

Form Unload:
(Main Form)

Form Unload Event

Unload Help form

End Form Unload

Begin Form Unload
Unload Help form
End Form Unload

Clear Click:
(Main Form)

Clear Click Event

Clear name text boxes
Title='Mr./Ms.'
Clear address text boxes
Clear letter label

End Clear Click

Begin Clear Click
  Clear name text boxes
  Title text box = "Mr./Ms."
    Clear address text boxes
    Clear letter label
End Clear Click

Compose Letter Click:
(Main Form)

Compose Letter Click Event

Combine FullName
Combine Title and FullName
Combine Title and last name
Combine City, State, Zip
Assemble personalized letter in label

End Compose Letter Click

Begin Compose Letter Click
  FullName = First and Last name
  TiFullName = FullName and Title
  TiLast = Title and Last name
  CityStZip = City and State and Zip
  LtrBody = Combine name, address,
        and words of letter body
  Letter label = LtrBody
End Compose Letter Click

continues

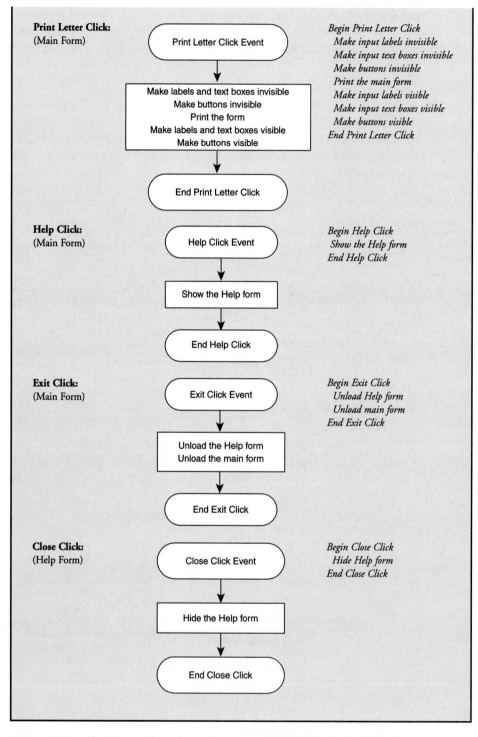

Print Letter Click:
(Main Form)

Print Letter Click Event

Make labels and text boxes invisible
Make buttons invisible
Print the form
Make labels and text boxes visible
Make buttons visible

End Print Letter Click

Begin Print Letter Click
Make input labels invisible
Make input text boxes invisible
Make buttons invisible
Print the main form
Make input labels visible
Make input text boxes visible
Make buttons visible
End Print Letter Click

Help Click:
(Main Form)

Help Click Event

Show the Help form

End Help Click

Begin Help Click
Show the Help form
End Help Click

Exit Click:
(Main Form)

Exit Click Event

Unload the Help form
Unload the main form

End Exit Click

Begin Exit Click
Unload Help form
Unload main form
End Exit Click

Close Click:
(Help Form)

Close Click Event

Hide the Help form

End Close Click

Begin Close Click
Hide Help form
End Close Click

Figure 2.48 *Flowcharts and pseudocode for each module of the* Marketing Letter *program.*

Step 3c: Develop a Test Plan (Table of Input with Sample Results)

After developing the logic for all the events, we are now thoroughly familiar with what this program should be able to do. This is a good time to develop a written test plan that will help later to confirm that our program works correctly. We should be sure to try each button in different orders, and enter names and addresses of differing lengths. The following is a list of test cases that we decide to use:

1. **Press the *Help* button.**

   Both the main form and the Help form are visible.

2. **Click the *Exit* button on the main form.**

   Both forms are unloaded and the program ends.

3. **Run the program again. Press the *Help* button.**

   Both the main form and the Help form are visible.

4. **Enter Joe, Doe, Mr., 15 Elm St., Boston, MA, 10203 in the text boxes of the main form and click *Compose Letter*.**

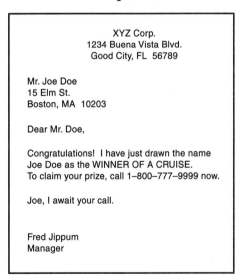

```
                    XYZ Corp.
                1234 Buena Vista Blvd.
                 Good City, FL  56789

Mr. Joe Doe
15 Elm St.
Boston, MA  10203


Dear Mr. Doe,


Congratulations!  I have just drawn the name
Joe Doe as the WINNER OF A CRUISE.
To claim your prize, call 1–800–777–9999 now.


Joe, I await your call.


Fred Jippum
Manager
```

5. Change the first name to Jon. Click the *Compose Letter* button.

XYZ Corp.
1234 Buena Vista Blvd.
Good City, FL 56789

Mr. Jon Doe
15 Elm St.
Boston, MA 10203

Dear Mr. Doe,

Congratulations! I have just drawn the name
Jon Doe as the WINNER OF A CRUISE.
To claim your prize, call 1–800–777–9999 now.

Jon, I await your call.

Fred Jippum
Manager

6. Press the *Print Letter* button.

The preceding letter, and surrounding space from the form, prints to the printer.

7. Press the *Clear* button.

The text boxes and letter label clear (the title says Mr./Ms.).

8. Press the *Close* button on the Help form.

The Help form is no longer visible.

9. Click the window's *Close* button in the upper-right corner of the form.

The program ends.

Step 4: Code the Program

After the logic has been designed for some or all modules, you can begin coding the program. It is often easier to code and test a program in small sections. You might code the *Help* button click event and test it, and then code the *Exit* button and test it. The *Form_Unload* (main form) and *Close* click (Help form) events would be good candidates to code next and test. Then code the *Clear* click event, run the program, type something in the text boxes, and click the *Clear* button. With relatively little coding, you now have five of the seven events coded and tested. Finally, code and test the *Compose Letter* click and the *Print Letter* click events. Don't forget to use meaningful names and to add comments to each event procedure. Code for the entire program, complete with comments, can be found in Figures 2.49 and 2.50.

```
' Program:    Chapter 2: Marketing Letter
' Form:       frmMain
' Uses forms: frmHelp
' Programmer: Ima Goodstudent
' Purpose:    Lets the user input client information, compose a letter
'             and print the letter if desired
Option Explicit

' Purpose: When the Clear button is clicked, the text boxes are cleared
'          (title is set to "Mr./Ms."), and the letter label is cleared
Private Sub cmdClearScreen_Click()
    txtFirstName.Text = ""
    txtLastName.Text = ""
    txtTitle.Text = "Mr./Ms."
    txtStreet.Text = ""
    txtCity.Text = ""
    txtState.Text = ""
    txtZip.Text = ""
    lblLetter.Caption = ""
End Sub


' Purpose: When the Compose Letter button is clicked, the contents of
'          the text boxes are used to assemble a personalized letter
Private Sub cmdComposeLetter_Click()
    Dim FullName   As String      ' Full name — first and last
    Dim TiFullName As String      ' Title and full name
    Dim TiLast     As String      ' Title and last name
    Dim CityStZip  As String      ' City, state and zip
    Dim LtrBody    As String      ' contents of letter

    FullName = txtFirstName.Text & " " & txtLastName.Text
    TiFullName = txtTitle.Text & " " & FullName
    TiLast = txtTitle.Text & " " & txtLastName.Text
    CityStZip = txtCity.Text & ", " & txtState.Text & "  " _
        & txtZip.Text
    LtrBody = ""
    LtrBody = LtrBody & "                    XYZ Corp." & vbLf
    LtrBody = LtrBody _
        & "              1234 Buena Vista Blvd." & vbLf
    LtrBody = LtrBody _
        & "              Good City, FL  56789" & vbLf & vbLf
    LtrBody = LtrBody & "   " & TiFullName & vbLf
    LtrBody = LtrBody & "   " & txtStreet.Text & vbLf
    LtrBody = LtrBody & "   " & CityStZip & vbLf & vbLf
    LtrBody = LtrBody & "   Dear " & TiLast & "," & vbLf & vbLf
    LtrBody = LtrBody & "   Congratulations!  I have just drawn the " _
        & "name " & vbLf
    LtrBody = LtrBody & "   " & FullName & " as the WINNER OF A " _
        & "CRUISE." & vbLf
    LtrBody = LtrBody & "   To claim your prize, call 1-800-777-9999" _
        & " now." & vbLf & vbLf
    LtrBody = LtrBody & "   " & txtFirstName.Text _
        & ", I await your call." & vbLf & vbLf & vbLf
    LtrBody = LtrBody & "   Fred Jippum" & vbLf
    LtrBody = LtrBody & "   Manager" & vbLf
    lblLetter.Caption = LtrBody
End Sub


' Purpose: When the Exit button is clicked, both forms are unloaded
'          from memory to end the program
Private Sub cmdExit_Click()
```

continues

```
        Unload frmMain       ' triggers Form Unload which unloads frmHelp
    End Sub

    ' Purpose: When the Help button is clicked, the Help form becomes
    '          visible
    Private Sub cmdHelp_Click()
        frmHelp.Show
    End Sub

    ' Purpose: When the Print Letter button is clicked, the labels, text
    '          boxes and buttons become invisible, the form is printed
    '          using the PrintForm method, and the controls are made
    '          visible again.
    Private Sub cmdPrint_Click()
        '    Make non-letter controls invisible
        PrintForm     ' Print the form with only the letter showing.
        '    Make non-letter controls visible again.
    End Sub

    ' Purpose: When the Close button in the upper-right corner of the form
    '          is clicked, the Help form is unloaded from memory to end the
    '          program.
    Private Sub Form_Unload(Cancel As Integer)
        Unload frmHelp
    End Sub
```

Figure 2.49   *Code for the* Marketing Letter *program, main form.*

```
    ' Form:    frmHelp
    ' Purpose: This form contains the instructions for the Marketing
    '          Letter program and a Close button.
    Option Explicit

    ' Purpose: When the Close button is clicked, the form is unloaded.
    Private Sub cmdCloseHelp_Click()
        Unload frmHelp
    End Sub
```

Figure 2.50   *Code for the* Marketing Letter *Program, Help form.*

Step 5: Test and Debug the Program

As suggested in step 4, coding and testing can be performed over and over on small segments of a program. After the entire program is coded, however, it is still important to test the final system, using the test plan that was created earlier. The outputs of the program should be carefully compared to the expected outputs to make sure that no problems exist.

1. Press the *Help* button.

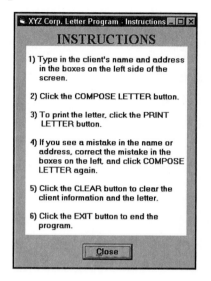

2. Click the *Exit* button on the main form.

   Both forms are unloaded and the program ends.

3. Run the program again. Press the *Help* button.

   Both the main form and the Help form are visible.

4. Enter Joe, Doe, Mr., 15 Elm St., Boston, MA, 10203 in the text boxes of
   the main form and click *Compose Letter.*

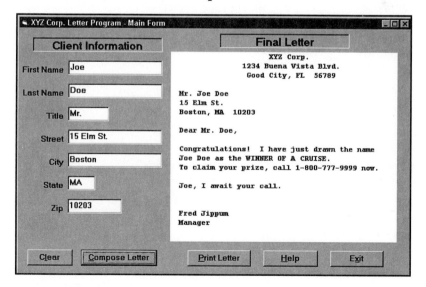

5. **Change the first name to Jon. Press the *Compose Letter* button.**

```
XYZ Corp. Letter Program - Main Form                           _ □ ✕

       Client Information              |        Final Letter
                                       |          XYZ Corp.
First Name  Jon                        |      1234 Buena Vista Blvd.
                                       |        Good City, FL   56789
 Last Name  Doe
                                           Mr. Jon Doe
     Title  Mr.                            15 Elm St.
                                           Boston, MA  10203
    Street  15 Elm St.
                                           Dear Mr. Doe,
      City  Boston
                                           Congratulations!  I have just drawn the name
     State  MA                             Jon Doe as the WINNER OF A CRUISE.
                                           To claim your prize, call 1-800-777-9999 now.
       Zip  10203
                                           Jon, I await your call.


                                           Fred Jippum
                                           Manager


     Clear    Compose Letter        Print Letter      Help         Exit
```

6. **Press the *Print Letter* button.**

   The preceding letter prints to the printer.

7. **Press the *Clear* button.**

```
XYZ Corp. Letter Program - Main Form                           _ □ ✕

       Client Information              |        Final Letter

First Name

 Last Name

     Title  Mr./Ms.

    Street

      City

     State

       Zip


     Clear    Compose Letter        Print Letter      Help         Exit
```

8. **Press the *Close* button on the Help form.**

   The Help form is no longer visible.

9. **Click the window's *Close* button in the upper-right corner of the form.**

   The program ends.

Step 6: Assemble the Final Documentation

Now that we have confirmed, to the best of our ability, that the program operates correctly, we can collect copies of our project documentation and place them in a notebook, and/or make them available online for people who will work with this program in the future. We have the Analysis Table, user interface, Object-Event Diagrams, flowcharts or pseudocode, test plan, code listings, and sample outputs that could all be included in the final documentation.

Summary

In this chapter, we started learning how to construct programming statements to create simple programs in Visual Basic. In general, a computer program consists of a sequence (or sequences) of *statements*. In an event-driven environment like Visual Basic, each event will have its own sequence of statements. Each program statement contains some combination of keywords, constants, variables, and special symbols. *Keywords* already have a meaning in the given programming language and must be used in the correct manner.

Constants are specific values that do not change during program execution. They may be represented in a program as a *numeric* or *string literal* (for example, 2.783 or "123 Main Street") or as a *symbolic constant*, defined in a *Const* declaration. *Variables* are named locations in memory used by the program to remember values during program execution. The purpose of using variables is to provide a way to store values that are likely to change during program execution. Variables must be declared in a *Dim* statement, where they are given a name and a type. Each type of data is stored in a different format. If you store data as one type and then try to use it as another type, you may get a type mismatch error. The four variable types primarily used in this book are String, Long, Currency, and Double.

We learned about several *special symbols* in this chapter, including the apostrophe that starts comments, the dot (period) used between a control name and a property name, the ampersand sign to indicate concatenation, the equal operator for assignment statements, and the underscore to continue long lines. *Comments* are statements that the computer ignores. They are for the benefit of programmers, and contain explanation or identification information for the program. The *dot notation* is used every time a program needs to work with values of a property of a control. The dot separates the control's name from the property's name (for example, *lblBlue.Caption*). *Concatenation* means the joining together of two (or more) strings into one longer string.

Assignment statements use the = operator to assign values to a variable or a property of a component. The assignment statement works from right to left, meaning that whatever is named to the left of the = will receive, or be set to, the value on the right.

The errors in a program can be classified as *syntax errors, Run Time errors,* and *logic errors.* Logic errors are the most difficult to find, so modern programming environments provide several tools to help programmers find defects in their code while the program is running. Four tools discussed in this chapter are *using breakpoints, watching variable values, viewing data tips,* and *single-stepping* through a section of code. *Breakpoints* mark stopping points in the code's execution. In addition, the programmer can carefully review, or *walkthrough,* the code by hand, or can add additional statements to display intermediate results or messages.

Large Windows programs may contain more than one form. This is readily implemented in Visual Basic by using the *Show* and *Unload statement* methods to control which form is visible. When a user requests an action that requires additional input, a Windows program often displays a dialog box in *modal* form, meaning that the dialog box must be closed before the user can perform actions in any other window of the project.

Key Terms

assignment statement	Dim *xxx* As *yyy*	real
Break mode	event procedures	reserved words
breakpoints	floating point	round-off error
code review	integer	Run Time errors
code walkthroughs	keywords	single-stepping
comments	literals	string
concatenate	logic errors	string literal
Const	methods	symbolic constant
constants	modal	syntax errors
data type	modeless	Unload
debugging	named constant	variable
delimiters	numeric	variable declarations
dialog box	numeric literal	Watch window

Test Your Understanding

1. What is the basic difference between string and numeric data?

2. What naming standard is suggested for controls that you place on a form?

3. Using the dot notation, how would your program refer to the BackColor property of label *lblAnswer*? What VB statement would cause your program to execute the *SetFocus* method of text box *txtCustName*?

4. What is the assignment operator in Visual Basic?

5. What statement assigns your name to the label *lblUserName*?

6. What character in Visual Basic indicates the start of a comment?

7. Write a Visual Basic statement that concatenates the contents in the text box *txtSize* with the characters *feet* and puts the result in label *lblAnswer*.

8. In Visual Basic, how do you continue a long statement on another line?

9. In Visual Basic, how do you declare a variable in an event procedure?

10. What are three rules for naming variables?

11. What statements declare *UserName* and *UserAge* to be variables of appropriate types? What statements store *Mary* and *21* in the variables *UserName* and *UserAge*, respectively?

12. What are two advantages of using symbolic constants in a program?

13. List five different techniques that could be used to locate a defect in a program.

14. If a telephone number, including area code, is stored without parentheses or dashes and has no decimal point, why can't it be stored in a variable of type Long?

15. Suppose you get an error message when you run your program. You set three breakpoints inside a certain procedure of the program, at lines 4, 12 and 20. When you run the program, you get the error message after clicking the Run button three times. What conclusion could you draw about the location of the error in the code?

16. When you run a program and it stops at a breakpoint, has it executed the line that is highlighted?

17. Give an example of a modal form in a common application such as Microsoft Word or Excel.

18. Write a more complete test plan for the case study program of this chapter. (For example, try longer names or street addresses, and buttons in different orders.)

Programming Exercises

1. Start up Visual Basic. Find and list five properties of a label.

2. Using Help:

   Look up the events of a text box. Describe five of them.
   List five methods of a command button.

Look up the Debug menu commands in Help.
Find out how to remove all breakpoints that are set.
Look up Dialog Boxes and select purpose in the Help index.
Summarize what it tells you about dialog boxes.

3. Create a form as shown below with six labels for name, phone, campus address, lecture and lab time, and interests. The form also has three buttons along the bottom. Give each label and button a meaningful name.

Write code for each button. Clicking the *Display* button should cause the program to display your name, and other information in the six labels as shown below. Clicking on *Hide* should cause it to look like the original form again, and clicking on *Quit* should cause the project to quit running. Save the project (CH2Ex3.frm and CH2Ex3.vbp), then run the program. Test the buttons in different orders. (Try clicking the *Display* button twice in a row.)

4. For the end-of-chapter *Marketing Letter* program, modify the *Print* click event to hide (make invisible) all controls on the form except the letter, and then make them visible again after the form is printed.

TRY A NEW CONTROL—Place two *frames* on the main form, one for all the input labels and text boxes, and the other for the command buttons.

Cut and paste the controls onto the frames (if you just drag the controls onto the frames they aren't made part of the frame). Then modify the *Print* button to make the two frames invisible, then visible, instead of making each separate control invisible, then visible.

5. Create a program that has a label that initially says GREETINGS !! and two buttons, one with the caption Formal and one with the caption Informal. Write code for each button that changes the label to Good day. How are you? or Hey dude. What's up?, respectively.

6. Create a program that has a label that says COLOR TEST and two buttons, one with the caption YELLOW and one with the caption BLUE. Pressing a button changes the label's back color to the corresponding color.

7. TRY A NEW CONTROL—Create a program that has a label that says Pick a color and three option buttons, one with the caption Green, one with the caption Yellow and one with the caption Blue. Clicking any option button changes the form to the corresponding color, as shown here.

8. TRY A NEW CONTROL—Create a program that has three command buttons and a frame. Place three shape objects inside the frame and pick the circle shape for each, as shown below. When the user clicks *Go,* the lower circle turns green. When the user clicks *Clear,* the middle circle turns yellow. When the user clicks *Stop,* the top circle turns red. Only one circle is colored at a time.

9. Create a form with three text boxes that are empty, as shown here. Code a *GotFocus* event for each text box that makes the background color of that text box yellow. Code a *LostFocus* event for each text box that makes the background color of that text box white. In other words, when the program runs, the text box with the focus will be yellow and the other two text boxes will be white.

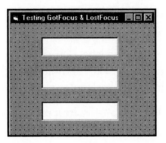

10. Create a program that has two labels that initially say HI and BYE, and a button that says SWITCH. Write code for the button click event that switches the locations of the words HI and BYE each time the button is clicked. Use a variable.

11. Create a program that has three labels that initially say Which came first?, the chicken, and the egg, and a button that says Change. Write code for the button click event that exchanges the locations of the words the chicken and the egg each time the button is clicked. Use a variable to store the word that is in one of the labels.

12. Write a program that has a form with two fixed labels, a text box, a large output label, and two buttons (see form image below). Name each component appropriately. Initially the text box and big label are empty. The user can type something into the text box. When the *Add New Text* button is pressed, the program concatenates the contents of the text box onto the end of the text in the large label and clears the text box. When the *Clear Contents* button is pressed, it clears the contents of the big label and the text box.

13. *About* forms—Most commercial applications have an About form accessed from the Help menu. The About form identifies the application with information such as the application name, author, copyrights, and version number. Add a button that says About, and add an About form to the end-of-chapter case study. Show the About form as a modal form when the user clicks the *About* button.

ARITHMETIC OPERATORS AND SCOPE

Introduction

Now that you have learned how to create, build, and execute simple Visual Basic programs, we can turn our attention to how to combine variables and constants in statements to perform mathematical calculations. We will also look at situations where a data item is used in only one portion of a program and situations where more than one event procedure needs access to the same data item. The extent to which other portions of your program can access a particular data item is determined by the data item's scope. This chapter teaches you the rules that Visual Basic uses to decide the scope of a data item.

Objectives

After working through this chapter, you should be able to:

- Convert between data types.
- Understand and use the arithmetic operators +, −, *, /, \, and Mod.
- Understand and use operator precedence.
- Distinguish between local, form, and global scope.
- Know and apply the basics of good coding style.

Data Conversion

As you write Windows programs, you often need to get information from the user and display answers or information to the user. When the user supplies information by typing at the keyboard, the information is frequently accessed through some property of a control on the form. When your program displays information, you will again use a control to display the information. In Chapter 1, "Introductory Programming Concepts and the Visual Basic Environment," you learned that a text box control is typically used to get information entered by the user via the keyboard, and a label control is typically used to display results to the user. Appendix A, "Visual Basic User Interface Objects," describes other controls that can also be used for input or output purposes.

In all the components just mentioned, the information displayed on the form, whether typed by the user or displayed by your program, is stored as a string in a property of the control. Information such as an address, part description, or name can be copied directly from the control to a string variable by using the assignment **operator**. The assignment operator can also be used to display new information on the screen by copying the contents of a string variable to one of the components previously mentioned. In Figure 3.1, the first assignment statement is an example of using the assignment operator to copy a String value from the Text property of a text box control to a String variable. The last assignment statement illustrates a copy in the opposite direction.

```
Dim TempName As String

TempName = txtFirst1.Text
txtFirst1.Text = txtFirst2.Text
txtFirst2.Text = TempName
```

Figure 3.1 *Assigning strings.*

The situation is somewhat more complicated when the information you want to display is stored in a numeric variable, because the information must be converted from its numeric form to a string before it can be displayed. Similarly, if the information that has been entered at the keyboard is numeric characters, it must be converted from string to numeric form before it can be stored in a numeric variable. If you try to perform arithmetic operations such as addition, subtraction, multiplication, and division using values that are in string form, it turns out that Visual Basic will sometimes try to do the conversions for you. Because this may have unexpected results, it is good programming practice to explicitly convert numeric data entered by the user from a string to numeric form before carrying out the arithmetic operation.

 TIP
Document your code by explicitly converting between data types.

Visual Basic has several type conversion **functions** that you can use to convert from one data type to another. We discuss functions in greater detail in a later chapter, but for now it is enough to know that a function is quite similar to the event procedures that you have already used. There are, however, two important differences:

- A function is activated, or *called*, by using the name of the function in an expression. An event procedure is activated by the occurrence of an event.

- A function returns a value back to the expression that called the function, and that value can then be used in a calculation or can be assigned to a variable or property.

String to Numeric Conversion

We will use several **type conversion functions,** shown in Figure 3.2, to convert numbers from string type to numeric type.

Function	Return Type	Rounds?
CCur	Currency	No
CDbl	Double	No
CInt	Integer	Yes
CLng	Long	Yes

Figure 3.2   *String to numeric conversion functions.*

These functions assume that the string passed to the function contains valid numeric characters, and that the return value from the function is within the range of the destination data type. If you attempt to use *CInt* to convert the string "33000," your program will have an error when it executes because 33000 is too large to be stored in an Integer. The following code fragment shows how the functions *CLng* and *CCur* are used to convert numbers from string form to numeric form:

```
Dim Quantity As Long
Dim Price As Currency

Quantity = CLng(txtQuantity.Text)
Price = CCur(txtPrice.Text)
```

If the user entered 33000 into txtQuantity and 5000 into txtPrice, the Text properties of the two text boxes contain the strings "33000" and "5000," respectively. In the first assignment statement, the numeric characters that have been entered by the user into the *txtQuantity* text box control are converted by the function *CLng* from a String into a Long and then stored in the variable *Quantity*. For our example, Quantity would now contain the long number 33000. In the second statement, the number that has been entered into the *txtPrice* text box control is converted by the function *CCur* from a String into a type Currency and then stored in the variable *Price*. For our example, Price would now contain the currency number 5000.00.

In both statements, the function is called by using the function's name and enclosing the value that needs converting within parentheses. Each function converts the data item's value from string type to numeric type and returns the converted value back to the statement for assignment to a variable of data type Long and Currency, respectively.

Numeric to String Conversion

We will use a function named *Format* to convert and round numeric data types such as Long, Double, or Currency to a String type. When we call *Format*, we will have to provide two values (called *arguments*) within the parentheses. The first value is the data item to be converted, and the second value specifies the appearance (or format) of the number after it has been converted into a string. The following code fragment shows how this function is used:

```
Dim Quantity As Long
Dim Price As Currency

Quantity = 123
Price = 3.69
txtQuantity.Text = Format(Quantity, "0")
txtPrice.Text = Format(Price, "0.00")
```

Both **Format functions** have a String constant as the second argument. We specified "0" for the format of *Quantity* because this item does not have a fractional value; in the case of *Price*, however, we specified "0.00" because we want *Price* to be displayed as a string rounded to two digits beyond the decimal point.

You can easily add a dollar sign to the display of a monetary figure by including it inside the quotation marks of the second argument. Appending units such as *cm* or *volts* to the end of a numeric display value is not quite as convenient and is done by following either of the following two procedures:

■ Precede each character of the unit with a backslash and insert the resultant string inside the quotation marks of the second argument.

■ Put the unit inside a set of quotation marks and concatenate the output of the *Format* function with the string containing the unit.

All three of the format enhancements are illustrated here:

```
txtPrice.Text = Format(Price, "$0.00")
txtLength.Text = Format(Length, "0.0 \c\m")
txtVoltage.Text = Format(Voltage, "0.000 ") & "volts"
```

Conversion Program Example

Program *Conversion 1*, shown in Figure 3.3, is a simple program that demonstrates the use of the three **data conversion** functions *CLng*, *CCur*, and *Format*.

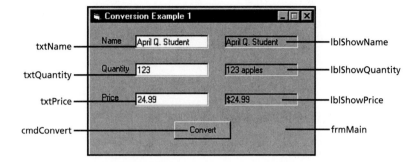

Figure 3.3   *Form for program* Conversion 1.

When the user clicks the *Convert* button, the data items stored in the *txtName*, *txtQuantity*, and *txtPrice* text boxes are copied to the local variables *Name*, *Quantity*, and *Price*, respectively. Note however, that *Quantity* is type Long and *Price* is type Currency. Therefore, as shown in Figure 3.4, *txtQuantity.Text* is converted by the *CLng* function to type Long and stored in the variable *Quantity*. Similarly, *txtPrice.Text* is converted by the *CCur* function to type Currency and then stored in the variable *Price*.

After the data items have been copied from the edit components on the left side of the form to the local variables, they are then copied from the three local variables to their corresponding labels on the right side of the form. Of course, *Quantity* and *Price* both have to be converted to string form before they can be stored in their respective labels. As shown in Figure 3.4, the *Format* function is used to carry out the conversion for both numeric data items. Note how the *Format* function has been used to insert a dollar sign in front of the *Price*. The last statement in the *cmdConvert_Click* event procedure is used to place the focus on the Name text box, which makes it easy for the user to type in a new name.

➤ Create the *Conversion 1* program.

1. Open a new project called Conversion 1. Design the form *frmMain* with a button, three identification labels along the left side, three text boxes in the center, and three destination labels on the right side.

2. Name the three text boxes txtName, txtQuantity, and txtPrice.

3. Name the three labels on the right lblShowName, lblShowQuantity, and lblShowPrice and set their properties as follows:

   ■   BorderStyle set to Fixed Single

   ■   Caption deleted

4. Type in the code for the button's *Click* event (see Figure 3.4).

5. Run the program with appropriate data values.

```
Private Sub cmdConvert_Click()
    Dim Name As String
    Dim Quantity As Long
    Dim Price As Currency

    ' Convert and copy to local variables
    Name = txtName.Text
    Quantity = CLng(txtQuantity.Text)
    Price = CCur(txtPrice.Text)
    ' Convert, copy to labels, and set focus on Name
    lblShowName.Caption = Name
    lblShowQuantity.Caption = Format(Quantity, "0 ") & "apples"
    lblShowPrice.Caption = Format(Price, "$0.00")
    txtName.SetFocus
End Sub
```

Figure 3.4 *Code for* Conversion 1 *program's* Convert *button click event.*

Expressions

Consider the following Visual Basic numeric expression:

```
(Quantity * Price) + .50
```

This expression, and any expression for that matter, is a collection of **operands** joined together by operators. In this example, the multiply operator (*) has two operands, *Quantity* and *Price*, and the addition operator (+) has two operands, the result of *(Quantity * Price)* and *.50*. Both * and + are called **binary operators** because they each have two operands. The parentheses inform Visual Basic that the multiplication of *Quantity* and *Price* is to occur prior to the addition.

A numeric expression can be evaluated to obtain a single numeric value, and that value can be stored in a variable by using the assignment operator. Some additional examples of expressions are as follows:

```
TotalPrice = Quantity * UnitPrice
LotPerimeter = 2.0 * (Frontage + Depth)
TotalQuantity = CLng(txtQtyAM.Text) + CLng(txtQtyPM.Text)
```

Arithmetic Operators

Visual Basic has seven **arithmetic operators**. Figure 3.5 shows the types of arithmetic operands and results for these seven binary arithmetic operators. You should notice several things while looking at this table:

- Visual Basic is less restrictive than highly typed languages such as C++, Java, and Pascal by allowing all seven operators to work with any of the numeric data types in any combination.

■ For / and ^, the result type is always Double.

■ For \ and Mod, the result type is either Integer or Long.

Operator	Operation	Allowed Operand Types	Usual Result Type	Notes
+	Addition	All	Same as most precise operand	1
–	Subtraction	All	Same as most precise operand	1
*	Multiplication	All	Same as most precise operand	2
/	Division	All	Double	
\	Integer division	All	Integer or Long	3
Mod	Remainder	All	Integer or Long	3
^	Exponentiation	All	Double	4

1. Order of precision from least to most precise is Integer, Long, Double, and Currency.
2. Order of precision from least to most precise is Integer, Long, Currency, and Double.
3. Prior to division, the dividend and divisor are rounded to Integer or Long types.
4. The base can be negative only if the exponent is an Integer value.

Figure 3.5   *Arithmetic operators: types of operands and results.*

You have probably learned in a math class that division by zero is undefined. On a computer, division by zero causes an error, and this caution applies to /, \, and Mod. Any program that you write should either prevent division by zero, or if it occurs, detect the error and take corrective action.

It is easy to confuse the two **divide operators** / (slash) and \ (backslash), but there is a significant difference between the two. The result of / division is always type Double; the result of \ division is rounded (truncated) in the direction of zero to an Integer or Long type value. As an example, 7/4 has the value 1.75, and 7\4 has the value 1.

The **Mod** operator, often called the **modulus operator**, returns the remainder from an integer division. Consider the following expression:

```
10 Mod 3
```

The number 10 is divided by 3, yielding a remainder of 1. Figure 3.6 displays the results of the Mod operation for several different operands. Notice that the maximum value returned by the Mod operator is 1 less than the divisor.

Expression	Value
0 **Mod** 3	0
1 **Mod** 3	1
2 **Mod** 3	2
3 **Mod** 3	0
4 **Mod** 3	1
5 **Mod** 3	2

Figure 3.6 *The Mod operator.*

Figure 3.7 contains expressions using all seven arithmetic operators with type Integer operands. Note that the results of division by the / operator and exponentiation by the ^ operators are always type Double.

Expression	Value
17 + 5	22
17 − 5	12
17 * 5	85
17 / 5	3.4
17 \ 5	3
17 Mod 5	2
17 ^ 5	1419857.0

Figure 3.7 *Results of arithmetic operations on Integer types.*

See Figure 3.8 for examples of using all seven arithmetic operators with type Double operands. Note that the results of division by the \ and Mod operators are always either type Integer or type Long.

Expression	Value
9.2 + 1.6	10.8
9.2 − 1.6	7.6
9.2 * 1.6	14.72
9.2 / 1.6	5.75
9.2 \ 1.6	4
9.2 Mod 1.6	1
9.2 ^ 1.6	34.84

Figure 3.8 *Results of arithmetic operations on Double types.*

Arithmetic Operators Program Example

Program *Arithmetic Operators 1*, shown in Figure 3.9, employs all seven of the arithmetic operators. All operators are used in expressions where both operands are type Long and also where both operands are type Double. When the program begins execution, I, J, X, and Y already have values entered into their text box controls. Clicking the *Calculate* button activates the *cmdCalculate_Click* event procedure (shown in Figure 3.10), the calculations are performed, and the results display in the label components. When the program is running, you can change one or more of the values in I, J, X, and Y, click the *Calculate* button, and examine the new results of the calculations.

➤ Create the *Arithmetic Operators 1* program.

1. Open a new project called Arithmetic Operators 1. Name the form frmMain, and set its Caption property to Arithmetic Operators Example 1.

2. Place a command button on the form, name it cmdCalculate, and set its Caption property to Calculate.

3. Add two text boxes at the top left and right.

4. On the left and right sides of the form, add nine label components down the left side that will be used for identification. Then add seven more label components on each side directly under the text box controls. These two sets of seven labels will be used to display the results of calculations.

5. Use the Properties window to set the controls' properties as follows:

   ■ For all output labels, set BorderStyle to Fixed Single, and delete the text in the Caption property.

   ■ Use Figure 3.10 to determine and then set the Name property of each text box. For example, the left text boxes are named txtI and txtJ.

   ■ Use Figure 3.9 to determine the value to store in the Text property of each edit component. For example, *txtI.Text* is set to 68 and *txtJ.Text* is set to 5.

   ■ Use Figure 3.9 to determine and then set the Name property of each output label. For example, the first two output labels on the left panel are named lblShowLongAdd and lblShowLongSub.

6. Double-click the *Calculate* button and use Figure 3.10 to enter the code in the event procedure.

7. Run the application by clicking the Run arrow.

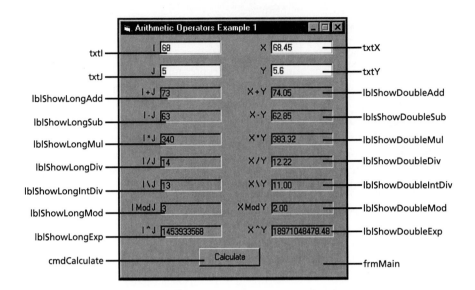

Figure 3.9 *Form for* Arithmetic Operators 1 *program.*

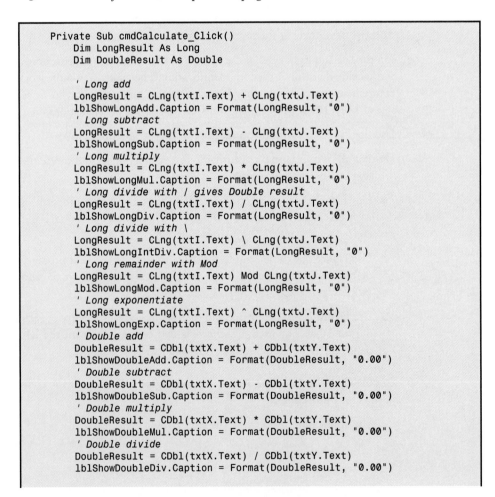

```
Private Sub cmdCalculate_Click()
    Dim LongResult As Long
    Dim DoubleResult As Double

    ' Long add
    LongResult = CLng(txtI.Text) + CLng(txtJ.Text)
    lblShowLongAdd.Caption = Format(LongResult, "0")
    ' Long subtract
    LongResult = CLng(txtI.Text) - CLng(txtJ.Text)
    lblShowLongSub.Caption = Format(LongResult, "0")
    ' Long multiply
    LongResult = CLng(txtI.Text) * CLng(txtJ.Text)
    lblShowLongMul.Caption = Format(LongResult, "0")
    ' Long divide with / gives Double result
    LongResult = CLng(txtI.Text) / CLng(txtJ.Text)
    lblShowLongDiv.Caption = Format(LongResult, "0")
    ' Long divide with \
    LongResult = CLng(txtI.Text) \ CLng(txtJ.Text)
    lblShowLongIntDiv.Caption = Format(LongResult, "0")
    ' Long remainder with Mod
    LongResult = CLng(txtI.Text) Mod CLng(txtJ.Text)
    lblShowLongMod.Caption = Format(LongResult, "0")
    ' Long exponentiate
    LongResult = CLng(txtI.Text) ^ CLng(txtJ.Text)
    lblShowLongExp.Caption = Format(LongResult, "0")
    ' Double add
    DoubleResult = CDbl(txtX.Text) + CDbl(txtY.Text)
    lblShowDoubleAdd.Caption = Format(DoubleResult, "0.00")
    ' Double subtract
    DoubleResult = CDbl(txtX.Text) - CDbl(txtY.Text)
    lblShowDoubleSub.Caption = Format(DoubleResult, "0.00")
    ' Double multiply
    DoubleResult = CDbl(txtX.Text) * CDbl(txtY.Text)
    lblShowDoubleMul.Caption = Format(DoubleResult, "0.00")
    ' Double divide
    DoubleResult = CDbl(txtX.Text) / CDbl(txtY.Text)
    lblShowDoubleDiv.Caption = Format(DoubleResult, "0.00")
```

```
     ' Store quotient from integer divide in DoubleResult
     DoubleResult = CDbl(txtX.Text) \ CDbl(txtY.Text)
     lblShowDoubleIntDiv.Caption = Format(DoubleResult, "0.00")
     ' Store remainder from integer divide in DoubleResult
     DoubleResult = CDbl(txtX.Text) Mod CDbl(txtY.Text)
     lblShowDoubleMod.Caption = Format(DoubleResult, "0.00")
     ' Double exponentiate
     DoubleResult = CDbl(txtX.Text) ^ CDbl(txtY.Text)
     lblShowDoubleExp.Caption = Format(DoubleResult, "0.00")
     txtI.SetFocus
  End Sub
```

Figure 3.10 *Code for* Arithmetic Operators 1 *program.*

Operator Precedence

In the following statement, assume that *A* has the value 7 and *B* has the value 2:

```
Result = A - 4 * B + 5
```

What will be the value of *Result*? If Visual Basic evaluates the expression by just proceeding from left to right, the statement would be the same as this:

```
Result = ((A - 4) * B) + 5
```

Because expressions within parentheses are evaluated first, 11 would be stored in *Result.*

If the addition and subtraction operations were performed before the multiplication operation, the statement would be the same as this:

```
Result = (A - 4) * (B + 5)
```

and 21 would be stored in *Result.*

Finally, if the multiplication is performed first, the subtraction second, and the addition last, the statement would be the same as this:

```
Result = (A - (4 * B)) + 5
```

and 4 would be stored in *Result.*

This last expression is the correct one. Therefore, it is very important that you know the criteria Visual Basic uses when it evaluates an expression.

In most computer languages, each operator is associated with a precedence (**operator precedence**), and the order in which operations are performed is specified by **rules of precedence**. Figure 3.11 specifies the precedence for the six arithmetic operators. Note that the negation operator is a unary operator—that is, it has only one operand—but all the other operators have two operands and are referred to as binary operators.

Operator	Precedence	Description
^	1 (highest)	Exponentiation
Unary −	2	Negation
*, /	3	Multiplication and division
\	4	Integer division
Mod	5	Modulus arithmetic
+, −	6 (lowest)	Addition and subtraction

Figure 3.11 *Precedence of arithmetic operators.*

The rules of precedence are as follows:

1. Expressions within parentheses are evaluated first. If there is more than one set of parentheses, the innermost set is evaluated first.

2. Operations with the highest precedence are evaluated prior to those with lower precedence.

3. Operations with equal precedence are performed from left to right.

If you apply these rules to the preceding statement

```
Result = A - 4 * B + 5
```

where *A* and *B* have the values 7 and 2, respectively, you know immediately that the multiplication operation of *4 * B* will occur first because * has a higher precedence than either + or −. Therefore, the statement can also be written as follows to yield the same result:

```
Result = A - (4 * B) + 5
```

Now apply the precedence rules to this latest statement. Because − and + have the same level of precedence, the left-to-right rule states that the subtraction will be performed before the addition and the statement becomes this:

```
Result = (A - (4 * B)) + 5
```

Filling in the actual numbers, the evaluation proceeds as follows:

```
Result = (7 - (4 * 2)) + 5      ' substitute actual values
         (7 -    8)    + 5      ' multiplication performed first
              -1       + 5      ' subtraction performed second
                   4            ' addition performed last
```

Another interesting example is the statement

```
Result = -A ^ B
```

where *A* and *B* have the values 7 and 2, respectively. Because there is no space between the minus sign and the variable A, we conclude that the person who wrote this code wanted to have the value of A negated (changed in sign) and then have the resulting value raised to the second power. Visual Basic ignores the differences in spacing, however, and is concerned only with the precedence of the two operators. Because the exponentiation operator has higher precedence than the negation operator does, the statement is the same as

```
Result = -(A ^ B)
```

which causes a value of -49 to be stored in the variable *Result*. This value is different from

```
Result = (-A) ^ B
```

which causes a value of $+49$ to be stored in *Result*.

Although you can always use the rules of precedence to evaluate a complex expression, a better approach is to break a complicated calculation into simpler pieces. This will help prevent you from making mistakes when you first write the code, and it will help other programmers when they have to maintain your programs. You can keep your expressions simple by doing the following:

- Use parentheses to make the expression more readable.

- Use intermediate variables to split a complicated expression into several simpler expressions

As an example, the algebraic formula for the current flow in an electronic circuit is

$$I_1 = \frac{E_2 R_3 + E_1(R_2 + R_3)}{(R_1 + R_3)(R_2 + R_3) - (R_3)^2}$$

If you write the exact Visual Basic statement for this formula, you will end up with a long, complex, and difficult-to-understand expression with many sets of parentheses:

```
I1 = (E2 * R3 + E1 * (R2 + R3)) / ((R1 + R3) * (R2 + R3) - R3 * R3)
```

Let us use the suggestion to keep our expressions simple by splitting the expression up into several simpler expressions. We can do this by introducing three additional variables: Num for the numerator, Denom for the denominator, and R23 for (R_2 + R_3). The Visual Basic code for this statement then becomes

```
R23 = R2 + R3
Num = (E2 * R3) + (E1 * R23)
Denom = (R1 + R3) * R23 - (R3 * R3)
I1 = Num / Denom
```

In the third code line, the parentheses around R3 * R3 are not required. Many experienced programmers would only use the required parentheses around R1 + R3 because they have become accustomed to the fact that * is higher in precedence than + and −. If in doubt, include parentheses in a statement. Unneeded sets of parentheses do not affect the processing efficiency of the computer instructions generated by Visual Basic, and they often improve the readability of a complex expression. If your programming statement has two or more levels of nested parentheses, you should consider the possibility of simplifying the expression by using additional variables to simplify the statement.

■ TIP
Keep expressions simple.

Variable Scope

In Chapter 2, "Data Types, Variables, and Assignment Statements," you learned about variables and how to declare them. Whenever possible, you should declare variables in the procedure that uses them. Situations arise, however, when variables must be accessed from more than one procedure. These variables must be declared outside the event procedure. The area in a program in which a variable is available for use is called the **scope** of the variable. Only a few programming languages require the scope of all variables to include the entire program. Most modern programming languages have definite scope rules, and a programmer must have a thorough understanding of these rules.

To learn what scope is and to understand Visual Basic's rules of scope, we will create the program shown in Figure 3.12. When this program begins execution, it displays two complete names. By clicking on the appropriate button, the user can swap either the first or last names. Clicking the *Original* button restores the original set of names, and a click on the *New* button shows a different set of names.

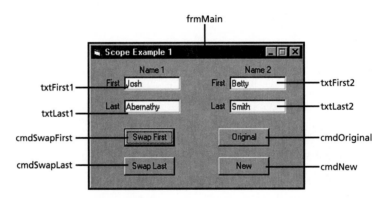

Figure 3.12 *Form for* Scope1 *program.*

➤ Create the *Scope1* program.

1. Open a new project called Scope1. Name the form frmMain, and set its Caption property to Scope Example 1.

2. Place three labels and two text boxes on both the top left and top right of the form.

3. Place four command buttons on the lower half of the form.

4. Use the Properties window to set the controls' properties as follows:

   ■ Use Figure 3.12 to set the Caption properties of the six labels.

   ■ Change the names of the two text box controls on the left to txtFirst1 and txtLast1 and the names of the text boxes on the right to txtFirst2 and txtLast2.

   ■ Name the left buttons cmdSwapFirst and cmdSwapLast, and the right buttons cmdOriginal and cmdNew.

   ■ Use Figure 3.12 to set the Caption properties of the four command buttons.

5. Create and code the four *Click* event procedures for the buttons by double-clicking on each button and adding the code shown in Figure 3.15. Observe that three assignment statements are used to achieve the swapping of contents. This is required because an assignment statement replaces the contents of the destination variable (right side of assignment). Therefore, if we left out the first line and immediately executed the second line

```
txtFirst1.Text = txtFirst2.Text
```

there would be no way to recover the original value in *txtFirst1*. To make the swap work, we need to create a temporary helper variable to save the value that was originally in *txtFirst1*.

6. Create and code the *Form_Load* event procedure. As shown in Figure 3.13, bring the Code Editor window to the foreground and select *Form* in the Object list box at the top left of the Code Editor. In the Procedure list box at the top right, select *Load*.

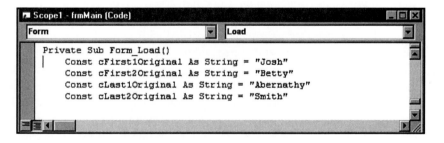

Figure 3.13 *Coding the* Form_Load *event procedure for program* Scope1.

Enter the code shown in Figure 3.15. The *Form_Load* procedure is executed the moment that the form is loaded into memory (each time the program starts). In this program, it initializes the text box controls with the *Original* group of names.

7. Run the application by clicking the Start button on the toolbar. To thoroughly test the program, you should select each button at least once. You can also type different names in the boxes and click the buttons again.

Procedure-Level Variables and Constants

If you study the procedures in Figure 3.15, you might wonder why *cmdSwapFirst_Click* and *cmdSwapLast_Click* both appear to have the same variable *TempName*. What would happen if *TempName* was declared in only one of those two procedures? If you change the declaration of *TempName* in the *cmdSwapFirst_Click* procedure to comments and run the project again, Visual Basic will display the error message Variable not defined. In addition, as shown in Figure 3.14, Visual Basic will also highlight *TempName* within procedure *cmdSwapFirst_Click* as the source of the error. Visual Basic displays the error message because a statement in procedure *cmdSwapFirst_Click* cannot access the variable *TempName* in procedure *cmdSwapLast_Click*.

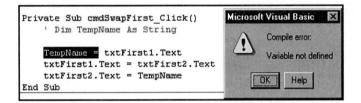

Figure 3.14 *Error from failure to declare* TempName.

More precisely, we say that the *scope* of variable *TempName* in procedure *cmdSwapLast_Click* is *local* to that procedure. This is the same as stating that only code in procedure *cmdSwapLast_Click* has access to or can change variables declared inside this procedure. Furthermore, although both variables have the same name, they are two distinct variables associated with two different memory locations. Variables and constants declared within procedures are called **local variables** and **local constants** because their scope is restricted to the procedure in which they were declared. Local variables are sometimes referred to as *procedure-level* variables because their scope is restricted to the procedure in which they are declared. Local variables declared with Dim do not exist in memory until the procedure begins execution, and they no longer exist after the procedure has finished execution. In Figure 3.15, all variables and constants are local.

You should notice one other thing about the code in Figure 3.15: The same set of constants is declared in procedures *cmdOriginal_Click* and *Form_Load*. From a program maintenance standpoint, this is unsatisfactory, because in the event that you want to change the *Original* names, you must make the same changes at two places in the program. In the next section, we show you how to declare constants and variables that have form-level scope. By using this feature, we will only have to declare one copy of *Original* constants.

```
' Project Scope1
Option Explicit

Private Sub cmdOriginal_Click()
    ' These constants have procedure-level scope
    Const cFirst1Original As String = "Josh"
    Const cFirst2Original As String = "Betty"
    Const cLast1Original As String = "Abernathy"
    Const cLast2Original As String = "Smith"

    txtFirst1.Text = cFirst1Original
    txtFirst2.Text = cFirst2Original
    txtLast1.Text = cLast1Original
    txtLast2.Text = cLast2Original
End Sub

Private Sub cmdNew_Click()
    Const cFirst1New As String = "Monica"
    Const cFirst2New As String = "Raymond"
    Const cLast1New As String = "O'Neal"
    Const cLast2New As String = "Hackman"

    txtFirst1.Text = cFirst1New
    txtFirst2.Text = cFirst2New
    txtLast1.Text = cLast1New
    txtLast2.Text = cLast2New
End Sub

Private Sub cmdSwapFirst_Click()
    Dim TempName As String

    TempName = txtFirst1.Text
    txtFirst1.Text = txtFirst2.Text
    txtFirst2.Text = TempName
End Sub

Private Sub cmdSwapLast_Click()
    Dim TempName As String

    TempName = txtLast1.Text
    txtLast1.Text = txtLast2.Text
    txtLast2.Text = TempName
End Sub

Private Sub Form_Load()
    Const cFirst1Original As String = "Josh"
    Const cFirst2Original As String = "Betty"
    Const cLast1Original As String = "Abernathy"
    Const cLast2Original As String = "Smith"

    txtFirst1.Text = cFirst1Original
    txtFirst2.Text = cFirst2Original
    txtLast1.Text = cLast1Original
    txtLast2.Text = cLast2Original
End Sub
```

Figure 3.15   *Code for program* Scope1.

Procedure-Level Variables with Persistence

In addition to scope, variables have a **lifetime**, the period of time during which they retain their value. The local variables that we previously discussed are created and initialized when the event procedure begins execution. Then when the procedure has finished executing, the memory used by the variables is reclaimed and the variables no longer exist. This cycle of variable creation, initialization, and destruction is repeated each time the procedure is called.

To make a procedure-level variable persist for the lifetime of a program, you must declare the variable as a **static variable**. Static variables are not re-initialized each time a procedure begins execution—that is, they "remember" or maintain their most recently assigned value for the lifetime of the program. To declare a static variable, use the keyword *Static* rather than *Dim* in your variable declaration:

```
Static PearsSold As Long
```

Static variables are useful for counters and for debugging purposes, but we will use them only sparingly in this textbook. Normally, when your variable must have persistence, it must also have a scope that is wider than procedure-level.

Form-Level Variables and Constants

We have seen that, except for the case of *static* variables, local variables cannot be used to store data that must stay in existence after the procedure has stopped execution. Furthermore, the scope of a local variable is restricted to the procedure in which it is declared. In many programs, procedures need to reference information that has been received or processed by other procedures. We can easily do this if our programming language has a category of variables with a scope that includes the entire form or even the project. In addition, this new category of variable also has to have a lifetime equal to that of the form or program itself; otherwise we will not be able to write programs that do anything useful.

In Visual Basic, variables and constants that can be accessed by other procedures in the same form, but are not accessible to other forms, are said to have **form-level scope**. In Visual Basic, *form-level* scope is also called **module-level scope**. Variables and constants that can be accessed from other forms have **project-level scope** and are called **global variables** and constants. Variables with *form-* and *project-level* scope also persist (stay in existence) for the life of the form or program.

Declaring Form-Level Variables and Constants

Variables and constants with *form-level* scope are declared outside the procedures using the **Private** keyword. In Figure 3.17, the four constants *cfFirst1Original*, *cfLast1Original*, *cfFirst2Original*, and *cfLast2Original* and the variable *fSwapCount* all have *form-level* scope. Notice that we are including the prefix "c" in the names for the constants and the prefix "f" in the names for the *form-level* variables and constants. This will enable us to distinguish constants and variables as well as to recognize their scope easily and quickly when we read code. Local variables will not have a prefix. Experience has shown that programs are easier to understand and maintain if a prefix convention for identifying scope is followed consistently.

TIP
Establish and faithfully follow variable naming conventions.

Form-level constants and variables are declared in the General Declaration section at the top of the form's Code window. The syntax you use is as follows:

```
Private Const constname As type = expression
Private varname As type
```

Note that when you declare a constant, *expression* may not include the names of other variables.

Program Example with Form-Level Scope

Suppose we want to modify the *Scope1* program, shown in Figure 3.12, so that a label will display the number of times a first or last name has been swapped. We can accomplish this by putting a *label* control on the form, and add code to the Swap button *Click* procedures so that a click of either Swap button causes the number displayed by the label to be incremented by one.

This is an example of counting, which will be discussed in more detail in the next section. At this point, however, it is useful to have some general programming guidelines that will help you use counters successfully:

1. Declare counters at the right scope (generally form-scope or global-scope).

2. Initialize counters (frequently zero) at the start before any of the repeating steps have been processed (possibly part of *Form_Load*).

3. Increment counters in the same event where the item or process being counted just changed (possibly a button *Click* event or menu *Click* event that signals the user is ready to process the next data set). The generic appearance of the assignment statement to increment a variable is: Variable = Variable + 1.

We will also add code to the *Original* and *New* click procedures to zero the counter when either of these buttons is clicked. Figure 3.16 shows the modified form for program *Scope2*.

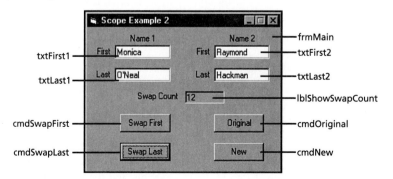

Figure 3.16   *Form for* Scope2 *program.*

Unlike program *Scope1*, where all the variables are local, we now need a variable that has *form-level* scope so that the program can keep track of the number of times that a first or last name has been swapped. Let us name this variable *fSwapCount*.

In addition to *form-level* scope, *fSwapCount* must have persistence (lifetime) for the duration of the program. In contrast to a local variable that only exists while the procedure to which it belongs is executing, a *form-level* variable will retain its value for the lifetime of the application. (Although a static variable does exist for the duration of the program, it does not have *form-level* scope.)

We can make an additional improvement to the program. As discussed previously, program *Scope1* has the same set of constants declared in procedures *cmdOriginal_Click* and *Form_Load*. If we declare these constants in the declaration section of the module, and use the keyword *Private*, they will have *form-level* scope and we can remove the redundant constant declarations from both modules.

➤ Create the *Scope2* program.

1. Start with the *Scope1* program and use File, Save Scope.frm As, Scope to create *Scope.frm* in a new directory. Use File, Save Project As, Scope2 to create project *Scope2* in the new directory.

2. Add two labels to the form. As shown in Figure 3.16, the label on the left has its Caption property set to Swap Count. The label on the right is named lblShowSwapCount and will be used to display the swap count.

3. Change the form's Caption property to Scope Example 2.

4. Use the Code Editor to modify the program's code so that it is the same as the code in Figure 3.17. The modifications are as follows:

   ■ Move (use Cut and Paste) the four constant declarations from procedure *cmdOriginal_Click* to the declaration section of the module. Add the keyword Private to the beginning of each line and the prefix f to each constant's name.

   ■ Delete the four constant declarations in procedure *Form_Load*. At this point, procedures *cmdOriginal_Click* and *Form_Load* should not contain any constant declarations.

   ■ Declare the *fSwapCount* form-level variable in the declaration section of the module.

   ■ Add the code

   ```
   fSwapCount = 0
   lblShowSwapCount.Caption = Format(fSwapCount, "0")
   ```

   to the *Form_Load, cmdOriginal_Click*, and *cmdNew_Click* procedures so that *fSwapCount* is assigned zero and *lblShowSwapCount* displays zero when the program starts or the *Original* or *New* buttons are clicked.

   ■ Add code that increments *fSwapCount* by one, uses Format to convert the value of *fSwapCount* to a string, and then assigns the string to the Caption property of *lblSwapCount*. This code should be added to the *SwapFirst* and *SwapLast* click procedures.

➤ Run and test the application.

```
' Project Scope2
Option Explicit

' These constants and variables have form-level scope
Private Const cfFirst1Original As String = "Josh"
Private Const cfFirst2Original As String = "Betty"
Private Const cfLast1Original As String = "Abernathy"
Private Const cfLast2Original As String = "Smith"
Private fSwapCount As Integer

Private Sub cmdOriginal_Click()
    txtFirst1.Text = cfFirst1Original
    txtFirst2.Text = cfFirst2Original
    txtLast1.Text = cfLast1Original
    txtLast2.Text = cfLast2Original
    fSwapCount = 0
    lblShowSwapCount.Caption = Format(fSwapCount, "0")
End Sub

Private Sub cmdNew_Click()
    ' These constants have procedure-level scope
    Const cFirst1New As String = "Monica"
    Const cFirst2New As String = "Raymond"
    Const cLast1New As String = "O'Neal"
    Const cLast2New As String = "Hackman"

    txtFirst1.Text = cFirst1New
    txtFirst2.Text = cFirst2New
    txtLast1.Text = cLast1New
    txtLast2.Text = cLast2New
    fSwapCount = 0
    lblShowSwapCount.Caption = Format(fSwapCount, "0")
End Sub

Private Sub cmdSwapFirst_Click()
    Dim TempName As String

    TempName = txtFirst1.Text
    txtFirst1.Text = txtFirst2.Text
    txtFirst2.Text = TempName
    fSwapCount = fSwapCount + 1
    lblShowSwapCount.Caption = Format(fSwapCount, "0")
End Sub

Private Sub cmdSwapLast_Click()
    Dim TempName As String

    TempName = txtLast1.Text
    txtLast1.Text = txtLast2.Text
    txtLast2.Text = TempName
    fSwapCount = fSwapCount + 1
    lblShowSwapCount.Caption = Format(fSwapCount, "0")
End Sub

Private Sub Form_Load()
    txtFirst1.Text = cfFirst1Original
    txtFirst2.Text = cfFirst2Original
    txtLast1.Text = cfLast1Original
    txtLast2.Text = cfLast2Original
    fSwapCount = 0
    lblShowSwapCount.Caption = Format(fSwapCount, "0")
End Sub
```

Figure 3.17   *Code for program* Scope2.

Project-Level Variables and Constants

When a program has two or more forms, procedures in one module may need to access variables or constants in one or more of the other modules. Variables and constants that meet these criteria have *project-level* or **global scope**.

Declaring Project-Level Variables and Constants

For programs with more than one form, use the keyword **Public** to declare *project-level* (global-scope) variables and constants in the declarations section at the top of a separate standard module. **Standard modules** (.BAS filename extension) contain declarations and procedures commonly accessed by other modules within the application. It is good programming practice to collect global variables and declare them in a standard module.

We will add the prefix "g" to the names of global variables and constants. The previous discussion showed that form-scope variables use the prefix "f" in the declaration, and local variables do not have any prefixes. Following this variable naming convention will enable us to immediately identify the scope of any variable or constant.

The declaration of *project-level* variables and constants is identical to the declaration of *form-level* variables, except for the use of the keyword *Public,* rather than *Private.* Global variables and constants are declared in the General Declaration section of a standard code module, and the syntax you use is as follows:

```
Public Const constname As type = expression
Public varname As type
```

Program Example with Project-Level Scope

The next example adds a second form to our *Scope2* program. We will call the new program *Scope3.* A *Swap Forms* button has been added to both forms and will be used to switch between the two forms. As in the single form program *Scope2,* each form in the *Scope3* program will store the number of name swaps in variable *fSwapCount.* This variable has form scope and its value will be used to display the number of name swaps performed on that particular form.

In addition, we will place the label *lblTotalSwapCount* on each form to display the sum of the name swaps performed on both forms. To keep track of the total number of name swaps, we will add the global-scope variable *gTotalSwapCount* to our program. By giving this variable global scope, both forms can access the variable to update its value each time a Swap button is clicked and use its value to display the total number of name swaps in label *lblTotalSwapCount.* The *Scope3* program has one additional difference. The text boxes on both forms will be blank when the program starts to execute.

In this two-form project, variable *gTotalSwapCount* and the eight *named* constants will be declared in a standard module named *basGlobal.* Figure 3.20 illustrates the declarations of the global variables and constants, and Figure 3.18 illustrates the appearance of *frmMain.*

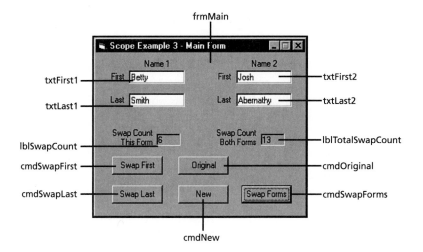

frmMain

txtFirst1

txtLast1

lblSwapCount

cmdSwapFirst

cmdSwapLast

cmdNew

txtFirst2

txtLast2

lblTotalSwapCount

cmdOriginal

cmdSwapForms

Figure 3.18   *Modified main form for* Scope3 *program.*

Except for the caption, the second form, *frmAlternate*, looks exactly like *frmMain*. Because the two forms are almost identical, we can save ourselves a lot of work by making a copy of the main form file. In the following steps, we will create a new project from *Scope2*, modify the form so that it looks like Figure 3.18, add a second form to the project, and then copy and paste all the controls from the first form to the second form in one copy-and-paste operation.

➤ Create the *Scope3* program files from *Scope2*.

1. Start with the *Scope2* program and click File, Save Scope.frm As, Main to create *Main.frm* in a new directory. Click File, Save Project As, Scope3 to create project *Scope3* in the new directory. At this point, the form is still named *frmMain*, and the project is still named *Scope2*.

2. Use the Properties window to make sure that the Text property for all four text boxes is blank.

3. Add a button and two label components to the form, and rearrange the components until the form's appearance is similar to Figure 3.18.

4. Change the button's Name property to cmdSwapForms and the Caption to Swap Forms.

5. Change the left label's Caption to Swap Count Both Forms. Change the right label's Name to lblTotalSwapCount and its BackColor to Window Background.

6. Click Project, Add Form, New Form, and then click Open. This creates a new blank *Form1* and adds it to the project.

7. Click File, Save Form1 As, Alternate to create the file *Alternate.frm*.

8. Double-click on frmMain in the Project Explorer window. Then make sure the form has been selected by clicking anywhere on the form background.

137

9. Click Edit, Select All and Edit, Copy.

10. Double-click on Form1 in the Project Explorer window. Then make sure the form has been selected by clicking anywhere on the form background.

11. Click Edit, Paste. If everything has worked correctly, *Form1* should look just like *frmMain*.

➤ Modify the properties of the two forms and the project.

1. In the Project Explorer window, double-click on Main.frm and change the Caption to Scope Example 3 – Main Form.

2. In the Project Explorer window, double-click on Alternate.frm and change its Name property to frmAlternate. Change the Caption to Scope Example 3 – Alternate Form.

3. In the Project Explorer window, click on Scope3.vbp and change its Name property to Scope3.

4. Click Project, Scope3 Properties and check to make sure that the Startup Object is *frmMain*. When the user starts our *Scope3* program, we want execution to begin with module *frmMain*.

➤ Create and add a standard module to the project.

1. Click Project, Add Module, New, select Module, and click Open.

2. Click File, Save Module1 As, and enter Global as the module filename. Make sure you save this file in the same directory that contains your other *Scope3* files.

3. In the Project Explorer window, click on Module1 and change its Name property to basGlobal.

4. Check to make sure the Project Explorer window is similar to Figure 3.19, although the order of listing may differ.

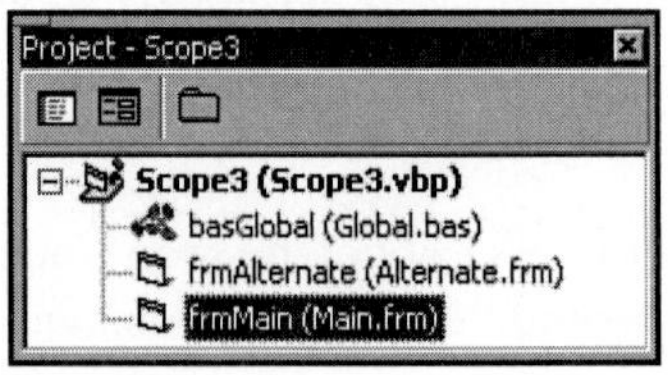

Figure 3.19 Scope3 *Project Explorer window.*

5. Enter the code displayed in Figure 3.20 into the standard module. Because all the constants and variables in this form are global, their names all include the prefix "g".

```
' Project Scope3 Standard Module
Option Explicit

' Global constants and variables for program Scope3
' Constants for names in original set
Public Const cgFirst1Original As String = "Josh"
Public Const cgFirst2Original As String = "Betty"
Public Const cgLast1Original As String = "Abernathy"
Public Const cgLast2Original As String = "Smith"

' Constants for names in new set
Public Const cgFirst1New As String = "Monica"
Public Const cgFirst2New As String = "Raymond"
Public Const cgLast1New As String = "O'Neal"
Public Const cgLast2New As String = "Hackman"

' Total number of first and last name swaps
Public gTotalSwapCount As Integer
```

Figure 3.20 *Code for program* Scope3 *standard module* (Global.bas).

➤ Use Figure 3.21 and modify the *frmMain* code. Note the following:

1. All constants have been moved to the standard module *basGlobal* and have global scope.

2. All text box controls are blank when the form first appears onscreen.

3. The *cmdSwapForms Click* event procedure is used to make *frmAlternate* visible and *frmMain* invisible.

4. In the *cmdSwapFirst* and *cmdSwapLast Click* event procedures, *Format* is used to convert the numeric value stored in global variable *gTotalSwapCount* to a string. This string is then assigned to the Caption property of label *lblTotalSwapCount*.

5. The *Form_Activate* event procedure is used to update the form's swap count and the total swap count for both forms. Form *frmMain* is activated (made visible) when the program begins execution and whenever the *Swap Forms* button on *frmAlternate* is clicked.

6. The *Form_Unload* event procedure is called when the user clicks the *Close* button on the title bar of *frmMain*. If we do not unload (remove from memory) *frmAlternate*, it will keep executing even though it is invisible and *frmMain* has been shut down.

➤ Modify the *frmAlternate* code.

1. Delete all the *frmAlternate* code. Copy and paste all the code from *frmMain* to *frmAlternate*.

2. Change the *cmdSwapForms* click event handler to make *frmMain* visible and *frmAlternate* invisible.

3. Delete the entire *Form_Load* procedure. The two initialization statements that were in this procedure will now be executed by the *Form_Load* procedure of module *frmMain*, because *frmMain* is the module that begins execution when the application is started.

4. Change the statement in the *Form_Unload* procedure to Unload frmMain. This procedure is called when form *frmAlternate* is visible, and the user clicks the Close button on the title bar. By unloading *frmMain*, our application ensures the program's complete shutdown.

➢ Run and test the application.

To summarize what we have learned from program *Scope3*:

■ Global variables and constants have project-level scope and are declared with the keyword *Public*. These constants can be accessed by code in either form.

■ We will add the prefix "g" to the names of all global variables and constants.

■ We will locate all global variables and constants in a standard module named *basGlobal*.

■ Form variables and constants have form-level scope and are declared with the keyword *Private*. These constants can be accessed only by code in the same form in which the variables and constants are declared.

■ We will add the prefix "f" to the names of all form variables and constants.

■ When a program has finished execution, all forms should be unloaded.

■ The *Form_Activate* event procedure is executed whenever the form is made visible.

When you are designing a program, you should always keep the scope of your variables and constants as small as you can. Local scope is better than form scope, for example, which is better than global scope. It is one of the principles of good software engineering practice that programs are easier to maintain (debug and modify) if information is hidden or encapsulated as much as possible. Information includes the names of constants, variables, and procedures.

TIP
Declare identifiers that are as local in scope as possible. Only when you need to share data or procedures among different procedures or forms should you consider using a more global scope.

```
    ' Project Scope3 code for frmMain
    Option Explicit

    Private fSwapCount As Integer       ' This variable has form-level scope

    Private Sub cmdOriginal_Click()
        txtFirst1.Text = cgFirst1Original
        txtFirst2.Text = cgFirst2Original
        txtLast1.Text = cgLast1Original
        txtLast2.Text = cgLast2Original
        fSwapCount = 0
        lblSwapCount.Caption = Format(fSwapCount, "0")
    End Sub

    Private Sub cmdNew_Click()
        txtFirst1.Text = cgFirst1New
        txtFirst2.Text = cgFirst2New
        txtLast1.Text = cgLast1New
        txtLast2.Text = cgLast2New
        fSwapCount = 0
        lblSwapCount.Caption = Format(fSwapCount, "0")
    End Sub

    Private Sub cmdSwapFirst_Click()
        Dim TempName As String
        TempName = txtFirst1.Text
        txtFirst1.Text = txtFirst2.Text
        txtFirst2.Text = TempName
        fSwapCount = fSwapCount + 1
        lblSwapCount.Caption = Format(fSwapCount, "0")
        gTotalSwapCount = gTotalSwapCount + 1
        lblTotalSwapCount.Caption = Format(gTotalSwapCount, "0")
    End Sub

    Private Sub cmdSwapForms_Click()
        frmAlternate.Show
        frmMain.Hide
    End Sub

    Private Sub cmdSwapLast_Click()
        Dim TempName As String
        TempName = txtLast1.Text
        txtLast1.Text = txtLast2.Text
        txtLast2.Text = TempName
        fSwapCount = fSwapCount + 1
        lblSwapCount.Caption = Format(fSwapCount, "0")
        gTotalSwapCount = gTotalSwapCount + 1
        lblTotalSwapCount.Caption = Format(gTotalSwapCount, "0")
    End Sub

    Private Sub Form_Activate()
        lblSwapCount.Caption = Format(fSwapCount, "0")
        lblTotalSwapCount.Caption = Format(gTotalSwapCount, "0")
    End Sub

    Private Sub Form_Load()
        fSwapCount = 0
        gTotalSwapCount = 0
    End Sub

    Private Sub Form_Unload(Cancel As Integer)
        Unload frmAlternate
    End Sub
```

Figure 3.21   *Code for program* Scope3 *main form* (Main.frm).

Investment Club Calculator Case Study

In this chapter, we discussed how to use counters and accumulators, determine the correct **variable scope**, and perform complex mathematical computations. To illustrate all these concepts in a single programming task, we will apply the program development process to the problem of computing the present value of one or more investments for an investment club, collectively and individually. The amount that must be initially invested, or present value (*PV*), can be found by using the following formula:

$$PV = \frac{FV}{(1 + Rate)^{Term}}$$

where future value (*FV*) is the amount of the future investment goal, *Rate* is the yearly interest rate, and *Term* is the length of the investment in years.

For each investment, the investor will provide the future investment goal, the term of the investment in years, and the yearly interest rate. The program will compute and display the initial amount that must be invested to attain the investment goal. The investor may wish to find the initial investment amount required for multiple investments, so after each calculation, the number of investments and the total initial investment amount required for all investments will also be displayed. If another investor wants to use the program, the program should provide the same type of information. Anytime after the investments of the first investor have been added to the club, the user may choose to see a summary of the total number of investors in the club, the total value of all initial investments, and the average initial investment per investor. The club summary information will be displayed on a second form.

Step 1: Analyze the Problem

This program will provide three different levels of summary output. For each investment, it will display the initial investment amount. For each investor, it will display the number of investments and the total initial investment amount. For the entire investment club, it will display the total number of investors in the club, the total value of all initial investments, and the average initial investment per investor.

The only input required for all these computations is the investment's future value, interest rate, and term in years. To make the program more conversational, you may also want to ask the user to enter a name.

The user can trigger many processes in this program. After the user has finished entering the three input items, the user will need to trigger the present value investment calculation. If the user likes the investment results, the user will need to trigger the updating of the investment counter and investor total. If any mistakes were made, it would be useful to allow the user to trigger the erasure of all input values, except the name. If the user decides to not add the investments to the club, the program must have provisions for another investor to enter data. When done with all investment options, the user will need to trigger the updating of the investor counter and club total. Anytime after the investments of the first investor have been added to the club, a trigger to view the club's summary results is needed. Finally, the user needs to be able to trigger when the program should terminate. Keeping all this in mind, we can construct a table of our input, processing, and output needs (Analysis Table), as shown in Figure 3.34.

Input Needs	Processing Needs	Output Needs
User's Name	Calculate Investment	Investment Amount
Investment Goal	Add to Portfolio	Number of Investments
Annual Growth Rate	Clear Inputs	Investor's Total
Term in Years	Add to Club	Number of Investors
	New Investor	Club's Total
	View Club Summary	Club's Average
	Return to Main Form	
	Exit Program	

Figure 3.34 *Analysis Table for* Investment Club Calculator.

Step 2: Design or Create the User Interface

Using the three basic controls to handle input (text box), processing (command button), and output (label) needs, we can revise our Analysis Table to identify how many and which types of controls our program needs (see Figure 3.35).

	Input Needs	Processing Needs	Output Needs
Main form	Text box and descriptive label to input each of the following: ■ User's Name ■ Investment Goal ■ Annual Growth Rate ■ Term in Years	Seven command buttons for each of the following: ■ Calculate Investment ■ Add to Portfolio ■ Clear Inputs ■ Add to Club ■ New Investor ■ View Club Summary ■ Exit Program	Descriptive label and blank label for each of the following: ■ Investment Amount ■ Number of Investments ■ Investor's Total
Summary form	None	One command button for: ■ Return to Main Form	Descriptive label and blank label for each of the following: ■ Number of Investors ■ Club's Total ■ Club's Average

Figure 3.35 *Controls required for* Investment Club Calculator *program.*

To complete the user interface design, we need to place the necessary controls in an organized, logical fashion on the two forms (see Figure 3.36). You can optionally add the three lines (see Appendix A for more information). Note that the main form (the form at the top) is displayed at about 75 percent of its actual size.

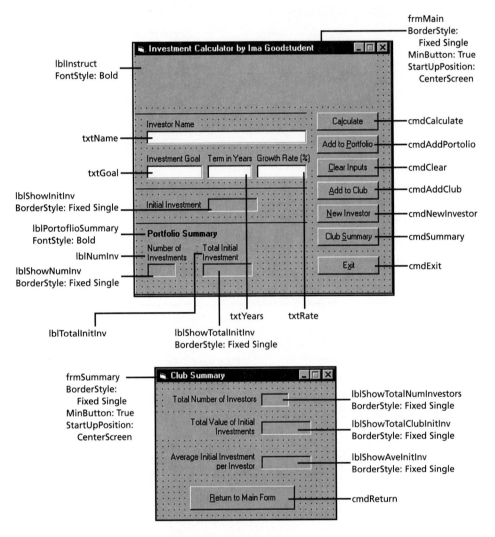

Figure 3.36   *Investment calculator user interface design.*

Step 3: Design the Logic for the Program

Now that the form is done, we can begin to think about how the program will actually function. Because we have not yet studied the programming control structure that allows our program to branch (make decisions about which portion of code to execute), our design will not be *user proof*. As an example, if the user clicks the *Calculate* button before entering valid data, the program will attempt to convert this data from string form to numeric form. This will cause the program to display a Run Time error message and then terminate execution. After you have studied a few more chapters in this text, you will be able to fix this problem.

Step 3a: Design the Macro-View (Object-Event Diagrams)

Because there are two forms, our macro logic will consist of three OEDs: the overall project, the main form, and the summary form. As you can see in Figure 3.37, our *Investment Calculator* program will consist of 13 events:

■ One for each of the eight command buttons

■ A **form load event** on the main form to assign lengthy captions, initialize counters and accumulators, clear labels and text boxes that are used for input/output, and disable several command buttons

■ A form activate event on the main form to set the focus

■ A form unload event on the main form to unload the summary form

■ A form activate event on the summary form to calculate and assign the summary data to the corresponding output labels.

■ A form unload event on the summary form to unload the main form

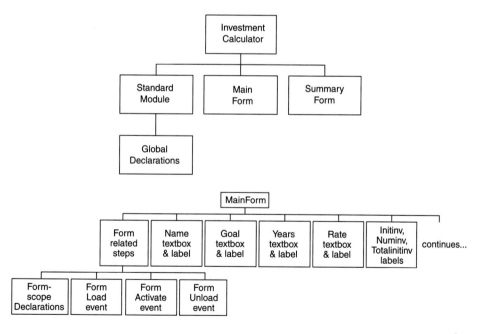

continues

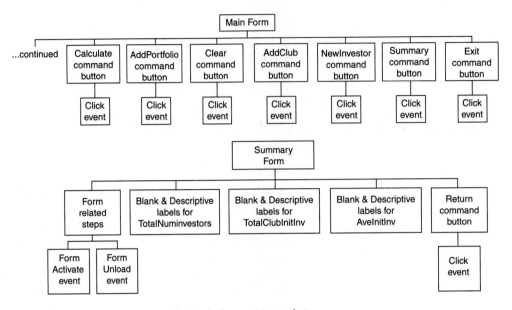

Figure 3.37 Investment Club Calculator *program design.*

Step 3b: Design the Micro-Level View (Flowcharts or Pseudocode)

We will consider each event procedure as a separate and distinct processing task. Figure 3.38 shows the flowcharts and pseudocode for each of the 13 event procedures. We will present each of the event procedures as they appear on the OED in order from left to right.

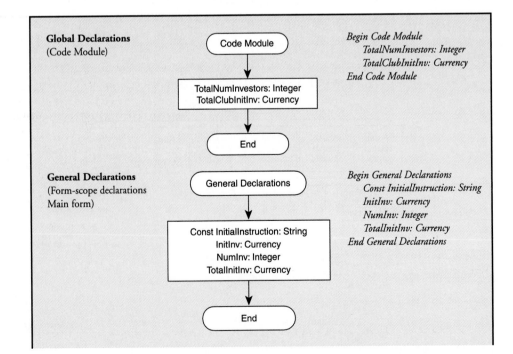

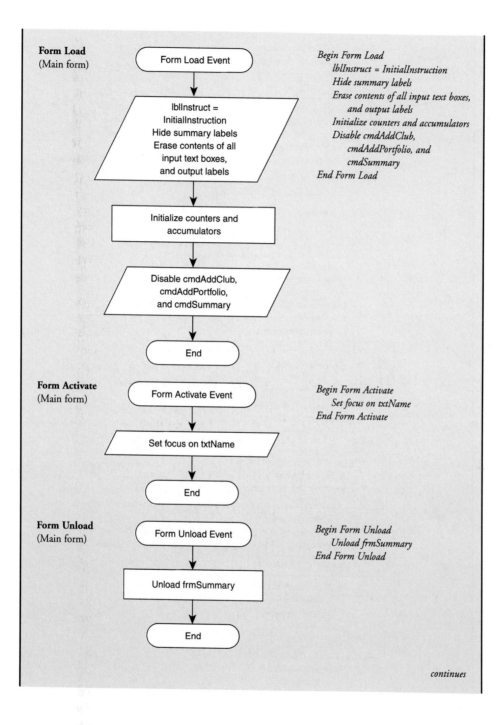

Form Load
(Main form)

Form Load Event

lblInstruct =
InitialInstruction
Hide summary labels
Erase contents of all
input text boxes,
and output labels

Initialize counters and
accumulators

Disable cmdAddClub,
cmdAddPortfolio,
and cmdSummary

End

Begin Form Load
lblInstruct = InitialInstruction
Hide summary labels
Erase contents of all input text boxes,
and output labels
Initialize counters and accumulators
Disable cmdAddClub,
cmdAddPortfolio, and
cmdSummary
End Form Load

Form Activate
(Main form)

Form Activate Event

Set focus on txtName

End

Begin Form Activate
Set focus on txtName
End Form Activate

Form Unload
(Main form)

Form Unload Event

Unload frmSummary

End

Begin Form Unload
Unload frmSummary
End Form Unload

continues

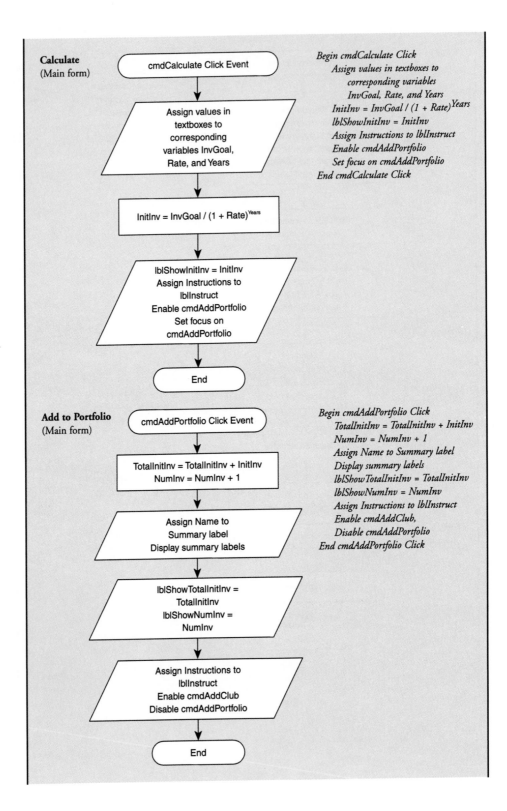

Calculate
(Main form)

cmdCalculate Click Event

Assign values in textboxes to corresponding variables InvGoal, Rate, and Years

InitInv = InvGoal / (1 + Rate)^{Years}

lblShowInitInv = InitInv
Assign Instructions to lblInstruct
Enable cmdAddPortfolio
Set focus on cmdAddPortfolio

End

Begin cmdCalculate Click
   Assign values in textboxes to
   corresponding variables
   InvGoal, Rate, and Years
   InitInv = InvGoal / (1 + Rate)^{Years}
   lblShowInitInv = InitInv
   Assign Instructions to lblInstruct
   Enable cmdAddPortfolio
   Set focus on cmdAddPortfolio
End cmdCalculate Click

Add to Portfolio
(Main form)

cmdAddPortfolio Click Event

TotalInitInv = TotalInitInv + InitInv
NumInv = NumInv + 1

Assign Name to Summary label
Display summary labels

lblShowTotalInitInv = TotalInitInv
lblShowNumInv = NumInv

Assign Instructions to lblInstruct
Enable cmdAddClub
Disable cmdAddPortfolio

End

Begin cmdAddPortfolio Click
   TotalInitInv = TotalInitInv + InitInv
   NumInv = NumInv + 1
   Assign Name to Summary label
   Display summary labels
   lblShowTotalInitInv = TotalInitInv
   lblShowNumInv = NumInv
   Assign Instructions to lblInstruct
   Enable cmdAddClub,
   Disable cmdAddPortfolio
End cmdAddPortfolio Click

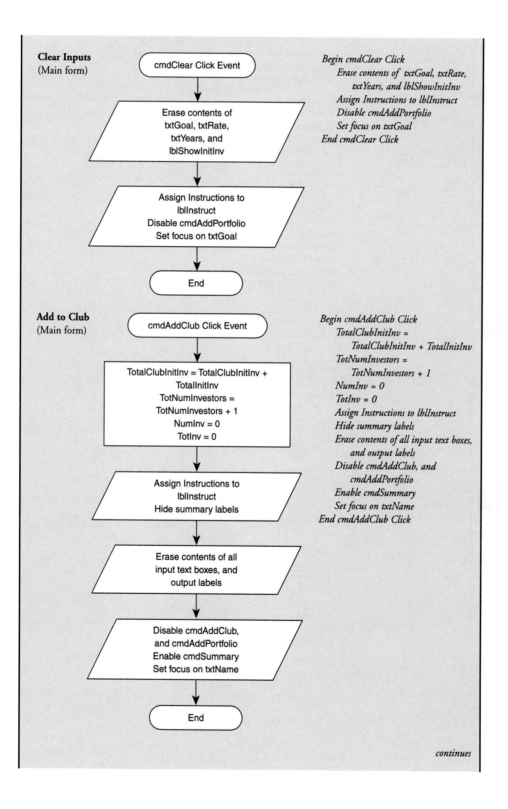

Clear Inputs
(Main form)

cmdClear Click Event

Erase contents of txtGoal, txtRate, txtYears, and lblShowInitInv

Assign Instructions to lblInstruct
Disable cmdAddPortfolio
Set focus on txtGoal

End

Begin cmdClear Click
Erase contents of txtGoal, txtRate, txtYears, and lblShowInitInv
Assign Instructions to lblInstruct
Disable cmdAddPortfolio
Set focus on txtGoal
End cmdClear Click

Add to Club
(Main form)

cmdAddClub Click Event

TotalClubInitInv = TotalClubInitInv + TotalInitInv
TotNumInvestors = TotNumInvestors + 1
NumInv = 0
TotInv = 0

Assign Instructions to lblInstruct
Hide summary labels

Erase contents of all input text boxes, and output labels

Disable cmdAddClub, and cmdAddPortfolio
Enable cmdSummary
Set focus on txtName

End

Begin cmdAddClub Click
TotalClubInitInv =
TotalClubInitInv + TotalInitInv
TotNumInvestors =
TotNumInvestors + 1
NumInv = 0
TotInv = 0
Assign Instructions to lblInstruct
Hide summary labels
Erase contents of all input text boxes, and output labels
Disable cmdAddClub, and cmdAddPortfolio
Enable cmdSummary
Set focus on txtName
End cmdAddClub Click

continues

161

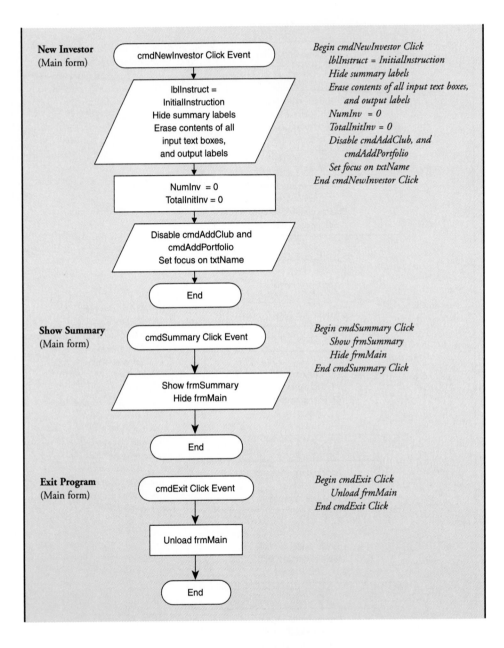

New Investor
(Main form)

cmdNewInvestor Click Event

lblInstruct =
InitialInstruction
Hide summary labels
Erase contents of all
input text boxes,
and output labels

NumInv = 0
TotalInitInv = 0

Disable cmdAddClub and
cmdAddPortfolio
Set focus on txtName

End

Begin cmdNewInvestor Click
lblInstruct = InitialInstruction
Hide summary labels
Erase contents of all input text boxes,
and output labels
NumInv = 0
TotalInitInv = 0
Disable cmdAddClub, and
cmdAddPortfolio
Set focus on txtName
End cmdNewInvestor Click

Show Summary
(Main form)

cmdSummary Click Event

Show frmSummary
Hide frmMain

End

Begin cmdSummary Click
Show frmSummary
Hide frmMain
End cmdSummary Click

Exit Program
(Main form)

cmdExit Click Event

Unload frmMain

End

Begin cmdExit Click
Unload frmMain
End cmdExit Click

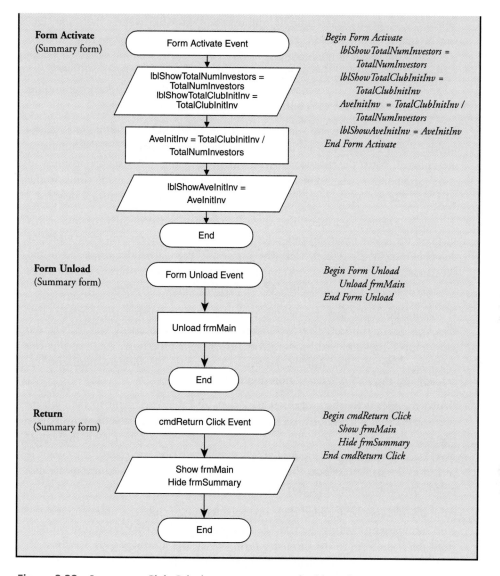

Form Activate
(Summary form)

Form Activate Event

lblShowTotalNumInvestors =
TotalNumInvestors
lblShowTotalClubInitInv =
TotalClubInitInv

AveInitInv = TotalClubInitInv /
TotalNumInvestors

lblShowAveInitInv =
AveInitInv

End

Begin Form Activate
  lblShowTotalNumInvestors =
    TotalNumInvestors
  lblShowTotalClubInitInv =
    TotalClubInitInv
  AveInitInv = TotalClubInitInv /
    TotalNumInvestors
  lblShowAveInitInv = AveInitInv
End Form Activate

Form Unload
(Summary form)

Form Unload Event

Unload frmMain

End

Begin Form Unload
  Unload frmMain
End Form Unload

Return
(Summary form)

cmdReturn Click Event

Show frmMain
Hide frmSummary

End

Begin cmdReturn Click
  Show frmMain
  Hide frmSummary
End cmdReturn Click

Figure 3.38   Investment Club Calculator *program micro-level logic design.*

When the form is loaded into memory, the *form load* event takes place. The procedure that handles this event will assign the instruction label at the top of the form a long, descriptive caption, ensure that the proper labels are either hidden or visible, erase the contents of all input text boxes and output labels, and initialize the counters and accumulators. Finally, this procedure will disable several buttons.

When the program begins running, the user will most likely enter the input data for the first investment and then click the *Calculate* button. This event procedure will assign the values in the input text boxes to their corresponding variables. These values will then be used to compute the initial investment amount required, based on the PV formula. The computed answer will be displayed in its corresponding label and the *Add to Portfolio* button enabled.

If the user is happy with this investment, it can be added to the portfolio by clicking the *Add to Portfolio* button. In this event, the investor's counter and accumulator are updated. Next, the investor's name, and current summary data are assigned to their corresponding labels. Finally, the portfolio summary data is made visible to the user, the *Add to Club* button is enabled, and the *Add to Portfolio* button is disabled.

To check another investment, the user can just change the desired input controls or press the *Clear Inputs* button. The *Clear Inputs* click event will clear all input controls (except the name), clear the previously calculated and displayed initial investment, and place the cursor in the *Investment Goal* text box. The summary labels will also be hidden and the *Add to Portfolio* button disabled.

If at some point the user decides not to make any investments, the user can click the *New Investor* button. The *New Investor* click event processing will include the same processing employed by the *Clear Inputs* event procedure. Additionally, the *Investor Name* text box will be cleared, the investor's accumulator and counter zeroed, and the *Add to Club* button disabled.

When the user is finished, the user may then add the investment to the club by pressing the *Add to Club* button. This event performs two main functions: It updates the summary data for the club and resets the summary data for an individual investor. Additionally, the input controls and answer label are erased, the cursor is placed in the name text box, the *Add to Portfolio* and *Add to Club* buttons are disabled, the *Club Summary* button is enabled, and the summary labels are hidden.

After all investors have added their investments to the club, the user can view the club summary by clicking the *Club Summary* button. This click event just switches from the main form to the summary form. When the summary form is activated, that form's activate event calculates and places the club's summary answers in their corresponding labels. The user may return to the main form by clicking the *Return* button.

At any time, the user can terminate the program by clicking the *Exit* button on the main form or the *X* on the summary form's title bar.

Step 3c: Develop a Test Plan (Table of Input with Sample Results)

The written test plan for this program should minimally test that each of the major computations works correctly. Figure 3.39 shows a list of the set of test cases we will use. FV (Future Value) denotes the investment goal and PV (Present Value), the initial investment.

Sample Input	Anticipated Output
Enter the following investments for John Doe, and click *Calculate* followed by *Add to Portfolio* for each investment: FV=1000; Term=1; Rate=5 FV=2000; Term=5; Rate=10 Click *Add to Club.*	The PV will appear after clicking *Calculate,* and the Number of Investments and Total Value will appear after clicking *Add to Portfolio*: PV=952.38; Number=1; Total=952.38 PV=1241.84; Number=2; Total=2194.22
Enter the following investment for Jane Smith, and click *Calculate* followed by *Add to Portfolio*: FV=5000; Term=2; Rate=8 Click *Add to Club.*	The PV will appear after clicking *Calculate,* and the Number of Investments and Total Value will appear after clicking *Add to Portfolio*: PV=4286.69; Number=1; Total=4286.69
Click *Club Summary.*	Number of Investors: 2 Total Value of Investments: 6480.92 Average Investment: 3240.46

Figure 3.39   *Test plan for* Investment Club Calculator *program.*

Step 4: Code the Problem

If you want to practice translating logic into Visual Basic code, you can refer to Appendix B to see how to translate each of the flowchart segments into their corresponding Visual Basic code. After you finish, compare your translation to the one shown in Figure 3.40 (which shows the contents of the Code window for our *Investment Calculator* program). If there are differences between our solution and your solution, you may want to discuss the differences with your instructor. If any errors are flagged, you can use our solution to help identify the lines that may need to be revised, and then debug your program.

```
MODULE

' Module:     basGlobal
' Purpose:    Contains global constants and variables

Option Explicit

Public gTotalNumInvestors As Integer   ' Total number of investors
Public gTotalClubInitInv As Currency   ' Total club initial investments
```

continues

```
MAIN FORM

' Program:    Chapter 3: Investment Calculator
' Form:       frmMain (Program starts with this form)
' Programmer: Ima Goodstudent
' Purpose:    This program computes initial investment for individual
'             club members & for the club as a whole. Given the future
'             goal, annual interest rate, & term in years, the initial
'             investment will be found & displayed. Additionally, for
'             multiple investments by a single investor, the number of
'             investments & their total value are found & displayed.
'             Finally, the number of investors, their total & average
'             initial investments, are displayed on a summary form.

Option Explicit

Private Const cfInitialInstruction As String = "Enter your invest" _
    & "ment goal, assumed annual percentage growth rate, and term " _
    & "in years. Click CALC to see the required initial investment."
Private fInitInv As Currency          ' Initial investment amount
Private fNumInv As Integer            ' Number of investments
Private fTotalInitInv As Currency     ' Total of all initial investments

' Purpose:    When Add to Club button is clicked, the club's summary
'             data and instructions are updated, the portfolio
'             summary labels are made invisible, the labels and text
'             boxes that are used for I/O are cleared, command buttons
'             are enabled/disabled, the counter and accumulator for
'             the individual are zeroed, & the focus is on the name.
Private Sub cmdAddClub_Click()
    gTotalClubInitInv = gTotalClubInitInv + fTotalInitInv
    gTotalNumInvestors = gTotalNumInvestors + 1
    fNumInv = 0
    fTotalInitInv = 0
    lblInstruct.Caption = "Click CLUB SUMMARY for club summary " _
        & "form. Otherwise - " & cfInitialInstruction
    lblPortfolioSummary.Visible = False
    lblNumInv.Visible = False
    lblShowNumInv.Visible = False
    lblTotalInitInv.Visible = False
    lblShowTotalInitInv.Visible = False
    txtName.Text = ""
    txtGoal.Text = ""
    txtRate.Text = ""
    txtYears.Text = ""
    lblShowInitInv.Caption = ""
    lblShowNumInv.Caption = ""
    lblShowTotalInitInv.Caption = ""
    cmdAddClub.Enabled = False
    cmdAddPortfolio.Enabled = False
    cmdSummary.Enabled = True
    Call txtName.SetFocus
End Sub

' Purpose:    When the Portfolio button is clicked, the investor's
'             investment summary data are updated and displayed,
'             instructions are displayed, and command buttons are
'             enabled/disabled.
Private Sub cmdAddPortfolio_Click()
    fTotalInitInv = fTotalInitInv + fInitInv
    fNumInv = fNumInv + 1
    lblPortfolioSummary.Caption = "Portfolio Summary-" & txtName.Text
```

```
        lblPortfolioSummary.Visible = True
        lblNumInv.Visible = True
        lblShowNumInv.Visible = True
        lblTotalInitInv.Visible = True
        lblShowTotalInitInv.Visible = True
        lblShowTotalInitInv.Caption = Format(fTotalInitInv, "currency")
        lblShowNumInv.Caption = Format(fNumInv, "0")
        lblInstruct.Caption = "Click CLEAR INPUTS to enter another " _
            & "investment. Click ADD TO CLUB to add your investments " _
            & "to the club and start a new investor.  Click NEW " _
            & "INVESTOR to cancel your investments and start a new " _
            & "investor."
        cmdAddClub.Enabled = True
        cmdAddPortfolio.Enabled = False
End Sub

' Purpose:    When the Calculate button is clicked, the initial
'             investment value is computed, the answer displayed, the
'             instructions are updated, & the Add to Portfolio button
'             is enabled and receives the focus.
Private Sub cmdCalculate_Click()
    Dim InvGoal As Currency    ' investment goal
    Dim Rate As Double         ' annual growth rate (percent)
    Dim Years As Integer       ' term of investment in years

    InvGoal = CCur(txtGoal.Text)
    Rate = CDbl(txtRate.Text) / 100
    Years = CInt(txtYears.Text)
    fInitInv = InvGoal / (1 + Rate) ^ Years
    lblShowInitInv.Caption = Format(fInitInv, "currency")
    lblInstruct.Caption = "Click ADD TO PORTFOLIO to add this " _
        & "investment to your portfolio. Click CLEAR INPUTS to " _
        & "cancel this calculation. Click NEW INVESTOR to cancel " _
        & "your investments and start a new investor."
    cmdAddPortfolio.Enabled = True
    Call cmdAddPortfolio.SetFocus
End Sub

' Purpose:    When Clear Inputs clicked, all input controls except
'             Investor Name are erased, the Initial Investment output
'             label is blanked, the Add Portfolio button is enabled, &
'             the cursor is placed in the Investment Goal text box.
Private Sub cmdClear_Click()
    txtGoal.Text = ""
    txtRate.Text = ""
    txtYears.Text = ""
    lblShowInitInv.Caption = ""
    lblInstruct.Caption = cfInitialInstruction
    cmdAddPortfolio.Enabled = False
    Call txtGoal.SetFocus
End Sub

' Purpose:    When the Exit button is clicked, the program terminates.
Private Sub cmdExit_Click()
    Unload frmMain
End Sub

' Purpose:    When New Investor clicked, the labels & text boxes that
'             are used for input/output are cleared, the counter
'             and accumulator for the individual are zeroed, the Add
'             Portfolio and Club buttons are disabled, and the focus
'             is put on the name.
```

continues

167

```vb
Private Sub cmdNewInvestor_Click()
    lblInstruct.Caption = cfInitialInstruction
    lblPortfolioSummary.Visible = False
    lblNumInv.Visible = False
    lblShowNumInv.Visible = False
    lblTotalInitInv.Visible = False
    lblShowTotalInitInv.Visible = False
    txtName.Text = ""
    txtGoal.Text = ""
    txtRate.Text = ""
    txtYears.Text = ""
    lblShowInitInv.Caption = ""
    lblShowNumInv.Caption = ""
    lblShowTotalInitInv.Caption = ""
    fNumInv = 0
    fTotalInitInv = 0
    cmdAddClub.Enabled = False
    cmdAddPortfolio.Enabled = False
    Call txtName.SetFocus
End Sub

' Purpose:    When Club Summary is pressed, the summary form
'             is displayed and the main form is hidden.
Private Sub cmdSummary_Click()
    Call frmSummary.Show
    Call frmMain.Hide
End Sub

' Purpose:    When the form is activated at start-up or when the user
'             returns here from summary, the focus is put on the name.
Private Sub Form_Activate()
    Call txtName.SetFocus
End Sub

' Purpose:    At start up the instructions are displayed, the labels &
'             text boxes that are used for input/output are cleared,
'             counters and accumulators are initialized, & the Add
'             Club, Add Portfolio, and Summary buttons are disabled.
Private Sub Form_Load()
    lblInstruct.Caption = cfInitialInstruction
    lblPortfolioSummary.Visible = False
    lblNumInv.Visible = False
    lblShowNumInv.Visible = False
    lblTotalInitInv.Visible = False
    lblShowTotalInitInv.Visible = False
    txtName.Text = ""
    txtGoal.Text = ""
    txtRate.Text = ""
    txtYears.Text = ""
    lblShowInitInv.Caption = ""
    lblShowNumInv.Caption = ""
    lblShowTotalInitInv.Caption = ""
    fNumInv = 0
    fTotalInitInv = 0
    gTotalNumInvestors = 0
    gTotalClubInitInv = 0
    cmdAddClub.Enabled = False
```

```
            cmdAddPortfolio.Enabled = False
            cmdSummary.Enabled = False
     End Sub

     ' Purpose:     When the Close button on the title bar is clicked, the
     '              program terminates execution.
     Private Sub Form_Unload(Cancel As Integer)
         Unload frmSummary
     End Sub
```

```
     SUMMARY FORM

     ' Form:        frmSummary
     ' Purpose:     This form displays the number of investors & their total
     '              initial investments & calculates & displays the average
     '              initial investment per investor.

     Option Explicit

     ' Purpose:     When Return to Main Form is clicked, the Summary
     '              form is hidden and the Main form is shown.
     Private Sub cmdReturn_Click()
         Call frmMain.Show
         Call frmSummary.Hide
     End Sub

     ' Purpose:     When the summary form is displayed, the number of
     '              investors & their total initial investments are
     '              displayed.  The average initial investment per investor
     '              is calculated and displayed.
     Private Sub Form_Activate()
         Dim AveInitInv As Currency   ' Average Initial Investment

         lblShowTotalNumInvestors.Caption = Format(gTotalNumInvestors, "0")
         lblShowTotalClubInitInv.Caption = Format(gTotalClubInitInv, _
             "currency")
         AveInitInv = gTotalClubInitInv / gTotalNumInvestors
         lblShowAveInitInv.Caption = Format(AveInitInv, "currency")
     End Sub

     ' Purpose:     When the Close button on the title bar is clicked, the
     '              program terminates execution.
     Private Sub Form_Unload(Cancel As Integer)
         Unload frmMain
     End Sub
```

Figure 3.40 *Code for* Investment Club Calculator *program.*

Step 5: Test and Debug the Program

Now that the program is written, we can test its accuracy by using the test data we developed in step 3c. Refer to Figure 3.41 for the actual program snapshots.

1. Startup screen:

Investment Calculator by Ima Goodstudent

Enter your investment goal, assumed annual percentage growth rate, and term in years. Click CALCULATE to see the required initial investment.

Investor Name

Investment Goal   Term in Years   Growth Rate [%]

Initial Investment

Calculate
Add to Portfolio
Clear Inputs
Add to Club
New Investor
Club Summary
Exit

2. John Doe's first investment calculation:

Investment Calculator by Ima Goodstudent

Click ADD TO PORTFOLIO to add this investment to your portfolio. Click CLEAR INPUTS to cancel this calculation. Click NEW INVESTOR to cancel your investments and start a new investor.

Investor Name
John Doe

Investment Goal   Term in Years   Growth Rate [%]
1000   1   5

Initial Investment $952.38

Calculate
Add to Portfolio
Clear Inputs
Add to Club
New Investor
Club Summary
Exit

3. Click *Add to Portfolio*:

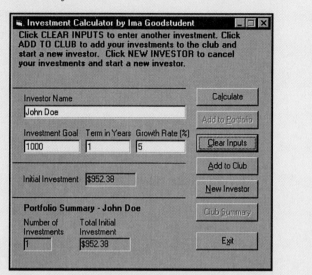

4. Click *Clear Inputs*:

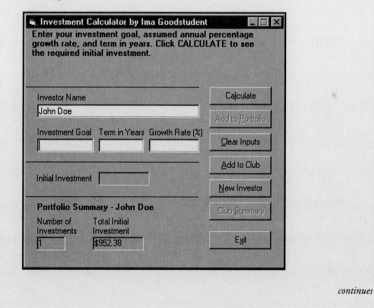

continues

5. Calculate second investment and add to portfolio:

6. Click *Add to Club*:

7. Calculate Jane's investment and add to portfolio:

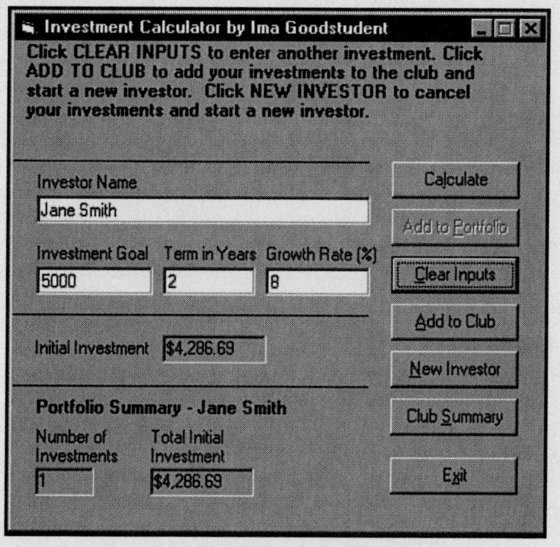

8. Add to club and then click *Club Summary.*

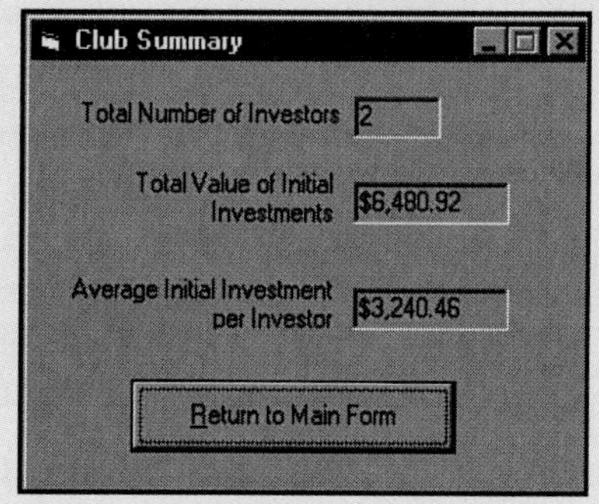

Figure 3.41   *Sample output using test data from design.*

Step 6: Assemble the Final Documentation

Now that the program has been tested and produced the expected results, you should gather all the documentation that describes the program and the problem it solves. This includes all the following deliverables (documents): Analysis Table, Object-Event Diagram, flowcharts/pseudocode, test plan, form image, form text, code, and output snapshots. Organize all these materials logically into a single folder or binder, keeping the needs of your user or teacher in mind.

Summary

The information that your program displays, whether typed by the user or displayed by your program, is often stored in a control as a string. If you want to perform arithmetic operations on the data item, it must be converted from a string representation to a numeric representation. The *CInt, CLng, CCur, and CDbl* functions are used in Visual Basic to convert a String to Integer, Long, Currency, and Double type values, respectively. You can use the *Format* function to convert Integer, Long, Currency, or Double data types to a String type. *Format* has two arguments (values inside parentheses): The first argument is the identifier, or name, of the data item to be converted; the second argument is a string constant and specifies the format or appearance of the string. Use "0" when you are converting any of these four data types and you want the result rounded to the nearest integer. Use "0.0" or "0.00" to convert Double or Currency to a string rounded to one or two decimal places, respectively.

To perform calculations on numeric data, Visual Basic has seven arithmetic operators. They include the four standard operations of + for addition, – for subtraction, * for multiplication, and / for division. There are three additional operators: ^, which is used for exponentiation; \, which is used for integer division; and Mod, which returns the remainder of an integer division. All these operators can be used with any combination of type Integer, Long, or Double numbers.

For the arithmetic operators, Visual Basic has six levels of precedence that control the order in which Visual Basic performs the operations in a calculation. Addition (+) and subtraction (–) have a lower precedence than the multiplication and division operators (*, /, \, Mod). The exponentiation operator (^) has the highest precedence. When an equation contains more than one operation from the same precedence level, they are performed left to right. You can use parentheses to alter the natural order of evaluation and to make an expression more readable.

Large programs will have many variables and constants. Scope is the area or extent of a program in which a variable or constant is recognized and can be used. There are several different levels of scope. Local variables and constants are declared inside a procedure, and can only be accessed by statements within that procedure. Local variables that are not static do not exist until the procedure begins execution, and they no longer exist after the procedure has finished execution. Variables and constants with form scope are declared Private in the General Declaration section at the top of the form's Code window. Global-level variables and constants are declared Public in the General Declaration section at the top of a standard module.

Good programmers generally follow coding style guidelines so that their programs will look neat and can be easily read by other programmers. Good coding style includes using meaningful names for identifiers, proper indentation, spaces around operators, and indentation of the continuation portions of statements that will not fit on one line.

Key Terms

accumulating	global variables	Private
arithmetic operators	incrementing	project-level scope
binary operators	lifetime	Public
coding style	local constants	rules of precedence
coding guidelines	local variables	scope
counting	Mod	standard modules
data conversion	module-level scope	static variable
divide operators	modulus operator	string to numeric con-version
form load event	numeric to string con-version	type conversion functions
form-level scope	operands	variable scope
Format functions	operator	vbNewLine
functions	operator precedence	
global scope		

Test Your Understanding

1. What is the result of 23.5 \ 6?

2. What is the purpose of using a type conversion function to display the result of a calculation on the screen?

3. Suppose you are writing a program to calculate the total number of books received by a bookstore in one day. When each box of new books is opened, the clerk will type into a text box on the screen the number of books received in that shipment. What data conversion function from Figure 3.2 would you use in this program to use the value entered by the clerk in the calculation by storing it in variable *BooksInBox*? Defend your answer.

4. Continuation of problem 3: The following statement appears in the *Add Books* button click event procedure: TotBooks = TotBooks + BooksInBox. Which variable is the accumulator? Which variable can be a local variable, and which variable should have form-level scope?

5. What are the seven arithmetic operators in Visual Basic?

6. What is the result of 23 Mod 6?

7. Apply the precedence rules to the following calculation. What is the answer?

15 – 10 + 10 / 5 * 2 – 5

Calling a Procedure

To execute this code, our program must specifically "call" this procedure because it has now been separated from its event. In contrast, event procedures are automatically invoked in response to events caused by the user or triggered by the system. At the point in our program where the *InitializeForm* procedure should be executed, we must insert a *Call* statement of the form

```
Call InitializeForm
```

where we had removed the 16 lines of duplicate code. When the *Call* statement is executed, control is transferred to the *InitializeForm* procedure. When *InitializeForm* has finished execution, control is transferred back to the calling procedure and execution resumes at the statement that follows the *Call*. Figure 4.2 illustrates three procedures, each calling a fourth procedure. The lines indicate how program flow passes from the calling procedure to the called procedure and then back to the statement following the *Call*.

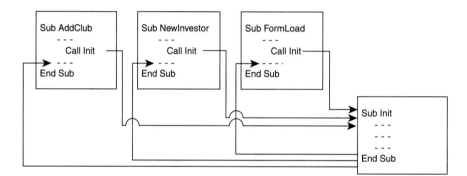

Figure 4.2   *Control flow between calling and called procedures.*

A Procedure Can Call Another Procedure

After looking at the program a bit more, we notice that the three text boxes used to enter investment goal, term, and rate are cleared in both the *cmdClear_Click* and *InitializeForm* procedures. We decide to remove the common code from both procedures and place them in a new procedure called *ClearInput*. See Figure 4.3 for a listing of *ClearInput* and our second version of *InitializeForm*. Although we have defined *ClearInput* prior to calling it from *InitializeForm*, Visual Basic does not require any particular ordering of functions and procedures. In general, it is a good idea to group the functions and procedures alphabetically.

TIP
Keep functions and procedures in alphabetic order so that they can be easily located.

```
Private Sub ClearInput()
    ' Does not clear name text box
    txtGoal.Text = ""
    txtRate.Text = ""
    txtYears.Text = ""
End Sub

Private Sub InitializeForm()
    txtName.Text = ""
    Call ClearInput
    lblShowInitInv.Caption = ""
    lblShowNumInv.Caption = ""
    lblShowTotalInitInv.Caption = ""
    lblPortfolioSummary.Visible = False
    lblNumInv.Visible = False
    lblShowNumInv.Visible = False
    lblTotalInitInv.Visible = False
    lblShowTotalInitInv.Visible = False
    fNumInv = 0
    fTotalInitInv = 0
    cmdAddClub.Enabled = False
    cmdAddPortfolio.Enabled = False
End Sub
```

Figure 4.3   *Code for procedure* InitializeForm, *version 2.*

Improving Understandability

We discussed earlier in this chapter that an important reason for using procedures and functions was to break down a complex program or module into several simpler and easier-to-understand subroutines. A rule of thumb for procedure length states that it should never be too large to fit on one screen. It is easier to understand a procedure or function if you can see the entire procedure without having to scroll up or down.

Our *InitializeForm* procedure in Figure 4.3 still appears to be a hodgepodge of unrelated lines of code; if we partition the code by functionality into one or more new procedures, however, we can make the resultant procedures shorter and easier to understand. After looking more closely at *InitializeForm*, we realize that three statements are used to clear the three output labels and five statements are used to hide summary-related labels. We can subdivide this procedure by creating two additional procedures with the descriptive names *ClearOutput* and *HideSummary*, and we should move the relevant code into each procedure.

We also notice that although we have matching procedures for *ClearInput* and *ClearOutput*, we do not have a match for *HideSummary*. A quick scan of the event procedures in the calculator program finds the matching five statements in *cmdAddPortfolio_Click* that are used to enable the display of the summary information. We decide to put these statements in a procedure named *ShowSummary*. Figure 4.4 displays the final version of our code for *InitializeForm*. Note that by using descriptive names for the procedures, we have made the *InitializeForm* procedure easier to understand.

```
Dim X as Double
Dim Result as Double

X = 20000
Result = Sqr(X)
lblShowResult.Caption = Format(Result, "0.000")
```

Using a Function's Returned Value to Determine the Flow of Code Execution

Some functions return a data type called *Boolean*, and your code can use such a function to branch to various tasks and routines based on whether the function returned *True* or *False*. We will be able to examine this use of a function as soon as we cover conditional statements.

Discarding a Function's Returned Value

Visual Basic enables you to treat a function call the same as a procedure call. This means you are discarding the returned value from a function call. Normally the function returns a value that will be used by the calling statement. In certain situations, however, the function performs some useful action and the returned result is not needed. When this situation occurs, Visual Basic allows the function to be treated as a procedure. The following statements both call the function *ProcessReading*, but they discard the returned value:

```
Call ProcessReading(CollectorVoltage, DeviceNumber)
ProcessReading CollectorVoltage, DeviceNumber
```

Example Program with Arguments

A local surveying firm is subdividing a section into triangular building lots. The firm sends out a surveying crew that measures two sides of a triangular lot and the included angle (the angle between the two sides). The lengths are measured in feet, and the angle is expressed in degrees. Using this information, the surveyors want to calculate the length of the third side and the area of the lot. You have been hired by the firm to design a program that will perform the desired calculations and display the results. The program's specifications state that the third side's length should be displayed rounded to one place beyond the decimal point and the area should be rounded to the nearest square foot.

After signing the contract to produce this program, you use a trigonometry book to locate the following mathematical formulae:

```
a2 = b2 + c2 - 2bcCos(A)
area = |bcSin(A)/2|
```

where b and c are the lengths of two sides of a triangle, and A is their included angle. The first formula is used to calculate the length a of the third side of the triangle, and the second formula is used to calculate the area. The vertical bars in the second formula mean that the *absolute value* is to be used.

Program *Function1* shown in Figure 4.9 uses several functions that are provided by Visual Basic. When the program begins execution, the user enters values for the base, adjacent side, and included angle, and then clicks the *Calculate* button. The program then calculates and displays the length of the third side and the area of the triangle.

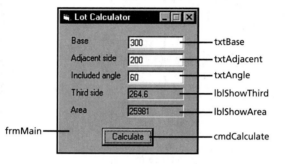

Figure 4.9   *Form for program* Function1.

To create the *Function1* program, follow these steps:

1. Open a new project called Function1. Name the form frmMain and set its Caption property to Lot Calculator.

2. Add five labels on the left side of the form. Add text box controls txtBase, txtAdjacent, and txtAngle on the upper-right of the form. Set their TabIndex properties to 0, 1, and 2, respectively.

3. Add the labels lblShowThird and lblShowArea. These labels will be used to display the results of the calculations. Set their BorderStyle properties to FixedSingle.

4. Add the button cmdCalculate.

5. Double-click on the *Calculate* button and use Figure 4.10 to enter the code for *cmdCalculate*.

6. Run and test the application.

Let's take a careful look at the code shown in Figure 4.10. This code is executed when the user clicks the *Calculate* button. Note the comments at the beginning of the procedure. This particular procedure uses some specialized formulae to calculate the included angle and area of the triangle. Without the comments, someone who has to modify this program would probably have a difficult time understanding what this procedure is supposed to do. Because we cannot put superscripts in our comments, we have to use terms such as a^2 to denote a^2.

Our program expects the user to enter the angle in degrees, but if we look in Visual Basic Help files, we find that the *Sin* and *Cos* functions require radians. By using a meaningful name when we defined the constant *cDegToRad*, we have made the code easier to read and maintain.

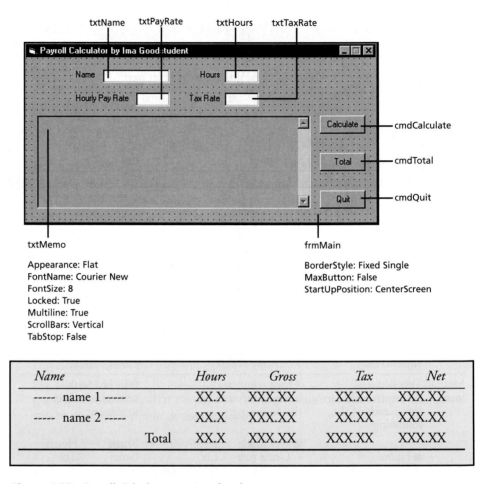

txtName   txtPayRate   txtHours   txtTaxRate

cmdCalculate

cmdTotal

cmdQuit

txtMemo

Appearance: Flat
FontName: Courier New
FontSize: 8
Locked: True
Multiline: True
ScrollBars: Vertical
TabStop: False

frmMain

BorderStyle: Fixed Single
MaxButton: False
StartUpPosition: CenterScreen

Name		Hours	Gross	Tax	Net
----- name 1 -----		XX.X	XXX.XX	XX.XX	XXX.XX
----- name 2 -----		XX.X	XXX.XX	XX.XX	XXX.XX
	Total	XX.X	XXX.XX	XXX.XX	XXX.XX

Figure 4.26 Payroll Calculator *user interface design.*

Step 3: Design the Logic for the Program

Now that the form is done, we can begin to think about how the program will actually function. Because we have not yet studied the programming control structure that allows our program to branch (make decisions about which portion of code to execute), our design will not be "user proof." As an example, if the user clicks the *Calculate* button before entering valid data, the program will attempt to convert this data from string form to numeric form. This will cause the program to display a Run Time error message and then terminate execution. After you have studied a few more chapters in this text, you will be able to fix this problem.

Step 3a: Design the Macro-View (Object-Event Diagrams)

Because there is only one form, our macro logic will consist of two OEDs: the overall project, shown in Figure 4.27; and the main form, shown in Figure 4.28. As you can see in Figure 4.28, our *Payroll* program will consist of four events:

- One for each of the three command buttons
- A form load event to initialize accumulators and format the report header in the output text box

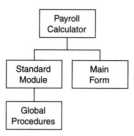

Figure 4.27   Payroll Calculator *Object-Event Diagram (overall view).*

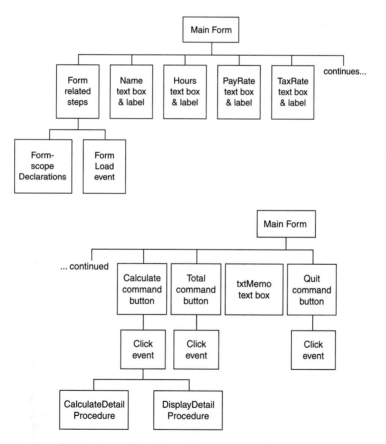

Figure 4.28   Payroll Calculator *Object-Event Diagram (main form).*

Step 3b: Design the Micro-Level View (Flowcharts or Pseudocode)

We will consider each event procedure as a separate and distinct processing task. Figure 4.29 shows the flowcharts and pseudocode for each of the five event procedures. We will present each of the event procedures as they appear on the Object-Event Diagram in order from left to right.

General Declarations
(Form-scope declarations Main form)

Form Load
(Main form)

Calculate
(Main form)

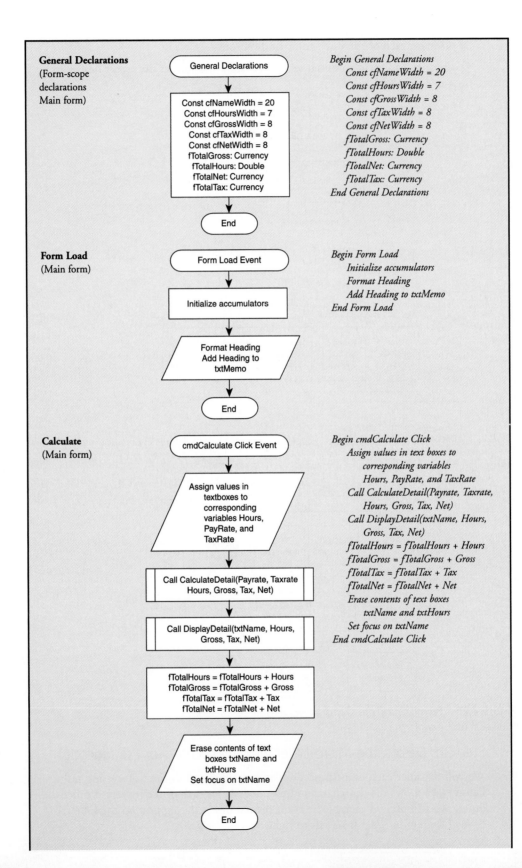

Begin General Declarations
Const cfNameWidth = 20
Const cfHoursWidth = 7
Const cfGrossWidth = 8
Const cfTaxWidth = 8
Const cfNetWidth = 8
fTotalGross: Currency
fTotalHours: Double
fTotalNet: Currency
fTotalTax: Currency
End General Declarations

Begin Form Load
Initialize accumulators
Format Heading
Add Heading to txtMemo
End Form Load

Begin cmdCalculate Click
Assign values in text boxes to corresponding variables Hours, PayRate, and TaxRate
Call CalculateDetail(Payrate, Taxrate, Hours, Gross, Tax, Net)
Call DisplayDetail(txtName, Hours, Gross, Tax, Net)
fTotalHours = fTotalHours + Hours
fTotalGross = fTotalGross + Gross
fTotalTax = fTotalTax + Tax
fTotalNet = fTotalNet + Net
Erase contents of text boxes txtName and txtHours
Set focus on txtName
End cmdCalculate Click

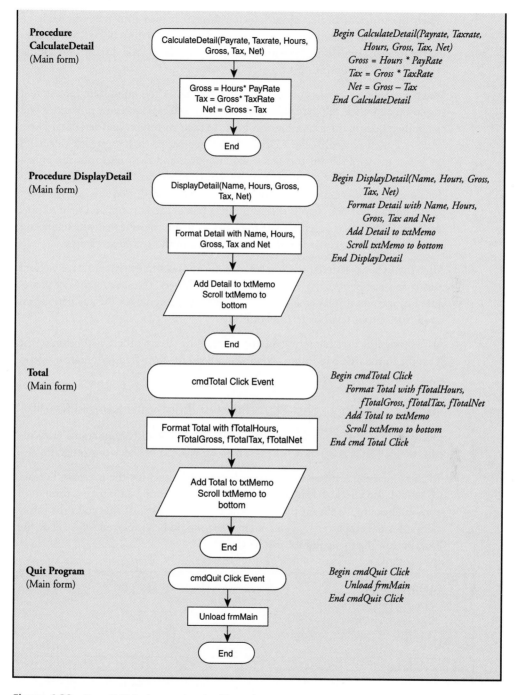

Figure 4.29 Payroll Calculator *micro-level logic design.*

When the program begins execution, the form is loaded into memory, and the *Form_Load* event is invoked. The *Form_Load* event procedure begins by initializing the total accumulators, formatting a heading for the payroll display, and adding the heading to the output text box.

When the form is visible onscreen, the user will enter the input data for the first employee and click the *Calculate* button. The *cmdCalculate Click* procedure will assign the values in the four input text boxes to their corresponding variables. These values are then passed to the *CalculateDetail* general procedure, which calculates the gross, tax, and net for this particular employee and then returnsto the procedure that called it. The employee's name, hours, gross, tax, and net are passed to the *DisplayDetail* general procedure, which formats and displays the information on the output text box, scrolls the output text box to the bottom, and then returns to the procedure that called it. The total accumulators are updated, the name and hours text boxes are cleared, and the focus is put on the *txtName* text box.

After the user has entered the information for those employees who have worked during this pay period, the *Total* button will be clicked. The *cmdTotal Click* procedure formats and displays the total hours, gross, tax, and net for the pay period and scrolls the output text box to the bottom.

At any time, the user can terminate the program by clicking the *Quit* button or the X on the form's title bar. Either action will unload the form and terminate program execution.

Step 3c: Develop a Test Plan (Table of Input with Sample Results)

Our written test plan for this program must check that all computations give correct results. Figure 4.30 shows the test data we will use to check our program.

To check that the text box scrolls to the bottom after clicking the *Calculate* button, we should also check the situation where we keep entering employee information until the heading scrolls off the top of the output text box. At this point the information for the employee that was entered last should be visible, and if we click the *Total* button the totals should also be visible.

Sample Input Hourly Pay Rate = 6.57 Tax Rate = 0.30	Anticipated Output			
Name	*Hours*	*Gross*	*Tax*	*Net*
Joseph Schmidt	34.0	223.38	67.01	156.37
Samuel Bennet	33.0	216.81	65.04	151.77
Total	67.0	440.19	132.05	308.14

Figure 4.30 *Test plan for* Payroll Calculator *program.*

Step 4: Code the Program

At this point you are ready to implement your design in Visual Basic. Most of the creative work has already been done, and in fact at some companies you would turn your design documentation over to a junior programmer who would code and test the program. The programmer will have to develop several implementation details, however. In the *Form_Load* event procedure, a heading has to be formatted; and in the *DisplayDetail* general procedure, a detail line has to be formatted. As shown in Figure 4.26, *formatted* means that the output columns must be exactly aligned with the names left-adjusted and the numeric data right-adjusted. In addition, we will have to use a font with fixed spacing in the output text box.

Figures 4.32a and 4.32b are listings of the code for our *Payroll Calculator* program. Because we have just been introduced to some of the string manipulating functions provided by Visual Basic, it may be instructive to take a look at the method by which this program constructs or builds a line of formatted output. Take a look at either the *Form_Load* or *DisplayDetail* procedure and you will notice that both procedures use general function procedures *LeftAlign* and *RightAlign*. These two functions are so useful that we expect to want to use them in other programs that we will write. We therefore put these functions in a standard module called *basTools*, and we will add *basTools* to any program that needs to left- or right-adjust strings. Because both functions are quite similar in the way they work, we will discuss only *LeftAlign*.

General function procedure *LeftAlign* is passed a string called *Source* and an integer called *Length*. *LeftAlign* creates a new string *Result*, which consists entirely of *Length* number of spaces (blanks). The string *Source* is then left-aligned within *Result*, and the resultant string is returned to the calling procedure. The Visual Basic code that does this is as follows:

```
Result = Space(Length)
LSet Result = Source
```

In the preceding code, the first line creates the string of blanks, and the second line uses Visual Basic's *LSet* statement to left-align *Source* within *Result*. See Figure 4.31 for a graphic representation of this procedure.

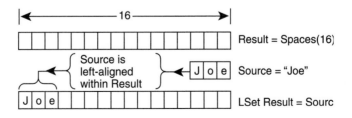

Figure 4.31 *Using* LSet *to left-align strings.*

Each time the user enters information for an employee and then clicks the *Calculate* button, a line of information is added to the bottom of the *txtMemo* text box. The same thing happens when the *Total* button is clicked. It is important that when the output text box fills up, it starts to scroll down as each line of payroll information is displayed. We make sure that this happens by taking the following steps:

- Set the MultiLine property of *txtMemo* to True. This can only be done at design time.

- Follow our design specifications as shown in Figure 4.29 and add the following line of code to the end of procedures *cmdTotal_Click* and *DisplayDetail.*

```
txtMemo.SelStart = Len(txtMemo.Text)
```

This line of code moves the selection point to the end of the text box and makes sure that the last line is visible.

As you implement this design in Visual Basic, you should keep in mind that one of the main reasons for using procedures is to reduce complexity. Because you now know how to create and call your own procedures, you should make sure you take advantage of this powerful development aid.

```
' Program:    Chapter 4: Payroll Calculator
' Form:       frmMain
' Programmer: Ima Goodstudent
' Date:       May 13, 1998
' Purpose:    This program uses the hours worked, hourly pay rate, and
'             tax rate to calculate the gross pay, tax, and net pay.
'             For each employee the name, hours, gross, tax and net are
'             displayed. When the Total button is clicked, totals are
'             displayed for the hours, gross, tax, and net.

Option Explicit

' Detail column width constants
Private Const cfNameWidth = 20
Private Const cfHoursWidth = 7
Private Const cfGrossWidth = 8
Private Const cfTaxWidth = 8
Private Const cfNetWidth = 8


' Accumulators
Private fTotalGross As Currency
Private fTotalHours As Double
Private fTotalNet As Currency
Private fTotalTax As Currency

' Purpose:    Calculate gross pay, tax, and net pay
'             Assumes no overtime (hours <= 40)
Private Sub CalculateDetail(ByVal PayRate As Currency, _
        ByVal TaxRate As Double, _
        ByVal Hours As Double, _
        ByRef rGross As Currency, _
        ByRef rTax As Currency, _
        ByRef rNet As Currency)

    rGross = Hours * PayRate
    rTax = rGross * TaxRate
    rNet = rGross - rTax
End Sub
```

```vb
' Purpose:    When the Calculate button is clicked gross, tax, and net
'             are calculated and displayed. Additionally, the total
'             accumulators are updated, Name and Hours text boxes are
'             cleared, and the focus is put on the Name text box.
Private Sub cmdCalculate_Click()
    Dim Gross As Currency
    Dim Hours As Double
    Dim Net As Currency
    Dim PayRate As Currency
    Dim Tax As Currency
    Dim TaxRate As Double

    Hours = CDbl(txtHours.Text)
    PayRate = CCur(txtPayRate.Text)
    TaxRate = CDbl(txtTaxRate.Text)
    Call CalculateDetail(PayRate, TaxRate, Hours, Gross, Tax, Net)
    Call DisplayDetail(txtName.Text, Hours, Gross, Tax, Net)
    fTotalHours = fTotalHours + Hours
    fTotalGross = fTotalGross + Gross
    fTotalTax = fTotalTax + Tax
    fTotalNet = fTotalNet + Net
    txtName.Text = ""
    txtHours.Text = ""
    Call txtName.SetFocus
End Sub

' Purpose:    When the Quit button is clicked, the program terminates.
Private Sub cmdQuit_Click()
    Unload frmMain
End Sub

' Purpose:    When the Total button is clicked, totals for hours, gross,
'             tax and net are displayed on the output text box, and the
'             text box is scrolled to the bottom.
Private Sub cmdTotal_Click()
    txtMemo.Text = txtMemo.Text & vbNewLine & _
        RightAlign("Total", cfNameWidth) & _
        RightAlign(Format(fTotalHours, "0.0"), cfHoursWidth) & _
        RightAlign(Format(fTotalGross, "0.00"), cfGrossWidth) & _
        RightAlign(Format(fTotalTax, "0.00"), cfTaxWidth) & _
        RightAlign(Format(fTotalNet, "0.00"), cfNetWidth)

    ' Force text box to display current line
    txtMemo.SelStart = Len(txtMemo.Text)
End Sub

' Purpose:    Format and display name, hours, gross, tax, and net on the
'             output text box. Scroll the textbox to the bottom.
Private Sub DisplayDetail(ByVal Name As String, _
        ByVal Hours As Double, _
        ByVal Gross As Currency, _
        ByVal Tax As Currency, _
        ByVal Net As Currency)

    txtMemo.Text = txtMemo.Text & vbNewLine & _
        LeftAlign(Name, cfNameWidth) & _
        RightAlign(Format(Hours, "0.0"), cfHoursWidth) & _
        RightAlign(Format(Gross, "0.00"), cfGrossWidth) & _
        RightAlign(Format(Tax, "0.00"), cfTaxWidth) & _
        RightAlign(Format(Net, "0.00"), cfNetWidth)
```

continues

213

```
        ' Force text box to display current line
        txtMemo.SelStart = Len(txtMemo.Text)
End Sub

' Purpose:    At start up the accumulators are initialized, and the
'             heading is displayed on the output text box.
Private Sub Form_Load()
    ' Initialize accumulators
    fTotalGross = 0
    fTotalHours = 0
    fTotalNet = 0
    fTotalTax = 0

    ' Display Report Heading
    txtMemo.Text = LeftAlign("Name", cfNameWidth) & _
        RightAlign("Hours", cfHoursWidth) & _
        RightAlign("Gross", cfGrossWidth) & _
        RightAlign("Tax", cfTaxWidth) & _
        RightAlign("Net", cfNetWidth)
End Sub
```

Figure 4.32a   *Code for* Payroll Calculator *form* frmMain.

```
' Module:     basTools
' Purpose:    Contains public procedures: LeftAlign
'                                         RightAlign

Option Explicit

' Purpose:    Left aligns a string
' Inputs:     Source: String to be left-aligned
'             Length: Length of returned string
' Returns:    Returns a string of length Length, with Source
'             left-aligned and padded with spaces on the right
Public Function LeftAlign(ByVal Source As String, _
        ByVal Length As Integer) As String

    Dim Result As String

    Result = Space(Length)
    LSet Result = Source
    LeftAlign = Result
End Function

' Purpose:    Right aligns a string
' Inputs:     Source: String to be Right-aligned
'             Length: Length of returned string
' Returns:    Returns a string of length Length, with Source
'             right-aligned and padded with spaces on the left
Public Function RightAlign(ByVal Source As String, _
        ByVal Length As Integer) As String

    Dim Result As String

    Result = Space(Length)
    RSet Result = Source
    RightAlign = Result
End Function
```

Figure 4.32b   *Code for* Payroll Calculator *module* basTools.

Step 5: Test and Debug the Program

Now that the program is written, we begin the testing phase by running the program and using the test data we developed in step 3c. Figure 4.33 shows the program output just after clicking the *Total* button.

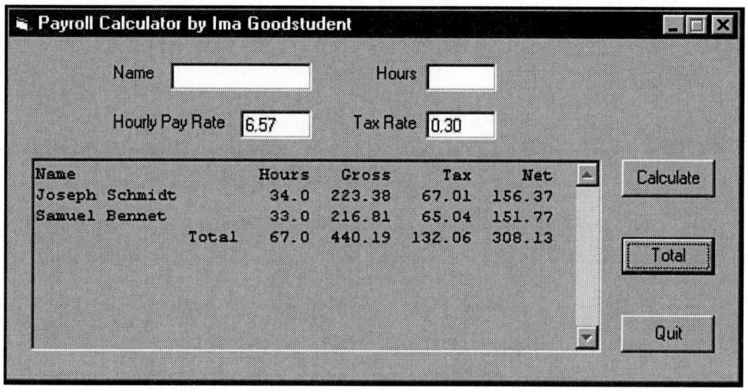

Figure 4.33   *Initial test results from* Payroll Calculator.

Now take a careful look at the Tax and Net columns in Figure 4.33. It looks like there is an error in the program because if you add the tax for Joseph and Samuel you find that the tax total is one cent too much. Similarly, if you add the net for Joseph and Samuel, the net total is one cent too little. There must be an error in the code we wrote to carry out the calculations. If you examine Figure 4.32, however, the code for the calculations seems to be correct. Furthermore, if you rerun the program with Joe's hours changed from 34 to 36, the totals are now correct! So it appears that the program sometimes gives the correct answer, but not always. Even though the error is only one penny, this is a serious error, and it is important that we understand why the error occurred and how we can fix it.

It probably didn't take you very long to figure out why our program sometimes gives the wrong answer. If you take your calculator and calculate the taxes, you find that Joe's tax is 67.014 and Sam's tax is 65.043. Because the smallest monetary unit is $0.01—that is, one penny—our program used the *Format* function to round Joe and Sam's taxes to 67.01 and 65.04, respectively. This in itself is not an error, but we should have written code so that the taxes added to the accumulator *fTotalTax* were exactly the same as the values displayed onscreen.

Rounding to the Nearest Cent

We now want to write some code that will enable us to take the values we have calculated for the taxes, round them to the nearest cent, and add the rounded values to *fTotalTax*. We would like to use the built-in function *Round*. As discussed earlier in this chapter, however, the *Round* function does not always round up. Let's try writing our own function. After a little research, we come up with the following lines of code to round the value stored in the variable *Tax*:

```
Tax = Int(Tax * 100 + 0.5) / 100
```

215

The *Int* function is listed in Appendix C, but you should also read about it in Visual Basic's Help. We will use a calculator and check each calculation in the calculation of *Tax* so that we understand how it works. Use the data for the first employee in our test example:

```
Initial value                              Tax =     67.014
Convert to cents                     Tax * 100 =  6701.400
Add 0.5 cents                  Tax * 100 + 0.5 =  6701.900
Truncate                  Int(Tax * 100 + 0.5) =  6701.000
Convert to dollars  Int(Tax * 100 + 0.5) / 100 =     67.010
```

Now that you know how to round to two decimal places, you should modify procedure *CalculateDetail* in the payroll program. The modification consists of adding one line of code so that after calculating the tax, the tax is rounded to two places beyond the decimal point. Figure 4.34 contains a listing of the modified procedure. You should run the program again and verify that the totals are now correct.

When a particular operation is performed in the body of a procedure, we say we are performing the operation inline. **Inline operations** are always faster than calling another procedure to perform the same operation, but many times we are willing to sacrifice a small amount of efficiency for a large reduction in complexity.

```
' Purpose:    Calculate gross pay, tax, and net pay
'             Assumes no overtime (hours <= 40)
Private Sub CalculateDetail(ByVal PayRate As Currency, _
        ByVal TaxRate As Double, _
        ByVal Hours As Double, _
        ByRef rGross As Currency, _
        ByRef rTax As Currency, _
        ByRef rNet As Currency)

    rGross = Hours * PayRate
    rTax = rGross * TaxRate
    rTax = Int(rTax * 100 + 0.5) / 100
    rNet = rGross - rTax
End Sub
```

Figure 4.34   *Procedure* CalculateDetail *with inline rounding.*

Adding a Custom Rounding Function

Because many of our programs will deal with dollars and cents, it seems reasonable for us to construct our own rounding function. By doing this, we don't have to remember the details of how to round every time we want to round a currency value to the nearest cent. We need to pass one data item, the currency value, to our function, so the function needs one parameter. Because we are going to use the return value of the function to return the rounded data item, the code will not need to change the value of the parameter, so we should pass the argument by value and use the *ByVal* keyword in our function definition. We will name our rounding function *RoundCur2* because it rounds a currency value to two places beyond the decimal.

Our *RoundCur2* function seems to be the kind of utility function that might be useful in other programs that we might write. We would like to make it easy to use this function. Of course, we could keep a listing of the function in our desk drawer, and because it is a short function it wouldn't take us too long to type it into any program that might need to use it. As you can guess, there has to be a better way to keep track of useful functions and procedures that you develop as you continue in your programming career.

In the course of working through this text, we will develop several useful software tools. We will save these tools in a standard module named *basTools*, and the standard module file will be named *Tools.bas*. By doing this, we can keep track of our tools and make it very easy for any program to use any of the functions or procedures. See Figure 4.35 for a listing of the *RoundCur2* function.

```
' Purpose:    Rounds Currency to 2 decimal places
' Inputs:     Money: Currency value to be rounded
' Returns:    Currency rounded to 2 decimal places
Public Function RoundCur2(ByVal Money As Currency) As Currency
    Dim Cents As Currency

    Cents = Int(Money * 100 + 0.5)
    RoundCur2 = Cents / 100
End Function
```

Figure 4.35   *Function* RoundCur2.

Now that we have our rounding function, we can modify our *CalculateDetail* procedure so that instead of performing the calculation inline, we call *CalculateDetail*. Figure 4.36 contains a listing of the up-to-date *CalculateDetail*. You should compare this version of *CalculateDetail* with the version displayed in Figure 4.34.

```
' Purpose:    Calculate gross pay, tax, and net pay
'             Assumes no overtime (hours <= 40)
Private Sub CalculateDetail(ByVal PayRate As Currency, _
        ByVal TaxRate As Double, _
        ByVal Hours As Double, _
        ByRef rGross As Currency, _
        ByRef rTax As Currency, _
        ByRef rNet As Currency)

    rGross = Hours * PayRate
    rTax = RoundCur2(rGross * TaxRate)
    rNet = rGross - rTax
End Sub
```

Figure 4.36   *Procedure* CalculateDetail *calling* RoundCur2.

It is important to understand that *anytime* you modify a program, you must again run the program through the full battery of tests. More than one programmer has been demoted as a consequence of his failure to follow this rule.

■■ TIP

Always test your program completely after any change.

Keeping the Documentation Current

Our program has not been released, and already we have made several changes. It is very important that when we make changes to the program, we must also make the corresponding changes to the documentation. If we do not do this, the documentation will lose its credibility and will be of little or no use to anyone. In fact, it is probably correct to state that the only thing worse than no documentation is invalid documentation.

■■ TIP

Keep the documentation current.

Because we have made changes to procedure *CalculateDetail*, and have added our rounding function to the *basTools* code module, we have to update our documentation to reflect the changes to the program code. For the case of *CalculateDetail*, it is a simple matter of adding the procedure call to the flowchart and pseudocode for *RoundCur2*. Function *RoundCur2* is a new addition to our program, and consequently we have to create a new flowchart and new pseudocode for this function. Finally, we have to be sure to test our program again with the test data from Figure 4.30. We make sure that this time the program output is correct, and we then generate a new copy of the test output. See Figures 4.37, 4.38, and 4.39 for the updated documentation.

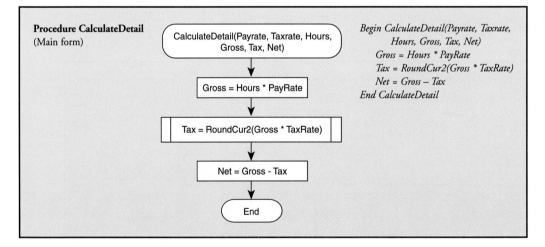

Figure 4.37 *Updated logic design for* CalculateDetail.

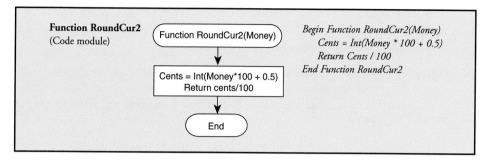

Figure 4.38   *Logic design for* RoundCur2.

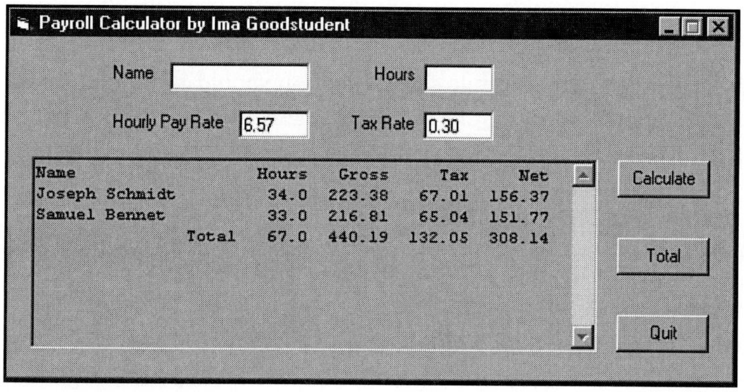

Figure 4.39   *Final test results from* Payroll Calculator.

Step 6: Assemble the Final Documentation

Now that the program has been tested and produced the expected results, you should gather all the documentation that describes the program and the problem it solves. This includes all the following deliverables (documents): Analysis Table, flowcharts/pseudocode, test plan, form image, form text, code, and output snapshots. Organize all these materials logically into a single folder or binder, keeping the needs of your user or teacher in mind.

Summary

Modularization, or breaking a program down into smaller and easier-to-understand segments, is a recommended approach to programming. Procedures and functions provide the programmer with ways to implement these modules. The difference between a function and a procedure is that a function returns a value when it stops executing, and a procedure doesn't. A procedure or function that is part of a control is called a *method.*

Functions and procedures can be passed arguments in two ways: by value and by reference. A by-value argument is preceded with the keyword *ByVal* and can only be used to send information to the called function or procedure. The default method of argument passing in Visual Basic is pass by reference, and is used when the called function or procedure must pass a value back to the calling function. The keyword *ByRef* may optionally precede a value parameter.

Visual Basic has a large number of useful functions and they can be grouped into several categories. These categories include mathematical, date and time, conversion and string functions, and statements. These functions are documented in Visual Basic's Help.

You might write your own functions and procedures for several reasons. You may be doing the same set of calculations at more than one place in your program, you may believe this set of calculations might be useful in another program, or you may want to reduce the complexity of your program by "factoring out" specific calculations.

A general guideline for module size is that you should keep procedures and functions small enough to fit on one screen. It is also a better programming practice to use parameters rather than global variables to communicate between modules.

Key Terms

arguments	method	predefined process
calling	modularity	procedure
event procedures	nested function call	property procedures
function procedures	parameter	scope visibility specifiers
general procedures	passed by reference	sub procedures
inline operations	passed by value	

Test Your Understanding

1. What is a nested function call?

2. What is the difference between a method and a procedure?

3. What is the difference between a function and a procedure?

4. List at least two reasons why you might want to write your own functions and procedures.

5. What is the meaning of *inline code*? How does it differ from a function or procedure?

6. In Visual Basic, is it safe for one event procedure to call another event procedure? Why would you ever want to do this?

7. Your friend tells you that he always names his variables with a letter followed by one number, such as *X1*. When you write programs, you use meaningful names like *Quantity* or *Salary*. Your friend claims that his programs will run faster than your programs. Is your friend correct?

8. Is it correct that when you call a function, your calling code must use the value returned by either assigning it to a variable or using it in a calculation?

9. What is an *argument*, and what is it used for?

10. Name the two types of procedure arguments, and explain their differences and how you decide which one to use.

Programming Exercises

1. Write the procedure *Swap(Volts1, Volts2)* which will swap the contents of the two variables which are passed to *Swap*. Assume that both arguments are type Double. Does it make a difference if you use pass by value, rather than pass by reference?

2. Write a function that takes a type Double argument, rounds it to three decimal places, and then returns the result to the calling procedure.

3. Construct a demo program, which uses the *QBColor* function to convert a slider control's Value property to an RGB color code. Assign the color code to the BackColor property of the demo program's form. Place the *BackColor* assignment statement in the *Change* event procedure associated with the slider control. You will have to use Help for the *QBColor* function, the slider control, and the BackColor property of a form to figure out the values for the Min and Max properties of the slider. The slider control shown here is part of the *Microsoft Windows Common Controls*. You should read about it in Appendix A, "Visual Basic User Interface Objects."

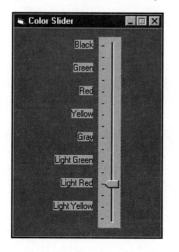

4. A polynomial approximation for sin(X)/X is $1 - .16605x^2 + .00761X^4$ for $0 \leq X \leq \pi/2$ and is accurate to about four decimal places. Write a Visual Basic function that uses this polynomial to calculate sin(X)/X.

5. Develop a Visual Basic Rand(L, H) that returns a random integer N, where $L \leq N \leq H$, each time it is called. Test your function for L = 100 and H = 1000.

6. Write a function that scans a string for an embedded comma and returns a string containing the portion of the original string that follows the comma. Hint: You probably will want to use the *InStr* and *Right* functions.

7. Write a function as in exercise 6, but this time the function should return the string that precedes the comma.

8. The force *f* between the plates of a parallel-plate capacitor with a separation distance *d* is given by the formula

$$f = \frac{1}{2d}CV^2$$

where *C* is the capacitance and *V* is the voltage. Write a Visual Basic function that is passed *d*, *C*, and *V* and returns the force. If you use *C* in Farads, *V* in volts, and *d* in meters, the force will be expressed in Newtons.

9. The equation of the normal (bell-shaped) probability density function used in statistical applications is

$$\frac{1}{\sqrt{2\pi}\,\sigma} \exp\left[-\frac{1}{2}\left(\frac{x-\mu}{\sigma}\right)^2\right]$$

where μ is the mean and σ is the standard deviation. Using this formula, write a function that calculates the probability density from x, μ, and σ.

Programming Projects

1. Design a simple editor that enables you to type text into a text box control and cut, copy, paste, and clear text as you want (see the following dialog box). When you click the *Copy* or *Cut* buttons, the Clipboard's *SetText* method is used. You can then paste back into the simple editor or paste into another application such as Notepad or Microsoft Word. When you click the *Paste* button, the Clipboard's *GetText* method is used. You should use Visual Basic's Help for details on these two methods. Be sure to clear the Clipboard before you put any text into the Clipboard. You are making things difficult for yourself if any of your event procedures have more than four lines of code.

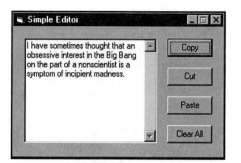

2. The resonant frequency of an inductor L and a capacitor C, connected in series or parallel, is given by the formula

$$f = \frac{1}{2\pi\sqrt{LC}}$$

where f is the frequency in hertz, L is the inductance in Henrys, and C is the capacitance in Farads. Develop an LCf calculator that uses this formula to calculate and display the value of the third component when the values of any two components are entered into the calculator. Your program should contain three user-written functions. One function returns f when L and C are passed, another function returns L when f and C are passed, and the third function returns C when f and L are passed. To make the calculator easy to use, you should assume that the following units are entered and displayed by your calculator: f in MHz, L in µH, and C in pF. The conversion factors are $1\text{Hz} = 10^{-6}\text{MHz}$, $1\text{H} = 10^{6}\text{µH}$ and $1\text{F} = 10^{12}\text{pF}$. The calculated results should be displayed to an accuracy of three decimal places. Your calculator's GUI should be similar to the following figure.

3. Modify the LCf Calculator in project 2 by using a progress bar to display the frequency f. To learn how to install the progress bar control on your Visual Basic Toolbox, you should read Appendix A. Name the progress bar control prgFMHz, set its Min property to 0 and its Max property to 100. Set the position of the progress bar by setting its Value property to the frequency in

223

MHz. Experiment with your program and find out what happens when f becomes greater than 100MHz. The modified calculator appears as follows:

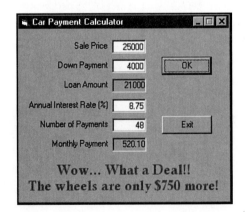

4. Design a monthly payment calculator for a used car salesman. The salesman enters the car sales price, the trade-in or down payment, the number of monthly payments, and the annual interest rate (entered as a percentage) of the loan. After the *OK* button is clicked, the calculator displays the loan amount and monthly payment along with a brief "sales pitch" in bold, red font. If any of the input text boxes are changed, the amounts displayed in the Loan Amount and Monthly Payment labels are erased, and the Sales Pitch label is made invisible. Your calculator should use the formula

$$Pmt = \frac{LoanAmt * IntRateMo}{1 - (1 + IntRateMo)^{-npmts}}$$

where *Pmt* is the monthly payment, *LoanAmt* is the amount of the loan, *IntRateMo* is the monthly interest rate (not a percentage), and *npmts* is the number of payments to pay off the loan. Write a function that uses this formula to calculate and return the monthly payment. Your calculator's appearance should be similar to the figure shown here.

5. Modify the monthly payment calculator by replacing the payment function you wrote with the *Pmt* function that comes with Visual Basic.

CHAPTER 5

DECISIONS AND DATA VALIDATION

Introduction

Many real-world problems involve some level of decision making. "Did an employee work more than 40 hours, and thereby qualify for overtime?" "Is the quantity the user wants to order greater than the number of items currently on the shelf?" As you analyze ordinary tasks, you are likely to find conditions that affect which processing steps will be completed. To find the average of several numbers, you need to divide the total of all values by the number of values. If a program tries to compute an average, but the user hasn't entered any values, a "division by zero" error will result. One way to prevent this problem is to bypass the computation if no values are entered. A program for a fitness center would need to collect information about its customers. If the user enters a gender of male, it is unnecessary to have the user specify pregnancy status.

Any time a user enters data that is later used in the program, the possibility for unreliable results or error messages due to bad input is introduced. The program may expect numeric input, but the user forgets to enter a value or accidentally enters non-numeric data. Without data validation, the program could display an error message and terminate, or give a wrong answer. The decision steps in a program often compare the user's input to the acceptable values. If the input values are missing or in error, the program can use a default value, ask for a new value, clear all input, or even terminate the program. Regardless of the action taken, it is a good idea to inform the user about the program's status. Well-planned data validation improves the user friendliness of your program and increases the chances of its acceptance by your intended users.

Chapter 1, "Introductory Programming Concepts and the Visual Basic Environment," introduced the three restricted control structures used in structured programming. Up until now, we have used only the sequential structure, where every step inside a procedure is processed one after the other starting with the first statement. In situations like the ones previously described, it is necessary to skip over some steps or choose one step from a set of choices. This chapter shows you how to use and code the *selection*, or *conditional*, structure. Virtually every programming language uses the same keywords to code this structure: *if* and *else*. Relational operators and expressions, and logical operators and expressions will be used to form the conditions to be evaluated in these decision statements.

After our programs have the capability to thoroughly check data inputs and make decisions, our test plans must expand to include test cases for all these situations. The end-of-chapter case study will bring all of these concepts together in a single Visual Basic program that will find the real roots of the quadratic equation.

Objectives

After completing this chapter, you should be able to:

- Recognize when a selection or conditional structure is needed in the logic of a program.

- Construct a flowchart segment containing simple or nested conditional structures.

- Translate the logic into a correct *If-Then-Else* statement in a Visual Basic program.

- Know the precedence of the arithmetic, relational, and logical operators in Visual Basic.

- Use relational and logical operators to form conditional expressions in Visual Basic.

- Select appropriate test data to test conditional statements.

- Find minimums and maximums using decision structures.

- Perform data validation to prevent program termination due to errors in user input.

Structured Programming

As you learned in Chapter 1, structured programming uses only combinations of the three restricted control structures, in which each structure has a single entry point and a single exit point. These three structures are the following:

- Sequential structure

- Conditional structure (selection structure)

- Repetitive structure (iterative structure)

In a **sequential structure**, the steps are each executed once, in the order they are listed, from top to bottom. The other two structures involve making a decision. In the **selection,** or **conditional, structure**, a decision marks a two-way branch point where either one or another set of steps will be processed, but both meet at the same point and continue together. With the **iterative structure**, or repetitive structure, a decision marks the beginning point or ending point of a series of steps that are processed repeatedly. This chapter focuses on the selection structure, and Chapter 7, "Repetitive Structures," shows you how to use the *repetitive structure.*

As you analyze a new problem, you need to determine what decision-making the program should do. Programs often enable the user to select the processing to be done. An investment analyzer program that can compute either the present value or future value of an investment would need some way of deciding which computation to perform. With event-driven programming, decisions made by the user do not always result in a decision structure within the program code. In the example just stated, if the user interface provides a *Calculate Present Value* button and a *Calculate Future Value* button, the user decides which button to click, but the program code just calculates and displays the appropriate value under each button click event procedure. On the other hand, if the user interface contains option buttons to select the desired calculation and a single *Calculate* button, the logic for the *Calculate* button click event would include a decision of which equation to use. Programmers must recognize when a decision structure is needed. The words *if* or *when* in the problem description are clues that a decision structure may be needed in the program's logic.

After the detailed logic has been fully planned, you can use the translation rules of the programming language to construct the program. In the case of Visual Basic, you can refer to the examples of this chapter or use Appendix B, "Program Design and Translation to VB Code," to see how specific decision structures should be written in a Visual Basic program.

Decisions: Logic Design Tools and the If Statement

In Chapter 1 (see Figure 1.24), we provided a set of standard flowcharting symbols and the corresponding pseudocode for a variety of statement types that are used in sequential control structures. Although programs involving decisions make use of these same logic constructs, we need to add some new constructs to depict the decision structure itself.

Logic Design Tools for Decisions

The diamond symbol is used in a flowchart to indicate a point where a decision is made. Inside the diamond is the decision criterion, usually stated to have a yes/no or true/false answer. The single arrow pointing down to the top of the diamond signifies the entry point into the selection structure. The left and right branches indicate the two choices that depend on the value of the condition inside the diamond. Both branches join together at a connector somewhere below the diamond. The single arrow pointing downward from the connector signifies the single exit point from the decision structure (see Figure 5.1). The "steps to process if condition is true" could consist of one or several statements. Similarly, the "steps to process if condition is false" could consist of one or several statements.

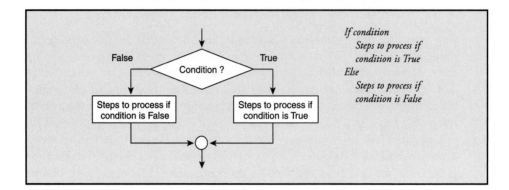

Figure 5.1 *General flowchart and pseudocode for a simple decision.*

When stating the logic of a problem with pseudocode, an *If* statement is used to indicate the starting point of the decision. Indentation is used to indicate the processing steps that should be performed if the condition is true. The keyword *Else* follows on the next line if there are separate processing steps when the condition is false, and those processing steps are also indented immediately below the *Else*. The right side of Figure 5.1 shows the general pseudocode structure for a decision with different steps to process if the condition is true or false.

Beginning programmers sometimes have trouble determining which statements are part of the decision structure, and which statements should be outside (before or after) the decision structure. Often the decision is a small part of a larger sequence of steps. If you notice that you have duplicated many of the same statements in the *true* block and the *false* block of a conditional structure, it is likely that those duplicated statements can be removed from the conditional structure. Place one copy of the statements before or after the conditional structure, as appropriate.

As you continue to program, you will find that in many valid situations no statements are processed on one branch of the decision structure. In this case, the decision condition is generally stated so that the statements are processed when the condition is true. This makes it easier to translate your logic into Visual Basic code. The flowchart or pseudocode can easily handle this situation, as illustrated in Figure 5.2.

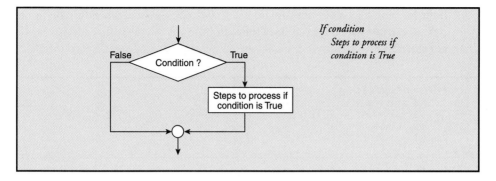

Figure 5.2   *General flowchart and pseudocode for a simple decision with no statements to process on the false branch.*

Coding the Selection Structure in Visual Basic

When translating decision logic into Visual Basic code, a block **If-Then-Else** statement is used. This statement looks very similar to the pseudocode just described, but an **End If** statement is required to indicate where the decision structure ends (see Figure 5.3). Another difference between pseudocode and the actual code is that the syntax of the condition in the actual code must be very precise. In the next section, we discuss many choices in forming conditional expressions. In Visual Basic code, this structure starts with a line that contains the keyword *If*, followed by a properly stated condition, followed by the word *Then*. On the lines that follow are Visual Basic statements that are to be executed only when the condition is true. The next line contains the keyword *Else*. Following this are the Visual Basic statements for the logic that is to be executed only when the condition is false. The decision structure code ends with the *End If* statement.

```
If condition Then
    VB statement
    VB statement       ' VB statement(s) to perform if condition is true
    VB statement
Else
    VB statement
    VB statement       ' VB statement(s) to perform if condition is false
    VB statement
End If
```

Figure 5.3   *Syntax of the* If-Then-Else *statement in Visual Basic.*

■■■ TIP
Always indent the processing steps on the True and False branches of a conditional structure.

If the decision logic does not contain any steps to be executed when the condition is false, the *Else* statement can be eliminated from the Visual Basic code, as shown in Figure 5.4.

```
If condition Then
    VB statement
    VB statement         ' VB statement(s) to perform if condition is true
    VB statement
End If
```

Figure 5.4 *Syntax of the* If-Then *statement in Visual Basic.*

Comparison Operators and Expressions

In Chapter 3, "Arithmetic Operators and Scope," we learned about arithmetic operators (+, −, *, /, ^, \, Mod) to indicate various mathematical calculations. The result of evaluating an arithmetic expression is a number. In all the decision structures just described, the *condition* is an expression that determines which branch to follow, or which block of statements to execute. In most cases, this *condition* is a comparison of two or more values, also called a **relational expression**. The computer evaluates the *condition*, and the result is a **Boolean value** of *true* or *false*. A **relational operator**, or comparison operator, is placed between the two values being compared to indicate which type of comparison to make. In some programming languages, you can use words (such as *equals* or *greater than*) for the comparison operators. In most languages, however, symbols are used. Figure 5.5 lists the Visual Basic relational operators.

Symbol	Meaning	Example
=	Equal to	LastName = "Smith"
<>	Not equal to	StateCode <> "MA"
<	Less than	TaxOwed < 1
>	Greater than	HrsWorked > 40.0
<=	Less than or equal to	Age <= 65.0
>=	Greater than or equal to	Cholesterol >= 200

Figure 5.5 *Relational, or comparison, operators.*

The values being compared may be literal or constant values, variables, or properties of controls on the form. They must be of compatible types, meaning that you must compare strings to strings and numbers to numbers. If the types are not compatible, a type mismatch error may cause your program to terminate. To make sure the types are compatible, you should use the appropriate conversion functions, as discussed in Chapter 3.

Comparing Numbers to Numbers

If you use compatible, but different, numeric types, you should be aware that Visual Basic will perform conversions before the actual comparison is made. If you are comparing a value of type Single to a type Double value, for example, the Double value will be rounded to the precision of the Single value. If a Currency value is compared with a type Single or Double value, the Single or Double is converted to type Currency.

You should also keep in mind that when you use any of the real number data types (Single, Double), some values will not have exact representations due to limitations of decimal accuracy. This requires you to use caution whenever comparisons of floating-point numbers are being performed—two values that are equal when computed manually may be unequal to the computer because they are stored as slightly different values. To compare two real numbers for equality, a suggested approach is to subtract the real values and compare the result to a very small fractional number (such as 0.0000001). This approach will be illustrated in this chapter's case study.

Comparing Strings to Strings

In most situations when you compare strings, the values are being compared alphabetically. If you imagine looking up the names in a phonebook or dictionary, you can determine what the result of the string comparison would be. You can think of "less than" as meaning "comes before alphabetically" and "greater than" as "comes after alphabetically." This means that the letter *A* is less than the letter *B* and *Andrews* is greater than *Anderson*. Uppercase letters and lowercase letters have different numeric codes in the computer, so *B* is not equal to *b*. Refer to the tear card in the front of this book for the ASCII codes that are assigned to various characters and symbols. The ASCII code values determine whether one character is greater than another in a string comparison. A general rule to remember the comparison order is this: 0 < 9 < A < Z < a < z. The ASCII code values have no effect on the comparison of numeric types of values. Hence, using numeric values, 123 is greater than 9. Using strings, "123" is less than "9", because the ASCII code for the character 1 is less than the ASCII code for the character 9. Some examples of string comparisons are

```
FirstName = "Ima"    (only people with the first name Ima)
State <> "IN"        (any state other than Indiana)
LastName < "M"       (all last names that start with A-L)
City > "L"           (all cities that start with L-Z except name="L")
LastName <= "M"      (all last names that start with A-L and name="M")
City >= "L"          (all cities that start with L-Z including name="L")
```

Evaluating Relational Expressions

The value (true or false) of a relational expression is determined during program execution, using the current value of any variables or properties in the expression. Figure 5.6 gives some examples of relational expressions and their resulting Boolean values. To determine whether the expressions are true or false, assume that at the time of execution, text box *txtName* is empty, and that the variables *Num1*, *Num2*, and *StuName* have been declared and assigned the values *12*, *0*, and *John Smith*, respectively.

Expression	*Boolean Value*
txtName.Text = ""	True
Num1 < 10	False
Num2 > 0	False
Num2 >= 0	True
StuName = "John"	False
StuName <> ""	True
StuName < "John Doe"	False
123 > 9	True
"123" > "9"	False
(Num1 * 3 – 25) > 0	True

Figure 5.6 *Examples of expressions using relational operators.*

Notice in the last example that you can use an arithmetic expression inside a relational expression. The parentheses are not required around the arithmetic expression, but may be used to clarify the order of the operations.

Operator Precedence

When several operations occur in an expression, each part is evaluated in a predetermined order called operator precedence. In Chapter 3, you learned that the arithmetic operators do not all have the same precedence levels. Comparison operators, on the other hand, have the same precedence, meaning that they are evaluated in order of appearance from left to right. As with arithmetic operators, parentheses can be used to change the order of evaluation. When both relational operators and arithmetic operators are present in one expression, all arithmetic operations will be performed before any comparisons, because arithmetic operators have higher precedence than relational operators.

The expression *0.25 * (WageRate * HrsWorked) > 1.00* would be evaluated in the following order, for example:

1. First the product WageRate * HrsWorked is computed.

2. Next the product of 0.25 and the result from step 1 are computed.

3. Finally, the result from step 2 is compared to 1.00 for the final Boolean result.

Take some time now to verify the values in the last three columns of the table shown in Figure 5.7.

WageRate	HrsWorked	After Step 1	After Step 2	After Step 3
6.00	0.5	3.0	0.75	False
5.75	40	230.0	57.5	True
8.00	0.5	4.0	1.0	False

Figure 5.7 *Evaluating combined arithmetic and conditional expressions.*

A Simple Comparison Program

To get a better idea of how these comparisons work, let's use each comparison operator in a program. Create the user interface shown in Figure 5.8. In this program, the user can enter two values of compatible types. If numbers are entered in each text box, the user should click the *Compare Numbers* button. The user can enter any characters (or no characters) in each text box and click the *Compare Strings* button.

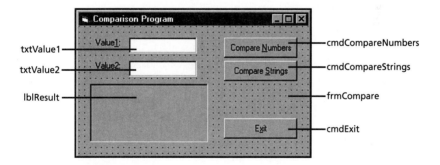

Figure 5.8 *User interface for a simple comparison program.*

The code for the *Compare Numbers Click* event will treat the first value as an Integer and the second value as type Single. It then calls a module that performs six comparisons to test the result of each comparison operator. The *Compare Strings Click* event is exactly the same, except that it assumes both values are strings. Figure 5.9 shows the logic for either button click. Notice that all the decision structures contain steps to execute when the condition is *True*, but the *False* branch is empty. Based on this logic, do you think that the result label will always contain at least one message? Could it contain more than one message?

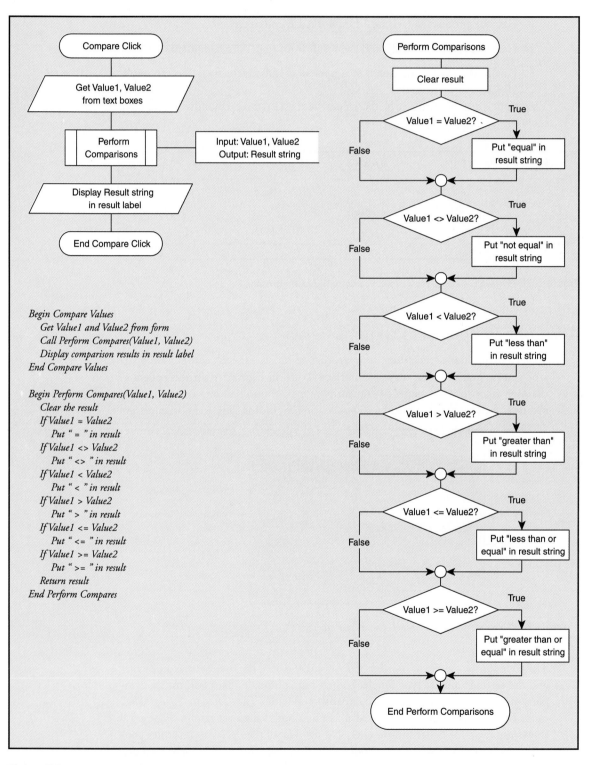

Figure 5.9 *Logic for* Compare Click *event.*

We decided to code the module as a function because it produces (or returns) one value, which is the string describing the comparison results. Type in the code for the *Compare Numbers* button click event and the *Compare Strings* button click event to match the logic of the given flowcharts or pseudocode. If you have any questions, refer to the code shown in Figure 5.10. Then run the program, enter a variety of values, and click an appropriate button to see how the computer compares numbers and strings. For numbers, you can enter various combinations with and without decimals, in both the first and second text box. For strings, compare upper- and lowercase values, and strings containing digits. After you have finished testing this program, you could easily modify it to compare other data types.

```
' Program:    Test Comparison Operators
' Form:       frmCompare
' Programmer: Ima Goodstudent
' Purpose:    This program illustrates how numeric and string
'             comparisons are evaluated.
Option Explicit

' Purpose: When the Compare Numbers button is pressed, convert the
'          first value to type Integer and the second to type Single
'          to see how they compare.
Private Sub cmdCompareNumbers_Click()
    Dim Value1 As Integer
    Dim Value2 As Single

    Value1 = CInt(txtValue1.Text)
    Value2 = CSng(txtValue2.Text)
    lblResult.Caption = PerformNumericCompare(Value1, Value2)
End Sub

' Purpose: When the Compare Strings button is pressed, convert both
'          values to type String to see how they compare.
Private Sub cmdCompareStrings_Click()
    Dim Value1 As String
    Dim Value2 As String

    Value1 = txtValue1.Text
    Value2 = txtValue2.Text
    lblResult.Caption = PerformStringCompare(Value1, Value2)
End Sub

' Purpose: When the Exit button is pressed, terminate the program.
Private Sub cmdExit_Click()
    Unload frmCompare
End Sub

' Purpose: This function compares FirstVal and SecondVal using the 6
'          relational operators and returns a string with the results
Function PerformNumericCompare(ByVal FirstVal As Integer, _
                               ByVal SecondVal As Single) As String
    Dim ResultWords As String

    ResultWords = ""
    If FirstVal = SecondVal Then
        ResultWords = ResultWords & "Value1=Value2" & vbCrLf
    End If
```

continues

235

```
        If FirstVal <> SecondVal Then
            ResultWords = ResultWords & " Value1<>Value2" & vbCrLf
        End If
        If FirstVal < SecondVal Then
            ResultWords = ResultWords & " Value1<Value2" & vbCrLf
        End If
        If FirstVal > SecondVal Then
            ResultWords = ResultWords & " Value1>Value2" & vbCrLf
        End If
        If FirstVal <= SecondVal Then
            ResultWords = ResultWords & " Value1<=Value2" & vbCrLf
        End If
        If FirstVal >= SecondVal Then
            ResultWords = ResultWords & " Value1>=Value2" & vbCrLf
        End If
        PerformNumericCompare = ResultWords
End Function

' Purpose: This function compares FirstVal and SecondVal using the 6
'          relational operators and returns a string with the results
Function PerformStringCompare(ByVal FirstVal As String, _
                              ByVal SecondVal As String) As String
    Dim ResultWords As String

    ResultWords = ""
    If FirstVal = SecondVal Then
        ResultWords = ResultWords & "Value1=Value2" & vbCrLf
    End If
    If FirstVal <> SecondVal Then
        ResultWords = ResultWords & " Value1<>Value2" & vbCrLf
    End If
    If FirstVal < SecondVal Then
        ResultWords = ResultWords & " Value1<Value2" & vbCrLf
    End If
    If FirstVal > SecondVal Then
        ResultWords = ResultWords & " Value1>Value2" & vbCrLf
    End If
    If FirstVal <= SecondVal Then
        ResultWords = ResultWords & " Value1<=Value2" & vbCrLf
    End If
    If FirstVal >= SecondVal Then
        ResultWords = ResultWords & " Value1>=Value2" & vbCrLf
    End If
    PerformStringCompare = ResultWords
End Function
```

Figure 5.10 *Code for a simple comparison program.*

We have provided a few sample results that you should be able to confirm with your program (see Figure 5.11). Some of the examples may appear to provide arbitrary results. You should be able to explain why the results seem unusual by using the debugger to display the data tips and to watch the program execute one line at a time. In the second *Compare Numbers* example, for instance, why does the result show that 5.1 is less than 5.000001? Recall that the first text box is converted to an Integer, and the second number is converted to a Single. Therefore, when the comparison is done, the actual values being compared turn out to be 5 (CInt(5.1)) and 5.000001 (CSng(5.000001)). In the case of the third *Compare Numbers* example, the user enters *5* and *5.0000001*. CInt(5) is obviously 5, but why is CSng(5.0000001) also 5? Because a Single data type has only a seven-digit decimal accuracy, the last 1 is ignored because it is beyond the precision maintained in a Single data type. For this reason, Cint(5) turns out to be equal to CSng(5.0000001), as illustrated by the example.

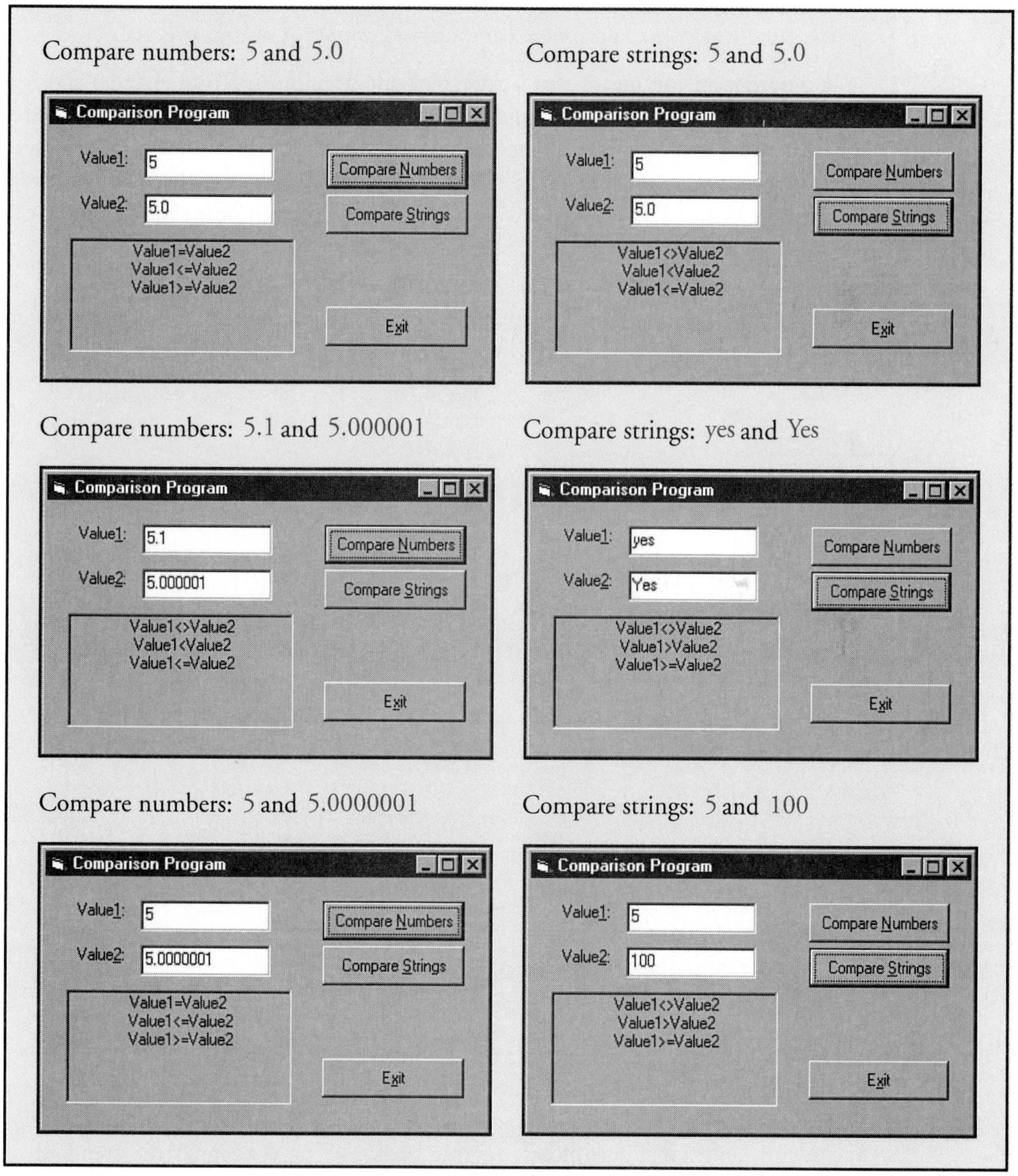

Figure 5.11   *Sample output from the comparison program.*

Nesting Decisions

You might wonder how you could state the logic of all programming problems with only three control structures. Think of each of these structures as a building block of programming logic. Each structure can contain a different sequence of basic steps, and you can combine them in a variety of ways. They can be stacked sequentially (one after another), and they can be nested one inside the other. The *True* branch or the *False* branch of a decision structure may involve additional decision-making. In this case, you can add a decision structure to a branch of a condition in the same way you add a simple computation, input, or output process.

A **nested decision** means that a branch of one decision structure includes another complete decision structure inside it. Structured programming requires that the inner structure be completely inside the outer structure. This means that the inner-most decision must always end (both branches meet) before the outer decision ends. In Figure 5.12, the nested decisions are enclosed in boxes in the flowchart, and highlighted in the pseudocode.

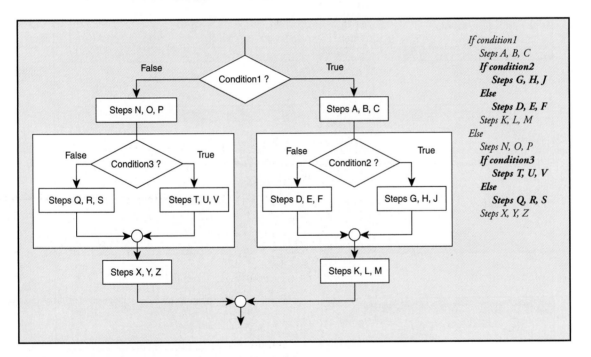

Figure 5.12 *General flowchart and pseudocode of nested decisions.*

As before, the translation of this nested decision logic into Visual Basic code looks very similar to the pseudocode. Notice in Figure 5.13 how the use of indentation makes it easier to see what statements are inside each condition. You should always indent conditional statements. In this book, we have adopted the standard of indenting four spaces.

```
If condition1 Then
    Steps A, B, C
    If condition2 Then
        Steps G, H, J
    Else
        Steps D, E, F
    End If
    Steps K, L, M
Else
    Steps N, O, P
    If condition3 Then
        Steps T, U, V
    Else
        Steps Q, R, S
    End If
    Steps X, Y, Z
End If
```

Figure 5.13   *General structure of Visual Basic code for nested decisions.*

Of course, the nested decision might only be on one branch of the outer decision. Appendix B contains additional variations on the nested structures, and explains how to translate them into Visual Basic code.

In this section's example program, we could check the input data when the user clicks the *Compare Numbers* button. The *Compare Numbers* code tries to convert the first value to type Integer. Because an Integer ranges in value from −32,768 to 32,767, any input of more than five digits is wrong. By setting the MaxLength property of the text box to *5*, we can prevent the user from entering longer numbers. Of course, the user could enter letters rather than numbers. Visual Basic provides an *IsNumeric* function that returns a Boolean value to indicate whether a string of characters is a legal number. Let's use this function to check whether the value in the second text box is a number. Using nested decisions, our logic for the *Compare Numbers Click* event looks like that in Figure 5.14.

You may recognize that there are still errors this logic won't catch, but this is just a trial program to practice using a nested decision. Try to modify your code for the *Compare Numbers Click* event to match this logic. If you have trouble, compare your code to the code of Figure 5.15.

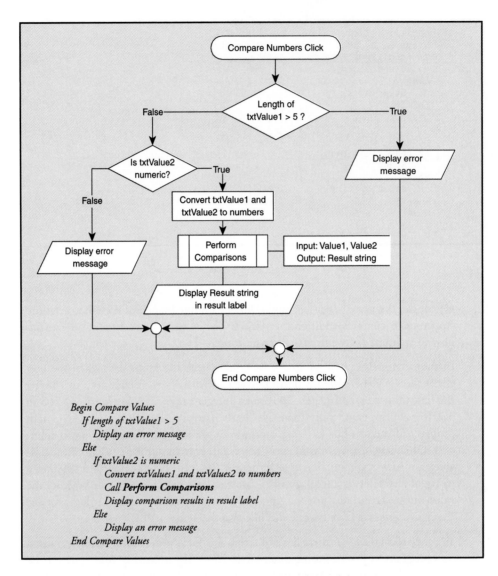

Figure 5.14 *Logic for* Compare Numbers Click *event with nested decisions.*

```
Private Sub cmdCompareNumbers_Click()
    Dim Value1 As Integer
    Dim Value2 As Single

    If Len(txtValue1.Text) > 5 Then
        MsgBox ("Value1 has too many digits for type Integer")
    Else
        If IsNumeric(txtValue2.Text) Then     ' both values pass the tests
            Value1 = CInt(txtValue1.Text)
            Value2 = CSng(txtValue2.Text)
            lblResult.Caption = PerformNumericCompare(Value1, Value2)
        Else
            Call MsgBox("Value2 does not contain a legal number")
        End If
    End If
End Sub
```

Figure 5.15 *Code for* Compare Numbers Click *event with nested* Ifs.

Logical Operators and Expressions

Sometimes a problem has one action to perform when two different conditions are true. Instead of nesting multiple decision structures, the conditions can be combined into a more complex condition, called a **logical expression**. The **logical operators** that combine the relational expressions are the words **And** or **Or**. Another logical operator, **Not**, acts on a single relational expression by reversing its Boolean value.

The words *And* and *Or* are used as we typically use them in the English language. If your mother says, "You can use the car if you wash it *and* vacuum it," the *and* means that both conditions must be true ("car washed" and "car vacuumed") to use the car. On the other hand, if your dad says, "I'll buy you a car if I win the lottery *or* strike oil," only one of the conditions needs to be true ("win lottery" or "strike oil") for you to get your car!

In the computer, the result of a logical expression is a Boolean value. When combining relational expressions with logical operators, each relational expression is evaluated first, and the logical operators are evaluated last. Because some logical expressions can get long and complicated, a **truth table** can be helpful in checking the expression results. Figure 5.16 shows the general truth table for the *And* operator. *Relation1* and *Relation2* are relational expressions such as *ClientCount < 100* and *ClientName <> ""*.

Notice that the result of the *And* operation is only true when both relational expressions are true. On the other hand, the *Or* operator gives true values as long as at least one of the relational expressions is true, as seen in the table of Figure 5.17. Figure 5.18 shows the truth table for the *Not* operator.

Relation1	Relation2	Relation1 And Relation2
True	True	True
True	False	False
False	True	False
False	False	False

Figure 5.16 *General truth table for the* And *operator.*

Relation1	Relation2	Relation1 Or Relation2
True	True	True
True	False	True
False	True	True
False	False	False

Figure 5.17 *General truth table for the* Or *operator.*

Relation1	Not Relation1
True	False
False	True

Figure 5.18 *General truth table for the* Not *operator.*

When you put a logical expression into a program, it is sometimes difficult to decide whether *And* or *Or* is the correct choice. The best way to resolve this question is to pick several representative values that cause each condition to be true and false, and set up a truth table for both *And* and *Or* in the expression. Then you can check the final result to see which one gives the results you want for the program. Figure 5.19 shows how to set up a truth table for the logical expression *(NumName<=100 And StuName<>"")* and the expression *(NumName<=100 Or StuName<>"")*. This example assumes that the program defines a numeric variable *NumName* and a string variable *StuName.* The first columns of the truth table contain values for the individual variables. The next columns evaluate the individual conditions, and the last two columns evaluate the two logical expressions. (Here we use *T* for true and *F* for false.)

NumName	StuName	NumName <=100	StuName <> ""	NumName<=100 AND StuName<>""	NumName<=100 OR StuName<>""
99	Mary	T	T	T	T
100	Joe	T	T	T	T
101	Ann	F	T	F	T
100		T	F	F	T
101		F	F	F	F

Figure 5.19 *Example of using a truth table to evaluate logical expressions.*

It is possible to devise longer and more complex expressions that combine more than two relational expressions in one statement. The precedence of the logical operators is *Not*, then *And*, and then *Or*. As with arithmetic operators, multiple logical operations at equal precedence are evaluated from left to right. Parentheses may be used to cause a different order of evaluation, however, and it is always okay to include extra parentheses if that helps you understand the statement better.

We have now discussed three different classes of operators— arithmetic, relational, and logical—as well as the string concatenation operator. In general, arithmetic operators are evaluated first, relational operators are evaluated next, and logical operators are evaluated last. The relational operators all have equal precedence. Two or more operations at the same precedence level are evaluated from left to right, but parentheses can always be used to modify the order of evaluation. Figure 5.20 contains an expanded **operator precedence** table for Visual Basic, from high to low, which includes all types of operators we have discussed.

Operator Symbols	Operator Names	Operator Type
^	Exponentiation	Arithmetic
–	Negation (unary minus)	Arithmetic
*, /	Multiplication and division	Arithmetic
\	Integer division	Arithmetic
Mod	Modulus	Arithmetic
+, –	Addition and subtraction	Arithmetic
&	String concatenation	Concatenation
=, <>, <, >, <=, >=	Equal, not equal, less than, greater than, less than or equal, greater than or equal	Relational or comparison
Not		Logical
And		Logical
Or		Logical

Figure 5.20   *Operator precedence table for Visual Basic.*

Data Validation

An important use of decisions in well-written programs is to verify the correctness of the input data prior to using it in the processing. In fact, entire programs have been written just to perform the data validation task of a large system. By now, you have seen that when certain errors occur in user input, Visual Basic displays an error message such as Type mismatch and may terminate the program. From a user's perspective, programs that terminate due to invalid input are poorly designed. A better program design is one that anticipates the kinds of problems that may exist in user input and then tests each input value before processing it. Even better is when the program prevents users from entering bad values by only offering them valid choices. If erroneous input is detected, a variety of solutions are available. Program termination should be the last resort.

For a given piece of input, it may be necessary to perform multiple tests to ensure the usability of the data. The data validation for other input items may be the same or very different. It is often helpful to have a typical user test your program to assess which checks are the most critical for a specific program. You may find that a simple change in the user interface to clarify the acceptable inputs will alleviate many problems. Nonetheless, even a well-planned interface cannot prevent all data-entry errors. Therefore, your programs should include some level of data validation for at least the more serious types of data-entry errors.

■■■ TIP
Always check user inputs for correctness.

A program can perform several different types of data validation. We can classify them as existence checks, type checks, range checks, reasonableness checks, code checks, and consistency checks.

Existence Check

Generally when a program requests input from the user, it is expected that the user will enter a value, but some inputs may be optional. If it is absolutely necessary that the user enter certain data before the processing can occur, the program should perform an existence check. An **existence check**, also called a presence check, makes sure that a value has been entered. If the input comes from a text box on the form, you should compare the contents of the text box to the empty or null string. A business may decide that a first and last name is required for each employee, for example, but that the middle initial is optional. Therefore, the program used to enter employee information should perform an existence check on the last name and first name values. This could be coded as one or more decision statements, as shown here:

```
If txtFirstName.Text = "" or txtLastname.Text = "" Then
    ' error processing: display message that name must be entered
Else
    ' process normally
End If
```

Textbox Change Event

The Textbox control has a **Change event** that recognizes when its contents have been altered. If the existence of a value is necessary for processing, one option available to the programmer is to disable the processing button (set the Enabled property to False) until a value is available. When a control is disabled, it is a lighter color. This provides a visual cue to the user that it is not possible to perform that processing. Often several values must be input before processing can occur. This requires a more complex logical expression to check for all values before enabling the button. For the employee example, if the program requires an ID number (always five characters), a first name, a last name, a start date, and a pay classification (always two characters), the *Change* event for all five text boxes might contain the following Visual Basic code:

```
If Len(txtID.Text) = 5 _
And txtFirstName.Text <> "" _
And txtLastname.Text <> "" _
And txtStartDate.Text <> "" _
And Len(txtClassif.Text) = 2 Then
    cmdCalculate.Enabled = True
Else
    cmdCalculate.Enabled = False
End If
```

There are two drawbacks to using the *Change* event in a program. The *Change* event is triggered each time the user types a character in or deletes a character from the text box. If the user is typing a long name, the *Change* event will occur many times. For this reason, the code in the *Change* event should be kept to a minimum. A bigger drawback is that the *Change* event can be triggered, often unintentionally, by other code. If any other statement in the program assigns a value to the Text property of the text box, it is changing the text box. This triggers the *Change* event. So long as no code has been written for the *Change* event, it doesn't cause a problem; as soon as you add code for a *Change* event, however, a number of unexpected side effects may show up. Therefore, anytime you have a *Change* event in your program, it is extremely important to review all other code and look for statements that would trigger this event.

Type Check

The most common use of the **type check** is to verify that the user has entered valid characters for a numeric value. A type mismatch error can occur if non-numeric characters are entered when a number is expected. In a program that does not check for wrong types, the user may see a type mismatch error message followed by program termination. To avoid this problem, you should add type checking to your program to verify that the data provided by the user is of the correct data type.

In Visual Basic, you can use the *IsNumeric* function to assess whether an expression can be evaluated as a number. The Boolean result from this function is true if the entire expression can be recognized as a number and false in all other cases, including if the expression is a date. This function was used in the code of Figure 5.15 as part of a decision structure. Additional testing could be performed to make sure the value does not contain a decimal point if it is supposed to be an Integer.

Another function called *IsDate* verifies that the expression passed to it can be evaluated as a legal date.

Range Check

Even if the user enters the correct type of data for a specific input item, the actual value of the input may be unacceptable because it is too large or too small. In a program without **range checking**, the user may see strange results or error messages, possibly followed by program termination.

Consider the case of a program that produces weekly paychecks for all employees. In the simplest case, a paycheck is the product of hours worked and the hourly wage rate. The range checks performed by this program could include the following:

- Verify that hours worked are between 0.5 and 75.

- Verify that wage rate is between minimum wage and $120/hour.

As with the other validation checks, a decision structure can be used to determine whether these conditions have been met. When checking for a range, the logical operators are often used. In the following code example, *Or* is used to check whether the value is outside the range:

```
If HoursWorked < 0.5 Or HoursWorked > 75 Then
    ' error processing: display message that hours worked must be
    ' between 0.5 and 75 hours
Else
    If WageRate < MinWage Or WageRate > 120 Then
        ' error processing: display message that wage rate must be
        ' between minimum wage and $120
    Else
        ' process normally
    End If
End If
```

If you reverse the relational operators and change *Or* to *And*, the code would check whether the value is within the range.

Reasonableness Check

Sometimes you want to perform a check on the range of values, but there isn't a specific limit on the range. You may know that by company policy an employee's age would not be over 70 or under 18 unless a special exception has been made, for example. Maybe the hourly pay for most employees is between the minimum wage and $20 per hour, but some skilled workers or consultants are paid more. When there is not a fixed upper or lower limit, the program can still test for a reasonable, or typical, limit. In the few cases where the value is outside this limit, the program could request verification or authorization (such as a password). If the entered value is incorrect, the user could hopefully recognize this fact and correct it.

Code Check

For some inputs, the program expects one of a specific set of values. A department code might be either "PAY" for Payroll, "MAR" for Marketing, or "PRO" for Production, for example. A series of nested decisions or one complex decision can check for a correct value:

```
If txtDeptCode.Text <> "PAY" _
And txtDeptCode.Text <> "MAR" _
And txtDeptCode.Text <> "PRO" then
     LblMessage.Caption = "Invalid department code"
Else

     ' Proceed with normal processing

End If
```

If this program is designed for casual users who are not familiar with the department codes, or are not good typists, the preceding example may suggest a poor user interface design choice. Controls are available in Visual Basic that show users the valid choices and do not let them enter a wrong value. Depending on how the data will be used, you may use a set of option buttons inside a frame, a combo box, or a list box. You can refer to Appendix A, "Visual Basic User Interface Objects," for more information on these controls.

Consistency Check

Often there are relationships between two or more values in a program. An employee's classification could affect whether the employee is paid hourly, biweekly, or monthly, for example, and what the acceptable pay ranges are. An employee whose marital status is single would not have a spouse. A hospital billing program should flag charges for maternity ward services when the patient's sex is male. The **consistency check** verifies that related values do not violate any processing rules. The logic may involve a decision that decides whether to request other related inputs, or it may involve more complex logical expressions or nested decisions that check all the related values for inconsistencies.

MsgBox Function

Whenever invalid data is detected, the user should be informed of the problem and resulting action taken by the program.

To display a message that a user is sure to notice, the Visual Basic *MsgBox* function can be used. The **MsgBox** function displays a modal dialog box that contains a custom message. If you need a simple Yes, No, OK, or Cancel response, the *MsgBox* function can provide optional buttons for this purpose. Several formats of the *MsgBox* function are as follows:

- MsgBox(*Message*)
- MsgBox(*Message, Icon*)
- MsgBox(*Message, Buttons*)
- MsgBox(*Message, IconAndButtons*)

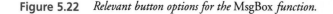 TIP

Inform the user of problems or corrective action taken.

The *Message* is the string variable or string constant that is displayed inside the message box. The optional *Icon* is the constant value that refers to the special icon that the message box should contain. Figure 5.21 lists some of the Visual Basic intrinsic constants that can be used to select this icon.

VB Intrinsic Constant	Icon Displayed
vbCritical	Critical Message (X)
vbQuestion	Warning Query (?)
vbExclamation	Warning Message (!)
vbInformation	Information Message (i)

Figure 5.21 *Relevant icon options for the* MsgBox *function.*

The optional *Buttons* parameter refers to the types of command buttons that the message box should contain. Figure 5.22 lists some of the VB constants that select which buttons appear.

VB Intrinsic Constant	Buttons Displayed
vbOKonly	OK button only
vbOKCancel	OK and Cancel buttons
vbAbortRetryIgnore	Abort, Retry, and Ignore buttons
vbYesNoCancel	Yes, No, and Cancel buttons
vbYesNo	Yes and No buttons

Figure 5.22 *Relevant button options for the* MsgBox *function.*

We recommend that you use the following message box format:

```
MsgBox(Message, IconAndButtons)
```

and restrict the *IconAndButtons* parameter to one of the following two combinations:

- vbOKOnly + vbInformation
- vbYesNo + vbQuestion + vbDefaultButton2

When the message box has more than one button, the constant *vbDefaultButton2* puts the focus on the second button and causes it to be the default in case the user presses the Enter key. Also, when there is more than one button, you can find out which button the user pressed by testing the return value of the *MsgBox* function. Figure 5.23 lists the VB constants that represent the possible return values. You can find the remaining options by looking up the *MsgBox* function under Visual Basic's online help.

VB Intrinsic Constant	Button Selected
vbOK	OK button
vbCancel	Cancel button
vbAbort	Abort button
vbRetry	Retry button
vbIgnore	Ignore button
vbYes	Yes button
vbNo	No button

Figure 5.23   *Return values from* MsgBox *function.*

The following examples contain various combinations of the *MsgBox* parameters. Notice that we use the word *Call* when *MsgBox* is being used by itself (and not as part of a longer statement).

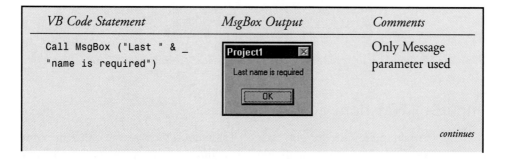

VB Code Statement	MsgBox Output	Comments
`Call MsgBox ("Last " & _` `"name is required")`	Project1 — Last name is required — OK	Only Message parameter used

continues

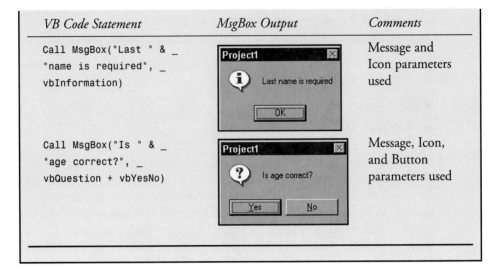

VB Code Statement	MsgBox Output	Comments

`Call MsgBox("Last " & _`
`"name is required", _`
`vbInformation)`
		Message and Icon parameters used

`Call MsgBox("Is " & _`
`"age correct?", _`
`vbQuestion + vbYesNo)`
		Message, Icon, and Button parameters used

Figure 5.24 *Examples using the* MsgBox *function.*

Let's practice using *Msgbox* with the Reasonableness Check from the beginning of this section. We use the *MsgBox* function to ask the user to verify the value input for Age if it is outside the range of 18 to 70. Figure 5.25 shows one possible decision structure using the *MsgBox* function with *Yes* and *No* buttons.

```
If CInt(txtAge.Text) < 18 Or CInt(txtAge.Text) > 70 Then
    BadInputs = False
    If MsgBox("Age is outside the usual range.  Is it correct?", _
            vbQuestion + vbYesNo + vbDefaultButton2) = vbNo Then
        lblMessage.Caption = "Enter correct age and click CALCULATE"
        BadInputs = True
    End If
    If Not BadInputs Then
        ' Proceed with processing for acceptable age
    End If
End If
```

Figure 5.25 *Example using the* MsgBox *function with multiple buttons.*

InputBox Function

If a certain input is needed only in special situations, then instead of having a text box on the form, you may want another way to get a new value from the user. If the user is married, for example, you may want the program to ask for the spouse's name. The Visual Basic **InputBox** function brings up an application modal dialog box that displays a specified message, includes a textual input area, and returns the value inside the text box when the user clicks the *OK* button. Several formats of the *InputBox* function are as follows:

- InputBox(*Prompt*)

- InputBox(*Prompt, TitleBar*)

- InputBox(*Prompt, TitleBar, DefaultValue*)

The *Prompt* is the string variable or string constant that is displayed in the InputBox window. The optional *TitleBar* is the string variable or string constant that appears as the title bar caption. The optional *DefaultValue* is the constant value that appears already highlighted inside the text box portion of the InputBox window. The default value is useful during program testing when you want to check that certain error messages are working, but you don't want to be forced to enter long input values. It is also useful when the likelihood of a particular value being entered is high. If you write a program to compute total purchases and need the user to enter the sales tax rate for the state of Indiana, for example, you can provide the value *5* for the default tax rate of 5 percent in Indiana.

Because the function returns a value, you will likely use it in an assignment statement. If the expected value is a string, you may use something like the following:

```
Dim UserInput As String
UserInput = InputBox("Enter tax rate", "Sales Tax", "5")
```

UserInput is a string variable that will receive the value entered by the user. If the value the user should enter is numeric (like in this case), the appropriate conversion function should be used around the *InputBox* function, and the result should then be assigned to a compatible type of variable, as illustrated here:

```
Dim UserInput As Double
UserInput = CDbl(InputBox("Enter tax rate", "Sales Tax", "5")) / 100
```

Figure 5.26 shows the input box that will appear when the preceding lines are executed.

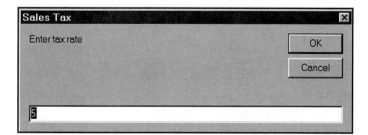

Figure 5.26 *Example using the* InputBox *function.*

You should use caution when using the *InputBox* function. Notice that the *OK* and *Cancel* buttons automatically appear. If the user clicks *OK* or presses Enter, whatever is in the text box will be returned. If the user clicks *Cancel,* a zero-length string ("") will be returned. In the preceding example, this would actually produce a type mismatch error because the *CDbl* function cannot accept a zero-length string. To prevent this problem, you must incorporate a selection structure to perform data validation on the string value entered by the user before converting it. A suggested solution to the problem is this:

```
Dim UserInput As String
Dim SalesTax As Currency
UserInput = InputBox("Enter tax rate", "Sales Tax", "5")
If UserInput = "" Then
    SalesTax = 0
Else
    If IsNumeric(UserInput) Then
        SalesTax = CDbl(UserInput)/100
    Else
        SalesTax = 0
    End If
End If
```

How Should Errors Be Processed?

We have illustrated how the decision structure is often used to test for the different types of errors. After a problem is uncovered, however, what action should the program take? Some options are to:

- Terminate the program
- Ask the user to reenter the data
- Use default values

Which error-handling method is best? It depends on the situation. In general, however, terminating the program should be the user's choice. At times, however, a program should terminate itself, such as when the program's security has been compromised (for example, the user fails to supply the correct password), or when major hardware or data errors are detected.

Asking the user to reenter a value is a friendlier approach because it gives the user the opportunity to get the needed results. To get a new value from the user, the program should be as helpful as possible. Often a message can explain the problem and the program bypasses remaining processing and returns control back to the form. Additionally, it could place the cursor in the erroneous text box. Sometimes the erroneous text is cleared or highlighted, but this is not always helpful because the user may only need to change or add one character. To put the focus on the erroneous text box, use the **SetFocus** method:

```
Call txtHours.SetFocus
```

Alternatively, a modal dialog box can be used to display a message, to ask a question, or to receive the corrected data. Be careful not to overuse modal dialog boxes, because doing so introduces extra mouse clicks for the user. When default values are used, it may be appropriate to put them in the text box from the beginning, or to have a brief message mentioning what default value is assumed.

Regardless of the type of error handling employed, the user should always be notified of both the problem and the corrective action taken by the program. You have seen two ways of using modal dialog boxes to notify the user of the problem. The *MsgBox* enables you to keep track of which button was pressed, and the *InputBox* provides a text box on a dialog box to retrieve a new value. You can also make error messages appear by making labels or other controls on the form visible; however, these can make your form more crowded. Whichever method you choose, always keep the user's needs in mind.

When Should Data Be Validated?

Keeping in mind that Visual Basic is event driven, deciding *when* data validation should occur is as important as the validation processing itself. The earliest opportunity to conduct data validation on an input text box is the *Change* event for that text box. As mentioned earlier, the *Change* event should be used sparingly. If the expected input consists of multiple characters, the error processing would be triggered more often than it should be. Suppose, for example, that a user is trying to enter *108* in a text box. If the text box's valid range is 100–999 and data validation is in the *Change* event, then when the user enters *1* (changing the previous value), the out-of-range error message displays even though the user is still typing the input value. The same thing happens again when the user enters the second character (current value of 10).

Another event where the data validation can be coded is the **LostFocus** event of the text box. This event is triggered when the user "leaves" the text box by pressing the Tab key or using the mouse to click on something else, or the system "leaves" the text box by processing the *SetFocus* method on another control in code. Figure 5.27 illustrates an example of a *LostFocus* event for a text box that contains the hours an employee worked. This value is supposed to be numeric and in the range 5–60. If an error is detected, the code displays an error message and then assumes a default value of 5 hours.

```
Private Sub txtHours_LostFocus()
    If Not IsNumeric(txtHours.Text) Then
        Call MsgBox ("Hours must be numeric - 5 hours assumed", _
                    vbInformation)
        Hours = 5
    Else
        If CDbl(txtHours.Text) < 5 Or CDbl(txtHours.Text) > 60 Then
            Call MsgBox ("Hours should be 5-60, 5 hours assumed", _
                        vbInformation)
            Hours = 5
        Else
            Hours = CDbl(txtHours.Text)
        End If
    End If
End Sub
```

Figure 5.27 *Example of using a default value in error handling in a* LostFocus *event.*

Alternatively, the same event could put the focus back to the text box when an error is detected, as illustrated in Figure 5.28.

```
Private Sub txtHours_LostFocus()
    If Not IsNumeric(txtHours.Text) Then
        Call MsgBox ("Hours must be numeric. Please correct", _
                    vbInformation)
        Call txtHours.SetFocus
    Else
        If CDbl(txtHours.Text) < 5 Or CDbl(txtHours.Text) > 60 Then
            Call MsgBox ("Hours must be in range 5 to 60", _
                        vbInformation)
            Call txtHours.SetFocus
        End If
    End If
End Sub
```

Figure 5.28 *Example of using* SetFocus *in error handling in a* LostFocus *event.*

As with the *Change* event, a potential for problems exists if you place the error handling in the *LostFocus* event of a text box. Suppose the user decides to exit the program when the focus is in a text box. This user action will trigger the *LostFocus* event right before the program termination process, causing the error message to be displayed when nothing was entered. Additionally, if you have several text boxes for user input, your program could get caught in an infinite loop due to cascading events. **Cascading events** means that while one event procedure is being processed, some of its processing steps trigger other events without any additional user action. Let's say we have a form with two text boxes, *txtHours* and *txtPay*. Both have *LostFocus* event procedures that require positive numeric values to be entered. When errors are found, the cursor (and focus) is placed back into the erroneous text box. If the user enters a negative value in *txtHours* and then tabs to *txtPay*, the focus has now shifted to *txtPay*, so the *LostFocus* event of *txtHours* would begin processing. The error message is displayed, and the focus is placed back in *txtHours*. Because the focus was just in *txtPay*, the *LostFocus* event of *txtPay* is triggered and begins processing. Because nothing was entered in *txtPay*, the error message is displayed, and the focus moves back to *txtPay*. Up to this point, the user has not had an opportunity to fix the original error. The moment the focus goes back to *txtPay*, the *LostFocus* event of *txtHours* will be triggered. This cycle repeats until the program's time limit expires, or the user halts program execution by pressing Control + Break or by shutting down the computer.

Despite this potential problem, the *LostFocus* event may be an acceptable place to code some error handling, as long as you remember the possibility of cascading events. Visual Basic 6.0 tries to address some of the problems of the *LostFocus* event by adding a CausesValidation property to many controls (which could be set to *False* on an *Exit* button), and a *Validate* event that can be used in place of the *LostFocus* event for data validation. However, there are a few situations that do not trigger this event, so it should be tested carefully if you decide to use it. A safer approach is to wait until all of the data have been entered and the user presses the processing button. Therefore, the *Click* event of the main processing button often includes the data validation processing for all input controls. Since the validation for even a single control can get lengthy, consider writing a separate validation procedure or function, possibly one for each input item, and then call the validation procedure or procedures at the beginning of the *Click* event for the main processing button.

An Example to Illustrate Decisions and Data Validation

Let's consider a simple calculator program as illustrated in Figure 5.29.

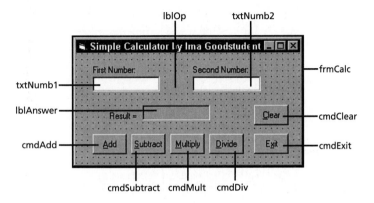

Figure 5.29   *Simple calculator user interface.*

The program gets two numbers from the user, performs the requested mathematical operation, and displays the result. In all cases, the values must be numeric. Figure 5.30 lists the code for a separate data validation procedure that receives two text boxes and two numeric variables as parameters, checks both text boxes, and returns the actual value if the number is valid or a default value of zero if an error is discovered.

```
Private Sub CheckNumbers(ByRef rtxtNum1 As TextBox, _
                         ByRef rtxtNum2 As TextBox, _
                         ByRef rNum1 As Double, _
                         ByRef rNum2 As Double)
    If IsNumeric(rtxtNum1.Text) Then
        rNum1 = CDbl(rtxtNum1.Text)
    Else
        Call MsgBox("First number must be numeric - zero assumed.", _
            vbOKOnly + vbInformation) ' Number 1 non-numeric
        rNum1 = 0
        rtxtNum1.Text = 0
    End If
    If IsNumeric(rtxtNum2.Text) Then
        rNum2 = CDbl(rtxtNum2.Text)
    Else
        Call MsgBox("Second number must be numeric - zero assumed.", _
            vbOKOnly + vbInformation) ' Number 2 non-numeric
        rNum2 = 0
        rtxtNum2.Text = 0
    End If
End Sub
```

Figure 5.30   CheckNumbers *procedure for simple calculator program.*

In the case of division, the second number cannot be zero. To avoid a "divide by zero" error, we will add more data validation to the *Click* event for the *Divide* button, as depicted in Figure 5.31. You should note that if the user enters invalid data for the second number, two error messages will be displayed. The first one results from the data validation in *CheckNumbers,* where the bad input is detected. The second one results from the "divide by zero" check, since our data validation assumed a zero value for the second number. We leave it as an exercise to improve the data validation further.

```vb
Private Sub cmdDiv_Click()
    Dim Number1 As Double
    Dim Number2 As Double
    Call CheckNumbers(txtNumb1, txtNumb2, Number1, Number2)
    lblOp.Caption = "/"
    If Number2 = 0 Then
        Call MsgBox("Second number must not be 0. Please re-enter.", _
            vbOKOnly + vbInformation)
        lblAnswer.Caption = ""
        Call txtNumb2.SetFocus
    Else
        lblAnswer.Caption = CStr(Number1 / Number2)
    End If
End Sub
```

Figure 5.31 Divide *button's* Click *event procedure for simple calculator program.*

Figure 5.32 shows the complete code for this program. You should create the form and write the code. Test the data validation for both text boxes for all arithmetic operations. Try stepping through the program to see the sequence that each step is processing.

```vb
Option Explicit

Private Sub cmdAdd_Click()
    Dim Number1 As Double
    Dim Number2 As Double

    Call CheckNumbers(txtNumb1, txtNumb2, Number1, Number2)
    lblOp.Caption = "+"
    lblAnswer.Caption = CStr(Number1 + Number2)
End Sub

Private Sub CheckNumbers(ByRef rtxtNum1 As TextBox, _
                         ByRef rtxtNum2 As TextBox, _
                         rNum1 As Double, _
                         ByRef rNum2 As Double)
    If IsNumeric(rtxtNum1.Text) Then
        rNum1 = CDbl(rtxtNum1.Text)
    Else
        Call MsgBox("First number must be numeric - zero assumed.", _
            vbOKOnly + vbInformation) ' Number 1 non-numeric
        rNum1 = 0
        rtxtNum1.Text = 0
    End If
    If IsNumeric(rtxtNum2.Text) Then
        rNum2 = CDbl(rtxtNum2.Text)
    Else
        Call MsgBox("Second number must be numeric - zero assumed.", _
```

```
                    vbOKOnly + vbInformation)  ' Number 2 non-numeric
            rNum2 = 0
            rtxtNum2.Text = 0

      End If
End Sub

Private Sub cmdClear_Click()
    txtNumb1.Text = ""
    txtNumb2.Text = ""
    lblAnswer.Caption = ""
    lblOp.Caption = ""
    Call txtNumb1.SetFocus
End Sub

Private Sub cmdDiv_Click()
    Dim Number1 As Double
    Dim Number2 As Double
    Call CheckNumbers(txtNumb1, txtNumb2, Number1, Number2)
    lblOp.Caption = "/"
    If Number2 = 0 Then
        Call MsgBox("Second number must not be 0. Please re-enter.", _
            vbOKOnly + vbInformation)
        lblAnswer.Caption = ""
        Call txtNumb2.SetFocus
    Else
        lblAnswer.Caption = CStr(Number1 / Number2)
    End If
End Sub

Private Sub cmdExit_Click()
    Unload frmCalc
End Sub

Private Sub cmdMult_Click()
    Dim Number1 As Double
    Dim Number2 As Double
    Call CheckNumbers(txtNumb1, txtNumb2, Number1, Number2)
    lblOp.Caption = "*"
    lblAnswer.Caption = CStr(Number1 * Number2)
End Sub

Private Sub cmdSubtract_Click()
    Dim Number1 As Double
    Dim Number2 As Double

    Call CheckNumbers(txtNumb1, txtNumb2, Number1, Number2)
    lblOp.Caption = "-"
    lblAnswer.Caption = CStr(Number1 - Number2)
End Sub
```

Figure 5.32   *Complete code for simple calculator program.*

Finding Minimums and Maximums

A common problem that involves decisions is deciding whether one value is smaller or larger than another value. This application can be extended further to decide which value is the minimum or maximum of all the values. Suppose that we want to check the price of our favorite stock many times a day, and want to know its highest and lowest price for the day. We set up a form like the one in Figure 5.33. Each time a new price is known, the user enters it and clicks the *Accept* button to update the *Low* or *High* value.

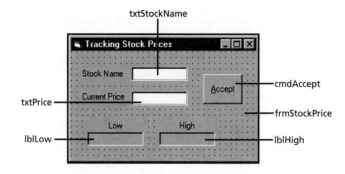

Figure 5.33 *Form for* Minimum/Maximum *program.*

Initialization Process

Two variables will be used to keep track of the current lowest (minimum) and highest (maximum) price. These variables need to have form-level scope, because their values must be retained between button clicks. Therefore these variables must be given an initial value when the program starts. There are two ways to initialize these variables. One way is to set the minimum and maximum value to the first actual value. In some applications, this value is known; in this program, however, the first price is unknown as the program starts. So we will use a different approach, which is to assign a high number to the minimum value and a low number to the maximum value. We initialize the maximum price to zero because the prices will all be greater than zero, and the minimum price to 200 because most of our stock prices will be less than $100.

```
Option Explicit
Private fMinPrice As Currency
Private fMaxPrice As Currency

Private Sub Form_Load()
    fMinPrice = 200
    fMaxPrice = 0
End Sub
```

Comparison Process

Ignoring data validation for now, the *Click* event for the *Accept* button will compare the price entered by the user to both the low and high price, and update either value when necessary. This involves two decision structures, as shown in the following code:

```
Private Sub cmdAccept_Click()
    Dim CurrPrice As Currency

    CurrPrice = CCur(txtPrice.Text)
    If CurrPrice < fMinPrice Then
        fMinPrice = CurrPrice
        lblLow.Caption = Format(fMinPrice, "Currency")
    End If
    If CurrPrice > fMaxPrice Then
        fMaxPrice = CurrPrice
        lblHigh.Caption = Format(fMaxPrice, "Currency")
    End If
End Sub
```

Code and run this program. To thoroughly test it, you should run the program more than once and enter the highest and lowest prices first, or last, or in the middle of other numbers.

Program Testing Guidelines

Now that we can test for special situations or errors, we must expand our program testing expectations. The following list provides some general guidelines for selecting data and procedures to test a program. Keep these in mind when testing future programs.

■ TIP
Test your programs thoroughly with a variety of good and bad values.

- *Execute all statements at least once*—In event-driven programming, this means we must be sure that every event occurs at least once during our test. In particular, the tester must click each button at least once.

- *Execute all branches of conditions*—If we know the program tests for certain situations, our testing should use data that causes both the true and false branches of each condition to execute at least once. When doing a "less than" or "greater than" type of comparison, your test should include a value above, below, and right at the boundary value.

- *Enter different lengths of string inputs*—This means you should enter short strings (one or two characters), long strings (as many characters as it will let you, or the longest possible value for the application), and "typical" strings.

- *Input various types of numeric values.*—For numeric inputs, try to enter typical values, negative numbers, positive numbers, zero, large numbers, and small numbers. If decimal numbers are allowed, vary the number of decimal digits entered. Enter the largest possible number and the smallest possible number. The actual values selected will depend on the application. A large value for a person's age might be 75 or 85, whereas the price of a new car would be considerably higher.

- *Test common error situations*—Keeping in mind the different types of data validation we discussed, you should enter the wrong type of value (characters rather than numbers), enter values that are too big or too small, and leave out one or more values. Also, try to type in areas of the screen that the user shouldn't be able to change.

- *Repeat the steps in different orders*—Be sure to click buttons twice in a row if they remain enabled. Often one click works the way it should, but the programmer did not expect the button to be clicked again. Try several different sequences of entering values and clicking buttons.

For all your selected test data, you should manually calculate (or determine from the specifications) what response you expect from the computer program. Otherwise you will not know whether the program is giving accurate information when you run it. It is helpful to document the selected test values and expected answers in a table format so that the tester doesn't have to recompute the expected answer(s) every time the program is tested.

When you discover problems while testing the program, you should follow the programming technique outlined here to locate and correct the logic errors in your program:

1. Decipher the error message given by Visual Basic. If it displays an error code, for example, look up the full description of the code to get some idea of the cause of the problem.

2. Try to remember which steps preceded the error, and which parts of the program seem to have executed correctly.

3. Use the approach outlined in Chapter 2, "Data Types, Variables, and Assignment Statements," to define breakpoints before, after, and/or inside selection structures and step through the program line-by-line to verify that the program follows the correct logic path. The goal with this step is to isolate where the problem area is.

4. At any point during the step-through program execution, use the Data Tips window to view the contents of specific variables and expressions by positioning the cursor over them. If the expression to be checked is not in view, use *Print* statements in the Immediate window to view the contents. The Immediate window can also be used to enter other executable VB code without affecting the actual program code. The goal of this step is to see the actual contents of specific memory locations before and after major control structures and computations to verify that they are what they should be.

5. When you isolate the problem area, carefully backtrack through the previous statements that were executed to further pinpoint the problem. Pay particular attention to statements that change the erronous memory locations.

6. Correct the error, and then retest the entire program. All too often, fixing one problem causes other problems to show up.

Quadratic Equation Case Study

In this chapter, we discussed how to add decision logic to our programs. This enables us to include data validation capabilities to enhance our programs. We now use many of these concepts in creating a program that can find the real roots of the quadratic equation

$$ax^2 + bx + c = 0$$

where a, b, and c are constants.

You may recall from algebra class that the formula for the roots of this equation is

$$\frac{-b \pm \sqrt{b^2 - 4ac}}{2a}$$

Step 1: Analyze the Problem

First the program needs to know the values of the three constants. The user could enter these values and click a button to signal that the roots should be computed. Before the actual roots are computed, the program must determine the number of real roots. There can be zero, one, or two real roots, depending on the value of b^2-4ac, as shown in Figure 5.34. If there are roots, one or both roots can be calculated and the answers displayed on the form. The program should verify that the three constant values are numeric. To be more user-proof, it should also check that the constant a is not zero (to avoid a "divide by zero" error). However, we will leave this as an exercise.

b^2-4ac	Number of Real Roots	Value(s) of Real Roots	
> 0	2	$\dfrac{-b+\sqrt{b^2-4ac}}{2a}$	$\dfrac{-b-\sqrt{b^2-4ac}}{2a}$
= 0	1	$\dfrac{-b}{2a}$	
< 0	0	Not applicable	

Figure 5.34   *Finding the real roots of the quadratic equation.*

The user may want to calculate roots for more than one problem, so there must be a way to clear the input areas and put the cursor back in the first text box. Optionally, the user may be interested in statistics on how many equations have been solved and how many problems had zero, one, or two roots. Finally, the user needs to be able to stop the program.

With this in mind, we construct a table of our input, processing, and output needs (Analysis Table), as shown in Figure 5.35.

Step 3: Design the Logic for the Program

With the initial form layout complete, we begin to plan what logic the program will actually perform in response to user actions and other events. Because you now know how to add decision structures to programs, this program will be as *user-proof* as possible. As an example, if the user clicks the *Calculate* button before entering valid data, the program should tell the user what values are missing or invalid, and take corrective action.

Step 3a: Design the Macro-View (Object-Event Diagrams)

Because there is really just one form and a summary message box, our macro logic will consist of one OED. We consider each control on the form, and whether there is an associated event. With our introduction to data validation in this chapter, we know that the text boxes used for input could be validated in the *Change* event, the *LostFocus* event, or a processing button *Click* event. Because only one processing button uses the input values, we elect to validate the inputs in the *Find Roots Click* event. As you can see in Figure 5.38, our initial design of the *Quadratic Equation Solver* program will consist of six event procedures and three other modules.

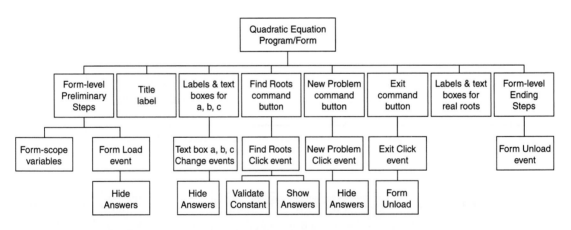

Figure 5.38   Quadratic Equation Solver *Object-Event Diagram.*

Step 3b: Design the Micro-Level View (Flowcharts or Pseudocode)

Now we must consider each event and module individually, and determine which steps go into that procedure and in what order. As we work on the *Find Roots Click* event procedure, we realize that the same validation needs to be performed on each of the three text boxes, but we would like the error message to be customized. We decide to write one validation module that is called three times, because a parameter can be used to provide the customized message information. Figure 5.39 contains the final list of form-scope variables that were identified as the logic was developed, followed by the logic for the six event procedures and three other modules.

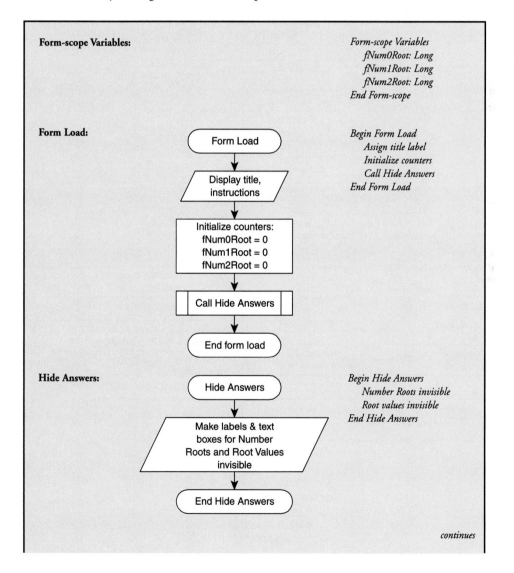

Form-scope Variables:

Form-scope Variables
fNum0Root: Long
fNum1Root: Long
fNum2Root: Long
End Form-scope

Form Load:

Form Load

Display title, instructions

Initialize counters:
fNum0Root = 0
fNum1Root = 0
fNum2Root = 0

Call Hide Answers

End form load

Begin Form Load
Assign title label
Initialize counters
Call Hide Answers
End Form Load

Hide Answers:

Hide Answers

Make labels & text boxes for Number Roots and Root Values invisible

End Hide Answers

Begin Hide Answers
Number Roots invisible
Root values invisible
End Hide Answers

continues

Text Box A, B, C Change:

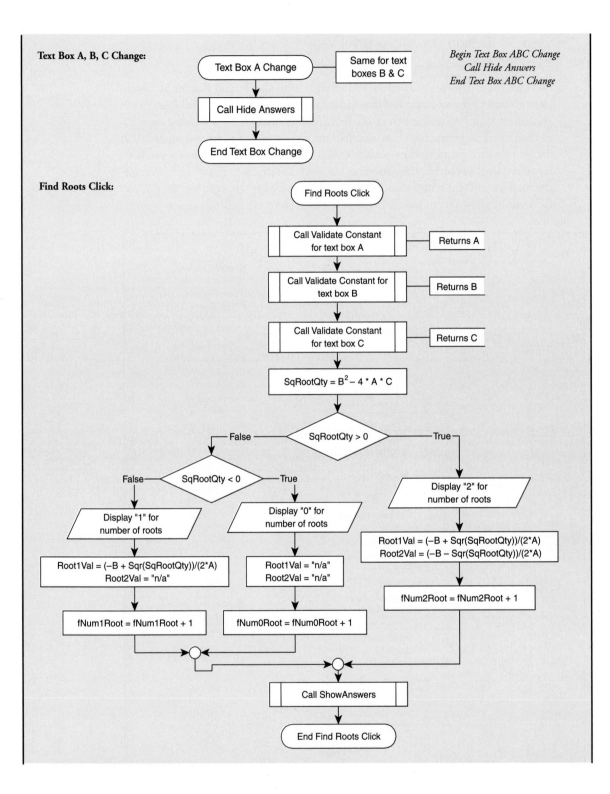

Begin Text Box ABC Change
Call Hide Answers
End Text Box ABC Change

Find Roots Click:

Begin Find Roots Click
    Call Validate Constant for A
    Call Validate Constant for B
    Call Validate Constant for C
    SqRootQty = B^2 – 4 * A * C
    If SqRootQty > 0
     Put "2" in NumRoots label
     Root1Val = (–B +
        Sqr(SqRootQty)) / (2 * A)
     Root2Val = (–B –
        Sqr(SqRootQty)) / (2 * A)
     fNum2Root =
           fNum2Root + 1
    Else
     If SqRootQty < 0
      Put "0" in NumRoots label
      Root1Val = "n/a"
      Root2Val = "n/a"
      fNum0Root =
           fNum0Root + 1
     Else   'zero => 1 root
      Put "1" in NumRoots
      Root1Val = –B / (2 * A)
      Root2Val = "n/a"
      fNum1Root =
           fNum1Root + 1
    Call Show Answers
End Find Roots Click

Validate Constant:

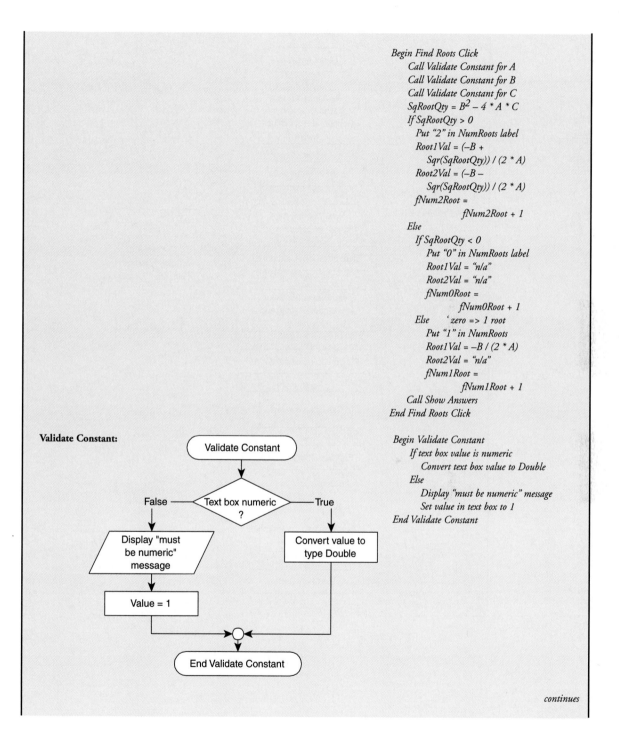

Begin Validate Constant
    If text box value is numeric
      Convert text box value to Double
    Else
      Display "must be numeric" message
      Set value in text box to 1
End Validate Constant

continues

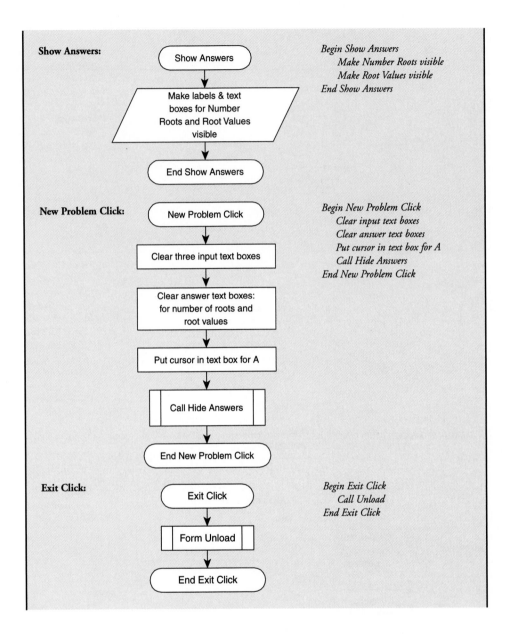

Show Answers:

Show Answers

Make labels & text boxes for Number Roots and Root Values visible

End Show Answers

Begin Show Answers
Make Number Roots visible
Make Root Values visible
End Show Answers

New Problem Click:

New Problem Click

Clear three input text boxes

Clear answer text boxes: for number of roots and root values

Put cursor in text box for A

Call Hide Answers

End New Problem Click

Begin New Problem Click
Clear input text boxes
Clear answer text boxes
Put cursor in text box for A
Call Hide Answers
End New Problem Click

Exit Click:

Exit Click

Form Unload

End Exit Click

Begin Exit Click
Call Unload
End Exit Click

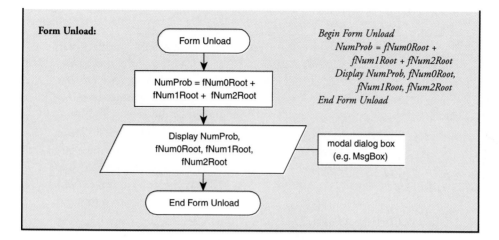

Figure 5.39 Quadratic Equation Solver *micro-level logic design.*

Step 3c: Develop a Test Plan (Table of Input with Expected Results)

Now that we have written the detailed logic for all events and other modules, we select appropriate test data to use in testing the finished program. Because our programs can now include decisions and provide data validation, we must be sure to include test cases for missing and non-numeric values for each of the equation constants. There should be at least one set of input values for equations with zero real roots, one real root, and two real roots. We must verify that the three buttons work correctly when clicked in various orders. And we should use different types of values for the constants (for example, negative with decimals). Figure 5.40 contains a list of a very minimal set of test cases. You should think about what test cases you would add to this. You may also want to confirm that the program is not yet "user-proof " by entering 0 for *A*.

Case	*User Input and Actions*	*Expected Results*
1	Run the program.	The title label displays a title and instructions. The three white boxes contain A, B, and C. The form is empty below the three command buttons.
2	Click *Exit Program.*	A message box displays saying 0 problems processed, 0 with zero roots, 0 with one root, 0 with two roots. When you click *OK,* the program ends.

continues

269

Case	User Input and Actions	Expected Results
3	Run the program. Click *New Problem. Click Exit* Program.	The form should start the same as in Case 1 and the text boxes clear after clicking *New Problem.* The summary message box should be the same as in Case 2.
4	Run the program. Click *Find Roots.*	Three message boxes will inform you that the constants must be *Numeric,* and substitute the value 1. The answer boxes appear with 0 roots and n/a in each root box.
5	Click *New Problem.*	The answer labels and boxes disappear. The input boxes clear. The instructions reappear in the title label.
6	Enter $-6, 45, -84$ in the three text boxes. Click *Find Roots.*	2 roots, values = 3.5 and 4.
7	Enter $12, 6, .75$ in the three text boxes. Click *Find Roots.*	1 root, values = -0.25, n/a.
8	Click *New Problem.* Enter nothing, -4.35, and letter O in the three text boxes. Click *Find Roots.*	Form resets (see Case 5). After *Find Roots,* a message box says Constant A must be numeric and substitutes 1 in the first box, says Constant C must be numeric and substitutes 1 in the third box. Answers are 2 roots, values = $4.106, 2.435$.
9	Change the value in the third box to 0. Click *Find Roots.*	Answers are 2 roots, values $4.35, 0$.
10	Click the *X* to close the program.	The summary message box displays saying 5 problems processed, 1 with zero roots, 1 with one root, 3 with two roots. When you click *OK,* the problem ends.

Figure 5.40   Quadratic Equation Solver *test plan.*

Step 4: Code the Program

After you thoroughly understand the logic for one or all modules in the program, you can start coding the program. As in the past, it is a good idea to code one event at a time and go on to test and debug it (see next section). Then come back and code another part of the program. Try to code this program yourself by referring only to the logic of Figure 5.39. If you have problems, check the complete code listing in Figure 5.41.

When you code the *Find Roots* event procedure, notice that it contains decisions that are comparing the quantity for the square root (*SqRootQty*) to the value zero. Because *SqRootQty* is a floating-point value of type Double, it is possible to have some results that are actually zero, but in the computer they are slightly above or below zero. Therefore, you should set up a very small constant that is almost zero to use in the comparison. See the code in Figure 5.41 if you can't figure out how to modify the comparisons.

Because the *ValidateConstant* module returns the numeric value of the characters in the text box, it can be coded as a function. It requires two parameters: one that is the custom words for the error message, and the other that is the text box itself. This module needs to check the value from the text box; if there is an error, it needs to change the text box to a default value.

```
' Program:     Quadratic Equation Solver
' Form:        frmQuadEqn
' Programmer:  Ima Goodstudent
' Purpose:     This program solves a quadratic equation. The user
'              inputs the 3 constants (a, b, c), the inputs are
'              validated and the real roots are calculated. A summary
'              of the number and types of problems solved will be
'              displayed as execution terminates.

Option Explicit

Private fNum0Root As Long     ' Number of equations with 0 roots
Private fNum1Root As Long     ' Number of equations with 1 root
Private fNum2Root As Long     ' Number of equations with 2 roots

' Purpose: When the Exit Program button is clicked, the summary
'          information is displayed right before the program ends.
Private Sub cmdExit_Click()
    Unload frmQuadEqn
End Sub

' Purpose: When the Find Roots button is clicked, it validates the
'          constants input by the user and computes the real roots of
'          the quadratic equation (0, 1 or 2 real roots). A counter
'          is updated and the answers are displayed.
Private Sub cmdFind_Click()
    Const cAlmostZero As Double = 0.00001
    Dim EqnConstantA As Double     ' Quadratic Equation Constant "A"
    Dim EqnConstantB As Double     ' Quadratic Equation Constant "B"
```

continues

271

Key Terms

And	InputBox	range checking
Boolean value	integration tests	relational expression
cascading events	iterative structure	relational operator
Change event	logical expression	selection structure
code check	logical operators	sequential structure
conditional structure	LostFocus	SetFocus
consistency check	MsgBox	system test
Else	nested decision	truth table
End If	Not	type check
existence check	operator precedence	unit coding and testing
If-Then-Else	Or	

Test Your Understanding

1. List the relational operators.

2. List the logical operators.

3. What flowchart symbol is used for decisions?

4. What type of value is obtained when evaluating a relational expression? When evaluating a logical expression? When evaluating an arithmetic expression?

5. Fill in the results of evaluating the expressions in the following table.

EmpAge	YrsWork	EmpAge <= 65	YrsWork < 20	EmpAge<=65 Or YrsWork<20	EmpAge>65 And YrsWork>20
64	19				
65	20				
66	15				
64	20				
65	13				
66	25				

the option buttons an
the last name is "Jone
Jones:. The program
clicked and there is no

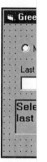

Variation—Modify the
there is no last name o

4. Design a program that
and tells the user whetl

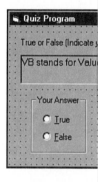

The form contains a la
False, a *Check Answer* b

5. Update the quiz progr
the answer is right, and
Use the ForeColor prope

6. Design a program that
this week, and parking
pay, as shown in the fo
working more than 40
pay $2 for "B" parking
more per hour pay $3
are a total of 23 percer
tions. Net pay is the gr

6. Fill in the results of evaluating the expressions in the following table:

EmpName	EmpStreet	EmpName < EmpStreet	EmpName = "" Or EmpStreet = ""	EmpName <> "" And EmpStreet <> ""
Joe	(empty)			
Mary	2 Elm St.			
(empty)	3 Main St.			
Jane Doe	Jane Blvd.			
(empty)	(empty)			

7. In Figure 5.12, what steps are executed if Condition1 is true, Condition2 is false, and Condition3 is true? If Condition1 is true, Condition2 is true, and Condition3 is false? If Condition1 is false, Condition2 is false, and Condition3 is false?

8. What logical expression would check whether a number is within the range 0.5–75?

9. What is the precedence of arithmetic operators, relational operators, and logical operators?

10. Name and define five different types of data validation a program can perform.

11. Suppose a program expects the user to type "Indianapolis", "Madison", "Boston", "San Francisco", or "Akron" into a text box. Why would you want to avoid using the *MsgBox* function in the *Change* event of this text box to inform the user that the input value is not acceptable? Suggest other types of controls (see Appendix A) that could be used instead of a text box.

12. What is a cascading event?

13. List five general guidelines for selecting test data for a program.

14. Write the Vi

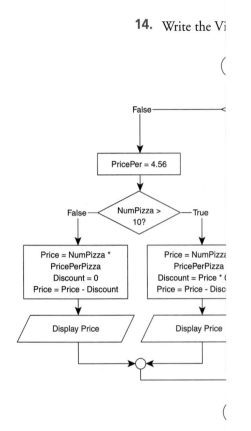

15. Redraw the

Programmin

1. Modify the
command b
power of th
ond numbe

2. Modify exer
ever, a messa
a negative
pressed, the
changed, th
computatio
message not

3. Create a for
last name,
instructions

7. Write a program that inputs resistance of a resistor and current, and computes the voltage across the resistor (voltage = current × resistance). Check that the values entered are legal positive numbers (decimals are allowed). Let the user select units. Convert kilo-ohms to ohms and milli-amps to amps.

8. Design and code a program that converts an angle measurement from degrees to radians or radians to degrees. The *Convert* button performs the selected conversion (360 degrees = 2 π radians). Verify that the angle is a legal number.

Variation—Only accept angles in the range from 0–360 degrees, or 0–6.3 radians

9. Design and code a program to troubleshoot problems with a robot. The user should be able to input the color of a status light (red, green, or none) and a voltage. If the status light is out, tell the user to replace the bulb and enter the color. For a red light, ask the person to measure the voltage at Test Point #1. For a voltage less than 30, the user should replace the circuit board. Otherwise, replace the power unit. For a green light, tell the user that no problem is indicated and to call the service man (make up a phone number) if something is not functioning properly.

10. Update the *Quadratic Equation* case study program to detect when the user enters *0* for *A* and add an appropriate response.

Programming Projects

All these projects should be designed to be as user-proof as possible. Therefore, all input data should be validated and any computations that may produce errors should be bypassed (for example, division by zero is undefined).

1. Write a program that will compute the present value for a future investment goal, future value for an investment made today, or monthly payment for a fixed-rate loan. The formulae for each of these values are listed here, where FV = future value, PV = present value, IR = yearly or monthly interest rate as a decimal, Terms = number of years or months, LA = loan amount, and NP = number of payments. Both IR and Terms should be for years, or both should be for months.

$$FV = PV * (1 + IR)^{Terms}$$

$$PV = \frac{FV}{(1 + IR)^{Terms}}$$

$$PMT = \frac{LA * IR}{1 - (1+IR)^{-NP}}$$

The following suggested form design employs the frame and line controls described in Appendix A.

2. Design a program to determine whether a loan applicant qualifies for a car loan. The criteria for assessing loan qualification are as follows:

- Individual applicant must be 21 or older. Applicants between 18 and 20 must either co-apply with a qualifying parent or must be enrolled in a college or university with a minimum overall GPA of 2.5.

- Take-home income must be at least $500 more than the monthly car payment.

- Credit rating must be average, good, or excellent.

A suggested form design is given here. Frames are used to group information, and the credit rating is shown with a combo box. Assume credit ratings can be poor, average, good, or excellent. You could also use option buttons for the credit rating. (Refer to Appendix A for more information on these controls.)

3. Design a computer program to determine whether a student qualifies for admission into a selected academic program. All academic programs have minimum criteria, but specialized programs have more selective criteria. When a student does not qualify for the selected program, but does qualify for other program(s), an appropriate message should be displayed that details the other programs. When a student does not meet minimum criteria, display a message advising the student of suggested strategies for future admission. The following suggested form designs employ new controls that are described in Appendix A.

Program Admission Requirements

Welcome to the Purdue University program admission requirements center. Please select the program which interests you.

Choose a program: ▼

Thank you. Now please indicate your qualifications by selecting the appropriate check-boxes and a recommendation based on your particular experience will be made.

Education (highest completed)
- ○ GED
- ○ High School Graduate
- ○ None of the above

College Education (highest completed)
- ○ Attended College (degree unfinished)
- ○ Bachelor's Degree
- ○ Master's Degree
- ○ Doctoral Degree

Additional Experience
- ☐ Work experience in industry
- ☐ Family business
- ☐ Laboratory research

Tests
- ☐ SAT Score:
- ☐ ACT Score:

Process

Clear

Exit

Please make an appointment with an academic counselor to begin scheduling your classes!

Thank You!

4. Write a quiz processor that enables a teacher to record quiz scores and then displays a statistical summary when all quizzes have been entered. The summary should include the highest score, the lowest score, the average score, and the total number of students who passed the quiz with a grade of C or better. Assume that the teacher uses straight scale for assigning grades (that is, 90 percent or better = A, 89 percent–80 percent = B, and so on).

Sample form designs follow. (See Appendix A for information on the line control.)

5. Write a survey processor program that will collect demographic information about students, including their gender, age, residency (in-state or out-of-state), marital status, number of dependents, and monthly income. When all students have been surveyed, a summary of the total number and average number in each category should be displayed. The following suggested form design employs new controls that are described in Appendix A.

6. Write a program for "Charge–A–Lot credit" card company that enables users to apply for credit and see whether they will be approved. Each user will input a name, address, annual income, monthly rent, and a total of current monthly payments from any other debts. The annual income, monthly rent, and monthly payments must be positive numbers. If the monthly income is more than 25 percent greater than rent and current debt payment, the user is approved for a credit card. In all other cases, the application is denied. The following user interface is suggested for the program.

Challenge 1: Validate the name. Check to make sure that each part begins with a capital letter and is followed by lowercase until a space or null occurs. A name can consist of two or three parts (the middle name is optional). Initials are permitted on the middle name, but not on the first or last.

Challenge 2: Determine a limit for each customer based on his or her income-to-debt ratio. The credit limits are as follows:

- *Platinum*—$5,000 (Monthly income exceeds payments by 50 percent or more.)

- *Gold*—$2,500 (Monthly income exceeds payments by 40 percent or more but less than 50 percent)

- *Silver*—$750 (Monthly income exceeds payments by 25 percent or more, but less than 40 percent.)

- *Secured*—Up to a $1,000 limit, based on equal-value security deposit (Monthly income exceeds monthly payments, but is less than 25 percent.)

7. Develop a program for the "ShirtHouse T–shirt" Company that will generate a total price for an order based on the type of artwork, shirt material, and quantity of shirts ordered. Pricing is as follows:

Shirt Material	Base Price	Type of Artwork	Artwork Cost
Poly-blend	$3.50/shirt	One color	$0.70/shirt
50/50	$5.00/shirt	12 colors	$1.50/shirt
All cotton	$7.00/shirt	High-res scan	$3.00/shirt

Add a sales tax of 5 percent to the subtotal to produce the final total. The following interface is suggested.

Challenge 1: Add a control that will ask whether the customer is a tax-exempt organization. If the input is yes, request the tax-exempt ID number. Tax-exempt organizations do not pay sales tax on purchases related to their tax-exempt status.

Challenge 2: Add a summary button to allow a user to see who currently has the most sales.

Challenge 3: ShirtHouse has decided to implement a tiered quantity discount to encourage greater sales quantities. For orders of 75 or more shirts, a 5percent percent discount will be offered; for 150 or more shirts, a 7.5 percent discount will be offered; and for 250 or more shirts, a 10 percent discount will be offered. Remember to apply the discount before sales tax is calculated. Modify the user interface to display the amount of the discount as well as the sales tax.

CHAPTER 6

THE CASE STRUCTURE AND ERROR HANDLING

Introduction

In Chapter 5, "Decisions and Data Validation," you learned about the decision structure and how to apply it in Visual Basic programs for data validation and processing. The basic decision structure is based on having the result of a comparison being true or false. As you continue to program, situations involving more complex decisions will frequently arise. Multiple nested decisions can become difficult to work with and follow. This chapter looks at two ways to simplify the nested structure. First, when the *Else* clause of each decision contains another *If* statement, Visual Basic has provided the combined keyword *ElseIf*. Second, when the variable used for making a decision can have multiple values (not just true or false), the *Case* structure can be used.

We have also talked about several different types of data validation that programs typically perform. If there are many values to validate and multiple types of validation are performed on each one, a program may ultimately become very complex with many nested conditions. These nested conditions maintain the "structured" nature of the program at the expense of many levels of indentation. Another approach that is often used is to incorporate error handling to exit that portion of the program as soon as an error is discovered. With error handling, the program execution immediately jumps to an error-handling section of the program when the computer detects certain types of errors.

Objectives

After completing this chapter, you should be able to:

- ☺ Know when to use the *ElseIf* keyword in statements with nested decisions.
- ☺ Recognize situations in which the *Case* structure can be used in place of *If* statements.

@ Apply Visual Basic error-handling statements appropriately during data validation.

@ State several applications for random numbers.

@ Use the *Rnd* function when random numbers are needed in a program.

Quiz Program with Multiple Decisions

We start this chapter with a program that incorporates decisions in several events. Suppose the instructor of an introductory programming class has asked us to create a quiz program that the students can use for short daily quizzes. The program is to ask a total of five questions. For each question, the program displays the question, lets a student type in a short answer, and tells the student whether his answer is right or wrong. It also keeps track of the total number of right answers. To make sure we understand what the instructor wants, we design a possible user interface for this program as shown in Figure 6.1.

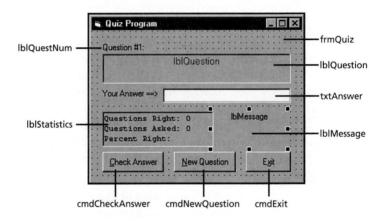

Figure 6.1 Quiz *program user interface.*

After the user interface is set, we proceed to design the logic for the program. When the program displays a question, the user will type in an answer and then click on the *Check Answer* button. Typing, just like clicking on a button, is an event that the computer can detect. So we, the programmers, must decide whether anything will happen while the user types in an answer or moves around the form. One approach is to put all the data validation and processing code under the *Check Answer* button. However, what if the user clicks on *Check Answer* without typing an answer? We have several alternatives. We could check for a missing answer in the *Check Answer* button click event, or we can disable the *Check Answer* button until an answer is entered. Let's follow the latter approach and disable the *Check Answer* button at the start of the program.

Next we consider whether a user should be able to skip a question by clicking on the *New Question* button without answering the current question. This is probably not desirable for a graded quiz, so we decide to disable this button also until the current question has been answered. The disabling of these two buttons are initial values, or settings, that we should be aware of. They should be included in our Initialization module while we are designing the logic, even though we may choose to set them in the Properties window in Visual Basic rather than in code. Figure 6.2 shows the initial Object-Event Diagram for this program.

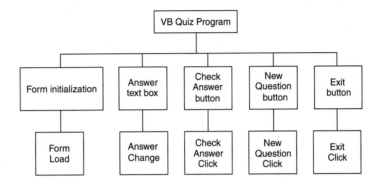

Figure 6.2 *OED for the* Quiz *program.*

Now that we have identified most of the events, we can proceed to design the logic for the individual events. At this point, the logic for the *Change* event of the answer text box is just to enable the *Check Answer* button if the user has typed something into the text box, and vice versa. Figure 6.3 shows this simple logic.

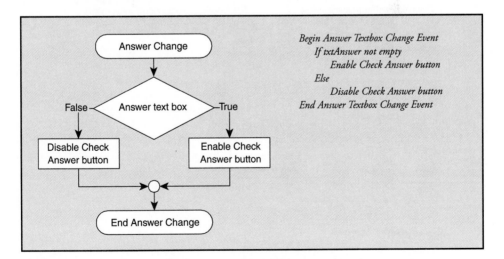

Figure 6.3 *Flowchart and pseudocode for the* Answer Change *event.*

We move on to the logic of the *Check Answer* button click event. This event procedure needs to determine whether the user's answer is right or wrong. It will contain a decision structure, as seen in Figure 6.4. In writing the logic for this event, we discover that the program must "know" what the right answer is to the current question. Because the answer is determined by the question that is asked, it makes sense to set the *RightAnswer* variable in the same place where the question is displayed. For the initial question, it would be set in the Initialization module(s).

If the user's answer is correct, it must be counted, so we need a "counter" variable (*NumRight*). Because *NumRight* must maintain its value between questions, this variable should have form scope. If *NumRight* is of form scope, it should be initialized in an event like the *Form Load* event procedure.

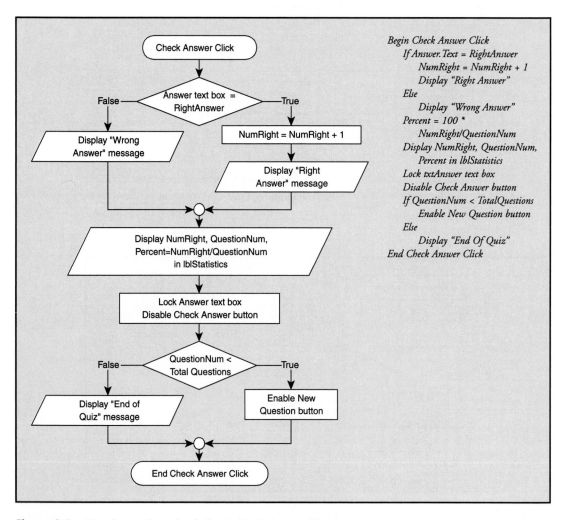

Figure 6.4 *Flowchart and pseudocode for the* Check Answer Click *event.*

We have now identified two form-scope variables (*NumRight* and *RightAnswer*), so we put them into the initialization (*Form Load*) logic. In so doing, we realize that to set initial the value of the *RightAnswer* variable, we must know what question is being asked. So we add Display 1st question to the *Form Load* process as well.

When the student clicks the *New Question* button, the program displays a different question and assigns the correct answer internally. How will this module know which question comes next? One way is to use a numeric variable that keeps track of which question the program is currently asking. This variable is incremented each time a new question is requested. Now we have another form-scope variable that should be initialized in the *Form Load* event procedure.

Note that we have been adding steps to the Initialization module (Form Load) as we think of them. This shows that logic design is a dynamic process where you must understand the interactions between different events to fully design the logic of one event. Hence you may find yourself updating details of the logic of one module while you are developing the logic of another module. Figure 6.5 shows the current logic of the Initialization module.

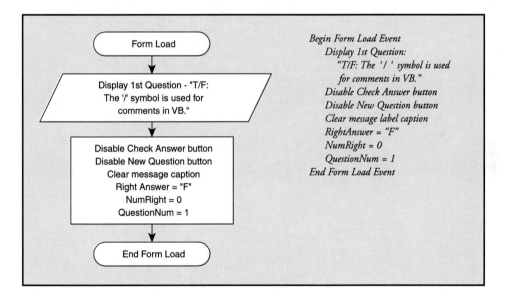

Figure 6.5   *Logic for the* Quiz *program initialization* (Form Load).

When the user clicks the *New Question* button, obviously a new question should display on the form. This program will use nested decisions and the current value of the *QuestionNum* variable to decide which question to display. At the same time, it will set the *RightAnswer*, clear old information from the screen, disable the *New Question* button, and put the focus on the answer box so that the program is ready to receive the user's input. Figure 6.6 shows the logic of the *New Question* button.

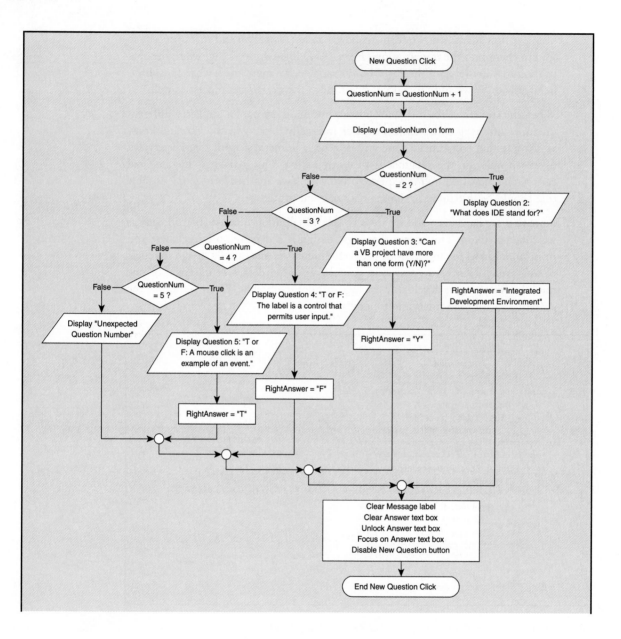

```
Begin New Question Click
    QuestionNum = QuestionNum + 1
    Display QuestionNum in lblQuestNum
    If QuestionNum = 2
        Display 2nd question in lblQuestion
        RightAnswer = (answer to 2nd question)
    Else
        If QuestionNum = 3
            Display 3rd question in lblQuestion
            RightAnswer = (answer to 3rd question)
        Else
            If QuestionNum = 4
                Display 4th question in lblQuestion
                RightAnswer = (answer to 4th question)
            Else
                If QuestionNum = 5
                    Display 5th question in lblQuestion
                    RightAnswer = (answer to 5th question)
                Else
                    Display error message
    Clear message label
    Clear Answer text box
    Unlock Answer text box
    Put focus on Answer text box
    Disable New Question button
End New Question Click
```

Figure 6.6   *Logic for the* New Question Click *event.*

With this analysis and documentation of the problem, it is time to proceed to the coding stage. The coding should be a smooth and straightforward process if we understand and follow our logic for each event. As mentioned in earlier chapters, it is usually easier for the programmer to code and test the project piece by piece, or event by event. Figure 6.7 presents the completed code for this program. If you are trying this example on the computer, however, follow the sequence of activities suggested here, refer to the appropriate flowcharts, and only look at the code if you get stuck.

A Suggested Coding Sequence

■ Start with the initializations. In Visual Basic, if the initialization step involves setting properties of controls, they can be set in the Properties window or in the code. On the other hand, variable initializations must be coded, typically in the *Form Load* event. Write the code for the *Form Load* event procedure and run the program to be sure there are no compile errors, that everything shows up correctly on the initial form, and that the two buttons are disabled as specified.

■ Next, code the Answer text box *Change* event and test the program to see whether the *Check Answer* button enables when a character is typed in the text box, and disables if the contents of the text box are deleted.

■ Now, code and test the *Check Answer* button. You should make sure that it gives a correct response to both right and wrong answers, and enables the *New Question* button. Why does the *Check Answer* logic set the Locked property of the Answer text box to *true*? Put a comment symbol at the beginning of this line and run the program again. Notice that the user can still type in the text box after the *Check Answer* button is disabled, which causes the *Check Answer* button to enable. Therefore, the program needs to "disable" the text box, using the Locked property of the text box.

If you disable the text box, you must also enable it somewhere. See whether you can decide which module this goes in and make sure the statement is there. If you are unsure, check the code listing of Figure 6.7.

■ Finally, code and test the *New Question Click* event.

■ Be sure to thoroughly test the program. Your test should include answering all questions correctly, answering all questions incorrectly, and various combinations of right and wrong answers. At each step, make sure the program gives the correct message for a right or wrong answer, and that the counts and percentage are updated accordingly.

The final code for this program, after following the logic design of all the previous flowcharts, is provided in Figure 6.7.

```
' Program:    Chapter 6: Quiz Program
' Form:       frmQuiz
' Programmer: Stew Dent
' Purpose:    This program displays 5 quiz questions, checks for a
'             right answer, notifies the user of the result and
'             displays statistics on the number and percent correct

Const cfTotalQuestions As Long = 5       ' Number of questions on quiz
Private fRightAnswer As String    ' Right answer to current question
Private fNumRight     As Integer  ' Number of right answers for user
Private fQuestionNum As Integer   ' Number of questions asked so far
Private fAllNums      As String
' Purpose: When the user clicks the Check Answer button, the answer
'          in the text box is compared to the right answer.  Right
'          answers are counted, an appropriate message is displayed,
'          and the statistics are updated.
Private Sub cmdCheckAnswer_Click()
    If txtAnswer.Text = fRightAnswer Then
        fNumRight = fNumRight + 1
        lblMessage.Caption = "You are right!!"
    Else
        lblMessage.Caption = "WRONG."
    End If
    lblStatistics.Caption = "Questions Right: " & Format(fNumRight) _
        & vbCrLf & "Questions Asked: " & Format(fQuestionNum) _
        & vbCrLf & "Percent Right: " _
        & Format(fNumRight / fQuestionNum, "Percent")
    txtAnswer.Locked = True
    cmdCheckAnswer.Enabled = False
    If fQuestionNum < cfTotalQuestions Then
        cmdNewQuestion.Enabled = True
    Else
        lblMessage.Caption = lblMessage.Caption & vbCrLf & vbCrLf & _
                    "END OF QUIZ."
```

```
      End If
End Sub

' Purpose: When the user clicks the Exit button, the form is unloaded.
Private Sub cmdExit_Click()
    Unload frmQuiz
End Sub

' Purpose: When the user clicks the New Question button, a new question
'          is displayed, the right answer is assigned, the question
'          number is updated, and old answers and messages are cleared.
Private Sub cmdNewQuestion_Click()
    fQuestionNum = fQuestionNum + 1
    lblQuestNum.Caption = "Question #" & CStr(fQuestionNum) & ":"
    If fQuestionNum = 2 Then
        lblQuestion.Caption = "What does IDE stand for?"
        fRightAnswer = "Integrated Development Environment"
    Else
        If fQuestionNum = 3 Then
            lblQuestion.Caption = _
                "Can a VB project have more than one form (Y/N)?"
            fRightAnswer = "Y"
        Else
            If fQuestionNum = 4 Then
                lblQuestion.Caption = "T or F: The label is a " _
                    & "control that permits user input."
                fRightAnswer = "F"
            Else
                If fQuestionNum = 5 Then
                    lblQuestion.Caption = "T or F: A mouse click is " _
                        & "an example of an event."
                    fRightAnswer = "T"
                Else
                    Call MsgBox("Unexpected error computing question #")
                End If   ' end Question 5
            End If    ' end Question 4
        End If     ' end Question 3
    End If      ' end Question 2
    lblMessage.Caption = ""
    txtAnswer.Text = ""
    txtAnswer.Locked = False
    Call txtAnswer.SetFocus
    cmdNewQuestion.Enabled = False
End Sub

' Purpose: When this form is loaded in memory, the first question
'          displays, the right answer is set, 2 buttons are
'          disabled and the form variables are initialized.
Private Sub Form_Load()
    cmdCheckAnswer.Enabled = False
    cmdNewQuestion.Enabled = False
    lblMessage.Caption = ""
    lblQuestion.Caption = _
                "T or F: The '/' symbol is used for comments in VB."
    fRightAnswer = "F"
    fNumRight = 0
    fQuestionNum = 1
End Sub

' Purpose: Whenever the user changes the contents of the answer text
'          box, the program enables or disables the Check Answer button.
Private Sub txtAnswer_Change()
```

continues

```
        If txtAnswer.Text <> "" Then
            cmdCheckAnswer.Enabled = True
        Else
            cmdCheckAnswer.Enabled = False
        End If
End Sub
```

Figure 6.7   *Visual Basic code for the* Quiz *program.*

Notice the comments on the *End If* statements of the *New Question Click* event. Adding comments like this helps document which structure is being ended by the statement. This makes it easier to see whether an *End If* is missing or in the wrong place.

Chained If-Then-Else Statements—The ElseIf Statement

In the previous example of nested decisions, each new *If* is inside the *Else* block of the previous *If*, so it is indented a new level. When there are too many levels of indenting, it becomes hard to see a complete statement on one line. Situations like the preceding example occur often enough that some programmers put the *Else* and the next *If* on the same line and continue indenting the same amount as the first *If* statement. Visual Basic provides a single **ElseIf** keyword for this situation. Using *ElseIf*, only one level of indenting is maintained throughout the nested *Ifs*, and only one *End If* statement is needed for the entire structure. If we use *ElseIfs* in our example from the preceding section, the *New Question* event procedure changes to the code of Figure 6.8.

```
Private Sub cmdNewQuestion_Click()
    fQuestionNum = fQuestionNum + 1
    lblQuestNum.Caption = "Question #" & CStr(fQuestionNum) & ":"
    If fQuestionNum = 2 Then
        lblQuestion.Caption = "What does IDE stand for?"
        fRightAnswer = "Integrated Development Environment"
    ElseIf fQuestionNum = 3 Then
        lblQuestion.Caption = _
            "Can a VB project have more than one form (Y/N)?"
        fRightAnswer = "Y"
    ElseIf fQuestionNum = 4 Then
        lblQuestion.Caption = _
            "T or F:The label is a control that permits user input."
        fRightAnswer = "F"
    ElseIf fQuestionNum = 5 Then
        lblQuestion.Caption = _
            "T or F: A mouse click is an example of an event."
        fRightAnswer = "T"
    Else
        Call MsgBox ("Unexpected error computing question number")
    End If
    lblMessage.Caption = ""
    txtAnswer.Text = ""
    txtAnswer.Locked = False
```

```
        Call txtAnswer.SetFocus
        cmdNewQuestion.Enabled = False
    End Sub
```

Figure 6.8   *Visual Basic code for the* Quiz *program using* ElseIf.

Don't forget to test the program again. It should run the same as the preceding version of the program, but a thorough test is still important.

Avoiding the "Dangling Else"

A potential problem with nested decisions is sometimes referred to as the "dangling else." This can occur when a program contains nested decisions and the inner decision does not have an *else* phrase, but the outer decision does have an *else*. This is illustrated in the following block of pseudocode:

```
if a>b then
  if c>d then
      lblMsg.Caption = "a>b, c>d"
else
  lblMsg.Caption = "a<=b"
```

Figure 6.9   *An example of a "dangling else" in pseudocode.*

The indentation clearly indicates that the programmer wants the *else* statement to go with the first (outer) *if* statement. If coded in this manner, however, the compiler will interpret the *else* as going with the second (inner) *if* statement. To achieve the desired result, you must remember to end the inner *If* with an *End If* statement *before* the *Else* of the outer *If* statement, as shown in Figure 6.10.

```
    If a > b Then
        If c > d Then
            lblMsg.Caption = "a>b, c>d"
        End If
    Else
        lblMsg.Caption = "a<=b"
    End If
```

Figure 6.10   *Avoiding a "dangling else" in Visual Basic code.*

The Case Structure

Our other special situation of the nested decision structure occurs when each decision is testing the *same* variable for several different values. This structure is called the **Case structure** and is available as a separate structure in most programming languages, including Visual Basic. The *Case* structure is typically flowcharted as shown in Figure 6.11, but is sometimes drawn with the choices to the right of the diamond as shown in Appendix B, "Program Design and Translation to VB Code."

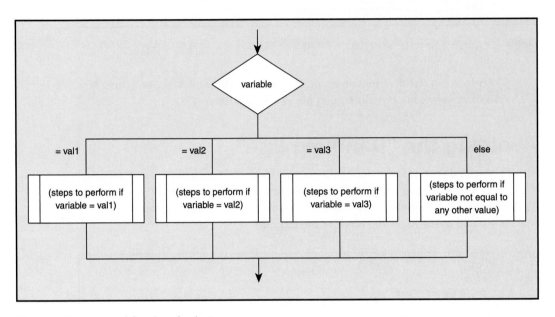

Figure 6.11 *General flowchart for the* Case *structure.*

This structure is equivalent to a series of nested decisions that successively check whether the variable is equal to *val1*, then *val2*, and then *val3*. Visual Basic offers additional flexibility to test whether the variable value falls within a range of values or is part of a list of several specific values.

TIP
Use a *Case* structure when the decision variable has more than two or three possible values.

Figure 6.12 shows the general form of the pseudocode for the *Case* structure, including a range and a list. Remember that pseudocode is not code, so the exact wording and layout can vary from one programmer to the next. After you pick a style, however, you should use it consistently in your logic documentation.

```
Case variable
  = val1
      (statements to do if variable = val1)
  = val2 to val3
      (statements to do if variable in range val2–val3)
  = val4, val5, val6
      (statements to do if variable =val4 or =val5 or =val6)
  else
      (statements to do if variable doesn't match any previous case)
End Case
```

Figure 6.12 *General pseudocode for the* Case *structure.*

In our problem of this chapter, the *QuestionNum* variable is tested in multiple decisions in the *New Question* procedure of our quiz program. Using the *Case* structure, the pseudocode for the *New Question Click* event would look like that of Figure 6.13. Figure 6.14 shows the corresponding flowchart.

```
Begin New Question Click
    QuestionNum = QuestionNum + 1
    Display QuestionNum in lblQuestNum
    Case QuestionNum
       =2
            Display 2nd question in lblQuestion
            RightAnswer = (answer to 2nd question)
       =3
            Display 3rd question in lblQuestion
            RightAnswer = (answer to 3rd question)
       =4
            Display 4th question in lblQuestion
            RightAnswer = (answer to 4th question)
       =5
            Display 5th question in lblQuestion
            RightAnswer = (answer to 5th question)
    Else
            Display error message
    Clear message label
    Clear Answer text box
    Unlock Answer text box
    Put focus on Answer text box
    Disable New Question button
End New Question Click
```

Figure 6.13   *Pseudocode for the* New Question Click *event with a* Case *structure.*

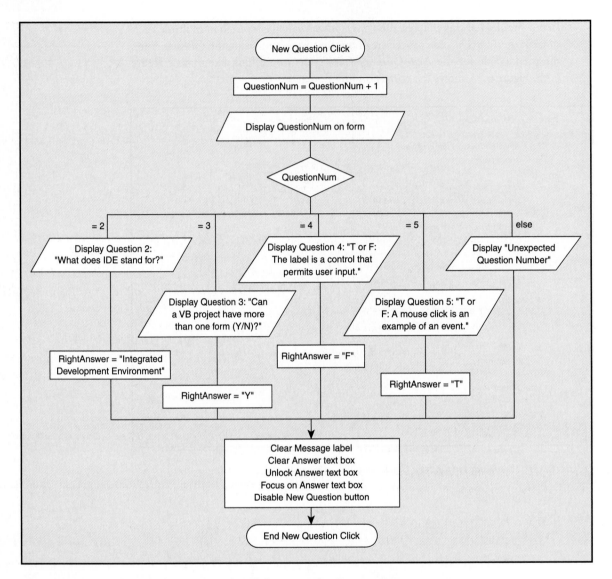

Figure 6.14 *Flowchart for the* New Question Click *event with a* Case *structure.*

The *Case* structure is implemented in Visual Basic with the **Select Case** statement. The general format of this statement is illustrated here with several of the main variations for the *Case* statement values:

```
Select Case test-expression
    Case value1                    ' single value
        statementA
        statementB
    Case Low-value To High-value   ' range of values
        statementM
        statementN
        statementO
    Case value2, value3, value4    ' list of values
        statementX
```

```
Case Else
      statementY
      statementZ
End Select
```

The first line of this Visual Basic *Case* structure is a *Select Case* statement that contains the variable or expression being tested. Many programming languages limit the data type of the *test-expression* and the values on the *Case* statements, but in Visual Basic it can be either a numeric expression or a string expression. The computer will first compare the value of this *test-expression* to the value or values on the first *Case* statement, *value1* in the above example. If equal, the program executes *statementA* and *statementB*, and then proceeds to the statement after the **End Select** statement. Otherwise, it checks whether the value of *test-expression* is in the range *Low-value* to *High-value* inclusive. If it is, *statementM*, *statementN*, and *statementO* are executed and execution continues on the statement after the *End Select* statement. If it hasn't found a match yet, the program next compares *test-expression* to the individual values *value2*, *value3*, and *value4*. If it equals any of these values, *statementX* is executed and execution continues on the statement after the *End Select* statement. Finally, if nothing has matched so far, *statementY* and *statementZ* are executed. Notice that the *Select Case* structure is terminated with an *End Select* statement.

From this general illustration, you can see that each **case** can involve a comparison for equality with one value, being within a range of values or being one of a list of values. One or several statements can follow each case, to be executed when that case is true. An optional **Case Else** is executed if no matching case is found. If the cases happen to overlap, only the statements in the first matching case will be executed.

Let's convert the *NewQuestion Click* procedure to a *Select Case* statement. It will look like the code in Figure 6.15. Now it would be easy to expand this code to ask more than five questions.

```
Private Sub cmdNewQuestion_Click()
    fQuestionNum = fQuestionNum + 1
    lblQuestNum.Caption = "Question #" & CStr(fQuestionNum) & ":"
    Select Case fQuestionNum
        Case 2
            lblQuestion.Caption = "What does IDE stand for?"
            fRightAnswer = "Integrated Development Environment"
        Case 3
            lblQuestion.Caption = _
                "Can a VB project have more than one form (Y/N)?"
            fRightAnswer = "Y"
        Case 4
            lblQuestion.Caption = "T or F:" _
                & "The label is a control that permits user input."
            fRightAnswer = "F"
```

continues

```
        Case 5
            lblQuestion.Caption = _
                "T or F: A mouse click is an example of an event."
            fRightAnswer = "T"
        Case Else
            Call MsgBox ("Unexpected error computing question number")
    End Select
    lblMessage.Caption = ""
    txtAnswer.Text = ""
    txtAnswer.Locked = False
    Call txtAnswer.SetFocus
    cmdNewQuestion.Enabled = False
End Sub
```

Figure 6.15 New Question Click *event using* Select Case.

Using Random Numbers

If this is a quiz that students might take multiple times, or if everyone in the class is taking the same quiz at different times, the instructor probably wants to mix up the order of the questions. Most programming languages have one or more random number generators that give programs a way to do things in random order, to generate random data values, or to select random numbers for game situations. Visual Basic has a function called **Rnd** that returns a floating-point number in the range zero to one (the range includes zero, but not one). For our quiz program, we want a number in the range one to five. To generate a random number in a range from *lowerBound* to *upperBound*, we can use the expression:

```
Int((upperBound - lowerBound + 1) * Rnd + lowerBound)
```

Using this expression, the statement to generate a new question number in our program becomes this:

```
QuestionNum = Int(5 * Rnd + 1)
```

Now another problem crops up. In a game, it may be expected that the same number will be selected more than once; in a quiz, however, we don't want to ask the same question twice. Our program needs a way to remove the question number after it has been selected. To do this, we will initially put our five question numbers together into one string and make use of several functions provided by Visual Basic to remove the selected question number from this string when it has been used. We assign the question numbers as an initialization step:

```
AllNums = "12345"
```

Because in the future we may have more than five questions, we will use the *Len* function to get the length of this string. The *Len* function returns the number of characters in a given string. In the following statement, the variable *AllNums* is passed to the *Len* function, which then returns a number and assigns it to the variable *QuestionRange*.

```
QuestionRange = Len(AllNums)
```

Knowing how many questions there are, we can get a random number that is in the range of this *QuestionRange* value. This random number will be used to extract the question number from the string of all question numbers:

```
RandQuestNum = Int(QuestionRange * Rnd + 1)
```

Now we use Visual Basic's *Mid* function to copy that question number out of the *AllNums* variable. The *Mid* function selects a substring, in this case one digit, out of a longer string. The *Mid* function has three parameters. The first is the entire string (*AllNums*), the second is the starting position of the substring, and the third is how many characters we want to copy out of the entire string. For this situation, the third parameter is always 1, because we want to copy out only one digit. The second parameter is our random number, *RandQuestNum*:

```
QuestionNum = Mid(AllNums, RandQuestNum, 1)
```

Finally we use the *Left* and *Right* functions provided in Visual Basic to remove the question number from *AllNums* so that it won't get asked again. The *Left* function extracts a specified number of characters from the left side of a longer string. It has two parameters: the string to extract from, and how many characters to extract. The *Right* function extracts a specified number of characters from the right side of a longer string. Just like the *Left* function, it has two parameters: the string to extract from, and the number of characters to extract.

```
AllNums = Left(AllNums, RandQuestNum - 1) & _
          Right(AllNums, QuestionRange - RandQuestNum)
```

Now, every time the *New Question* button is clicked, it can randomly select a question number from the remaining questions.

If we want the first question to be randomly selected also, we should include question number 1 in our *Case* statement and include the *New Question* code in the *Form Load* event also. To avoid duplicating this code in both events, we can instead put the "random question selection" code in a separate procedure and call the new procedure from both the *Form Load* and *New Question Click* events. The code for this procedure, named *GetQuestionAndAnswer*, is shown in Figure 6.16. It has three parameters. The first parameter is the string of available question numbers, the second is the text of the selected question, and the third is the correct answer for this question. All three parameters are changed by the procedure, so they are passed by reference.

```
Private Sub GetQuestionAndAnswer(ByRef rAllNums As String, _
    ByRef rQuestion As String, ByRef rAnswer As String)

    Dim RandNum As Integer
    Dim QuestRange As Integer
    Dim QuestNum As String

    QuestRange = Len(rAllNums)
    RandNum = Int(QuestRange * Rnd + 1)
    QuestNum = Mid(rAllNums, RandNum, 1)
    rAllNums = Left(rAllNums, RandNum - 1) & _
               Right(rAllNums, QuestRange - RandNum)
    Select Case QuestNum
        Case "1"
            rQuestion = "T or F: The symbol '/' starts a comment in VB."
            rAnswer = "F"
```
continues

```
            Case "2"
                rQuestion = "What does IDE stand for?"
                rAnswer = "Integrated Development Environment"
            Case "3"
                rQuestion = _
                    "Can a VB project have more than one form (Y/N)?"
                rAnswer = "Y"
            Case "4"
                rQuestion = "T or F:" _
                    & " The label is a control that permits user input."
                rAnswer = "F"
            Case "5"
                rQuestion = _
                    "T or F: A mouse click is an example of an event."
                rAnswer = "T"
            Case Else
                Call MsgBox ("Unexpected error computing question number")
        End Select
End Sub
```

Figure 6.16 *Visual Basic code for* GetQuestionAndAnswer *procedure using* Rnd.

Figure 6.17 shows the code for the *Form_Load* event, with the call to the *GetQuestionAndAnswer* procedure.

```
    Private Sub Form_Load()
        Dim FirstQuestion As String

        fAllNums = "12345"
        fNumRight = 0
        fQuestionNum = 1
        Randomize
        cmdCheckAnswer.Enabled = False
        cmdNewQuestion.Enabled = False
        lblMessage.Caption = ""
        Call GetQuestionAndAnswer(fAllNums, FirstQuestion, fRightAnswer)
        lblQuestion.Caption = FirstQuestion
    End Sub
```

Figure 6.17 *Visual Basic code for* Form_Load *using* Randomize.

Notice in Figure 6.17 that the statement **Randomize** has been added to the *Form_Load* event. If you run the program without using the *Randomize* statement, you would soon realize that every time you start running the program, it gives you the same sequence of questions. That is because the *Rnd* function is really a *pseudo-random* number generator, and it generates the same sequence of values every time the program starts over. This can be helpful during program testing, but is generally unacceptable for actual program operation. The *Randomize* statement initializes, or "seeds," the *Rnd* function with a new starting value, based on the clock time. Because the time will be different every time the program runs, a different sequence of numbers will be generated. *Randomize* is an initialization operation, so it only needs to be called one time. Therefore, we place it in the *Form_Load* event.

Figure 6.18 contains the updated code for the *New Question Click* procedure, with the call to *GetQuestionAndAnswer*.

```
Private Sub cmdNewQuestion_Click()
    Dim NextQuestion As String

    fQuestionNum = fQuestionNum + 1
    lblQuestNum.Caption = "Question #" & CStr(fQuestionNum) & ":"
    Call GetQuestionAndAnswer(fAllNums, NextQuestion, fRightAnswer)
    lblQuestion.Caption = NextQuestion
    lblMessage.Caption = ""
    txtAnswer.Text = ""
    txtAnswer.Locked = False
    Call txtAnswer.SetFocus
    cmdNewQuestion.Enabled = False
End Sub
```

Figure 6.18   New Question Click *event with questions in random order.*

The rest of the program is the same, except for adding a declaration of *fAllNums* at the beginning of the program as a string variable that has form scope.

Error Handling

In Chapter 5 we talked about several types of data validation and suggested ways to check the program's data to prevent processing errors. The decision structure is a big part of data validation routines. A complete program will always try to anticipate errors that a user is likely to make and help the user avoid making these errors as well as provide a way to correct the error. Sometimes, however, it is not possible or feasible to separately test for all possible errors that may occur in a program. Certain calculations may produce underflow (number too small) or overflow (number too large) errors, and other code may be subject to hardware errors (no disk in a drive, for example). Most programming languages provide a way for a program to detect these errors and let the program handle the error in a nice way.

Visual Basic has a built-in **Err object** that exists in all VB programs. When an error occurs, the properties of the *Err* object are updated with information about the error. Three of these properties are *number, source,* and *description,* as seen in Figure 6.19.

Property	Data Type	Description
Number	Long	VB's internal error number
Source	String	Name of VB file in which error occurred
Description	String	Error message text describing the error

Figure 6.19   *Properties of the VB* Err *object.*

After an error occurs, you can test for specific error numbers, or display some or all of the property values in an error message. The following call to the *MsgBox* function would display all three of these property values, for example:

```
Call MsgBox(CStr(Err.Number) & ": " & Err.Description & " - " _
     & Err.Source)
```

The properties of *Err* receive new values at the time the error occurs and are available until

- Another error is reported

- The procedure ends

- The error-handler is reinitialized with a *Resume* or *On Error* statement

Error handlers in Visual Basic are "turned on" with an "**On Error GoTo** *program-label*" statement, often at the beginning of a procedure or function. This statement tells Visual Basic what statements to execute if an error occurs on a following statement. If a statement following the "On Error" statement causes an error, processing will jump to the line labeled *program-label*. The *program-label* is a programmer-selected name that marks the beginning of the error-handler code. Suppose we select the name "GeneralErrHandler" for our label. Then the statement to "turn on" **error handling** is as follows:

```
On Error GoTo GeneralErrHandler
```

Next, you must provide the code to be executed when the error occurs. This code follows a line containing the *program-label*. The code in the error handler could specifically check for various types of errors and display appropriate error messages or attempt to correct the problem. Or the error-handler code could just display a message, no matter what error occurred, that shows the error number and error description supplied by the Err object, as shown here:

```
GeneralErrHandler:
     Call MsgBox("[" & CStr(Err.Number) & "] " & Err.Description)
```

Finally, Visual Basic needs to know when it has finished handling this error. You can exit from an error handler using the **Resume**, **Resume Next**, or **Resume** statements, or with an **Exit Sub** statement.

The *Resume* statement returns execution to the statement that caused the error and tries to execute it again. Hence, you would only use this statement if the program or the user were somehow able to fix the problem immediately. If the user forgot to put a disk in the drive, for example, the error handler could test for this error and display a message with the *MsgBox* function. The user could react to the message by inserting the disk and clicking the appropriate button provided by *MsgBox*. Depending on which button was clicked, the *Resume* statement could then retry the statement that required a disk. If the error is due to a missing value for a calculation, the error handler could assign a "typical value" and the calculation could continue by using the *Resume* statement.

The *Resume Next* statement returns to execute the statement following the one that caused the error. This can be used when the error handler can "fix" the problem and the rest of the program should then continue to be executed. If a data conversion operation causes a "Type Mismatch" error, for example, it might be appropriate for the program to assign a default value to the variable and continue processing.

The *Resume label* statement jumps to the line containing the specified *label* and continues execution. This label could be at a statement before or after the one that originally caused the error.

Using Error Handling in a Sample Program

Assume we want a program to multiply two numbers. Start a new project in Visual Basic. Put two text boxes, a *Multiply* button, and an answer label on the form. The form shown in Figure 6.20 also contains two additional labels with the multiplication sign (×) and the equal (=) sign. Add code to the *Multiply* button that converts the text box values to numbers, multiplies them, and displays the result in the answer label. Save and run the program. You should be able to enter two numbers and get the correct multiplication result.

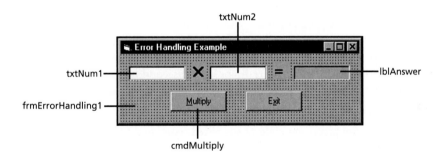

Figure 6.20   *Form design for the* Multiply *program.*

Without data validation, a number of errors could occur while this program executes. The user may forget to enter a number, accidentally enter an invalid number, or enter a very large number that causes an overflow error when the numbers are multiplied. We learned in Chapter 5 how to add decisions to a program to catch some of these errors. In this program, we will use error handling instead. The easiest way to add error handling to this program is to display the same error message for any error that occurs. Figure 6.21 illustrates one way to do this.

```
Private Sub cmdMultiply_Click()
    Dim Answr As Long

    On Error GoTo MultErrHandler
    Answr = CLng(txtNum1.Text) * CLng(txtNum2.Text)
    lblAnswer.Caption = CStr(Answr)
    Exit Sub

MultErrHandler:
    Call MsgBox ("Error while trying to multiply")
    Exit Sub

End Sub
```

Figure 6.21 *Visual Basic code for the* Multiply Button Click *event, with error handling.*

After entering this code, run the program with missing data values, illegal numbers, and extremely large numbers to generate errors. You could also replace the *MsgBox* statement of Figure 6.21 with the one presented earlier in this section that displays the error's number, description, and source (shown here).

```
Call MsgBox(CStr(Err.Number) & ": " & Err.Description & " - " _
    & Err.Source)
```

If you then run the program and try to generate the same types of errors, you can see what error numbers are generated for missing values, illegal numbers, and very large numbers that cause overflow errors. The first message, Error while trying to multiply, is more general and user-friendly. The second message is more helpful to the programmer when debugging the program. You must decide which is more appropriate for the types of errors you are trapping.

If you tested the preceding code as suggested, you would have seen that an overflow error generates error number 6 and a Type Mismatch error generates error number 13. You can find additional error numbers in the Visual Basic Help facility by looking up "Trappable Errors." We now take advantage of this information to make the error handler smarter in how it handles certain types of errors. The error messages can be more informative for specific errors, for example. Figure 6.22 shows a revised version of our *Multiply* program that makes use of the *Select Case* statement to test for specific error numbers.

```
Private Sub cmdMultiply_Click()
    Dim Answr As Long

    On Error GoTo MultErrHandler
    Answr = CLng(txtNum1.Text) * CLng(txtNum2.Text)
    lblAnswer.Caption = CStr(Answr)
    Exit Sub

MultErrHandler:
    Select Case Err.Number
        Case 6
            Call MsgBox ("Overflow while multiplying." & vbCrLf _
                & "Numbers too large.  Try again.")
            Exit Sub
        Case 13
            Call MsgBox ("Error converting numbers." & vbCrLf _
                & "Correct and try again.")
            Exit Sub
        Case Else
            Call MsgBox (Err.Number & " - " & Err.Description)
            Exit Sub
    End Select

End Sub
```

Figure 6.22   *Visual Basic code for the revised* Multiply *program, with error handling.*

In this error handler, because the *Exit Sub* statement appears at the end of each case, it could instead be coded one time immediately after the *End Select* statement. In many programs that use this approach of testing for separate errors, however, the program or the user can fix the errors in some cases and not in others, so the program may be able to use *Resume* or *Resume Next*, which don't need to exit the procedure.

Error handling is often used with file processing, so you will see it again in Chapter 9, "Sequential Files."

Unstructured Exits from Decisions

The preceding section introduced a new statement, *Exit Sub*, which causes the program execution to exit out of the current sub procedure. The *Exit Sub* statement does not just apply to error handling, but can be used in any situation where immediate exit from the current procedure is the best solution. Using *Exit Sub* results in more than one exit path from the function or procedure. This violates the single entry-single exit criterion of structured programming. As a beginning programmer, you should look for a structured way to code the module first, and only use *Exit Sub* to avoid making the logic vastly more complex.

One common use of *Exit Sub* is when errors are found in a processing module. You are working on a module whose primary purpose is a series of calculations to display a result, for example. But in the module there are several tests to determine whether processing can continue (for example, testing for zero or negative values or values out of range). Instead of many levels of nested decisions, the program could instead use *Exit Sub* to leave the module when an error condition is found.

Order Price Calculation Case Study

Suppose that a company needs a program to look up an item's price, description, and weight, and then to calculate the total price of an order for the desired quantity, including sales tax and shipping costs. (For now, each order can only have one item of any quantity.) Because the ordering business is just getting started, they currently have six items that can be ordered, which are listed in Figure 6.23.

Item Code	Item Description	Unit Cost	Weight (ounces)
173AJ-247	"Farm Scene" Quilt	522.49	168
182K-304A	Platinum Cuff Links	299.99	15.99
206B7-55H	"Eagle in Flight" Wood Carving	105.75	16.1
499GN-801	Hand-crafted Bird Feeder	29.55	65.7
499GN-801X	Deluxe Hand-crafted Bird Feeder	39.99	78
626T-71W	Hand-woven Straw Placemats	10.00	4

Figure 6.23 *Item data for the* Order Calculation *program.*

The company will ship items to customers within a limited region of neighboring states. Assume that the current law says customers pay the sales tax of their own states. Indiana, Michigan, Kentucky, and Tennessee residents pay 6 percent sales tax; Illinois residents pay 6.25 percent; and Ohio and Wisconsin residents pay 5 percent sales tax. Shipping costs are $3.00 for the first pound or less. Each additional ounce is 12 cents if shipped to a location in Indiana and 15 cents if shipped to a neighboring state. When determining shipping costs, a fraction of an ounce counts as a whole ounce. The quantity on most orders is less than 10, so the program should question the reasonableness of quantities that are 100 or more.

Step 1: Analyze the Problem

For this program, the user needs a way to enter an item code or item name. We ask the company representatives how they usually identify an item, and learn that they would normally use the item code, which is a sequence of 8 to 10 digits and capital letters with a dash in the middle. So the program will give the user a way to enter the item code. Other user inputs are the quantity desired and a two-letter state abbreviation. Next we need to decide what event causes the program to look up the item price, description, and weight. If a bad item code is entered, there is no need for the user to enter the quantity and state abbreviation. But calculations cannot be performed until all three values have been entered. We start by putting this information into our Analysis Table, as shown in Figure 6.24.

Input Needs	Processing Needs	Output Needs
Item code	Search for item code	Item description
Quantity	Check for valid inputs	Item price
State abbreviation	Calculate item total	"Bad Item Code" message
	Calculate sales tax	"Bad Quantity" message
	Calculate shipping weight	"Bad State" message
	Calculate shipping total	Item total
	Calculate order total	Shipping price
	Clear inputs	Sales tax
	Clear outputs	Order total
	Exit program	

Figure 6.24 *Analysis Table for the* Order Calculation *program.*

Step 2: Design or Create the User Interface

Using our three basic controls, we revise the preceding table to identify which controls our program needs (see Figure 6.25).

Input Needs	Processing Needs	Output Needs
Text boxes and descriptive labels to input:	Four command buttons to:	Labels for each of:
Item Code	Search for Item Code	Item Description
Quantity	Validate and Calculate	Item Price
State Abbreviation	Check for Valid Inputs	Item Total
	Calculate Item Total	Shipping Price
	Calculate Sales Tax	Sales Tax
	Calculate Shipping Weight	Order Total
	Calculate Shipping Total	Label or MsgBox for:
	Calculate Order Total	"Bad Item Code" message
	Clear Inputs and Outputs	"Bad Quantity" message
	Exit Program	"Bad State" message

Figure 6.25 *Controls required for the* Order Calculation *program.*

With these requirements in mind, we arrange the needed controls on the form. One possibility appears in Figure 6.26.

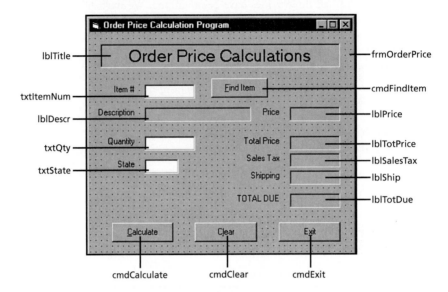

Figure 6.26 *Possible user interface for* Price Calculation *program.*

The gray boxes are labels with the border style changed to *1 – Fixed Single*. The Alignment property of the numeric labels should be set to *1 – Right Justify*.

Step 3: Design the Logic for the Program

Now we must further identify the events to be used by our program. One way some programs help the user is to disable buttons that don't currently apply. We know, for example, that the program won't be able to find an item if no item number has been typed in. Similarly, the program can't calculate the order total if the item, quantity, and state aren't available. If you explore the events of a text box, you find *KeyPress* and *Change* events in the list. Look up the *KeyPress* event in the Visual Basic Help files. It tells us that the *KeyPress* event has a parameter, *keyascii*, that contains the numeric ASCII code value of the key the user pressed, and that setting this parameter to zero cancels the keystroke. The Help file also mentions the Visual Basic *Chr* and *Asc* functions, which are used to convert ASCII values to characters and characters back to numeric code values. The *KeyPress* event can be used to screen out illegal characters as the user is typing. The *Change* event can be used to enable or disable the command buttons, depending on whether there is a value in the text box. *Change* events can also be used to clear other calculated portions of the screen that are supposed to go with the input values. If the program finds an item, for example, it displays the description and price for that item. If the user then changes the item number, the description and price will not be for the item number showing, so the description and price should be cleared. If you want to read more about these events, refer to Appendix A, "Visual Basic User Interface Objects."

Step 3a: Design the Macro-View (Object-Event Diagram)

Because there is just one form, our macro logic will consist of one OED. We consider each control on the form, and whether there is an associated event. In considering the various kinds of data validation for this problem, we decide to use the *KeyPress* events to check for invalid characters in the Item Number, Quantity, and State text boxes. We will use the *Change* events to decide whether certain results should be cleared, and to enable or disable the command buttons. As we think about the sequence of events, we notice that several controls are always cleared at the same time, and in more than one place, so we identify several "clear" procedures to eliminate duplicate code. Figure 6.27 shows our initial design of the *Order Price* program, which contains 10 event procedures and three other modules.

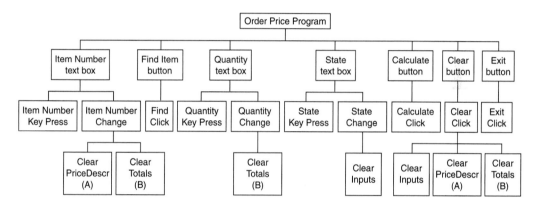

Figure 6.27 *OED for* Order Price *program.*

Step 3b: Design the Micro-Level View (Flowcharts and Pseudocode)

Let's work on the data validation modules first. We will use the text box *KeyPress* event to make sure that only valid characters are placed in the text boxes. Valid characters for the Item Number are capital letters, digits, and a dash. Remember that the *KeyPress* event will give us the ASCII code for the key the user pressed, so we can either look up the ASCII values of these characters in the table on the tearcard of this book, or we can use the *Chr* function to convert the input to a character. Because a good program should try to help the user whenever possible, the program can automatically convert lowercase letters to capital letters, instead of forcing the user to retype them. There is more than one way to do this, depending on whether we choose to work with the numeric code value or the character itself. We can subtract a numeric amount from the code of lowercase letters to convert them to the code for uppercase letters, for example, or we can use the *UCase* function to convert lowercase characters to uppercase. The other user inputs have slightly different sets of valid characters. The quantity contains only digits, and the state abbreviation consists of two uppercase letters. We can set the MaxLength property of the text box to prevent the user from typing more than two characters for the state abbreviation.

The *Item Number Change* event performs one additional validation to make sure the first character is not a dash. It then decides whether to enable the *Find Item* button and it clears previous results from the form.

The *Quantity Change* event determines whether to enable or disable the *Calculate* button; because enabling depends on both quantity and state, however, a Boolean variable (*StateOK*) is introduced. This module also clears the price totals.

The *State Change* event validates the state abbreviation by using a *Case* structure, and then enables or disables the *Calculate* button and clears any previous price totals.

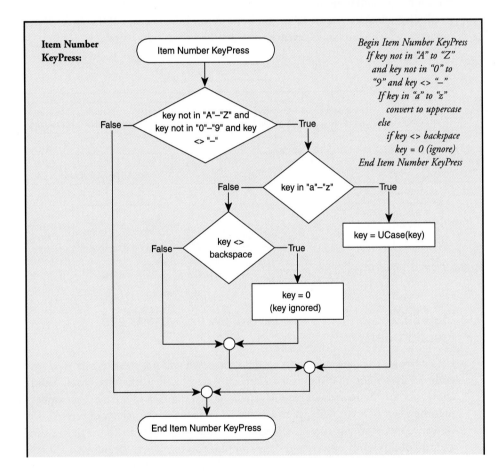

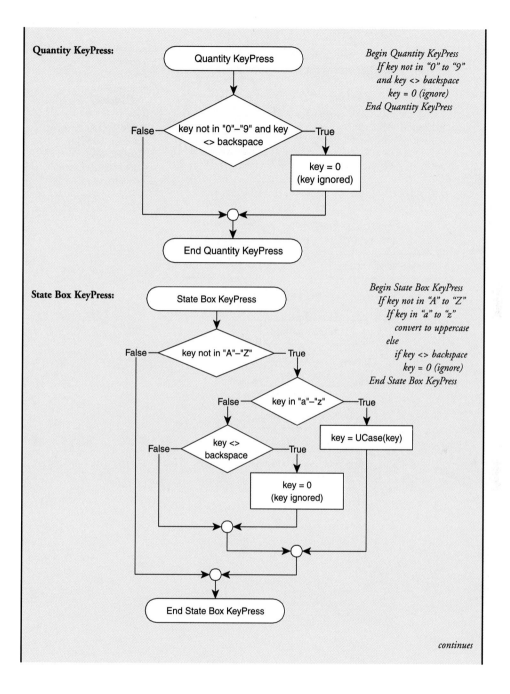

Begin Quantity KeyPress
  If key not in "0" to "9"
    and key <> backspace
      key = 0 (ignore)
End Quantity KeyPress

Begin State Box KeyPress
  If key not in "A" to "Z"
    If key in "a" to "z"
      convert to uppercase
    else
      if key <> backspace
        key = 0 (ignore)
End State Box KeyPress

continues

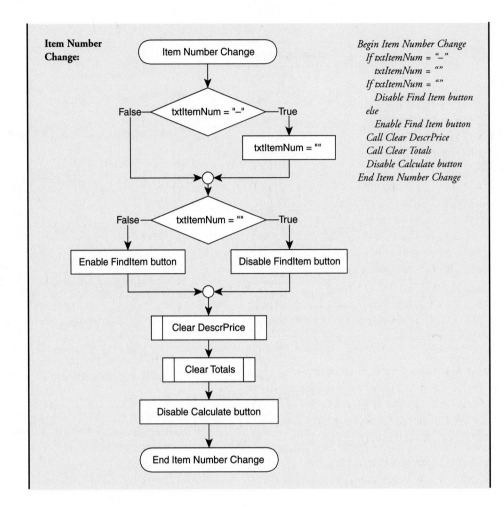

Item Number Change:

Item Number Change

False — txtItemNum = "–" — True

txtItemNum = ""

False — txtItemNum = "" — True

Enable FindItem button   Disable FindItem button

Clear DescrPrice

Clear Totals

Disable Calculate button

End Item Number Change

Begin Item Number Change
If txtItemNum = "–"
   txtItemNum = ""
If txtItemNum = ""
   Disable Find Item button
else
   Enable Find Item button
Call Clear DescrPrice
Call Clear Totals
Disable Calculate button
End Item Number Change

Quantity Change:

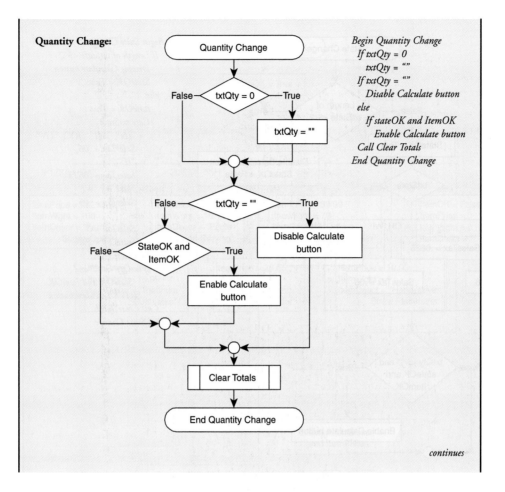

Quantity Change

False — txtQty = 0 — True

txtQty = ""

txtQty = ""   False — True

StateOK and ItemOK   False — True

Disable Calculate button

Enable Calculate button

Clear Totals

End Quantity Change

Begin Quantity Change
 If txtQty = 0
  txtQty = ""
 If txtQty = ""
  Disable Calculate button
else
  If stateOK and ItemOK
   Enable Calculate button
Call Clear Totals
End Quantity Change

continues

319

Test Case	User Input and/or Action	Expected Results
1 (No item #)	Click *Find Item*. Click *Calculate*.	Nothing happens. The buttons are disabled.
2 (No item #)	Enter 5 in Quantity, IN in State. Click *Calculate*.	Nothing happens. The button is disabled.
3 (Find button not clicked)	Enter 499GN–801 in Item per Fig. 6.26. Click *Calculate*.	*Find Item* button is enabled. The *Calculate* button is disabled.
4 (Find middle item)	Click *Find Item*.	Descr: Hand-crafted Bird Feeder Price: $29.55 *Calculate* button is enabled.
5 (Calculate with all inputs, "IN", over 16 oz.)	Click *Calculate*.	Tot Pr: $147.75 Tax: $8.87 Ship: $40.56 Tot Due: $197.18
6 (Change quantity)	Click in Quantity. Highlight the current value. Type 2 in Quantity.	Total Price, Tax, Shipping, and Total Due clear. *Calculate* button is enabled.
7 (Delete quantity using backspace)	Use backspace to delete Quantity.	Quantity box is empty. *Calculate* button is disabled.
8 (Recalculate with new Qty)	Type 1 in Quantity. Click *Calculate*.	*Calculate* button is enabled. Tot Pr: $29.55 Tax: $1.77 Ship: $9.00 Tot Due: $40.32
9 (Change state)	Click in State. Highlight the current value. Type IL in State.	Total Price, Tax, Shipping, and Total Due clear. *Calculate* button is enabled.
10 (Delete state using backspace)	Use backspace to delete the State.	*Calculate* button is disabled when one letter is deleted. State box is empty.
11 (Calculate button for "WI")	Type WI in State. Click *Calculate*.	Tot Pr: $29.55 Tax: $1.48 Ship: $10.50 Tot Due: $41.53
12 (*Clear* button)	Click *Clear*.	All input text boxes and output labels clear. *Find Item* and *Calculate* buttons are disabled.

Test Case	User Input and/or Action	Expected Results
13 (Item # errors)	Try to type !, @, #, $, %, ^, &, *, (,), –, =, +,], [, ', /, ., ? in Item #. Enter a mixture of letters, numbers, and other characters.	None of these characters can be entered, except the dash (if not the first character). The letters and numbers will appear in Item #.
14 (Type lowercase in Item #)	Type abc3–4jkl into Item #.	ABC3–4JKL appears in Item #. *Find Item* button enabled.
15 (Quantity errors)	Try to type letters and other non-numeric characters in Quantity.	No characters except 0–9 will appear in Quantity. Zero is not allowed as the first character.
16 (State errors)	Try to type numbers and other nonalphabetic characters in State.	Only letters A–Z will appear in State.
17 (Type lower-case state)	Type any lowercase letters in the State box.	All letters convert to uppercase. Only allows two letters to be entered.
18 (Find with bad Item #)	Click *Find Item*.	Descr: ** NO SUCH ITEM **
19 (Change Item #)	Type 626t–71w in Item #. Type 4 in Qty, IL in State.	626T–71W appears in Item #. Description clears.
20 (Find last item #, price ends in zeroes)	Click *Find Item*.	Descr: Hand-woven Straw Placemats Price: $10.00 *Calculate* button is enabled.
21 (Calculate for "IL", exactly 16 oz.)	Click *Calculate*.	Tot Pr: $40.00 Tax: $2.50 Ship: $3.00 Tot Due: $45.50

Figure 6.31 *Test plan for the* Order Calculation *program.*

As you can see, a complete test plan can get quite lengthy for even this small program, especially when it includes data validation. If you don't take the time to develop the test plan now, however, you may forget to test some of the cases in the rush to finish the program. We leave it as an exercise to find other test cases to add to this test plan.

Step 4: Code the Program

With the logic worked out, we now proceed to the coding step. Because the user must first enter an item number to perform any processing, the *Find Item* button click event is a logical place to start. Once coded, you should test *Find Item* by typing in each of the actual item numbers and a bad item number to see whether the proper messages appear.

A typical user of this program would next type in a quantity and a state, and then click the *Calculate* button; therefore, the *State Change* and *Calculate* button click events are good modules to code next. In looking at the logic, we notice several numbers related to shipping costs and reasonable quantity, and decide to create named constants for these. The *Calculate Click* procedure makes use of an *Exit Sub* statement when the quantity is very large and the user wants to make a correction. After these procedures are coded, you should perform a long set of tests to make sure the tax is calculated correctly for each valid state and the shipping is calculated correctly for a variety of quantities for each item.

Next you can start adding the data validation code that is performed in the *KeyPress* and other *Change* events, and the remaining button click events.

```
' Program:    Chapter 6: Order Price
' Form:       frmOrderPrice
' Programmer: Cal Q. Laytor
' Purpose:    Looks up an item and calculates the order total
'             for the specified quantity and state.

Option Explicit

Const cfReasonableQty    As Long = 100
Const cfBaseShipPrice    As Currency = 3#
Const cfInStateShipRate  As Currency = 0.12
Const cfOutStateShipRate As Currency = 0.15

Private fItemOK       As Boolean    ' true if Item Number is valid
Private fItemPrice    As Currency   ' current item's price
Private fItemDescr    As String     ' current item's description
Private fItemWght     As Double     ' current item's weight in ounces
Private fSalesTaxFrac As Double     ' current state's sales tax fraction
Private fStateOK      As Boolean    ' true if valid two-letter state code

' Purpose: Clears the text boxes and form variables for
'          item description and item price.
Private Sub ClearDescrPrice()
    lblDescr.Caption = ""
    lblPrice.Caption = ""
    fItemDescr = ""
    fItemPrice = 0
    fItemWght = 0
End Sub

' Purpose: Clears the input text boxes
Private Sub ClearInputs()
    txtItemNum.Text = ""
    txtQty.Text = ""
    txtState.Text = ""
End Sub
```

```
' Purpose: Clears the text boxes containing the item totals.
Private Sub ClearTotals()
    lblTotPrice.Caption = ""
    lblSalesTax.Caption = ""
    lblShip.Caption = ""
    lblTotDue.Caption = ""
End Sub


' Purpose: Calculates the order's total price, including tax and
'          shipping.  Assumes the state code has been validated,
'          but asks user to verify quantities over 100.  Performs
'          error trapping for problems such as numeric overflow
'          while converting or multiplying.
Private Sub cmdCalculate_Click()
    Dim Qty As Long            ' numeric quantity ordered
    Dim TotItemPrice As Currency ' qty*price of item
    Dim Tax As Double          ' sales tax on item
    Dim Weight As Double       ' total weight of order
    Dim OuncesOver16 As Double ' ounces over 1 lb.
    Dim ShipCost As Currency   ' shipping cost of order
    Dim PerOz As Currency      ' shipping per ounce
    Dim TotDue As Currency     ' total amount due

    On Error GoTo MathErr    ' Turn on error handling
    Qty = CLng(txtQty.Text)
    If Qty > cfReasonableQty Then
        If MsgBox("Large quantity -- Is it correct?", vbYesNo, _
                "Large Quantity Verification") = vbNo Then
            Call txtQty.SetFocus
            Exit Sub  ' exit so user can enter new quantity
        End If
    End If
    ' quantity is OK
    TotItemPrice = Qty * fItemPrice
    Tax = TotItemPrice * fSalesTaxFrac
    Weight = Qty * fItemWght
    ShipCost = cfBaseShipPrice
    If Weight > 16 Then                 ' 16 ounces per pound
        If txtState.Text = "IN" Then
            PerOz = cfInStateShipRate
        Else
            PerOz = cfOutStateShipRate
        End If
        OuncesOver16 = Int(Weight - 16 + 0.99) ' go to next whole ounce
        ShipCost = ShipCost + OuncesOver16 * PerOz
    End If
    TotDue = TotItemPrice + Tax + ShipCost
    lblTotPrice.Caption = Format(TotItemPrice, "Currency")
    lblSalesTax.Caption = Format(Tax, "Currency")
    lblShip.Caption = Format(ShipCost, "Currency")
    lblTotDue.Caption = Format(TotDue, "Currency")
    Exit Sub      ' end of regular processing

MathErr:
    MsgBox ("Error in calculations.  Check inputs.")
    Exit Sub
End Sub
```

continues

```
' Purpose: Clears all text boxes on the form (and disables '
the Find and Calculate buttons as a result).
Private Sub cmdClear_Click()
    ClearInputs          ' Also disables Find Item and Calculate buttons
'   ClearDescrPrice   Not needed. ClearInputs triggers this
'   ClearTotals       Not needed. ClearInputs triggers this
End Sub

' Purpose: Ends the program
Private Sub cmdExit_Click()
    Unload frmOrderPrice
End Sub

' Purpose: Searches for the item number.  If found, it
'          displays the item description and price, and
'          sets form variables for price and weight.
Private Sub cmdFindItem_Click()
    fItemOK = True
    Select Case txtItemNum.Text
        Case "173AJ-247"
            fItemPrice = 522.49
            fItemWght = 168
            fItemDescr = "'Farm Scene' Quilt"
        Case "182K-304A"
            fItemPrice = 299.99
            fItemWght = 15.99
            fItemDescr = "Platinum Cuff Links"
        Case "206B7-55H"
            fItemPrice = 105.75
            fItemWght = 16.1
            fItemDescr = "'Eagle in Flight' Wood Carving"
        Case "499GN-801"
            fItemPrice = 29.55
            fItemWght = 65.7
            fItemDescr = "Hand-crafted Bird Feeder"
        Case "499GN-801X"
            fItemPrice = 39.99
            fItemWght = 78
            fItemDescr = "Deluxe Hand-crafted Bird Feeder"
        Case "626T-71W"
            fItemPrice = 10#
            fItemWght = 4
            fItemDescr = "Hand-woven Straw Placemats"
        Case Else
            fItemOK = False
            fItemPrice = 0
            fItemWght = 0
            fItemDescr = ""
    End Select
    If fItemOK Then
        lblDescr.Caption = fItemDescr
        lblPrice.Caption = Format(fItemPrice, "Currency")
        Call txtQty.SetFocus
        If fStateOK And (txtQty.Text <> "") Then
            cmdCalculate.Enabled = True
        End If
    Else
        lblDescr.Caption = " ** NO SUCH ITEM ** "
        Call txtItemNum.SetFocus
    End If
End Sub
```

```
' Purpose:  Initializes form-scope variables and
'           disables the Find Item and Calculate buttons.
Private Sub Form_Load()
    cmdFindItem.Enabled = False
    cmdCalculate.Enabled = False
    fStateOK = False
    fItemOK = False
    txtState.MaxLength = 2
End Sub

' Purpose:  Decides whether the Find Item button should be
'           enabled, and clears the item description, price
'           and all totals.  Disables the Calculate button.
Private Sub txtItemNum_Change()
    If Left(txtItemNum.Text, 1) = "-" Then   ' dash invalid at start
        txtItemNum.Text = ""
    End If
    If txtItemNum.Text = "" Then
        cmdFindItem.Enabled = False
    Else
        cmdFindItem.Enabled = True
    End If
    Call ClearDescrPrice
    Call ClearTotals
    cmdCalculate.Enabled = False
End Sub

' Purpose:  Verifies that only A-Z, 0-9, and dash are entered.
'           Converts lowercase letters to uppercase.
Private Sub txtItemNum_KeyPress(KeyAscii As Integer)
    Dim KeyChar As String    ' Character form of key pressed

    KeyChar = Chr(KeyAscii)
    If (KeyChar < "0" Or KeyChar > "9") _
            And (KeyChar < "A" Or KeyChar > "Z") _
            And KeyChar <> "-" Then
        If KeyChar >= "a" And KeyChar <= "z" Then
            KeyAscii = Asc(UCase(KeyChar))
        ElseIf KeyAscii <> 8 Then       ' ASCII for backspace is 8
            KeyAscii = 0                ' Discard this key
        End If
    End If
End Sub

' Purpose:  Decides whether the Calculate button should
'           be enabled and clears the total boxes.
Private Sub txtQty_Change()
    If Left(txtQty.Text, 1) = "0" Then   ' No zero in first character
        txtQty.Text = ""
    End If
    If txtQty.Text = "" Then
        cmdCalculate.Enabled = False
    ElseIf fStateOK And fItemOK Then
        cmdCalculate.Enabled = True
    End If
    Call ClearTotals
End Sub
```

continues

```
' Purpose:  Verifies that only 0-9 are entered.
Private Sub txtQty_KeyPress(KeyAscii As Integer)
    If (KeyAscii < 48 Or KeyAscii > 57) And KeyAscii <> 8 Then
        ' ASCII for "0"-"9" is 48-57, backspace is 8
        KeyAscii = 0                    ' Discard this key
    End If
End Sub
' Purpose:  Checks for a valid state abbreviation, decides
'           whether the Calculate button should be enabled,
'           and clears the total boxes.
Private Sub txtState_Change()
    If Len(txtState.Text) <> 2 Then
        cmdCalculate.Enabled = False
        fStateOK = False
    Else
        fStateOK = True
        Select Case txtState.Text
            Case "IN", "MI", "KY", "TN"
                fSalesTaxFrac = 0.06
            Case "IL"
                fSalesTaxFrac = 0.0625
            Case "OH", "WI"
                fSalesTaxFrac = 0.05
            Case Else
                fSalesTaxFrac = 0
                fStateOK = False
        End Select
        If txtQty.Text <> "" And fStateOK And fItemOK Then
            cmdCalculate.Enabled = True
        End If
    End If
    Call ClearTotals
End Sub

' Purpose:  Verifies that only A-Z are entered.
'           Converts lowercase to uppercase.
Private Sub txtState_KeyPress(KeyAscii As Integer)
    Dim KeyChar As String     ' Character form of key pressed

    KeyChar = Chr(KeyAscii)
    If KeyChar < "A" Or KeyChar > "Z" Then
        If KeyChar >= "a" And KeyChar <= "z" Then
            KeyAscii = Asc(UCase(KeyChar))
        ElseIf KeyAscii <> 8 Then       ' ASCII for backspace is 8
            KeyAscii = 0                 ' Discard this key
        End If
    End If
End Sub
```

Figure 6.32   *Visual Basic code for the* Order Calculation *program.*

If you tried to type 10.00 for the price of the straw placemats, you noticed that VB changed this to 10#. Because there are no digits to the right of the decimal, VB doesn't keep them, but it uses the "#" to signal that this literal constant is a decimal value, not an integer. The *Case* structure of the *Find Item Click* event can easily be extended to handle more items. One disadvantage of using the *Case* structure is that each time the price of one item changes, the code in this event must be updated. As you continue on with future chapters that cover loops, arrays, and sequential files, you will be able to see that there are better ways to handle a large number of items and frequent price changes.

Step 5: Test and Debug the Program

After the program is entirely coded, we can perform a complete system test using our test plan developed earlier. A few of the output screens have been captured and displayed in Figure 6.33.

Test Case	User Input and/or Action	Screen Output
2–4 Find middle item	Enter 5 in Quantity, IN in State, 499GN–801 in Item #. Click *Find Item*.	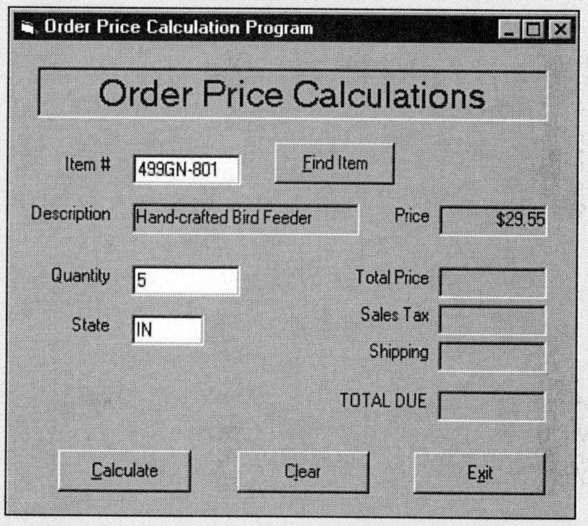
5 Calculate with all inputs, IN, over 16 oz.	Click *Calculate*.	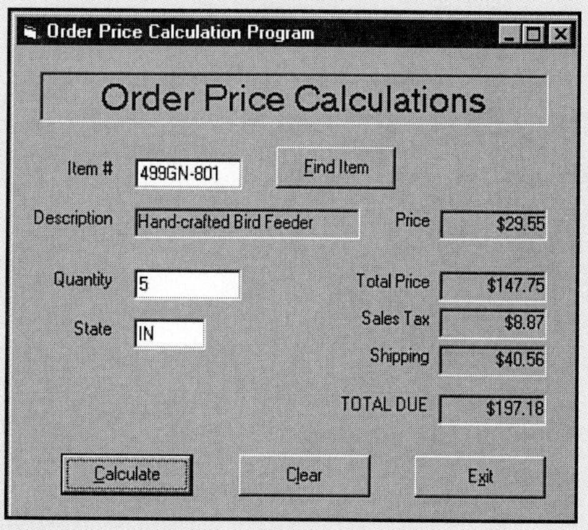

continues

Test Case	User Input and/or Action	Screen Output
8 Recalculate with new quantity	Type 1 in Quantity. Click *Calculate*.	
11 *Calculate* button for "WI"	Type WI in State. Click *Calculate*.	
12 *Clear* button	Click *Clear*.	

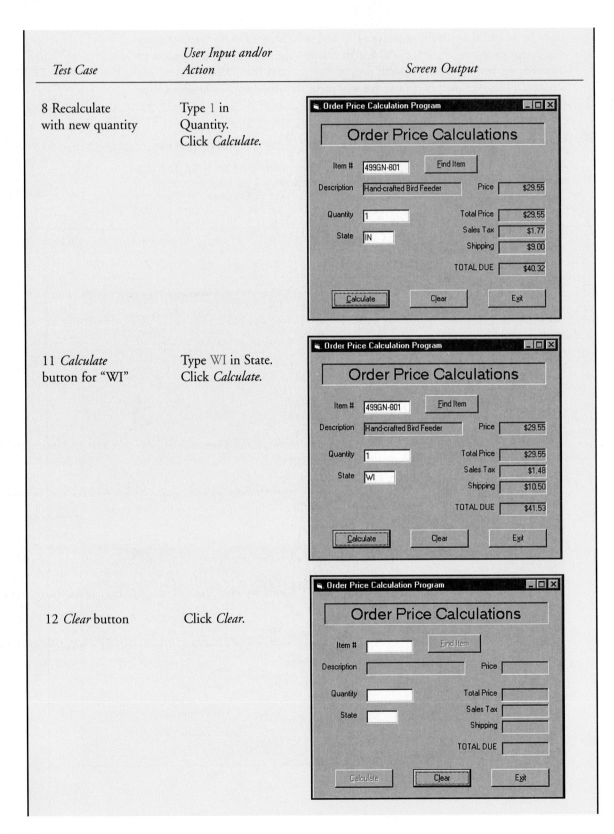

Test Case	User Input and/or Action	Screen Output
14, 18 Find with bad item #	Type abc3–4jkl into Item #. Click *Find Item*.	
19, 20 Find last item #, price ends in zeroes	Type 626t–71w in Item #. Type 4 in Qty, IL in State. Click *Find Item*.	

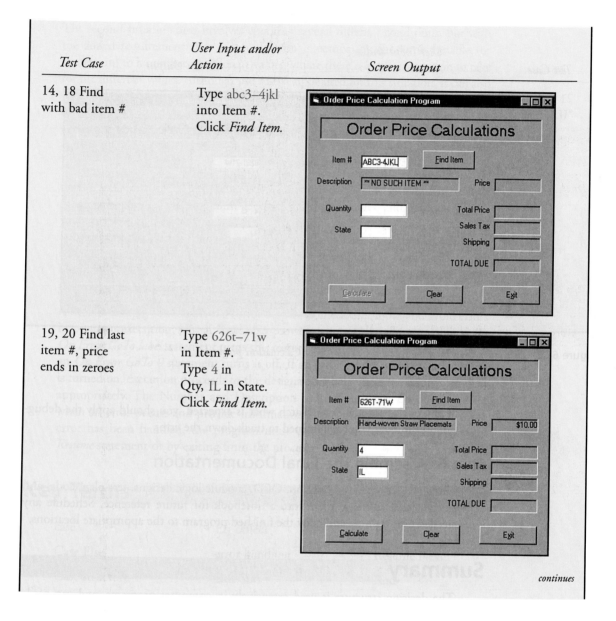

continues

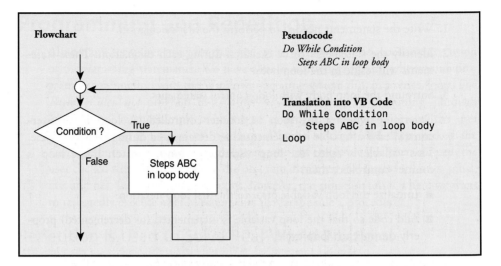

Figure 7.2 *Flowchart, pseudocode, and VB code for pre-test loop structure.*

In Visual Basic, the **Do While/Until Loop** statement is used to write code for a pre-test loop, and its syntax is shown here with optional items enclosed in brackets:

```
Do [{While|Until} condition]
    [body-statements]
    [Exit Do]
    [body-statements]
Loop
after-statement
```

Figure 7.3 gives detailed information about each part of the *Do...Loop* statement.

Part	Description
While|Until	Optional—If *While* is present, repetition continues as long as *condition* is true. If *Until* is present, repetition continues as long as *condition* is false. If neither *While* nor *Until* is present, the loop is infinite unless an *Exit Do* statement is executed.
[body-statements]	Optional—These statements make up the loop body.
Exit Do	Optional—Used as alternative method to exit the loop. May be placed anywhere in the loop body and is usually used in conjunction with a conditional statement to transfer control to the first statement following the loop.
after-statement	After the loop is exited, execution continues with this after-statement.

Figure 7.3 *Description of* Do...Loop *statement parts.*

condition is any variable, comparison, or complex condition that results in a true or false value. When the *Do While...Loop* executes, *body-statements* are repeated as long as *condition* is true. When *condition* is false, execution continues with *after-statement*. If *condition* is not true to begin with, *body-statements* are never executed, not even once.

Similarly, when the *Do Until...Loop* executes, the loop body is repeatedly executed as long as *condition* is false. When *condition* is true, execution continues with *after-statement*. If *condition* is not false to begin with, *body-statements* are never executed, not even once.

It is important to understand that when the loop body is entered, the entire group of statements in the loop is executed before *condition* is tested again. This means that even if a statement in the loop body does something to change *condition*, the following statements in the loop body will still be executed. The only exception to this statement is when *Exit Do* is used to prematurely exit the loop.

SumSquares Program with Pre-Test Loop

Suppose we want a computer program that will add up the squares of all the even or odd integers between two numbers. Figure 7.4 shows the program interface, and Figure 7.5 shows the logic for the calculation.

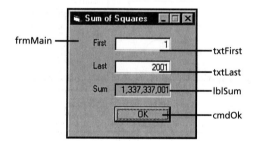

Figure 7.4 *Program* SumSquares.

Set up a simple form for this problem with a button named *cmdOK*, input text boxes *txtFirst* and *txtLast*, and output label *lblSum*. If you convert the flowchart to Visual Basic code, your *cmdOK_Click* event procedure will look like one of the two listings in Figure 7.6, depending on whether you use the *Do While* or *Do Until* version of the *Do...Loop*. This example also illustrates that to switch a *Do While* into an equivalent *Do Until*, you need to use the opposite condition (Num<=Last becomes Num>Last). Both programs are equivalent, and there is no particular advantage of one loop over the other. You should look closely at both listings and make sure you understand the differences between the two programs.

Figure 7.1 listed six steps that should be followed during the loop design process. If we compare this figure with our flowchart in Figure 7.5 and either set of programming code in Figure 7.6, we notice immediately that the loop body consists of the statements

```
Sum = Sum + Num * Num
Num = Num + 2
```

351

```
' Return the first prime number >= Start
Private Function GetPrimeNum(ByVal Start As Long) As Long
    Dim Cntr As Long
    Dim FoundPrime As Boolean
    Dim LastTrial As Long
    Dim Num As Long

    Num = Start
    ' The outer loop generates odd numbers until a prime is found
    Do
        ' Determine if Num is Prime
        LastTrial = Sqr(Num)
        Cntr = 3
        ' The inner loop checks to see if Num is prime
        Do Until Cntr > LastTrial Or Num Mod Cntr = 0
            Cntr = Cntr + 2
        Loop
        If Cntr <= LastTrial Then
            FoundPrime = False
        Else
            FoundPrime = True
        End If
        Num = Num + 2
    Loop Until FoundPrime
    GetPrimeNum = Num - 2
End Function
```

Figure 7.21   *Function* GetPrimeNum *with nested loops.*

Loan Payment Calculator Case Study

In this chapter, we discussed how to use several different types of repetitive logic in our programs. In the last part of this chapter, we will apply our knowledge of repetitive logic and use our program development process to develop a loan payment calculator.

You have been retained as a consultant by a finance company. The marketing manager of this company asks you to develop a program that can be used to calculate the monthly payment that will pay off a loan. In addition, the manager wants the program to be able to calculate and display a table of payments.

The manager envisions a program that will be simple enough for a prospective customer to run. The customer would enter the amount of the loan, the annual percentage interest rate, the term of the loan in years, and then press the Enter key or click the *Payment* button. At this point, the monthly payment displays. The customer may want to change one or more of the loan parameters and again calculate the monthly payment. Some customers may want to know the details of the repayment schedule, and they would click the *Amortize* button. The manager wants the repayment schedule to display the principal and interest payments for each monthly payment.

Step 1: Analyze the Problem

To find the monthly payment, we will use the standard formula:

$$pmt = \frac{loanamt * intmo}{1 - (1 + intmo)^{-npmts}}$$

where *pmt* is the monthly payment (constant except for possibly the last payment), *loanamt* is the amount of the loan, *intmo* is the monthly interest rate (annual interest rate percentage divided by 12), and *npmts* is the number of payments. Because the monthly payment is made in dollars and cents, the program will have to round *pmt* to the nearest cent before it is used in any additional calculations. We anticipate that the user will enter the loan amount, annual percentage interest rate, and the number of years during which the loan will be repaid. After entering this amount, the user would probably click a button to signal that the monthly payment should be calculated.

After the monthly payment has been computed, the user may want to have a payment or amortization schedule displayed and would signal this by clicking a button. To calculate and display the amortization schedule, the program will have to repetitively perform the following calculations:

- *intpmt* = *bal* * *intmo* where *intpmt* is the monthly interest payment and *bal* is the balance remaining. Because the interest payment is made in dollars and cents, we will have to round *intpmt* to the nearest cent before it is used in any additional calculations.

- *prinpmt* = *pmt* – *intpmt* where *prinpmt* is the principal payment. Note that this calculation is not used for the last payment.

- *prinpmt* = *bal* for the last payment.

- *totalpmt* = *intpmt* + *prinpmt* is valid for all payments.

Finally, the user needs to be able to exit or stop the program. We can now construct a table of our input, processing, and output needs (Analysis Table) as shown in Figure 7.22.

Input Needs	Processing Needs	Output Needs
Loan amount	Validate the three inputs	Payment number
Annual interest rate (%)	Calculate payment	Monthly payment
Term (years)	For each month calculate:	Interest payment
	Interest payment	Principal payment
	Principal payment	Balance
	For last month calculate:	Error message if
	Principal payment	nonnumeric input
	Final payment	Error message if input
		is zero or negative
		Error message if loan
		term contains a
		decimal point

Figure 7.22   *Analysis Table for* Loan Payment Calculator.

Step 2: Design or Create the User Interface

Using the three basic controls to handle input (text box), processing (command button), and output (label and text box) needs, we can revise our Analysis Table to identify how many and what types of controls our program needs (see Figure 7.23).

Input Needs	Processing Needs	Output Needs
Text boxes and descriptive labels for:	■ Payment command button to:	■ Label to show payment
■ Loan amount	Validate three inputs	■ Text box for repayment schedule displaying:
■ Annual interest rate (%)	Calculate payment	Payment number
■ Term (years)	■ Amortize command button to:	Monthly payment
	Calculate for each month:	Interest payment
	Interest payment	Principal payment
	Principal payment	Balance
	Calculate for last month:	Will use system message
	Principal payment	boxes for error messages
	Final payment	
	■ Exit command button to terminate processing	

Figure 7.23   *Controls required for* Loan Payment Calculator.

To complete the user interface design, we need to place the necessary controls in an organized and logical fashion on the form. In addition, we must specify the format in which the repayment schedule should be displayed in the output text box. After some preliminary sketching, we come up with the desired user interface design as shown in Figure 7.24.

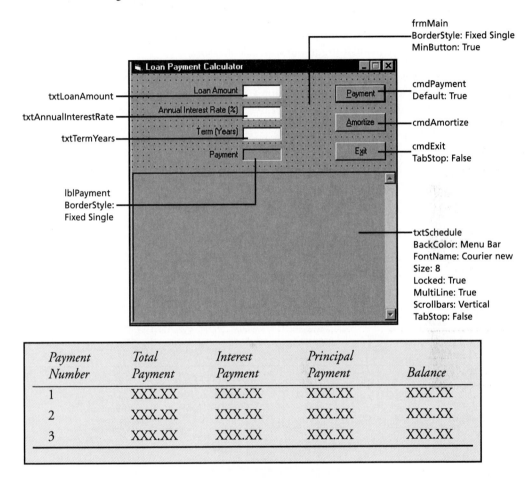

Payment Number	Total Payment	Interest Payment	Principal Payment	Balance
1	XXX.XX	XXX.XX	XXX.XX	XXX.XX
2	XXX.XX	XXX.XX	XXX.XX	XXX.XX
3	XXX.XX	XXX.XX	XXX.XX	XXX.XX

Figure 7.24 Loan Payment Calculator *user interface design.*

Step 3: Design the Logic for the Problem

Now that the user interface has been designed, we can plan how the program should respond to various user actions and program-generated events. In particular, we want to make this program easy to use and "user-proof." As an example, if the user enters unreasonable information such as nonnumeric data or numbers that are not positive, we want the program to inform the user which value is invalid and set the focus on the incorrect entry. Similarly, if the calculator is displaying the results of a calculation and the user changes any of the input data, we want the program to immediately clear the output controls to prevent the display of incorrect information.

369

Step 3a: Design the Macro-View (Object-Event Diagrams)

Because our program consists of only one form, our macro logic will consist of two OEDs: the overall project, Figure 7.25; and the main form, Figure 7.26. The code module is the same *basTools* module we put together and used in the *Payroll Calculator* program in Chapter 4. The module contains global procedures *LeftAlign* and *RightAlign* and currency-rounding function *RoundCur2*. We will be using *RightAlign* to right adjust the header and detail lines in the amortization table, and we will need *RoundCur2* in our loan calculations.

As you can see in Figure 7.26, our *Loan Payment* program will consist of seven event and seven general procedures. Note that there are three change event procedures—one each for the Amount, Rate, and Term text boxes.

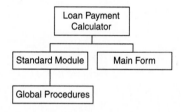

Figure 7.25 Loan Payment Calculator *Object-Event Diagram (overall view)*.

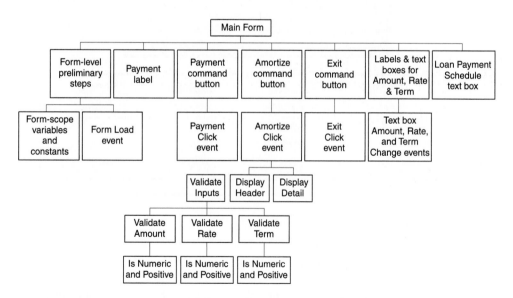

Figure 7.26 Loan Payment Calculator *Object-Event Diagram (main form)*.

Step 3b: Design the Micro-Level View (Flowcharts or Pseudocode)

Our plan is to consider each procedure as a distinct processing task. Because Amount, Rate, and Term all must be numeric and positive, we decide to write a validation routine that will be called three times. In addition to this validation test, Term must also evaluate to an integer, and we will test for this property in the

Validate Term module. Figure 7.27 shows the flowcharts and pseudocode for each of the seven event and seven general procedures. Our order of presentation will follow their left-to-right, top-to-down order of appearance in the Object-Event Diagram.

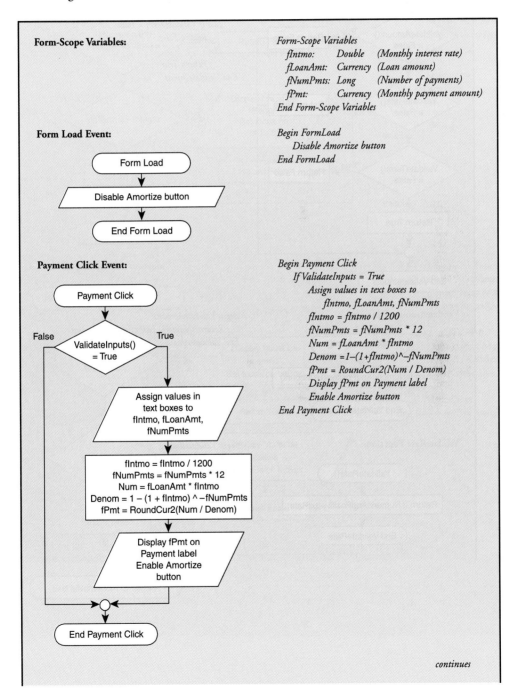

Form-Scope Variables:

Form-Scope Variables
    fIntmo: *Double*   *(Monthly interest rate)*
    fLoanAmt: *Currency* *(Loan amount)*
    fNumPmts: *Long*   *(Number of payments)*
    fPmt: *Currency* *(Monthly payment amount)*
End Form-Scope Variables

Form Load Event:

Begin FormLoad
    Disable Amortize button
End FormLoad

Form Load

Disable Amortize button

End Form Load

Payment Click Event:

Begin Payment Click
    If ValidateInputs = True
       Assign values in text boxes to
          fIntmo, fLoanAmt, fNumPmts
       fIntmo = fIntmo / 1200
       *fNumPmts = fNumPmts * 12*
       *Num = fLoanAmt * fIntmo*
       Denom = 1–(1+fIntmo)^–fNumPmts
       fPmt = RoundCur2(Num / Denom)
       Display fPmt on Payment label
       Enable Amortize button
End Payment Click

Payment Click

False   ValidateInputs()
= True   True

Assign values in
text boxes to
fIntmo, fLoanAmt,
fNumPmts

fIntmo = fIntmo / 1200
fNumPmts = fNumPmts * 12
Num = fLoanAmt * fIntmo
Denom = 1 – (1 + fIntmo) ^ –fNumPmts
fPmt = RoundCur2(Num / Denom)

Display fPmt on
Payment label
Enable Amortize
button

End Payment Click

continues

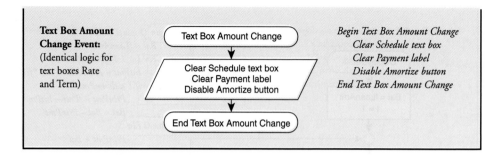

Figure 7.27   Loan Payment Calculator *micro-level logic design.*

Step 3c: Develop a Test Plan (Table of Input with Expected Results)

Our written test plan for this program must check that all computations give correct results. Because our programs can now include decisions and provide data validation, we must be sure to include test cases for missing, nonnumeric and negative values for the amount, interest rate, and term of the loan. We must also verify that the three buttons work correctly when clicked in different sequences. It is very important that we make sure that every line of code we have written is executed at least once.

TIP

During testing, execute every line of your program at least once.

Figure 7.28 contains a list of test cases that we want to use to test our program. You should expand this list with several sets of your own test data

Case	User Input and Actions	Expected Results
1	Run the program.	The three input text boxes are blank and the focus is on Loan Amount. The Payment label and payment schedule text box are blank. Only the *Amortize* button is disabled.
2	Click *Exit Program*.	The program stops running.
3	Run the program. Click the *X* in the right side of the title bar.	The program stops running.
4	Run the program. Click *Payment*.	A message box displays Loan amount must be numeric . Click *OK*, and the focus is put on the Amount text box.

Case	User Input and Actions	Expected Results
5	Enter 10000 and click *Payment*.	A message box displays Interest rate must be numeric. Click *OK*, and the focus is put on the Interest text box.
6	Enter 18.5 and click *Payment*.	A message box displays Term must be numeric. Click *OK*, and the focus is put on the Term text box.
7	Enter 1 and click *Payment*.	919.18 appears in the payment label, and the *Amortize* button is enabled.
8	Make the loan amount negative by entering −10000 in Amount. Click *Payment*.	As soon as the loan amount is changed, the Payment label is cleared, and the *Amortize* button is disabled. A message box displays Loan amount must be positive. Click *OK*, and the focus is put on the Amount text box.
9	Change the Amount back to 10000 and repeat Case 8 for Interest and Term.	The results are the same as Case 8. Make sure that the correct text box is named in the message box and that the focus is returned to the correct text box.
10	Enter 10000, 18.5, and 1.1 for Amount, Rate, and Term. Click *Payment*.	A message box displays Term must be an integer. Click *OK*, and the focus is put on the Term text box.
11	Enter 10000, 18.5, and 1 for Amount, Rate, and Term. Click *Payment*, and then click *Amortize*.	The *Amortize* button is disabled, and a loan payment schedule is displayed. Compare the program's output with the anticipated output given in Figure 7.29.

Figure 7.28   Loan Payment Calculator *test plan.*

Payment Number	Total Payment	Interest Payment	Principal Payment	Balance
1	919.18	154.17	765.01	9234.99
2	919.18	142.37	776.81	8458.18
3	919.18	130.40	788.78	7669.40
4	919.18	118.24	800.94	6868.46
5	919.18	105.89	813.29	6055.17
6	919.18	93.35	825.83	5229.34
7	919.18	80.62	838.56	4390.78
8	919.18	67.69	851.49	3539.29
9	919.18	54.56	864.62	2674.67
10	919.18	41.23	877.95	1796.72
11	919.18	27.70	891.48	905.24
12	919.20	13.96	905.24	0.00

Figure 7.29   *Anticipated loan payment schedule for Test Case 11.*

Step 4: Code the Program

Your coding effort will be more interesting and you can demonstrate progress to your manager by implementing this program in several steps. After each step, you should test the program to make sure that it is working properly before proceeding with the next step. One possible set of implementation steps is as follows:

- Code the data validation functions and test them by calling *ValidateInputs* from the *cmdPayment_Click* event procedure.

- Add the code to *cmdPayment_Click* to calculate and display the monthly payment.

- Code the header format and display statements and test them by calling *DisplayHeader* from *cmdAmortize_Click*.

- Code the statements that calculate and display the schedule of payments and test them by calling *DisplayDetail* from *cmdAmortize_Click*.

- Add and test the change event procedures for Amount, Rate, and Term.

Several properties for the Payment Schedule test box must be set correctly; otherwise, the payment schedule will either not work properly or the columns will not be neatly aligned. Make sure you select a fixed-size font such as *Courier New*. The MultiLine property must be set to *true* or the *vbNewLine* string will not be interpreted properly by the text box. To have a vertical scrollbar appear on the text box when it can't display all of its lines of text, you must set its ScrollBars property to Vertical. The MultiLine and ScrollBars properties must be set at Design Time.

Now you can proceed with the implementation of your program in Visual Basic. Try to write the code for this program by using the logic in Figure 7.27 and the Visual Basic Help files. If you get stuck, you can always refer to the complete code listing in Figure 7.30.

```
' Program:    Chapter 7: Loan Payment Calculator
' Form:       frmMain (Program starts with this form)
' Programmer: Ima Goodstudent
' Date:       June 24, 1998
' Purpose:    Compute and displays a table of loan payments.
'             The user enters the loan amount, annual percentage
'             interest rate, and the term of the loan in years. When
'             the Payment button is clicked the input items are
'             validated and the monthly payment is calculated and
'             displayed. When the Amortize button is clicked, a table
'             of payments is calculated and displayed. For each
'             monthly payment, the total payment, interest payment,
'             principal payment, and loan balance are displayed.

Option Explicit

' Detail column width constants
Private Const cfPmtNumWidth As Long = 7
Private Const cfTotPmtWidth As Long = 11
Private Const cfIntPmtWidth As Long = 11
Private Const cfPrnPmtWidth As Long = 11
Private Const cfBalWidth    As Long = 11

Private fIntmo As Double        ' Monthly interest rate
Private fLoanAmt As Currency    ' Loan amount
Private fNumPmts As Long        ' Number of payments
Private fPmt As Currency        ' Monthly payment amount (except last
                                ' payment)

' Purpose: When the Amortize button is clicked, calculate and display
'          the table of payments. For each monthly payment, the total
'          payment, interest payment, principal payment, and loan
'          balance are displayed. The Amortize button is disabled.
Private Sub cmdAmortize_Click()
    Call DisplayHeader
    Call DisplayDetail
    cmdAmortize.Enabled = False
End Sub

' Purpose: Terminate the program when the Exit button is clicked.
Private Sub cmdExit_Click()
    Unload frmMain
End Sub

' Purpose: When the Payment button is clicked, the input items are
'          validated and the monthly payment is calculated and
'          displayed.
Private Sub cmdPayment_Click()
    Dim Num As Double
    Dim Denom As Double
```

continues

```vb
        If ValidateInputs Then
            ' Get the input values.
            ' Divide by 100 to convert interest rate from a percentage.

        ' Divide by 12 to convert interest rate from annual to monthly
            fIntmo = CDbl(txtAnnualInterestRate.Text) / 1200
            fLoanAmt = CCur(txtLoanAmount.Text)
            fNumPmts = CLng(txtTermYears.Text) * 12   ' 12 months in a year

            ' Calculate and display the monthly payment
            Num = fLoanAmt * fIntmo
            Denom = 1 - (1 + fIntmo) ^ -fNumPmts
            fPmt = RoundCur2(CCur(Num / Denom))
            lblPayment.Caption = Format(fPmt, "0.00")
            cmdAmortize.Enabled = True
        End If
End Sub

' Purpose: Create a formatted string containing payment number, total
'          payment, principal payment, and balance. Concatenate the
'          string to the end of the txtSchedule text property.
Private Sub DisplayDetail()
    Dim I As Long
    Dim Bal As Currency
    Dim IntPmt As Currency
    Dim PrinPmt As Currency
    Dim TotPmt As Currency

    ' Calculate and display detail
    Bal = fLoanAmt
    For I = 1 To fNumPmts
        IntPmt = RoundCur2(Bal * fIntmo)
        If I < fNumPmts Then
            PrinPmt = fPmt - IntPmt
            Bal = Bal - PrinPmt
        Else
            ' Different calculations for last payment
            PrinPmt = Bal
            Bal = 0
        End If
        TotPmt = IntPmt + PrinPmt

        ' Build the formatted detail line and add to the text box.
        txtSchedule.Text = txtSchedule.Text & vbNewLine & _
            RightAlign(Format(I, "0"), cfPmtNumWidth) & _
            RightAlign(Format(TotPmt, "0.00"), cfTotPmtWidth) & _
            RightAlign(Format(IntPmt, "0.00"), cfIntPmtWidth) & _
            RightAlign(Format(PrinPmt, "0.00"), cfPrnPmtWidth) & _
            RightAlign(Format(Bal, "0.00"), cfTotPmtWidth)
    Next I
End Sub

' Purpose: Create a formatted string containing two lines of header for
'          the loan payment display. Assign the string to the text
'          property of the txtSchedule text box.
Private Sub DisplayHeader()
    txtSchedule.Text = RightAlign("payment", cfPmtNumWidth) & _
        RightAlign("total", cfTotPmtWidth) & _
        RightAlign("interest", cfIntPmtWidth) & _
        RightAlign("principal", cfPrnPmtWidth) & _
        RightAlign("balance", cfBalWidth) & vbNewLine & _
        RightAlign("number", cfPmtNumWidth) & _
```

```
            RightAlign("payment", cfTotPmtWidth) & _
            RightAlign("payment", cfIntPmtWidth) & _
            RightAlign("payment", cfPrnPmtWidth)
    End Sub


    ' Purpose: Disable the Amortize button when the form is loaded
    Private Sub Form_Load()
        cmdAmortize.Enabled = False
    End Sub


    ' Purpose: Validate the entry in the text box parameter. Return true
    '          if the entry is numeric and positive, otherwise place the
    '          focus on the text box, display an error message and return
    '          false. The second parameter is used to construct the error
    '          message.
    Private Function IsNumericAndPositive(ByVal txtBox As TextBox, _
        ByVal Item As String) As Boolean

        If Not IsNumeric(txtBox.Text) Then
            Call MsgBox(Item & " must be numeric", vbExclamation)
            txtBox.SetFocus
            IsNumericAndPositive = False
        ElseIf CDbl(txtBox.Text) <= 0 Then
            Call MsgBox(Item & " must be positive", vbExclamation)
            txtBox.SetFocus
            IsNumericAndPositive = False
        Else
            IsNumericAndPositive = True
        End If
    End Function


    ' Purpose: Clear the contents of the payment label and the payment
    '          schedule text box when the annual interest rate entry is
    '          changed.
    Private Sub txtAnnualInterestRate_Change()
        txtSchedule.Text = ""
        lblPayment.Caption = ""
        cmdAmortize.Enabled = False
    End Sub


    ' Purpose: Clear the contents of the payment label and the payment
    '          schedule text box when the loan amount entry is changed.
    Private Sub txtLoanAmount_Change()
        txtSchedule.Text = ""
        lblPayment.Caption = ""
        cmdAmortize.Enabled = False
    End Sub


    ' Purpose: Clear the contents of the payment label and the payment
    '          schedule text box when the term entry is changed.
    Private Sub txtTermYears_Change()
        txtSchedule.Text = ""
        lblPayment.Caption = ""
        cmdAmortize.Enabled = False
    End Sub


    ' Purpose: Validate the entry in the loan amount text box.
    '          The item is valid if it is numeric and positive.
    Private Function ValidateAmount() As Boolean
        ValidateAmount = IsNumericAndPositive(txtLoanAmount, "Loan amount")
    End Function
```

continues

381

```vb
' Purpose: Validate the information entered for loan amount, annual
'          interest rate, and term. Returns true if all entries are
'          valid, otherwise returns false. If an entry is invalid, an
'          error message is displayed and the focus is placed on the
'          text box containing the invalid data.
Private Function ValidateInputs() As Boolean
    If Not ValidateAmount Then
        ValidateInputs = False
    ElseIf Not ValidateRate Then
        ValidateInputs = False
    ElseIf Not ValidateTerm Then
        ValidateInputs = False
    Else
        ValidateInputs = True
    End If
End Function

' Purpose: Validate the entry in the interest rate text box.
'          The item is valid if it is numeric and positive.
Private Function ValidateRate() As Boolean
    ValidateRate = _
        IsNumericAndPositive(txtAnnualInterestRate, "Interest rate")
End Function

' Purpose: Validate the entry in the term text box.
'          The item is valid if it is numeric, positive and integral.
Private Function ValidateTerm() As Boolean
    If Not IsNumericAndPositive(txtTermYears, "Term") Then
        ValidateTerm = False
    ElseIf CDbl(txtTermYears.Text) <> Int(txtTermYears.Text) Then
        Call MsgBox("Term must be an integer", vbExclamation)
        txtTermYears.SetFocus
        ValidateTerm = False
    Else
        ValidateTerm = True
    End If
End Function
```

```vb
' Module:    basTools
' Purpose:   Contains public procedures: LeftAlign
'                                        RightAlign
'                                        RoundCur2

Option Explicit

' Purpose:   Left aligns a string
' Inputs:    Source: String to be left-aligned
'            Length: Length of returned string
' Returns:   Returns a string of length Length, with Source
'            left-aligned and padded with spaces on the right
Public Function LeftAlign(ByVal Source As String, _
        ByVal Length As Integer) As String
    Dim Result As String

    Result = Space(Length)
    LSet Result = Source
    LeftAlign = Result
End Function
```

```
' Purpose:    Right aligns a string
' Inputs:     Source: String to be Right-aligned
'             Length: Length of returned string
' Returns:    Returns a string of length Length, with Source
'             right-aligned and padded with spaces on the left
Public Function RightAlign(ByVal Source As String, _
        ByVal Length As Integer) As String
    Dim Result As String

    Result = Space(Length)
    RSet Result = Source
    RightAlign = Result
End Function

' Purpose:    Rounds Currency to 2 decimal places
' Inputs:     Money: Currency value to be rounded
' Returns:    Currency rounded to 2 decimal places
Public Function RoundCur2(ByVal Money As Currency) As Currency
    Dim Cents As Currency

    Cents = Int(Money * 100 + 0.5)
    RoundCur2 = Cents / 100
End Function
```

Figure 7.30   *Code for* Loan Payment Calculator.

Step 5: Test and Debug the Program

Unit Coding and Testing

In Chapter 5, "Decisions and Data Validation," we discussed performing *unit coding and testing* followed by *integration testing*. Unit coding and testing is accomplished by coding and testing the program in sections. Integration testing occurs when the tested units are combined, in one or more steps, and tested after each successive combination.

In the preceding section of this chapter, "Step 4: Code the Program," we listed one possible sequence of integration testing. Your testing and debugging will be greatly simplified if you assemble and test the program in successive steps as opposed to the alternative method of coding and testing the program as a whole. In addition, integrating the development and testing phases has the advantage of your being able to present your manager or client with visible evidence that you are indeed making progress toward producing a high-quality useful product. Finally, most programmers have less stress and more fun while working on a project that alternates coding, testing, and integration.

Final System Test

At this stage, the program has been written, and we can perform the final system test by running the program and using the test data we developed in Step 3c. When we developed our test plan, we made sure that the test data would check every part of the program. Figure 7.31 contains several screen captures from the test cases.

Case	User Input and Actions	Results
1	Run the program.	
4	Run the program. Click *Payment*.	
7	Enter 1 and click *Payment*.	
8a	Make the loan amount negative by entering −10000 in Amount.	As soon as the loan amount is changed, the Payment label is cleared and the *Amortize* button is disabled.

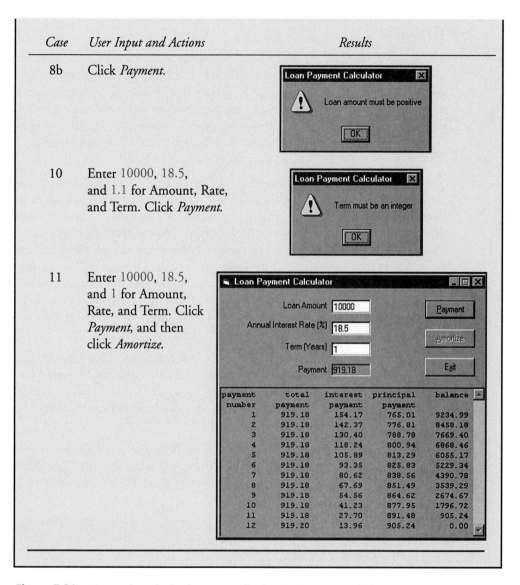

Case	User Input and Actions	Results
8b	Click *Payment*.	
10	Enter 10000, 18.5, and 1.1 for Amount, Rate, and Term. Click *Payment*.	
11	Enter 10000, 18.5, and 1 for Amount, Rate, and Term. Click *Payment*, and then click *Amortize*.	

Figure 7.31   *Output from the final system test for the* Loan Payment Calculator.

Step 6: Assemble the Final Documentation

Now that the program has been tested and produces the expected results, you should gather all the documentation that describes the program and the problem it solves. This includes all the following deliverables (documents): IPO Analysis Table, Object-Event Diagram(s), flowcharts/pseudocode, test plan, form image, form text, code, and output snapshots. Organize all these materials logically into a single folder or binder.

Summary

The repetitive structure provides a way for programmers to write a group of statements once and have them executed many times in succession. Every loop has some sort of loop control condition, and a loop body that consists of the statements to be repeated. We have learned how to use flowcharting and pseudocode to write three types of loops: pre-test, post-test, and the counting loop. For each type of loop, we found out how to convert our flowchart or pseudocode logic into Visual Basic code.

The *Do While/Until...Loop* statement is used by Visual Basic to implement a pretest loop and the *Do...Loop While/Until* is used to implement a post-test loop. Both loops repeat a group of statements as long as the loop condition is true or false, depending on whether the loop condition is type *While* or *Until*. In Visual Basic, the counting loop is implemented by the *For...Next* statement, which repeats the statements in the loop body a specified number of times. This type of loop is a specialized form of the pre-test loop and contains a counting variable that is initialized to a starting value by the *For...Next* statement. After each repetition of the loop body, the counter variable is automatically incremented, and the loop is exited when the counting variable exceeds the specified ending value.

A programmer can state the logic of very complex problems by using selection structures and repetitive structures combined in various sequences, or nested one inside another. As an example of nested structures, the *DisplayDetail* procedure used in the *Loan Payment Calculator* contains an *If Else* decision structure inside the body of a counting loop.

Testing and debugging of programs is simplified if programs are assembled and tested in successive steps. Integrating the development and testing phases produces visible evidence of progress toward the development of a reliable useful product.

Key Terms

counter-controlled loop	For...Next	nested loops
Do...Loop While/Until	infinite loop	post-test loops
Do While/Until Loop	iteration	pre-test loops
early exit	loop body	repetition
Exit Do	loop counter	sentinel
Exit For	loop control condition	
flag	loop variable	

Test Your Understanding

1. What is a counting loop?

2. What is the difference between a pre-test and a post-test loop?

3. Does Visual Basic implement the counting loop as a pre- or post-test loop?

4. After deciding that your program needs a loop, how do you decide whether the loop should be a counting loop?

5. What is an infinite loop?

6. In Visual Basic, is it possible to write a loop that will never terminate?

7. In Visual Basic, is it possible to write a counting loop that subtracts 10 from the counting variable on each loop iteration?

8. What is meant by this expression: "This loop contains code for an early exit."?

9. Should you routinely write loops that contain early exits? Why or why not?

10. What is the meaning of the expression "nested loops"?

11. Is it possible to nest a pre-test loop inside a post-test loop?

12. Consider the following Visual Basic code fragment:

```
For I = 1 To 5
    Call MsgBox("Hail Purdue")
Next I
```

- How many times is the message Hail Purdue displayed?

- What is the value of the loop counter *I* after the loop has been exited?

Programming Exercises

1. Analyze and test the early exit version of program *TrimRight* and verify that the program works correctly for the following three special cases:

   - No text is entered before clicking the *Trim* button.

   - The text that is entered consists entirely of spaces, asterisks, and dashes.

   - The entered text does not have any trailing spaces, asterisks, and dashes.

2. Analyze and test the normal exit version of program *TrimRight* and verify that the program works correctly for the same three special cases listed in programming exercise 1.

3. Using the listings in Figures 7.20 and 7.21, simplify function *GetPrimeNum* by moving the inner loop to a function *IsPrime(Num)*, which returns *true* if *Num* is prime. Use the following code for *GetPrimeNum*:

```
' Return the first prime number >= Start
Private Function GetPrimeNum(ByVal Start As Long) As Long
    Dim FoundPrime As Boolean
    Dim Num As Long

    Num = Start
    Do
        FoundPrime = IsPrime(Num)
        Num = Num + 2
    Loop Until FoundPrime
    GetPrimeNum = Num - 2
End Function
```

Is the modified program more or less complex than the original program? If you were given the assignment of modifying program *NextPrime*, which version of the program would you want to work on?

4. In the *Loan Payment Calculator* program, rounding function *RoundCur2* is called from two different places. It is used in event procedure *cmdPayment_Click* to round *fPmt* and in general procedure *DisplayDetail* to round *IntPmt*. Remove these two calls to *RoundCur2* and run the *Loan Payment Calculator* program with the same set of test data that was used previously. Are there any differences in the repayment schedules for the two versions of the programs? Which repayment schedule is correct, or are they both correct?

5. Check your answer to question 12 of "Test Your Understanding," by creating a Visual Basic program that keeps track of how many times Hail Purdue is displayed and displays the value of *I* after the loop has been exited. You may want to use the following code fragment in the event procedure *cmdStart_Click*:

```
' Display Hail Purdue
    Count = 0
    For I = 1 To 5
        Count = Count + 1
        lblCount.Caption = CStr(Count)
        Call MsgBox("Hail Purdue")
    Next I
lblI.Caption = CStr(I)
```

6. Your friend wants to work for your consulting company as a Visual Basic programmer. While looking at some of the code he has written at his previous job, you come across the following code fragment:

```
Qty = 5
TotalQty = 0
I = Qty
For I = 1 To I
    TotalQty = TotalQty + I
Next I
```

You ask your friend what this loop is supposed to do. He tells you that the loop body will execute exactly *Qty* times. You tell your friend that he is wrong and that the loop will probably be an infinite loop. Settle this argument by writing a simple program. If this is a representative example of your friend's code, should you hire him?

7. Draw the flowchart corresponding to the *TrimRight* program code displayed by Figure 7.17.

8. Write a Visual Basic function *Factorial(N)* that returns *N* factorial when passed the integer *N*. The factorial of the number *N* is $N! = 1 * 2 * 3 * \ldots * (N{-}1) * N$. As an example $1! = 1$, $2! = 2$, $3! = 6$, $4! = 24$, $5! = 120$. Because the factorials increase very rapidly, you should have *Factorial(N)* return a data type of Double.

9. The value of 1/e can be calculated from the series

    $$1/e = 1 - 1/1! + 1/2! - 1/3! + 1/4! - 1/5! + \ldots$$

    Write a Visual Basic program that calculates the value *e* by using a loop to sum this series. Your program should use the *Factorial* function you developed in exercise 8. You may terminate your series with the term that includes the evaluation of 18!. You should compare your result with the value provided by the Visual Basic *Exp* function.

Programming Projects

1. Design a temperature conversion calculator that will generate a table of temperatures with two columns, one for Fahrenheit and the other for Celsius, in one-degree increments. The user uses an option button to select the desired conversion and enters the temperature range into two text boxes. The table is displayed in a locked text box containing a vertical scrollbar, as shown here.

2. Develop a program that produces a straight-line depreciation table for a capital asset, as shown in the following figure. The user enters the purchase price and the term in years over which the asset is to be depreciated. The depreciation table should display the year, yearly depreciation (constant except for possibly the last year), end-of-year value, and the accumulated depreciation. All values should be rounded to the nearest dollar.

3. Create a program that reverses and displays the name that a user enters into a text box, as shown here. The reversed name is displayed in an output label. Your program should call the function *Reverse*, which you will have to write. *Reverse* is passed a string and returns a new string, which is the same as the original string, but with the characters of the string reversed.

4. When data is sent between different computers, it is useful to know whether the data has been transferred correctly. A very common method of checking for transmission errors is for the sending computer to calculate a checksum of the data that will be sent and then send the checksum along with the data. The receiving computer also calculates a checksum from the received data and compares this locally generated checksum with the checksum transmitted with the data. If the two checksums agree, the data has almost certainly been transferred without an error.

Develop a program with a multiline text box and a label to display the checksum of the text that has been entered in the text box. When the user clicks the *Checksum* button, the checksum is calculated and displayed. You should use modulo 2^{16} addition to calculate the checksum by summing the ASCII codes of all the characters in the text box. For example, if the characters "ABC" were entered into the text box, the checksum would be 198 (65 + 66 + 67). The program should have a *Clear* button to clear the text box and output label. The results should look like the following figure.

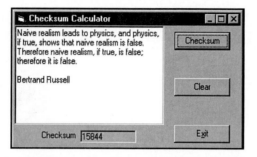

5. Produce a program that animates a bouncing ball (see the following figure). Use a Shape control configured as a red circle to simulate the ball. When the user clicks the *Start* button, the ball appears to bounce around the form and behind the two buttons. Use a loop to change the Top and Left properties of the Shape by 10 units during each iteration. You will have to test for the inside boundary of the form, as given by the form's ScaleHeight and ScaleWidth properties, and change directions when the position of the Shape is outside this boundary. Set the loop up for about 5,000 iterations. If you want your user to be able to stop the application, you should call the *DoEvents* function from inside the loop.

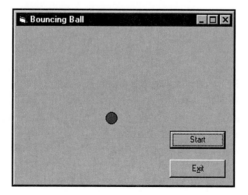

6. Write a multiplication table program that accepts a multiplication base number, as well as the low and high values for the range of multipliers. It then constructs a multiplication table for the base number from the low number to the high number. If the base number is 5, the low number is 3, and the high number is 15, for example, the multiplication table would display all multiples of 5 from 3 × 5 up to 15 × 5. Use a list box or text box with a vertical scrollbar to enable the user to see all possible products. Include a test to make sure the number is not zero or negative. A sample interface is shown here.

CHAPTER 8

ARRAYS, SEARCHING, AND SORTING

Introduction

In all our programs so far, we have named a separate variable every time we needed to remember a value in memory. But what if a program asks the user to enter multiple values of similar types, such as the scores for every student in a class? If one variable is used, each new score replaces the preceding score in the variable. This works for some programs, but other programs need to go back and use previous scores after other scores have been entered. A user would not like having to enter the same scores over and over again.

One solution could be to make a separate variable for each student's score. This is not very practical, because some courses might have several hundred students. It would be very tedious to declare hundreds of separate variable names, especially if we want to store the students' names, IDs, test scores, quiz scores, and lab scores. The program would also get very lengthy because it would have to have separate sections of code to work with each different variable. It wouldn't take long to notice that the code contains a lot of repetition. The only difference would be the different variable names being used. It would be nice to be able use a repetitive structure in situations like this.

Fortunately, programming languages provide a data structure to store multiple values of one type under one name so that the values can be processed using a loop. This data structure is called an array. These arrays can be easily searched for particular values, or sorted into a new order. If the data is more naturally arranged in a two-dimensional table format, we can declare a two-dimensional array.

When we understand array notation, we find that we can designate certain controls on a form to be part of a control array. Also, some controls in Visual Basic contain multiple lines, or strings, of information, and can be processed using the array notation and loops. Two other language elements, enumerations and user-defined types, can be useful when working with arrays.

Objectives

Upon completion of this chapter, you should be able to:

- Explain what an array is.

- Declare arrays.

- Reference a particular position of an array.

- Design and code an algorithm to sequentially search an array for a particular value.

- Design and code an algorithm to utilize a binary search of an array for a particular value.

- Decide whether a sequential or binary search is more appropriate for a given application.

- Design and code an algorithm to sort the elements of an array in ascending or descending order.

- Create and use control arrays in Visual Basic.

- Recognize and use properties of controls that are implemented like arrays.

- Define and use an enumeration and a user-defined type.

What Is an Array?

An **array** is a data structure in the computer's memory that has one name to reference multiple contiguous memory locations that all contain the same type of value. Each position of this structure is numbered, typically starting at zero or one. To use this structure, the program references the individual locations by using both the name of the array and the position number. This position number is usually called a **subscript** or *index*. If a program to work with student scores declares an array to hold 10 integers, starting with position one, for example, we could visualize the array in memory as shown in Figure 8.1. According to this figure, the test score of the third person is a 79. If the array's name is *StuScore*, the program's reference to the third person's score would be *StuScore(3)*.

1	98
2	67
3	79
4	82
5	90
6	81
7	76
8	60
9	99
10	84

Figure 8.1 *An array of test scores.*

Why Use Arrays?

Data in the real world includes large sets of similar data that all need to be processed in the same manner. An instructor has many students in a course, and every student's scores are processed the same way to determine grades. A bank has many customer accounts, and at the end of the month, the deposits and withdrawals for every account must be added and subtracted. The repetitive structure presented in the preceding chapter provides the control structure to code a process once and perform it multiple times. But how does a loop access *different* data values on each iteration of the loop when the variable names stay the same? The answer up to now has been that new values must be placed in the variables for each repetition, through calculation or keyboard input, replacing the previous values.

Suppose the program must use the same set of data more than once. The instructor may want to calculate grades, then sort the student scores by grade, and then print the grades in order by student ID. The bank may list all the transactions for an account in the order they were received, then separately list all the checks in check number order, and then list all the deposits. Obviously the user shouldn't have to type the values in more than once. Therefore the first time the values are entered, they must each be stored in a separate variable (or memory location). To use the repetitive structure, however, the variable names must be the same. This is precisely why arrays are needed. The multiple elements of the array allow all the different values to be retained in memory, and the fact that the array has *one* name allows the repetitive structure to be used. Adjusting the array index, using a numeric variable that is incremented each time through the loop, accesses the different values in the array.

Use arrays to store values that must be processed more than once by a
program.

In general, when you design an application that performs the same processing for
multiple sets of data values, you will write the process once using an array reference,
and surround these statements with a loop that adjusts the array index on each
iteration.

Declaring Arrays

Arrays are declared in Visual Basic in the same type of statements as variables. If the
array will be used only locally in a procedure, it is declared in a *Dim* statement. For
both variables and arrays, the declaration establishes a name and a data type. In
addition, the array declaration indicates how many memory locations are needed.
The general format of a local array declaration is this:

```
Dim arrayName(lowerBound To upperBound) As dataType
```

The *arrayName* is any valid name the programmer selects for the array. It must follow the same rules used in naming a variable. Within the parentheses are the starting and ending values for the array's subscripts, separated by the keyword *To*.
The subscript values are integers that must fall within the range of a Long type. The
value *lowerBound* is the index number to reference the first value in the array.
The value *upperBound* is the position number of the last position in the array. These
two numbers represent a range of values, starting with *lowerBound*, ending with
upperBound, and including all integer values in between. Recall that we also saw
this range notation used in the *Case* statement for a case that applies to a range of
values.

If the array will be used in multiple events, it can be declared to have form scope
by declaring it at the top of the file and substituting the word *Private* for the
word *Dim*.

Using the student test score example, we can declare an array named *StudentScore*
to hold 10 scores, starting with position one, with one of the following statements:

```
Dim StudentScore(1 to 10) as Long
```
or
```
Private fStudentScore(1 to 10) as Long
```

It is also possible to omit the lower bound from an array declaration, in which case
Visual Basic assumes a lower bound of zero (unless the *Option Base 1* statement is
included in the General Declarations section). In this book, we will always declare
both the lower and upper bound for the array subscript.

Declare both the lower and upper bound for array subscripts.

Using Arrays

Within the code of a Visual Basic program, specifying both the array name and the position number references a particular location of an array. The general notation is as follows:

```
arrayName(subscript)
```

If we need to reference the seventh student score in the *StudentScore* array (assuming the array starts with a subscript value of one), we could use *StudentScore(7)* in our code statements in the same manner that we would use a variable. It is more common, however, to use a numeric variable for the subscript. Typically this subscript variable will be initialized to one and incremented on each pass through a loop. Therefore, if the code refers to *StudentScore(StuCnt)* in a loop, it would cause the first student's score to be used when *StuCnt* is *1*, the second student's score to be used when *StuCnt* is *2*, and so on. It is also possible to use a numeric expression for the subscript. Hence, if *StuCnt* currently has the value *3*, *StudentScore(StuCnt – 1)* refers to the second position of the Student Score array, and *StudentScore(StuCnt + 1)* refers to the fourth position of the array.

The following block of statements illustrates the use of an array named *Nm* in several types of statements. See whether you can determine the resulting contents of the array and variables.

```
Dim Nm(3 To 6) As String
Dim Nbr As Long
Dim NewName As String

Nbr = 3
Nm(Nbr) = "Bob"                        ' statement A
Nm(Nbr + 1) = "Jim"                    ' statement B
Nbr = 5
If Nm(Nbr) <> "Bob" Then               ' statement C
    Nm(Nbr) = "Slim" & Nm(Nbr - 1)     ' statement D
Else
    Nm(Nbr) = "XXX"                    ' statement E
End If
NewName = Nm(4) & Nm(Nbr - 2)          ' statement F
lblTest.Caption = NewName
```

It is often helpful to try new statements in a short practice program. To quickly test the preceding code, put a label (*lblTest*) and a command button on a form, and enter the code under the button click event. Then put the array and the variables in a Watch window, set a breakpoint on the first executable statement, and run the program. After you click the button, you can single-step through the rest of the code to see whether you are right. You will see a plus sign (+) in the Watch window next to the array name. Click it to see the contents of each array position.

In the preceding code, the first statement declares an array with four locations in it, numbered from 3 to 6. Statement A assigns the name "Bob" to array position 3. Statement B assigns the name "Jim" to array position 4. Statement C tests whether the name "Bob" is in position 5 of the array. Statement D then takes the value in array position 4 ("Jim"), concatenates it with "Slim", and assigns the result to array position 5. Statement E is not executed, and Statement F takes the name in array position 4 ("Jim"), concatenates it with the name in position 3 ("Bob"), and assigns the result to variable *NewName*. The Watch window in Figure 8.2 shows the result of executing this code. The name "JimBob" should appear in the label on the form.

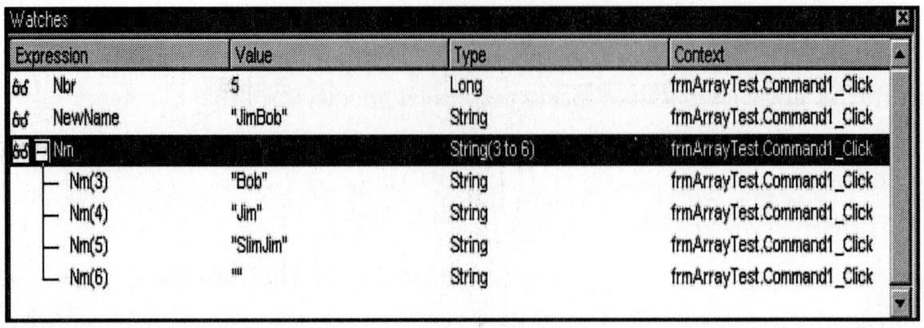

Watches			☒
Expression	Value	Type	Context
🔍 Nbr	5	Long	frmArrayTest.Command1_Click
🔍 NewName	"JimBob"	String	frmArrayTest.Command1_Click
🔍 ⊟ Nm		String(3 to 6)	frmArrayTest.Command1_Click
├ Nm(3)	"Bob"	String	frmArrayTest.Command1_Click
├ Nm(4)	"Jim"	String	frmArrayTest.Command1_Click
├ Nm(5)	"SlimJim"	String	frmArrayTest.Command1_Click
└ Nm(6)	""	String	frmArrayTest.Command1_Click

Figure 8.2 *Watch window results from single-stepping through the button click event.*

■ **TIP**
Practice your debugging skills regularly.

There is no need to save this program; it was just a quick test to help us understand array notation.

Parallel or Corresponding Arrays

Instead of only one array, you often need to store multiple pieces of information about each object or item in a computer application. In addition to each student's score, for example, the instructor may want to keep track of the student names and student IDs. Hence, instead of needing one array, the program actually needs several arrays to hold the corresponding values for each item. This is very easily accomplished by selecting an appropriate name for each array, declaring each array to have the same range of subscript values, and selecting the appropriate data type for each array. Figure 8.3 shows how we might visualize three arrays—for Student ID, Student Name, and Test Score—in memory.

	Student ID	Student Name	Test Score
1	11-22	Joe	98
2	13-08	Frank	67
3	13-22	Mary	79
4	15-66	Bill	82
5	16-44	Nancy	90
6	16-77	Jean	81
7	20-02	Pat	76
8	20-03	Ann	60
9	20-14	Tom	99
10	39-47	Don	84

Figure 8.3 *Three corresponding arrays for Student ID, Student Name, and Test Score.*

The declarations for our student arrays look like this:

```
Private fScoreArray(1 To 10) As Long
Private fNameArray(1 To 10)  As String
Private fIDArray(1 To 10)    As String
```

Even though the arrays are separate arrays in memory, the program should treat them as if they go together. When values are stored in the arrays, the student's ID, name, and score are stored in the same location number of the different arrays. Later, when the program finds the name "Bill" in position 4 of the *StudentName* array, the program "knows" that Bill's student ID is in position 4 of the *StudentID* array, and Bill's test score is in position 4 of the *TestScore* array.

Storing Values in an Array

Let's develop a program that creates and works with these arrays. The first thing the program needs is a way to enter the student IDs, names, and test scores. The form shown in Figure 8.4 provides three text boxes for this purpose. Clicking the Insert Student button will store the information into the arrays and clear the text boxes. A label for error messages is also included. For now, we will assume that the teacher enters the students in the desired order. Hence, we will place the first student in position 1 of the arrays, the second student in position 2, and so on.

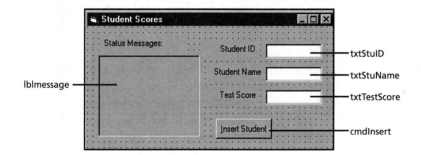

Figure 8.4   *Initial form for array example.*

The program also needs to count how many students are entered, to know whether the arrays are full, and for use in later processing. We previously discussed counters when learning about loops, so we know that every counter should be initialized somewhere in the program. In this case, the counter needs to start at zero. Because the *Insert Student* button will be clicked once for each student, we don't want to set the counter to zero in that event; otherwise, it would be reset every time the button is clicked. We need an event that is only executed once when the program starts. One such event is the *Form Load* event that we have used in previous chapters.

The main code for the *Insert Student Click* event must increment the counter, and place the data from the three text boxes into the three arrays at the location indicated by the counter. Try to write your own code for this part of the program, and then compare your code to that of Figure 8.5.

When using the *Preserve* keyword, only the upper bound of the array can be changed.

In our student scores program, class sizes could vary greatly in a university setting. Figure 8.9 contains the updated code using *ReDim* statements for the arrays.

```
' Program:    Chapter 8: Student Scores
' Form:       frmStudentScores
' Programmer: Joe Veyall
' Purpose:    Input and store student IDs, names, and scores
Option Explicit

Private fIDArray()    As String ' student ID array
Private fNameArray()  As String ' student name array
Private fScoreArray() As Long   ' student score array
Private fNumStudents  As Long   ' total number entered

' Purpose: Neatly display all student IDs, names, and scores from arrays
Private Sub cmdDisplay_Click()
    Dim StuCntr As Long         ' Student counter for loop
    Dim NewLine As String       ' Contents of next display line

    lblMsgLabel.Caption = "Student Listing"
    lblMsg.Caption = "    ID              Name                    Score Grade" _
        & vbCrLf & " --------------------------------------------------"
    For StuCntr = 1 To fNumStudents
        NewLine = "   " & Format(fIDArray(StuCntr), "!@@@@@@@@@@@") _
            & " " _
            & Format(fNameArray(StuCntr), "!@@@@@@@@@@@@@@@@@@@") _
            & " " & Format(fScoreArray(StuCntr), "000")
        lblMsg.Caption = lblMsg.Caption & vbCrLf & NewLine
    Next StuCntr
End Sub

' Purpose: Store student IDs, names, and scores in arrays
Private Sub cmdInsert_Click()
    fNumStudents = fNumStudents + 1
    ReDim Preserve fIDArray(1 To fNumStudents)
    ReDim Preserve fNameArray(1 To fNumStudents)
    ReDim Preserve fScoreArray(1 To fNumStudents)
    fIDArray(fNumStudents) = txtStuID.Text
    fNameArray(fNumStudents) = txtStuName.Text
    fScoreArray(fNumStudents) = CLng(txtTestScore.Text)
    lblMsg.Caption = "Student " & Format(fNumStudents) & " added."
    txtStuID.Text = ""
    txtStuName.Text = ""
    txtTestScore.Text = ""
    Call txtStuID.SetFocus
End Sub

' Purpose: Initialize number of students to zero
Private Sub Form_Load()
    fNumStudents = 0
End Sub
```

Figure 8.9   *Code for the* Student Scores *program using* ReDim *statements.*

Notice that the constant *cfMaxStudents* was removed, because the array size now matches the number of students (*fNumStudents*). In the *Insert Click* procedure, the arrays are expanded one additional space before storing the new student. The *Preserve* keyword is used to keep the previous data values.

Searching

Think about the many different ways that you search for various kinds of things. To find a sheet of instructions in a messy stack of papers, you will probably start with the first paper and check each piece of paper in the stack until you find the instructions. If you are looking up a word in the dictionary, you definitely will not start with page one and check each page. Instead, you may make a mental estimate of the position of the starting letter in the alphabet, open the book, and turn multiple pages at a time using the letter combinations at the top of each page. If you need to look up a topic in a reference book, you usually check the index, and then go directly to the indicated page number(s). If you are on a game show guessing the price of an expensive prize where they tell you whether your guess is high or low, you can quickly zero in on the exact price by first guessing a high and low price and then always guessing halfway in between.

In a programming context, **searching** means that a program determines whether a specific value is contained in a list of multiple values, and usually the location of that specific value in the list. A variety of standard search algorithms have been developed over the years. Finding the sheet of instructions in the unordered stack of papers is analogous to the **sequential search** algorithm used often in programming problems. The halving strategy for guessing the price on a game show is the basic idea behind the **binary search** algorithm. We will look at the algorithms for both of these search strategies in this section, and compare the advantages and disadvantages of each one.

Sequential or Serial Search

A sequential search, or **serial search**, for a particular value in a list starts by looking at the first item in the list to see whether it is the desired value. If not, the next item in the list is checked to see whether it matches. The process continues to look at successive items in the list until the value is found or it reaches the end of the list. Figure 8.10 shows the flowchart and pseudocode for a sequential search of a *Name* array. The search itself, depicted by dotted lines on the flowchart, is very short. Following the search, however, the program has specific actions to take if the item is found, and different actions (or no action) if the item is not in the list.

Let's add a *Lookup Name* button to the main form of our *Student Scores* program, as shown in Figure 8.11, and make use of this algorithm. If the teacher enters a name in the Name text box and clicks the *Lookup Name* button, the program should put that student's ID and score in the large label. A Not Found message displays if the name is not in the array. Refer to Figure 8.12 for the code for this button click event. Notice how it follows the logic of the flowchart, using the value in the *txtName* text box for the *SearchName* of the flowchart.

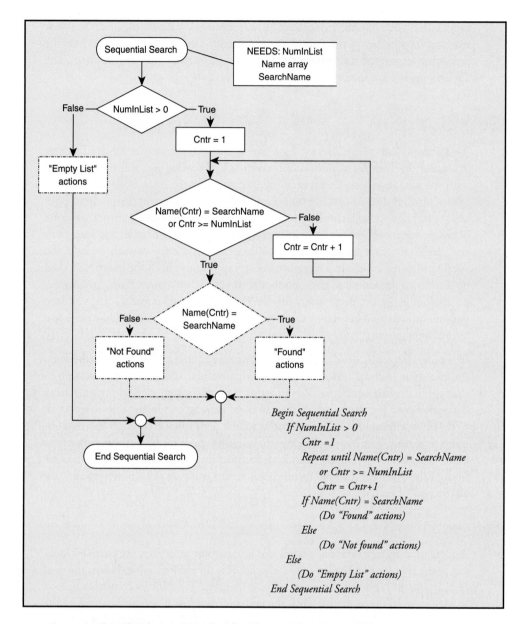

Figure 8.10 *Flowchart and pseudocode of the sequential search algorithm.*

If you carefully evaluate what the computer must do when performing a sequential search, you can come up with valuable statistics for estimating the time or work involved in performing a sequential search. Suppose the value you are searching for is the first one in the list. Then on the very first comparison, the program will find the value you are looking for. On the other hand, if you are searching for the value that happens to be the last one in the list, this algorithm will look at every item in the list before locating the matching value. For a list of 2,000 items, therefore, it might take anywhere from a minimum of one to a maximum of 2,000 comparisons to find the desired value. If the program will be performing a number of searches, we would find that the average of all the searches would be half the list, or 1,000 elements for this example. These numbers give us a way to compare the sequential search with other search methods, or to estimate the time a particular algorithm will usually take to execute (if we know the speed of the machine).

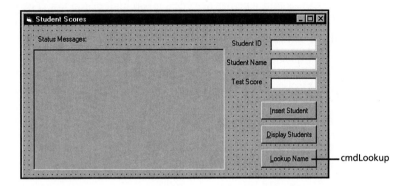

Figure 8.11   Lookup Name *button added to* Student Scores *program.*

```
' Purpose: See whether the name the user entered in the text box is in the
'          fNameArray.  If so, display the student's ID and score.
Private Sub cmdLookup_Click()
    Dim StuCntr As Long

    lblMsgLabel.Caption = "Lookup Results:"
    If fNumStudents > 0 Then
        StuCntr = 1
        Do Until fNameArray(StuCntr) = txtStuName.Text _
        Or StuCntr >= fNumStudents
            StuCntr = StuCntr + 1
        Loop
        If fNameArray(StuCntr) = txtStuName.Text Then
            lblMsg.Caption = "   ID: " & fIDArray(StuCntr) & vbCrLf _
                & "Score: " & CStr(fScoreArray(StuCntr))
        Else
            lblMsg.Caption = " *** Student not in list ***" _
                & vbCrLf & "  *** Check spelling.    ***"
        End If
    Else
        lblMsg.Caption = " *** LIST IS EMPTY.  ADD STUDENTS FIRST. ***"
    End If
End Sub
```

Figure 8.12   *Code for the* Lookup Name *button click event.*

Binary Search

Although the sequential search algorithm may be the simplest to understand and code, it is also very inefficient for large lists. A much faster algorithm, and not too difficult either, is the binary search. Perhaps in earlier years you had a math problem that asked when a rabbit will make it home if it starts 50 feet from its home, and with each hop goes half the remaining distance. The main idea of the binary search is to repeatedly cut a list in half with every comparison.

High/Low Guessing Game

If you have watched a game show where contestants must guess the price of an item, you may have noticed that some contestants can guess the price with time to spare, and others don't come close even though they talk very fast. With each guess, the contestant is told whether her guess is too high or too low. The successful contestants probably use something similar to the binary search technique to guess the price. If the contestant thinks the price of the stereo is between $200 and $1,000 (a difference of $800), for example, their first guess should be the number right in the middle ($600). If this is too low, then she guesses the number halfway between $600 and $1,000 ($800). When told this is too high, she guesses the number halfway between $600 and $800 ($700). This process continues a few more times to reach the correct price (see Figure 8.13).

Low Price	High Price	Guess in Middle	Answer
$200	$1,000	$600	Too low
$600	$1,000	$800	Too high
$600	$800	$700	Too low
$700	$800	$750	Too low
$750	$800	$775	Too high
$750	$775	$762	Too high
$750	$762	$756	Too low
$756	$762	$759	RIGHT!!

Figure 8.13   *Guessing game—Illustrating the power of the binary search method.*

In eight guesses, the contestant reached the correct price out of 800 possible values. Try this technique for other prices and the results will be similar. In 10 guesses or less, you can guess the correct price in a range of 1,000, as long as you know how to divide in half each time. Compare this to our previous discussion of the sequential search algorithm. For this game example, the sequential search would have an average of 400 guesses and a maximum of 800 guesses. Quite a difference!

Binary Search Limitations

So why did we even learn about the sequential search if the binary search is so much more efficient? Unfortunately, the binary search can only be applied if the list we are searching is *in order*. In looking back at Figure 8.3, we see that the student IDs are in order, but the names and scores are not. Hence, we could do a binary search for a student ID, but not for a particular name or score. The binary search also requires *random access* to the individual values of the list so that we can go directly to the middle position of the list.

■■■ TIP
Use a binary search when the list is in order on the search field and stored in an array or random access file.

Binary Search Example for an ID That Is in the List

Let's add a few more students to our arrays, as shown in Figure 8.14, and try a binary search for student ID 39-47.

		Student ID	Student Name	Test Score
	1	11–22	Joe	98
	2	13–08	Frank	67
	3	13–22	Mary	79
	4	15–66	Bill	82
	5	16–44	Nancy	90
	6	16–77	Jean	81
	7	20–02	Pat	76
Middle Location →	8	20–03	Ann	60
	9	20–14	Tom	99
	10	39–47	Don	84
	11	39–55	Gert	71
	12	42–08	Harry	80
	13	47–33	Sam	73
	14	55–06	Brett	79
	15	58–11	Dixie	93

Figure 8.14 *Student arrays with more data.*

Because there is now data for 15 students in the arrays, the variable *NumStudents* will have the value *15*. We can use this variable to calculate the position of the middle student, which would be position 8. Then we compare the search value (*39–47*) to the student ID at position 8 (*20–03*). Because the ID we are searching for comes *after* *20–03*, and we know that the IDs are in order, we can eliminate array positions 1 through 8 from the search, and look in positions 9 to 15. Now we repeat the process. We determine the middle location of array positions 9 to 15, which would be 12. Again, we compare our search value (*39–47*) to the student ID at this middle position (*42–08*). This time, the ID we are searching for comes *before 42–08*, so we can now eliminate array positions 12 through 15 from the search.

This leaves array positions 9 to 11. Repeating the process again, we calculate the middle location of positions 9 to 11, and get 10. When comparing our search value (*39–47*) to the student ID at position 10 (*39–47*), we see the IDs are equal, so we can stop the search. Knowing that we found the ID at position 10, we also know that the name and score are in position 10 of the other two arrays.

Binary Search Example for an ID That Is Not in the List

This time, let's try the binary search for student ID *39–50*, which is not in the student ID array. The search process starts the same way. We determine that array location 8 is the middle position of the array, so we compare *39–50* to *20–03*. Because *39–50* comes after *20–03*, we next look at the middle position of the last half of the array (positions 9 to 15). The ID at array position 12 (*42–08*) comes after the ID we are looking for, so our search narrows down to array positions 9 to 11. The midpoint here is position 10, which contains *39–47*. This comes before the ID we want, so our search narrows to positions 11 to 11. Obviously, the midpoint should be location 11, which contains *39–55*. Because this is not what we are looking for, and we can't shrink the search section down anymore, the ID must not be in the list. Now we need an algorithm for this process we just walked through.

Binary Search Algorithm

We will assume that the ID we are searching for has been placed in the variable *SearchID*, that the array starts at position 1, and that the last student is in position *NumStudents* of the array. We can calculate the middle value between two numbers (like the average) by adding them up and dividing by two. (When coded, this should be integer division to drop any remainder.) Figure 8.15 contains a flowchart and pseudocode for a binary search of the *StudentID* array. If the desired ID is located, the name and test score are displayed on the form. If the ID is not found, an error message displays.

To make sure you understand this algorithm, add a *Lookup ID* button to the *Student Scores* program and translate the preceding logic into code. We leave the coding of a *Lookup ID* button click event as an exercise for you to complete.

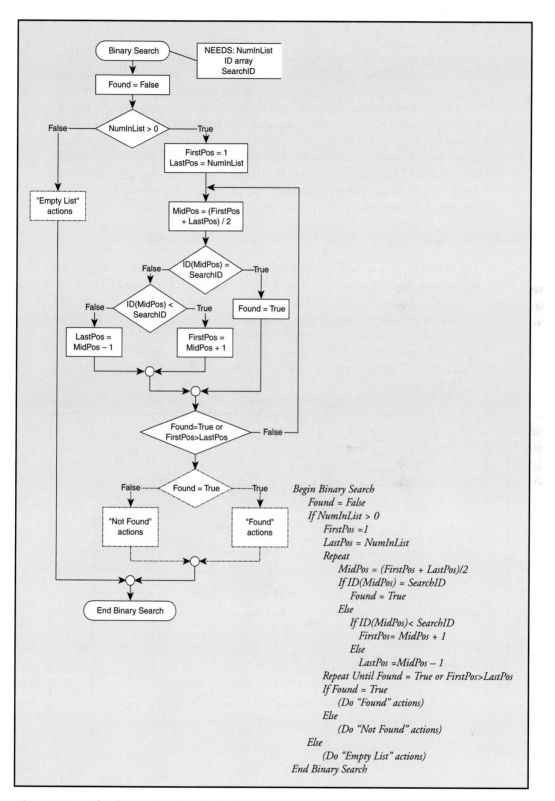

Figure 8.15   *Flowchart and pseudocode of a binary search.*

Sorting

Sorting means that you rearrange the elements of a list so that they are in order, numeric or alphabetic, depending on the type of values in the list. This order can further be specified as ascending or descending. Ascending order means that the values go from small to large numbers, or in alphabetic order (from A to Z) for strings. Descending order means that the order goes from largest to smallest numbers or in reverse alphabetic order. Almost all programming texts include at least one sort algorithm, even though you can usually find an efficient sort routine that has already been written. There are several reasons for this. First, a sort algorithm provides a good example of using nested loops with arrays. Second, it gives you some idea of the amount of work the computer is doing when performing a sort command.

Sort Algorithms

The algorithm that we will look at is called a **selection sort**. If we are sorting a list into ascending order, for each array position, the algorithm finds (selects) the smallest remaining value and moves it into position. Let's look at the specific example of wanting to sort the student scores into descending order. For the first "pass," we find the largest value and put it into the first array position. For the second "pass," we find the next largest value and put it into the second array position. This process continues until the entire list is in order. Figure 8.16 shows the results at the end of the first four passes.

	Original Test Scores	After Pass 1	After Pass 2	After Pass 3	After Pass 4
	98	99	99	99	99
	67	67	98	98	98
	79	79	79	90	90
	82	82	82	82	84
	90	90	90	79	79
	81	81	81	81	81
	76	76	76	76	76
	60	60	60	60	60
Largest →	99	98	67	67	67
	84	84	84	84	82

Figure 8.16 *Illustration of several passes of a selection sort.*

The algorithm for one pass through the array to find the largest value uses a loop. Because there are multiple passes, the sort algorithm will contain a loop inside a loop. The inner loop performs one pass, and the outer loop counts the passes until all have been completed. Figure 8.17 shows one possible flowchart for this algorithm.

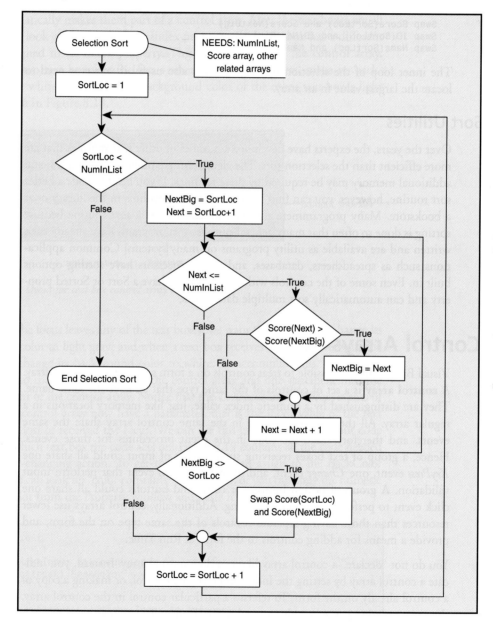

Figure 8.17   *Flowchart of a selection sort, in descending order, on student scores.*

Try adding a user-defined type for ID, name, and score to the *Student Scores* program we worked on earlier in this chapter. Then define one array, using this new type, and update the processing code as necessary. Figure 8.33 contains one possible solution.

```
' Program:     Chapter 8: Student Scores
' Form:        frmStudentScores
' Programmer: Joe Veyall
' Purpose:     Input and store student IDs, names, and scores
Option Explicit

Private Type StudentDataType
    StuID    As String
    StuName  As String
    TestScore As Long
End Type

Private fStuArray()   As StudentDataType   ' student data array
Private fNumStudents  As Long    ' total number entered


' Purpose: Neatly display all student IDs, names, and scores from arrays
Private Sub cmdDisplay_Click()
    Dim StuCntr As Long       ' Student counter for loop
    Dim NewLine As String     ' Contents of next display line

    lblMsgLabel.Caption = "Student Listing"
    lblMsg.Caption = "    ID           Name                    Score Grade" _
        & vbCrLf & "    --------------------------------------------------"
    For StuCntr = 1 To fNumStudents
        NewLine = "  " _
            & Format(fStuArray(StuCntr).StuID, "!@@@@@@@@@@") & " " _
            & Format(fStuArray(StuCntr).StuName, _
              "!@@@@@@@@@@@@@@@@@@@") & " " _
            & Format(fStuArray(StuCntr).TestScore, "000")
        lblMsg.Caption = lblMsg.Caption & vbCrLf & NewLine
    Next StuCntr
End Sub

' Purpose: Store student IDs, names, and scores in arrays
Private Sub cmdInsert_Click()
    fNumStudents = fNumStudents + 1
    ReDim Preserve fStuArray(1 To fNumStudents)
    fStuArray(fNumStudents).StuID = txtStuID.Text
    fStuArray(fNumStudents).StuName = txtStuName.Text
    fStuArray(fNumStudents).TestScore = CLng(txtTestScore.Text)
    lblMsgLabel.Caption = "Insert Results:"
    lblMsg.Caption = "Student " & Format(fNumStudents) & " added."
    txtStuID.Text = ""
    txtStuName.Text = ""
    txtTestScore.Text = ""
    Call txtStuID.SetFocus
End Sub

' Purpose: See whether the name the user entered in the text box is in the
'          fNameArray.  If so, display the student's ID and score.
```

```
Private Sub cmdLookup_Click()
    Dim StuCntr As Long

    lblMsgLabel.Caption = "Lookup Results:"
    If fNumStudents > 0 Then
        StuCntr = 1
        Do Until fStuArray(StuCntr).StuName = txtStuName.Text _
        Or StuCntr >= fNumStudents
            StuCntr = StuCntr + 1
        Loop
        If fStuArray(StuCntr).StuName = txtStuName.Text Then
            lblMsg.Caption = "   ID: " & fStuArray(StuCntr).StuID & _
                vbCrLf & "Score: " & CStr(fStuArray(StuCntr).TestScore)
        Else
            lblMsg.Caption = " *** STUDENT NOT IN LIST ***" _
                & vbCrLf & "  *** Check spelling.      ***"
        End If
    Else
        lblMsg.Caption = " *** LIST IS EMPTY.  ADD STUDENTS FIRST. ***"
    End If
End Sub

' Purpose: Initialize number of students to zero
Private Sub Form_Load()
    fNumStudents = 0
End Sub
```

Figure 8.33 Student Scores *program with a user-defined type.*

Order Price Calculation Case Study—Making Improvements

At the end of Chapter 6, "The Case Structure and Error Handling," we developed a program that could look up an item code to get its description, price, and weight and then calculate an order cost. At that time we used a *Case* structure to implement the search. The problem with that approach is that each item requires its own case condition. Not only do we have to update the program code for each new item, but also the code increases in length with each additional item. If we convert this problem to use arrays to store the item data and a search loop, the search code stays the same length whether we have five items or 500 items. Often problems that can be solved with *If* statements or *Case* statements when there are a few choices, should instead be solved with arrays and loops so that the problem is expandable and the code doesn't have to be changed every time the data changes.

Hence, as in Chapter 6, we want a program in which the user enters an item code and the program looks up its price, description, and weight. After the user enters a quantity, the program calculates the total price of the order, including tax and shipping. In addition, we will add the capability to store new items, delete current items that are no longer sold, and update prices, weights, or descriptions of existing items. For now, we will keep the same sales tax and shipping rules as we used in Chapter 6.

Step 1: Analyze the Problem

From the user's point of view, this program will operate in almost the same way as the program at the end of Chapter 6. The user enters an item code, quantity, and state; and the program finds the item's description, price, and weight, and then calculates the total due on the order. The new capability we are giving the user is to be able to add or delete items and update prices. Because these updates won't be performed on a regular basis, a modal form can be used to handle updates to the items.

Step 2: Design or Create the User Interface

We start with the form designed for the program in Chapter 6. The changes to our user interface include a button on the main form to initiate an update, and a second form to actually perform the item updates. The second form contains four text boxes to input item code, description, price, and weight and five command buttons to add an item, delete an item, modify an item, clear the text boxes, and close the update form. We can also add an extra label for messages. Figure 8.34 shows a possible layout for this new form, and Figure 8.35 shows the main form with the added *Update Items* button.

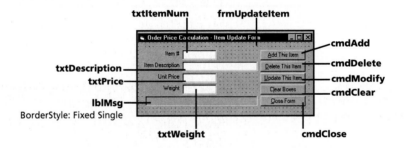

Figure 8.34 *Order program update form.*

Figure 8.35 *Order program main form.*

Step 3: Design the Logic for the Program

We are going to replace the *Case* structure of Chapter 6 with an array for the items. This provides a better structure for expandability if more items will be added. For now, we load some of the array values in the *Form Load* event, but in the next chapter you will learn how to store these values in a data file so that the program can load the array from a file.

Step 3a: Design the Macro-Level View (Object-Event Diagrams)

We need to add the *Update Items* button to the Object-Event Diagram for the main form, and create an OED for the update form, as shown in Figures 8.36 and 8.37.

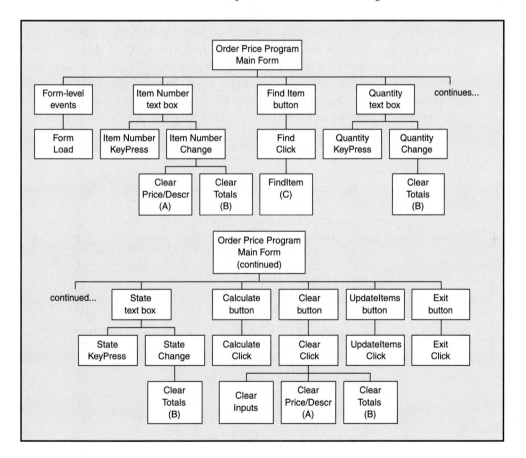

Figure 8.36   *OED for main form of* Order Price *program.*

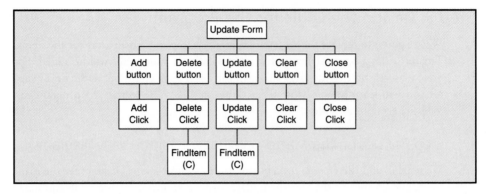

Figure 8.37 *OED for update form of* Order Price *program.*

In thinking about the processing of the *Delete* and *Update* buttons on the update form, and the *Find Item* button on the main form, we realize that they all need to search the *Items* array for a particular item. If we designate this logic as a separate procedure, it will need to be coded only in one place. (Actually, the *Add Item* button could also use this procedure to verify that it is not adding a duplicate item number to the list. We leave this as an exercise.) The OEDs include this *FindItem* procedure.

Step 3b: Design the Micro-Level View (Flowcharts and Pseudocode)

Because the logic of many of these procedures was developed in Chapter 6, only the ones that are new or changed will be presented here. Let's first look at the *FindItem* procedure used by several of the new events. It contains a simple loop to look through the *Items* array for the designated *ItemCode*.

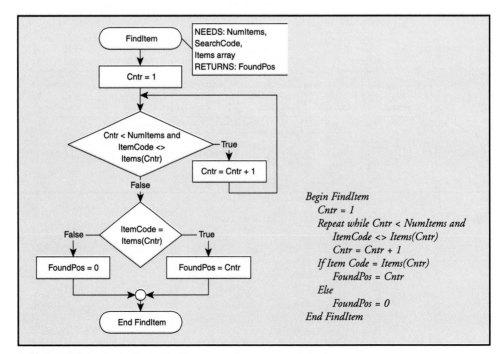

Figure 8.38 *Logic for the* FindItem *procedure.*

The *Find Item* button click event uses the preceding procedure to locate an item, and then displays the description and price from the arrays.

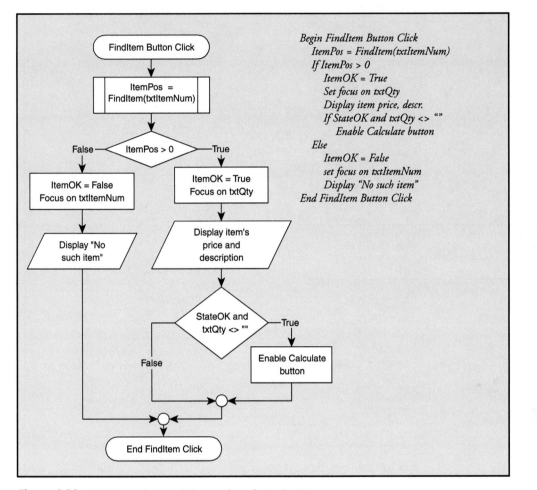

Figure 8.39   Find Item *button click event logic for* Order Price *program.*

The *Calculate* button uses the item arrays to get the item price and weight.

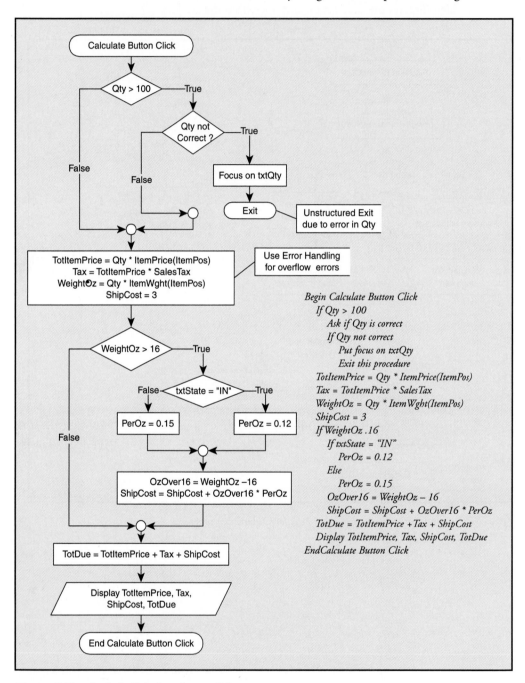

Figure 8.40   *Logic for* Calculate *button click event.*

The *Update Items* button click event merely shows the update form modally, so we omit its flowchart. The straightforward *Clear* and *Close* buttons on this form are also left for the reader to figure out. Let's look at the logic for the *Add Item, Delete Item,* and *Update Item* click events from the second form, shown in Figure 8.41.

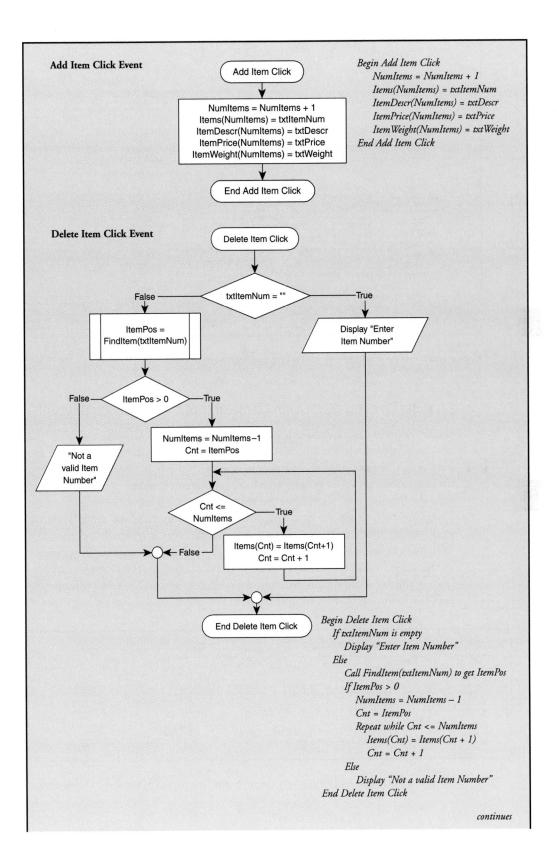

Add Item Click Event

Add Item Click

NumItems = NumItems + 1
Items(NumItems) = txtItemNum
ItemDescr(NumItems) = txtDescr
ItemPrice(NumItems) = txtPrice
ItemWeight(NumItems) = txtWeight

End Add Item Click

Begin Add Item Click
NumItems = NumItems + 1
Items(NumItems) = txtItemNum
ItemDescr(NumItems) = txtDescr
ItemPrice(NumItems) = txtPrice
ItemWeight(NumItems) = txtWeight
End Add Item Click

Delete Item Click Event

Delete Item Click

txtItemNum = "" — False / True

Display "Enter Item Number"

ItemPos = FindItem(txtItemNum)

ItemPos > 0 — False / True

"Not a valid Item Number"

NumItems = NumItems−1
Cnt = ItemPos

Cnt <= NumItems — True / False

Items(Cnt) = Items(Cnt+1)
Cnt = Cnt + 1

End Delete Item Click

Begin Delete Item Click
If txtItemNum is empty
Display "Enter Item Number"
Else
Call FindItem(txtItemNum) to get ItemPos
If ItemPos > 0
NumItems = NumItems − 1
Cnt = ItemPos
Repeat while Cnt <= NumItems
Items(Cnt) = Items(Cnt + 1)
Cnt = Cnt + 1
Else
Display "Not a valid Item Number"
End Delete Item Click

continues

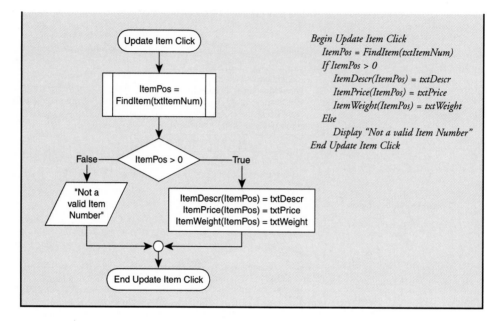

Figure 8.41 *Logic for* Add, Delete, *and* Update *button click events.*

Step 3c: Develop a Test Plan (Table of Input with Expected Results)

We developed a fairly extensive test plan for this program in Chapter 6. Besides the test cases listed there, we should add some to check the search and updates of the item arrays. A good rule of thumb is to search for the first, last, and at least one middle element of an array. Also search for a nonexistent element that would precede the first element, come after the last element, or fall between elements of the array. Similarly, delete the first, last, and a middle element of the array. Then try to delete one that would precede the first element, come after the last element, or fall between elements of the array. Use the same guidelines to test modifying items. In this program, we are adding to the end of the array only, rather than maintaining a sequence, so no special decisions are needed to add an item. We will initially load the following four items into the item arrays during the *Form_Load* event.

Item Code	Item Description	Unit Cost	Weight (ounces)
173AJ–247	"Farm Scene" quilt	522.49	168
182K–304A	Platinum cuff links	299.99	15.99
499GN–801	Hand-crafted bird feeder	29.55	65.7
626T–71W	Hand-woven straw placemats	10.00	4

We can add several additional test cases to our test plan. Figure 8.42 shows these.

436

Test Case	User Input and/or Action	Expected Results
1 (Find last item #.)	Enter 626T–71W in Item#. Click *Find Item*.	Descr: Hand-woven Straw Placemats Price: $10.00
2	Enter 6 in Quantity, WI in State. Click *Calculate*.	Tot Pr: $60.00 Tax: 3.00 Ship: 4.20 Tot Due: 67.20
3 (Find first item.)	Enter 173AJ–247 in Item#. Click *Find Item*.	Descr: "Farm Scene" Quilt Price: $522.49 *Calculate* button enabled.
4 (Find non- existent item after last item.)	Enter 777J–77 in Item#. Click *Find Item*.	Not found. *Calculate* button disabled. Focus on item number.
5 (Find non- existent item before first item.)	Enter 111Q–22 in Item#. Click *Find Item*.	Not found. *Calculate* button disabled. Focus on item number.
6 (Delete first item.)	Click *Update Items* button. Enter 173AJ–247 in Item#. Click *Delete Item*. Return to main form. Enter 173AJ–247 in Item#. Click *Find Item*.	Item is deleted. Find Item says not found.
7 (Delete last item.)	Click *Update Items* button. Enter 626T–71W in Item#. Click *Delete Item*. Return to main form. Enter 626T–71W in Item#. Click *Find Item*.	Item is deleted. Find Item says not found
8 (Add new item.)	Click *Update Items* button. Enter 678Y–99 in Item#, New Item in Description, 9.99 in Price, and 11 in Weight. Click *Add Item*. Return to main form. Enter 678Y–99 Item#. Click *Find Item*.	Descr: New Item Price: $9.99 *Calculate* button enabled.
9 (Modify first item.)	Click *Update Items* button. Enter 182K–304A in Item#, Pewter Cuff Links in Description, 111.11 in Price, and 5.5 in Weight. Click *Update Item*. Return to main form. Enter 182K–304A in Item#. Click *Find Item*.	Descr: Pewter Cuff Links Price: $111.11 *Calculate* button enabled.

Figure 8.42 *Additional test cases for* Order Price *program.*

Step 4: Code the Program

In coding the program, we try several of the new language elements introduced in this chapter. First, because there are multiple pieces of information about an item, we create a user-defined type called *ItemType*. Then we declare a dynamic *Items* array of type *ItemType*. Because both forms must access the *Items* array, we set them up with Public access in a separate standard module (see Figure 8.43). The *FindItem* function is also included in this standard module, because it is called from both forms.

```
' Program:    Chapter 8: Order Price
' Module:     basGlobal
' Programmer: Cal Q. Laytor
' Purpose:    Contains global items definition and array and the
'             FindItem function.

Option Explicit

Public Type ItemType
    Code      As String
    Descr     As String
    Price     As Currency
    WeightOz  As Double
End Type

Public gNumItems     As Integer     ' current number of items
Public gItems()      As ItemType

' Purpose:  Searches for an item number in the gItems array and
'           returns the position found (0 if not found).
Public Function FindItem(ItemCode As String) As Long
    Dim Cntr As Integer

    Cntr = 1
    Do While Cntr < gNumItems And ItemCode <> gItems(Cntr).Code
        Cntr = Cntr + 1
    Loop
    If ItemCode = gItems(Cntr).Code Then
        FindItem = Cntr
    Else
        FindItem = 0
    End If
End Function
```

Figure 8.43 *Global code for* Order Price *program.*

We use the *Form_Load* event to load a few items into the *Items* array (presumably items that are always available).

```
Private Sub Form_Load()
' Load basic items into Items array
    gNumItems = 4
    ReDim gItems(1 To gNumItems)
    gItems(1).Code = "173AJ-247"
    gItems(1).Descr = "'Farm Scene' Quilt"
    gItems(1).Price = 522.49
```

```
            gItems(1).WeightOz = 168
            gItems(2).Code = "182K-304A"
            gItems(2).Descr = "Platinum Cuff Links"
            gItems(2).Price = 299.99
            gItems(2).WeightOz = 15.99
            gItems(3).Code = "499GN-801"
            gItems(3).Descr = "Hand-crafted Bird Feeder"
            gItems(3).Price = 29.55
            gItems(3).WeightOz = 65.7
            gItems(4).Code = "626T-71W"
            gItems(4).Descr = "Hand-woven Straw Placemats"
            gItems(4).Price = 10
            gItems(4).WeightOz = 4
            ' Other initialization
            cmdFindItem.Enabled = False
            cmdCalculate.Enabled = False
            txtState.MaxLength = 2
            fStateOK = False
            fItemOK = False
            fCurrItem = 0
        End Sub
```

Figure 8.44 *Code for the* Form_Load *event.*

The code for the *Calculate* button must be updated to get the item price and weight from the array. The *Find Item* button calls the *FindItem* function, and also accesses the *Items* array. The *Update Items* button click event contains one statement to show the second form modally.

```
    ' Purpose:  Calculates the order's total price, including tax and
    '           shipping.  Assumes the state code has been validated,
    '           but asks user to verify quantities over 100.  Performs
    '           error trapping for problems such as numeric overflow
    '           while converting or multiplying.
    Private Sub cmdCalculate_Click()
        Dim Qty As Long                 ' numeric quantity ordered
        Dim TotItemPrice As Currency    ' qty*price of item
        Dim Tax As Double               ' sales tax on item
        Dim WeightOz As Double          ' total weight of order in oz.
        Dim OuncesOver16 As Double      ' ounces over 1 lb.
        Dim ShipCost As Currency        ' shipping cost of order
        Dim PerOz As Currency           ' shipping per oz.
        Dim TotDue As Currency          ' total amount due

        On Error GoTo MathErr    ' Turn on error handling
        Qty = CLng(txtQty.Text)
        If Qty > cfReasonableQty Then
            If MsgBox("Large quantity — Is it correct?", vbYesNo, _
                    "Large Quantity Verification") = vbNo Then
                Call txtQty.SetFocus
                Exit Sub  ' exit so user can enter new quantity
            End If
        End If
        ' Quantity is OK
        TotItemPrice = Qty * gItems(fCurrItem).Price
        Tax = TotItemPrice * fSalesTaxFrac
```

continues

```
        ' Find weight category, get shipping cost
        WeightOz = Qty * gItems(fCurrItem).WeightOz
        ShipCost = cfBaseShipPrice
        If WeightOz > 16 Then              ' 16 ounces per pound
            If txtState.Text = "IN" Then
                PerOz = cfInStateShipRate
            Else
                PerOz = cfOutStateShipRate
            End If
            ' Go to next whole oz
            OuncesOver16 = Int(WeightOz - 16 + 0.99).
            ShipCost = ShipCost + OuncesOver16 * PerOz
        End If
        ' Calculate Total Due and Display Results
        TotDue = TotItemPrice + Tax + ShipCost
        lblTotPrice.Caption = Format(TotItemPrice, "Currency")
        lblSalesTax.Caption = Format(Tax, "Currency")
        lblShip.Caption = Format(ShipCost, "Currency")
        lblTotDue.Caption = Format(TotDue, "Currency")
        Exit Sub       ' end of regular processing

MathErr:
    MsgBox ("Error in calculations.  Check inputs.")
    Exit Sub
End Sub


' Purpose:  Searches for the item number.  If found, it
'           displays the item description and price, and
'           sets form variables for price and weight.
Private Sub cmdFindItem_Click()
    fCurrItem = FindItem(txtItemNum.Text)
    If fCurrItem > 0 Then
        fItemOK = True
        lblDescr.Caption = gItems(fCurrItem).Descr
        lblPrice.Caption = Format(gItems(fCurrItem).Price, "Currency")
        Call txtQty.SetFocus
        If fStateOK And (txtQty.Text <> "") Then
            cmdCalculate.Enabled = True
        End If
    Else
        fItemOK = False
        lblDescr.Caption = " ** NO SUCH ITEM ** "
        Call txtItemNum.SetFocus
    End If
End Sub


Private Sub cmdUpdateItems_Click()
    Call frmUpdateItem.Show(vbModal)
End Sub
```

Figure 8.45 *Code for the* Calculate, Find Item, *and* Update Items *button click events.*

In Figure 8.46, you will find the code for the new form, which performs the various updates to the *Items* array.

```
' Program:   Chapter 8: Order Price
' Form:      frmUpdateItem
' Programmer: Cal Q. Laytor
' Purpose:   A modal dialog to add a new item, delete an item or
'            update an existing item.
```

```
Option Explicit

' Purpose:  Adds values from text boxes to new position at end of
'           gItems array.
Private Sub cmdAdd_Click()
    gNumItems = gNumItems + 1
    ReDim Preserve gItems(1 To gNumItems)
    gItems(gNumItems).Code = txtItemNum.Text
    gItems(gNumItems).Descr = txtDescription.Text
    gItems(gNumItems).Price = txtPrice.Text
    gItems(gNumItems).WeightOz = txtWeight.Text
    lblMsg.Caption = " *** Item Added ***"
End Sub

' Purpose:  Clears the text boxes and puts focus on top text box.
Private Sub cmdClear_Click()
    txtItemNum.Text = ""
    txtDescription.Text = ""
    txtPrice.Text = ""
    txtWeight.Text = ""
    lblMsg.Caption = ""
    Call txtItemNum.SetFocus
End Sub

' Purpose:  Unloads update form and returns to main form.
Private Sub cmdClose_Click()
    Unload frmUpdateItem
End Sub

' Purpose:  Searches for Item Number and deletes that item from the
'           gItems array.
Private Sub cmdDelete_Click()
    Dim ItemPosition As Long
    Dim Cntr As Long
    If txtItemNum.Text = "" Then
        lblMsg.Caption = "Enter Item Number that you want deleted."
    Else
        ItemPosition = FindItem(txtItemNum.Text)
        If ItemPosition > 0 Then
            gNumItems = gNumItems - 1
            For Cntr = ItemPosition To gNumItems
                gItems(Cntr) = gItems(Cntr + 1)
            Next Cntr
            ReDim Preserve gItems(1 To gNumItems)
            lblMsg.Caption = " *** Item Deleted ***"
        Else
            lblMsg.Caption = " XXXX Not a valid Item Number. XXXX"
        End If
    End If
End Sub

' Purpose:  Locates the item and updates its description, price,
'           and/or weight using values in the text boxes.
Private Sub cmdModify_Click()
    Dim ItemPosition As Long

    ItemPosition = FindItem(txtItemNum.Text)
    If ItemPosition > 0 Then
        gItems(ItemPosition).Descr = txtDescription.Text
        gItems(ItemPosition).Price = CCur(txtPrice.Text)
```

continues

```
            gItems(ItemPosition).WeightOz = CDbl(txtWeight.Text)
            lblMsg.Caption = " *** Item Updated ***"
        Else
            lblMsg.Caption = " XXXX Not a valid Item Number. XXXX"
        End If
End Sub
```

Figure 8.46 *Code for the* Update Form *button click events.*

Step 5: Test and Debug the Program

After everything is coded, we must run the final system test. Because we are updating an existing program, the temptation is to skip testing the old portions of the program, because we know they work. This is a bad idea. There have been too many cases where a seemingly simple change to a program had unexpected effects on other parts of the program. Hence, we must run all the test cases for the original program (see Chapter 6), as well as the new test cases that add, delete, and modify items. Your supervisors and users will also expect that you have carefully checked that the resulting calculations are still accurate to the penny.

Step 6: Assemble the Final Documentation

As always, we draw our project to a close by assembling our updated OED, flowcharts, code, and test output, and incorporating them into the notebook for this program. In addition, we should include a summary of the changes that were just made. This is helpful in case a problem is detected and someone else must try to fix it, because a new problem is often caused by the most recent changes that were made.

Summary

An *array* is a structure in memory that consists of multiple storage locations storing values of the same type and having one name. The multiple locations are numbered consecutively. This number is called a *subscript* or *index*. An individual array location is referred to using both the name of the array and a subscript value enclosed in parentheses. Using a numeric variable as the subscript makes it easy to process all the elements of an array inside a loop.

Initially, the programmer needs to determine how many positions will be needed in the array, and specify this in the array declaration. Arrays are declared in *Dim* or *Private* statements, just like variables, except that the range of the subscript is also indicated. The programmer can even specify the starting and ending numbers for the array subscripts, although arrays typically start with position zero or one. If an application needs varying array sizes that are not known at compile time, the programmer can choose to create dynamic arrays, which can be redimensioned by using the *ReDim* statement while the program is executing.

After an array has been assigned some data values, programs can perform a variety of processing. This includes displaying some or all of the values in the array, searching for particular values, and sorting the array values. There is more than one way to conduct a search for a particular value. The *sequential search* checks each value, starting from the first position, until the desired value is found. The *binary search* does not check every value in sequence, but instead jumps to the middle value in each section of the array. The binary search can be much faster than a sequential search, but it only works if the list is in order.

The dimensions of an array may correspond to values such as the months of the year or the days of the week. To show this in the code, it is possible to define a sequence of meaningful names in an *Enum* statement to take the place of a sequence of numbers. This is called an *enumeration*.

Applications often require more than one array of related data values. This situation can be handled by declaring multiple arrays, declaring *multidimensional arrays,* or declaring an array using a user-defined type. *User-defined types* provide a way to declare a structure that contains more than one value of different types. Certain component properties in Visual Basic make use of the array structure, such as the List property of a list box or combo box.

Key Terms

array	enumerations	serial search
binary search	Format	sorting
control array	Preserve	static array
Dim array (low to high) As type	ReDim	subscript
	searching	two-dimensional array
dynamic array	selection sort	Type statement
End Type	sequential search	user-defined type
Enum		

Test Your Understanding

1. What are the main characteristics of an array?

2. If the array reference NewEmpl(5) appears within a code statement, what is the array name? What is the subscript value?

3. What is the difference in meaning of the values between parentheses in an array *declaration* versus an array *reference* in an event procedure?

4. How would you declare a dynamic array for employee names? How would you redimension this array in the *Add Employee* event?

5. Describe the general process of performing a sequential search.

6. On the average, how many array locations are checked during a sequential search?

7. What are the requirements for being able to perform a binary search?

8. Make a list of the prices you would guess for the price of a refrigerator, applying the binary technique in the "High/Low" guessing game (assume actual price is $948).

9. If *Preserve* is needed in the *ReDim* statement in Figure 8.29, why isn't it needed in the *ReDim* statement in Figure 8.27?

10. Define an enumeration for the days of the week.

11. Define a user-defined type for a product that has an ID code, a category, a description, a color, a weight, and a price.

Programming Exercises

1. Add a *Lookup ID* button to the student grade program of this chapter. Code the binary search algorithm found in Figure 8.15. List the test data you would use to test your program.

2. For the *SalesData* array program of this chapter, store the city names in an array. Display the city names at the start of each row in the output label on the form.

3. For the *SalesData* array program, define an enumeration for the city names and use it for the first dimension of the *SalesData* array.

4. For the *SalesData* problem, put the month names in a combo box that becomes visible when the user clicks the *Month Total* button. Code the *Click* event of the combo box to calculate the total of the selected month.

5. For the *SalesData* problem, change the *Store Total* button to show totals of each of the seven cities instead of asking which city. Change the *Month Total* button to show the totals of each of the 12 months instead of asking which month.

6. Modify the end-of-chapter problem by adding a search to the *Add* button to verify the item is not currently in the array.

7. Modify the end-of-chapter case study by declaring one or more arrays for the state abbreviations and sales tax rates. Assign values to the state array(s) in the *Form_Load* event. Modify the *txtState Change* event to search the state array.

Programming Projects

1. Design and code a complete program for Ye Old Ice Cream Shoppe (see Figure 8.20). Store the ice cream prices in an array. You will need to store the price for a single and a double scoop. Add a frame and use check boxes for toppings. Assume that hot fudge and chopped nuts are always available, but other toppings are offered each day. Store the topping prices in an array. The manager should be able to enter new ice cream flavors with prices, and new toppings with prices. Assume there is no difference in the cost of a cone versus a cup, and the sales tax is 7.25 percent. Decide on the test data you will use and create a thorough test plan.

2. Using the end-of-chapter case study as a guide, design and code a program that uses arrays to hold item data for a company (item code, description, price, and weight); state data (state abbreviation, state name, state sales tax, and shipping zone); and shipping rate data (rates by weight and by distance) (see the following table). The user should be able to add, delete, or modify item data (perform reasonable data validation on all inputs). The user should be able to look up item numbers and calculate total prices. The user should be able to request several different items in an order.

Weight ↓	To → IN	IL/OH/MI	KY/TN	WI
0–16 oz	1.85	2.00	2.50	2.55
Over 1, up to 2 lb. 2.25	2.25	2.35	2.65	2.65
Over 2, up to 5 lbs. 2.65	2.65	2.82	3.08	3.11
Over 5, up to 10 lbs.	3.03	3.24	3.57	3.66
Over 10, up to 20 lbs.	3.50	3.75	4.02	4.04
Over 20, up to 35 lbs.	4.35	4.56	4.88	5.01
Over 35, up to 50 lbs.	4.90	5.00	5.25	5.28

3. A program is needed to analyze the failure data of various machines in a manufacturing plant. Each time a machine fails, data is gathered as to which machine, during which shift it fails, how long the machine is down in *hours* and *minutes*, and the cost to repair it. Your program should input the data into one or more arrays. It should be able to calculate the number of times each machine is down, the total length of time each machine is down, the average amount of time the machine is down per failure, the total repair costs, and the average cost per failure. The user should be able to view the results for one machine, for each machine, and the company totals and averages for all machines. An example of the paper report the company assembles is shown here.

```
                            date
                    MACHINE FAILURE REPORT
                          TOTAL    AVERAGE   TOTAL    AVG.
   MACHINE  SHIFT  NBR.TIMES MINUTES  MINUTES   COST     COST
   =============================================================
      A       1       3       640     213.3   $707.60  $235.87
              2       1        15      15.0    $45.00   $45.00
   ...........................................................
   MACHINE A TOTALS:    4       655     163.8   $752.60  $188.15

      B       2       2        77      38.5   $101.94   $50.97
   ...........................................................
   MACHINE B TOTALS:    2        77      38.5   $101.94   $50.97


   OVERALL TOTALS ==>    6       732     122.0   $854.54  $142.42
```

4. Code a program that enables a person to input names, phone numbers, and categories (Friend, Relative, Business) of acquaintances (maximum of 25). Input the first names, last names, and phone numbers into text boxes. Use option buttons for the category. When the user clicks an *Add to List* button, the program stores the name, number, and category in arrays, displays how many names are saved, and clears the input values from the screen. A message label is used for error messages and to indicate how many names have been added to the arrays. When the user clicks the *Clear* button, the text boxes, message, category, and list box clear. When the user clicks the *Display List* button, all the values from the arrays are displayed in the list box at the bottom. Display a special message if *Display List* is clicked before any names are in the arrays. A rough layout of the form is shown here.

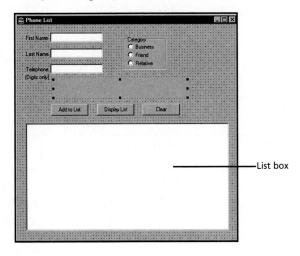

5. Write a Visual Basic program in which prospective home buyers could enter information about what type of home they are looking for so that the system will display the homes that meet a buyer's preferences. For each available home, you need to store the list price, number of bedrooms, number of bathrooms, whether the home has a fenced yard, whether the home includes any farmland, and whether the home has a garage. Assign this available homes data to an array of a user-defined type in the *Form Load* event. Create a message box that displays the addresses and list prices (one home entry per line) for all matching homes. A suggested form is shown here.

CHAPTER 9

SEQUENTIAL FILES

Introduction

In Chapter 8, "Arrays, Searching, and Sorting," we learned how to work with the array structure. For a program that is run often or that stores many values in arrays, however, it would be useful to get values into the arrays without making the user type them over and over again. A common solution is to store these data values in a data file. In many computer applications, the computer must process data stored in external storage. Nowadays this often means the data is maintained in a database. At times, however, data can be stored in files, rather than databases. In this chapter we will work with one particular type of file, the *sequential file*. Techniques for retrieving data from files and creating new files will be explored, as well as the Visual Basic statements used to work with these files.

Objectives

After completing this chapter, you should be able to:

- Understand the basic difference between sequential and random file access.
- Understand the difference between text and binary formats.
- Carry out the basic operations of opening and closing files.
- Create and process comma-delimited text files.
- Create and process report files.
- Create and process fixed record-length text files.
- Create and process fixed record-length binary files.

File Details

You are already familiar with the concept of a **file**. You create files when you save a word processing document or a spreadsheet. Throughout the book, we work with files every time we open and save our programs. A file is just a collection of related data stored in one unit (under one name) on a disk. In the same way that a word processor can access files that have been saved in certain formats, programs that you write can access data that has been stored in a file by another program. Or a program that you write can store (write) new data into a file. The files that a program accesses are often called **data files**, or sometimes **report files**, depending on their format and purpose. Data files may be formatted for space savings, or to make them readily accessible to a program, and not necessarily to look nice to a person reading through them. Report files, on the other hand, are formatted so that they can be printed out, and provide useful information to a person making decisions. The values stored in a data file are generally organized into individual units called **records**. When displaying the contents of a file, typically each record displays as one line of data.

Programs use files for several reasons:

- Data generated by one program can be read by other programs.

- Data used in one run of a program will be available the next time the program is executed.

- Reports can be generated and saved in the form of a file. The report can be viewed at any time just by displaying or printing the file.

Logical Structure

Although a file is just a sequence of bytes located on a disk, your program must make certain assumptions about what these bytes represent, how they are organized, and how they are accessed. The bytes might represent the characters that make up a person's name, or they might be the binary representation of this person's hourly wage rate in the form of the Currency numeric data type. These individual data items are called **fields**. In a file, a group of related fields for a particular employee, department, patient, and so on is called a *record*. Finally, a file consists of a collection of related records. In this context, related records means that the records are all similar in the sense that they are all employee records, or all department records, or all patient records, and so forth.

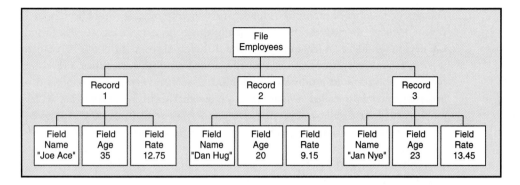

Figure 9.1   *Example of file data hierarchy.*

As shown in Figure 9.1, fields, records and a file form a hierarchy. In this example, the *Employees* file has three records. Each record has fields for the employee's name, age, and pay rate.

Physical Details

Although Figure 9.1 shows the logical relationship between the file, records, and fields, we need a certain amount of information about their physical relationships before we can write the computer programs that can read and write a file of this type. We need to know the answers to the following questions:

- Can the records be accessed in a sequential fashion?
- Can the records be accessed in an arbitrary order?
- Do all the records have the same length?
- What is the order of the fields in a record?
- What is the data type of each field?
- Is the length of a particular field the same on each record?
- How are the fields separated?

Access Methods

A file's records can usually be accessed sequentially, that is, when a record is read or written, the next read or write will refer to the following record. In the case of reading from a file, successive reads can continue until the end of the file has been reached and there are no more unread records. In the case of writing to a file, successive writes can continue until the unused space on the physical medium has been exhausted. This method of accessing records is called **sequential access**. Sequential access is the method most often used to access files.

In many cases, it is necessary to access the records in an arbitrary order. Suppose, for example, that a company has information about its 5,000 employees stored in an Employees file. If a clerk in the personnel department has been requested to change the number of exemptions for a particular employee, it would be very inefficient to have to read the file sequentially until the correct record was found. Clearly, it would be much more efficient if the employee's ID could be used to directly access the correct record. Some files, called **random access files**, allow their records to be accessed randomly in addition to sequentially, and this method of accessing records is called *random access*. Now that database systems are widely employed, files that allow random access are not as prevalent as they used to be. This chapter concentrates on reading and writing records sequentially.

Common Record Formats

A file is composed of records, and if a computer program is going to process records sequentially, the records have to be formatted so that two adjacent records can be differentiated from each other. Similarly, within a given record, there has to be some method of distinguishing between the different fields. Keep these two requirements in mind as we study four common methods of formatting records in a file. Note that within a given file, all the records must have the same format. As we discuss these different formatting schemes, you should refer to Figure 9.2, where the same information is stored in each type of record. Each record has three fields, one each for name, age, and hourly pay rate.

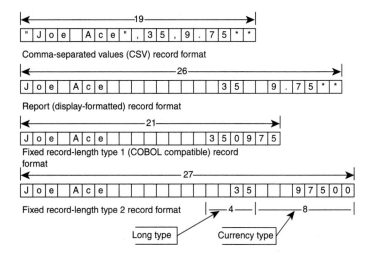

Figure 9.2 *Common record formats.*

Comma-Separated Values (CSV) Record Format

A very common method of formatting a file is to use the comma as a field delimiter. This type of file, sometimes also called **comma-separated values (CSV)**, can be used to exchange information with spreadsheet programs such as Microsoft Excel. Fields that might contain an embedded comma are surrounded by quotation marks ("). Within a field surrounded by quotation marks, an embedded quotation mark is represented by two consecutive quotation marks. Fields that contain numbers are not surrounded by quotation marks. All data are stored as ANSI characters—that is, the ANSI code for a particular character is stored in each byte. The end of record (EOR) is marked by the carriage return-linefeed pair of characters (ANSI codes 13 and 10) at the end of each record and is marked by the "**" in Figure 9.2. In this type of file, a record is the same as a line.

This type of file contains **variable-length records** because the fields and the records have variable lengths. This type of record is usually space efficient because each field is just long enough to contain the required number of characters. The commas, quotation marks, and end of record marker are, of course, overhead and may be significant if a record contains many short fields. See the first sample record in Figure 9.2 for an example of a comma-delimited (comma-separated) record. Note that the comma-delimited record can store data that can be represented as ANSI characters.

Report-Record (Display-Formatted) Format

This *display-formatted* record is used to store information that may be used to produce reports. The file records are formatted so that the file can be sent directly to a printer. Typically, this file might contain a multipage report complete with page headings, footers, and detail, or it might contain a short "read me" type of file that could be displayed by a text editor. The carriage return-linefeed pair of characters is used to mark the end of each line (record) and is marked by the "**" in Figure 9.2. Because this type of file is viewed in a text editor or word processor or printed, no special character is used to delimit the fields.

The primary purpose of a report-record format file is to have a printable file that is understandable to humans. Consequently, it would be unusual to read data from this type of file for purposes other than printing. If a computer reads a file with report-record format, it would normally read the entire line as a string. The string would have to be parsed to extract the values of each field embedded in the record. Extracting each field would involve string manipulation and knowledge of both the order of fields and the exact columnar locations of the fields. See the second sample record in Figure 9.2 for an example of a display-formatted record.

Fixed Record-Length Type 1 (COBOL-Compatible) Format

On occasion you may have to read or write files that are compatible with programs written in the COBOL language. COBOL is one of the oldest, but still popular, programming languages. Alternatively, you may have to develop an application that has to read or write files compatible with COBOL programs. As shown in the third sample record in Figure 9.2, this type of record has the following characteristics:

- Fields have fixed length.
- Records have fixed length.
- All data is stored as ANSI characters.

- Numeric data has leading zeros.

- Numeric data with fractional values is not stored with a decimal point, and the computer programs that read and write this format have to account for the decimal position.

- No special character (or characters) marks the end of the record.

Except for the use of ANSI character codes to represent the data, none of these statements apply to the comma-delimited and display-formatted records.

Fixed Record-Length Type 2 Format

This format is similar to the COBOL-compatible format, except the numeric data is stored in its binary representation. Unlike the other formats, this format may not be compatible with programs written in other languages. This format is useful for programs that have to read or write large amounts of numeric data, because the numeric data will not have to be converted from binary form to ANSI character form during input or output.

Figure 9.3 contains a summary of some of the characteristics of these four different types of formats. In this chapter, we will develop sample programs for each of these file formats.

Format	Fixed Record Length	Fixed Field Lengths	EOR Mark	Input and Output	ANSI Numeric
CSV	No	No	Yes	Yes	Yes
Report	No	No	Yes	Output only	Yes
COBOL	Yes	Yes	No	Yes	Yes
Fixed Type 2	Yes	Yes	No	Yes	No

Figure 9.3 *Characteristics of record formats.*

File Operations

Most programming languages classify file operations in the four categories of *open, read, write,* and *close.* The open operation is used to inform the operating system which file is to be accessed and to associate this file with the appropriate read and write statements in the program. The read and write operations are used to perform input and output operations on the file. Finally, when the program no longer needs access to this file, the close operation is used to inform the operating system that the program has finished processing the file.

Opening a File

You must open a file before you can read from the file or write to the file. In Visual Basic, you use the **Open statement** to open a file. As part of the file open operation, the operating system will allocate a memory storage area, called a **buffer**. Because input and output operations to an external storage device are much slower than internal memory access operations, the operating system will temporarily store input and output data in a buffer.

The *Open* statement along with its syntax is shown here, with optional items enclosed in brackets:

```
Open pathname For mode [Access access] [lock] As [#]filenumber _
    [Len = reclength]
```

Figure 9.4 gives detailed information about each part of the *Open* statement.

Part	Description
pathname	Required. A string that specifies the name of the file including its full path.
mode	Required. Keyword specifying the file mode: *Append, Binary, Input, Output,* or *Random.*
access	Optional. Keyword specifying the operations permitted on the open file: *Read, Write,* and *Read Write.*
lock	Optional. Keyword specifying the operations permitted on the open file by other processes: *Shared, Lock Read, Lock Write,* and *Lock Read Write.*
filenumber	Required. A valid filenumber in the range 1–511, inclusive. Use the *FreeFile* function to obtain the next available file number.
reclength	Optional. Number <= 32,767 (bytes). For files opened for random access, this value is the record length. For sequential files, this value is the number of characters buffered.

Figure 9.4   Description of Open *statement parts.*

It is important to understand the various parts of the *Open* statement listed in Figure 9.4. The *pathname* is used to give the operating system the name of the file that we want to perform input or output operations on. *pathname* can be a string surrounded by quotation marks, but it is good programming practice to use a string variable containing the filename. Some examples of *pathname* are as follows:

```
"Report.txt"
"A:\Sales\Customer.dat"
SalesFileName
```

Input # Statement

The **Input # statement** reads data from an open sequential file and assigns the data to variables. This is the statement that you would use to read information from a file containing records with comma-delimited fields (see Figure 9.2). Normally, the file being read with the *Input #* statement has been written with the *Write #* statement. The *Input #* statement is shown here, and Figure 9.9 gives detailed information about each part of the statement.

```
Input #filenumber, varlist
```

Part	Description
filenumber	Required. Filenumber of the input file.
varlist	Required. One or more variables separated by commas. These variables are assigned values read from the file. No error is generated if a variable is numeric and the data being read is not numeric. Data items in a file must appear in the same order as the variables in varlist, and their type must match.

Figure 9.9   *Description of* Input # *statement parts.*

The following is an example of using the *Input #* statement to read one record from a file formatted, as shown in the first record of Figure 9.2:

```
Input #FileNumber1, Name, Age, HourlyRate
```

Line Input # Statement

The statement you normally use to read information from a report file is the **Line Input # statement** (see Figure 9.2). As its name indicates, this *Line Input* reads a line from an open sequential file and assigns it to a String variable. The *Line Input # statement* is shown here, and Figure 9.10 gives detailed information about each part of the statement.

```
Line Input #filenumber, varname
```

Part	Description
filenumber	Required. Filenumber of the input file.
varname	Required. String variable name. This variable is assigned the line read from the file, but does not include the line terminators.

Figure 9.10   *Description of* Line Input # *statement parts.*

Normally, a file being read with the *Line Input #* statement has been written with the *Print #* statement (described later in the section regarding output). Note that the carriage return-linefeed pair, which marks the end of each line of a report file, is not stored in *varname*. In the example that follows, a line is read from a report file, formatted as shown in the second record of Figure 9.2, and appended to a text box.

```
Line Input #FileNumber2, ReportLine
txtReport.Text = txtReport.Text & ReportLine & vbNewLine
```

Get Statement

When we want to read from a file with fixed record-length format and no CR/LF characters (the last two records in Figure 9.2), we have to use the **Get statement**. We cannot use the *Input* and *Line Input* statements in this situation because they expect the end of each record to be marked by the carriage return-linefeed pair of characters. Normally, the file being read with the *Get* statement has been written with the *Put* statement (described later in the section regarding output). The *Get* statement is shown here, and Figure 9.11 gives detailed information about each part of the statement.

```
Get [#]filenumber, [recnumber], varname
```

Part	Description
filenumber	Required. Filenumber of the input file.
recnumber	Optional. Not needed when reading records sequentially, but the commas must be present.
varname	Required. A variable name into which the record is read.

Figure 9.11   *Description of Get statement parts.*

The following is an example of using of the *Get* statement to read one record from a file with fixed record-length format (the last two records in Figure 9.2) into variable *Employee*:

```
Get #FileNumber3, , Employee
```

Detecting the End of a File (EOF Function)

When your program is reading records sequentially from a file, it has to know when there are no more records to read from the file. Your program can use several techniques to detect the end of the file. One method is to use a special record whose contents differ from the normal records. A record of this type is called a **data sentinel**. If a data sentinel is going to be used, the program that creates the file must add the data sentinel as the last record of the file. In addition, all programs that read from this file must know that the file contains a data sentinel record, and they must know how to identify the record that is the data sentinel.

A more common method of detecting the end of a file is to use a function that indicates when the end of a file has been reached. Typically this function is called after each file read statement has been executed. The function's return value indicates whether the end of a file has been reached. In Visual Basic, this function's name is *EOF*.

The syntax of the **EOF function** is

```
EOF(filenumber)
```

where *filenumber* is the file number of the file being read. The *EOF* function returns *True* when the end of the file has been reached.

In the following code fragment, a report file is read, and each line is appended to the *txtReport* text box. When the last line has been read from the file, the *EOF* function returns *True* and execution will continue with the first statement following *Loop*.

```
Do Until EOF(FileNumber2)
    Line Input #FileNumber2, Line
    txtReport.Text = txtReport.Text & Line & vbNewLine
Loop
```

A final method of detecting the end of a file is to utilize the fact that a Run Time error will be raised if the program attempts to read a nonexistent record. To use this method in Visual Basic, your program must enable an error-handling routine by executing the *On Error* statement. When your program attempts to read a record that follows the end of file, an error is generated and program execution will transfer to the error-handling routine. This routine must check to make sure that the error was caused by the attempt to read beyond the end of file and then take appropriate action. In this chapter, we will use the *EOF* function to detect the end of a file.

Writing to a File (Write)

After a file has been opened, your program can begin writing to the file. Visual Basic has several statements that are used to perform file output, and Figure 9.12 lists the Visual Basic file output statements that can be used to write a file sequentially. In later sections of this chapter, sample programs use each of these statements.

File Output Statements	Used with Record Format
Write #	Comma-delimited (CSV)
Print #	Report (display-formatted)
Put	Fixed record-length (COBOL-compatible)
	Fixed record-length (type 2)

Figure 9.12 *Visual Basic file input statements.*

Write # Statement

The **Write # statement** writes data to an open sequential file. This is the statement that you should use to write information to a file that contains records with comma-delimited fields (see Figure 9.2). Normally, the file being written with the *Write #* statement will be read by the *Input #* statement. The *Write #* statement is shown here, and Figure 9.13 gives detailed information about each part of the statement.

```
Write #filenumber, [outputlist]
```

Part	Description
filenumber	Required. Filenumber of the output file.
outputlist	Required. One or more variables separated by commas. The values of these variables are written as comma-delimited fields to the file in the same sequence as they are listed in the *Write* statement. If a particular variable is type String, the field will be enclosed by quotation marks.

Figure 9.13 *Description of* Write # *statement parts.*

The first record of Figure 9.2 shows an example of the use of the *Write #* statement to write one record with comma-delimited fields to a file formatted as shown here:

```
Write #FileNumber1, Name, Age, HourlyRate
```

Print # Statement

The **Print # statement** writes display-formatted data to a sequential file. This corresponds with the second record in Figure 9.2. Because this type of file may be printed, you must format the data so that it is easy to read. Data written with *Print #* is usually read from a file with the *Line Input #* statement. The *Spc* and *Tab* functions can be used with the *Print #* statement to position output at the desired column. The *Print #* statement along with its syntax is shown here, with optional items enclosed in brackets. The "|" between the *Spc* and *Tab* functions means that one or the other may be used. Figure 9.14 gives detailed information about the statement and its parts

```
Print #filenumber, [outputlist]
```

where *outputlist* is one or more of the following:

```
[{Spc(n) | Tab[(n)]}] [expression] [charpos]
```

cmdAdd_Click Event Procedure

Each time the user clicks the *Add* button, the variable *fMaxID*, which keeps track of the number of employees, is incremented by one. The *fEmp* array has its size increased by one element, and the value of *fMaxID* is converted to a String and stored in the *txtID* text box. The information that has been entered into the text boxes for name, age, and hourly rate is stored into the array, using *fMaxID* as the subscript.

cmdChange_Click Event Procedure

After the user has selected a particular employee by clicking the *Find* button, it is very easy to change any of the information. The user just makes changes to one or more of name, age, and hourly rate, and then clicks the *Change* button. The entry in the *txtID* text box is used as a subscript, and the employee information is copied to the array.

There is a problem with this particular implementation of *Change*. In addition to the lack of validation on the individual items, the user could change the *ID* entry; then when the *Add* button is clicked, the data might be copied to the wrong employee. It would be better to lock the text box after a *Find* so that this error could not be made. This improvement will be an exercise at the end of the chapter.

cmdSave_Click Event Procedure

After the user has finished adding information about new employees and made changes to existing employees, the *Save* button is clicked. As shown in Figure 9.17, this causes the contents of the array to be written to an output file. If the user wants to use a different file for output, the user must be sure to change the entry in the *File Name* text box prior to clicking the *Save* button.

When the *Save* button is clicked, the *Open* statement is executed. Because the mode option is *Output*, an existing file with the same name as the name entered in the *File Name* text box will be overwritten without any warning. This "feature" is probably not desirable, and one of the end-of-chapter exercises asks you to correct this problem.

After the file has been opened, a *For...Next* loop is used to copy the contents of the array to the output file. The loop iterates *EmpID* times, and its body has only one statement, the *Write #* statement. Notice how the *Write #* statement has been specifically designed to make writing to a CSV file a very simple operation. This file output statement automatically encloses string fields within quotation marks and converts numeric data items to their ANSI character representation. After the last record has been written, the output file is closed.

```vb
' Program CSV, Chapter 9
Option Explicit

Private Type EmployeeType
    Name As String
    Age As Long
    HourlyRate As Currency
End Type

Private fEmp() As EmployeeType  ' Array of employees
Private fMaxID As Long          ' Number of employees

Private Sub cmdAdd_Click()
    ' Enlarge the array
    fMaxID = fMaxID + 1
    ReDim Preserve fEmp(1 To fMaxID)

    ' Add the information to the array
    txtID.Text = Format(fMaxID, "0")
    lblMaxID.Caption = Format(fMaxID, "0")
    fEmp(fMaxID).Age = CLng(txtAge.Text)
    fEmp(fMaxID).HourlyRate = CCur(txtHourlyRate.Text)
    fEmp(fMaxID).Name = txtName.Text
End Sub

Private Sub cmdChange_Click()
    Dim EmpID As Long

    ' Get the EmpID and carry out the change
    EmpID = CLng(txtID.Text)
    fEmp(EmpID).Age = CLng(txtAge.Text)
    fEmp(EmpID).HourlyRate = CCur(txtHourlyRate.Text)
    fEmp(EmpID).Name = txtName.Text
End Sub

Private Sub cmdExit_Click()
    Unload frmMain
End Sub

Private Sub cmdFind_Click()
    Call FindEmployee
End Sub

Private Sub cmdLoad_Click()
    Dim EmpFileNum As Long
    Dim EmpID As Long

    ' Open the Employee file for input
    EmpFileNum = FreeFile
    Open txtFileName.Text For Input As #EmpFileNum

    ' Read the file into the array, enlarging the array on-the-fly
    EmpID = 0
    Do Until EOF(EmpFileNum)
        EmpID = EmpID + 1
        ReDim Preserve fEmp(1 To EmpID)
        Input #EmpFileNum, fEmp(EmpID).Name, fEmp(EmpID).Age, _
            fEmp(EmpID).HourlyRate
    Loop
    fMaxID = EmpID
```

continues

```
        ' Display the number of employees and the first employee
        lblMaxID.Caption = Format(fMaxID, "0")
        txtID.Text = "1"
        Call FindEmployee

        Close #EmpFileNum
End Sub

Private Sub cmdSave_Click()
    Dim EmpFileNum As Long
    Dim EmpID As Long

        ' Open the Employee file for output
        EmpFileNum = FreeFile
        Open txtFileName.Text For Output As #EmpFileNum

        ' Write contents of array to the output file
        For EmpID = 1 To fMaxID
            Write #EmpFileNum, fEmp(EmpID).Name, fEmp(EmpID).Age, _
                fEmp(EmpID).HourlyRate
        Next EmpID

        ' Close the file
        Close #EmpFileNum
End Sub

Private Sub Form_Load()
    fMaxID = 0
    lblMaxID.Caption = Format(fMaxID, "0")
End Sub

' Use entry in txtID to find and display the employee
Private Sub FindEmployee()
    Dim EmpID As Long

    EmpID = CLng(txtID.Text)
    txtName.Text = fEmp(EmpID).Name
    txtAge.Text = Format(fEmp(EmpID).Age, "0")
    txtHourlyRate.Text = Format(fEmp(EmpID).HourlyRate, "0.00")
End Sub
```

Figure 9.17 *Code for program* CSV.

Add a Report to Program CSV

We will now modify the *CSV* program so that when the *Save* button is clicked, in addition to the creation of the CSV file, a report file is also created. This report file will contain the same information that is in the CSV file; unlike the CSV file, however, it will be formatted in a form suitable for printing. In particular, we will neatly line up the data in columns and add a title, a date, and column headings to the beginning of the report. The name for the report file will be the same as the CSV file except the report file will have the file extension .TXT. The name of the modified program will be *CSV with Report*, but the user interface will be unchanged and appear as shown in Figure 9.16.

Report File Layout

The first step we must take is to decide how the information should be displayed. Because the printer we are using normally prints 80 columns wide, and the information we are displaying for each employee is limited to employee ID, name, age, and hourly rate, we can display the information for two employees on each line of the report. The person in the organization that will be reading the report wants the report arranged so that the employee IDs are in ascending order down the left column and then continue starting with the top of the right column.

A report for a company with 51 employees would have the first several lines of the report appear as shown in Figure 9.18. The left column lists employees 1 through 26, and the right column lists employees 27 through 51. Because the total number of employees is odd, the left column contains one more employee than the right column.

E M P L O Y E E   R E P O R T

As of 9/30/98

Emp ID	Name	Age	Hourly Rate	Emp ID	Name	Age	Hourly Rate
1	Thomas O Whitten	20	10.76	27	Gerald Hummer	22	20.99
2	Ralph J Alderfer	34	17.33	28	Donald D King	18	18.37
3	Owen F Detweiler	27	7.90	29	James F Lyman	49	8.69
4	Stephen Donneger	26	21.50	30	Susan O Moyer	19	13.20

Figure 9.18   *Report file layout.*

To prevent having to do a lot of "trial-and-error" programming, we can assign widths to the different columns and, where needed, spacing between columns. Figure 9.19 shows our sketch of the left column of the report. Because the layout for both columns is the same, there is no need to prepare a sketch for the right column. As you can see in Figure 9.19, the width of each column is 35 characters. Therefore, starting the right column at the middle of the page, character position 40 for a page with 80 columns should yield a balanced-looking, two-column report.

In Figure 9.19 we have identified each width and spacing with a symbolic name. Each name is preceded with the prefix "cf", because these symbols will become constants in our program with form scope. Note that while the name is left adjusted, all the numeric items in the report are right adjusted. We are also making the assumption that the report will be printed with a font, such as Courier, which has fixed character spacing. If the report is printed with a font that has proportional spacing, the numbers will not be neatly aligned.

```
                   cfIDWidth
                       cfIDNameSpacing           cfRateWidth
                           cfNameWidth      cfAgeWidth
        |-3-| /                          |    |      |——7——|
        Emp|-2-|——————————20——————————|—3—|Hourly
           ID  Name                     Age    Rate
            1  Thomas O Whitten           20   10.76
            2  Ralph J Alderfer           34   17.33
            3  Owen F Detweiler           27    7.90
```

Figure 9.19   *Detailed report file layout of left column.*

Description of Program Code

One advantage of event-driven programming is that your program is automatically split up into procedures. This oftentimes leads to easier modification of your program, because the program already consists of many procedures, each associated with an event. To produce our new program, we make a copy of the folder containing the program *CSV* name it (and the program) CSV with Report. Now open the copy, add several constants to the General Declarations section and add one line at the end of the *cmdSave_Click* event procedure. All the additional code will be in new functions and procedures that we add to the program, as displayed in Figure 9.21.

The first thing we do is add constants for the widths and spacing that are listed in Figure 9.19. Because most of these constants are used by more than one procedure, we add them to the General Declarations section of the form file, as shown in Figure 9.20. In addition to the constants from Figure 9.19, we include *cfPageWidth*, which specifies the total number of character positions in the page; *cfReportExtension*, which specifies the file extension of the report file; and *cfReportTitle*, which specifies the title of the report.

The only other modification of existing code is to insert the *Call* statement

```
Call GenerateReport
```

just before the *End Sub* statement in event procedure *cmdSave_Click*.

```
Const cfAgeWidth As Long = 3
Const cfIDNameSpacing As Long = 2
Const cfIDWidth As Long = 3
Const cfNameWidth As Long = 20
Const cfPageWidth As Long = 80
Const cfRateWidth As Long = 7
Const cfReportExtension As String = "txt"
Const cfReportTitle As String = "E M P L O Y E E    R E P O R T"
```

Figure 9.20   *Constant declarations in program CSV with Report.*

GenerateReport Procedure

When the user clicks the *Save* button in program *CSV with Report*, the contents of the existing arrays are written to the CSV file. After the CSV file is closed, the general procedure *GenerateReport* is called. As shown in Figure 9.21, this procedure is a *driver*, or coordinator, of several other modules that it calls in the process of producing the report file. We could have written all the code in one procedure, but then we would have had a monstrously large routine that would be difficult to understand and modify as the need arises. As it is currently written, the *GenerateReport* procedure is short and easy to understand. Notice the use of descriptive names for the functions and procedures that it calls. The complexity of producing the report has been reduced to five simple tasks:

- Invoke function *GetReportFileName*, which returns the name of the report file.

- Open the report file using the string returned by *GetReportFileName*.

- Call procedure *WriteHeader* that writes the title, date, and two-column header lines to the open file.

- Call procedure *WriteDetail*, which writes the rest of the report.

- Close the report file.

GetReportFileName Function

The task of function *GetReportFileName* is to take the filename that has been entered in *txtFileName* and return a string that is the same filename but with the extension of .TXT. The code can also handle the situation where the filename that has been entered into the text box does not have an extension.

As it stands, this routine has a few problems. If the CSV file has an extension of .TXT, this program will not warn the user; instead, it will silently overwrite the CSV file. If the filename has two or more embedded periods, this routine will find only the leftmost period. Both of these shortcomings would have to be fixed before this program could be considered suitable for release to a user.

WriteHeader Procedure

The *WriteHeader* procedure is passed the filenumber of the report file. The procedure formats each header line, and using the filenumber it then writes the header lines to the report file using the *Print #* statement. The individual fields of the column headers are precisely aligned by using the *LeftAlign* and *RightAlign* functions that are part of our programming tool kit, *basTools*. These functions were introduced in Chapter 4. Using the *Space* function generates the spaces between the right-aligned employee ID and the left-aligned name.

Because the report is a two-column report, each header line consists of two identical strings. Note the use of the *Tab* function in the *Print #* statements, which makes it very easy to start the right column of each header line at exactly the center of the page.

WriteDetail Procedure

Procedure *WriteDetail* is the most complex of our procedures. We have designed it in such a way that it can be modified to add several features that would normally have to be present. As currently written, column headings are only written at the beginning of the report. Many reports are longer than one page, and usually you want a header at the top of each new page. If the report will be longer than one page, the user will probably want a page number on each page. As we start adding features to our simple report, we will want to put some of these items in a *footer* at the bottom of each page.

Actually producing reports can turn out to be quite complex, but you may want to use special programs called *report writers* instead of spending a lot of effort on writing customized programs to produce reports.

TIP

Consider purchasing standard packages such as report writers, sort utilities, and database systems.

The most complicated part of designing the *WriteDetail* procedure is to compose an algorithm to handle reports with varying numbers of employees. We have this problem because our user wants a report with the employee IDs arranged in ascending order down the left column and then continue at the top of the right column. Naturally, the user wants both columns to have the same number of rows when the number of employees is even. When the number of employees is odd, the user wants the left column to have one more row than the right column. We will, of course, need some special logic to handle the last line, because the right-hand column will not have an entry when the number of employees is odd.

We keep in mind the fact that the ID of an employee is also the subscript used to access the array containing their name, age, and hourly rate. If we were just printing out the employees' names, a particular *Print #* statement would have the general form

```
Print #Filenumber Name(ID); Tab(40); Name(ID + Delta)
```

and this statement would be inside a *For...Next* loop. *Delta* is the integer (constant for any particular report) that must be added to the left-column subscript to generate the subscript for the right column. *Delta* depends only on the total number of employees, *fMaxID*, and will be approximately equal to one half of *fMaxID*.

When the number of employees is even, *Delta* is exactly one half of *fMaxID*. When the number of employees is odd, we still want to divide by two, but we have to round the result of the division up to the next nearest integer. Because Visual Basic does not have a function that performs this calculation, we decide that we will write our own function. Using the analogy that the ceiling of a room is higher than our desk, we decide to name our function *Ceiling*. By choosing this name, we will be reminded that our new function rounds up, rather than down. Furthermore, if at some future date we learn to program in the programming languages C++ or Java, we will find that we are already familiar with an identical function in both of those languages called *Ceil* (short for *Ceiling*).

Now that we are able to calculate *Delta*, we can call the function *GetDetail* twice from inside the *For...Next* loop. *GetDetail* takes the employee ID and returns a string properly formatted for the *Print #* statement. As shown in Figure 9.21, the *Tab* function is used to position string *DetailR* at the beginning of the right column.

When all lines, except the last line have been written, execution leaves the *For...Next* loop and enters the logic that writes the last line. If the total number of employees (*fMaxID*) is even, both halves of the last line are written. Otherwise, only the left-column entry is written.

GetDetail Function

The *GetDetail* function is passed an employee ID, and uses the ID's value as a subscript to access the elements of the array that contain information about the particular employee. The spacing and width constants along with the *Left-* and *RightAlign* functions are used to prepare a string formatted properly for either column of the report. This formatted string is returned to the calling procedure.

```
Private Sub GenerateReport()
    Dim ReportFile As Long
    Dim ReportFileName As String

    ' Open the report file
    ReportFileName = GetReportFileName
    ReportFile = FreeFile
    Open ReportFileName For Output As #ReportFile

    ' Write the two header lines
    Call WriteHeader(ReportFile)

    ' Write the detail lines
    Call WriteDetail(ReportFile)

    Close #ReportFile
End Sub

Private Function GetDetail(ByVal EmpID As Long) As String
    GetDetail = RightAlign(Format(EmpID, "0"), cfIDWidth) & _
        Space(cfIDNameSpacing) & _
        LeftAlign(fEmp(EmpID).Name, cfNameWidth) & _
        RightAlign(Format(fEmp(EmpID).Age, "0"), cfAgeWidth) & _
        RightAlign(Format(fEmp(EmpID).HourlyRate, "0.00"), cfRateWidth)
End Function

Private Function GetReportFileName() As String
    Dim Point As Long
```

continues

```
        ' Replace the file extension with ReportExtension
        Point = InStr(txtFileName.Text, ".")
        If Point = 0 Then
            GetReportFileName = txtFileName.Text & "." & cfReportExtension
        Else
            GetReportFileName = Left(txtFileName.Text, Point) & _
                cfReportExtension
        End If
End Function

Private Sub WriteDetail(ByVal File As Long)
    Dim DetailL As String   ' Left half of detail line
    Dim DetailR As String   ' Right half of detail line
    Dim Delta As Long       ' Subscript difference between the 2 columns
    Dim EmpID As Long

    ' Write the detail lines except for the last line
    Delta = Ceiling(fMaxID / 2) ' Ceiling rounds up to next integer
    For EmpID = 1 To Delta - 1
        DetailL = GetDetail(EmpID)
        DetailR = GetDetail(EmpID + Delta)
        Print #File, DetailL; Tab(cfPageWidth \ 2); DetailR
    Next EmpID

    ' Last line depends upon whether fMaxID is even or odd
    DetailL = GetDetail(EmpID)
    If fMaxID Mod 2 = 0 Then      ' fMaxID is even
        DetailR = GetDetail(EmpID + Delta)
    Else
        DetailR = ""
    End If
    Print #File, DetailL; Tab(cfPageWidth \ 2); DetailR
End Sub

Private Sub WriteHeader(ByVal File As Long)
    Dim Header1 As String
    Dim Header2 As String
    Dim Title2 As String

    ' Write the title, date, and one blank line
    Print #File, Tab((cfPageWidth - Len(cfReportTitle)) / 2); _
        cfReportTitle
    Title2 = "As of " & Format(Date, "General Date")
    Print #File, Tab((cfPageWidth - Len(Title2)) / 2); Title2; _
        vbNewLine

    ' Build the two headers and then write them
    Header1 = RightAlign("Emp", cfIDWidth) & Space(cfIDNameSpacing) & _
        RightAlign("Hourly", cfNameWidth + cfAgeWidth + cfRateWidth)
    Header2 = RightAlign("ID", cfIDWidth) & Space(cfIDNameSpacing) & _
        LeftAlign("Name", cfNameWidth) & _
        RightAlign("Age", cfAgeWidth) & _
        RightAlign("Rate", cfRateWidth)
    Print #File, Header1; Tab(cfPageWidth \ 2); Header1
    Print #File, Header2; Tab(cfPageWidth \ 2); Header2
End Sub
```

Figure 9.21 *Additional code for program* CSV with Report.

Ceiling Function

Figure 9.23 contains the code for the *Ceiling* function. This function is stored in the standard module *basTools* and is part of our programming toolbox. We have already discussed why this function is needed by program *CSV with Report*. The function is passed a type Double number X, and if the fractional part of X is zero (that is, X is an integer), X is returned without change. Otherwise, X is rounded up to the next nearest integer. A more technical, precise, and briefer explanation of what this function does is as follows: The *Ceiling* function returns the smallest integer not less than X. See Figure 9.22 for examples of how the function processes negative and positive numbers.

X	$Ceiling(X)$
−4.3	−4.0
−4.0	−4.0
4.0	4.0
4.3	5.0

Figure 9.22   *Sample calculations performed by* Ceiling *function.*

As shown in Figure 9.23, if X is equal to or less than zero, *Ceiling* uses the Visual Basic function *Fix* to perform the calculation. For numbers greater than zero, X is tested to see whether its fractional value is already zero. If X is not an integer, one is added to X and the resulting value is processed by the *Fix* function and returned. If X is already an integer, no further processing is needed and X is returned unchanged.

```
' Purpose:    Returns the smallest integer not less than the argument
' Input:      Double value to have its ceiling calculated
' Returns:    Double value with zero fractional part
Public Function Ceiling(ByVal X As Double) As Double
    If X <= 0 Then
        Ceiling = Fix(X)
    Else
        If X <> Fix(X) Then
            Ceiling = Fix(X + 1)
        Else
            Ceiling = X
        End If
    End If
End Function
```

Figure 9.23   *Code for function* Ceiling.

Programming with Fixed Record-Length Type 1

We now turn our attention to modifying our *CSV* program so that it will read and write fixed-length records. In particular, we are interested in the format that is read and written by COBOL programs. This format was discussed earlier and is depicted as the third record type in Figure 9.2.

Employee File Record Layout

A record is fixed length because all its fields are fixed length. Unlike the situation with CSV records, programs that read and write files with fixed-length records need specific information about the length of each field of the record. We recall from our discussion earlier in this chapter that numeric data with fractional values is not stored with a decimal point. Therefore, if a field contains a numeric value that is not an integer, the programs must know the position of the assumed decimal point. What this all means is that programs that read and write numeric data must manipulate the data so that the decimal point is removed before writing and inserted after reading.

After discussions with our user about the nature of the employee data, we can prepare the record layout table shown in Figure 9.24. The *99.99* entry for Rate in the Decimal Point column is a notation borrowed from the COBOL programming language to document the position of the assumed decimal point.

Name	Description	Length	Position	Decimal Point
Name	Alphabetic	20	1–20	n/a
Age	Long	2	21–22	n/a
Rate	Currency	4	23–26	99.99

Figure 9.24   *Record layout table, type 1.*

Figure 9.25 shows how the information for three employees is stored on the disk. Note that the third employee's hourly rate of $7.90 is stored with a leading zero. This is a general characteristic of numeric data in this type of format—that is, all the characters in a numeric field must themselves be numeric.

Although Figure 9.25 is useful for visualization purposes, you should not be misled by the illustration and conclude that each record is stored as a separate line. As shown in Figures 9.2 and 9.25, no special characters mark the end of each record. Because each record has the same length and the program reading or writing the file knows this length, the program and operating system can successfully access consecutive records.

Figure 9.25   *File with three records, type 1.*

Description of Program Code

To create program *Fixed Record Length Type 1*, you should start with program *CSV*, copy the program, and name it Fixed Record Length Type 1. Just like the preceding program, we will not be making any changes to the form, but we will modify the program so that it can read and write type 1 fixed record-length files. In the discussion that follows, we cover only those parts of the modified program that differ from program *CSV*. Modification of the program consists of the following steps:

- Defining the record type
- Modifying the *cmdLoad_Click* event procedure
- Modifying the *cmdSave_Click* event procedure

Defining the Record Type

Because all the records in our *Employee* file must have the same length, we will create a user-defined type and give it the name *EmployeeRecordType*. We will then use this new type to declare a record variable with the name *fEmpRec*. The data stored in this variable is an exact image of how the data is stored in the file as a record. *fEmpRec* will be used in the *Put* statement when we write records and in the *Get* statement when we read records. All of this will become clear as we develop our program. Figure 9.26 contains code that should be inserted in the General Declarations section of the program.

Note that all fields, even the numeric ones, are composed of fixed-length strings. First, they are String type because all the data is stored in the file as ANSI characters. Second, the strings are fixed length because each field must be fixed length, which in turn guarantees that the record itself is fixed length. Look at the notation used to define a fixed-length string in Figure 9.26. You should compare this code with Figure 9.25 and note the agreement between the lengths of the strings in the record definition and the field lengths in the diagram.

In actual use, there is little difference between variable- and fixed-length strings, except for the following behavior when assigning a string to a fixed-length string:

- If the source string is too long for the fixed-length string, truncation occurs.
- If the source string is shorter than the fixed-length string, the resultant string is padded with enough trailing spaces to fill the string.

```
Private Type EmployeeRecordType
    Name As String * 20
    Age As String * 2
    HourlyRate As String * 4
End Type

Private fEmpRec As EmployeeRecordType
```

Figure 9.26 *Record definition for program* Fixed Record Length Type 1.

Modifying the cmdLoad_Click Event Procedure

If you compare the *cmdLoad_Click* event procedure for program *CSV* in Figure 9.17 with the version shown in Figure 9.27, you will see many similarities. Both procedures open the file, size the arrays, copy the contents of the *Employee* file into the arrays, and close the file. The details do differ, however, and you should pay attention to these differences.

The Open Statement

We open the file in *Random* mode even though we will be processing the input file sequentially. We have to use this mode because we want the value specified in the *Len* clause to be interpreted as the record length. The somewhat misleading portion of the *Open* statement

```
Len = Len(fEmpRec)
```

is interpreted as follows. The *Len* on the right of the assignment statement is the same *Len* function we have previously used to find the length of a string. As used here, the *Len* function calculates the number of characters in the record variable *fEmpRec*. The value returned by the *Len* function is assigned to the *Len* on the left and is interpreted as the record length by the *Open* statement.

Sizing the Array and Reading the File

Unlike program *CSV*, in this program we can determine how many records are contained in the *Employee* file. We can do this because each record has the same length. After the file has been opened, we use the *LOF* function to find the length of the input file. Dividing the file length by the record length gives the number of records, and this result is assigned to variable *fMaxID*. Now that we know the number of employees, we can size the dynamic array to its final size with only one execution of the *ReDim* statement.

Next we use a *For...Next* loop to read records from the file and store the data in the array. Unlike program *CSV*, we do not need to use the *EOF* function to determine when to stop reading from the file. In the body of the loop, the *Get* statement reads a record from the file into the record variable *fEmpRec*. Then three assignment statements extract the data from the fields of the record. Note that we have to divide the hourly rate by 100, because the rate is stored without a decimal point in the file.

```
Private Sub cmdLoad_Click()
    Dim EmpFile As Long
    Dim EmpID As Long

    ' Open the Employee file for input
    EmpFile = FreeFile
    Open txtFileName.Text For Random Access Read As #EmpFile _
        Len = Len(fEmpRec)

    ' Calculate the number of records in the file and size the array
    fMaxID = LOF(EmpFile) \ Len(fEmpRec)
    ReDim fEmp(1 To fMaxID)

    ' Read the file into the array
    For EmpID = 1 To fMaxID
        Get #EmpFile, , fEmpRec
        fEmp(EmpID).Name = fEmpRec.Name
        fEmp(EmpID).Age = CLng(fEmpRec.Age)
        fEmp(EmpID).HourlyRate = CCur(fEmpRec.HourlyRate) / 100
    Next EmpID

    ' Display the number of employees and the first employee
    lblMaxID.Caption = Format(fMaxID, "0")
    txtID.Text = "1"
    Call FindEmployee

    Close #EmpFile
End Sub
```

Figure 9.27   *Code for procedure* cmdLoad_Click *in program* Fixed Record Length Type 1.

Modifying the cmdSave_Click Event Procedure

Again, there are a lot of similarities between the *cmdSave_Click* event procedure for program *CSV* in Figure 9.17 and the version shown in Figure 9.28. Both procedures erase any existing file with the same name as the output file, open the file, copy the contents of the array to the *Employee* file, and close the file. The details do differ, however, and you should pay attention to these differences.

Delete the Old Output File

In the *CSV* program, when the user clicks the *Save* button the entry in the *File Name* text box is used as the name of the output file. If a file by this name already exists, the file is deleted and a new file is created with the same name. We mentioned earlier that during the design period you should discuss this topic with the user. In most cases, your program should act as follows: If the file exists, the program queries the user and gets his permission before deleting the file.

We want the program we are currently working on to have the same behavior as the *CSV* program. When the *Open* statement is executed in *Random* mode, however, an existing file is not deleted, but it is just reused. Normally, this is not the kind of behavior we want, because some of the data in the existing file may still be present when we close the file. This unwanted situation will occur when the existing file is longer than the file that would normally be created when we click the *Save* button.

477

The solution to this problem is to erase any existing file with the same name as our output file. We can easily do this by opening the file with mode *Output* and then immediately close the file.

Writing the File

Just like the *CSV* program, we use a *For...Next* loop to copy the contents of the array to the file. Inside the body of the loop, we copy the employee information from the array to the fields in the *fEmployee* record variable. Note that all numeric information must be written with leading zeroes and cannot contain a decimal point. We use the *Format* function to format our data with leading zeros, and in the case of the hourly rate, we have to multiply by 100 so that the rate is stored in the file as cents rather than dollars. The contents of *fEmployee* are written to the file by using the *Put* statement.

You should test program *Fixed Record Length Type 1* thoroughly by using it to create a file through a series of Adds, one for each new employee. After you have added several employees, click the *Save* button. Then click the *Load* button and make sure that all employees are present with the same information that you originally entered. The files on the CD that accompanies this book include a type 1 data file containing 51 records.

```
Private Sub cmdSave_Click()
    Dim EmpFile As Long
    Dim EmpID As Long

    ' If the output file exists, erase it
    EmpFile = FreeFile
    Open txtFileName.Text For Output As #EmpFile
    Close #EmpFile

    ' Open the Employee file in random mode
    EmpFile = FreeFile
    Open txtFileName.Text For Random Access Write As #EmpFile _
        Len = Len(fEmpRec)

    ' Write contents of array to the output file
    For EmpID = 1 To fMaxID
        fEmpRec.Name = fEmp(EmpID).Name
        fEmpRec.Age = Format(fEmp(EmpID).Age, "00")
        fEmpRec.HourlyRate = Format(fEmp(EmpID).HourlyRate * 100, _
            "0000")
        Put #EmpFile, , fEmpRec
    Next EmpID

    ' Close the file
    Close #EmpFile
End Sub
```

Figure 9.28 *Code for procedure* cmdSave_Click *in program* Fixed Record Length Type 1.

Programming with Fixed Record-Length Type 2

The fourth type of file organization we are concerned with also has records with constant length; unlike the type 1 file type, however, numeric data is stored in its binary representation in the file. A record of this type is depicted as the fourth sample record in Figure 9.2. To produce a program that can read and write records of this type, we will again modify the *CSV* program. Our new program will actually be somewhat simpler than the preceding program we developed to read the type 1 record format. The program is simpler because there will be no need for the program to keep track of the decimal point in numeric data. In addition, the program will not need to convert numeric data in the age and hourly rate arrays to ANSI character codes prior to writing data or the opposite conversion when reading data.

Employee File Record Layout

Figure 9.29 shows the record layout for the type 2 file. You should compare this layout with the layout for the type 1 file in Figure 9.24. The main difference is that a numeric field stored as a Long will always require four character positions in the type 2 file and a Currency field will always require eight character positions. Contrast this with the type 1 file situation where a large integer might require as many as 10 characters, and a large currency value might require as many as 17 character positions. In general, numeric data stored in the type 2 format will require less disk storage than the type 1 format, and input and output operations should be somewhat more efficient because the numeric data do not have to be converted to or from their binary representations during file I/O.

Name	Description	Length	Position
Name	Alphabetic	20	1–20
Age	Long	4	21–24
Rate	Currency	8	25–32

Figure 9.29 *Record layout table, type 2.*

Figure 9.30 is an illustration of how information for three employees is stored on the disk. You should compare this figure with Figure 9.25. The only difference between the two types of records is the way that numeric data is stored on the disk. The cross hatching in Figure 9.30 for the age and hourly rate fields indicates that the data is stored on the disk exactly as the same data is stored in memory.

Unlike the situation with the type 1 file format in which you can display the contents of the file by just printing the file or by loading the file into a text editor, a type 2 file should not be printed. You should not print a type 2 file because the numeric data is not converted to ANSI character codes before being stored in the file. If you persist and do print the file, you will not be able to read the numeric

Form-scope Variables:

Form-scope Variables

fEmpFile	Long	(File number for Employee file)
fName	String	(Employee name)
fPayFile	Integer	(File number for Pay file)
fPayRate	Currency	(Employee hourly pay rate)
fSSN	Long	(Employee Social Security number)
fIncomeTable()	Currency	(Array of income levels to match with tax rates)
fTaxRateTable()	Double	(Array of tax rates to match with income levels)

End Form-scope Variables

Form Load Event:

```
Begin FormLoad
    NumArgs = ParseCmdLine(CmdLineArgs)
    If NumArgs = 3
        If IOFilesOK(CmdLineArgs) = True
            Call LoadTaxTables(CmdLineArgs(1))
            fEmpFile = 2
            Open CmdLineArgs(2) for Input as #fEmpFile
            fPayFile = 3
            Open CmdLineArgs(3) for Output as #fPayFile
            Call LoadEmployee
        Else
            Unload frmMain
    Else
        Display "Not enough args"
        Unload frmMain
End FormLoad
```

ParseCmdLine Function:

```
Begin ParseCmdLine(CmdLineArgs())
    CmdLineLen = Len(CmdLine)
    MaxArgs = MaxSub(CmdLineArgs)
    InArg = False
    NumArgs = 0
    I = 1
    Do While I <= CmdLineLen
        Ch = CmdLine(I)
        If Ch <> " " And Ch <> Tab
            If InArg = False
                If NumArgs = MaxArgs
                    Display "Too many arguments on command line"
                    Exit Loop
                NumArgs = NumArgs + 1
                InArg = True
            CmdLineArgs(NumArgs) = CmdLineArgs(NumArgs) + Ch
        Else
            InArg = False
        I = I + 1
    Loop
    Return NumArgs
End ParseCmdLine
```

IOFilesOK Function:

```
Begin IOFilesOK(CmdLineArgs())
    Result = False
    If FileExists(CmdLineArgs(1)) <> 0
        Display "No tax table file"
    Else If FileExists(CmdLineArgs(2)) <> 0
        Display "No employee file"
    Else If FileExists(CmdLineArgs(3)) = 0
        Display "Pay file exists. Continue?"
        If Response = "Yes"
            Result = True
    Else If FileExists(CmdLineArgs(3)) = 1
        Display "Pay file path error"
    Else
        Result = True
    Return Result
End IOFilesOK
```

FileExists Function:

```
Begin FileExists(FileName)
    Open FileName for Input as #1
    If Open Was Successful
        Result = 0
        Close #1
    Else If file path error
        Result = 1
    Else
        Result = -1
    Return Result
End FileExists
```

LoadTaxTables Procedure:

```
Begin LoadTaxTables(TaxFile)
    Open TaxFile for Input as #1
    I = 0
    Do Until EOF(#1) = True
        I = I + 1
        Input #1, fIncomeTable(I), fTaxRateTable(I)
    Loop
    Close #1
End LoadTaxTables
```

LoadEmployee Procedure:

```
Begin LoadEmployee
    Clear Hours text box
    IF EOF(fEmpFile)
        Display "No more employees to process"
        Clear Name label
        Clear SSN label
        Disable Next button
    Else
        Input #fEmpFile, fSSN, fName, fPayRate
        Display fSSN on SSN label
        Display fName on Name label
End LoadEmployee
```

continues

Next Click Event:
```
Begin Next Click
    If txtHours <> ""
        If HoursIsValid
            Assign Hours text box to Hrs
            Call CalcPay(Hrs, Gross, Tax, Net)
            Write #fPayFile, fSSN, Hrs, Gross, Tax, Net
            Call LoadEmployee
    Else
        Call LoadEmployee
    Set focus on Hours text box
End Next Click
```
HoursIsValid Function:
```
Begin HoursIsValid()
    If Hours text box is numeric
        Assign Hours text box to Hrs
        If Hrs >= 5 And Hrs <= 100
            Result = True
        Else
            Result = False
            Display "Invalid value for Hours"
    Else
        Result = False
        Display "Hours must be numeric"
    Return Result
End HoursIsValid
```
CalcPay Procedure:
```
Begin CalcPay(Hrs, Gross, Tax, Net)
    If Hrs > 40
        Gross = fPayRate * (40 + (Hrs – 40) * 1.5)
        Gross = RoundCur2(Gross)
    Else
        Gross = RoundCur2(fPayRate * Hrs)
    I = 1
    Do Until Gross * 52 < fIncomeTable(I)
        I = I + 1
    Loop
    Tax = Gross * fTaxRateTable(I)
    Tax = RoundCur2(Tax)
    Net = Gross – Tax
End CalcPay
```
RoundCur2 Function:
```
Begin RoundCur2(Money)
    Cents = Int(Money * 100 + .5)
    Return Cents / 100
End RoundCur2
```
Exit Click Event:
```
Begin Exit Click
    Unload frmMain
End Exit Click
```
Form Unload Event:
```
Begin Form Unload
    Close files
End Form Unload
```

Figure 9.43 Payroll *program micro-level logic design.*

Step 3c: Develop a Test Plan (Table of Input with Expected Results)

Our written test plan for this program must check that all numeric computations give correct results. The only input item we have to validate is the hours worked, but we also have to detect and deal with the following file-related exceptions:

- Invalid command line (too many or too few filenames on the command line)
- Missing *Tax* file
- Missing *Emp* file
- *Pay* file still present
- End-of-file for *Emp* file

To test our program, we need two input files. All files have CSV records, so we can use a spreadsheet to prepare and edit the files. Following the format for the *Tax* file given in Figure 9.42 and the tax table information in Figure 9.35, we create the *Tax* file A:\Tax.csv, which we will use to test our program. Figure 9.44 contains the listing of the *Tax* file.

```
5000,0
10000,.10
25000,.15
75000,.25
150000,.33
9E+12,.40
```

Figure 9.44   Tax *file for* Payroll *program.*

The *Tax* file we are using has six different tax rates, so for testing purposes we decide we will use two employees for each tax rate. Figure 9.45 contains a list of test cases that we want to use to test our program. You should expand this list with several sets of your own test data.

SSN	Name	Hrs	Rate	Gross	Gross*52	Tax	Net
241341521	Thomas O Whitten	8	10.75	86.00	4472	0.00	86.00
492735055	Owen F Detweiler	11	17.30	190.30	9896	19.03	171.27
533479537	Stephen Donneger	32	15.00	480.00	24960	72.00	408.00
639170707	Dirk Gehman	38	37.00	1406.00	73112	351.50	1054.50
690371986	Edward S Eastman	38	75.00	2850.00	148200	940.50	1909.50
761236124	Michael L Aiman	9	10.75	96.75	5031	9.68	87.07
785720348	Tony A Edison	12	17.30	207.60	10795	31.14	176.46
790184316	Grace J Ebermann	35	15.00	525.00	27300	131.25	393.75
826687434	Carol C Banana	40	37.00	1480.00	76960	488.40	991.60
841182276	Ralph J Alderfer	40	75.00	3000.00	156000	1200.00	1800.00
949744067	Harold U Bates	45	10.95	520.13	27047	130.03	390.10
987493232	Candice F Carter	50	15.65	860.75	44759	215.19	645.56

Figure 9.45   *Test data for* Payroll *program.*

Following the format for the *Emp* file given in Figure 9.42 and using the data in Figure 9.45, we generate the *Emp* file, A:\Emp.csv, displayed in Figure 9.46.

```
241341521,Thomas O Whitten,10.75
492735055,Owen F Detweiler,17.30
533479537,Stephen Donneger,15.00
639170707,Dirk Gehman,37.00
690371986,Edward S Eastman,75.00
761236124,Michael L Aiman,10.75
785720348,Tony A Edison,17.30
790184316,Grace J Ebermann,15.00
826687434,Carol C Banana,37.00
841182276,Ralph J Alderfer,75.00
949744067,Harold U Bates,10.95
987493232,Candice F Carter,15.65
```

Figure 9.46 Emp *file for* Payroll *program.*

Figure 9.47 contains a list of test cases that we want to use to test our program. You should expand this list with several sets of your own test data. In the following instructions, it is assumed that you have put a copy of the *Payroll* executable file in the root directory of the A: drive as A:\Payroll.exe, a copy of the *Tax* test data from Figure 9.44 in the file A:\Tax.csv, and a copy of the *Emp* test data from Figure 9.46 in the file A:\Emp.csv.

Case	User Input and Actions	Expected Results
1	Run the program with the following command line: a:payroll a:\tax.csv a:\emp.csv a:\pay.csv	The main form appears. The SSN and Name labels display 241-34-1521 and Thomas O Whitten, respectively. The Hours text box is blank and has the focus.
2	Click *Exit Program.*	The program stops running.
3	Run the program.	A message box displays Pay file already exists. Do you want to continue? Click *No,* and the program stops running.
4	Run the program.	A message box displays Pay file already exists. Do you want to continue? Click *Yes,* and the main form appears exactly as described in Case 1 above.
5	Enter 4.5 hours and click *Next.*	A message box displays Invalid value for Hours. Click *OK,* and the focus is put on the Hours text box.
6	Enter 100.5 hours and click *Enter.*	A message box displays Invalid value for Hours. Click *OK,* and the focus is put on the Hours text box.
7	Enter 8A and click *Enter.*	A message box displays Hours must be numeric. Click *OK,* and the focus is put on the Hours text box.
8	Enter 8 and click *Next.*	The SSN and Name labels display 492-73-5055 and Owen F Detweiler, respectively. The Hours text box is blank and has the focus.

Case	User Input and Actions	Expected Results
9	Click *Exit*, and then run the program with the following command line: a:payroll	A message box displays Not enough arguments on command line. Notify MIS department. Click *OK*, and the program stops running
10	Run the program with the following command line: a:payroll a:\Hax.csv a:\emp.csv a:\pay.csv	A message box displays Tax table file does not exist. Notify MIS department. Click *OK* and the program stops running.
11	Run the program with the following command line: a:payroll a:\tax.csv a:\Rmp.csv a:\pay.csv	A message box displays Employee file does not exist. Notify MIS department. Click *OK*, and the program stops running
12	Run the program with the following command line: a:payroll a:\tax.csv a:\emp.csv a:\ABCD\pay. csv	A message box displays Pay file path error. Notify MIS department. Click *OK*, and the program stops running
13	Run the program with the following command line: a:payroll a:\tax.csv a:\emp.csv a:\pay.csv a:\abc.csv	A message box displays Too many arguments on command line. Notify MIS department. Click *OK*, and the program continues running normally.
14	Use the test data in Figure 9.45 and enter the hours for 12 employees.	A message box displays No more employees to process. Click *OK*, and the main form reappears with the SSN and Name labels and the Hours text box all cleared. In addition, the *Next* button is disabled.
15	Click *Exit*.	The program stops running. Compare the program's output, which has been written to file A:\Pay.csv, with the anticipated output given in Figure 9.48.

Figure 9.47   Payroll *program test plan*

writing to the file. Depending on the file format, you use the VB *Input #*, *Line Input #*, or *Get statements* to read from a file. The *EOF function* is used to determine when you have reached the end of file. Visual Basic has several statements used to perform file output. They are the *Write #*, *Print #*, and *Put statements*.

When your program no longer needs access to a file, it uses the *Close statement* to inform the operating system to close the file. In the case of an output file, this is important so that any data still stored in a memory buffer will be written to the output device.

Key Terms

access methods	fields	Print # statement
buffer	file	Put statement
Close statement	filenumber	random access files
comma-separated values (CSV)	fixed-length records	records
data files	flushing the buffers	report files
data sentinel	Get statement	sequential access
disk dump utility	Input # statement	variable-length records
EOF function	Line Input # statement	Write # statement
	Open statement	

Test Your Understanding

1. What is the difference between a file and a record?

2. For any particular file, which is greater: the number of records or the number of fields?

3. What three types of statements can be used to get data from a file?

4. A programmer wants to use a comma-separated values file type to store information about engine parts. However, some of the part descriptions, such as *Injector, Bosch*, have embedded commas. Can the programmer safely store this type of data in a CSV file? Explain why or why not.

5. Another programmer also wants to use a CSV file to store information about electronic devices. In this case, some of the part descriptions contain embedded quotation marks. An example is *Pin Line Sockets with "Break" Feature*. Can the programmer safely store this type of data in a CSV file? Explain why or why not.

6. Describe three different methods programs could use (depending on the file format) to know when the last record of a sequential text file has been read.

7. The documentation for a fixed record-length file lists the following fields along with their lengths. This file contains address labels, and the company has just purchased a mailing list with 350,000 names. How many megabytes will be needed to store the new mailing list?

Field Name	Length
Name	25
Street	20
City	15
State	2
Zip	5
ExpireDate	8

8. Suppose you have two open files, and you want to close the files because your program no longer needs to access these two files. What is the difference, if any, between *Close #1, #2*, and *Close*? Does your answer change if you have a third file open, but you only want to close files #1 and #2?

9. What is the *FreeFile* function, and why is it useful?

10. Does the *EOF* function return *True* before or after the last record of a file has been read?

11. Which of the following will cause a Run Time error in Visual Basic?

   ■ Open an already open file.

   ■ Close an already closed file.

   ■ Attempt to read the last record of a file for a second time.

12. Suppose that your program has finished reading all the records of a sequential file. At a later point in the program, you want the program to again read the same file. Can this be done, and, if so, how is it done?

13. Which of the following will cause a Run Time error in Visual Basic?

   ■ Open an existing file for Output.

   ■ Open an existing file for Input.

   ■ Open a nonexistent file for Output.

   ■ Open a nonexistent file for Input.

Programming Exercises

1. Determine how much overhead there is when a dynamic array of type Currency has its size increased. You can do this by writing a simple Visual Basic program that includes the following *For...Next* loop:

```
For I = 2 To MaxSize
    ReDim Preserve fHourlyRate(1 To I)
Next I
```

505

You should time your program with different values for *MaxSize*, such as *MaxSize* = 50000, 100000, and 200000. You can use your wristwatch, or your program can call the *Timer* function before and after the loop, subtract the two values given by *Timer*, and display the result. Does there seem to be any significant Run Time overhead when you increase the size of an array?

```
┌─────────────────────────────────────────┐
│ ▄. ReDim Overhead with Preserve  _ □ ✕   │
│ ┌─Dual 150 MHz Pentium Pro ───────────┐  │
│ │                                      │  │
│ │        Max Size  [200,000        ]   │  │
│ │                                      │  │
│ │     Elapsed Time [10 seconds     ]   │  │
│ │                                      │  │
│ │          ┌──────────────┐            │  │
│ │          │    Check     │            │  │
│ │          └──────────────┘            │  │
│ └──────────────────────────────────────┘ │
└─────────────────────────────────────────┘
```

2. Remove the *Preserve* option from the loop in programming exercise 1, and check to see whether the *ReDim* overhead becomes greater or smaller. Can you explain the difference?

3. In program *CSV*, during the process of making a change to name, age, or hourly rate, the user might inadvertently change the ID. Then when the *Change* button is clicked, the wrong employee's information might be changed. Make modifications to the *CSV* program to prevent the user from making this type of error.

4. In program *CSV*, when the *Save* button is clicked, an existing file with the same name as the name entered in the *File Name* text box will be overwritten without any warning. Modify the program so that if the output file exists, the user is given the choice to either continue or cancel when he clicks the *Save* button.

5. Write a program that creates a CSV file, A:\Random.csv, with 100,000 random integers, 10 numbers per line. The random numbers should be in the range of 0 to 20,000, inclusive. Approximately how long does it take this program to run?

6. Write a program that creates a report file, A:\Random.rpt, with 100,000 random integers, right adjusted in 10 columns, with one space between each column. The first row contains the first 10 numbers, the second row contains the next 10 numbers, and so on. The random numbers should be in the range of 0 to 20,000, inclusive.

7. Modify the end-of-chapter pay program so that the three filenames are stored in three lines of a sequential text file rather than as command-line arguments. When the program begins, the filenames are input and displayed in text boxes, which the user can update. Add a *Load Employees* button to the form that loads the employee and tax data. The file is rewritten when the program ends, in case the user changed the files being used.

Programming Projects

1. Write a program that creates a CSV file containing 10 random integers per line. The form for the program enables the user to select the quantity and range of the random numbers. The program should use the common dialog control to provide the user with a Save As dialog box. Specify a "*.rnd" file filter that is displayed in the *Files of type* list box. See Appendix A, "Visual Basic User Interface Objects," for a discussion of the common dialog control set of standard dialog boxes for operations such as opening and saving files. Appendix A also contains instructions on how to add the common dialog control to the toolbox.

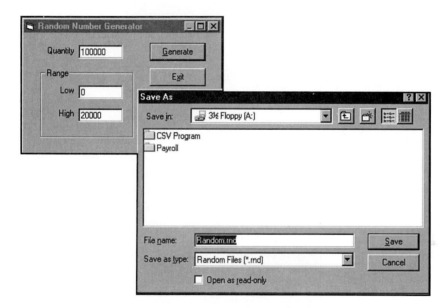

2. Develop a program that reads the file created by programming project 1 and displays the quantity of numbers that were read, the largest and smallest numbers, and the mean. Your program should use the Open dialog box, which is provided by the common dialog control.

3. Design a program that is used to store data produced by a trucking fleet. The program is used to enter truck number, miles driven, and gallons of fuel. The trucking company runs this program weekly, but the data is only analyzed quarterly. Your program should open the file in *Append* mode so that the data will be added to the end of an existing file. If the file does not exist, it should be created. You should use the Open dialog box, which is provided by the common dialog control. Because the company may want to access the data with a spreadsheet program, you should generate a file with CSV format.

4. Write a program that analyzes the data produced by the program described in programming project 3. The program should calculate and display the total miles driven by all the trucks, the total number of gallons of fuel that was used, and the average miles per gallon (rounded to one place beyond the decimal point) for the entire fleet. You should use the Open dialog box, which is provided by the common dialog control.

5. Create a program that searches a CSV file sequentially for a record containing a specific Social Security number. If the record is found, additional data from the record is displayed. If the record is not found, display NOT FOUND in the Name label. Because the search is sequential, you will have to close and reopen the file each time a search is performed. The file contains the following fields: SSN, Name, Department, Building, Age, and Hourly Pay Rate. Use a spreadsheet program to prepare the data file.

6. Write a Visual Basic program where prospective home buyers can enter information about the type of home they are looking for and then the system will display the homes that meet the buyer's preferences. Use a spreadsheet

program to create a CSV file to record data on each available home that includes the address, list price, number of bedrooms, number of bathrooms, whether the home has a fenced yard, whether the home includes any farmland, and whether the home has a garage. Load this data from the CSV file into an array of a user-defined type in the *Form Load* event. Create a message box that displays the addresses and list prices (one home entry per line) for all matching homes. A suggested form is shown here.

Challenge 1: Instead of the message box with basic information, display all the data on the matching houses in a list box. Instruct the prospective buyer to select all desired houses to schedule a showing. Each selection should be written to a nicely formatted SHOW.TXT file that includes descriptive headers and all detailed information on the selected, matching homes.

CHAPTER 10

INTRODUCTORY DATABASE PROGRAMMING

Introduction

Most businesses these days maintain considerable data in computer-readable format. It is too much trouble to have to reenter the same information over and over again on a daily, weekly, monthly, or even yearly basis. It is also important to be able to maintain a historical record to track progress in specific areas and make crucial business decisions. In Chapter 9, "Sequential Files," you learned how to store data in external files for future retrieval as well as how to retrieve data from files that already exist. What if some of the data needed by your program already exists in a company or departmental database? You could re-create a sequential file with data from the database, and then apply the concepts learned in Chapter 9. However, you can also develop a program that accesses the database data directly.

This chapter shows you how to use the data control to access data in a database. Techniques for retrieving and modifying database data will be presented, as well as the Visual Basic statements used to work with these databases. You will learn how to create an application that navigates a database by setting specific properties of the data control and data-bound controls without writing any code. You will also learn how to write code to customize the database access to search, add, delete, and modify information in the database. Chapter 11, "Database Programming with Data Objects and SQL," will then show you how to integrate rudimentary Structured Query Language (SQL) within your code to perform similar database processing.

Objectives

After completing this chapter, you should be able to:

@ Define relational database.

@ Explain database organization.

511

@ Provide reasons for using databases.

@ Understand how to connect to a database using the data control.

@ Understand how to navigate a database.

@ Understand how to search for specific data in a database.

@ Understand how to add, modify, and delete database records.

Why Use Databases?

In the early days of programming, people developed external data files to store program data for future retrieval. The nature of these programs would result in the creation of a new data file for each new program. Because many of the programs used the same data, this file approach resulted in enormous amounts of duplicated data. Although storage media is relatively cheap today, the unnecessary duplication of data in those days was a significant storage problem. Despite the low cost of storage, it is always smart to make efficient use of space, when possible.

Related to the wasted storage was a more critical problem: The same data stored in different files did not always have the same values. Suppose, for example, that a local bank maintains several program applications, each with its own data file. When a customer sends in a name or address change, the data entry person makes the change in one file. But what if the person has several different types of accounts? In this situation, we would have contradictory data in different files for the same person's record. How would we know which version is right? This **data integrity** problem is a more important reason for using a database approach over a group of sequential files for each separate application.

Another reason that you may need to use the database approach is that the data you need to process may already exist in a company or department database. If so, it would certainly be easier and faster to write a Visual Basic program that accesses the data in the database instead of going to the trouble of re-creating just the data you need in a sequential file and applying the concepts from Chapter 9. Furthermore, accessing database data through a Visual Basic program can be a fairly straightforward task. This chapter shows you how to use the data control and data-bound controls to access database data. In the next chapter, you learn how to use data access objects (DAOs) to do more direct, easier-to-customize programming to process database data and even create a database.

Relational Databases: A Collection of Tables

Before we can use a database, we need to understand what a database actually is. When people use the term **database** these days, they usually mean a relational database. A **relational database** is a collection of organized, related tables. It gets its name from how different tables can be related together through sharing the same data. As shown in Figure 10.1, a database table stores data in rows and columns.

A given row represents a single record in the table. Each column represents a different field. These fields can be used to relate different tables together by replicating the same data in these shared fields.

Column = Field

EmpID	EmpName	BirthDate	PayRate
1	Thomas O Whitten	1/1/78	$10.76
2	Ralph J Alderfer	5/4/64	$17.33
3	Owen F Detweiler	12/1/70	$7.90
4	Stephen Donneger	11/4/71	$21.50
5	Edward S Eastman	3/27/77	$20.36
6	Grace J Ebermann	7/29/38	$20.10
7	Michael L Aiman	4/30/71	$15.90
8	George F Carter	10/5/71	$15.32
9	Carol C Banana	9/20/59	$17.83
10	Harold U Bates	7/15/48	$14.47
11	Tony A Edison	11/25/38	$10.97
12	Dirk Gehman	2/28/57	$15.66
13	John A Gifford	8/30/54	$9.27
14	Rick R Gleason	3/3/76	$10.67
15	Robert J Glick	7/15/36	$9.29
16	Anna V Grolier	4/20/53	$16.19
17	Mildred K Hale	6/15/39	$17.81
18	Addie K Everley	4/13/74	$15.21
19	Donna Feldman	5/5/49	$17.55
20	Eric C Fontaine	6/10/40	$8.57
21	Ruth B Gellslay	8/12/37	$17.72

Employee : Table

Row = Record

Record: 1 of 51

Figure 10.1   *An example of a database table.*

If you review Figure 9.1 in Chapter 9, you will see that the data hierarchy of files is similar to the data hierarchy of databases. When using a file approach, related fields make up a record, and related records make up files. When using a database approach, related fields make up a record, related records make up a table, and related tables make up a database. If you consider a single database table as illustrated in Figure 10.1, a **database field,** or **attribute**, is represented as a column of data that includes the same information for all records, such as all Social Security numbers, all names, all birth dates, all hourly wage rates, and so on. A **database record** is represented as a row of related information containing multiple fields of data for a single person, product, transaction, and so forth. Each table needs to have a way of uniquely identifying a single record. This is accomplished by identifying a **key field**—a special field or combination of fields that uniquely identifies each record.

Consider this example. Figure 10.2 partially illustrates the database organization for the Northwind Microsoft Access database shipped with Visual Basic. For our purposes, it is not necessary to be able to load the Northwind database in Access. If you have Access on your computer, however, you may want to load the database so that you can identify the various elements described here. Otherwise, just follow along with us using the figure alone.

From the top portion of the figure, you can see that the database contains eight tables. You can also see that two of these tables are related by having a common field—*Category Name* in the *Categories* table and *Category* in the *Products* table. By looking at related records, you can surmise that *Aniseed syrup* (in the *Products* table) is a *sweet and savory sauce, relish, spread, and seasoning* (in the *Categories* table).

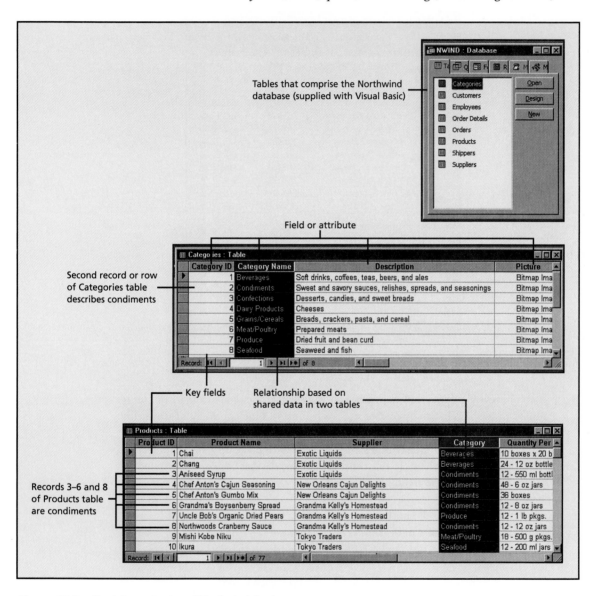

Figure 10.2 *Partial organization of Northwind database.*

To access the related information, you have to look up data in both tables for a match on the category name. You may be wondering why several related database tables are used rather than just one large file—it would certainly simplify the task of getting all the information we want about Aniseed syrup (or any other product). The answer requires us to recall the earlier discussion of why we should use databases. If we only have one large file, every condiment record would have to repeat the same information on condiments. If we have thousands of products that could be categorized into 10 areas, it would result in considerable data being repeated in the file. When any changes are made to specific data, extra precautions would be required to ensure that this same data was consistent in all occurrences. Therefore, the duplicated data would not only take up extra space, but could also lead to data integrity problems. Now if you examine the database approach more closely, you should see that some data is in fact repeated in multiple tables; however, this controlled redundancy is necessary to relate tables together and is preferred to having to replicate all the data for thousands of records or more.

Database Management System (DBMS)

Although you can create databases programmatically, typically a software product called a **database management system (DBMS)** is used to initially create the database (as well as maintain the database). Several popular database management systems are available commercially. Visual Basic is equipped with the Microsoft Jet database engine (the same database engine that powers Microsoft Access, a popular microcomputer DBMS). The Jet engine handles the mechanics of storing, retrieving, and updating data in the database. Visual Basic also provides the data control as a simplified bridge to the Jet engine for elementary database programming. After you move beyond the basics, you can develop elaborate, customized Visual Basic programs using built-in **database objects**.

In addition to its native format, the Jet database engine can also read and write dBASE, Lotus, Excel, FoxPro, Paradox, and text files. The Professional version of Visual Basic includes Open Database Connectivity (ODBC) drivers that enable you to access SQL Server, Oracle, and DB2 databases as well. For the purposes of this text, it is not important to understand how to use a DBMS to access the database; however, you must know the name of the DBMS for which the database was written.

Before you can retrieve and manipulate the data in the database, you also need to know the organization of the database. Just like with file access, you need to know the database filename, the names of the tables, and the names and types of fields that comprise a table's records. With this information, you can quickly create a database navigation program with little to no code.

The Data Control

If you need to create a quick database navigation program, you can use the combination of the intrinsic data control along with one or more data-bound controls. The **data control** enables you to view database data, change data in an individual record, and navigate database records. It includes buttons to provide navigation functionality that consists of moving to the first record, moving to the previous record, moving to the next record, and moving to the last record. The current record's information can be viewed through **data-aware controls** that have been bound to individual fields in the database through the data control. Without a data control on the form, the **data-bound controls** cannot automatically access data in the database.

Depending on the type of data in the field, any of the following data-aware, intrinsic controls can be used:

- Label (for display of textual data only—cannot be changed by the user)
- Text box (for display or input of textual data)
- Check box (for display or input of Boolean data)
- Image and picture (for display of image data)
- List box and combo box (for input and display of a list of textual choices)
- OLE

The Professional and Enterprise editions of Visual Basic have additional data-aware controls including the *MaskedEdit* and *RichTextBox*, which can also be used to view or manipulate field data from the current record. If you want to view or manipulate data from multiple records simultaneously, you can use alternative data-aware controls such as the *DBList*, *DBCombo*, and *MSFlexGrid* controls.

Data Control Properties

To implement the navigation functionality previously described, you need to review certain data control properties. These properties include Connect, DatabaseName, ReadOnly, RecordSource, BOFAction, and EOFAction. We will illustrate the use of these properties by designing a form to navigate the *Products* table in the Northwind database. To display and possibly change the contents of the current product record, the field data should appear in text boxes. Like our other GUI designs, descriptive labels should precede each text box to let the user know what information is being displayed. A data control is needed to handle the navigation process. Finally, like all our other programs, an *Exit* button should be included for convenient program termination. See Figure 10.3 for a suggested interface of our first database navigation program.

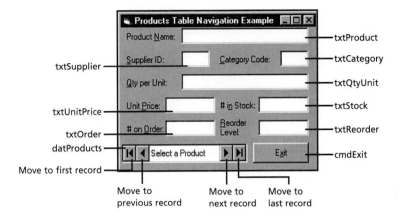

Figure 10.3   *Database navigation user interface and data control.*

Throughout this text, we have discussed various three-character prefixes for naming different types of controls. In the case of the data control, the recommended three-character prefix standard is *dat*. Therefore, for our example program, we assign datProducts to the Name property. Also like other controls, the caption property contains the textual information that you want displayed on the form. For our example, we assign Select a Product to the Caption property.

Next, you need to check the properties that provide information about the database. The **Connect property** identifies the DBMS source of the database. Because Access is Visual Basic's native format, you should keep the default value. If your database source is different, you can select the appropriate source from the list of choices under the Connect property. In our case, the default of Access is correct.

The **DatabaseName property** identifies the filename, including the full path, of the physical database. To set this property at Design Time, click on the Settings button. When the Open File dialog box displays, identify the drive, path, and filename of the database. When you install Visual Basic 6.0, a copy of Microsoft's Northwind database is copied to the following location: C:\Program Files\ Microsoft Visual Studio\VB98\Nwind.mdb.

Alternatively, we illustrate some examples using a subset of this database that is on the CD that accompanies this textbook. If you copy it to a folder named Chapter10 on a disk, you would identify A:\Chapter10\Northwind.mdb as the filename (see Figure 10.4).

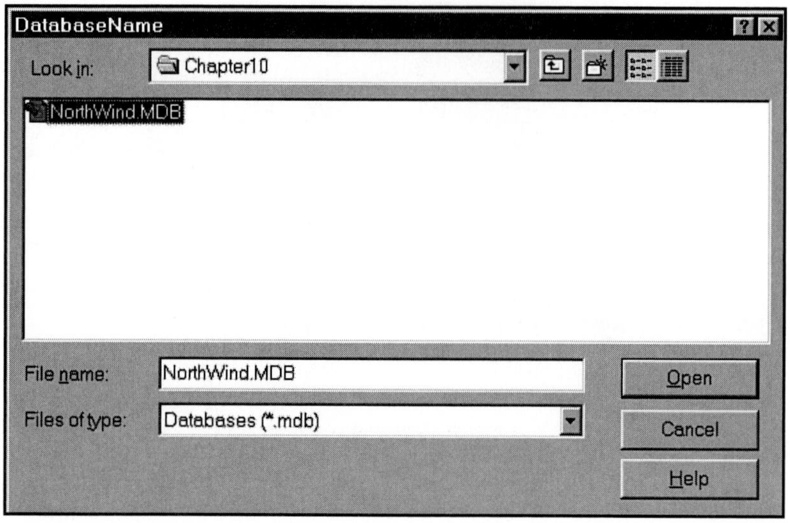

Figure 10.4   *Data control—DatabaseName property's Open File dialog box.*

The **ReadOnly property** determines whether changes can be made to the database or not. Notice that the default is *False*. If you do not change the value of this property and you use editable controls like text boxes to display record data, any changes that the user makes at Run Time will automatically and permanently change the database's contents. To avoid accidental modifications by a user who is just navigating the database, it would be safer to change this property to True. A side benefit is faster access as well. Another alternative is to use noneditable controls such as labels to display the data.

The **RecordSource property** is the last property we need to set at Design Time. Here, we specify what subset of the database we wish to access. For now, we will just select from the list of choices that appear. Because we want to navigate the results of the *Products* table, select that name from the drop-down list as shown in Figure 10.5.

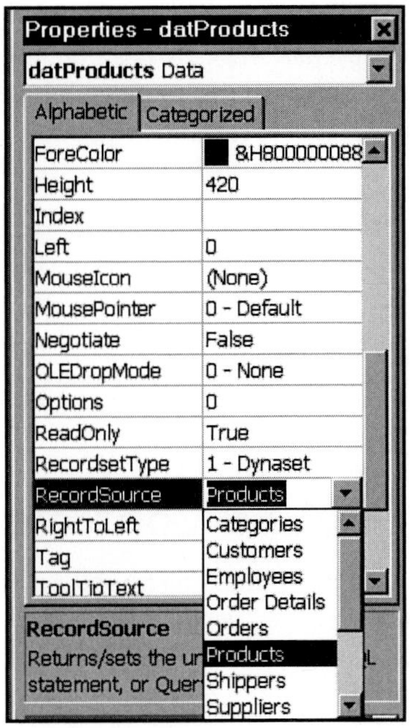

Figure 10.5 *Data control—assigning the RecordSource property.*

You may want to change two additional properties. When you navigate a database table, a pointer keeps track of where the current record is located in the table. If you attempt to access an invalid record, you could potentially trigger an error. If the current record is the first record, and the user clicks on the *move previous* arrow, then the current record pointer will be positioned before the start of the first record. This action causes the **BOF property** to be set to *True*. The data control's **BOFAction** property can be used to prevent this error. This property has two setting choices. To merely force the current record pointer to remain at the first record without any other actions, set it to 0–Move First. To stay at the first record and disable the *previous* button to give the user a visual cue that there was an attempt to go past the beginning of the database table, set it to 1–BOF.

Likewise, if the current record is the last record, and the user clicks on the *move next* arrow, then the current record pointer will point to after the last database record, causing the **EOF property** to be set to *True*. The **EOFAction property** can be used to prevent an error due to the EOF property being set to *True*. To keep the current record pointer fixed at the last record, set the EOFAction property to 0–Move Last. To stay at the last record as well as disable the *next* button, set it to 1–EOF. To automatically allow record additions, set it to 2–Add New.

For our program, we will keep the default values of BOFAction set to *0–Move First* and EOFAction set to *0–Move Last*. At this point, you could try to run the program; however, you would not see any results. We still need to relate the individual fields in the database table to their corresponding display controls on our form. We describe this process in the next section.

After you complete the next section and run this navigation program, we leave it as an exercise for you to select the other options for BOFAction and EOFAction. As you might expect, if you set the ReadOnly property to *True*, adding a new record is not a valid choice for the EOFAction. If you select this combination, you will get an error message when you run the program and try to add a new record to the read-only database.

Creating Data-Bound Controls

Before our program can display anything from the database, we need to create data-bound controls by making a few changes to the controls that will display each individual field's data. Labels and text boxes are data-aware controls in that they can be bound to a database by setting two properties: DataSource and DataField. The **DataSource property** is used to identify the name of the data control connected to the desired subset of the database. In our example, set the DataSource property of all the text boxes to *datProducts*, the name of the data control on our form. If you have already placed the data control on the form, you can select the name from the drop-down list instead of possibly typing it incorrectly. You can even do this in one step by selecting all the text boxes, and then selecting *datProducts* from the DataSource list.

After all the display controls have been bound to the *Products* database table, you need to specify the field in the *Products* table that should be linked to its corresponding text box. To do this, select one of the text boxes. Next, once the DataSource property has been assigned, you can select the appropriate database field from the list in the **DataField property** list. For our example, make the following selections.

User Interface Control	DataField Property Selection
txtProduct	ProductName
txtSupplier	SupplierID
txtCategory	CategoryID
txtQtyUnit	QuantityPerUnit
txtUnitPrice	UnitPrice
txtStock	UnitsInStock
txtOrder	UnitsOnOrder
txtReorder	ReorderLevel

You are now ready to see whether anything happens when you run your program. Keep in mind that your program consists of an interface with no code in it. Do you expect the program to produce the desired results?

Figure 10.6 shows the screen at different points during execution. Notice that at startup the first record shows on the form. This happens because the current record pointer will start at the first table record. Can you explain why nothing happens when we click the *Exit* button? Remember that we have not written any code. Therefore, when the *Exit* button is clicked, there is no code to be processed for that button's click event. To correct this, you will need to add one line of code to your program. We leave that as an exercise.

At this point, you may be wondering why our program produced results despite the fact that we wrote no code. Unlike the previous chapters where code was necessary to make the program do something, this program allowed navigation of the *Products* table in the Northwind database one record at a time. What made all this possible? First, we had to place a data control on the form and set a few properties to identify the type of database, the location of the database, and the subset of the database we wanted to view. Second, we had to bind the text box display controls to their corresponding fields in the database. The rest of the navigation functionality is provided automatically through the data control. For more practice, we recommend that you create simple database navigation programs for other tables in the Northwind database or for tables in other databases.

Form at startup:

Click on the *last record* button:

continues

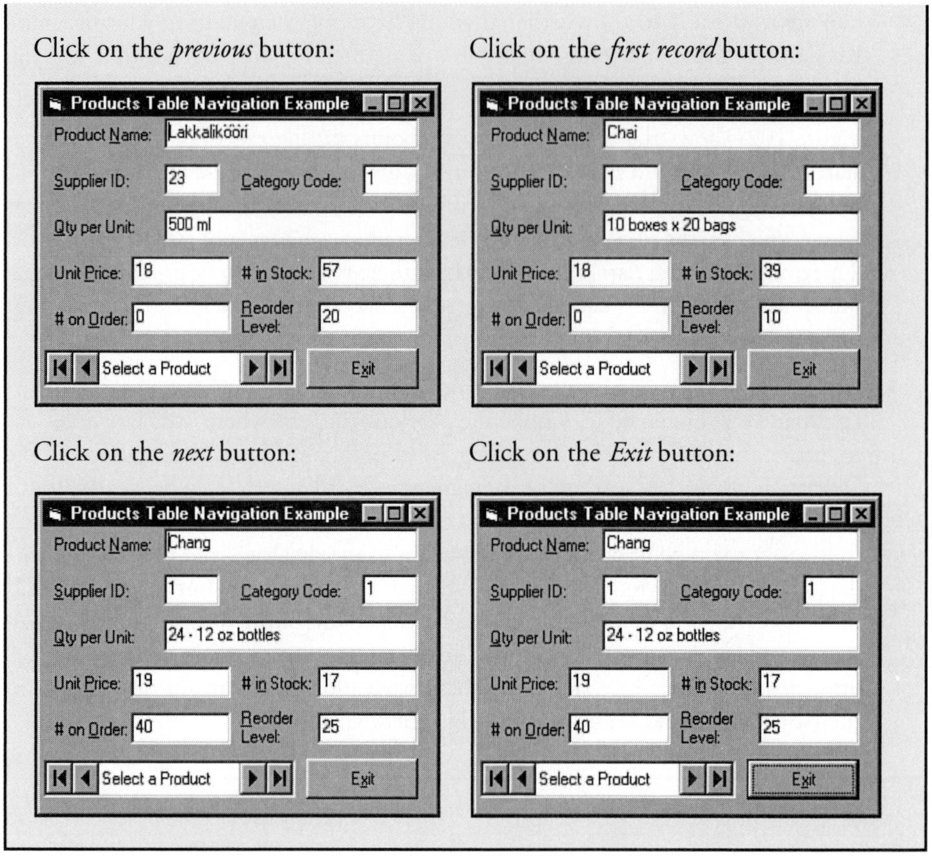

Click on the *previous* button:

Click on the *first record* button:

Click on the *next* button:

Click on the *Exit* button:

Figure 10.6 *Output screens of no-code database navigation program.*

Later in this chapter, we will use the *Employee* database that contains data similar to the file examples in Chapter 9. To facilitate understanding of other examples, you should create the navigation program for the *Employee* table in the *Employee* database that is included on the CD that accompanies this text. For your information, the design of the *Employee* table in the *Employee* database is described in Figure 10.7. A suggested interface is shown in Figure 10.8. We opted to keep the database read-only. Consequently, to prevent the user from attempting to make changes to the database data, we locked the display text boxes, as well as set the TabStop property to *False*.

Field Name	Description
EmpID	Long Integer that uniquely identifies each employee
EmpName	The full name of the employee (up to 30 characters)
BirthDate	The employee's date of birth stored as a short date (used to determine age)
PayRate	The hourly pay rate stored as Currency

Figure 10.7   *Employee database design.*

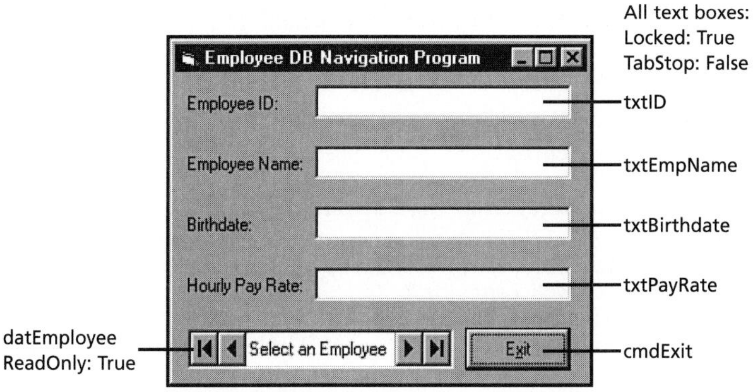

Figure 10.8   *GUI for* Employee *database navigation program.*

Programming the Data Control

Although the data control provides considerable navigation capability, if you need to do any processing beyond what has been illustrated, you must write code. Before describing any of the code, we need to cover more fundamental concepts regarding database programming in Visual Basic.

The data control is initialized before the *Form Load* event of the form holding the data control. If any errors occur during initialization, a nontrappable error results. If you copy the project folder to a different location that can no longer access the path and filename that was assigned to the DatabaseName property, for example, an error message would be displayed to the user and the program would not work correctly. In this situation, you could remove the assignment of the path and filename at Design Time, and then add a line of code in the *Form Load* event to assign them during form load.

When programs are installed on the computer, external files are typically stored at the same path. Visual Basic provides a global object called *App* that you can use to reference application-level information about the project, including the project's path. Then regardless of the location of a particular Visual Basic project, you can write code that will locate the database file using the application's path. The *App* object is also used to determine or specify information about the application's title, version information, the name of its executable file and Help files, and whether a previous instance of the application is running. Therefore, after you copy the database to the same location as the project, you can use the *App* object's Path property in code to ensure that the correct path is used to locate the database.

To test this, make a copy of your *Employee* database navigation program folder, including the database. Next, open the program in Visual Basic. Now, erase the DatabaseName property of the data control using the Properties window. Finally, add the code in the code window as shown in Figure 10.9. The program should work as before, but now the assignment of the database occurs when the *Form_Load* event executes.

```
' Purpose: This function safely appends the passed filename
'          to the passed path by making sure the last character
'          in the path contains a "\"
Private Function AppendFileToPath(ByVal Path As String, _
    ByVal File As String) As String

    If Path = "" Then      ' the path was not supplied
        AppendFileToPath = File
    ElseIf Right(Path, 1) = "\" Then
        AppendFileToPath = Path & File
    Else
        AppendFileToPath = Path & "\" & File
    End If
End Function

Private Sub Form_Load()
    Dim FileName As String
    FileName = AppendFileToPath(App.Path,"EmployeeDB.MDB")
    ' Add optional error checking to make sure the file exists
    datEmployee.DatabaseName = FileName
End Sub
```

Figure 10.9 Employee *database navigation program with DB assignment in form load.*

The preceding example illustrates how to use the *AppendFileToPath* function to return the correct file specification for the database file. After you have written the function, you add a few lines of code to the *Form Load* event to call the function. The value returned from the function is a complete file specification assigned to the *FileName* string variable. This, in turn, is assigned to the DatabaseName property of the associated data control. Then, when the program is loaded, the correct database is accessed. You can watch when this happens by setting a breakpoint and watching the execution a line at a time.

The *AppendFileToPath* function is used to account for three situations that could occur depending on the exact values of the *Path* and *File* parameters passed to it. The path will be the empty string if it is not supplied by the calling procedure. In our case, we used *App.Path* for the *Path* parameter. If the file happens to be at the root, the path will end with a "\" symbol. Otherwise, it will not. To ensure that the filename with path is constructed correctly, we check each of these situations in the function and return the appropriate file specification. Because we will use this function in the problem-solving case study at the end of this chapter, you should add it to your *Tools.Bas* module file.

The **Validate event** of the data control may also contain code to change values and update data. It is triggered just before a different database record becomes current. You can also choose to save data or stop whatever action is causing the event to occur and substitute a different action.

The Recordset Object

Visual Basic code accesses database data through a **Recordset object**. When you set the data control's RecordSource property to the name of a database table, a *Recordset* object is created. A *Recordset* object is used to manipulate database data at the record (row) level. Once defined, the Microsoft Jet database engine automatically populates the *Recordset* object. Then, it can be manipulated independently of the data control. In this chapter, we will continue to access the Recordset through the data control.

The five types of *Recordset* objects are as follows:

A **table-type Recordset** is used to reference a specific database table. It allows records to be added, deleted, or modified from the table, unless the file is locked or is read-only. Table Recordsets require you to use Seek methods to search for specific records. To use the Seek methods, indexes must be predefined in the database. If you have the Professional or higher version of Visual Basic, you can also create indexes using data access objects (DAO). Because DAO will not be covered until Chapter 11, we will omit further discussion of the *table-type Recordset*.

A **dynaset-type Recordset** is a dynamic set of records consisting of fields from one or more database tables for purposes of adding, deleting, or modifying records. It can be a stored query, a single table, part of a table, or a collection of data from multiple tables. As long as the file is not locked or read-only, it can also be updateable. When a dynaset is comprised of multiple tables, it will not be updateable unless the tables were joined properly. To search for specific records when using a *dynaset Recordset*, you need to use the Find methods. Our examples will use *dynaset-type Recordsets* that consist of single tables that are updateable. Later in this chapter, we will illustrate the four Find methods to search for specific records in the defined dynaset.

A **snapshot-type Recordset** is a static copy of a set of records consisting of fields from one or more database tables. Because it is not updateable, it is used primarily for finding data or generating reports. *Snapshot Recordsets* also use the Find methods for searching for specific records. The navigation and searching illustrations we present in this chapter will also work if the *snapshot-type Recordset* is selected. You can test this now by loading the *Employee* database navigation program and changing the Recordset property of the data control to snapshot in place of dynaset. When you run the program, the results should appear the same.

A **forward-only Recordset** is identical to a snapshot, but you can only progress forward through records. It is used for viewing or reporting purposes when only one pass through the records is necessary.

A **dynamic-type Recordset** is a query that represents a dynamic set of records consisting of fields from one or more database tables for purposes of adding, deleting, or modifying record data. Additionally, records updated by other users also appear in your Recordset.

When using the data control's *Recordset* object, you can use three of the five types: table, dynaset, and snapshot. If you don't specify the type of Recordset, Visual Basic will default to dynaset. The remaining discussion focuses on the *dynaset-type Recordset* object.

Recordset Properties

Several Recordset properties are useful when accessing the database programmatically. The Bookmark, RecordCount, BOF, EOF, and NoMatch properties are illustrated here. Because the Recordset is being accessed through the data control, the notation to reference the Recordset's properties is *datName.Recordset.PropertyName*. Because a property represents a value, it would appear as part of a statement, and not on a line by itself.

The **Bookmark property** can be used to set or track the current database record. If you move to a different record, but you want to keep track of the current record, you can assign the Bookmark to a Variant or String variable. Then to return to that record, you can assign the Bookmark property back to the value stored in the variable:

```
Dim CurRecord As Variant
CurRecord = datProducts.Recordset.Bookmark
' Code to move to a different record
datProducts.Recordset.Bookmark = CurRecord ' Return to previous record
```

Sometimes it is useful to know exactly how many records the Recordset contains. After all records have been accessed, the **RecordCount property** returns a Long integer equal to the count of total records in the Recordset. If you have just opened the database, you will need to move to the last record before using the RecordCount property for an accurate record count. If the value of RecordCount is zero, you know that the Recordset has no records.

Because trying to access the last record in an empty Recordset can trigger an error, a better way to determine that the Recordset contains no records is by simultaneously using the Boolean BOF and EOF properties. As described earlier, these properties are set to *True* when the current record moves before the beginning of the database or past the end of the database. Therefore, if you find that both BOF and EOF are true at the same time immediately after creating the Recordset, the Recordset has no records in it:

```
If datProducts.Recordset.BOF And datProducts.Recordset.EOF Then
    ' There are no records in the Recordset
Else
    ' There are records in the Recordset
End If
```

In the event that the program accesses a database with no records, an error would be triggered in the *Form Load* procedure. Therefore, it would be a good idea to modify the *Form_Load* procedure as shown in Figure 10.10.

```
Private Sub Form_Load()
    Dim FileName As String
    FileName = AppendFileToPath(App.Path, "EmployeeDB.MDB")
    ' Add optional error checking to make sure the file exists
    datEmployee.DatabaseName = FileName
    datEmployee.Refresh
    If datEmployee.Recordset.BOF And datEmployee.Recordset.EOF Then
    ' There are no records
        Call MsgBox("The database is empty. Program exiting.", _
            vbOKOnly + vbInformation)
        Call cmdExit_Click
    End If
End Sub
```

Figure 10.10 Employee *database navigation program with DB updated form load.*

After assigning the filename to the DatabaseName property, we need to explicitly open the database using the *Refresh* method. Anytime we change a data-control property that changes how we view the data, the *Refresh* method should be called again. Just in case there are no records, we simultaneously check the BOF and EOF properties. If both are true, this indicates that the database is empty. To prevent a Visual Basic error, we display a descriptive message and then terminate program execution.

Sometimes, you will use the Recordset to search for a record that meets specific criteria. When you do this, it is important to know if the search was successful. The **NoMatch property** holds a Boolean value that is true if the search was not successful and false if it was successful:

```
If datProducts.Recordset.NoMatch Then
    ' The search was unsuccessful
Else
    ' The current record pointer is pointing to the matching record
End If
```

After the search is done, you may want to see the contents of a particular field of the current record. To accomplish this, use either of these notations:

```
datName.Recordset!FieldName
```

or

```
datName.Recordset("FieldName")
```

where *FieldName* is the name of the corresponding database field name. In this chapter, we will illustrate the first notation. In the next chapter, we will illustrate the second notation.

Recordset Methods

The Recordset object has several methods that enable you to perform useful processes on the data. The general notation is *Call datName.Recordset.Method.* Because a method is a process, this code appears on a line by itself.

Move Methods

The first group of methods enables you to move the current record pointer. When you call one of these methods, the contents of the new record display automatically in data-bound controls. These four Move methods are shown here:

```
' Move to the first record regardless of current position in DB
Call datProducts.Recordset.MoveFirst

' Move to the last record regardless of current position in DB
Call datProducts.Recordset.MoveLast

' Move to the record immediately following the current record
Call datProducts.Recordset.MoveNext

' Move to the record immediately preceding the current record
Call datProducts.Recordset.MovePrevious
```

What do you think happens if the current record is the first record and the *MovePrevious* method is executed, or if the current record is the last record and the *MoveNext* method is executed? As described in the section titled "The Data Control," the BOF or EOF properties will be set to *True,* triggering an error. To prevent an error, your procedure's code should check the BOF or EOF property immediately after executing a *MovePrevious* or *MoveNext* method. If there is a potential for error, you can circumvent it by moving the record pointer to a valid record before that procedure is done.

To test the Move methods, make a copy of the folder containing the most recent version of the database navigation program. Open the program in Visual Basic, and add four command buttons labeled &First Record, &Last Record, &Next Record, and &Previous Record. Hide the data control by setting its Visible property to False. This setting will limit the user to navigating the database only through the customized code behind each of these buttons. Figure 10.11 shows the updated GUI. Figure 10.12 shows the Visual Basic code for handling the four different Move functions through code.

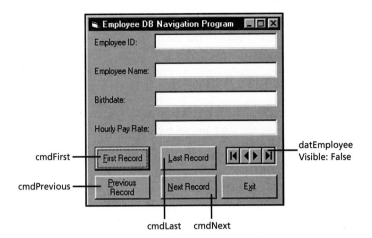

Figure 10.11   *Updated GUI for* Employee *database navigation program with Move methods.*

```
MoveFirst:

  Private Sub cmdFirst_Click()
      Call datEmployee.Recordset.MoveFirst
  End Sub

MovePrevious:

  Private Sub cmdPrevious_Click()
      Call datEmployee.Recordset.MovePrevious
      If datEmployee.Recordset.BOF Then
          Call datEmployee.Recordset.MoveLast
      End If
  End Sub

MoveLast:

  Private Sub cmdLast_Click()
      Call datEmployee.Recordset.MoveLast
  End Sub

MoveNext:

  Private Sub cmdNext_Click()
      Call datEmployee.Recordset.MoveNext
      If datEmployee.Recordset.EOF Then
          Call datEmployee.Recordset.MoveFirst
      End If
  End Sub
```

Figure 10.12   *Code for Move operations.*

If your display controls are not data aware or data bound, they cannot automatically display the contents of the current database record. You can achieve the same results, however, through additional code. Recall that you can reference the content of a specific field of the current record. By assigning each field to its corresponding display control as soon as the record pointer has moved, you will effectively accomplish the same result.

Another benefit of displaying the field data through code instead of using data-bound controls is that you can control the format of the display. Our current program shows the hourly pay rate as a number, for example. If you display that field through code, you can use the currency format so that the number appears as a monetary figure.

Because each Move operation must repeat the same steps, we should write a single procedure and call it before the *End Sub* in each Move *Click* event. During form load, we need to explicitly open the database using the **Refresh method** as well as move to and show the first record by calling the *cmdFirst_Click* event. Figure 10.13 shows the code for the updated procedures in our *Employee* database program with the changes emphasized in bold in code. To try this yourself, do the following:

1. Using Windows Explorer, make another copy of your *Employee* database navigation program folder and its contents.

2. Open the program by double-clicking on the project file.

3. Erase the values in the DataSource and DataField properties of the four text boxes.

4. Make any changes to the procedures shown here so that they match Figure 10.13. (You need to leave the *cmdExit_Click* event and *AppendFileToPath* function alone.)

5. Click the disk icon to save everything in the new folder.

```
Private Sub Form_Load()
    Dim FileName As String
    FileName = AppendFileToPath(App.Path, "EmployeeDB.MDB")
    ' Add optional error checking to make sure the file exists
    datEmployee.DatabaseName = FileName
    datEmployee.Refresh
    If datEmployee.Recordset.BOF And datEmployee.Recordset.EOF Then
    ' There are no records
        Call MsgBox("The database is empty. Program exiting.", _
            vbOKOnly + vbInformation)
        Call cmdExit_Click
    Else
        Call cmdFirst_Click
    End If
End Sub

Private Sub cmdFirst_Click()
    Call datEmployee.Recordset.MoveFirst
    Call ShowDBData
End Sub

Private Sub cmdLast_Click()
    Call datEmployee.Recordset.MoveLast
    Call ShowDBData
End Sub

Private Sub cmdPrevious_Click()
    Call datEmployee.Recordset.MovePrevious
```

```
If datEmployee.Recordset.BOF Then
        Call datEmployee.Recordset.MoveLast
    End If
    Call ShowDBData
End Sub

Private Sub cmdNext_Click()
    Call datEmployee.Recordset.MoveNext
    If datEmployee.Recordset.EOF Then
        Call datEmployee.Recordset.MoveFirst
    End If
    Call ShowDBData
End Sub

Private Sub ShowDBData()
    txtID.Text = datEmployee.Recordset!EmpID
    txtEmpName.Text = datEmployee.Recordset!EmpName
    txtBirthdate.Text = Format(datEmployee.Recordset!Birthdate, _
        "short date")
    txtPayRate.Text = Format(datEmployee.Recordset!PayRate, "currency")
End Sub
```

Figure 10.13   *Updated code for Move operations without data-bound controls.*

In addition to using the Move methods to customize database navigation, we can use the Move methods to fill an array with all the data in the Recordset. Then we can process all the data in the array instead of having to search the database every time for each new record. Figure 10.14 shows code for filling an array of a user-defined type with the values inside a Recordset.

To try this, you should make a copy of the folder containing the latest database navigation program. After opening the program in Visual Basic, add a command button called cmdFillArraywithDB. Finally, add the code for this button's *Click* event shown in Figure 10.14. To see how this code works, you will need to use the Visual Basic debugger. Step through the program one line at a time, and use the Data Tips or the Immediate window to see the contents of various array elements.

```
Private Type DBRecord
    ID As Long
    Employee As String
    BirthDate As Date
    HrRate As Currency
End Type
Private fDBArray() As DBRecord
Private fTotRec As Integer

Private Sub cmdFillArrayWithDB_Click()
    Dim CurRec As Integer
    ReDim fDBArray(datEmployee.Recordset.RecordCount) As DBRecord
    ' Move to first DB record & set CurRec to 1
    CurRec = 1
    Call datEmployee.Recordset.MoveFirst
    Do
        ' Copy current DB record to CurRec subscript of fDBArray
```

continues

```
            fDBArray(CurRec).ID = datEmployee.Recordset!empid
            fDBArray(CurRec).Employee = datEmployee.Recordset!empname
            fDBArray(CurRec).BirthDate = datEmployee.Recordset!BirthDate
            fDBArray(CurRec).HrRate = datEmployee.Recordset!payrate
            Call datEmployee.Recordset.MoveNext
            CurRec = CurRec + 1
        Loop Until datEmployee.Recordset.EOF
        fTotRec = CurRec - 1
        Call datEmployee.Recordset.MoveFirst
        CurRec = 1
        ' Replace with desired processing on filled array
    End Sub
```

Figure 10.14 *Code for filling an array with values from a Recordset.*

Find Methods

The four Find methods sound similar to the Move methods: *FindFirst, FindLast, FindNext,* and *FindPrevious.* These Find methods require that you define a search criterion that is represented as a string. The difference between the four Find methods is the direction of the search and the starting point of the search.

Specifying the Search Criteria

To use any of the Find methods, you must stipulate a search criterion that identifies both the specific database field(s) in the current Recordset to be checked as well as the precise comparison(s). This will be written as a relational expression stored inside a string. In addition to the typical relational operators discussed in Chapter 5, "Decisions and Data Validation," the database *Like* operator may be used for a similar match rather than an exact match. When using the *Like* operator, you would generally use the "*" wildcard character to denote that any characters at that position are acceptable.

The general format of the search criteria is

```
<DBFieldName> <relational operator> <search criteria>
```

When writing the search condition, its syntax must follow the required format. In particular, the entire condition must be type String, the field names must match the names in the database, and single quotation marks must surround the matching values when comparing for string literal equivalency. Some examples of valid search criteria for the *Employee* table are shown here. In these examples, *SearchCriteria* is the name of a string variable. Note that all these search conditions are surrounded by double quotation marks to denote string data.

- ■ `SearchCriteria = "EmpID < 57"`

- ■ `SearchCriteria = "EmpID < " & InputBox("Enter ID to find:")`

- ■ `SearchCriteria = "EmpID < " & txtIDToFind`

- ■ `SearchCriteria = "EmpName = 'John Doe'"`

■ SearchCriteria = "EmpName Like 'John*'"

■ MinWage = 25
   SearchCriteria = "PayRate >= " & Format(MinWage)

After the search criterion has been assigned, you can use any one of the four Find methods as shown here:

```
Dim SearchCriteria As String
' Assign a string value to SearchCriteria here by
' using any of the above examples

' Starting at record 1, search forwards for the first matching record
Call datProducts.Recordset.FindFirst(SearchCriteria)

' Starting at the current record, search forwards for the first match
Call datProducts.Recordset.FindNext(SearchCriteria)

' Starting at the last record, search backwards for the first match
Call datProducts.Recordset.FindLast(SearchCriteria)

' Starting at the current record, search backwards for the first match
Call datProducts.Recordset.FindPrevious(SearchCriteria)
```

The Find methods are appropriate when you need to allow the user to go directly to a particular record rather than navigating through single records until the desired record is located. To illustrate this, we will add a *Find ID* button on our form. When the button is clicked, the user will be prompted via an InputBox to enter an employee ID for the record to be located. The matching record then displays on the form.

To try this yourself, make a copy of the folder containing the most recent version of the database navigation program. Open the program in Visual Basic. Replace the *Fill Array* button with the Find ID button, and change its name to cmdFindID. Figure 10.15 shows the GUI for this enhancement. Next, delete the code for the *cmdFillArrayWithDB_Click* procedure, along with the general declarations for the user-defined type array. Finally, write the code for the *cmdFindID_Click* event as shown in Figure 10.16.

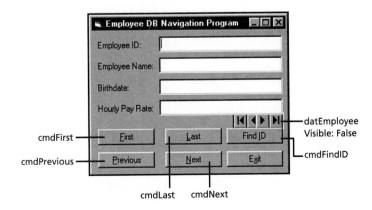

Figure 10.15 *Updated GUI for* Find ID *process.*

```
Private fTotRec As Integer

Private Sub cmdFindID_Click()
    Dim UserResp As String
    Dim SearchID As Integer
    Dim ErrorFlag As Boolean
    Dim SearchStr As String

    ErrorFlag = True
    Do While ErrorFlag
        UserResp = InputBox("Enter the Employee ID of the Employee" _
            & " you are seeking")
        If IsNumeric(UserResp) Then
            SearchID = CInt(UserResp)
            If SearchID >= 1 And SearchID <= fTotRec Then
                ErrorFlag = False
            Else
                Call MsgBox("Employee ID must be between 1 and " & _
                    Format(fTotRec) & ". Please re-enter.", _
                    vbOKOnly + vbInformation)
            End If
        Else
            Call MsgBox("Employee ID must be a number. " _
                & "Please re-enter.", vbOKOnly + vbInformation)
        End If
    Loop
    SearchStr = "EmpID = " & UserResp
    Call datEmployee.Recordset.FindFirst(SearchStr)
    Call ShowDBData
End Sub

Private Sub Form_Load()
    Dim FileName As String
    FileName = AppendFileToPath(App.Path, "EmployeeDB.MDB")
    ' Add optional error checking to make sure the file exists
    datEmployee.DatabaseName = FileName
    datEmployee.Refresh
    If datEmployee.Recordset.BOF And datEmployee.Recordset.EOF Then
        Call MsgBox("The database is empty. Program terminating.", _
            vbOKOnly + vbInformation)
        Call cmdExit_Click
    Else
        Call datEmployee.Recordset.MoveLast
        fTotRec = datEmployee.Recordset.RecordCount
    End If
End Sub
```

Figure 10.16   *Updated code for* Find ID *process.*

If you examine the code closely, you will notice that we added several checks on the ID entered by the user to make sure it was a number within the required range. If we assume that the user provides valid data, these checks are not needed. As you have probably realized by now, however, even knowledgeable users make errors when entering data. Therefore, well-written programs need to anticipate as many user-input errors as possible. Consequently, your programs should include appropriate data validation or error checking to prevent the program from terminating.

In this particular case, we keep requesting a new ID if the user enters an ID outside the valid range. After an ID within the valid range is specified, the matching record is sought. When found, the database record pointer will be positioned to the location of that first match. Unfortunately, if the database had some deleted records within the valid range, searching for these nonexistent records will actually create an error. Our next Find example will show how to use the NoMatch property to prevent errors on any Find operation.

What if you wanted to search for the match starting with the current record or in a backward fashion? The code for the other search options is exactly the same except for the specific Find method used. To search from the last record in a backward fashion, for example, you would just replace the

```
Call datName.Recordset.FindFirst(SearchString)
```

statement with this statement:

```
Call datName.Recordset.FindLast(SearchString)
```

Likewise, to search forward for the first match starting with the current record, use the following:

```
Call datName.Recordset.FindNext(SearchString)
```

Finally, to search backward for the first match starting with the current record, use this:

```
Call datName.Recordset.FindPrevious(SearchString)
```

Now we will consider the case of a record that is no longer in the database. If a few of the employees are fired or leave their jobs, for example, their IDs would not exist in the database. Then checking for numeric input within a certain range is not sufficient. In this situation, you should use the NoMatch property to determine whether the search was successful, and then process accordingly. Also, you should use the Bookmark property to keep track of the current record before initiating the search. Then, if the search was unsuccessful, you could move the record pointer back to that record.

To practice this, make another copy of the folder containing the latest database program. Open the Visual Basic program and delete the *cmdFindID_Click* procedure. Add an Employee Name text box to the form and replace the *Find ID* command button with a Find Name command button that is positioned next to the text box. The user will need to enter a name in the *Employee Name* text box and then click on *Find Name* to locate the matching record. If found, the matching record is displayed. If not, a message is displayed and the record that was displayed before the search will be displayed again. Figure 10.17 shows the updated GUI to search for employees by name. Figure 10.18 shows the code for the updated *cmdFindName_Click* procedure.

```
Private Sub cmdAddRec_Click()
    If cmdAddRec.Caption = "&Add" Then
        Call DisableNavigation
        Call datEmployee.Recordset.MoveLast
        txtID.Text = Format(datEmployee.Recordset!empid + 1)
        Call datEmployee.Recordset.AddNew
        txtEmpName.Text = ""
        txtBirthdate.Text = ""
        txtPayRate.Text = ""
        ' Change caption to Save and disable other buttons
        cmdAddRec.Caption = "&Save"
        cmdDeleteRec.Enabled = False
        Call txtEmpName.SetFocus
    Else ' the caption must be &Save Record
        Call WriteDBData
        datEmployee.Recordset!empid = txtID.Text
        Call datEmployee.Recordset.Update
        ' Change caption to Add and enable other buttons
        cmdAddRec.Caption = "&Add"
        cmdDeleteRec.Enabled = True
        Call EnableNavigation
    End If
End Sub
```

Figure 10.24   *Code for* Delete Record *operation.*

To try this out, copy the folder that contains the last program we discussed with the *Add* operation. Open the program in Visual Basic and add a Delete Record command button. Add the *cmdDeleteRec_Click* code shown in Figure 10.24. Additionally, make a slight modification to the *cmdAddRec_Click* procedure by adding the lines highlighted in bold.

The last type of record change is to modify an existing record. As with the *Delete* operation, you need to move to the desired record to make it the current record using a Find operation or by navigating through the database one record at a time. Once the record to be changed is current, apply the **Edit method**. This will copy the contents of the current record to the copy buffer. After the user has finished making changes, you need to apply the *Update* method to save the changes. If this step is omitted, the changes will be lost. Like with the *Add*, we will not allow the key field to be changed such that it creates duplicate keys. See Figure 10.25 for code to modify the current database record. Note that two more lines should be added to the *cmdAddRec_Click* procedure, as shown in bold.

```
Private Sub cmdModifyRec_Click()
    ' The current record will be the one to be modified
    If cmdModifyRec.Caption = "&Modify" Then
        Call DisableNavigation
        Call datEmployee.Recordset.Edit
        ' Change caption to Save and disable other buttons
        Call txtEmpName.SetFocus
        cmdModifyRec.Caption = "&Save"
        cmdDeleteRec.Enabled = False
        cmdAddRec.Enabled = False
    Else ' the caption must be &Save
        Call WriteDBData
        Call datEmployee.Recordset.Update
        ' Change caption to modify and enable other buttons
        cmdModifyRec.Caption = "&Modify"
        cmdDeleteRec.Enabled = True
        cmdAddRec.Enabled = True
        Call EnableNavigation
    End If
End Sub

Private Sub cmdAddRec_Click()
    If cmdAddRec.Caption = "&Add" Then
        Call DisableNavigation
        Call datEmployee.Recordset.MoveLast
        txtID.Text = Format(datEmployee.Recordset!empid + 1)
        Call datEmployee.Recordset.AddNew
        txtEmpName.Text = ""
        txtBirthdate.Text = ""
        txtPayRate.Text = ""
        ' Change caption to Save and disable other buttons
        cmdAddRec.Caption = "&Save"
        cmdDeleteRec.Enabled = False
        cmdModifyRec.Enabled = False
        Call txtEmpName.SetFocus
    Else ' the caption must be &Save Record
        Call WriteDBData
        datEmployee.Recordset!empid = txtID.Text
        Call datEmployee.Recordset.Update
        ' Change caption to Add and enable other buttons
        cmdAddRec.Caption = "&Add"
        cmdDeleteRec.Enabled = True
        cmdModifyRec.Enabled = True
        Call EnableNavigation
    End If
End Sub
```

Figure 10.25 *Code for* Modify Record *operation.*

Figure 10.26 shows a sample GUI for implementing all these operations in our *Employee* database program. To implement the final change, make another copy of the folder containing the *Delete* operation. Open the program in Visual Basic, and add a command button for *Modify Record*. Like the *Add* button, the caption on the

Modify button will change midway to *Save*, and the other buttons will be disabled to force the user to complete the change. After the interface has been updated, you should enter the remaining code as shown in Figure 10.25.

Before trying it out, you should make a backup copy of the database so that you can compare the original database to the modified database. When you are ready, run the program and practice various operations. After you have finished, you can go back to the original *Employee* database navigation program and view all the records. Then you can change the DatabaseName property to the other database and navigate again to compare the contents.

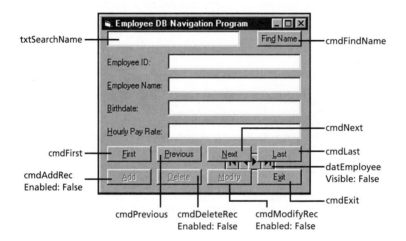

Figure 10.26 *New GUI for* Add, Delete, *and* Modify *operations.*

Preventing Errors

As stated earlier, the data control has a *Validate* event that is triggered just before the next record becomes current. To prevent the display of error messages and program termination due to these errors, you can add code to the *Validate* event to check for specific errors, correct them, and reset the error condition to prevent program termination. You can also add error handlers to some of the preceding procedures to trap for potential errors. In fact, it is a good idea to include error handlers in any procedure that accesses database data.

In the *Form Load* event where you assign the DatabaseName property, for example, you may want to add an error handler to trap for an invalid file reference due to a nonexistent database, file, or path (Err.Number = 3004, 3024, 3044, respectively). Likewise, in the *Add Record Click* event, you may want to trap for a blank primary key (Err.Number = 3058 or 3315) or duplicate primary key (Err.Number= 3022). Additionally, in the *Validate* event, you may want to verify that all data is of the correct type and length.

As shown in previous chapters, you need to make use of the *Err* object's Number property to identify the actual error. If there is one error to check, you can use a simple decision. If several errors must be checked, you need to use a nested *If* or *Select Case*. In all these situations, you may want to use the Description property to display Visual Basic's description of the error. Finally, to resume processing, you need to use the appropriate *Resume* statement as described in Chapter 6, "The Case Structure and Error Handling."

Figure 10.27 illustrates a revision that you can make to the *Form Load* procedure in the first program that assigned the database filename through code. To test this, change the name of the database file and run the program. When the program is loaded, the File Not Found error is detected. The error handler causes a descriptive error message to be displayed right before the program terminates.

```
Private Sub Form_Load()
    Dim FileName As String
    On Error GoTo FileError
    FileName = AppendFileToPath(App.Path, "EmployeeDB.MDB")
    ' Add optional error checking to make sure the file exists
    datEmployee.DatabaseName = FileName
    datEmployee.Refresh     ' needed to open the db & recognize the error
    Exit Sub
FileError:
    Select Case Err.Number
        Case 3004, 3024, 3044
            Call MsgBox(FileName & " not found. " & vbCrLf & vbCrLf & _
                "Once this program exits, " & _
                "make sure that the database is in the same " _
                & "location as the application. Then, you may run " _
                & "the program again." & vbCrLf & vbCrLf & "Error #" _
                & Err.Number & " and VB error description: " & _
                Err.Description, vbOKOnly + vbInformation)
        Case Else
            Call MsgBox(Err.Number & " - " & Err.Description, _
                vbOKOnly + vbInformation)
    End Select
    Unload frmMain
End Sub
```

Figure 10.27   *Database error handler for* Form Load *event.*

Payroll Database Case Study

The company you are consulting with was able to outsource the development of the employee payroll database. Now the company wants you to modify the program created in Chapter 9 to retrieve the accounting and payroll database data to create the weekly payroll file. As before, programs will be run weekly to produce the payroll file. The company's payroll database has an employee table that contains the Social Security number (SSN), name, and pay rate for all hourly employees, and a tax table that contains the salary cutoffs for each tax rate. In addition to processing all employees, you should also allow the user to quickly look up a specific employee's pay information by entering his or her name. The existing program that updates the company's records and prints payroll checks will still use the Pay file. This file must be in the CSV format and contain SSN, hours worked, gross pay, tax, and net pay for each employee who has worked during the pay period. Finally, the manager tells you that the program must be designed so that when the IRS tax rates change, the modifications to the database can be done through the program. This includes adding or deleting tax records if the number of categories change, as well as modifying existing tax records in the event the cutoffs change.

Step 1: Analyze the Problem

Because this sounds very similar to the file-oriented program we just wrote in the preceding chapter, we decide to review that program again in more detail. Next, we need to outline the similarities and differences. Primarily, the data is now coming from a database rather than a file. In addition, we are adding more options to peruse the employee database table one record at a time or to jump to a specific record. Finally, we need to add features that will allow record-level changes to the tax table.

We can now construct a table of our input, processing, and output needs (Analysis Table) as shown in Figure 10.28. Because we are really doing two separate problems, we have two rows in the Analysis Table. The first row identifies the IPO needs of the paycheck processing, and the second row identifies the IPO needs of the tax table navigation and updating.

The input and output needs that are read from or written to a database table are marked by "(dbt)." Note that all output will be written to the same CSV pay file as in the previous chapter. Like before, for security reasons it will not be displayed on the user interface.

Major Function	Input Needs	Processing Needs	Output
Process employee paychecks	SSN (Emp dbt)	Load tax tables.	SSN (Form & Pay file)
	Name (Emp dbt)	Read Emp record.	Name (Form)
	Hours worked (Form)	Validate the	Hourly pay rate (Form)
	Hourly pay rate	hours.	Hours worked (Pay file)
	(Emp dbt)	Calculate:	Gross pay (Pay file)
	Income levels	Gross pay	Tax (Pay file)
	(Tax dbt)	Tax	Net pay (Pay file)
	Tax rates (Tax dbt)	Net pay	Error message if nonnumeric
	Name of pay file	Write Pay record.	hours.
		Find Emp record.	Error message if hours are not
		Return to main	within allowed range.
		form.	Error message if database
		Exit program.	files do not exist.
			Notify user if output file
			exists.

Major Function	Input Needs	Processing Needs	Output
Navigate tax table and update as needed	Income levels Tax rates	Load tax tables. Write tax record. Read tax record. Find tax rate for given income level.	Income levels (Tax dbt) Tax rates (Tax dbt)

Figure 10.28 *Analysis Table for* Payroll Database *program.*

Step 2: Design or Create the User Interface

Using the three basic controls to handle input (text box), processing (command button), and output (label and text box) needs, we can revise our Analysis Table to identify how many and which types of controls our program needs (see Figure 10.29). Because there are two separate functions, we use separate forms to distinguish each function. In addition, we add a third "main" form to select whether to process paychecks or to navigate the tax tables. Each form needs to provide fast program termination. In addition, the two functional forms need to be able to return to the main form.

Function	Input Needs	Processing Needs	Output Needs
Main form		■ Command buttons to decide which process is desired: ● Input employee pay data ● Navigate tax tables ● Exit program	
Process employee paycheck	■ Text box and descriptive label for hours worked ■ Retrieve pay file name via system (Note that the other input is from the database table, so no controls are needed on the form for input.)	■ Next command button to: ● Validate the hours ● Calculate: Gross pay Tax Net pay ● Write Pay record ■ Find command button to locate specific employee by name ■ Main command button to return to main form ■ Exit command button to terminate processing	■ Display and descriptive labels for: ● SSN (Emp dbt) ● Name (Emp dbt) ● Hourly pay rate (Emp dbt) ■ Error messages displayed using system message boxes (Note that the other output is to the pay file, so no controls are needed on the form for output.)

continues

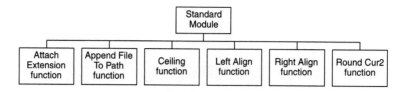

Figure 10.32   Payroll Database *program standard module Object-Event Diagram.*

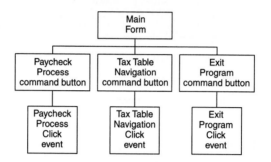

Figure 10.33   Payroll Database *program main form Object-Event Diagram.*

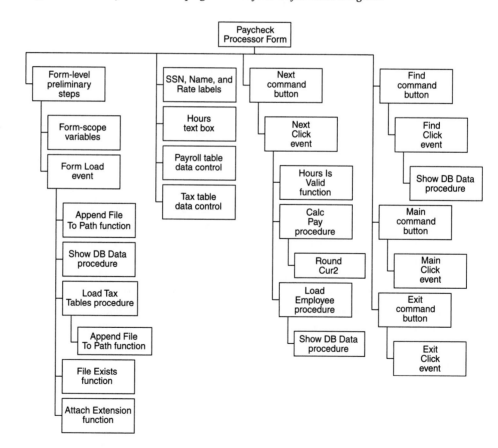

Figure 10.34   Payroll Database *program paycheck processor form Object-Event Diagram.*

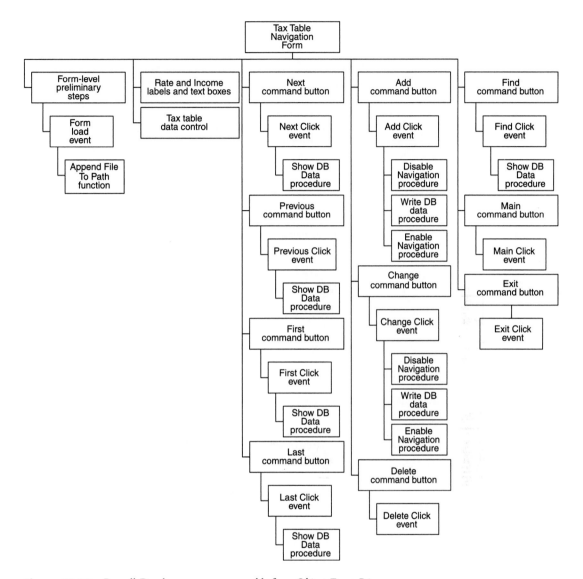

Figure 10.35   Payroll Database *program tax table form Object-Event Diagram.*

Because our program will be interfacing with several files, we need to document the organization of each file and the association of the files with the program. As depicted in Figure 10.36, the *Payroll Database* is both an input and output file and the Pay file is only an output file. Figure 10.37 documents the organization of both tables in the *Payroll Database.* Figure 10.38 repeats the organization of the pay CSV file—that is, the fields are separated by commas.

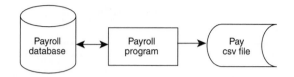

Figure 10.36 Payroll Database *program with files.*

Table	Field Name	Description
EmpInfo	SSN	11-character identification code that uniquely identifies each employee (999-99-9999)
	EmpName	The full name of the employee (up to 30 characters)
	HourlyRate	The hourly pay rate stored as Currency
TaxTable	AnnualIncome	The maximum income for a particular tax rate stored as Currency
	TaxRate	The tax rate stored as a percent

Figure 10.37 Payroll Database *design.*

Field Names and Data Types in Pay CSV File				
SSN	Hours	Gross Pay	Tax	Net Pay
(Long)	(Double)	(Currency)	(Currency)	(Currency)

Figure 10.38 *Payroll CSV file record layout.*

The payroll program from the preceding chapter was written to allow the user to identify the filenames on the command line. This version of the program will assume that there is only one companywide *Payroll* database. Consequently, the name of the *Payroll* database file is "hard-coded" in the program with an assumption that it will be stored at the same location as this program. Because the payroll CSV file will change each week, however, the user will be prompted to enter the filename.

Step 3b: Design the Micro-Level View (Flowcharts or Pseudocode)

Our job now is to design the logic for each procedure displayed in the Object-Event Diagrams, Figures 10.31 through 10.35. Because this program is an enhancement to the one from Chapter 9, we will only discuss the new procedures or old procedures that have been changed. Refer to Figure 10.39 for the detailed program logic of the new procedures. If you have questions about the other procedures, you should refer to the logic discussion in the preceding chapter. Our order of presentation will follow their left-to-right, top-to-down order of appearance in the Object-Event Diagrams.

Standard Module: Attach Extension Function
Begin AttachExtension(Filename, Extension)
    Temp = position of "." in Filename
    If Temp > 1 (there is a "." after one or more characters in Filename)
       File = Filename with everything after "." cropped off
    Else If Temp = 1 (the first character is ".")
       Display message that filename is invalid & "Backup" will be used
       File = "Backup"
    Return File & Extension
End AttachExtension

Standard Module: AppendFileToPath Function
Begin AppendFileToPath(Pathname, Filename)
    If Pathname was not supplied
       Return Filename
    Else If Pathname ends in "\"
       Return Pathname & Filename
    Else
       Return Pathname & "\" & Filename
End AppendFileToPath

Main Form: Paycheck Process Click Event
Begin PaycheckClick
    Unload the Main form
    Show the Paycheck form
End PaycheckClick

Main Form: Tax Table Navigation Click Event
Begin TaxClick
    Unload the Main form
    Show the Tax form
End TaxClick

Main Form: Exit Click Event
Begin Exit Click
    Unload the Main form
End Exit Click

continues

Paycheck Form: Form-Scope Variables
Begin Form-scope Variables
    fName: *String*   *(Employee name)*
    fPayRef   *Long*   *(File Reference number for Pay file)*
    fPayFile: *String*   *(File name for Pay file)*
    fPayRate: *Currency*   *(Employee hourly pay rate)*
    fSSN: *Long*   *(Employee social security number)*
    fIncomeTable():   *Currency*   *(Array of income levels for tax rates)*
    fTaxRateTable():   *Double*   *(Array of tax rates for income levels)*
End Form-scope Variables

Paycheck Form: Form Load Event
Begin FormLoad
    Filename = AppendFileToPath(App.Path, "Payroll.MDB")
    datPayroll Database file = Filename
    Move to first table record
    Call ShowDBData
    Call LoadTaxTables
    Get fPayFile from User
    If nothing entered Then
        fPayFile = "Paycheck"
        Display message
    fPayFile = AttachExtension(fPayFile, "csv")
    fPayFile = AppendFileToPath(App.Path, fPayFile)
    Open fPayFile for Output as #1
End FormLoad

Paycheck Form: ShowDBData Procedure
Begin ShowDBData
    lblSSN = value of SSN field in current table record
    lblName = value of EmpName field in current table record
    lblRate = value of HourlyRate field in current table record
    fSSN = lblSSN
    fName = lblName
    fPayRate = lblRate
End ShowDBData

Paycheck Form: LoadTaxTables Procedure
Begin LoadTaxTables
    Filename = AppendFileToPath(App.Path, "Payroll.MDB")
    datPayroll Database file = Filename
    Move to first table record
    I = 0
    Do Until past end of DB table
        I = I + 1
        fIncomeTable(I) = value of AnnualIncome in current DB record
        fTaxRate(I) = value of TaxRate field in current DB record
        Move to next table record
    Close database
End LoadTaxTables

Paycheck Form: FileExists Function

Begin FileExists(FileName)
    Open FileName for Input as #1
    If Open Was Successful
        Result = True
        Close #1
    Else
        Result = False
    Return Result
End FileExists

Paycheck Form: LoadEmployee Procedure

Begin LoadEmployee
    Clear Hours text box
    Move to next table record
    IF EOF
        Display "No more employees to"
          "process"
        Clear Name label
        Clear SSN label
        Disable Next button
    Else
        Call ShowDBData
End LoadEmployee

Paycheck Form: Find Click Event

Begin Find Click
    CurRecord = current table record pointer
    Get SearchName from User
    If SearchName = "" Then
        Display "Find canceled"
    Else
        SearchString = "EmpName Like "" & SearchName & """*
        Find first table record that matches SearchString
        If search was unsuccessful Then
            Display "No such employee"
            Reset current record pointer to CurRecord
        Else
            Call ShowDBData
            Display instructions message
End Find Click

Paycheck Form: Main Click Event

Begin Main Click
    Close all files
    Unload the Paycheck form
    Show the Main form
End Main Click

Paycheck Form: Exit Click Event

Begin Exit Click
    Close all files
    Unload the Paycheck form
End Exit Click

continues

Name	Hrs
Thomas O Whitten	8
Owen F Detweiler	11
Stephen Donneger	32
Dirk Gehman	38
Edward S Eastman	38
Michael L Aiman	9
Tony A Edison	12
Grace J Ebermann	35
Carol C Banana	40
Ralph J Alderfer	40
Harold U Bates	45
Candice F Carter	50

Figure 10.41 *Test data for* Payroll Database *program.*

After the program terminates, you should be able to view the contents of the pay-check file and compare with the anticipated results illustrated in Figure 10.42.

SSN	Name	Rate	Hrs	Gross	Gross*52	Tax	Net
241341521	Thomas O Whitten	10.75	8	86.00	4472	0.00	86.00
492735055	Owen F Detweiler	17.30	11	190.30	9896	19.03	171.27
533479537	Stephen Donneger	15.00	32	480.00	24960	72.00	408.00
639170707	Dirk Gehman	37.00	38	1406.00	73112	351.50	1054.50
690371986	Edward S Eastman	75.00	38	2850.00	148200	940.50	1909.50
761236124	Michael L Aiman	10.75	9	96.75	5031	9.68	87.07
785720348	Tony A Edison	17.30	12	207.60	10795	31.14	176.46
790184316	Grace J Ebermann	15.00	35	525.00	27300	131.25	393.75
826687434	Carol C Banana	37.00	40	1480.00	76960	488.40	991.60
841182276	Ralph J Alderfer	75.00	40	3000.00	156000	1200.00	1800.00
949744067	Harold U Bates	10.95	45	520.13	27047	130.03	390.10
987493232	Candice F Carter	15.65	50	860.75	44759	215.19	645.56

Figure 10.42 *Anticipated results with test data for* Payroll Database *program.*

Figure 10.43 contains a list of test cases that we want to use to test our program. You should expand this list with several sets of your own test data.

Case	User Input and Actions	Expected Results
1	Run the program and click *Exit*.	The program stops running.
2	Run the program and click *Input Employee Hours*.	An InputBox requesting the file name appears.
3	Click *Cancel*.	A message box displays Invalid filename. Paycheck.csv will be used.
4	Click the *OK* button on the message box.	The Payroll form appears, showing the first employee's information.
5	Enter all the sample data shown in Figure 10.41 and click *Next* after each entry.	After the last employee's hours have been entered, a message stating that no more employees exist is displayed.
6	Click *OK* on the message box and then click *Main* on the payroll form.	The main form is displayed. At this point, the Paycheck.csv file should match the anticipated results shown in Figure 10.42.
7	Click *Input Employee Hours*. Enter paycheck in the filename InputBox.	A message asking whether the file should be rewritten is displayed.
8	Click *No*.	The program terminates. At this point, the Paycheck.csv file should be unchanged.
9	Run the program and click *Input Employee Hours*. Enter pay2 for the filename.	The payroll form appears showing the first record.
10	Click *Find* and enter Doris in the InputBox.	A message box stating there is no such employee is displayed.
11	Click *OK* and then click *Find* again. This time enter Grace.	A message box instructing us to enter Grace's hours and then click *Next* is displayed.
12	Enter 50 and click *Next*.	Carol's record appears (because she follows Grace).
13	Enter 15 and click *Next*. Then click *Main*.	The main form appears. (At this point, the pay2.csv file should contain two payroll records. See Figure 10.44.)

continues

Case	User Input and Actions	Expected Results
14	Click *Edit Tax Rates*.	The tax tables form appears, displaying the first record.
15	Try to change the data in the text boxes.	Nothing should happen because the text boxes should be locked.
16	Click *Change*, make the income level 4000, and click *Save*.	The updated record should be displayed.
17	Click *Last*.	The last record is displayed.
18	Click *Delete*.	The 33% tax rate record is displayed (the new last record).
19	Click *First* and then click *Previous*.	The 33% tax rate record is displayed (the new last record).
20	Click *Add* and enter .5 for rate and 900000000 for income. Click *Save*.	The 33% tax rate record is displayed (the new last record).
21	Click *FindRate* and enter 1000000.	The 50% rate just entered is displayed
22	Click *Exit*.	The program terminates.

Figure 10.43 Payroll Database *test plan*.

SSN	Hrs	Gross	Tax	Net
790184316	50	825	206.25	618.75
826687434	15	555	138.75	416.25

Figure 10.44 *Anticipated contents of Pay2.csv for Test Case 13.*

Step 4: Code the Program

Figure 10.45 shows the complete code listing for the program, and you can refer to it as needed. This program is large enough that it makes sense for you to implement this program incrementally. At the end of each step, you should make sure that the program works properly before proceeding to the next step. One possible set of implementation steps is as follows:

- Write all the code for the main form (*cmdExit_Click*, *cmdPay_Click*, *cmdUpdate_Click*) and the *cmdExit_Click* and *cmdMain_Click* procedures on the other two forms. Make sure that you can switch back and forth between forms as well as exit for any form.

- Copy the *AttachExtension* and *AppendFileToPath* functions in the *basTools* module.

- Write the *Form Load* procedure in the tax form. Write the *cmdFirst_Click* and *ShowDBData* procedures. Test with different databases to make sure the error handling prevents errors and the first record displays at the start.

- Implement the code in the tax form to perform the other navigation operations (*cmdLast_Click*, *cmdNext_Click*, and *cmdPrevious_Click*). Test to make sure each works correctly.

- Implement the code in the tax form to locate the applicable tax rate (*cmdFind_Click*). Test by locating the rates for a really low income, a really high income, the exact incomes for each range, and incomes within each category.

- Implement the code in the tax form to add, delete, and modify records (*cmdAdd_Click*, *cmdDelete_Click*, *cmdModify_Click*, *DisableNavigation*, *EnableNavigation*, and *WriteDBData*). Test each of the button processes.

- Write the *Form Load* procedure in the employee form. Write the form-scope declarations, the *ShowDBData* and *LoadTaxTables* procedures, and the *FileExists* function. Test with different databases to make sure the error handling prevents errors and the first record displays at the start.

- Write the code to locate a specific employee record (*cmdFind_Click*). Test by looking up the first employee (Thomas), the last employee (Candice), an employee in the middle (Tony), and a nonexistent employee (Mike).

- Write the remaining code to process the paycheck information (*cmdNext_Click*, *HoursIsValid* function, *LoadEmployee* procedure, and *CalcPay* procedure). Test with the sample data shown in Figure 10.41.

```
' Program:    Payroll
' Form:       frmMain
' Programmer: Ima Goodstudent
' Date:       October 25, 1998
' Purpose:    Manage tax table in payroll database & create payroll
'             csv file of paid employees. The processing for each
'             function is handled in two separate forms accessible
'             from this form.
Option Explicit

' Purpose: When the Exit button is clicked, the files the program
'          stops executing.
Private Sub cmdExit_Click()
    Unload frmMain
End Sub

' Purpose: When the Pay button is clicked, the Main form is unloaded
'          and the employee paycheck processing form is shown.
Private Sub cmdPay_Click()
    Unload frmMain
    Call frmCalcPay.Show
End Sub
```

continues

```vb
' Purpose: When the Edit Tax Rates button is clicked, the main form
'          is unloaded and the tax table form is shown.
Private Sub cmdUpdate_Click()
    Unload frmMain
    Call frmTax.Show
End Sub


' Program:    Payroll
' Form:       frmCalcPay
' Programmer: Ima Goodstudent
' Date:       October 25, 1998
' Purpose:    Access payroll database & create payroll csv file. The
'             employee table contains the SSN, name, and hourly pay rate
'             for each employee. The tax table contains cutoff income
'             levels and their corresponding tax rates. The user can
'             enter hours for all/most employees or look up individual
'             employees and enter the hours worked. A CSV pay file is
'             created that includes the employee's gross pay, tax, and
'             net pay, along with the SSN and hours worked. If all
'             employees are being processed and a particular employee
'             has not worked, the user presses Enter. No information
'             is written to the pay file. In all cases, the SSN and
'             name of the next employee are displayed. After all the
'             employees have been processed, the user can click Exit or
'             return to the main form.
' Input:      Payroll database with tax table and employee table
' Output:     Pay CSV file with fields: SSN, hours, gross, tax, net


Option Explicit

' The range of valid hours is
Private Const cfMaxHrs As Long = 100
Private Const cfMinHrs As Long = 5

' Overtime-related constants
Private Const cfOTHrs  As Double = 40
Private Const cfOTRate As Double = 1.5

Private Const cfAnnualPayFactor As Long = 52

Private fName As String
Private fPayRef As Long
Private fPayFile As String
Private fPayRate As Currency
Private fSSN As Long

' Tax table arrays
Private fIncomeTable() As Currency
Private fTaxRateTable() As Double

' Purpose: Pass hours worked to calculate gross pay, tax, and net pay.
Private Sub CalcPay(ByVal Hrs As Double, ByRef rGross As Currency, _
    ByRef rTax As Currency, ByRef rNet As Currency)

    Dim I As Long

    ' Calculate the Gross and then round to the nearest cent
    If Hrs > cfOTHrs Then
        rGross = fPayRate * (cfOTHrs + (Hrs - cfOTHrs) * cfOTRate)
        rGross = RoundCur2(rGross)
    Else
        rGross = RoundCur2(fPayRate * Hrs)
    End If
```

```
    ' Find the tax rate, calculate the tax, and then round
    I = 1
    Do Until rGross * cfAnnualPayFactor < fIncomeTable(I)
        I = I + 1
    Loop
    rTax = RoundCur2(rGross * fTaxRateTable(I))
    rNet = rGross - rTax
End Sub

' Purpose: When the Exit button is clicked the files are closed and the
'          program stops executing.
Private Sub cmdExit_Click()
    Close
    Unload frmCalcPay
End Sub

' Purpose: When the Find button is clicked, the user is asked for a
'          name. This name is used to lookup corresponding information
'          in the database and display it on the form.
Private Sub cmdFind_Click()
    Dim CurRecord As Variant
    Dim SearchString As String
    Dim SearchName As String

    ' Save location of current record
    CurRecord = datPayroll.Recordset.Bookmark
    SearchName = InputBox("Enter the name of the employee " & _
        "to be found:")
    If SearchName = "" Then ' Cancel pressed or nothing entered
        Call MsgBox("No name entered. Find canceled.", vbOKOnly + _
            vbInformation)
    Else
        SearchString = "EmpName Like '" & SearchName & "*'"
        Call datPayroll.Recordset.FindFirst(SearchString)
        If datPayroll.Recordset.NoMatch Then
            Call MsgBox("No such employee", vbOKOnly + vbInformation)
            ' Move pointer to previously saved location
            datPayroll.Recordset.Bookmark = CurRecord
        Else
            Call ShowDBData
            Call MsgBox("To add a paycheck record for " & _
                datPayroll.Recordset!EmpName & _
                ", enter hours worked and press Next.", _
                vbOKOnly + vbInformation)
        End If
    End If
End Sub

' Purpose: When the Main button is clicked, this form is unloaded
'          and the main form is shown.
Private Sub cmdMain_Click()
    Close
    Unload Me
    frmMain.Show
End Sub

' Purpose: When the Next button is clicked, the gross pay, tax, and net
'          pay are calculated and, along with the SSN, are written to
'          the pay file.
```

continues

```
                            & vbCrLf & vbCrLf & "Error #" & Err.Number & _
                            " and VB error description: " & Err.Description, _
                            vbOKOnly + vbInformation)
                Case 3021  ' empty database
                    Call MsgBox("Database table is empty. " & vbCrLf & vbCrLf & _
                            "Once this program exits, copy the correct database " & _
                            "with the employee names, SSNs, and rates in the " _
                            & "employee table, and then run the program again." _
                            & vbCrLf & vbCrLf & "FYI: Error #" & Err.Number & _
                            " and VB error description: " & Err.Description, _
                            vbOKOnly + vbInformation)
                Case Else
                    Call MsgBox("Unexpected error #" & CStr(Err.Number) & _
                            " occurred: " & Err.Description, vbCritical)
            End Select
            Stop
    End Sub

    ' Purpose: The current record's data is displayed in the corresponding
    '          labels on the form as well as assigned to form-scope
    '          variables for later processing.
    Private Sub ShowDBData()
        lblSSN.Caption = datPayroll.Recordset!ssn
        lblName.Caption = datPayroll.Recordset!EmpName
        lblRate.Caption = Format(datPayroll.Recordset!HourlyRate, _
            "currency")
        fSSN = CLng(lblSSN.Caption)
        fName = lblName.Caption
        fPayRate = CCur(lblRate.Caption)
    End Sub

    ' Purpose: Returns true if FileName exists, and false if not.
    Private Function FileExists(ByVal FileName As String) As Boolean
        Dim File As Integer

        File = FreeFile
        ' Enable error checking and see whether file is present
        On Error GoTo HandleErrors
        Open FileName For Input As File
        ' There was no error so file must exist
        FileExists = True
        Close File
    Exit Function

    HandleErrors:    ' Handle any errors here
        Const ErrFileNotFound As Long = 53
        Const ErrPathFileAccessError As Long = 75
        Const ErrPathNotFound As Long = 76

        ' There was an error during open: file doesn't exist or path error
        Select Case Err.Number
            Case ErrFileNotFound, ErrPathNotFound, ErrPathFileAccessError
                FileExists = False
                Exit Function
            Case Else
                Call MsgBox("Unexpected error #" & CStr(Err.Number) & _
                        " occurred: " & Err.Description, vbCritical)
                Stop
        End Select
    End Function
```

```
' Program:    Payroll
' Form:       frmTax
' Programmer: Ima Goodstudent
' Date:       October 25, 1998
' Purpose:    Manage tax table in payroll database by allowing
'             navigation and modifications at the record level.
'             Individual records can be looked up by identifying an
'             income. The user can exit directly or return to the main
'             form. The tax table contains cutoff income levels and
'             their corresponding tax rates.
' Input:      Tax table of payroll database.
' Output:     Updated tax table in payroll database
Option Explicit

' Purpose: When the user clicks on Exit, the program terminates.
Private Sub cmdExit_Click()
    Unload frmTax
End Sub

' Purpose: When the form is loaded, the database filename is
'          assigned and the database is opened to the first record.
Private Sub Form_Load()
    Dim FileName As String
    On Error GoTo HandleErrors
    FileName = AppendFileToPath(App.Path, "Payroll.MDB")
    ' Add optional error checking to make sure the file exists
    datPayroll.DatabaseName = FileName
    Call datPayroll.Refresh
    Call cmdFirst_Click
    ' There was no error so file must exist
    Exit Sub

HandleErrors:    ' Handle any errors here
    Select Case Err.Number
        Case 3004, 3024, 3044 ' DB file does not exist
            Call MsgBox(FileName & " not found. " & vbCrLf & vbCrLf & _
                "Once this program exits, make sure that the " & _
                "database is in the same location as the " _
                & "application. Then, you may run the program again." _
                & vbCrLf & vbCrLf & "FYI: Error #" & Err.Number & _
                " and VB error description: " & Err.Description, _
                vbOKOnly + vbInformation)
        Case 3021 ' empty database
            Call MsgBox("Database table is empty. " & vbCrLf & vbCrLf & _
                "Once this program exits, copy the correct " & _
                "database with the minimum income levels and rates " _
                & "in the tax table, and then run the program again." _
                & vbCrLf & vbCrLf & "FYI: Error #" & Err.Number & _
                " and VB error description: " & Err.Description, _
                vbOKOnly + vbInformation)
        Case 58 ' File already exists
            Call MsgBox(FileName & " already exists. " & vbCrLf & _
                vbCrLf & "The program is terminating to avoid over-" _
                & "writing the file. Run it again and enter a new " & _
                "name.", vbOKOnly + vbInformation)
        Case Else
            Call MsgBox("Unexpected error #" & CStr(Err.Number) & _
                " occurred: " & Err.Description, vbCritical)
    End Select
    Stop
End Sub
```

continues

```vb
' Purpose: When the Find button is clicked, the user enters
'          the income level. This data is used to look up the
'          appropriate tax record to be displayed on the form.
Private Sub cmdFind_Click()
    Dim CurRecord As Variant
    Dim SearchString As String
    Dim SearchRate As String

    ' Save location of current record
    CurRecord = datPayroll.Recordset.Bookmark

    SearchRate = InputBox("Enter the yearly income to " & _
        "look up the corresponding tax rate:")
    If SearchRate = "" Then ' Cancel pressed or nothing entered
        Call MsgBox("Nothing entered for income. Find canceled.", _
            vbOKOnly + vbInformation)
    ElseIf Not IsNumeric(SearchRate) Then
        Call MsgBox("Income must be numeric. Find canceled.", _
            vbOKOnly + vbInformation)
    Else
        SearchString = "AnnualIncome >= " & SearchRate
        Call datPayroll.Recordset.FindFirst(SearchString)

        If datPayroll.Recordset.NoMatch Then
            Call MsgBox("No rate found", vbOKOnly + vbInformation)
            ' Move pointer to previously saved location
            datPayroll.Recordset.Bookmark = CurRecord
        Else
            Call ShowDBData
        End If
    End If
End Sub

' Purpose: When the First button is clicked, the db pointer is set
'          to the first record & its data is displayed on the form.
Private Sub cmdFirst_Click()
    Call datPayroll.Recordset.MoveFirst
    Call ShowDBData
End Sub

' Purpose: When the Last button is clicked, the db pointer is set
'          to the last record & its data is displayed on the form.
Private Sub cmdLast_Click()
    Call datPayroll.Recordset.MoveLast
    Call ShowDBData
End Sub

' Purpose: When the Previous button is clicked, the db pointer is
'          set to the previous record & its data is displayed.
Private Sub cmdPrevious_Click()
    Call datPayroll.Recordset.MovePrevious
    If datPayroll.Recordset.BOF Then
        Call datPayroll.Recordset.MoveLast
    End If
    Call ShowDBData
End Sub
```

```
' Purpose: When the Next button is clicked, the database pointer is
'          set to the next record and its data is displayed on the form.
Private Sub cmdNext_Click()
    Call datPayroll.Recordset.MoveNext
    If datPayroll.Recordset.EOF Then
        Call datPayroll.Recordset.MoveFirst
    End If
    Call ShowDBData
End Sub


' Purpose: Displays the current record's data in the corresponding
'          text boxes on the form.
Private Sub ShowDBData()
    txtTaxRate.Text = datPayroll.Recordset!TaxRate
    txtIncome.Text = datPayroll.Recordset!AnnualIncome
End Sub


' Purpose: When the Add buton is clicked, the display controls are
'          cleared, and the copy buffer is cleared to accept data
'          for a new record. The caption is changed to Save so the
'          user can indicate when the record data has been entered
'          and should be written to the database. Other controls
'          are disabled to limit the user's choices until the Save
'          has been processed.
Private Sub cmdAddRec_Click()
    If cmdAddRec.Caption = "&Add" Then
        Call DisableNavigation
        Call datPayroll.Recordset.AddNew
        txtTaxRate.Text = ""
        txtIncome.Text = ""
        ' Change caption to Add and disable other buttons
        cmdAddRec.Caption = "&Save"
        cmdDeleteRec.Enabled = False
        cmdModifyRec.Enabled = False
    Else ' the caption must be &Save
        Call WriteDBData
        Call datPayroll.Recordset.Update
        ' Change caption to Add and disable other buttons
        cmdAddRec.Caption = "&Add"
        cmdDeleteRec.Enabled = True
        cmdModifyRec.Enabled = True
        Call EnableNavigation
    End If
End Sub


' Purpose: Called when the user is in the middle of an add/change,
'          so this procedure disables several controls and unlocks
'          text boxes so the user can change the data.
Private Sub DisableNavigation()
    Dim CurRec As Variant
    CurRec = datPayroll.Recordset.Bookmark
    cmdFirst.Enabled = False
    cmdLast.Enabled = False
    cmdPrevious.Enabled = False
    cmdNext.Enabled = False
    datPayroll.ReadOnly = False
    txtIncome.Locked = False
    txtTaxRate.Locked = False
    Call datPayroll.Refresh
    Call datPayroll.Recordset.MoveLast
    datPayroll.Recordset.Bookmark = CurRec
    Call txtTaxRate.SetFocus
End Sub
```

continues

```
' Purpose: Called when the user has just completed an add or change
'          to let this procedure enable the disabled controls and
'          lock the text boxes again so the user cannot change the
'          data accidentally.
Private Sub EnableNavigation()
    Dim CurRec As Variant
    CurRec = datPayroll.Recordset.Bookmark
    cmdFirst.Enabled = True
    cmdLast.Enabled = True
    cmdPrevious.Enabled = True
    cmdNext.Enabled = True
    datPayroll.ReadOnly = True
    txtIncome.Locked = True
    txtTaxRate.Locked = True
    Call datPayroll.Refresh
    Call datPayroll.Recordset.MoveLast
    datPayroll.Recordset.Bookmark = CurRec
    Call txtTaxRate.SetFocus
End Sub

' Purpose: This procedure copies the contents of the text boxes
'          to corresponding fields in the current database record.
Private Sub WriteDBData()
    datPayroll.Recordset!AnnualIncome = txtIncome.Text
    datPayroll.Recordset!TaxRate = txtTaxRate.Text
End Sub

' Purpose: When the Delete button is clicked, the current database
'          record being displayed is deleted from the database.
Private Sub cmdDeleteRec_Click()
    Dim CurRec As Variant
    CurRec = datPayroll.Recordset.Bookmark
    ' The current record will be the one to be deleted
    datPayroll.ReadOnly = False
    Call datPayroll.Refresh
    Call datPayroll.Recordset.MoveLast
    datPayroll.Recordset.Bookmark = CurRec
    Call datPayroll.Recordset.Delete
    datPayroll.ReadOnly = True
    Call datPayroll.Refresh
    ' Move to the last record
    Call cmdLast_Click
    If datPayroll.Recordset.EOF Then ' The last record was deleted
        Call cmdFirst_Click
        If datPayroll.Recordset.BOF Then ' There are no records
            Call MsgBox("There are no records left-the DB is" _
                & " empty", vbOKOnly + vbInformation)
        End If
    End If
End Sub

' Purpose: When the Change buton is clicked, the database is ready
'          to accept changes for the modified record. The caption
'          is changed to Save to let user indicate when the record
'          data has been entered and should be written to the db.
'          Other controls are disabled to limit the user's choices
'          until the Save has been processed.
Private Sub cmdModifyRec_Click()
```

```
        ' The current record will be the one to be modified
        If cmdModifyRec.Caption = "&Change" Then
            Call DisableNavigation
            Call datPayroll.Recordset.Edit
            ' Change caption to Save and disable other buttons
            cmdModifyRec.Caption = "&Save"
            cmdDeleteRec.Enabled = False
            cmdAddRec.Enabled = False
        Else ' the caption must be &Save
            Call WriteDBData
            Call datPayroll.Recordset.Update
            ' Change caption to Change and disable other buttons
            cmdModifyRec.Caption = "&Change"
            cmdDeleteRec.Enabled = True
            cmdAddRec.Enabled = True
            Call EnableNavigation
        End If
End Sub


' Purpose: When the Main button is clicked, this form is unloaded
'          and the main form is shown.
Private Sub cmdMain_Click()
    Unload Me
    frmMain.Show
End Sub



' Module:      basTools
' Purpose:     Contains public procedures: AttachExtension
'                                          AppendFileToPath
'                                          Ceiling
'                                          LeftAlign
'                                          RightAlign
'                                          RoundCur2


Option Explicit

' Purpose: This function safely appends desired extension to the
'          passed filename
' Inputs:  Filename and desired extension as strings
' Returns: Filename with desired extension
Public Function AttachExtension(ByVal File As String, _
    ByVal Ext As String) As String
    Dim Temp As Integer

    Temp = InStr(1, File, ".")
    If Temp > 1 Then
        File = Left(File, Temp - 1) ' crop off after period
    ElseIf Temp = 1 Then
        Call MsgBox("The filename entered is not acceptable. " & _
            "File renamed to Backup", vbOKOnly + vbInformation)
        File = "Backup"
    End If
    AttachExtension = File & Ext
End Function

' Purpose: This function safely appends the passed filename
'          to the passed path by making sure the last character
'          in the path contains a "\"
' Inputs:  Path name and filename as strings
' Returns: Complete filename with path as a string
Public Function AppendFileToPath(ByVal Path As String, _
ByVal File As String) As String
```

continues

```
        If Path = "" Then      ' the path was not supplied
                AppendFileToPath = File
            ElseIf Right(Path, 1) = "\" Then
                AppendFileToPath = Path & File
            Else
                AppendFileToPath = Path & "\" & File
            End If
    End Function

    ' Purpose:    Returns the smallest integer not less than the arg.
    ' Input:      Double value to have its ceiling calculated
    ' Returns:    Double value with zero fractional part
    Public Function Ceiling(ByVal X As Double) As Double
        If X <= 0 Then
            Ceiling = Fix(X)
        Else
            If X <> Fix(X) Then
                Ceiling = Fix(X + 1)
            Else
                Ceiling = X
            End If
        End If
    End Function

    ' Purpose:    Left aligns a string
    ' Inputs:     Source: String to be left aligned
    '             Length: Length of returned string
    ' Returns:    Returns a string of length Length, with Source
    '             left aligned and padded with spaces on the right
    Public Function LeftAlign(ByVal Source As String, _
            ByVal Length As Integer) As String
        Dim Result As String

        Result = Space(Length)
        LSet Result = Source
        LeftAlign = Result
    End Function

    ' Purpose:    Right aligns a string
    ' Inputs:     Source: String to be Eight aligned
    '             Length: Length of returned string
    ' Returns:    Returns a string of length Length, with Source
    '             right aligned and padded with spaces on the left
    Public Function RightAlign(ByVal Source As String, _
            ByVal Length As Integer) As String
        Dim Result As String

        Result = Space(Length)
        RSet Result = Source
        RightAlign = Result
    End Function

    ' Purpose:    Rounds Currency to two decimal places
    ' Inputs:     Money: Currency value to be rounded
    ' Returns:    Currency rounded to two decimal places
    Public Function RoundCur2(ByVal Money As Currency) As Currency
        Dim Cents As Currency

        Cents = Int(Money * 100 + 0.5)
        RoundCur2 = Cents / 100
    End Function
```

Figure 10.45   *Code for* Payroll Database *program.*

Step 5: Test and Debug the Program

At this stage, the program has been written, and we can perform the final system test by running the program and using the test data we developed in step 3c. When we developed our test plan, we made sure that the test data would check every part of the program. Figure 10.46 contains several screen captures from the test cases.

Case	User Input and Actions	Results
1	Run the program and click *Exit*.	The following screen is displayed followed by program termination.
2	Run the program and click *Input Employee Hours*.	An InputBox requesting the filename appears.
3	Click *Cancel*.	A message box displays Invalid filename. Paycheck.csv will be used.

continues

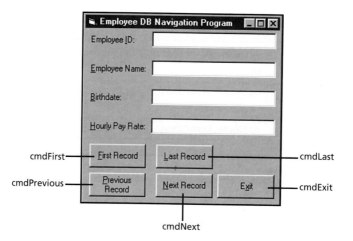

Figure 11.6 *Updated GUI for* DAO Employee DB *program.*

```
Option Explicit
Private fUserWS As Workspace
Private fEmpDB As Database
Private fEmpRS As Recordset

Private Function AppendFileToPath(ByVal Path As String, _
    ByVal File As String) As String
    If Path = "" Then                       ' The path is at the root
        AppendFileToPath = File
    ElseIf Right(Path, 1) = "\" Then
        AppendFileToPath = Path & File
    Else
        AppendFileToPath = Path & "\" & File
    End If
End Function


Private Sub Form_Load()
    Dim FileName As String                  ' File & path of DB file
    Dim SQL As String                       ' SQL will hold the query

    Set fUserWS = DBEngine.Workspaces(0)    ' Use default workspace
    FileName = AppendFileToPath(App.Path, "EmployeeDB.MDB")
    Set fEmpDB = fUserWS.OpenDatabase(FileName)    ' Open Employee DB
    SQL = "SELECT * FROM Employee"          ' The Employee table
    Set fEmpRS = fEmpDB.OpenRecordset(SQL)  ' Open Products RS
    If fEmpRS.BOF And fEmpRS.EOF Then        ' There are no records
        Call MsgBox("The database is empty. Program exiting.", _
            vbOKOnly + vbInformation)
        Call cmdExit_Click
    Else
        Call cmdFirst_Click
    End If
End Sub


Private Sub cmdExit_Click()
    Unload frmMain
End Sub
```

```
Private Sub cmdFirst_Click()
    Call fEmpRS.MoveFirst
    Call ShowDBData
End Sub

Private Sub cmdLast_Click()
    Call fEmpRS.MoveLast
    Call ShowDBData
End Sub

Private Sub cmdPrevious_Click()
    Call fEmpRS.MovePrevious
    If fEmpRS.BOF Then
        Call fEmpRS.MoveLast
    End If
    Call ShowDBData
End Sub

Private Sub cmdNext_Click()
    Call fEmpRS.MoveNext
    If fEmpRS.EOF Then
        Call fEmpRS.MoveFirst
    End If
    Call ShowDBData
End Sub

Private Sub ShowDBData()
    txtID.Text = fEmpRS("EmpID")
    txtEmpName.Text = fEmpRS("EmpName")
    txtBirthdate.Text = Format(fEmpRS("BirthDate"), "short date")
    txtPayRate.Text = Format(fEmpRS("PayRate"), "currency")
End Sub

' Purpose: Close all DB connections
Private Sub Form_Unload(Cancel As Integer)
    On Error Resume Next          ' In case connections already closed
    Call fEmpRS.Close             ' The Employee table connection
    Call fEmpDB.Close             ' Close connection to Employee DB
End Sub
```

Figure 11.7   *Updated code for* DAO Employee DB *program.*

RDO and ADO also have object hierarchies that expose properties, methods, and events. You can find out more about each model's object hierarchy by checking Visual Basic's online help. These object hierarchies can be difficult to understand, and the object hierarchies of DAO, RDO, and ADO are not the same. As a result, modifying a program that was written for one object hierarchy for the purposes of using another can be quite a chore if you used the full-blown object methods for that object type.

Luckily the DAO, RDO, and ADO objects all have methods to execute an SQL statement. As you already know, SQL is an industry standard language. Hence, if you develop your applications using SQL statements to access database data, your programs can be changed easily from one database object to another.

SQL Fundamentals

SQL is a powerful language for defining your exact needs for database processing. To take greater advantage of the DAO approach, we therefore need to present some fundamental SQL statements. The discussion in this section describes SQL syntax for select queries as well as action queries. **Select queries** are used to specify criteria that describe a desired subset of database data. The result of a select query is one or more fields of one or more records in one or more tables. **Action queries** are used to copy or change the data in a database. Valid actions that we will present include adding, deleting, and modifying fields in a database record.

In all our queries, we will use the convention of uppercase to denote SQL keywords. Keep in mind that when you implement SQL in Visual Basic, you need to define a string that contains a syntactically correct SQL statement. For a select query, the string is assigned to the Recordset object using the **OpenRecordset method**. For an action query, the string holding the SQL statement is processed using the *Execute* method of the database object. Both methods will be illustrated in the examples in this section.

Retrieving Records (Performing Queries)

The SQL **SELECT statement** provides considerable control over specifying the exact subset of data that you need. In Visual Basic, you can use this to create a Recordset dynamically (during execution). Because you have already written a program with an SQL query, we will begin with a brief discussion of the SQL *SELECT* statement. From our earlier discussion, you know that the SQL *SELECT* statement is used to perform queries that retrieve only specific records. You can use several optional clauses with the *SELECT* statement. We will illustrate each of these individually by presenting the general format followed by specific examples. In some cases, we will combine multiple clauses in a single query to give you an idea of the level of control you have when using the SQL *SELECT* statement.

The SQL SELECT Statement

The minimum syntax of the SQL *SELECT* statement is shown here:

```
SELECT [DISTINCT] fieldlist FROM tablename
```

You should replace *tablename* with the name of the desired database table and *fieldlist* with a list of desired field names within that table separated by commas. You may use the DISTINCT option in cases where the selected field may have duplicate values. If you want every field in the selected table, you can use an asterisk, the **wildcard character** (*), instead of having to list every field by name. The following examples show a few variations of the basic SELECT statement.

Examples

The following query will retrieve all the employee names in the employee table:

```
SELECT EmpName FROM Employee
```

If several employees have the same name, you may not want to see the same name listed several times. To retrieve only unique occurrences of employee names, use the **DISTINCT predicate** as shown here:

```
SELECT DISTINCT EmpName FROM Employee
```

Likewise, if you want a list of all unique birth dates among the employees in the database, you should use this query:

```
SELECT DISTINCT BirthDate FROM Employee
```

If you want several related fields for each employee record, you should list multiple fields separated by commas. The following query, for example, returns the employee ID, Social Security number, and name for every employee in the employee table:

```
SELECT EmpID, SSN, EmpName FROM Employee
```

If you have several fields in the table and you want to retrieve all of them, you can list every field name by expanding the preceding example, or you can just use the wildcard character as shown here:

```
SELECT * FROM Employee
```

The WHERE Clause

Sometimes, you need just a small subset of records in a specific table rather than all the records in the entire table. To limit which records are returned, you should add the **WHERE clause** to the SQL *SELECT* statement, as shown here:

```
SELECT [DISTINCT] fieldlist
FROM tablename
[WHERE searchcriteria]
```

The rules for specifying the search conditions are the same as the rules presented in the preceding chapter in the *Find methods* section. Basically, you need to identify the specific database field(s) in the selected table as well as the precise comparison(s). The comparison can use the relational operators discussed in Chapter 5, "Decisions and Data Validation," or the database **Like operator** discussed in Chapter 10. When using the *Like* operator, the "*" wildcard character provides a way of matching zero or more characters in the same relative position as the asterisk symbol. For example, "*s" will match on anything that ends in the letter *s*, "q*" will match anything that starts with *q*, and "*x*" will match anything with an *x* in it. Logical operators can be used to combine multiple search criteria as needed. Remember that the field names must exactly match the names in the database, and single quotation marks must surround the matching values when comparing for string literal equivalency.

On large databases, the *WHERE* clause should include an "indexed" field for performance reasons. It is much more efficient for the DBMS to search an index than it is for it to search every row in the entire table.

The following examples illustrate the SQL *SELECT* statements with a *WHERE* clause.

Examples

To retrieve the names of all employees who earn more than $10.00 per hour, use the following query:

```
SELECT EmpName
FROM Employee
WHERE PayRate > 10
```

What would you need to change to retrieve both the names and hourly pay of all employees earning more than $10.00 per hour? What if you wanted to retrieve all fields for every employee who passed the $10.00-per-hour test?

To try this yourself, make a copy of the program from Figure 11.7. Open the copy in Visual Basic and change the *Form_Load* event as highlighted in Figure 11.8. When you run the program, you should notice that only those employees whose hourly rates are more than $10.00 appear. The first three employees who are excluded from the Recordset have IDs 3, 13, and 15, for example. Their exclusion is due to their hourly rates being $7.90, $9.27, and $9.29, respectively, all of which are less than the required $10.00 per hour.

```
Private Sub Form_Load()
    Dim FileName As String              ' File & path of DB file
    Dim SQL As String                   ' SQL will hold the query

    Set fUserWS = DBEngine.Workspaces(0)    ' Use default workspace
    FileName = AppendFileToPath(App.Path, "EmployeeDB.MDB")
    Set fEmpDB = fUserWS.OpenDatabase(FileName)     ' Open Employee DB
    ' More restrictive query
    SQL = "SELECT * FROM Employee WHERE PayRate > 10"
    Set fEmpRS = fEmpDB.OpenRecordset(SQL) ' Open Products RS
    If fEmpRS.BOF And fEmpRS.EOF Then       ' There are no records
        Call MsgBox("The database is empty. Program exiting.", _
            vbOKOnly + vbInformation)
        Call cmdExit_Click
    Else
        Call cmdFirst_Click
    End If
End Sub
```

Figure 11.8 DAO DB *program—all employees earning more than $10 per hour.*

To further restrict the records returned, you can combine multiple conditions such as the following one. Here, we are interested in seeing all the field data only for those employees who earn at least $10.00 per hour and who are managers.

```
SELECT *
FROM Employee
WHERE PayRate >= 10
AND Manager = True
```

Again, to try this yourself, make a copy of the Figure 11.8 program and open the copy. Change the *Form_Load* event code to match Figure 11.9. The database has 11 managers, but only one (EmpID = 31) earns less than $10.00 per hour. When you navigate the Recordset, you should notice that only 10 different records comprise the Recordset. This is due to the dual restriction of a minimum hourly salary and management status.

```
Private Sub Form_Load()
    Dim FileName As String              ' File & path of DB file
    Dim SQL As String                   ' SQL will hold the query

    Set fUserWS = DBEngine.Workspaces(0)    ' Use default workspace
    FileName = AppendFileToPath(App.Path, "EmployeeDB.MDB")
    Set fEmpDB = fUserWS.OpenDatabase(FileName)    ' Open Employee DB
    ' Even more restrictive query
    SQL = "SELECT * FROM Employee WHERE" _
        & " PayRate >= 10 AND Manager = True"
    Set fEmpRS = fEmpDB.OpenRecordset(SQL) ' Open Products RS
    If fEmpRS.BOF And fEmpRS.EOF Then       ' There are no records
        Call MsgBox("The database is empty. Program exiting.", _
            vbOKOnly + vbInformation)
        Call cmdExit_Click
    Else
        Call cmdFirst_Click
    End If
End Sub
```

Figure 11.9 DAO DB *program—all managers earning at least $10 per hour.*

The Like Comparison Operator

Sometimes, the search criterion involves looking for string literal matches (whole or partial). For whole matches, you would use the equality (=) operator and a string literal. For partial matches, you would use the *Like* operator with a wildcard search, as you did in Chapter 10. Both examples are shown in the following section.

Examples

To return all field values for all employees in the *Employee* table whose name is equal to "Tom Jones," use the following query. Notice that the single quotation marks must surround the string literal. Also note that if you add extraneous spaces inside the single quotation marks, your search will yield no matches.

```
SELECT *
FROM Employee
WHERE EmpName = 'Tom Jones'
```

If you knew the first name or the beginning part of the first name was "Tom," you could modify the preceding example by using the *Like* operator and a trailing wildcard as shown here:

```
SELECT *
FROM Employee
WHERE EmpName LIKE 'Tom*'
```

Likewise, if you knew the ending part of the employee name, you could use a leading wildcard as shown here:

```
SELECT *
FROM Employee
WHERE EmpName LIKE '*Jones'
```

Finally, you could use wildcards on both sides and search for any employee who had a specific set of contiguous letters in the name field. A variation for this query that looks for all employees with an *x* in the name field is shown below:

```
SELECT *
FROM Employee
WHERE EmpName LIKE '*x*'
```

To illustrate how you may want to use this type of search criterion in our employee database program, consider Figure 11.10. First, we ask the user to enter the search characters using an *InputBox* function. We use the result of that input to form a query that searches for all employees who have the selected letters anywhere in their name. To try this yourself, make a copy of the Figure 11.9 program. When you open the copy, change the code in the *Form_Load* event to match what is shown in Figure 11.10. If you test the program with *en*, you should see four different employees in the Recordset.

```
Private Sub Form_Load()
    Dim FileName As String            ' File & path of DB file
    Dim SQL As String                 ' SQL will hold the query
    Dim UserName As String

    Set fUserWS = DBEngine.Workspaces(0)    ' Use default workspace
    FileName = AppendFileToPath(App.Path, "EmployeeDB.MDB")
    Set fEmpDB = fUserWS.OpenDatabase(FileName)     ' Open Employee DB
    ' Ask user for text in name and use it to form query
    UserName = InputBox("Enter the partial names for all desired employees")
    If UserName = "" Then ' Nothing entered or Cancel clicked
        SQL = "SELECT * FROM Employee"
    Else
        SQL = "SELECT * FROM Employee WHERE" _
            & " EmpName Like '*" & UserName & "*'"
    End If
    Set fEmpRS = fEmpDB.OpenRecordset(SQL) ' Open Products RS
    If fEmpRS.BOF And fEmpRS.EOF Then       ' There are no records
        Call MsgBox("The database is empty. Program exiting.", _
            vbOKOnly + vbInformation)
        Call cmdExit_Click
    Else
        Call cmdFirst_Click
    End If
End Sub
```

Figure 11.10 DAO DB *program—find similar employee names.*

The Order By Clause

In all the preceding examples, the records appeared in the same order in which they were stored in the database (ascending order by employee ID). However, there may be a need to specify a different order on a different field. To accomplish this, use the **ORDER BY clause** as shown here:

```
SELECT [DISTINCT] fieldlist
FROM tablename
[WHERE searchcriteria]
[ORDER BY fieldlist [ASC¦DESC]]
```

The optional **ASC** and **DESC keywords** are used to cause the resulting sort to be in ascending order and descending order, respectively. If the order is not specified, ascending is assumed.

Examples

To return the employee ID, SSN, and employee name field values for all employees in the *Employee* table sorted in ascending order by SSN, use the following query:

```
SELECT EmpID, SSN, EmpName
FROM Employee
ORDER BY SSN
```

To return the employee name and hourly rate values for all employees in the *Employee* table sorted in descending order by hourly rate, use the following query:

```
SELECT EmpName, PayRate
FROM Employee
ORDER BY PayRate DESC
```

In Figure 11.11, we illustrate how you can retrieve all employee records so that all managers are shown first, ordered by pay rate from high to low, followed by all non-managers, also ordered by pay rate from high to low. To try this, copy the Figure 11.10 folder and open the new copy in Visual Basic. Change the code in *Form_Load* to match Figure 11.11. When you run the program, you should notice that the employees are displayed in the order just described.

```
Private Sub Form_Load()
    Dim FileName As String          ' File & path of DB file
    Dim SQL As String               ' SQL will hold the query
    Dim UserName As String

    Set fUserWS = DBEngine.Workspaces(0)    ' Use default workspace
    FileName = AppendFileToPath(App.Path, "EmployeeDB.MDB")
    Set fEmpDB = fUserWS.OpenDatabase(FileName)     ' Open Employee DB
    SQL = "SELECT * FROM Employee ORDER BY Manager, PayRate DESC"
    Set fEmpRS = fEmpDB.OpenRecordset(SQL)  ' Open Products RS
    If fEmpRS.BOF And fEmpRS.EOF Then        ' There are no records
        Call MsgBox("The database is empty. Program exiting.", _
             vbOKOnly + vbInformation)
        Call cmdExit_Click
    Else
        Call cmdFirst_Click
    End If
End Sub
```

Figure 11.11   DAO DB *program*—ORDER BY *clause.*

Aggregate Queries

All the previous queries returned one or more records consisting of one or more fields of information. If you were interested in summary-type information, one option is to use a loop to move through each record and compute the summary results; however, there is an easier way. You can add an **aggregate function** to the *SELECT* statement as shown here:

```
SELECT aggregatefunction(fieldname) AS newdbfield
FROM tablename
[WHERE searchcriteria]
```

Any of the following functions shown in Figure 11.12 can be used in place of *aggregatefunction*. The resulting value is then stored in *newdbfield*.

Function	Purpose
AVG	Returns the average of the values in the selected field
COUNT	Returns the number of records in the selected fields
SUM	Returns the sum of all the values in the selected field
MAX	Returns the highest value in the selected field
MIN	Returns the smallest value in the selected field

Figure 11.12 *SQL* SELECT *aggregate functions.*

Examples

To return the average hourly pay rate for all employees in the *Employee* table, use the following query:

```
SELECT AVG(PayRate) AS AvgPayRate
FROM Employee
```

To return the highest salary earned by a manager in the *Employee* table, use this query:

```
SELECT MAX(PayRate) AS MaxPayRate
FROM Employee
WHERE Manager = True
```

To return the number of non-managers in the *Employee* table, use the following query:

```
SELECT COUNT(EmpID) AS NbrEmpl
FROM Employee
WHERE Manager = False
```

Let's try an example that will display the average salary of all managers and the average salary of all non-managers. Start by copying the Figure 11.11 program folder and open the new copy in Visual Basic. Add a label called lblSummary that will display the summary information returned by the aggregate query. Make the initial caption for this label blank. Add another label and text box to display whether the employee is a manager or not. Name the text box txtMgr and set its Text property to blank. Figure 11.13 shows how the form should look.

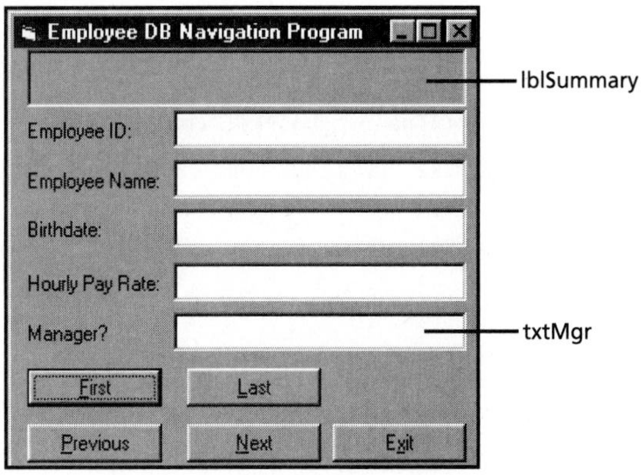

Figure 11.13 *Updated form to demonstrate aggregate function results.*

Next, change the code in the *Form_Load* event and the *ShowDBData* subprocedure to match Figure 11.14. When you run the program, you should notice that the summary information is displayed in the summary label as soon as the program loads and stays there throughout program execution. In addition, *txtMgr* will show the word *Yes* or *No*, depending on whether the employee is a manager. Because the final query from the preceding program returns all records ordered by their manager status, you should see all the manager records before seeing all the nonmanager records.

```
Private Sub Form_Load()
    Dim FileName As String            ' File & path of DB file
    Dim SQL As String                 ' SQL will hold the query
    Dim TempRS As Recordset           ' Rec'set for aggregate info
    Dim UserName As String

    Set fUserWS = DBEngine.Workspaces(0)   ' Use default workspace
    FileName = AppendFileToPath(App.Path, "EmployeeDB.MDB")
    Set fEmpDB = fUserWS.OpenDatabase(FileName)    ' Open Employee DB

    SQL = "SELECT AVG(PayRate) AS AvgPayMgr FROM Employee" _
        & " WHERE Manager = True"
    Set TempRS = fEmpDB.OpenRecordset(SQL)
    lblSummary.Caption = "Managers earn an average " & _
        Format(TempRS("AvgPayMgr"), "currency") _
        & " weekly, while" & vbNewLine
    Call TempRS.Close

    SQL = "SELECT AVG(PayRate) AS AvgPayNon FROM Employee " _
        & "WHERE Manager = False"
    Set TempRS = fEmpDB.OpenRecordset(SQL)
    lblSummary.Caption = lblSummary.Caption & "Non-Managers earn " & _
        "an average " & Format(TempRS("AvgPayNon"), "currency") & _
        " weekly."
    Call TempRS.Close
```

continues

```
SQL = "SELECT * FROM Employee ORDER BY Manager, PayRate DESC"
    Set fEmpRS = fEmpDB.OpenRecordset(SQL)  ' Open Products RS
    If fEmpRS.BOF And fEmpRS.EOF Then        ' There are no records
        Call MsgBox("The database is empty. Program exiting.", _
            vbOKOnly + vbInformation)
        Call cmdExit_Click
    Else
        Call cmdFirst_Click
    End If
End Sub

Private Sub ShowDBData()
    txtID.Text = fEmpRS("EmpID")
    txtEmpName.Text = fEmpRS("EmpName")
    txtBirthdate.Text = Format(fEmpRS("BirthDate"), "short date")
    txtPayRate.Text = Format(fEmpRS("PayRate"), "currency")
    txtMgr.Text = Format(fEmpRS("Manager"), "Yes/No")
End Sub
```

Figure 11.14 *Updated code for* Aggregate Function Results *program.*

SQL SELECT Statement for Multiple Tables

In Chapter 10, we illustrated how a database can consist of multiple tables. If your program needs to retrieve related data from multiple tables, you would use a broader form of the basic SQL statement as shown here:

```
SELECT [DISTINCT] fieldlist
FROM tablelist
[WHERE searchconditions]
```

Replace *tablelist* with the names of the desired database tables separated by commas and replace *fieldlist* with a list of desired field names within the tables separated by commas. If multiple tables have fields with the same names, you will need to precede the field name with the table name using our familiar dot notation. To reference the *EmpID* field in the *Employee* table, for example, use the notation *Employee.EmpID* in the *SELECT* statement. To make sure you only get related records from the multiple tables, you should include search conditions that identify which fields should match from different tables.

A preferred alternative to using the *WHERE* clause to match related fields is the newer option of **INNER JOIN** as shown here:

```
SELECT [DISTINCT] fieldlist
FROM table1 INNER JOIN table2 ON table1.field1 = table2.field2
[WHERE searchconditions]
```

Examples

To illustrate this, let's write a program to display related fields in the *Suppliers* and *Products* tables of the *Northwind* database. To simplify things, we will retrieve all fields from both tables where the two tables share common *SupplierID* values. To be able to view all products from the same supplier consecutively, we will order the records by the suppliers' names (*CompanyName* field in *Suppliers* table). Finally, we want a summary label to display the total number of products.

The following query will return the total number of products in the *TotProd* field:

```
SELECT COUNT(*) AS TotProd FROM Products
```

The following query will return the desired records ordered by company name:

```
SELECT * FROM Suppliers, Products
WHERE Suppliers.SupplierID = Products.SupplierID
ORDER BY CompanyName
```

Figure 11.15 depicts the GUI. Note that we did not display all the fields even though we wrote the query such that every field in both tables is returned. The source code for form-scope variables, the *Form_Load* event, and the *ShowDBData* subprocedure is listed in Figure 11.16. The code for the other procedures matches the previous examples, with the Recordset's name changed from *fEmpRS* to *fSupRS*.

When you run the program, you should notice that the total number of product records appears in the summary label. When you navigate records using the next or previous buttons, you should also see that the products for a given supplier are displayed in sequence. This is due to the *ORDER BY* clause in the query.

We leave as an exercise changing the *fSupRS* query to the following for comparison purposes:

```
SELECT * FROM Suppliers INNER JOIN Products
ON Suppliers.SupplierID = Products.SupplierID
ORDER BY CompanyName
```

Would you expect the same number of records to be returned? Would they be ordered the same way?

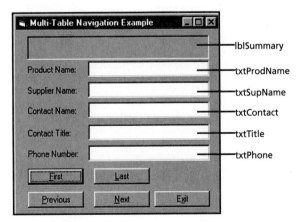

Figure 11.15 *Updated GUI for Northwind multitable query.*

```
Option Explicit
Private fUserWS As Workspace
Private fNWindDB As Database
Private fSupRS As Recordset

Private Sub Form_Load()
    Dim     FileName As String              ' File & path of DB file
    Dim SQL As String                       ' SQL will hold the query
    Dim TempRS As Recordset                 ' RS for aggregate info
    Dim UserName As String

    Set fUserWS = DBEngine.Workspaces(0)    ' Use default workspace

    FileName = AppendFileToPath(App.Path, "Northwind.MDB")
    Set fNWindDB = fUserWS.OpenDatabase(FileName)    ' Open NWind DB

    SQL = "SELECT COUNT(*) AS TotProd FROM Products"
    Set TempRS = fNWindDB.OpenRecordset(SQL)
    lblSummary.Caption = "We have " & _
        Format(TempRS("TotProd")) & " total products."
    Call TempRS.Close

    SQL = "SELECT * FROM Suppliers, Products WHERE " & _
        "Suppliers.SupplierID = Products.SupplierID ORDER BY" & _
        " CompanyName"
    Set fSupRS = fNWindDB.OpenRecordset(SQL) ' Open Recordset
    If fSupRS.BOF And fSupRS.EOF Then       ' There are no records
        Call MsgBox("The database is empty. Program exiting.", _
            vbOKOnly + vbInformation)
        Call cmdExit_Click
    Else
        Call cmdFirst_Click
    End If
End Sub

' Purpose: Show the current DB record's field contents in text boxes.
Private Sub ShowDBData()
    txtProdName.Text = fSupRS("ProductName")
    txtSupName.Text = fSupRS("CompanyName")
    txtContact.Text = fSupRS("ContactName")
    txtTitle.Text = fSupRS("ContactTitle")
    txtPhone.Text = fSupRS("Phone")
End Sub
```

Figure 11.16 *Source code for Northwind multitable query.*

Minimizing Problems

Although our *Employee* database has valid values for all fields of all records, it is possible that the data in a particular field may contain a Null value. A Null value represents something that is missing or not known, and is not the same as spaces or **zero values.** If you try something like *txtProdName.Text = fSupRS("ProductName")* and the field is Null in the database, for example, you would get a Run Time error. To avoid problems due to Null fields, you can make use of the *IsNull* function to detect Null fields. Figure 11.17 shows a function that you should use when retrieving data from database fields. The function expects two *ByVal* parameters: a Recordset object and a database field name as a String, and it returns the corresponding value in the database (processing as needed in the case of Null values).

To use the same function for all data types, we assign a **Variant** type to the function's return value. The Variant data type behaves like a chameleon. It allows Visual Basic to determine what the appropriate type should be, based on the operations used to assign it a value. Therefore, if the database field value is a String, a String will be returned. If it is a Long, a Long will be returned. The same is true for any other type as well.

The chapter case study will use this function, so we recommend that you add it to the *basTools* module.

```
' Purpose: Safely returns a usable field value from a Recordset object.
'          If the field contains a Null value, it is substituted with
'          an empty string or zero depending on the field's data type.
Public Function DBGetField(rRS As Recordset, _
    ByVal FieldName As String) As Variant

    If IsNull(rRS(FieldName)) Then
        Select Case rRS(FieldName).Type
            Case dbText, dbMemo
                DBGetField = ""
            Case Else
                DBGetField = 0
        End Select
    Else
        DBGetField = rRS(FieldName)
    End If
End Function
```

Figure 11.17 *Function to avoid problems due to Null database fields.*

If you add this function to the program illustrated in Figure 11.16, the *ShowDBData* subprocedure should be revised as shown in Figure 11.18.

```
' Purpose: Show the current DB record's field contents in text boxes.
Private Sub ShowDBData()
    txtProdName.Text = DBGetField(fSupRS, "ProductName")
    txtSupName.Text = DBGetField(fSupRS, "CompanyName")
    txtContact.Text = DBGetField(fSupRS, "ContactName")
    txtTitle.Text = DBGetField(fSupRS, "ContactTitle")
    txtPhone.Text = DBGetField(fSupRS, "Phone")
End Sub
```

Figure 11.18 *Updated source code for multitable query with* DBGetField *calls.*

Modifying Database Records

All the examples thus far have illustrated only database navigation. Although text boxes were used to display data, any changes made by the user were ignored by the database because no code was written to copy the data from the Visual Basic controls to their corresponding database fields. This section shows you how you can add, delete, and update database records using action queries.

To process each of these action queries in Visual Basic, use the **Execute method** as shown here:

```
Dim SQL As String                ' String that holds the action query
Dim DBObject As Database         ' Name of DB Object

SQL = "the action query"
Call DBObject.Execute(SQL)
```

Type Compatibility

When you write SQL queries, you often refer to specific fields. Because each field has a specific type, it is important for you to make sure that the values assigned to each field are compatible to avoid type mismatch errors. The following sections discuss some specific rules to keep in mind about type compatibility.

String Data Type

When assigning string data to textual database fields, you need to make sure that the string is surrounded by single quotation marks. If the string contains a single quotation character, you actually need to insert an extra single quotation mark so that the DBMS interprets it correctly. To assign *Bill's Car* to a textual database field, for example, you must use the literal string *"'Bill''s Car'"*. Notice that the entire string is enclosed in single quotation marks (inside the double quotation marks that Visual Basic uses to denote string data). Furthermore, where the final string literal would contain a single quotation mark (the apostrophe in *Bill's*), our Visual Basic string has two single quotation marks in succession.

Because embedded single quotation marks could become a potential problem in many database applications, it would be a good idea to develop a general function to handle this consistently and correctly. Figure 11.19 illustrates a function called *DBTextFmt* that accomplishes this purpose. Note that it employs the new Visual Basic 6 *Replace* function. You can get more information on the Replace function by consulting Visual Basic help. The chapter case study will use the *DBTextFmt* function, so we recommend that you add it to the *basTools* module.

```
' Purpose: Used to format string variables that are being included in
'          SQL statements.  The argument is wrapped in single quotation marks
'          and any embedded quote marks are changed to two quotation marks.
'          For example, if the argument contains "Bill's Car", it will
'          return "'Bill''s Car'".
Public Function DBTextFmt(ByVal Str As String) As String
    DBTextFmt = "'" & Replace(Str, "'", "''") & "'"
End Function
```

Figure 11.19 DBStr *function to handle embedded quotation marks problem.*

Date Data Type

When using date formats in SQL statements in Visual Basic, you must use English (United States) notation. To avoid ambiguities, use the format #mm/dd/yyyy#. For the same reason that we created a function to format strings correctly, we recommend that you use the function shown in Figure 11.20 to format date data correctly. Although the chapter case study does not use date data types in SQL statements, you may still want to add this to your general *basTools* module.

Keep in mind that after the date is in the correct format, you still need to convert it to a string to concatenate it in the SQL query.

```
' Purpose: Used to format date variables that are being included in
'          SQL statements.  The dates are always formatted in
'          the U.S. date format of #mm/dd/yyyy#.
Public Function DBDateFmt(ByVal DateArg As Date) As String
    DBDateFmt = "#" & Format(DateArg, "mm\/dd\/yyyy") & "#"
End Function
```

Figure 11.20   DBDateFmt *function to handle date data types.*

Numeric and Boolean Data Types

Numeric values can be stored in a variety of numeric formats; Boolean values, on the other hand, are limited to *True* or *False*. In either case, because the query is stored as a string, you must remember to convert the data to a string data type before concatenating it with the rest of the SQL statement. The best approach is to just use the *CStr* function in these cases.

Inserting Records

To add new records to a database table, you use the **INSERT INTO SQL statement**. The general syntax of this append query is shown here:

```
INSERT INTO tablename [(field1[, field2[, ...]])]
VALUES (value1[, value2[, ...]])
```

An **append query** writes the new record to the end of the database table. If you omit a field in the table, a Null value is written for that field. If the table has a primary key, you must supply a unique, non-Null value for the primary key field. Otherwise, the Jet database engine will not append the record. When the table was first created, a numeric field may have been included whose value was automatically updated. If the table has such an AutoNumber field and you want to renumber the appended records, do not include the AutoNumber field in your query. If you want to retain the original values from the field, be sure to include this AutoNumber field.

Example

The following append query inserts a single record to the end of the *Employee* table by providing specific values for each field:

```
INSERT INTO Employee
(EmpID, SSN, EmpName, BirthDate, PayRate, Manager)
VALUES
(1, '555-66-7777', 'Whitten, Thomas O', #12/03/1961#, 10.15, False)
```

```
        If fEmpRS.BOF And fEmpRS.EOF Then        ' There are no records
            Call MsgBox("The database is empty. Program exiting.", _
                vbOKOnly + vbInformation)
            Call cmdExit_Click
        Else
            Call cmdFirst_Click
        End If
End Sub
```

Figure 11.22   *Code to perform adds using DAO on* Employee DB.

Updating Records

To update fields in an existing record of a database table, you use the **UPDATE SQL statement**. The general syntax of this update query is shown here:

```
UPDATE tablename
SET fieldname = value [,fieldname = value]
[WHERE criteria]
```

An **update query** is an action query that changes a set of records according to criteria you specify. You can use it to change individual fields of single records as well as to perform bulk updates when you want to change field values for many records.

Single Record Update Example

The following example shows how to change the values for the fields *EmpName, BirthDate, PayRate,* and *Manager* for the second employee. Because *EmpID* is a key field, using this in the *WHERE* clause restricts the update to just the employee whose *EmpID* field is equal to *2.*

```
UPDATE Employee SET
EmpName = 'Whitten, Thomas O',
BirthDate = #12/03/1961#,
PayRate = 10.15,
Manager = False
WHERE EmpID = 2
```

Bulk Update Examples

If the *WHERE* clause uses a broader comparison or uses a field with non-unique values, all records that meet the criteria will be updated. The following update query gives all employees who are managers a $10.00 raise, for example:

```
UPDATE Employee SET
PayRate = PayRate + 10
WHERE Manager = True
```

To make all employees managers if their employee ID is less than *10,* use the following update query:

```
UPDATE Employee SET
Manager = True
WHERE EmpID < 10
```

If the *WHERE* clause is omitted entirely, the change is made to all records. The following example illustrates how to give all employees a $5.00 raise:

```
UPDATE Employees SET
HourlyRate = HourlyRate + 5
```

To practice performing bulk updates to records in a database table, we will revise the program illustrated in Figure 11.13. This program will be used at the end of the year to assign all managers and all non-managers an end-of-year raise. You will need to add another command button called *cmdRaise*, which will serve as the trigger to begin the bulk update process. Each raise will be input as a percentage via an InputBox, and then applied to all appropriate employee records. Just as with the *Add* example, we close the database and reopen it again to ensure that the Recordset contains current data. Figure 11.23 shows the source code for the *cmdRaise_Click* event. Figure 11.24 shows four sample screen shots that illustrate the average hourly pay rates before changes were made, the values entered by the user, and the resulting new averages after the bulk updates.

```
Private Sub cmdRaise_Click()
    Dim TempRS As Recordset
    Dim MgrRaise As Single
    Dim NonRaise As Single
    Dim SQL As String
    MgrRaise = CSng(InputBox("Enter the raise for all managers " & _
        "(1-100%):"))
    NonRaise = CSng(InputBox("Enter the raise for all non-managers " _
        & "(1-100%):"))
    If MgrRaise > 0 Then
        SQL = "UPDATE Employee SET " & _
            "PayRate = PayRate * " & Format(1 + (MgrRaise / 100)) & _
            " Where Manager = True"
        Call fEmpDB.Execute(SQL)
    End If
    If NonRaise > 0 Then
        SQL = "UPDATE Employee SET " & _
            "PayRate = PayRate * " & Format(1 + (NonRaise / 100)) & _
            " Where Manager = false"
        Call fEmpDB.Execute(SQL)
    End If
    Call fEmpRS.Close          ' The Employee table connection
    Call fEmpDB.Close          ' Close connection to Employee DB
    Call ReOpenDB

    SQL = "SELECT AVG(PayRate) AS AvgPayMgr FROM Employee " & _
        "WHERE Manager = True"
    Set TempRS = fEmpDB.OpenRecordset(SQL)
    lblSummary.Caption = "Managers earn an average " & _
        Format(TempRS("AvgPayMgr"), "currency") & " weekly, while" _
        & vbNewLine
    Call TempRS.Close

    SQL = "SELECT AVG(PayRate) AS AvgPayNon FROM Employee " & _
        "WHERE Manager = False"
    Set TempRS = fEmpDB.OpenRecordset(SQL)
    lblSummary.Caption = lblSummary.Caption & "Non-Managers earn an " _
        & "average " & Format(TempRS("AvgPayNon"), "currency") & _
        " weekly."
    Call TempRS.Close

End Sub
```

Figure 11.23   *Code to perform end-of-year bulk updates on hourly pay.*

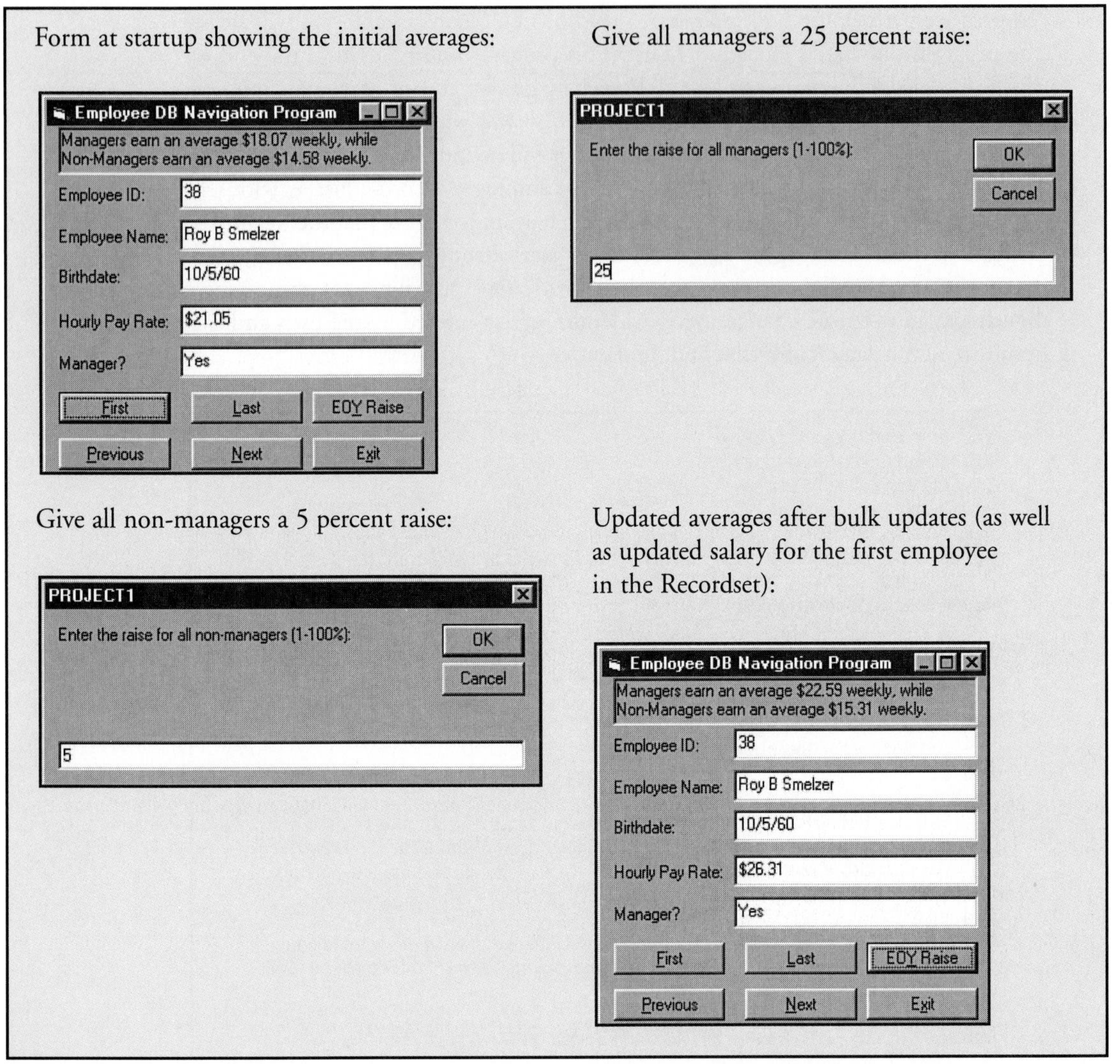

Form at startup showing the initial averages:

Give all managers a 25 percent raise:

Employee DB Navigation Program

Managers earn an average $18.07 weekly, while
Non-Managers earn an average $14.58 weekly.

Employee ID: 38

Employee Name: Roy B Smelzer

Birthdate: 10/5/60

Hourly Pay Rate: $21.05

Manager? Yes

[First] [Last] [EOY Raise]

[Previous] [Next] [Exit]

PROJECT1

Enter the raise for all managers (1-100%):

[OK] [Cancel]

25

Give all non-managers a 5 percent raise:

Updated averages after bulk updates (as well as updated salary for the first employee in the Recordset):

PROJECT1

Enter the raise for all non-managers (1-100%):

[OK] [Cancel]

5

Employee DB Navigation Program

Managers earn an average $22.59 weekly, while
Non-Managers earn an average $15.31 weekly.

Employee ID: 38

Employee Name: Roy B Smelzer

Birthdate: 10/5/60

Hourly Pay Rate: $26.31

Manager? Yes

[First] [Last] [EOY Raise]

[Previous] [Next] [Exit]

Figure 11.24 *Sample output screens from* End-Of-Year Bulk Update *program.*

Deleting Records

To delete records in a database table, you use the **DELETE SQL statement**. The general syntax of this delete query is shown here:

```
DELETE FROM tablename
[WHERE criteria]
```

A **delete query** is an action query that removes a set of records from a database table according to criteria you specify. As with the *UPDATE* statement, you can use *DELETE* to remove single records as well as for performing bulk deletes.

Single Record Delete Example

The following example shows how to delete the second employee. Because *EmpID* is a key field, using this in the *WHERE* clause restricts the delete to just the employee whose Employee ID field is equal to *2*.

```
DELETE FROM Employee
WHERE EmpID = 2
```

Bulk Delete Examples

As with the *UPDATE* statement, if the *WHERE* clause uses a broader comparison or uses a field with non-unique values, all records that meet the criteria will be deleted. The following delete query removes all employees who are managers, for example:

```
DELETE FROM Employee
WHERE Manager = True
```

To delete all employees whose employee ID is less than *10*, use the following delete query:

```
DELETE FROM Employee
WHERE EmpID < 10
```

If the *WHERE* clause is omitted entirely, all records are deleted. The following example illustrates how to accomplish this for the *Employee* table:

```
DELETE FROM Employee
```

To practice deleting individual records from a database table in a Visual Basic program using DAO, revise the program illustrated in Figure 11.7. First, update the GUI by adding a button named *cmdDelete*. Next, add the new code shown in Figure 11.25. The program is used primarily for navigating the records in the *Employee* table. At any time, if the *Delete* button is clicked, the record that was in view when the button was clicked is deleted.

```
Private Sub cmdDelete_Click()
    Dim SQL As String
    SQL = "DELETE FROM Employee Where EmpID = " & _
        fEmpRS("EmpID")
    Call fEmpDB.Execute(SQL)
    Call fEmpRS.Close
    Call fEmpDB.Close
    Call ReOpenDB
End Sub
```

Figure 11.25   *Code to perform individual deletes.*

Creating a New Database

Thus far, we have created applications that assume the database already exists. If it does not, the missing database file will trigger a Visual Basic error and cause our program to terminate. It would be nice to make the application more robust so that when the database cannot be located, the user would have the option to create a new one. After the new database is created, additional instructions are used to define its structure and content. Minimally, this includes creating or removing tables as well as creating or removing indexes.

DAO CreateDatabase Method

The first step in creating a new database in code is to use the **CreateDatabase method**. The general syntax is shown here:

```
Set DBObject = WSObject.CreateDatabase(FileName, Locale[, options])
```

FileName should be replaced with the full path and filename of the database file to be created. In Chapter 10, we created an *AppendFileToPath* function that you can use here to append the path of the application (*App.Path*) to the filename. This method applies to MDB files; if the extension is not supplied, however, .MDB is automatically added. Finally, before processing this method, it would be a good idea to make sure that the specified file does not exist. In Chapter 9, "Sequential Files," we created a *FileExists* function that can be used here, too. If the file does exist, you can ask the user whether it should be replaced. If so, the **Kill FileName statement** can be used to delete the specified file.

Locale refers to the collating order of text for string comparisons. This string value generally specifies the language used as well as an optional password that you can create for the new database. For example, using

```
dbLangGeneral & ";pwd=SecretPassword"
```

in place of *Locale* allows the database to handle English, German, French, Portuguese, Italian, and Modern Spanish collating order and requires the *SecretPassword* to open the database. Omitting the password part just assigns the same collating order without assigning any password to the database.

If desired, you can add options to encrypt the database for added security as well as to specify the Jet database engine version file format. Our examples will not include these options. Consult Visual Basic help for more information on how to implement these options in your programs.

Example

The code in Figure 11.26 illustrates how to create a new database using general language syntax and no password:

```
Option Explicit
Private fUserWS As Workspace
Private fNewDB As Database

Private Sub CreateDB()
    Dim FileName As String

    Set fUserWS = DBEngine.Workspace(0)
    FileName = AppendFileToPath(App.Path, "NewTestDB.mdb")
```

```
    If FileExists(FileName) Then
        If MsgBox("The database exists. Do you want to replace it?", _
            vbYesNo + vbQuestion) = vbYes Then
            Kill FileName
    Else
            Exit Sub            ' Do not create the DB-already exists
        End If
    End If
    Set fNewDB = fUserWS.CreateDatabase(FileName, dbLangGeneral)
End Sub
```

Figure 11.26   *Code to create a new database.*

Data Definition Language (DDL)

After a new database has been created with the CreateDatabase method, the next step involves using some SQL **data definition language** (**DDL**) commands to create, delete, or modify database tables, fields, and indexes.

Adding a Table

To add a table to the database, use the **CREATE TABLE statement** syntax shown here:

```
CREATE TABLE tablename (field1 type [(size)] [, field2 type [(size)]...])
```

The types must correspond to valid SQL data types. Figure 11.27 shows the association between several Visual Basic data types and corresponding SQL data types.

Visual Basic Data Type	SQL Data Type
Boolean	BIT
Byte	BYTE
Currency	CURRENCY
Date	DATETIME
Double	DOUBLE
Integer	SHORT
Long	COUNTER[1]
Long	LONG
Single	SINGLE
String	TEXT
String	LONGTEXT

[1]*A number automatically incremented by the Microsoft Jet database engine whenever a new record is added to a table. If the table contains a counter field (sometimes called an Autonumber field), do not include it in an SQL Insert statement.*

Figure 11.27   *Visual Basic-to-SQL data types cross-reference.*

AppendFileToPath Function
Begin AppendFileToPath(Path, Filename)
   If Path = ""
      Return Filename
   Elseif Right(Path, 1) = "\"
      Return Path & FileName
   Else
      Return Path & "\" & FileName
End AppendFileToPath

FileExists Function
Begin FileExists(FileName)
   Call FileLen(FileName)
   If Run Time error did not occur
      Return True
   Else
      Return False
End FileExists

CreatePaychecksDatabase(FileName) Procedure
Begin CreatePaychecksDatabase
   Call CreateDatabase(FileName)
   Format CREATE TABLE SQL statement
   Execute CREATE TABLE SQL statement
   Create index for SSN
   Close database
   Display "File created successfully"
End CreatePaychecksDatabase

DBGetField (FileName) Function
Begin DBGetField(Recordset, FieldName)
   If IsNull(FieldName)
      If field type = text or memo
         Return ""
      Else
         Return 0
   Else
      Return Recordset(FieldName)
End DBGetField

OpenPayrollDatabase Function
Begin OpenPayrollDatabase
   FileName = AppendFileToPath(App.Path, PayrollName)
   If FileExists(FileName) = False
      Display "Database does not exist. Notify MIS"
      Return False
   Open Paychecks database
   Return True
End OpenPayrollDatabase

LoadTaxTables Procedure
Begin LoadTaxTables
   Format query to select all TaxRate records
   Open recordset
   I = 0
   Do until recordset.EOF
      I = I + 1
      ReDim IncomeTable
      ReDim TaxRateTable
      IncomeTable(I) = DBGetField("Income")
      TaxRateTable(I) = DBGetField("TaxRate")
   Loop
   Close recordset
End LoadTaxTables

LoadEmployee Procedure

Begin LoadEmployee
   If employee recordset.EOF = True
      Display "No more employees"
      Clear lblName
      Clear lblSSN
      Disable cmdNext
   Else
      fSSN = DBGetField(employee recordset, "SSN")
      fPayRate = DBGetField(employee recordset, "PayRate")
      EmpName = DBGetField(employee recordset, "EmpName")
      Display fSSN on lblSSN
      Display EmpName on lblEmpName
End LoadEmployee

FormUnload Event

Begin FormUnload
   Close employee recordset
   Close Payroll database
   Close Paychecks database
End FormUnload

Next Click Event

Begin Next Click
   If txtHours <> ""
      If HoursIsValid
         Assign Hours text box to Hrs
         Call CalcPay(Hrs, Gross, Tax, Net)
         Call InsertPaycheckRecord(fSSN, Hrs, Gross, Tax, Net)
         Get next employee
         Call LoadEmployee
   Else
      Get next employee
      Call LoadEmployee
   Set focus to Hours text box
End Next Click

HoursIsValid Function

Begin HoursIsValid
   If Hours text box is numeric
      Assign Hours text box to Hrs
      If Hrs ≥ 5 And Hrs ≤ 100
         Result = True
      Else
         Result = False
         Display "Invalid value for Hours"
   Else
      Result = False
      Display "Hours must be numeric"
   Return Result
End HoursIsValid

continues

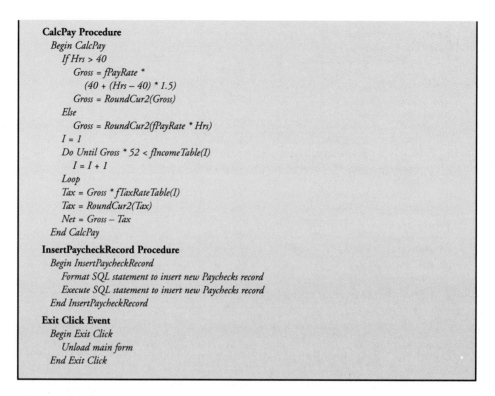

```
CalcPay Procedure
    Begin CalcPay
        If Hrs > 40
            Gross = fPayRate *
                (40 + (Hrs – 40) * 1.5)
            Gross = RoundCur2(Gross)
        Else
            Gross = RoundCur2(fPayRate * Hrs)
        I = 1
        Do Until Gross * 52 < fIncomeTable(I)
            I = I + 1
        Loop
        Tax = Gross * fTaxRateTable(I)
        Tax = RoundCur2(Tax)
        Net = Gross – Tax
    End CalcPay

InsertPaycheckRecord Procedure
    Begin InsertPaycheckRecord
        Format SQL statement to insert new Paychecks record
        Execute SQL statement to insert new Paychecks record
    End InsertPaycheckRecord

Exit Click Event
    Begin Exit Click
        Unload main form
    End Exit Click
```

Figure 11.34   Payroll DAO *program pseudocode.*

Step 3c: Develop a Test Plan (Table of Input with Expected Results)

In this version of the *Payroll* program, we have changed the mechanism for storing information—databases rather than CSV files. The user interface and the data values for this program are exactly the same as those used in the version from Chapter 9, however, so we can use the same test data. Figure 11.35 shows the list of test cases that we can use to test the calculations. Of course, you should feel free to extend this list with some of your own test cases.

SSN	Name	Hrs	Rate	Gross	Gross*52	Tax	Net
241341521	Thomas O Whitten	8	10.75	86.00	4472	0.00	86.00
492735055	Owen F Detweiler	11	17.30	190.30	9896	19.03	171.27
533479537	Stephen Donneger	32	15.00	480.00	24960	72.00	408.00
639170707	Dirk Gehman	38	37.00	1406.00	73112	351.50	1054.50
690371986	Edward S Eastman	38	75.00	2850.00	148200	940.50	1909.50
761236124	Michael L Aiman	9	10.75	96.75	5031	9.68	87.07
785720348	Tony A Edison	12	17.30	207.60	10795	31.14	176.46

```
' Purpo
'
Private
    ByR

    Dim

    SQL

    SQL
    SQL
    SQL
    SQL
    SQL

    SQL

    SQL
    SQL
    SQL
    SQL
    SQL

    Cal
End Sub

' Purpos
'
'
Private
    txt

    If

    Els

    End
End Sub

' Purpos
'
Private
    Dim
    Dim
    Dim

    ' F
    SQL
    SQL
    SQL

    ' O
    Set
```

SSN	Name	Hrs	Rate	Gross	Gross*52	Tax	Net
790184316	Grace J Ebermann	35	15.00	525.00	27300	131.25	393.75
826687434	Carol C Banana	40	37.00	1480.00	76960	488.40	991.60
841182276	Ralph J Alderfer	40	75.00	3000.00	156000	1200.00	1800.00
949744067	Harold U Bates	45	10.95	520.13	27047	130.03	390.10
987493232	Candice F Carter	50	15.65	860.75	44759	215.19	645.56

Figure 11.35   *Test data for* Payroll DAO *program.*

In addition to the test data, we also need to test for exceptions. For example, database files may be missing, the *Paychecks* database may exist and contain data from a previous run, and the user may enter an invalid information. Figure 11.36 contains some of the cases we should include during our testing. As before, extend this list with some of your own test cases.

Case	User Input and Actions	Expected Results
1	Run the program and make sure no database files are present in the same folder as the program.	A message displays that says the *Paychecks* database does not exist and asks us whether it should be created. Click *No* and the program ends.
2	Run the program and make sure no database files are present in the same folder as the program.	A message displays that says the *Paychecks* database does not exist and asks us whether it should be created. Click *Yes* and a message is displayed that says the database was created successfully. Click *OK.* A message displays that says the Payroll database does not exist. Click *OK* and the program ends.
3	Run the program and make sure the *Payroll* database file is present but that the *Paychecks* file is not present.	A message displays that says the *Paychecks* database does not exist and asks us whether it should be created. Click *No* and the program ends.
4	Run the program and make sure the *Payroll* database file is present but that the *Paychecks* file is not present.	A message displays that says the *Paychecks* database does not exist and asks us whether it should be created. Click *Yes* and a message is displayed that says the database was created successfully. Click *OK.* The main form appears. The SSN and Name labels display 241–34–1521 and Thomas O Whitten, respectively. The Hours text box is blank and has the focus.

continues

```
Privat
   Di

   Se

   If

   Er

   If

   Er
   Ca

   '
   SC

   SC
   SC

   '
   Se
   ' (
   Ca
End Sul
.
' Purp
'
Private
   '
   '
   '

   On
   Ca
   Ca
   Ca
End Sul

' Purp
Private
   Di

   If

   El:

   En
End Fur
```

5. Develop a program that enables the user to manage the *Employee* table in the *Payroll* database. Minimally, the user needs to navigate through all employee records, add employees, delete employees, change employee data, and search for employees by entering the first few letters of the employee's name or by entering the first few digits of the SSN. Do not allow the user to enter duplicate employee numbers (for add and change).

6. Create a *Contacts* database within a Visual Basic program. Add features that enable you to manage your personal contacts after the database has been created. Contact information should include name, street address, city, state, zip code, phone number, fax, and email. You should be able to look up a contact quickly by specifying a similar name, city, phone number, or email. If the wrong person shows up, searching again with the same request will bring up the next match. Searches may continue until no more matching records can be found. You should also be able to add, delete, and change contact information.

OBJECT-ORIENTED PROGRAMMING

Introduction

As you have worked your way through the various case studies at the end of each chapter in this text, you should have noticed the programs getting larger and larger. The length of the source code increases because, as you gain a broader knowledge of computer programming, you can write software to solve more complex problems.

Software developers have historically tried many different programming tricks and techniques to help deal with the continually increasing complexity of today's software. In Chapter 4, "Simplifying Programming Through Modularity," you learned how modularity is used to break large chunks of code into small procedures to help improve understandability and facilitate reusability. This practice allows the procedure to be reused without having to know the exact details of how it has been implemented. Instead, you need to know only which arguments it expects and which values it might return.

Object-Oriented Programming (OOP, rhymes with *loop*) is also an attempt to simplify the process of developing software by providing another mechanism that allows pieces of previously developed software to be reused. Be warned that much of the terminology commonly used when discussing OOP may sound overly academic and intimidating. The concepts of OOP are founded on common sense, however—much like many other processes involved in computer programming.

This chapter discusses the principles of OOP as well as how you apply them in Visual Basic. Additionally, we will introduce Visual Basic *collections*, which can make working with lists of objects a bit easier.

Objectives

After completing this chapter, you should be able to:

- List the advantages and disadvantages of programming with objects.

- Define the difference between an object and a class.

- List and describe the three requirements of an Object-Oriented Programming language.

- Define your own classes, complete with properties and methods.

- Know the conditions under which to use Property procedures.

- Create objects from your own classes.

- Understand how to communicate errors between objects.

- Know how to use Visual Basic collections.

Why Use Objects?

Almost everything in our world can be thought of as a type of object. Chairs are objects, computers are objects, electronic documents are objects, a bank checking account is an object, and even people are objects. Therefore, it should seem natural that we would prefer to write computer programs using tools that enable us to more closely model things as they exist in the real world. OOP provides the tools for us to do just that.

Visual Basic provides you with many intrinsic objects, some of which you have already used. Forms are types of objects, for example, and so are the controls you have drawn on them. Therefore, you have already used objects in every program for which you designed a GUI. Additionally, Visual Basic contains many other nonvisual types of objects. You used the *Screen* object in Chapter 1, "Introductory Programming Concepts and the Visual Basic Environment," the *Err* object in Chapter 6, "The Case Structure and Error Handling," and Database objects in Chapter 11, "Database Programming with Data Objects and SQL." Visual Basic also contains many other intrinsic objects for programming such tasks as printing information (the *Printer* object), and copying data to and from the Windows Clipboard (the *Clipboard* object). You can even purchase objects from third-party vendors and add them to your Visual Basic projects (see the section titled "ActiveX Components" in Appendix A, "Visual Basic User Interface Objects," for more information).

With all these different types of objects around, you might guess that there is some advantage to programming with objects. The advantage of using OOP is its promise of increasing programming productivity by allowing large amounts of previously written and tested code to be easily reused. As the theory goes, reusing components should result in increased productivity. Increased productivity should lead to lower software development costs, which should lead to increased profits for the company doing the development.

In Chapter 11, for example, you didn't have to code your own relational database engine. You didn't even have to understand how the database engine was implemented. Instead, you had a much simpler task of only learning how to use the properties and methods of the Database objects that someone else had developed.

The disadvantage of using OOP is that the initial development time for a reusable object is usually longer than if traditional programming techniques were used. The extra development time results because of the syntax for creating objects and because of the extra design and testing time needed to ensure an object can be reused effectively. Even with this increased development time, the advantages most often outweigh the disadvantages.

OOP languages have been around for quite some time, but have gained in popularity only in the past 10 years or so. Software reusability has been a much sought-after goal, but it has seldom been achieved successfully. Such is the case with Object-Oriented Programming languages. Although OOP technologies have helped to increase productivity, they have not been the "silver-bullet" fix to today's software problems as had once been predicted.

Principles of Object-Oriented Programming

To be labeled a *true* Object-Oriented Programming language, the language must support three fundamental concepts: **encapsulation**, **polymorphism**, and **inheritance**. Visual Basic is generally not considered a *true* Object-Oriented Programming language because it does not support the concept of inheritance.

Some programming languages (for example, SmallTalk) are considered truly object oriented because they were designed to be object oriented from their inception. History has shown, however, that programmers prefer to use something they are already familiar with rather than switch to a completely different development tool. C++ is considered an OOP language, but is really just OOP extensions added to the C programming language. Similarly, Microsoft continually adds new OOP features to Visual Basic; these features have helped it to remain popular even though it is not considered truly OOP.

Classes and Objects

When we discuss OOP, we will use the terms *object* and *class*, so it is important that you understand the difference between the two.

The controls in the Visual Basic toolbox represent **classes**. A command button object does not exist until one is drawn on a form. All command button objects are created from the same command button class. Each button shares the exact same set of properties, methods, and events that are defined by the command button class. After you place a control on the form and customize its properties, you have created an object that is an instance of that class. Each command button object can be made distinct by setting various property values such as its name, position, and caption.

When you create a class, you are defining a new type of data. When you declare a variable of this new data type, you are creating an object. Therefore, an **object** is said to be an **instance** of a class. Classes are often described as the "blueprints" or templates for objects. In summary:

Classes = Object blueprints

Objects = Class instances

In Chapter 8, "Arrays, Searching, and Sorting," you learned how to create user-defined data types (UDTs) and then how to declare variables of this new type. Think of classes as an enhancement to UDTs. A UDT contains only data items. Procedures that act on their data must be written in different sections of the program code. Classes enhance the UDT concept by enabling the programmer to define *both* the data items *and* the procedures that act on them in a single module.

Encapsulation

Encapsulation is arguably the biggest benefit of OOP. Encapsulation uses a concept sometimes referred to as **data hiding**. Think of encapsulation as the ability to define a "black-box" view of an object. In other words, you do not need to know what is going on inside an object. You need to know only how to work with its properties, methods, and events. The "black-box" should do everything that it was designed to do, should do it well, and should do nothing else.

When we call a text box's *SetFocus* method, for example, we don't know exactly how the cursor gets moved to the text box. Likewise, when we reference a command button's Height property, we don't know how that number is actually being stored internally in the command button. The command button may indeed have a variable of type Long to store the height, but it may just as well have a variable that stores the bottom position of the form and then uses this value with the Top property to calculate the button's height whenever the Height property is requested. The point is that the exact implementation of an object is not important if we are just using it.

Like forms and controls, the objects you create can have properties, methods, and even events (although events are used much less frequently than properties and methods). The variables and procedures your class exposes (by declaring them with the *Public* keyword) become its properties and methods. The public properties and methods are sometimes referred to as the class's *interface*.

Encapsulation makes program maintenance easier than with traditional ways of writing code because you have to look in only one place for both the data and procedures. Traditional ways require data declarations to be changed in one place, and the procedural code in another. Encapsulation also allows the internals of an object to be changed without adversely affecting any other parts of the programs that use it.

Polymorphism

The term *polymorphism* literally means "many shapes." When used in the context of OOP, it just means that many classes can provide a property or method with the same name. Most controls provide a Height property and a Move method. Polymorphism allows properties to be set and methods to be called without regard to the object's class.

Suppose, for example, that you have a form that contains many text boxes and combo boxes that should contain valid numeric values. You might write a general-purpose function as shown here to ensure that the text property of a control contains a numeric value and displays a message, and sets the focus to the control if it does not:

```
Private Function IsTextNumeric(rCtl As Object) As Boolean
    If IsNumber(rCtl.Text) = True Then
        IsTextNumeric = True
    Else
        Call MsgBox("Text must be numeric.", _
            vbOKOnly + vbInformation)
        Call rCtl.SetFocus
        IsTextNumeric = False
    End If
End Function
```

You can then pass either a text box or combo box to the function because they both provide a Text property and a *SetFocus* method, as follows:

```
If IsTextNumeric(txtHoursWorked) = False Then Exit Sub
If IsTextNumeric(cboPayRate) = False Then Exit Sub
```

Note that the data type for the argument in the *IsTextNumeric* function is declared as type *Object*. *Object* is a Visual Basic keyword. As used in this example, it will allow the function to be passed any type of object as the argument. As long as the object being passed provides a Text property and the *SetFocus* method, everything will work as planned. Otherwise, a Run Time error will be generated.

Inheritance

The concept of *inheritance* is best explained by way of example. Suppose you are writing an employee database application for your company. Your company has only two types of employees: managers and laborers.

The managers and laborers share many of the same properties. They both have Social Security numbers, names, job codes, and dates of hire. They also have some differences, however. Managers might have annual salaries; the laborers might have hourly pay rates. You would like to create classes to encapsulate these two types of employees so that you design the two classes as shown in Figure 12.1.

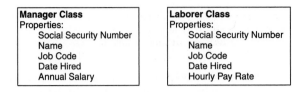

Figure 12.1   Manager *and* Laborer *classes without inheritance.*

With inheritance, you can choose an alternative design that enables you to share the coding for the properties that both classes have in common. You can define a class called *Employee* that contains the common properties, and then specify that the *Manager* and *Laborer* classes "inherit" the properties from the *Employee* class. Using OOP terms, we would call the *Employee* class a **base class** and say that the *Manager* and *Laborer* classes are **derived** from the *Employee* class. Figure 12.2 shows the classes designed using inheritance.

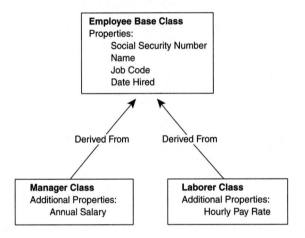

Figure 12.2   Manager *and* Laborer *classes with inheritance.*

Suppose that later every employee in the company is assigned an email address. Inheritance allows an email property to be added to the base *Employee* class, and since the *Manager* and *Laborer* classes are derived from the *Employee* class, they both will automatically "inherit" the new property.

This notion of inheritance can be extended to many levels. Suppose that your company further classifies the *Laborer* class into two more distinct *Laborer* classes. You might then have to define a *Skilled Laborer* and an *Unskilled Laborer* class, each of which is derived from the *Laborer* class (see Figure 12.3).

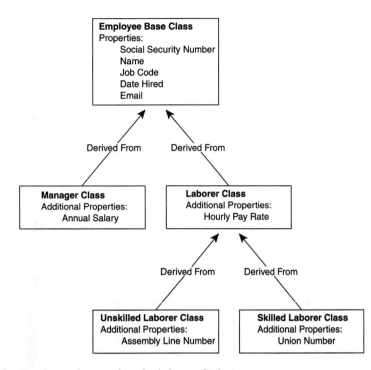

Figure 12.3   Employee *classes with multiple layers of inheritance.*

Inheritance allows different data types to share the same code, leading to a reduction in code size and an increase in functionality. It is a powerful technique that is sometimes used when developing classes, but at the same time can expand the complexity of the source code. Multiple levels of inheritance particularly become a problem. Using our sample classes as an example, if a bug is reported with the *Unskilled Laborer* class, you might have to debug the *Unskilled Laborer and* the *Laborer and* the *Employee* base classes.

Recall that OOP was developed as a tool to help resolve the difficulties of understanding and maintaining the always-increasing complexity of today's software. Overuse of inheritance has often replaced one form of complexity with another. Perhaps this is the reason Microsoft has chosen not to include inheritance in Visual Basic.

Defining and Using Your Own Objects

Now that you have an understanding about the basic principles of Object-Oriented Programming, it is time to discover how you create objects of your own. Throughout this section, we will be creating an *Employee* class for example purposes.

Property Procedures

Property procedures enable you to write code that is executed when a property is set or retrieved. This code allows an object to "protect" itself from bad data values. Property procedures also enable you to selectively "expose" private data members; private data members enable you to create read-only or write-only properties. We again illustrate with an example.

Suppose we have a need to know how many years an employee has worked for our company. Because the *Employee* class contains a DateHired property, we could use this value to calculate the number of years employed whenever the value is needed. However, a better alternative is to have the *Employee* class expose a YearsEmployed property, as shown in Figure 12.10. Property procedures enable us to create this property without having to define yet another Public variable. Instead, the value is calculated whenever the property is retrieved. Note that the syntax for *Property Get* procedures is almost the same as for functions.

```
Property Get YearsEmployed() As Long
    YearsEmployed = DateDiff("d", DateHired, Date) / 365.25
End Property
```

Figure 12.10 *Example* Property Get *procedure.*

The syntax for using the new YearsEmployed property is the same as usual. However, this time, retrieving the property value will cause our property procedure to be called. For example:

```
Dim Emp As New clsEmployee
...
If Emp.YearsEmployed > 25 Then
    Call MsgBox("Give this employee a gold watch.", _
        vbOkOnly + vbInformation)
Else
    Call MsgBox("Give this employee our thanks.", _
        vbOkOnly + vbInformation)
End If
```

The preceding example illustrates using a *Property Get* procedure that causes code to be executed whenever the property value is retrieved. We can also write a *Property Let* procedure that causes code to be executed whenever the property value is set.

Suppose the valid range of values for the JobCode property of our *Employee* class is 1, 2, 3, and 4. Anything else is assumed to be invalid. Because the JobCode property is currently implemented as a Public variable, there is no guarantee that it will be set to only valid values. If we want to ensure only valid values are set for JobCode, we should change the job code variable to be Private and write property procedures so that the object can control how its values are set. If an invalid value is attempted, we will instead use a default value of *1*. (In the next section, we will show how to generate a Run Time error when an invalid property value is set.)

Figure 12.11 shows the changes made to the *Employee* class. Note that the syntax for *Property Let* procedures is the same as for general sub procedures. A single argument is declared that contains the value we want to assign to the property. Also note that if we want to allow the JobCode property value to be retrieved, we have to define a *Property Get* procedure because the *mJobCode* variable is declared Private and cannot be directly accessed.

```
Public SSN      As String
Public EmpName   As String
Public DateHired As Date

Private mJobCode As Long

Property Get JobCode() As Long
    ' Nothing special is required when getting the JobCode value
    ' so just return it.
    JobCode = mJobCode
End Property

Property Let JobCode(ByVal JobCodeArg As Long)
    ' If the value attempting to be set is out of the range,
    ' assume a value of 1.
    If JobCodeArg < 1 Or JobCodeArg > 4 Then
        mJobCode = 1
    End If
End Property
```

Figure 12.11   *Example* Property Let *procedure.*

If we now try to assign an invalid value to the JobCode property, our *Property Let* procedure is called and passed the invalid value. Our code then sets the internal variable to the assumed value of *1*. For example:

```
Dim Emp As New clsEmployee
...
Emp.JobCode = 10
' Job code now actually has a value of 1, since 10 is out of range.
```

You learned that properties can be added to a class using two techniques: by declaring *Public* variables or by using property procedures. You might wonder which technique you should use and under what circumstances. The following lists show the rules for how to declare properties:

■■■ **TIP**

Use Public variables when the property is read-write and

- Any value in the range supported by the property's data type is valid. This is the case with many properties.
- The property is a String data type, which has no size limitations.
- The property is a Boolean data type, which can only have a value of *True* or *False*.

Use property procedures when

- The property is read-only or write-only.
- The property has a range of valid values that need to be validated when the property is set.
- Setting the property causes a change in other property values or in private member variables. Setting an *Employee* object's HoursWorked property, for example, might recalculate the employee's NetPay amount.
- You need to change the data type of the internal variable that represents the property, but you do not want to change the **class interface.**

Communicating Errors from a Class

Think about what happens when you set an invalid property value to one of Visual Basic's intrinsic objects. Set a form's Height property to -1, for example. Doing so causes an Invalid property value Run Time error. Because we want our classes to behave like other objects, our classes should also cause Run Time errors when something unexpected occurs.

In Chapter 6, you learned how to "trap" Run Time errors and use the properties of the *Err* object to display a description of the Run Time error to the user. Additionally, the *Err* object has a **Raise method** that you can call to cause your own Run Time errors to be generated.

The simplified syntax for the *Err* object's *Raise* method is as follows:

```
Call object.Raise(errornumber, source, description)
```

where *errornumber* is some unique number, *source* is the class name of the object, and *description* is descriptive text of what caused the error.

Visual Basic includes the **vbObjectError** keyword that you can use to ensure your object is raising errors with unique numbers. You typically add a sequential number to *vbObjectError* for each error your class raises. Experience has shown, however, that the error description is usually more helpful than the error number when tracking down errors raised by classes.

Now that you know how to raise errors from a class, we should revisit the JobCode property procedures we created in the previous section. A better alternative to just ignoring the invalid value is to raise an error if an invalid value is trying to be set. Figure 12.12 shows our new and improved version of the JobCode property procedures.

```
Property Get JobCode() As Long
    ' Nothing special is required when getting the JobCode value
    ' so just return it.
    JobCode = mJobCode
End Property

Property Let JobCode(ByVal JobCodeArg As Long)
    ' If the value attempting to be set is out of the range of
    ' valid values, raise a Run Time error.
    If JobCodeArg < 1 Or JobCodeArg > 4 Then
        Call Err.Raise(vbObjectError + 1, "clsEmployee", _
            "Invalid JobCode property value.")
    End If
    mJobCode = JobCodeArg
End Property
```

Figure 12.12   Property Let *procedure raising a Run Time error.*

One more step is required to communicate Run Time errors from class modules. Visual Basic contains an option that determines how errors are handled when raised from class modules. By default, raising an error in a class module causes execution to pause as soon as the error is raised, even if an error handler has been declared in the procedure that is using the class. To cause Visual Basic to honor the error handler, you have to change Visual Basic's Error Trapping option.

From the Tools menu, select Options, select the General tab, and select the *Break on Unhandled Errors* option (see Figure 12.13). The case study at the end of this chapter uses error handlers in all *Form Event* procedures to catch errors raised from the classes.

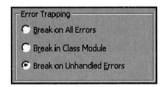

Figure 12.13   *Visual Basic error trapping options.*

Using Collections

Creating Arrays of Objects

In Chapter 8, you used the array data structure to create lists of the same data type. You were shown how arrays could be declared for simple data types (for example, Strings and Integers) as well as for UDTs. Similarly, you can declare arrays of objects or object references. For example:

```
' Declare 10 Employee objects.
Private fEmps(1 To 10) As New clsEmployee
' Declare 10 Employee object references.
Private fEmps(1 To 10) As clsEmployee
```

Although arrays work fine in many circumstances, most developers use a more advanced structure when working with lists of objects: *collections*.

What Are Collections?

Visual Basic **collections** are similar in concept to an array in that they are used to store lists of objects. Collections are much more powerful and flexible than arrays, however. A collection allows objects to be added at any position; an array allows objects to be added only to its end. Collections allow objects to be deleted from the middle of the collection; arrays have no easy way to allow an object to be removed. Collections allow objects to be retrieved by using a "key" value; arrays require you to write code to explicitly search the array.

With most software, more power and flexibility usually means less efficient processing. Such is the case with collections in comparison to arrays. You never have to indicate the number of occurrences a collection might need, however, and you never have to *ReDim* a collection just to add a new value. Therefore using collections results in simpler, easier-to-read, and easier-to-maintain source code.

Creating a Collection

To create a collection, just define a variable with data type Collection. A collection is actually an object itself, so you must use the *New* keyword in the declaration statement. If you omit the *New* keyword, you get a reference to a collection and no *Collection* object is created.

The following statement defines a form-scope collection that we will use to add references to *Employee* objects:

```
Private fEmployees As New Collection
```

After a *Collection* object is created, you add object references to it using the collection's *Add* method. An event procedure in a form might create a new *Employee* object and add it to the form's *Employee* collection using code similar to the following:

```
Dim Emp As New clsEmployee
Call fEmployees.Add(Emp)
```

The *Add* method also enables you to supply an optional *Key* argument. The key value can then be used at a later point to directly retrieve the object reference from the collection. Note that the key value must be unique within the collection, and must be a string that cannot be evaluated as a number. "Bob" and "B14" are valid collection key values, for example, but "123" is not.

To add an *Employee* object to a collection using the employee's name as a key value, you can use code similar to the following:

```
Dim Emp As New clsEmployee
Call fEmployees.Add(Emp, Emp.EmpName)
```

Retrieving an Object Reference from a Collection

Object references are retrieved from a collection using the collection's *Item* method with either a position index value or a key value. The first object in the collection uses an Index value of *1*. The following example retrieves the reference to the first employee in the *fEmployees* collection and assigns it to a local variable:

```
Dim Emp As clsEmployee ' Declare an Employee object reference.
Set Emp = fEmployees.Item(1)
```

Alternatively, you can retrieve an object reference using a key value—no searching is required! The following example retrieves a reference to the *Employee* object with a key value of "Bob."

```
Dim Emp As clsEmployee ' Declare an Employee object reference.
Set Emp = fEmployees.Item("Bob")
```

In either example, if an object reference with the specified index or key value is not found in the collection, a Run Time error is generated.

Iterating Through a Collection

In Chapter 8, you used *For...Next* loops to iterate through the items in an array. You can use the same technique with collections. The collection object provides a Count property that indicates the number of objects in the collection. The following code iterates through the collection and calls each *Employee* object's *DebugPrint* method:

```
Dim Emp  As clsEmployee ' Declare an Employee object reference.
Dim Indx As Long        ' Declare a variable to use as an index.

For Indx = 1 To fEmployees.Count
    Set Emp = fEmployees.Item(Indx)
    Call Emp.DebugPrint
Next Indx
```

Visual Basic provides an alternative technique for working with collections, which is both easier to code and executes significantly faster. You can use the *For Each...Next* looping structure to process each object in a collection. The *For Each...Next* structure is easier to use because it doesn't require an index variable to be declared, and the object reference is automatically set to a variable.

The following example shows an alternative style of iterating through our *Employee* collection:

```
Dim Emp As clsEmployee ' Declare an Employee object reference.

For Each Emp In fEmployees
    Call Emp.DebugPrint
Next Emp
```

■ TIP
For better performance, use *For Each...Next* to iterate through the objects in a collection.

Deleting an Object Reference from a Collection

Objects can be deleted from a collection using the collection's *Remove* method. Just as with the *Item* method, you can supply either an index position or a key value to the *Remove* method. The following examples remove the first employee and the employee named "Bob" from the *Employee* collection.

```
Call fEmployees.Remove(1) ' Removes the first employee.

Call fEmployees.Remove("Bob") ' Removes employee named Bob.
```

Whenever an object reference is removed from a collection, the collection's Count property is decreased by *1*. Note that if an object reference with the specified index or key value is not found in the collection, a Run Time error is generated; therefore, you may need to define an error handler.

Deleting a Collection

In the preceding section, you were shown how to explicitly destroy an object by setting the object reference to *Nothing*. Because a collection is itself an object (an instance of the built-in *Collection* class), you can explicitly destroy it using the same technique, as follows:

```
Set fEmployees = Nothing
```

OOP Case Study

In Chapter 9, "Sequential Files," we developed a *Payroll* application that used CSV files for data storage. In Chapter 10, "Introductory Database Programming," and Chapter 11, we enhanced the program to use databases for data storage instead of using CSV files. In the last section of this chapter, we will once again enhance the *Payroll* application. This time the logical components that make up the application will be encapsulated into classes so that they can be reused in future projects.

Step 1: Analyze the Problem

Because your conversion of the *Payroll* program to DAO and SQL was such a success, the project manager has asked you to perform further enhancements. The *Payroll* program is working correctly and requires no user-interface or processing changes. Instead, it seems the manager has been reading up on current programming trends and has declared that all new applications will be developed using Object-Oriented Programming techniques.

The manager has recognized that OOP can help make programmers more productive, and, because he has a backlog of software development projects, he has decided to give it a try. For the pilot project, you have been asked to rewrite the *Payroll* application using OOP techniques so that its components can be reused in future projects.

The *Payroll* program requires no input, output, or processing changes, so we can use the Analysis Table from Chapter 11. It is repeated in Figure 12.14 for completeness.

Input Needs	Processing Needs	Output Needs
SSN (*Emp* table)	Load tax tables.	SSN (*Paychecks* table)
Name (*Emp* table)	Initialize *Paychecks*	Hours worked (*Paychecks* table)
Hours worked	database (create	Gross pay (*Paychecks* table)
Hourly pay rate (*Emp*	if necessary).	Tax (*Paychecks* table)
table)	Validate the hours.	Net pay (*Paychecks* table)
Income levels (*Tax* table)	Calculate:	Error message if nonnumeric hours
Tax rates (*Tax* table)	Gross pay	Error message if hours is not within
	Tax	allowed range
	Net pay	Error message if *Payroll* database does
	Write *Paychecks*	not exist
	record.	Notify user if *Paychecks* database does
	Read *Emp* record.	not exist and give option to create it
		Notify user if *Paychecks* table already
		contains records

Figure 12.14 *Analysis Table for* Payroll *program.*

Step 2: Design or Create the User Interface

As mentioned earlier, the *Payroll* program doesn't require any user-interface changes. We will again show the user-interface design from Chapter 9 in Figure 12.15 for completeness.

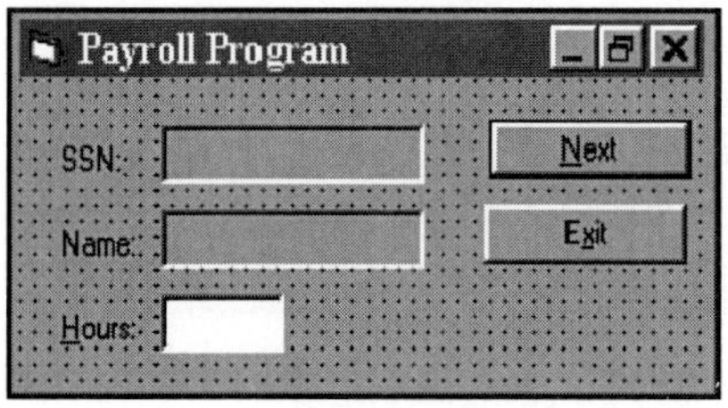

Figure 12.15 Payroll *program user-interface design.*

Step 3: Design the Logic for the Program

In previous chapters, the logic for the application was contained almost entirely within the form modules. With OOP, most of an application's logic is contained in the classes used by the application. As a result, we have to modify our design steps to identify the appropriate objects that will be used by the application and to identify their interface—their Public properties and methods.

In the case of our *Payroll* program, the logic has mostly been developed. Our task is then to identify the necessary classes and use them to encapsulate the logic that was previously contained in the main form.

Step 3a: Define the List of Classes

One goal of OOP is to separate the user-interface logic from the business processing logic. We know that VB forms act as a kind of visual object, so we can assume that one "class" we need is the main user-interface form.

By reviewing the processing requirements for the *Payroll* application, you decide on three more main classes. A list of employees is used as input, a tax rate table is used as input for computing paycheck amounts, and a file of paycheck records is created as output. Two of the classes actually encapsulate a list of other objects, so you add two more classes to your design document: an *Employee* class and a *Tax Rate Item* class.

Figure 12.16. shows the complete list of objects for the payroll application.

Class	Class Name	Description
Main User Interface	frmMain	Acts as the controller of the other objects used in the project
Employee List	clsEmpList	Encapsulates the details of retrieving individual employees from the database file
Employee	clsEmployee	Encapsulates a single employee in the *Employee List* class
Paychecks File	clsPaychecks	Encapsulates the *Paychecks* file that is created as output
Tax Rate Table	clsTaxRates	Encapsulates the details of retrieving and searching of the tax rates from the database
Tax Rate Item	clsTaxRateItem	Encapsulates a single tax rate record used in the *Tax Rates Table* class

Figure 12.16 *List of objects used by the* Payroll *program.*

Step 3b: Define the Interfaces for the Classes

After you have the list of classes identified, the next step is to identify the interface each class exposes. Recall that each class should be treated as a "black box," meaning that the "users" of the objects should not "know" how the internals of the class are actually implemented. This approach suggests that the classes should make public only those properties and methods necessary to achieve the desired functionality.

The *Employee List* class encapsulates the details of how employee records are stored, for example, so the main form should not contain any code that directly references an employee file or database. Any additional data members or procedures required by the classes should be kept private so that they can be changed at a later date, guaranteeing the changes will not damage other portions of the program.

Because the *Payroll* project has only one form and this form will act as the controller for the other objects, it is not necessary to add any new public properties or methods to it. Of course all our other classes do require an interface. After some thought about how the classes will be used, you develop the interface list shown in Figures 12.17 through 12.21 for the classes used in this project. All properties should be considered read/write unless otherwise noted.

clsEmpList Properties	Description
FileName	Sets or returns a string that specifies the name of the database or file that contains the list of employee records.
EOF	Read-only property that returns a Boolean value that indicates whether the end of the employee list has been reached. The value should be checked before calling the *GetNext* method.
clsEmpList Methods	**Description**
GetFirst	Gets and returns the first employee in the list. Employees are returned in ascending SSN order.
GetNext	Gets and returns the next employee in the list. Call the *GetFirst* method before calling this method.

Figure 12.17   clsEmpList *interface*.

clsEmployee Properties	Description
EmpName	A String data type that contains the employee's full name.
Gross	Read-only property that returns a Currency data type containing the employee's payroll gross pay amount.
Hrs	The number of hours worked by the employee, returned as Double data type. Setting this property causes the employee's gross pay, tax amount, and net pay to be recalculated.
MaxHrs	Read-only constant Long value that indicates the maximum number of hours an employee is allowed to work.

continues

Exists Property
Begin Exists
    Call FileLen(FileName)
    If run-time error did not occur
      Return True
    Else
      Return False
End Exists

InsertRecord Method
Begin InsertRecord
    Format SQL statement to insert new Paychecks record
    Execute SQL statement to insert new Paychecks record
End InsertRecord

RecordsExist Property
Begin RecordsExist
    Query to see how many records exist
    If records exist
      Return True
    Else
      Return False
End RecordsExist

Figure 12.26 Paychecks *File* (clsPaychecks) *pseudocode.*

Class Terminate Event
Begin Class_Terminate
    Close database if open
End Class_Terminate

DBGetField Function
Begin DBGetField(Recordset, FieldName)
    If IsNull(FieldName)
      If field type = text or memo
        Return ""
      Else
        Return 0
    Else
      Return Recordset(FieldName)
End DBGetField

FindRate Method
Begin FindRate(AnnualPayAmt)
    If tax tables are not loaded
      Call LoadTaxTables
    For each TaxItem
      If AnnualPayAmt < TaxItem.IncomeAmount
        ItemFound = True
        Return TaxItem.TaxRate
    Next TaxItem
    If ItemFound = False
    Raise Error
End FindRate

```
LoadTaxTables Procedure
Begin LoadTaxTables
    If database is closed
        Call DBOpen
    Format query to select all TaxRate records.
    Open recordset
    Do until recordset.EOF
        Create new TaxItem object
        TaxItem.IncomeAmount = DBGetField("Income")
        TaxItem.TaxRate = DBGetField("TaxRate")
        Add TaxItem to collection
        Call recordset.MoveNext
    Loop
    Close recordset
End LoadTaxTables
```

Figure 12.27   Tax Rates *table* (clsTaxRates) *pseudocode.*

Note that encapsulating logic into the class modules actually requires more overall code than just coding everything in the form. This extra coding is a byproduct of encapsulation and of making the classes as easy to use as possible. Instead of relying on code in the form, for example, the *Employee List* class (*clsEmpList*) now contains logic to open its own database connection and its *Class_Terminate* event ensures the Recordset and database connections are closed

You should also note, however, that the logic contained in the main form is now greatly simplified. Remember that the payoff of Object-Oriented Programming is not during initial development. Rather the gains in productivity are realized during program maintenance and when a previously developed class is reused in another project. If we have designed our objects correctly, we can change their implementation without adversely affecting other portions of the applications that use them so long as we don't change their interface. Likewise, we can reuse them in future projects without regard to how they are implemented.

Step 3e: Develop a Test Plan (Table of Input with Expected Results)

Remember that this version of the *Payroll* program has been an exercise in Object-Oriented Programming, not in adding new features to the program. We did make changes to the program, however, so it must be retested. We can use the same test data that has been used in previous versions (shown in Figure 12.28 for completeness). Also, don't forget to test for any exceptions that may occur (for example, a missing *Payroll* database file and invalid user input).

SSN	Name	Hrs	Rate	Gross	Gross*52	Tax	Net
241341521	Thomas O Whitten	8	10.75	86.00	4472	0.00	86.00
492735055	Owen F Detweiler	11	17.30	190.30	9896	19.03	171.27
533479537	Stephen Donneger	32	15.00	480.00	24960	72.00	408.00
639170707	Dirk Gehman	38	37.00	1406.00	73112	351.50	1054.50
690371986	Edward S Eastman	38	75.00	2850.00	148200	940.50	1909.50
761236124	Michael L Aiman	9	10.75	96.75	5031	9.68	87.07
785720348	Tony A Edison	12	17.30	207.60	10795	31.14	176.46
790184316	Grace J Ebermann	35	15.00	525.00	27300	131.25	393.75
826687434	Carol C Banana	40	37.00	1480.00	76960	488.40	991.60
841182276	Ralph J Alderfer	40	75.00	3000.00	156000	1200.00	1800.00
949744067	Harold U Bates	45	10.95	520.13	27047	130.03	390.10
987493232	Candice F Carter	50	15.65	860.75	44759	215.19	645.56

Figure 12.28 *Test data for* Payroll *program.*

Step 4: Code the Program

A special note should be made about the changes to the event procedures in the main form. Remember that objects communicate exceptions to each other by raising errors. You learned in Chapter 6 how to create error handlers using the *On Error* keywords. Now that the main form delegates most of the processing to the methods of the objects we have created, you have to be diligent with the use of error handlers. Review the form's code again and make sure that any event procedure that uses objects also has an error handler defined.

Remember that the user interface and some of the code is copied directly from the *Payroll* program developed in earlier chapters. So you might start developing this version by modifying a copy of the project files from Chapter 11.

The complete source code listing for the new *Payroll* program is shown in Figures 12.29 through 12.34.

```
' Program:    Payroll
' Form:       frmMain
' Programmer: Bill Goodcoder, III
' Date:       September 23, 1998
' Purpose:    To create the paychecks data.  This program gets
'             employee and tax rate information from EmplList and
'             TaxRates objects and uses it to calculate paycheck
'             amounts.  The paycheck data is sent to the Paychecks
'             object to be saved for later processing.  The user is
'             presented with the SSN and name of an employee and, if
'             that employee has worked, enters the hours and presses
'             Enter.  The gross pay, tax, and net pay are calculated
'             and along with the SSN are passed to the Paychecks
```

```
'             database. If the employee has not worked, the user
'             presses Enter, and the employee is skipped.  In either
'             case, the SSN and name of the next employee are
'             displayed. After all the employees have been processed,
'             the user clicks Exit.
' Input:      EmpList, Employee and TaxRates objects.
' Output:     Paychecks object.

Option Explicit

' Database filenames
Private Const cfPayrollDBName As String = "Payroll.mdb"
Private Const cfPaychecksDBName As String = "Paychecks.mdb"

' The current employee
Private fCurrEmp As clsEmployee

' Payroll objects
Private fEmpList As New clsEmpList
Private fTaxRates As New clsTaxRates
Private fPaychecks As New clsPayChecks

' Purpose: This function safely appends the passed filename
'          to the passed path by making sure the last character
'          in the path contains a "\".
Private Function AppendFileToPath(ByVal Path As String, _
    ByVal File As String) As String

    If Path = "" Then
        AppendFileToPath = File
    ElseIf Right(Path, 1) = "\" Then
        AppendFileToPath = Path & File
    Else
        AppendFileToPath = Path & "\" & File
    End If
End Function

' Purpose: Unload the form to cause the program to end.
Private Sub cmdExit_Click()
    Unload frmMain
End Sub

' Purpose: When the Next button is clicked, the gross pay, tax, and
'          net pay are calculated and along with the SSN are passed
'          to the Paychecks object to be saved.
Private Sub cmdNext_Click()
    On Error GoTo ErrHandler

    If txtHours.Text <> "" Then
        If HoursIsValid Then

            ' Set the employee object's reference to the TaxRates
            ' object before setting the Hrs property so that its
            ' Gross, Tax, and Net properties can be properly
            ' calculated.
            Set fCurrEmp.TaxRates = fTaxRates

            fCurrEmp.Hrs = CDbl(txtHours.Text)
            Call fPaychecks.InsertRecord(fCurrEmp)

            Set fCurrEmp = fEmpList.GetNext
            Call LoadEmployee
        End If
```

continues

2. Appendix A includes a simple illustration of how to use graphic methods to draw circles on a picture box control (see PictureBox Example 1 in Appendix A). Circles of random sizes and colors are drawn whenever the user clicks on the picture box with the mouse. The circles are not saved when the application ends, however. Enhance this example program using OOP techniques to save the circles when the application closes, and to redraw them when the application restarts.

You should define a *Circle* class and a *Circle List* class. The *Circle* class will need properties for its center point, color, and radius. It will also need a *Draw* method that can be called to cause the circle to be drawn on the object that is passed as an argument.

The *Circle List* class should contain a collection of *Circle* objects. It will need methods to:

- Clear the contents of the circles collection.

- Create a new random-colored and random-sized circle at the specified location.

- Save the collection of circles to a CSV or database file.

- Load the collection of circles from a CSV or database file.

- Draw the collection of circles on the object passed as an argument.

3. Enhance the program developed in project 2 to enable the user to determine whether a circle or square should be drawn on the picture box when clicked. Add option buttons to the toolbar to let the user select which shape to be drawn. Create a new *Square* class that behaves much the same as the *Circle* class. It should use the picture box's *Line* method to draw the square. Change the *Circles List* class to a more general sounding name like *Shapes List*. Add a new method for it to create a new *Square* object and add it to its collection of shapes. Both the list of circle and square objects should be saved in the same collection.

4. Your friends and relatives always complain that you constantly forget their birthdays. Now that you have knowledge of computer programming, you finally decide to solve this problem by developing some software that you can use to remind you of these important dates. The following form shows how the UI might look.

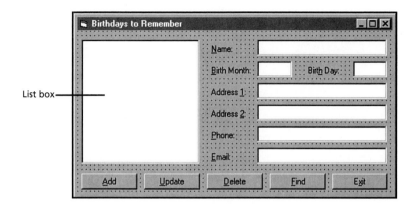

Begin the project by designing a *BirthdayList* class and a *BirthdayItem* class. The *BirthdayList* class should contain a collection of *BirthdayItem* objects. The *BirthdayList* class should save the collection of its *Brithday Item* objects to a simple CSV file during its terminate event and should load its contents from the same CSV file during its initialize event. The *BirthdayItem* class should have properties for each of the values shown on the sample form. Additionally, it should have a read-only property that returns the number of days until the person's birthday. When the main form first loads, it should call a method in the *BirthdayList* class to display a message for each person who has a birthday in the next 10 days. The *BirthdayList* class should also have methods that allow *BrithdayItem* objects to be added, updated, deleted, found, and a method to fill a list box with the names from the collection of *BrithdayItem* objects.

The list box on the form should show the name for each person in the list. Clicking a name in the list box should cause that person's information to be displayed in the text boxes. Buttons on the form should allow items to be added, updated, and deleted from the *BirthdayList* object. When the *Find* button is selected, code in the event procedure should call a method in the *BirthdayList* class to search for the name specified in the Name text box.

Remember the rule of encapsulation. The main form should only work with the *BirthdayList* and *BirthdayItem* classes' interface. It should not "know" that the birthday information is stored in a collection and CSV files. Likewise, the *BirthdayList* and *BirthdayItem* classes should not contain any reference to the form.

VISUAL BASIC USER INTERFACE OBJECTS

Overview

The purpose of this appendix is to list commonly used Graphical User Interface (GUI) objects and their properties, events, and methods. Forms, intrinsic controls, menus, and ActiveX controls are all discussed. It may seem overwhelming at first because these objects sometimes have hundreds of properties, events, and methods. In most applications, however, only a small subset is commonly used, and that subset consists of the ones that you will find here. Additionally, this appendix includes brief coding examples so that you can see how these objects are typically used. The complete code for all examples at the end of each section is included with the sample code that accompanies this book.

Each new version of Visual Basic includes enhancements and changes to these objects, so you should always consult the Visual Basic Help files for the most complete and up-to-date description of objects, properties and property values, events, and methods.

Common Object Properties, Events, and Methods

Visual Basic GUI objects contain many of the same properties, events, and methods. This section lists some of the more common ones. Not all the listed properties, events, and methods are available for all objects, and some behave slightly differently depending on the object. Check the Visual Basic Help file if you are unsure.

Common Properties	Description
Appearance	This property determines whether the object is drawn with three-dimensional effects. This property was added because of the Windows 95 user interface changes, so you should probably leave this property set to its default 3D setting.
BackColor, ForeColor	You can use these properties to get or set the background or foreground colors of an object. Because Windows allows the user to use the Display Control Panel applet to select color schemes, it is advised that you normally leave these properties set to their default values of *vbWindowBackground* and *vbWindowsText*.
Enabled	The Enabled property is used to determine whether an object can respond to events. If this property is set to *True*, the control is enabled. If it is set to *False*, the control is disabled and typically displays a "gray" appearance to give the user a visual cue.
	Setting this property to *True* or *False* for a group of controls at Run Time is commonly done to indicate whether the controls apply to the current input values.
Font	You can use the Font property to change the font used to display text on an object. The Font property actually refers to a Font object, which contains its own set of properties. The Font object contains font name, size, bold, italic, and underline properties.
	For example, this code changes a text box's font property:

```
txtName.Font.Name = "Arial"
txtName.Font.Size = 14
txtName.Font.Bold = True
txtName.Font.Italic = True
txtName.Font.Underline = False
```

	Because Windows enables the user to use the Display Control Panel applet to select font schemes, and because not all font characteristics are contained in your application when you make an executable (EXE), you should normally leave the font properties set to their default values to ensure that they will display correctly on the user's PC.
Width, Height	These properties set the horizontal and vertical dimensions of an object. Height and Width are normally set at Design Time when you draw the user interface, but they can also be set at Run Time to give the effect of resizing an object.
Left, Top	These properties are used to indicate an object's horizontal and vertical position in its container. Left and Top are normally set at Design Time when you draw the user interface, but they can also be set at Run Time to give the effect of moving an object.

Common Properties	Description
Name	The Name property is used in code to identify an object. To reference a particular object in code, you will need to use its name. Therefore, from a programming perspective, using descriptive names that follow accepted standards will facilitate your programming. This property is set in the Properties window at Design Time and is read-only at Run Time.
TabIndex, TabStop	These properties are typically set at Design Time to control how the focus is moved from control to control when the user presses the Tab and Shift+Tab keys.
	When the user presses the Tab key, Visual Basic checks the TabIndex property of the control that has the focus, finds the control with the next sequential TabIndex value on the form that can receive the focus, and moves the focus to that control. Pressing Shift+Tab works the same except that the focus is moved to the control with the preceding sequential TabIndex value.
	TabIndex is usually set to zero for the first control (upper left) and to the highest number for the last control (lower right). The TabStop property is used to indicate whether the user can use the Tab and Shift+Tab keys to give focus to a control. Setting TabStop to *True* will cause the cursor to stop on the control, and setting it to *False* will cause the control to be skipped.
	The TabIndex property for a control is automatically assigned when it is added to the form. The first control added to the form gets TabIndex = 0, the second control gets TabIndex = 1, and so on. If you add controls to the form in the desired tab order, you might never have to change the TabIndex property. Because many Visual Basic programs are developed iteratively and the GUI is likely to change during the iterations, your final interface is not likely to have the desired tab sequence. Therefore, one final step in good user interface construction is to set the tab order for all controls on a form in a logical sequence.
	When you change the TabIndex property of one control on a form, Visual Basic automatically renumbers the TabIndex property of other controls on the same form. Because of this behavior, you can easily set the TabIndex property for all controls to the desired value by following this trick:
	■ Select the last control on the form.
	■ Select the TabIndex property in the Properties Window. (When you click on another object, its TabIndex property will already be selected.)

continues

Common Properties	Description
	■ Press *0* with one hand while keeping your other hand on the mouse.
	■ Then, work your way from the last control to the first control by alternately clicking a control and pressing *0* for that control's TabIndex property value. When you reach the first control, all controls should now have the correct tab order set.
Tag	Unlike all other properties, the Tag property is not used by Visual Basic, so you can use it to store any extra data you need. Experienced programmers have used this property to circumvent limitations imposed by Visual Basic.
	A PictureBox control can be used to display an image from a variety of graphics file formats, for example. PictureBox does not have a "filename" property, however, so you might store the graphics filename in the Tag property instead.
ToolTipText	If you set the ToolTipText property to a short string and the user hovers the mouse over the object for about one second, the string will display in a small rectangle just below the object. This property gets its name because this feature was originally added to buttons on a toolbar, but is now available for almost all controls.
Visible	This property just determines whether an object is visible or hidden at Run Time. Using a form's Show or Hide method is the same as setting the form's Visible property to *True* or *False*.

Common Events	Description
Click, DblClick	These common events normally occur when the user clicks or double-clicks the mouse over an object. However, the *Click* event can also occur for many other reasons. For example:
	■ Pressing the Spacebar when a command button, option button, or check box has the focus
	■ Setting the Value property for a command button, option button, or check box
	■ Selecting a new item in a list box using the up- and down-arrow keys
GotFocus, LostFocus	The *GotFocus* event occurs when an object receives the focus and the *LostFocus* event occurs when an object loses the focus. Focus is typically changed by a user action such as tabbing to an object, clicking it, or by pressing an access key. Focus can also be manipulated by your program using an object's *SetFocus* method. An object will not get the focus if it is disabled or hidden.

Common Events	Description
	GotFocus is sometimes used to enable/disable other controls that are dependent on the control that has the focus. *LostFocus* is sometimes used to validate a control's contents. To avoid infinite loops due to cascading events, you should never set the focus in the *GotFocus* or *LostFocus* events.
	Imagine a form with several text boxes in sequential tab sequence, for example. Each text box has a *LostFocus* event that performs data validation as well as changes the focus back to the erroneous text box (using the *SetFocus* method). The *LostFocus* for the first text box occurred when the second text box received the focus. If the first text box has an error, the *SetFocus* would move the focus from the second text box to the first text box. This will, in turn, trigger the *LostFocus* event of the second text box. But the user never had the opportunity to enter the second data item, so it is likely that its data validation will cause the focus to return to the second text box from the first one. This process will continue until the user realizes that there is no way out and cancels the application.
KeyPress, KeyDown, KeyUp	These three events are triggered by the user's action with the keyboard.
	KeyPress is triggered when the user presses any of the printable keyboard character keys. An argument passed to the event procedure enables you to determine which key was pressed. Pressing keys such as function keys and navigation keys will *not* cause a *KeyPress* event to occur.
	This event is sometimes used to test each key as it is typed and ignore the key if it is invalid, or to automatically capitalize the contents of a text box. You can code an event procedure for a text box to limit input to numeric digits, for example. A user can also "paste" alphabetic characters into the text box, however, so you can't rely on this method alone to guarantee the text box contains a valid number.
	KeyDown and KeyUp occur when the user presses and releases a key, respectively; they provide more detailed information than the *KeyPress* event. *KeyDown* and *KeyUp* events are triggered when the user presses and releases a function key or navigation key, for example. Additionally, arguments passed to the event procedure enable you to determine whether the Shift, Ctrl, and Alt buttons were also pressed.

continues

Common Events	Description

MouseDown, MouseUp, MouseMove	These events are similar to *KeyDown* and *KeyUp* except they occur when the user presses and releases a mouse button. Arguments passed to the event procedure enable you to determine
	■ Which mouse buttons (left, middle, right) are pressed
	■ Whether the Shift, Ctrl, and Alt buttons are also pressed
	■ The X and Y coordinates of the mouse pointer
	Because the click event doesn't indicate which mouse button was pressed, the *MouseUp* event is sometimes used instead of the click event. If you want to pop up a menu when the user clicks the right-mouse button, for example, you could use code similar to this:
	<pre>Private Sub Form_MouseUp (_
	    Button As Integer, _
	    Shift As Integer, _
	    X As Single, Y As Single)
	
	    If Button = vbRightButton Then
	        Call Me.PopupMenu(mnuFile)
	    End If
	End Sub</pre>The *MouseMove* event is triggered each time the mouse pointer passes over a new pixel. Because the user can generate hundreds of *MouseMove* events just by moving the mouse a few inches, you should never add lengthy code to this event procedure.

Common Methods	Description
Move	The *Move* method allows an object to be moved to a new location at Run Time. Arguments can be passed to specify new Left, Top, Width, and Height property values, although only the Left property is required. Executing this method is generally more efficient than setting each of the Left, Top, Width, and Height properties in separate statements.

Common Methods	Description
Refresh	Executing this method will cause the form or control to be redrawn immediately. Normally, Windows will wait for idle time before redrawing controls, but sometimes you may need an object to be redrawn without waiting for idle time.
	Using a label control to indicate the status of a long running loop is one such example. In the following code segment, the label's caption will not show each time it is changed if you remove the call to its *Refresh* method.

```
Dim SubX As Long
For SubX = 1 To 10000"
    lblExample.Caption = Format(SubX)
    Call lblExample.Refresh
Next SubX
```

SetFocus	Call the *SetFocus* method to move the cursor to the named control. The SetFocus method is normally used in an input validation procedure to move the cursor to a control that contains invalid data.
	You cannot use the *SetFocus* method to move the cursor to a control that is not visible or that does not have its Enabled property set to *False*. Likewise, you cannot set the focus to a control in a form's load event. Instead, set the TabIndex property to zero for the control that should get the initial focus.
ZOrder	In Windows graphic programming, coordinates are specified using an X, Y, and Z coordinate system. The X coordinate refers to the horizontal position, the Y coordinate refers to the vertical position, and the Z coordinate refers to the back-to-front position. You can use the ZOrder method to move an object to the front or back within its graphical level. For example:

```
' Moves the form to the front.
Call frmMain.ZOrder(0)
' Moves the form to the back.
Call frmMain.ZOrder(1)
```

Form Objects

Visual Basic forms are the main building blocks of the Graphical User Interface and are typically the first thing you see when you start a new project. Forms are used in Visual Basic applications to create the main user interface, to create modal dialog

Command Button Properties	Description
Value	This property can only be set to True and can only be set at Run Time. Setting the Value property to *True* will cause the click event to be triggered. This technique is generally undesirable because it is more straightforward to call a Public form procedure. In versions of Visual Basic previous to version 4.0, it was impossible to have a Public form procedure. So, code in one form could set the Value property of a command button on another form to *True* to cause a procedure in the other form to be executed.

Command Button Events	Description
Click	This is the primary event used when programming with command buttons. If a button does not have a *Click* event coded, the button is probably not needed on the form. The *Click* event is triggered when ■ The command button is clicked with the left mouse button. ■ The command button has the focus and the Spacebar or Enter key is pressed. ■ The button's access key is pressed. See the examples at the end of this section for more information.

CommandButton Examples

Using the standard command button is as simple as drawing it on the form, setting its name and caption properties, and writing some code for its Click event procedure. In this example, you will learn how to use the graphics-style buttons to create a low-budget toolbar. Additionally, you will use the button's Tag property, its ToolTipText property, and the form's Controls collection.

You can use many techniques and third-party products to give your application a toolbar with varying degrees of sophistication. The technique in the *CommandButton Example 1* project is very simple. It provides most of the functionality of a good toolbar, but includes none of the overhead and dangers of using ActiveX controls.

➢ **Begin CommandButton Example 1.**

Create a new project called CommandButton Example 1. Add five command button controls to the default form and set the following properties:

NOTE
Note the .BMP files used to set the picture properties are included with Visual Basic and should be found in the Microsoft Visual Studio\Common\ Graphics\Bitmaps\TlBr_W95. They are also included in the sample projects that accompany this text.

Object	Property	Value
Command Button 1	Name	cmdToolOpen
	Caption	Open
	Left, Top, Width, Height	0, 0, 555, 555
	Picture	Open.BMP
	Style	Graphical
Command Button 2	Name	cmdToolSave
	Caption	Save
	Left, Top, Width, Height	630, 0, 555, 555
	Picture	Save.BMP
	Style	Graphical
Command Button 3	Name	cmdToolPrint
	Caption	Print
	Left, Top, Width, Height	1260, 0, 555, 555
	Picture	Print.BMP
	Style	Graphical
Command Button 4	Name	cmdCaptions
	Caption	Captions
	Left, Top, Width, Height	90, 1620, 1200, 315
Command Button 5	Name	cmdNoCaption
	Caption	No Captions
	Left, Top, Width, Height	1440, 1620, 1200, 315

Figure A.5 CommandButton Example 1 *sample form.*

When finished, the form should look similar to Figure A.5.

At this point, you have a simple toolbar with three buttons. All you have to do is add code to implement the des ired tasks in the toolbar buttons' *Click* events.

One feature common in toolbars is the option to show button descriptions as captions or as ToolTip-style pop-up windows. You might like to offer this feature in your application, so write some event code to implement it.

You will need a place to store the button's Caption property when it is not displayed. Therefore, in the *Form_Load* event, use the form's Controls collection property to loop through all the controls on the form and find the toolbar buttons. Because all toolbar buttons are named with a prefix of "cmdTool," you can check the left seven characters of each control. When one is found, copy its Caption property to its Tag property. Recall that the Tag property is provided for programmer use only and is not used by Visual Basic.

For example:

```
' Purpose: This procedure will loop through all controls on
'          the form looking for toolbar command buttons and
'          will store their captions in the Tag property because
'          an option exists that allows the captions to be hidden.
Private Sub Form_Load()

    Dim Index As Long
    Dim Ctl   As Control

    For Index = 0 To Me.Controls.Count - 1
        Set Ctl = Me.Controls(Index)
        If Left(Ctl.Name, 7) = "cmdTool" Then
            Ctl.Tag = Ctl.Caption
        End If
    Next Index
End Sub
```

Next you need to implement code that can remove the captions, set the ToolTipText property, and change the buttons to a smaller size. To make the code easier to follow, include the following constants in the form's General Declaration section:

```
Private Const fcNoCaptionHeight = 315
Private Const fcCaptionHeight = 555
```

The toolbar-style option might be found on a dialog box or as a menu option in a commercial application. For the sake of simplicity, however, this example shows and hides the toolbar captions as a result of clicking the Captions and No Captions buttons. Implement their *Click* events as shown here:

```
' Purpose: This procedure will loop through all controls on
'          the form looking for toolbar command buttons.
'          When one is found, its Caption is set to the
'          caption saved in the Tag property and its height
'          is adjusted taller.
Private Sub cmdCaptions_Click()
    Dim Index As Long
    Dim Ctl   As Control

    For Index = 0 To Me.Controls.Count - 1
        Set Ctl = Me.Controls(Index)
        If Left(Ctl.Name, 7) = "cmdTool" Then
            Ctl.Caption = Ctl.Tag
            Ctl.ToolTipText = ""
            Ctl.Height = fcCaptionHeight
        End If
    Next Index
End Sub
' Purpose: This procedure will loop through all controls on
'          the form looking for toolbar command buttons.
'          When one is found, its Caption is set to an
'          empty string and its height is adjusted smaller.
Private Sub cmdNoCaptions_Click()
    Dim Index As Long
    Dim Ctl   As Control

    For Index = 0 To Me.Controls.Count - 1
        Set Ctl = Me.Controls(Index)
        If Left(Ctl.Name, 7) = "cmdTool" Then
            Ctl.Caption = ""
            Ctl.ToolTipText = Ctl.Tag
            Ctl.Height = fcNoCaptionHeight
        End If
    Next Index
End Sub
```

Note the code in the procedures is nearly identical. If the captions are to be shown, the Caption property is set to the Tag property and the ToolTipText property is set to an empty string. If the captions are to be hidden, the Caption property is set to an empty string and the ToolTipText property is set to the Tag property. In either case, the heights of the buttons are changed appropriately.

Run and test the application to make sure the captions can be hidden and shown correctly. More toolbar buttons can be added by just including more command buttons with pictures and naming them with a "cmdTool" prefix.

The Frame Control

The Frame control is typically used to group related controls together on a form (see Figure A.6). The Frame control acts as a "container" control, meaning that other controls can be drawn *inside* the frame.

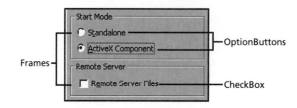

Figure A.6 *Frames, OptionButtons, and CheckBox controls.*

To draw a control inside the frame, you can't just move a frame over a group of controls or drag controls from the form onto the frame. Instead, draw the frame first, and then draw the other controls on top of it. You can easily tell whether a control is actually inside the frame (not just showing through from behind) by dragging the frame around the form. If the other controls move with the frame, you can be assured they are contained inside it. If the other controls don't move, they are not contained in the frame. To get them inside, delete and redraw them. Or, you can select the controls, copy them to the Clipboard, click the frame that is to contain them, and select Paste.

Frame Properties	*Description*
Caption	Used to specify the text that displays on the upper-left corner of the frame.

The CheckBox Control

The CheckBox control (refer to Figure A.6) is used to restrict the user to only two choices: to select or not select.

CheckBox Properties	*Description*
Alignment	If the Alignment property is set to left justified (*vbLeftJustify*), the check box is drawn to the left of its caption. If set to right justified (*vbRightJustify*), the check box is drawn to the right of its caption. Check boxes normally are left aligned.
Caption	This property is used to indicate the text displayed next to the check box. Include an ampersand (&) in the caption string to assign an access key for the control.
Value	Unfortunately, the Value property doesn't have two values of *True* and *False*. Instead, it has three values of unchecked (*vbUnchecked*), checked (*vbChecked*), and grayed (*vbGrayed*). You can't use simple assignment statements to map this control to a Boolean variable.
	See the examples at the end of this section for more information.

CheckBox Events	Description
Click	The *Click* event occurs whenever the Value property changes. The event is triggered when ■ The control is clicked with the left mouse button. ■ The control has the focus and the Spacebar is pressed. ■ The button's access key is pressed. ■ The Value property is changed in code at Run Time.

CheckBox Examples

The *CheckBox Example 1* project contains code in just two event procedures to illustrate the different methods of transferring the value of a Boolean variable to and from a checkbox control. Recall that the Value property actually has three values, so an assignment statement alone will not be enough.

➤ **Begin CheckBox Example 1.**

1. Create a new project called CheckBox Example 1.

2. Add two CheckBox control button controls to the default form. Because this example is illustrating coding techniques, you can leave the default property values for the check boxes.

3. Add a single command button and change its Caption property to &OK and its name to cmdOK.

4. Add two Boolean variables to the General Declarations section and name them fBool1 and fBool2.

At this point you can add the code to map the variables to the control. With the case of a dialog box, the values of the variables are typically assigned to the controls during the *Form_Load* event, and then copied back from the controls to the variables when the user clicks the OK button.

One technique for mapping a Boolean variable to a check box is to use an *If* condition. This technique is very clear, but requires five lines of code. The other technique is based on the fact that the numeric values for the intrinsic constants are as follows:

Constant	Numeric Value
True	−1
False	0
vbUnchecked	0
vbChecked	1
vbGrayed	2

By reviewing the preceding table, you can see that it is possible to assign a Boolean variable to a check box's Value property if you ignore the sign and assume the check box will never be "grayed." Likewise, you can assign the value of a check box to a Boolean variable if you always add a negative sign. This technique requires much less code, but is also more confusing to the casual reader.

The following code shows both methods of copying a Boolean variable's value to and from a check box control:

```
' Purpose: To show the two techniques commonly used to copy
'          the value of a Boolean variable to a check box control.
Private Sub Form_Load()
    If fBool1 = True Then
        Check1.Value = vbChecked
    Else
        Check1.Value = vbUnchecked
    End If

    Check2.Value = Abs(fBool2)
End Sub

' Purpose: To show the two techniques commonly used to copy
'          the value of a check box control to a Boolean variable.
Private Sub cmdOK_Click()
    If Check1.Value = vbChecked Then
        fBool1 = True
    Else
        fBool1 = False
    End If

    fBool2 = -(Check2.Value)
End Sub
```

The OptionButton Control

Option buttons (sometimes called *radio buttons*) are typically used to display a set of choices, of which the user may only select one. They are also sometimes used for a data value when there are just two values and you want to provide more descriptive captions than a single check box control would allow (refer to Figure A.6). If the number of choices is more than about 10 values, you should consider using an alternative GUI control, such as a combo box or list box.

When the user selects an option button, it gets selected and all other option buttons in the same group are automatically deselected. Option buttons must be grouped together inside a container control (for example, a frame control). In fact, their behavior may not work correctly if they are not properly grouped inside a container. See the section titled "The Frame Control" for instructions on making sure controls are drawn inside the container.

■■■ NOTE

Note that the form object can act as a container. Therefore, a single group of option buttons can be placed directly on the form.

Option Button Properties	Description
Caption	This property is used to indicate the text displayed just to the right of an option button's selection indicator. Include an ampersand (&) in the caption string to assign an access key for the control.
Value	The Value property for the option button is *True* if it is selected and *False* if it is not selected.

Option Button Events	Description
Click	The *Click* event occurs whenever the Value property changes. The event is triggered when
	■ The control is clicked with the left mouse button.
	■ The control has the focus and the Spacebar is pressed.
	■ The button's access key is pressed.
	■ The Value property is changed in code at Run Time.

OptionButton Examples

Like the programming example for check boxes, this example will show how to transfer the value of a variable to and from a group of option buttons. In this example, we will use an enumerated data type and a control array to indicate the seven days of the week.

➤ **Begin OptionButton Example 1.**

1. Create a new project called OptionButton Example 1.

2. Add a single frame.

3. Create a control array for the seven option buttons by drawing the first option button *inside* the Frame control. Make sure the option button is inside the frame by dragging the frame around the form. The option button should move with the frame. Set the option button's name property to optWeekday.

4. Select the option button and choose Copy from Visual Basic's Edit menu.

5. Make sure the frame is selected and choose Paste from the Edit menu. Visual Basic should display a message box asking you whether you want to create a control array. Answer Yes. Continue selecting Paste from the Edit menu until you have a total of seven option buttons in the frame.

6. Add a single command button and change its Caption property to &OK and its name to cmdOK.

7. Set the following properties:

Object	Property	Value
Frame	Caption	Weekday
OptionButton 1	Name	optWeekday
	Caption	&Sunday
	Index	0
OptionButton 2	Name	optWeekday
	Caption	&Monday
	Index	1
OptionButton 3	Name	optWeekday
	Caption	&Tuesday
	Index	2
OptionButton 4	Name	optWeekday
	Caption	&Wednesday
	Index	3
OptionButton 5	Name	optWeekday
	Caption	T&hursday
	Index	4
OptionButton 6	Name	optWeekday
	Caption	&Friday
	Index	5
OptionButton 7	Name	optWeekday
	Caption	S&aturday
	Index	6
CommandButton	Name	cmdOK
	Caption	&OK

Arrange the controls on the form and set a proper tab order. When finished, your form should look similar to Figure A.7.

Figure A.7 OptionButton Example 1 *sample form.*

You need to declare the matching enumerated data type and a variable to hold the actual data value, so add the following code to the form's General Declaration section:

```
Private Enum Weekdays
    Sunday = 0
    Monday = 1
    Tuesday = 2
    Wednesday = 3
    Thursday = 4
    Friday = 5
    Saturday = 6
End Enum

Private fWeekday As Weekdays
```

As before, variables are typically assigned to the controls during the *Form_Load* event, and then copied back when the user clicks the OK button. Because the seven option buttons were created as a control array, setting the Value property to *True* for the correct one is easy—just use the value of the variable as the Index property:

```
' Purpose: To copy the variable's value to one of the
'          Weekday option buttons.
Private Sub Form_Load()
    fWeekday = Sunday
    optWeekday(fWeekday).Value = True
End Sub
```

Determining which option is selected and getting that value back into the variable is a little more involved. You could use an *If* or a *Select Case* statement; however, you can also use a looping structure to iterate through the option buttons looking for the one selected. Because a group of option buttons can have only one button selected, the loop can be exited as soon as the selected one is found. Add the following code to the *cmdOK_Click* event:

```
' Purpose: To determine which option button is selected and
'          set the Weekday variable accordingly.

Private Sub cmdOK_Click()
    Dim Index As Long

    For Index = Sunday To Saturday
        If optWeekday(Index).Value = True Then
            fWeekday = Index
            Exit For
        End If
    Next Index
End Sub
```

You can now run and test your code. You will have to set breakpoints and step through the statements to make sure they work correctly. Experiment with different starting values for the *fWeekday* variable to test the *Form_Load* logic. Also make sure the GUI works properly and that only one of the option buttons in the group can be selected.

The ListBox Control

ListBox controls are used frequently in Windows applications because they can show a long list of items. If the list contains too many items to show in the list, a vertical scrollbar will be automatically added. A ListBox is also a good control to use when the user needs to select one or more items from a predefined list. See Figure A.8 for some samples.

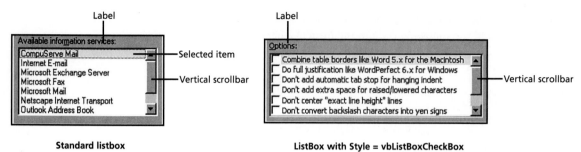

Figure A.8 *Sample ListBox controls.*

ListBox Properties	Description
Columns	This property determines whether the list box should scroll vertically or horizontally. The default value of zero indicates that the items are listed in a single column and the list scrolls vertically. Any other value indicates the items are arranged in snaking columns that scroll horizontally (even for single columns). The first column is filled, then the second, and so on. You cannot use this property to create a "grid" where each column contains different data.
ItemData	This property enables you to store a Long integer number for each item in the list. This property is frequently used to store a subscript for an associated array, or a database record key (if the key is a number) for the item shown in the list. See the examples at the end of this section for more information.

List	The List property is an array of strings that correspond to the text for the items shown in the list. Because this property is actually an array, you must include a subscript value when referencing it. For example:
	
	 `Index = 5`
	 `TempService = lstAvailServices.List(Index)`

ListCount	This property returns the number of items in the list. ListCount will return *zero* when the list is empty.
ListIndex	The ListIndex property returns or sets the item that is currently selected in the list. The valid range for this property is *zero* to *ListCount –1*. Therefore, if the fourth item in the list is selected, *ListIndex* will equal *3*. A *ListIndex* value of *–1* indicates no items are selected. See the examples at the end of this section for more information.
MultiSelect	This Boolean property indicates whether more than one item in the list box can be selected. To determine which items are selected, you have to use the Selected property mentioned on the next page.

ListBox Properties	Description
NewIndex	This property is changed each time a new item has been added to the list using the *AddItem* method (discussed in the Methods table) and indicates the position of the last item in the list. This property is frequently used when a ListBox has its Sorted property set to *True* and you need to synchronize it with an array using the ItemData property.
	See the examples at the end of this section for more information.
SelCount	This property returns the number of items that are currently selected and will return *zero* if no items are selected.
Selected	You can use this Boolean property to return or set the selection status of an item in the list.
Sorted	This property is used to indicate whether the items shown in the list are sorted. Setting Sorted to *True* causes them to be automatically sorted in alphabetic order. Setting Sorted to *False* causes each new item to be added to the end of the list.
	See the examples at the end of this section for more information.
Style	This property is used to indicate whether the ListBox control displays a check box beside each entry in the list. Valid values are *vbListBoxStandard* (the default) and *vbListBoxCheckBox*.

ListBox Events	Description
Click	Occurs when a user selects an item from the list either by clicking it with the mouse or by using the arrow keys.

ListBox Methods	Description
AddItem	Adds an item to the list. You can optionally pass the *AddItem* method a parameter to indicate the position for the new item.
	See the examples at the end of this section for more information.
Clear	The *Clear* method clears the entire contents of the list box.
	See the examples at the end of this section for more information.
RemoveItem	Use this method with an index argument to remove a single item from the list.
	See the examples at the end of this section for more information.

ListBox Examples

This example will use a ListBox control to

- Show the contents of an array containing people's names.

- Synchronize it with an array using the ItemData property.

- Show how to write code that clears the list.

- Remove selected items from the list.

➤ **Begin ListBox Example 1.**

1. Create a new project called ListBox Example 1.

2. Add a ListBox control and three command buttons to the default form.

3. Set the following properties:

Object	Property	Value
ListBox	Name	lstNames
	Sorted	True
CommandButton 1	Name	cmdShow
	Caption	&Show
CommandButton 2	Name	cmdRemove
	Caption	&Remove

You will need an array to store the names. Define an array in the General Declaration section of the form and populate it with a list of names in the *Form_Load* event. Make sure to populate the array with names that are not sorted alphabetically.

```
Option Explicit

Private fNameArray(1 To 12) As String

' Purpose: To populate the array with an arbitrary
'          list of names.
Private Sub Form_Load()
    fNameArray(1) = "Sally"
    fNameArray(2) = "Kameron"
    fNameArray(3) = "Keith"
    fNameArray(4) = "Janet"
    fNameArray(5) = "Jodi"
    fNameArray(6) = "Jesi"
    fNameArray(7) = "Bob"
    fNameArray(8) = "Cindy"
    fNameArray(9) = "Chris"
    fNameArray(10) = "Brittany"
    fNameArray(11) = "Pat"
    fNameArray(12) = "Lisa"
End Sub
```

The next step is to add code to show the array in the list box. This processing is relatively simple. Begin by clearing the contents of the list using the *Clear* method, and then call the *AddItem* method for each name in the array. After each name is added, set the ItemData property so that we can use it later to link the selected item back to the array.

Implement the *cmdShow_Click* event as shown here:

```
' Purpose: To load the array with the list of names
'          from the array.
Private Sub cmdShow_Click()
    Dim Index As Long

    Call lstNames.Clear

    For Index = 1 To UBound(fNameArray)
        Call lstNames.AddItem(fNameArray(Index))
        lstNames.ItemData(lstNames.NewIndex) = Index
    Next Index
End Sub
```

Run and test the program. After you click the Show button, you should see the names sorted in alphabetic order and your form should look similar to the one shown in Figure A.9.

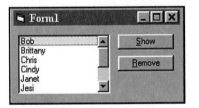

Figure A.9   ListBox Example 1 *sample form.*

The final task is to implement the Remove button. When it is clicked, the general processing should be as follows:

1. Use the ListIndex property to make sure an item is selected.

2. Use the ItemData property of the selected item to reference back to the original array element and ask the user for confirmation.

3. Call the *RemoveItem* method to remove the item from the ListBox.

The completed code is shown here:

```
' Purpose: To allow the selected item to be removed from
'          the ListBox.
Private Sub cmdRemove_Click()
    Dim Index As Long

    ' Make sure an item has been selected.

    If lstNames.ListIndex = -1 Then
        Call MsgBox("No items are selected.", _
            vbOKOnly + vbInformation)
```

```
        Call lstNames.SetFocus
        Exit Sub
    End If

    ' Get the array subscript from the selected item.

    Index = lstNames.ItemData(lstNames.ListIndex)

    ' Ask the user for confirmation and remove the item
    ' if he answers Yes.

    If MsgBox("Are you sure you want to remove " & _
        fNameArray(Index) & "?", _
        vbYesNo + vbQuestion) = vbYes Then

        Call lstNames.RemoveItem(lstNames.ListIndex)
    End If
End Sub
```

The ComboBox Control

The ComboBox control combines the features of a text box and a list box into a single control. As shown in Figure A.10, it consists of three parts: a text box, a drop-down button, and a list box. A user can type into the text box, or can click the drop-down button and select a value from the list. You can also set properties so that the user can't type in the text box and instead *must* select an item from the list.

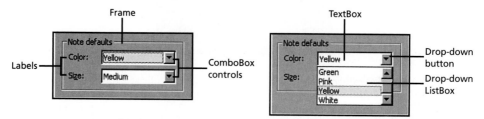

Figure A.10 *Sample combo box.*

Because the user can select an item from the list, the ComboBox control can help reduce data entry errors. It is typically used to allow the user to enter information when there are many valid items to choose from and the number is too great to use OptionButton controls (for example, selecting a U.S. state code).

If you are familiar with the ListBox control, the ComboBox should present no problems because it shares most of the same properties, events, and methods.

ComboBox Properties	*Description*
ItemData	This property enables you to store a Long integer number for each item in the list. This property is frequently used to store a subscript for an associated array, or a database record key (if the key is a number) for the item shown in the list.

List	The List property is an array of strings that correspond to the text for the items shown in the list. Because this property is actually an array, you must include a subscript value when referencing it. For example:
	
	```Index = 5```
	```TempColor = cboAvailColors.List(Index)```

ListCount	This property returns the number of items in the list. ListCount will return *zero* when the list is empty.
ListIndex	The ListIndex property returns or sets the item currently selected in the list. The valid range for this property is *zero* to *ListCount – 1*. Therefore, if the fourth item in the list is selected, *ListIndex* will equal *3*. A *ListIndex* value of *–1* indicates no items are selected. See the examples at the end of this section for more information.
Locked	Setting the Locked property to *True* will stop the text box from being changed and will prevent an item from being selected from the list, even though the user can still drop down the list.
NewIndex	This property is changed each time a new item has been added to the list using the *AddItem* method (discussed later) and indicates the position of the last item in the list.
Sorted	This property is used to indicate whether the items shown in the list are sorted. Setting Sorted to *True* causes them to be automatically sorted in alphabetic order. Setting Sorted to *False* causes each new item to be added to the end of the list.
Style	This property determines the style of the combo box and can only be set at Design Time. There are actually three styles, although only two of them are commonly used. *vbComboDropDown* enables the user to type in the text box or select from the list box. *vbComboDropDownList* requires the user to select from the list box only. The third style, *vbComboSimple*, is rarely used and enables the user to type in the text box or select from the list; the list box is always visible, however, and takes up more form space.
Text	The Text property contains the text displayed in the text box. This property is read-only at Run Time if Style = vbComboDropDownList.

ComboBox Events	Description
Change	The event occurs when the text in the text box portion of the control is changed and only when Style is set to *vbComboDropDown*. This event is not triggered when the text is changed due to the user selecting a new value from the drop-down list.
Click	Occurs when the user selects an item from the drop-down list.

ComboBox Methods	Description
AddItem	Adds an item to the list. You can optionally pass the *AddItem* method a parameter to indicate the position for the new item.
	See the examples at the end of this section for more information.
Clear	The *Clear* method clears the contents of the combo box's list.
	See the examples at the end of this section for more information.
RemoveItem	Use this method with an index argument to remove an item from the list.

ComboBox Examples

You were previously shown how you might use seven option buttons to allow the user to select a day of the week. This example shows how you might use a ComboBox control to do the same thing. The advantage of using a ComboBox is that it takes up much less form space.

> **Begin ComboBox Example 1.**

1. Create a new project called ComboBox Example 1.

2. Add a single ComboBox control and a single command button to the default form.

3. Set the following properties:

Object	Property	Value
ComboBox	Name	cboWeekday
	Sorted	False
	Style	vbComboDropDownList
CommandButton	Name	cmdOK
	Caption	&OK

As with the option button example, you need to declare the matching enumerated data type and a variable to hold the actual data value. Add the following code to the form's General Declaration section:

```
Private Enum Weekdays
    Sunday = 0
    Monday = 1
    Tuesday = 2
    Wednesday = 3
    Thursday = 4
    Friday = 5
    Saturday = 6
End Enum

Private fWeekday As Weekdays
```

The next step is to populate the combo box with the days of the week. You can do this at Design Time by setting the List property using the Properties window. This method is sometimes awkward because you must press Ctrl+Enter to add a new item and you have only a small box to type in. In earlier versions of Visual Basic, you had to populate the combo box's list in code using its *AddItem* method. Because this technique is still very common, we will use it in this example during the *Form_Load* event.

After the list box is populated, we can set its initial value based on the value of the enumerated type form variable. Note that the values for the enumerated type exactly match the items that were added to the combo box. The first enumerated value is zero for Sunday, for example. The first item in the combo box's list is also Sunday, and the combo box will have ListIndex = 0 if Sunday is selected. If you always number the enumerated values starting with zero and add matching descriptions to an *unsorted* combo box, converting the data value back and forth is easy.

As before, set the initial value of the control to the variable in the *Form_Load* event. The complete procedure is as follows:

```
' Purpose: To load the combo box with the seven days of the week
'          and set its initial value.
Private Sub Form_Load()
    Call cboWeekday.Clear
    Call cboWeekday.AddItem("Sunday")
    Call cboWeekday.AddItem("Monday")
    Call cboWeekday.AddItem("Tuesday")
    Call cboWeekday.AddItem("Wednesday")
    Call cboWeekday.AddItem("Thursday")
    Call cboWeekday.AddItem("Friday")
    Call cboWeekday.AddItem("Saturday")

    cboWeekday.ListIndex = fWeekday
End Sub
```

And finally, copy the control's value back to the variable in the OK button's *Click* event. First make sure the combo box has an item selected (ListIndex <> –1). If an item has been selected, ListIndex is guaranteed to have a value between *0* and *6* (because there are seven items in the list), so we can assign the ListIndex property back to the variable.

```
' Purpose: To determine which weekday is selected.
Private Sub cmdOK_Click()

    ' Make sure an item has been selected.

    If cboWeekday.ListIndex = -1 Then
        Call MsgBox("You must select a day of the week.", _
            vbOKOnly + vbInformation)
        Call cboWeekday.SetFocus
        Exit Sub
    End If

    ' Set the variable = to the ListIndex.

    fWeekday = cboWeekday.ListIndex
End Sub
```

You can now run and test the code. You will have to set breakpoints and step through the statements to make sure they work correctly. Experiment with different starting values for the fWeekday variable to test the *Form_Load* logic.

The Image Control

The Image control is a simple control that has just one purpose: to display graphics files. It can display a graphic from a bitmap, icon, metafile, GIF, or JPEG file.

The Image control is similar to the PictureBox control except that it contains only a small subset of the PictureBox's properties, methods, and events. Therefore, the Image control is sometimes called a "lightweight" control like the Label, Shape, and Line controls. If all you need to do is display an image from a graphic file, you should always use the Image control rather than a PictureBox to save system resources.

Image Properties	Description
BorderStyle	The BorderStyle can be set to either no border (*vbBSNone*) or a 3D border (*vbFixedSingle*).
Picture	This property indicates the graphics file that should be drawn on the control and can be set to any valid bitmap, icon, metafile, GIF, or JPEG file.
	When you set the picture property at Design Time, the image is saved with your form and compiled into the .EXE file, so you don't have to distribute the image file with your executable. Setting this property to a very large graphics file is a sure way to greatly increase the size of the executable and also to slow down the form's load time; therefore, care should be taken to choose an image of an acceptable size. You can also set this property at Run Time using the *LoadPicture* statement.
Stretch	Setting this property to *True* causes the graphics file to always be resized to fit in the control. If the value is set to *False* (the default), the image control will be resized to fit the graphic. The Stretch property is not available in the PictureBox control.

The PictureBox Control

As its name implies, the PictureBox control can be used to display graphics images on a form. However, you can use it for much more than that. The PictureBox control has the most properties, events, and methods of all the Visual Basic intrinsic controls and is sometimes called a "heavyweight" control because of the additional computer resources it uses. If all you need to do is display a graphics image, you should use the Image control instead.

Like the Frame control, the PictureBox control can be used as a container for other controls. It can also be made to automatically align itself at the top, bottom, left, or right of a form; therefore, it can be used to make toolbars and status bars.

The PictureBox control contains many graphic methods that you can use at Run Time to draw circles, rectangles, and lines on it. If you are developing an application similar to the Windows Paint program, you might use a PictureBox control as the "canvas" the user draws on.

PictureBox Properties	Description
Align	This property determines whether the PictureBox should automatically align itself to the top, bottom, left, or right of the form. Use this property when using a PictureBox control to make toolbars and status bars.
	When this property is set, the PictureBox will automatically change its width whenever the form is resized. The default value is no automatic alignment.
AutoRedraw	If your program has code that uses graphics methods to draw on the PictureBox at Run Time, you probably need to either set AutoRedraw to *True* or write code for the control's Paint event. If AutoRedraw is set to *True*, Windows will reserve a chunk of memory large enough to store a bitmap image of the PictureBox. Windows will then "redraw" the picture box from this bitmap in memory when necessary—when the form is resized, for example, or when it is minimized and then restored. Setting AutoRedraw to *True* is generally easier than writing complex code in the Paint event, but it uses significantly more memory and other computer resources. The default value is *False*.
	See the examples at the end of this section for more information.
AutoSize	Setting this property to *True* will cause the PictureBox to resize to fit the image assigned to its Picture property. This property should not be confused with the Stretch property of the Image control.

continues

745

PictureBox Properties	Description
BorderStyle	This property just determines whether the PictureBox should have borders drawn around it.
CurrentX, CurrentY	These properties determine the current drawing position on the PictureBox control. Some graphics methods require that these properties be set prior to calling the method, and others enable you to pass the X and Y coordinates to the method as arguments.
FillColor, FillStyle	These properties determine how the interior of shapes created with the *Circle* and *Line* methods are drawn. For example, FillColor is used to indicate the color of the interior, and FillStyle is used to indicate whether the interior should be solid, transparent, crossed lines, and so on.
FontTransparent	Setting this property to *True* before using the *Print* method will allow the background graphics to show around the spaces in the text.
Picture	This property indicates the graphics file that should be drawn on the control. It can be set to any valid bitmap, icon, metafile, GIF, or JPEG file. See the Picture property for the Image control for more information.
ScaleMode	This property enables you to change the ScaleMode from the default of twips to other values such as pixels, inches, centimeters, and so forth. See the examples at the end of this section for more information.

PictureBox Events	Description
Paint	This event is triggered whenever Windows has determined that the control needs to be redrawn. See the AutoRedraw property and the examples at the end of this section for more information.

PictureBox Methods	Description
Circle	Call this method to draw a circle, ellipse, or an arc on the PictureBox.
	See the examples at the end of this section for more information.
Cls	The *Cls* method can be used to clear all the graphics that have been drawn on the PictureBox.
	See the examples at the end of this section for more information.
Line	This method can be use to draw lines and rectangles on the PictureBox.
Point	The *Point* method returns a long integer representing the color of the pixel at a specified point.
Print	Use this method to print text at the CurrentX and CurrentY location.
Pset	The *PSet* method sets the color of a pixel at a specified point.
TextHeight, TextWidth	These methods are typically used with the *Print* method to determine the height and width of text printed on the PictureBox.

PictureBox Examples

Although developing a full-fledged graphics drawing program can certainly be done using Visual Basic, it is beyond the scope of this appendix. This simple example is a program that draws circles and illustrates many of the concepts you need to know to create such a program.

> **Begin PictureBox Example 1.**

1. Create a new project called PictureBox Example 1.

2. Add two PictureBox controls to the default form.

3. Draw a command button on the first picture box (make sure the button is drawn on top of it).

4. Set the following properties:

Object	Property	Value
PictureBox 1	Name	picToolbar
	Align	vbAlignTop
	AutoRedraw	False
	BackColor	vbButtonFace or &H8000000F
	BorderStyle	vbBSNone
	Height	315
	ScaleMode	vbPixel
PictureBox 2	Name	picCanvas
	Align	vbAlignNone
	AutoRedraw	True
	BackColor	vbWindowBackground or0x80000005
	BorderStyle	vbFixedSingle
	FillStyle	**Solid**
	ScaleMode	vbPixel
CommandButton 1	Name	cmdClear
	Caption	&Clear
	Height	21 *
	Width	80 *

* Note the height and width values are specified in pixels because that is the ScaleMode for the button's container (the first PictureBox).

When finished, your form should look similar to Figure A.11.

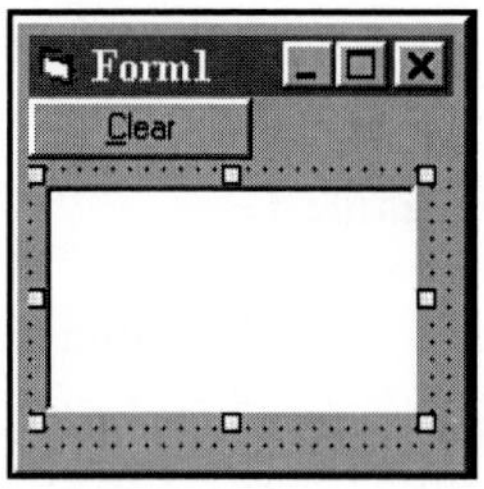

Figure A.11   PictureBox Example 1 *sample form.*

(For simplicity sake, this example uses a command button with a simple caption on the toolbar. In a real application, you would probably use the techniques described in the CommandButton section to include a picture on the toolbar button.)

You should also make the canvas picture box resize to always fill the form's client area. In the section titled "Form Examples," you wrote code for the form's *Resize* event to do this with a TextBox control. You can easily modify this code to use a picture box and to account for the additional space required by the toolbar as follows:

```
' Purpose: To resize the canvas PictureBox so that it
'          always fills the interior of the form.
Private Sub Form_Resize()
    Dim Left   As Single
    Dim Top    As Single
    Dim Width  As Single
    Dim Height As Single

    ' Exit the procedure if the form is being minimized since
    ' the user can't see anything anyway.

    If Me.WindowState = vbMinimized Then
        Exit Sub
    End If

    ' Size the text box to fill the form unless the form is
    ' sized so small it won't be seen.

    Left = 0
    Top = picToolbar.Height
    Width = Me.ScaleWidth
    Height = Me.ScaleHeight - picToolbar.Height

    If Width > 0 And Height > 0 Then
        Call picCanvas.Move(Left, Top, Width, Height)
    End If
End Sub
```

You can now run the application and make sure the canvas always fills the form's client area.

Also notice that the appearance of the top of the toolbar appears "flat." Windows programs typically draw lines around controls to give them a 3D effect. You can do the same by using the PictureBox's *Line* method in its *Paint* event. The following code will add a single highlighted line to the top of the toolbar:

```
' Purpose: To draw a highlight line across the top of the
'          toolbar.
Private Sub picToolbar_Paint()
    picToolbar.ForeColor = vb3DHighlight
    picToolbar.Line (0, 0)-(picToolbar.ScaleWidth, 0)
End Sub
```

Now run the application. The line makes a slight but noticeable difference. Also try setting a break point in the *Paint* event when running the program. Notice how the *Paint* event is triggered every time you change the size of the form. This is a good indication that the code inside the *Paint* event should be fairly small. If your drawing logic is rather large, set the AutoRedraw property to *True* and code it outside of the *Paint* event.

To illustrate another of the graphics methods, add code to draw a circle whenever the user clicks the mouse on the canvas. The circle should be drawn at the point where the mouse is clicked. The *Click* event doesn't give you these coordinates, so you must use the *MouseDown* or *MouseUp* event. Also, to make this example more interesting, have your program generate a random radius and a random color for the circle.

Add the following code to the *MouseUp* event procedure:

```
' Purpose: To draw a circle of random radius and random
'          color on the canvas PictureBox at the point
'          where the mouse was "clicked."
Private Sub picCanvas_MouseUp(Button As Integer, _
    Shift As Integer, X As Single, Y As Single)

    Dim Radius As Long
    Dim Color  As Long

    ' Generate a random radius between 1 and 50.

    Radius = 50 * Rnd

    ' Generate a random color between 1 and 16 million (255 ^3).

    Color = CLng(255 ^ 3) * Rnd

    ' Draw the circle.

    picCanvas.FillColor = Color
    picCanvas.Circle (X, Y), Radius, Color
End Sub
```

When using the *Rnd* function, initialize the random number generator in the *Form_Load* event.

```
' Purpose: To initialize the random number generator.
Private Sub Form_Load()
    Randomize
End Sub
```

The last feature to implement is to allow the user to clear the screen. Recall that the PictureBox control has a *Cls* method to do just that.

```
' Purpose: To clear the canvas PictureBox.
Private Sub cmdClear_Click()
    Call picCanvas.Cls
End Sub
```

Now run and test the application. Make sure circles are drawn whenever you click the mouse on the canvas. Because the canvas PictureBox has the AutoRedraw property set to *True*, you should also be able to minimize and restore the form without losing the circles. Experiment with different values for the AutoRedraw property to see its effect on the drawing methods.

You might also modify this application to draw the circle in the *MouseMove* event, rather than the *MouseUp* event. Consider changing to draw boxes, rather than circles, and allow the user to select the color using the method described in the ScrollBar controls section.

The Line Control

The Line control is another "lightweight" control that you can use to add decorations to your form. It has only a few properties, and no special methods or events.

Line Properties	Description
BorderColor	This property determines the color of the line.
BorderStyle	The BorderStyle property allows the line to be drawn as solid, dashed, dotted, and so on.
BorderWidth	When BorderStyle is set to solid, you can set the BorderWidth property to determine the width of the line.
X1, Y1, X2, Y2	These properties determine the coordinates of the line control in two-dimensional space where the X coordinates are horizontal and the Y coordinates are vertical. The X1, Y1 pair are one end of the line, and the X2, Y2 are the other end.

Line Control Example

Line controls are sometimes used to separate a form into different sections. For example, you can use two Line controls to achieve an effect similar to that shown in Figure A.12.

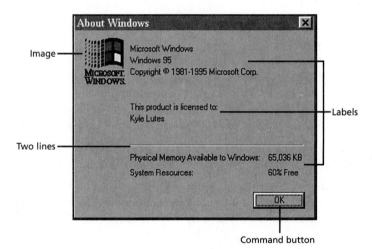

Figure A.12   *Line Control sample form.*

Set the BorderColor of the first line to *vbButtonShadow* and *vb3DHighlight* for the second. Next, set the Y1 and Y2 properties of the second line to always be 30 twips (or two pixels) greater than those of the first line.

The Shape Control

The Shape control can be used to add simple rectangles, squares, ovals, circles, rounded rectangles, or rounded square shapes to a form. Experimenting with these controls is easy. Just draw one on a form and use the Properties window to change the values.

This control has limited use, but is preferred to using PictureBox controls if all you need is a simple shape.

Shape Properties	Description
BackColor, FillColor, BorderColor	These properties enable you set the color of the shape.
BackStyle	This property enables you to determine whether the shape is transparent or opaque.
BorderStyle	The BorderStyle property is used to specify whether the border of the shape should be solid, dashed, dotted, and so on.
BorderWidth	This property determines the thickness of the border on the shape.
FillStyle	FillStyle can be used to make the shape draw transparent, solid, or shaded lines of various angles.
Shape	This is the actual property you set to make the Shape control draw a rectangle, square, oval, circle, rounded rectangle, or rounded square.

The Timer Control

You can use the Timer control to cause an event procedure to be called at regular intervals. Timer controls are used to display the current system time, for animation purposes, and to implement "autosave" features in applications that save data to files. The Timer can be programmed to trigger an event in a range as small as once every millisecond to as large as approximately once every minute.

The Timer control belongs to a class of controls that are invisible at Run Time. At Design Time, a small icon appears on the form just so that you can change its properties using the Properties window. You can't change the height and width of the Timer control and its position on the form really isn't important because it won't be visible to the user at Run Time. Figure A.13 shows a Timer control at Design Time.

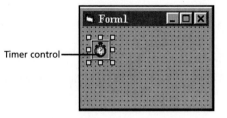

Timer control

Figure A.13 *Timer control at Design Time.*

Timer Properties	Description
Enabled	The Enabled property must be *True* before the control's Timer event will be triggered.
Interval	Set this property to determine how frequently the control's Timer event gets triggered. A value of *1* will trigger it every millisecond, a value of *1,000* will trigger it once a second, and a value of *60,000* will trigger it once a minute. The maximum value you can specify is *65,535*. A value of *zero* is the same as disabling the Timer control.

See the examples at the end of this section for more information. |

Timer Events	Description
Timer	This is the only event the Timer control has. It is triggered when the time period in the Interval property has elapsed. Use this event to do processing that occurs at a regular interval.

See the examples at the end of this section for more information. |

Timer Control Examples

This example will use Timer controls to

- Display the current date and time in a Label control

- Do some simple animation by setting an Image control's Picture property at Run Time

- Show how to implement a timer that occurs for more than one minute

➤ **Begin Timer Example 1.**

1. Create a new project called Timer Example 1.

2. Add a single Label control, an Image control, and three Timer controls. *(Their sizes and positions are not important for this example.)*

3. Set the following properties:

Object	Property	Value
Label	Name	lblClock
	Caption	Empty string
	Autosize	True

continues

Object	Property	Value
Image	Name	imgAnimate
	Picture	None
	Stretch	False
Timer 1	Name	tmrClock
	Interval	1000 (about one second)
	Enabled	True
Timer 2	Name	tmrAnimate
	Interval	100
	Enabled	True
Timer 3	Name	tmrAutosave
	Interval	60000 (about once per minute)
	Enabled	True

First begin by implementing the clock timer. This requires that you add only one statement to the first timer's *Timer* event procedure to update the label control with the current date and time:

```
' Purpose: To show the current date and time
'          in the clock label control.
Private Sub tmrClock_Timer()
    lblClock.Caption = Format(Now, "short date") _
        & " " & Format(Now, "hh:mm:ss AM/PM")
End Sub
```

Run and test the application to verify that you can't see the Timer controls and that the clock label is updated each second. Note that you will have to wait until about one second after the form has loaded before the first *Timer* event is triggered. Alternatively, you could call the *tmrClock_Timer* procedure during the *Form_Load* event to make sure the clock is available as soon as the form can be seen.

Next implement the animation timer. This simple animation works by periodically displaying a series of graphics images at the same position on the form, where each image is just slightly different from the previous one. The sample code that accompanies this text includes the following 16 globe icon files shown in Figure A.14.

Figure A.14   TimerExample 1 *sample form.*

The way this example achieves the animation effect is by loading these 16 images into an image control approximately once every 1/10th of a second. After Globe16.ico has been loaded, the process is started over again with Globe1.ico. You will need a static variable to act as an image counter, and you can use the *LoadPicture* statement to load the icon images into the image control at Run Time.

```
' Purpose: To load the globe icon files into image control
'          approximately once every 10th of a second.
Private Sub tmrAnimate_Timer()
    Static ImageCounter As Long

    ImageCounter = ImageCounter + 1
    If ImageCounter > 16 Then
        ImageCounter = 1
    End If

    imgAnimate.Picture = _
        LoadPicture(App.Path & "\Globe" & _
        CStr(ImageCounter) & ".ico")
End Sub
```

Note how the *LoadPicture* statement dynamically creates the image filename using the static counter variable. Also, App.Path is used because it is assumed the icon files are in the same folder as the rest of the project files.

Run and test the application and make sure the globe appears to spin. Experiment with different values for the Timer's Interval property and the size and Stretch property of the image control.

Loading pictures at Run Time is a slow process. This same effect could be achieved more efficiently if you loaded all the icon files into an Image control array at Design Time. During the *Form_Load* event, you move all images to the exact same location, and in the *Timer* event you just set the Zorder of the current globe.

The final example illustrates how to overcome the Timer's maximum interval of about once per minute. Suppose that you need an event to be triggered over a longer duration (for example, once every 15 minutes). One technique is to set the Timer's interval property to occur once every minute (Interval = 60000). Then in the *Timer* event procedure, you use a static variable to count the number of times the event has been triggered. When the counter has reached your desired interval, you execute the necessary code. In this example, a simple message box is displayed. Don't forget to reset the counter variable back to *zero* so that the process can repeat.

The following code uses the third Timer control in the example to simulate an "autosave every 15 minutes" feature:

```
' Purpose: To illustrate how an AutoSave feature might
'          be implemented.
Private Sub tmrAutosave_Timer()
    Static MinuteCounter As Long

    MinuteCounter = MinuteCounter + 1
    If MinuteCounter >= 15 Then
        MinuteCounter = 0
        Call MsgBox("Its now time to save your file.", _
            vbOKOnly + vbInformation)
    End If
End Sub
```

Run and test the program. If you have programmed the timer correctly, you will have to wait 15 minutes to see the message box reminding you to save your file.

HScrollBar (Horizontal Scrollbar) and VScrollBar (Vertical Scrollbar)

The horizontal scrollbar (HScrollBar) and the vertical scrollbar (VScrollBar) controls have the same properties, events, and methods. Their only difference is the way they appear on the form. Figure A.15 shows some examples.

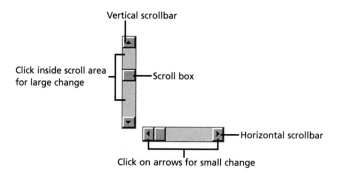

Figure A.15 *Sample scrollbars.*

These controls are *not* used with text boxes and list boxes because those controls have properties that will automatically add scrollbars at Run Time when necessary.

The use of horizontal and vertical scrollbar controls has been reduced significantly, beginning with the use of the Windows 95 GUI and its Slider control (see the ActiveX section later in this appendix). In previous versions of Windows, these controls were sometimes used as input mechanisms for numbers that were in a discrete range of values (for example, the volume control for your PC's sound card).

ScrollBar Properties	Description
LargeChange, SmallChange	These properties set or return the amount to change the Value property by when the user clicks the corresponding area on the scrollbar.
	See the examples at the end of this section for more information.
Max, Min	These properties are used to indicate the maximum and minimum values of the Value property.
	See the examples at the end of this section for more information.
Value	The Value property is changed when the user clicks the large change or small change areas on the scrollbar, or drags the scroll box. The Value property is always in a range between the values set using the Max and Min properties. Your program can change the position of the scroll box by changing the Value property at Run Time.
	See the examples at the end of this section for more information.

ScrollBar Events	Description
Change	This event is triggered when the Value property is changed either by the user, or by setting the Value at Run Time in code.
	See the examples at the end of this section for more information.
Scroll	The *Scroll* event occurs while the user is dragging the scroll box. Because this event can be triggered hundreds of times if the user moves the scroll box just a few inches, you shouldn't add any long-running code to this event.
	See the examples at the end of this section for more information.

Scrollbar Examples

Proper GUI design now suggests that the ActiveX Slider control be used rather than scrollbars, but scrollbars are sometimes more convenient for the programmer to use because they are built in to Visual Basic and you may need to avoid the problems associated with ActiveX controls. Therefore, in this example, you will use scrollbars to build a GUI component that will allow the user to choose a custom color.

Almost all colors that can be displayed on a computer screen can be specified using a combination of the red, green, and blue primary colors. Color properties in Visual Basic are always a Long integer data type and are sometimes explicitly specified using the hexadecimal notation of &*HBBGGRR* where *BB* specifies the amount of blue, *GG* specifies the amount of green, and *RR* specifies the amount of red. Therefore, a statement such as

```
picSample.BackColor = &HFF0000
```

will set the background color of the picture box to blue. Visual Basic also includes the *RGB* function, which allows colors to be specified using more friendly decimal values. To set the background color of a picture box to blue using the *RGB* function, for example, use the following code:

```
picSample.BackColor = RGB(0, 0, 255)
```

The values for the arguments to the *RGB* function can be in the range from *0* to *255*. This means the *RGB* function can be used to specify more than 16 million colors! RGB(0, 0, 0) will return black, and RGB(255, 255, 255) will return white.

The following example uses ScrollBar controls to allow the user to specify the amount of red, green, and blue for a color, and gives the user visual feedback by setting the background color of a PictureBox control.

➤ **Begin ScrollBar Example 1.**

1. Create a new project called ScrollBar Example 1

2. Add a Frame control. Inside the frame, add three horizontal scrollbars, a picture control, and five label controls.

3. Set the following properties:

Object	Property	Value
Frame	Caption	Color Selector
HScrollBar 1	Name	hsbRed
	LargeChange	25
	Max	255
	Min	0
	SmallChange	1
HScrollBar 2	Name	hsbGreen
	LargeChange	25
	Max	255
	Min	0
	SmallChange	1

Object	Property	Value
HScrollBar 3	Name	hsbBlue
	LargeChange	25
	Max	255
	Min	0
	SmallChange	1
Label 1	Caption	&Red:
Label 2	Caption	&Green:
Label 3	Caption	&Blue:
Label 4	Caption	Sample:
Label 5	Name	lblRGB
	Caption	RGB(0,0,0)
PictureBox	Name	picSample

Also arrange the controls on the form so it looks similar to Figure A.16.

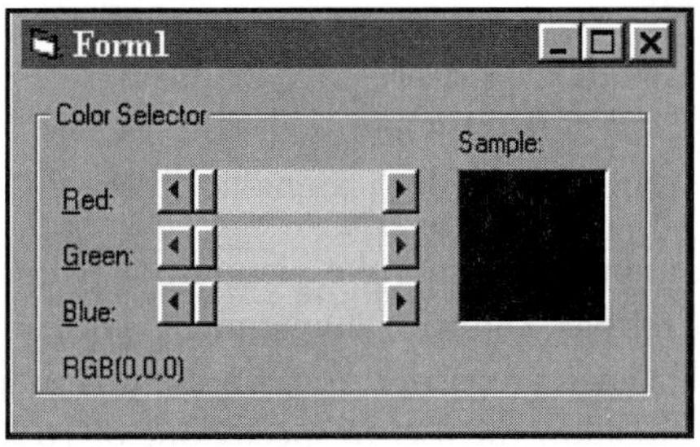

Figure A.16   ScrollBar Example 1 *sample form.*

Whenever the user changes the value of one of the ScrollBar controls, you should update the picture box so the user can see the new color. Also update the RGB label so that the user can see the decimal values used to create the color. Because there are two events a user can trigger when changing the value of a scrollbar, add the following general sub procedure to the form that updates the GUI:

```
' Purpose: To update the sample color and RGB values
'          label with the current scrollbar values.
Private Sub UpdateSample()
    picSample.BackColor = _
        RGB(hsbRed.Value, hsbGreen.Value, hsbBlue.Value)
    lblRGB.Caption = "RGB(" & Format(hsbRed.Value) & "," & _
        Format(hsbGreen.Value) & "," & _
        Format(hsbBlue.Value) & ")"
End Sub
```

Now call the UpdateSample procedure whenever the scrollbars change. Remember that the *Change* event is triggered whenever the user clicks the small change or large change area. Additionally, when the user drags the scroll box, it triggers the *Scroll* event. In this

File Control Events	Description
Change (DriveListBox, DirListBox)	The *Change* event is triggered whenever the Drive property or the Path property is changed at Run Time using code, or when the user changes them by clicking on the controls. See the examples at the end of this section for more information.
Click (FileListBox)	Occurs when a user selects an item from the list either by clicking it with the mouse or by using the arrow keys. See the examples at the end of this section for more information.

File Controls Examples

The code in this example will use the three file system controls and an image control to create a graphic file preview application. This is a great example of how you can use Visual Basic to quickly create nontrivial applications.

➤ **Begin File Controls Example 1.**

1. Create a new project called File Controls Example 1
2. Add two Frame controls.
3. In the first frame, add a DriveListBox, a DirListBox, and a FileListBox.
4. In the second frame, add a CheckBox control and an Image control.
5. Set the following properties:

Object	Property	Value
Frame 1	Caption	File
Frame 2	Caption	Picture
DriveListBox	Name	drvGraphic
DirListBox	Name	dirGraphic
FileListBox	Name	filGraphic
	Pattern	*.BMP; *.ICO; *.WMF; *.JPG; *.GIF
CheckBox	Name	chkStretch
	Caption	&Stretch Graphic
Image	Name	imgGraphic

At this point, you can run the application and see that the file controls are already functioning. However, they all default to the current drive and folder. Changing the DriveListBox does not cause the other two controls to be updated. You have to provide that functionality by adding some code. Fortunately, it's just a couple of lines:

```
' Purpose: Update the FileListBox's path with the new value
'          of the DirListBox's path.
Private Sub dirGraphic_Change()
    filGraphic.Path = dirGraphic.Path
End Sub

' Purpose: Update the DirListBox's path with the new drive
'          letter from the DriveListBox.
Private Sub drvGraphic_Change()
    dirGraphic.Path = drvGraphic.Drive
End Sub
```

If you run the application now, you should notice that if you select a new drive letter from the DriveListBox control (drvGraphic), its *Change* event will be triggered; and because you added code to the drvGraphic_Change event procedure, the DirListBox will get its Path property set to the new drive. Setting the Path property of dirGraphic in turn triggers its own Change event, which causes the FileListBox (filGraphic) to be updated with the new path.

The following procedure checks to make sure a file has been selected in the FileListBox, and then uses the *LoadPicture* statement to cause the file to be shown in the Image control:

```
' Purpose: Loads the currently selected graphic file into the
'          image control.
Private Sub filGraphic_Click()
    If filGraphic.ListIndex <> -1 Then
        imgGraphic.Picture = _
            LoadPicture(filGraphic.Path & "\" _
            & filGraphic.filename)
    End If
End Sub
```

The only problem remaining is to allow the user to select whether the graphic should be stretched to exactly fit the image control, or whether the image control should be resized to fit the graphic. The check box will allow the user to decide; therefore, whenever the check box is changed, you need to appropriately set the Stretch property on the Image control. If the Stretch property is set to *False*, however, the Image control will change its size and lose its original Height and Width property values. If the user changes the Stretch property back to *True*, you need to restore its height and width to the values set at Design Time.

If, at Run Time, you need to save properties set at Design Time, you typically declare form-scope variables and assign values to them in the *Form_Load* event. For example:

Keep in mind the following rules when designing menu structures:

- Menu commands that appear on the menu bar should be one word only.

- Commands on menus and submenus should be one to three words.

- If selecting the menu command will show a modal dialog box (including a message box), include an ellipsis at the end of the menu's caption.

- The first (leftmost) menu should include an Exit menu command as the last entry on the menu.

- Assign each menu command an access key that is unique within its hierarchical level.

- Assign shortcut keys to commonly used menu commands.

- A single submenu is sometimes appropriate, but avoid it if possible. Instead, show a dialog if your program needs further information.

- Make your menu structure similar to other Windows programs.

Menu Examples

In this example, you use the Menu Editor dialog box to add a simple menu structure to a form and use the form's PopupMenu method to implement a pop-up menu when the user clicks the right mouse button.

The menu structure that will be added to the form is shown in its finished form in Figure A.18.

Figure A.18   Menu Example 1 *sample form.*

> **Begin Menu Example 1.**

1. Create a new project called Menu Example 1

2. Make sure the default form is selected and choose Menu Editor from Visual Basic's Tools menu, or right-click on the form and choose Menu Editor from the pop-up menu. The Menu Editor dialog box will display similar to the one shown in Figure A.19.

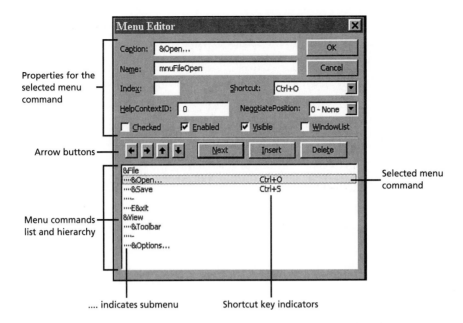

Figure A.19   *Menu Editor dialog box.*

To define a menu command, follow these steps:

1. Select a menu command in the list. The last item in the list is always blank, so you can select it to add a new menu command.

2. Type a caption for the menu command. As with other controls, use an ampersand (&) to specify an access key.

3. Type a Name property. Menu names should be prefixed with "mnu".

4. If needed, assign a shortcut key by selecting one from the Shortcut drop-down combo box. Shortcut keys must be unique for all menu commands on the form.

5. Set the Checked, Enabled, and/or Visible properties as necessary.

6. Specify the menu command's order in the menu hierarchy by using the arrow buttons.

7. Repeat steps 1 through 6 for each menu command required.

8. Click the OK button to close the Menu Editor dialog.

Even though you are still in Design Time mode, you can now click the commands on the menu bar to make sure the menu hierarchy is defined correctly. Additionally, you can use the Insert button on the Menu Editor to insert a new menu command before the selected command, and you can use the Delete button to delete the selected command. To delete the entire menu structure, use the Delete button repeatedly to delete *each* menu command. Use the up- and down-arrow buttons to move the selected command's position in the menu structure.

Separator bars are created by using the nonintuitive method of typing a dash (–) for the Caption property. You also have to specify a Name property even though you will never reference it in code.

Using the previously described steps, add the following menu structure to the default form:

Menu Level	Caption	Name	Shortcut Key	Checked
1	&File	mnuFile		False
2	&Open...	mnuFileOpen	Ctrl+O	False
2	&Save	mnuFileSave	Ctrl+S	False
2	-	mnuFileSep1		False
2	E&xit	mnuFileExit		False
1	&View	mnuView		False
2	&Toolbar	mnuViewToolbar		True
2	-	mnuViewSep1		False
2	&Options	mnuViewOptions		False

You can now run and test the menus. The menus should all work, but selecting a menu command won't cause anything to happen because you didn't write code for their *Click* events. Writing code for a menu command's *Click* event is the same as writing code for any other event.

Previously, the PictureBox example showed how to use a PictureBox control as a container for command buttons when creating a simple toolbar. The following code sample shows how you might allow the user to show or hide the toolbar using a menu command:

```
Private Sub mnuViewToolbar_Click()
    mnuViewToolbar.Checked = Not mnuViewToolbar.Checked
    picToolbar.Visible = mnuViewToolbar.Checked
End Sub
```

To create a pop-up menu, call the form's *PopupMenu* method and pass it the name of the menu to be displayed. The name of the menu to be displayed must have at least one submenu. Your first guess might be to add this code to the form's *Click* event; in that case, however, you can't determine which mouse button was clicked. Instead, you add code to the *MouseUp* event. For example:

```
Private Sub Form_MouseUp(Button As Integer, Shift As Integer, _
    X As Single, Y As Single)

    If Button = vbRightButton Then
        Call Me.PopupMenu(Me.mnuFile)
    End If
End Sub
```

If you want to create a special menu that is only used to show as a pop-up (that is, one that doesn't show on the menu bar), define the menu as normal but set the highest level menu command's Visible property to *False*. This prevents it from showing on the menu bar, but it will still show if you pass it to the *PopupMenu* method.

Run and test the program. Make sure the menu structure displays correctly. You should be able to right-click on the form to pop up the File menu. Make sure you can toggle the View toolbar check mark on and off.

ActiveX Components

History of ActiveX Components

When Microsoft released the first version of Visual Basic in 1991, it was immediately recognized as a revolutionary software development tool. One of the reasons for its popularity was that the creators of Visual Basic included a mechanism that allowed components written by third-party vendors to be added to Visual Basic to extend its usefulness. These Visual Basic extensions (or VBXs as they were commonly called, because of their file type extension) became hugely popular and quickly became the best example of commercially successful reusable components—a key goal of Object-Oriented Programming.

Other software development tools (such as Microsoft's Visual C++) soon added support for VBXs. When Microsoft migrated the Windows operating system to 32-bits, it also enhanced the VBX technology to include portions of its Object-Linking and Embedding (OLE) technology and so renamed the VBX file type to OCX.

The popularity of OCX components continued to rise, so Microsoft once again enhanced the technology to fix some problems and to make them more compatible with Internet technologies. During this last revision, Microsoft gave them the new name of ActiveX components, even though their file type is still OCX.

Literally thousands of ActiveX components are currently on the market, and they are an important tool for any Windows software developer. ActiveX components are usually GUI controls. They exist for specialty tasks such as word processing, spell checking, graphing, calendar functions, spreadsheet grids, database interfaces, multimedia and game programming, email functions, and Internet protocol interfaces. If there is any functionality you wish your application could provide, chances are somebody somewhere has "wrapped" that functionality into an ActiveX control of some type. Visual Basic comes bundled with many popular examples from Microsoft. If you search your PC's disk drives, you will likely find many OCX files in your Windows System folder that are being used by the applications you have installed.

Pitfalls of Using ActiveX Components

Depending on the ActiveX control, it might save you anywhere from a few hours of coding to a few years. ActiveX controls can greatly reduce your development time, but all this timesaving is not free.

First, you must find a control that fits your needs, learn how to use it, and pay for it. You can easily find ActiveX controls by surfing the Internet and downloading a trial version. If it serves your purpose, you can purchase it from the author and you will receive a

File Open dialog box

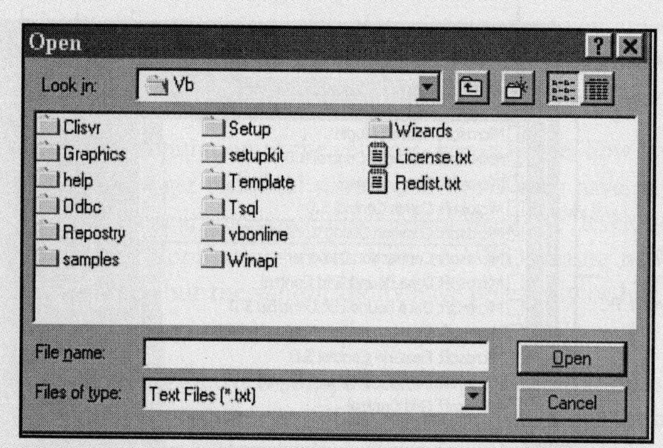

File Save dialog box

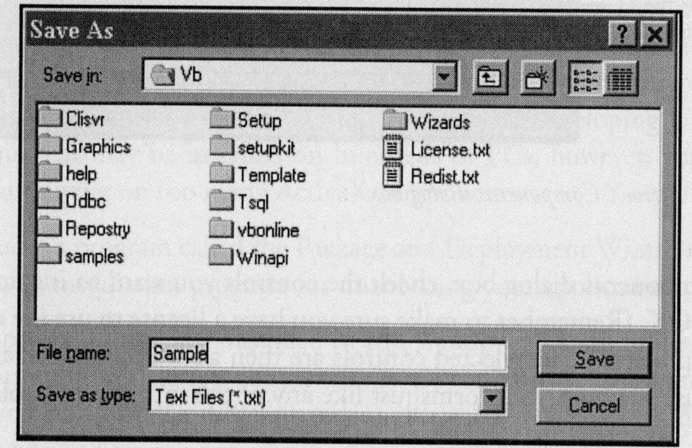

Color dialog box

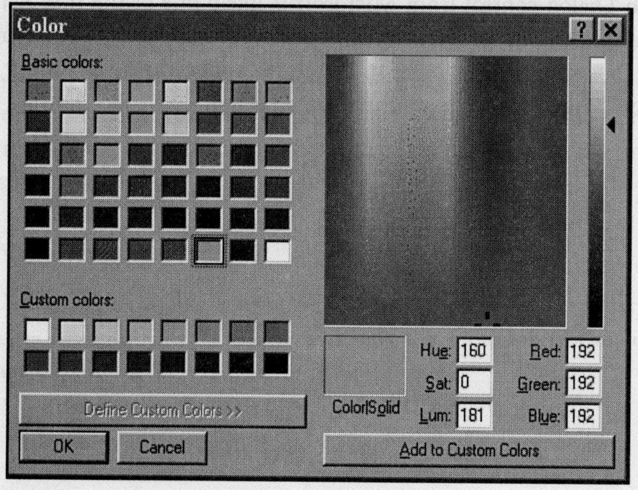

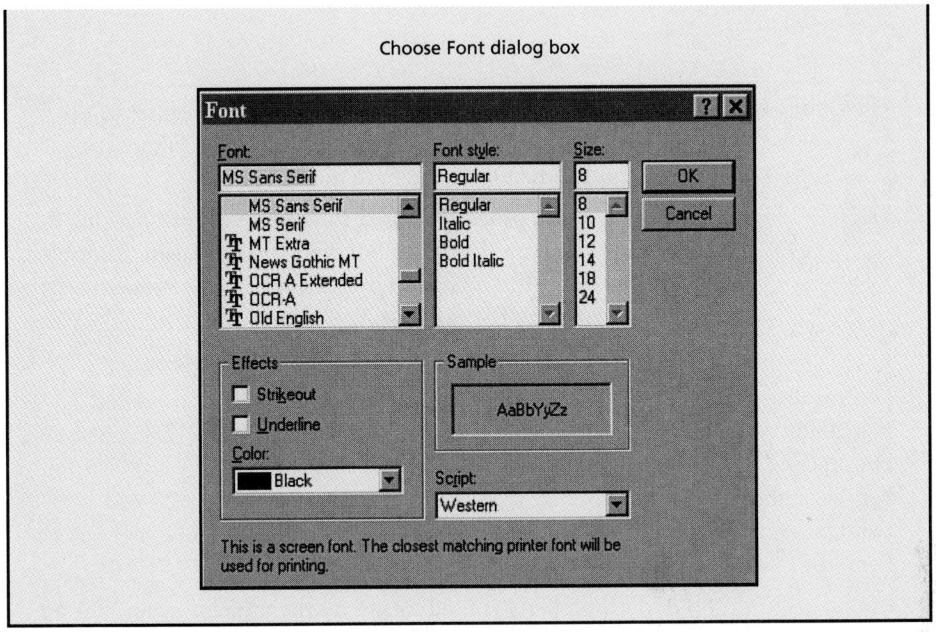

Figure A.21   *Sample common dialog boxes.*

Additionally, the Common Dialog control allows your programs to show a Printer Setup dialog box and to interface with the Windows help engine. The Common Dialog control has several useful properties and methods.

Common Dialog Properties	Description
CancelError	Setting this property to *True* will cause the Common Dialog control to raise a Run Time error when the user presses the Cancel button on the dialog box.
Color	This property is used both for the Color and Font dialog boxes. It indicates the selected color.
DialogTitle	Set the DialogTitle property to override the default title shown on the common dialog boxes.
FileName	This property indicates the fully qualified name of the file selected in either the Open or Save dialog boxes.
FileTitle	This property is similar to the FileName property except that it doesn't include the path information of the selected file.

Filter	The Filter property is used to specify the list of file types shown on the Open and Save dialog boxes. You indicate multiple arguments by separating them with pipe (|) characters. For example:
	
	```dlgSample.Filter = _```
	``` "Text Files (*.txt)|*.txt|All Files (*.*)|*.*"```

continues

Common Dialog Properties	Description
FilterIndex	This property is used to indicate the default filter to use (index corresponds to desired choice in the Filter property) for the Open and Save dialog boxes.
Flags	This single property is used to indicate various options depending on the dialog box that will be shown. Multiple arguments can be passed by "OR'ing" many property values together. For example:
	`dlgSample.Flags = cdlCCFullOpen Or cdlCCRGBInit`
FontName, FontBold, FontItalic, FontStrikethru, FontUnderline, FontSize	These properties specifies the various font properties selected by the user when showing the Font dialog box.
InitDir	This property is used to specify the initial directory for an Open or Save As dialog box. If this property isn't specified, the current directory is used.

Common Dialog Methods	Description
ShowOpen, ShowSave, ShowColor, ShowFont, ShowPrinter, ShowHelp	These methods show the corresponding common dialog box, allow the user to make a selection, and return the values to your application.

Common Dialog Control Examples

This example shows how to use the Common Dialog control to display the four most common dialog boxes seen in Figure A.21.

> **Begin Common Dialog Control Example 1.**

1. Create a new project called Common Dialog Control Example 1.

2. Add a single label and four command buttons to the default form.

3. Select Components from the Project menu and make sure the control named *Microsoft Common Dialog Control 5.0* is checked (your version number may be different) and click OK.

4. Draw a single Common Dialog control on the form. Note that this control behaves like the Timer control in that it shows only an icon at Design Time and is invisible at Run Time.

5. Set the following properties:

Object	Property	Value
Label	Name	lblSample
	Caption	Sample
CommandButton 1	Name	cmdOpen
	Caption	&Open...
CommandButton 2	Name	cmdSave
	Caption	&Save...
CommandButton 3	Name	cmdColor
	Caption	&Color...
CommandButton 4	Name	cmdFont
	Caption	&Font...
Common Dialog	Name	dlgSample

When finished, your form should look similar to Figure A.22.

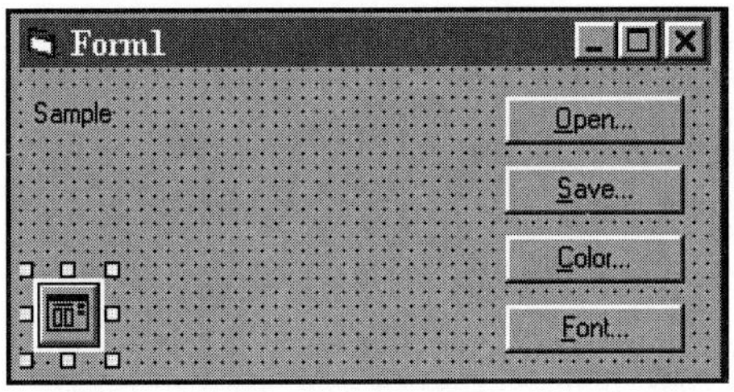

Figure A.22   Common Dialog Control Example 1 *sample form.*

Although it is possible to set all the properties for the Common Dialog control at Design Time using the Properties windows, it is also very common to set them at Run Time in code. This allows a single Common Dialog control to serve as an Open, Save, Color, or Font dialog box.

The following code shows some typical procedures that can be used to show the various dialog boxes. Add them to the event procedures for the command buttons and review it to make sure you understand the properties being set. Refer to the Visual Basic Help file if you need further information. Finally, run and test the application to make sure the dialog boxes are displayed correctly and the sample label is updated with your choices.

```vb
' Purpose: To show the common color dialog and assign
'          the selected color to the background of
'          the label sample.
Private Sub cmdColor_Click()
    dlgSample.Color = lblSample.BackColor
    dlgSample.Flags = cdlCCFullOpen Or cdlCCRGBInit
    dlgSample.CancelError = True
    On Error Resume Next
    dlgSample.ShowColor

    If Err.Number <> 0 Then
        Exit Sub ' Cancel was pressed.
    End If

    lblSample.BackColor = dlgSample.Color
End Sub

' Purpose: To show the common font dialog and assign
'          the selected font properties to the sample
'          label.
Private Sub cmdFont_Click()

    ' Set the font properties to the label's current values.

    dlgSample.FontName = lblSample.Font.Name
    dlgSample.FontSize = lblSample.Font.Size
    dlgSample.FontBold = lblSample.Font.Bold
    dlgSample.FontItalic = lblSample.Font.Italic
    dlgSample.FontUnderline = lblSample.Font.Underline
    dlgSample.FontStrikethru = lblSample.FontStrikethru
    dlgSample.Color = lblSample.ForeColor

    ' Show the dialog and check for cancel being pressed.

    dlgSample.Flags = cdlCFEffects Or cdlCFBoth
    dlgSample.CancelError = True
    On Error Resume Next
    dlgSample.ShowFont

    If Err.Number <> 0 Then
        Exit Sub ' Cancel was pressed.
    End If

    ' Assign the font properties to the sample label.

    lblSample.Font.Name = dlgSample.FontName
    lblSample.Font.Size = dlgSample.FontSize
    lblSample.Font.Bold = dlgSample.FontBold
    lblSample.Font.Italic = dlgSample.FontItalic
    lblSample.Font.Underline = dlgSample.FontUnderline
    lblSample.FontStrikethru = dlgSample.FontStrikethru
    lblSample.ForeColor = dlgSample.Color
End Sub

' Purpose: To show the common File Open dialog and
'          set the sample label's caption to the
'          file name selected.
Private Sub cmdOpen_Click()
    dlgSample.filename = ""
    dlgSample.Flags = cdlOFNFileMustExist _
        Or cdlOFNNoChangeDir Or cdlOFNHideReadOnly
    dlgSample.Filter = _
        "Text Files (*.txt)|*.txt|All Files (*.*)|*.*"
    dlgSample.FilterIndex = 1
    dlgSample.CancelError = True
```

```
    On Error Resume Next
    dlgSample.ShowOpen

    If Err.Number <> 0 Then
        Exit Sub ' Cancel was pressed.
    End If

    lblSample.Caption = dlgSample.filename
End Sub

' Purpose: To show the common File Save dialog and
'          set the sample label's caption to the
'          file name selected.
Private Sub cmdSave_Click()
    dlgSample.filename = lblSample.Caption
    dlgSample.Flags = cdlOFNNoChangeDir _
        Or cdlOFNHideReadOnly Or cdlOFNOverwritePrompt _
        Or cdlOFNPathMustExist
    dlgSample.Filter = _
        "Text Files (*.txt)|*.txt|All Files (*.*)|*.*"
    dlgSample.FilterIndex = 1
    dlgSample.CancelError = True
    On Error Resume Next
    dlgSample.ShowSave

    If Err.Number <> 0 Then
        Exit Sub ' Cancel was pressed.
    End If

    lblSample.Caption = dlgSample.filename
End Sub
```

Microsoft Windows Common Controls

With Windows 95 (and Windows NT 4.0), Microsoft added a new 3D look to the GUI and also added several new common controls. To enable Visual Basic to use these new controls, Microsoft bundled them together into a single ActiveX control (or OCX file). If you add the Microsoft Windows Common Controls component to your project, eight new controls will be added to the Visual Basic toolbox. These controls are

- A TabStrip control to enable you to create tabbed dialog boxes

- A Toolbar control that enables you to create more sophisticated toolbars than those shown in the CommandButton and PictureBox control examples

- A StatusBar control

- A ProgressBar control that can be used to give visual feedback on the state of a long-running task

- A TreeView control that enables you to create a GUI component similar to that found in the left pane of the Windows Explorer

- A ListView control that enables you to create a GUI component similar to that found in the right pane of the Windows Explorer

- An ImageList control used by the other common controls to save lists of images

- A Slider control similar to the intrinsic ScrollBar controls

The properties for the various controls are too numerous to list here. Consult the Visual Basic Help file for more information.

Windows Common Controls Examples

This example modifies the ScrollBars example to use the more appropriate Slider control. As you work with the Slider control, you will notice that it has been designed with many of the same properties, methods, and events as the ScrollBar control, which makes it easy to update existing projects.

(If you haven't yet completed the ScrollBars example, you should do so now.)

> **Begin Common Controls Example 1.**

1. Copy the ScrollBars Example 1 to a new folder named Common Controls Example 1.

2. Open the project.

3. Use the Components dialog box to make sure the Microsoft Windows Common Controls component is included in your project.

4. Delete the three horizontal scrollbars from the form.

5. Inside the frame, add three new Slider controls.

6. Set their properties as follows:

Object	Property	Value
Slider 1	Name	sldRed
	LargeChange	25
	Max	255
	Min	0
	SmallChange	1
	TickFrequency	25
Slider 2	Name	sldGreen
	LargeChange	25
	Max	255
	Min	0
	SmallChange	1
	TickFrequency	25
Slider 3	Name	sldBlue
	LargeChange	25
	Max	255
	Min	0
	SmallChange	1
	TickFrequency	25

Leave all other controls and their properties unchanged, but be sure to set the tab order. Your form should now look like the one shown in Figure A.23.

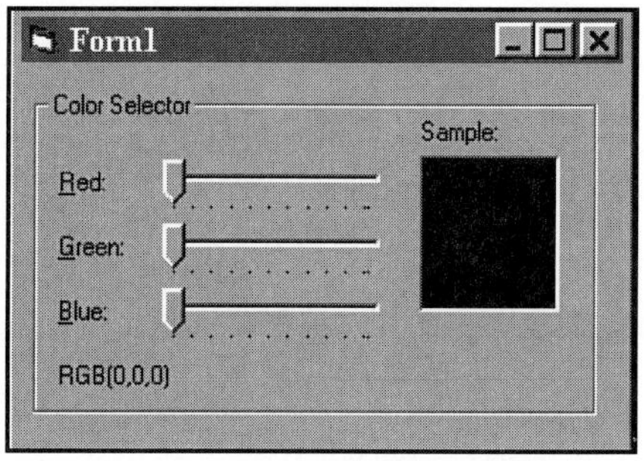

Figure A.23 Common Controls Example 1 *sample form.*

Now change the code in the event procedures. As previously mentioned, the Slider control shares most of the same properties and events as ScrollBars. Therefore, if you have followed these directions correctly, you should be able to use Visual Basic's Edit menu to change all occurrences of "hsb" (the horizontal scrollbar's prefix) to "sld" (the Slider control's prefix). This converts all the ScrollBar code to Slider control code. After you've done that, run and test the application and make sure it works similarly to the one you created with ScrollBars.

Microsoft Internet Transfer Control

The Microsoft Internet Transfer (Inet) control allows programs to transfer files over an Internet connection using two of the most widely used Internet protocols: HTTP and FTP. Using the HTTP protocol, programs can connect to World Wide Web servers to download HTML and image files. By using the FTP protocol, you can connect to FTP servers to download *and* upload files. Like the Timer control, the Inet control is visible only at Design Time.

Inet Properties	Description
AccessType	Used to indicate whether the control should communicate through a proxy server. The default is to use the values found in the system Registry.
Password	Indicates the password used when logging on to remote computers. Sometimes needed when using the FTP protocol.
Protocol	Indicates the protocol used when connecting to remote computers.
Proxy	Used to specify the name of the proxy server when connecting to remote computers through a proxy.
RequestTimeout	Indicates the number of seconds to wait for the remote computer to respond to a request before a "timeout" Run Time error occurs. See the examples at the end of this section for more information.
UserName	Indicates the username used when logging on to remote computers. Sometimes needed when using the FTP protocol.

Inet Events	Description
StateChanged	This event occurs whenever the state of the connection changes. This event can be used to determine the status of the file transfer request.
	See the examples at the end of this section for more information.

Inet Methods	Description
Cancel	Cancels the current request and closes any connections currently established.
Execute	This method can be used to execute commands on the remote computer. For example, you could use this method to delete a file on a remote FTP server.
OpenUrl	Use this method to retrieve a file from a remote computer. An argument enables you to specify whether the file being transferred is a text file (for example, an HTML document) or a binary file (for example, an image or sound file). This method uses the file's URL to determine which protocol to use.
	See the examples at the end of this section for more information.

Microsoft Internet Transfer Control Example

This example illustrates the simplicity and power of the Internet Transfer Control *and* the tremendous capabilities of the Internet. We will use them to quickly create an application that can download an image file located anywhere on the Internet and show it in an Image control.

To complete the example, your computer must be connected to the Internet. If connected through a proxy server, you may have to additionally set the control's AccessType and Proxy properties. See your network administrator for more information.

> **Begin Internet Example 1.**

1. Create a new project called Internet Example 1.

2. Use the Components dialog to make sure the Microsoft Internet Transfer Control component is included in your project.

3. Add a text box, a command button, a label, an image, and an Inet control to the default form.

4. Set the following properties:

Object	Property	Value
TextBox	Name	txtFileName
	Text	Empty string
CommandButton	Name	cmdRefresh
	Caption	&Refresh
Label	Name	lblStatus
	Autosize	True
	Caption	Waiting…
Image	Name	imgMain
	Stretch	False
Inet	Name	netMain
	RequestTimeout	120

Make sure to set the Image controls Stretch property to *False* to cause the Image control to automatically resize itself to the size of the image file that is downloaded. When finished, your form should look similar to Figure A.24.

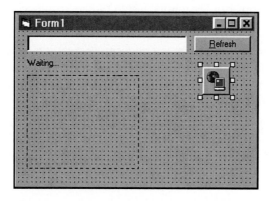

Figure A.24   Internet Example 1 *sample form.*

Now add the code to download the file specified in the text box when the *Refresh* button is clicked. The amount of code required is really quite small considering all that is being accomplished.

```
' Purpose: To download the file indicated in the text box
'          and show it in the image control.
Private Sub cmdRefresh_Click()
    Dim FileName As String
    Dim ByteArray() As Byte

    ' Enable error handling because it's not uncommon
    ' for internet requests to fail.
    On Error GoTo ErrHandler

    ' Let the user know this may take awhile.
    Screen.MousePointer = vbHourglass
```

```
' Create a temporary file name to store the image.
    FileName = App.Path & "\~temp.dat"

    ' Tell the Inet control to get the image and save
    ' it in our byte array.
    ByteArray = netMain.OpenURL(txtFileName.Text, icByteArray)

    ' Write the byte array to disk so it can be loaded
    ' into the image control.
    Open FileName For Binary Access Write As #1
    Put #1, , ByteArray()
    Close #1

    ' Try to load the image into the image control.
    imgMain.Picture = LoadPicture(FileName)

    ' Reset the mouse pointer.
    Screen.MousePointer = vbDefault
    Exit Sub

ErrHandler:
    Call MsgBox(Err.Description, vbOKOnly + vbInformation)
    Screen.MousePointer = vbDefault
End Sub
```

The Internet is a constantly changing and busy place. You can never be sure whether the OpenUrl request will actually return the image file you requested. Therefore, our code includes a minimal error-handler routine just in case something goes wrong.

Depending on the type of network connection, Internet transfers can be one of the slowest operations you can make a computer perform. Because it is generally a good idea to give your user a visual cue that your program is processing, the code changes the system's mouse pointer to an hourglass during the download operation and then back to the default arrow after the transfer is complete.

Also note that the *OpenUrl* method of the Inet control returns an array of bytes that contain the file that was just received. This array of bytes has to be written to a temporary file before it can be loaded into the Image control using the *LoadPicture* method.

To test the program, find an interesting image file on the Internet that you would like to download. Use a Web browser to navigate to your favorite Web site and find the name of one of the image files included on the Web page. Image files are generally in JPEG or GIF format.

Some interesting images that were active at the time this book was published include the following:

http://www.purdue.edu//Purdue/Images/PurdueImage.jpg	The Purdue Boilermaker Special
http://www.tech.purdue.edu/facilities/live/gte.jpg	Live picture of Purdue's CPT–GTE WAN Laboratory
http://weather.yahoo.com/graphics/satellite/usa.jpg	Live satellite image of the United States

http://www.tech.purdue.edu/cpt/ facstaff/arharriger/harriger.jpg	Photos of this book's authors
http://www.tech.purdue.edu/cpt/ facstaff/sklisack/lisack.jpg	
http://www.tech.purdue.edu/cpt/ facstaff/jkgotwals/gotwals.jpg	
http://www.tech.purdue.edu/cpt/ facstaff/kdlutes/lutes.jpg	

Remember that transfer speed depends greatly on the speed of your Internet connection. You may need to adjust the Inet control's RequestTimeout property to a larger value if you frequently receive "timeout" errors.

Recall that the Inet control has a single event: the *StateChanged* event, which can be used to give the user even more feedback during the download process. Therefore, you should add the following event procedure to show the transfer status in the label control.

```
' Purpose: To show the Inet control's current status
'          as a file is being downloaded.
Private Sub netMain_StateChanged(ByVal State As Integer)
    Dim Status As String
    Select Case State
        Case 0: Status = ""
        Case 1: Status = "Resolving host"
        Case 2: Status = "Host resolved"
        Case 3: Status = "Connecting"
        Case 4: Status = "Connected"
        Case 5: Status = "Requesting"
        Case 6: Status = "Request sent"
        Case 7: Status = "Receiving response"
        Case 8: Status = "Response received"
        Case 9: Status = "Disconnecting"
        Case 10: Status = "Disconnected"
        Case 11: Status = "Error " & _
            netMain.ResponseCode & " : " & netMain.ResponseInfo
        Case 12: Status = "icResponseCompleted"
        Case Else: Status = "Unknown status " & CStr(State)
    End Select
    lblStatus.Caption = Status
End Sub
```

You might try adding some features to this application such as a Timer control to cause a live image to automatically reload every few minutes, or downloading a text file and displaying it in a TextBox control.

PROGRAM DESIGN AND TRANSLATION TO VB CODE

Introduction

Programming is about solving problems with the help of a computer. Therefore, to better understand programming, we need to really understand what problem solving entails. A formal definition of **problem solving** is *a systematic approach for overcoming an obstacle*. A given problem may have several solutions, and one or some of these solutions may be faster, less expensive, more reliable, more precise, or easier to implement than the alternative solutions. Additionally, similar problems occur frequently in many disciplines. Therefore, people can save time and money by documenting their proven solutions to common problems.

Documented solutions are useful only if they are easy to understand. Solutions are more understandable if standardized notation is used. Graphical solutions are easier to follow, but are more time-consuming to develop than textual solutions. If the intended users of the documented solution are novices who will need to be able to read and follow the solution, a graphical solution is recommended.

Graphical flowcharts are one type of tool used by program designers to visually document their program's logic. This appendix defines standardized, graphical flowcharting notation for depicting the logic for program solutions. Furthermore, it provides a set of translation rules to convert the graphical flowchart solutions into working Visual Basic code.

Objectives

After completing this appendix, you should be able to:

- Describe when graphical solutions should be used.
- Identify fundamental flowcharting symbols.
- Describe the use of various flowcharting symbols.

@ List Visual Basic code translation rules for various flowchart constructs.

@ Convert graphical flowcharts into equivalent Visual Basic code.

The Ubiquitous Flowchart

The **flowchart** has become a universal standard for representing complex processes in a graphical manner to novice users. The Internal Revenue Service documents various qualification tax rules using flowcharts. The insurance industry uses flowcharts to help its agents determine whether potential customers should be offered insurance. Medical references use flowcharts to help parents assess whether to take their child to the doctor's office. Hundreds of businesses and individuals have documented various processes using flowcharts on the World Wide Web. The graphical nature of the flowchart makes reading it intuitive. This attribute of the flowchart explains why so many businesses and individuals employ it for their documentation needs. Refer to Figure B.1 for some sample flowcharts found on the Web.

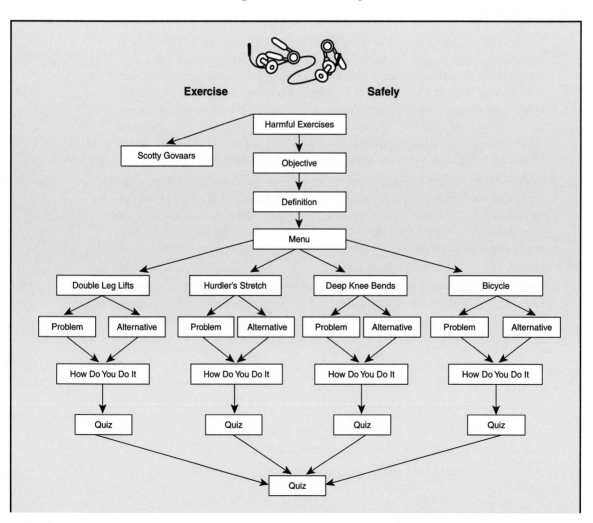

URL of Exercise Safety flowchart as of 8/10/98: **http://www.coe.uh.edu/courses/ cuin7305/flow/harmful_exercises.html**
Reprinted by permission of the creator, Scotty Govaars, DODDS Italy, DSO Educational Technologist.

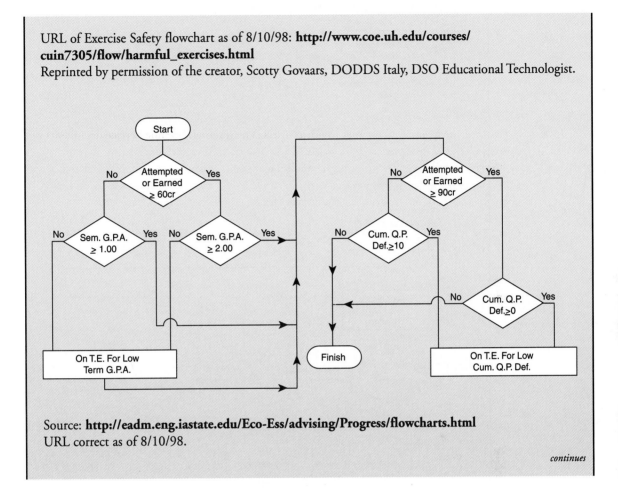

Source: **http://eadm.eng.iastate.edu/Eco-Ess/advising/Progress/flowcharts.html**
URL correct as of 8/10/98.

continues

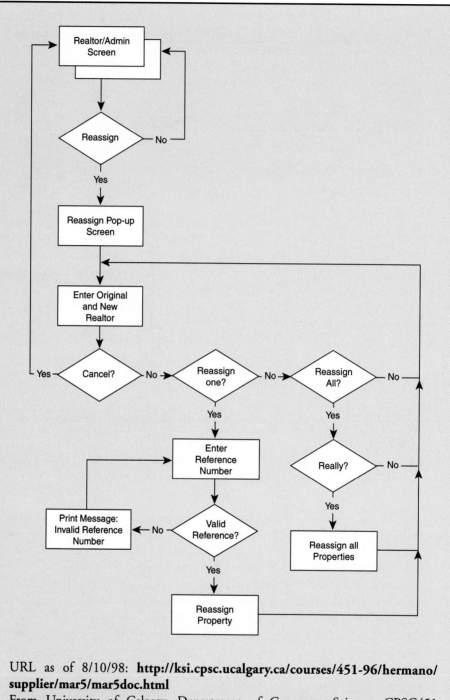

URL as of 8/10/98: **http://ksi.cpsc.ucalgary.ca/courses/451-96/hermano/supplier/mar5/mar5doc.html**
From University of Calgary, Department of Computer Science, CPSC451 "Practical Software Engineering," Class of 1996. Reprinted by permission of Professor Mildred L.G. Shaw.

Figure B.1 *Sample public flowcharts.*

Common Features

By comparing several of these flowcharts, you should be able to identify several common features:

- They generally have a single starting point and a single exit point.
- They use a somewhat standardized symbology.
- They may incorporate decisions for the following:
  - Selective processing
  - Repetitive processing
- When a process requires data, it is solicited *before* any computations and subsequent displays.

The very layout of the flowchart makes identifying where the process begins and ends apparent. Generally, the starting point is at the very top for downward flowing designs or at the extreme left for rightward flowing designs, and the ending point is at the opposite end. Sometimes the symbology alone can identify the starting point and ending point. The **oval** is a commonly accepted **terminal symbol** used for these purposes. To guide the user through the process between the beginning and ending points, separate steps are placed inside distinct symbols, and single directional lines are used to identify the flow of control from one point to the next.

Some flowcharts may incorporate decisions where multiple, outgoing, directional lines signify a modification in the process for different situations. These decision points may mark the beginning of a **selective process** where only one of the branches will be processed, but all will continue toward the same goal. Other decision points may serve as part of a repetitive process where one or more steps are repeated and control returns to the same decision point to determine whether the *loop* process is finished or should be repeated again. The **diamond** is a commonly accepted **decision symbol**.

In nearly all flowcharts, the generalized **IPO approach (input-process-output)** is used in the overall sequencing of the processing steps. Before answers can be provided to the user, certain computations must be performed. Before computations can be performed, the user may need to provide some input data. Therefore, when you review the overall sequencing of steps, you will see major input steps before the computations that use the input data, and these computations will come before the display of the desired results. If you have segments of flowchart logic, you should be able to put them together in the correct sequence by remembering this generalized approach.

Reading Flowcharts

Let's look at the temporary enrollment flowchart shown in Figure B.2. For each of the situations listed here, use the flowchart to explain what would happen and why.

1. As a freshman, Johnny performed quite well, earning a 3.5 GPA. In his first semester as a sophomore, however, he received four Fs and one D. When he was placed on temporary enrollment status this past semester, he improved his grades to all Cs. He has earned 40 credit hours.

2. Sarah has been on temporary enrollment due to a cumulative quality point deficiency of 10. During the past semester's classes, her cumulative quality point deficiency stayed the same. She now has 93 credits.

3. Douglas stayed on temporary enrollment status due to a cumulative quality point deficiency (currently 8). Last semester, his cumulative quality point deficiency went up to 10.

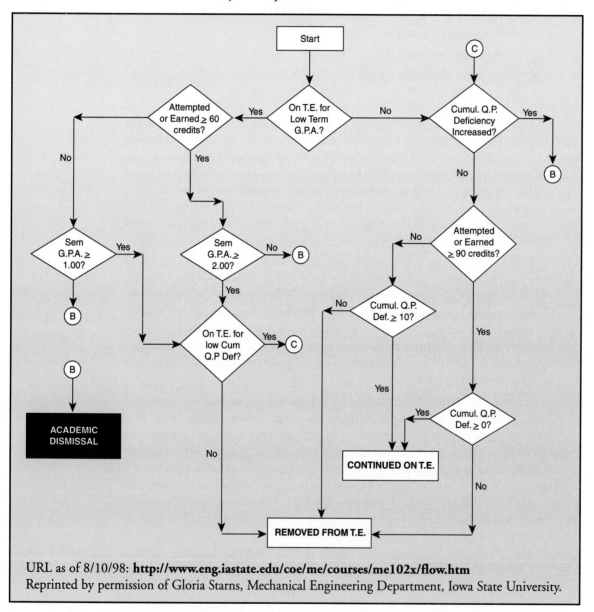

URL as of 8/10/98: **http://www.eng.iastate.edu/coe/me/courses/me102x/flow.htm**
Reprinted by permission of Gloria Starns, Mechanical Engineering Department, Iowa State University.

Figure B.2   *Temporary enrollment flowchart.*

Let's do the first case together. We start by asking whether Johnny has been on *temporary enrollment* status due to a *low term GPA*. Because the problem description clearly states that he was on temporary enrollment, we next follow the branch to the left labeled *Yes*. Our next question is whether Johnny has *attempted or earned at least 60 credits*. Again, the problem states that he has only earned 40 credits. Therefore, we now follow the branch on the left side and downward labeled *No*. Our next question is whether his *current semester's GPA* is at least 1.0. In the problem description, it states that he earned all Cs. Most schools use a 4.0 scale (or higher). On the 4.0 scale, straight Cs equal a semester GPA of 2.0, so we would follow the branch to the right labeled *Yes*. The next question asks whether Johnny was placed on temporary enrollment status due to a *low cumulative quality point deficiency*. Although we don't know exactly how the cumulative quality point deficiency is tabulated, we do know that he performed quite well the first semester. This suggests that he was not placed on temporary enrollment status for this reason. Therefore, we would follow the downward branch labeled *No* and come up with the final recommendation of *Removal from Temporary Enrollment*.

If you were able to follow along with us, you should be able to complete the remaining two cases on your own.

Not All Flowcharts Are Created Equal

Why were you able to find the answers for each case? Part of it is due to the fact that reading a flowchart is somewhat intuitive; however, the labeling used and the use of directed flow lines guides you from start to finish. Although you were able to read the flowchart, do you think that another design may have been easier to follow?

Previously, we discussed the fact that a single problem can have multiple solutions; however, even if there is only one solution, the documented solutions can appear to differ if the same standards are not followed. Consider the two Travel Authorization flowcharts shown in Figure B.3.

The first flowchart was found on the Web. It describes an approach for authorizing a request for travel. The second flowchart was created by applying specific flowcharting standards to the Web flowchart. The flowcharts are equivalent because they depict the same logic and will produce the same solutions in the same manner; however, one of the flowcharts is a little easier to follow.

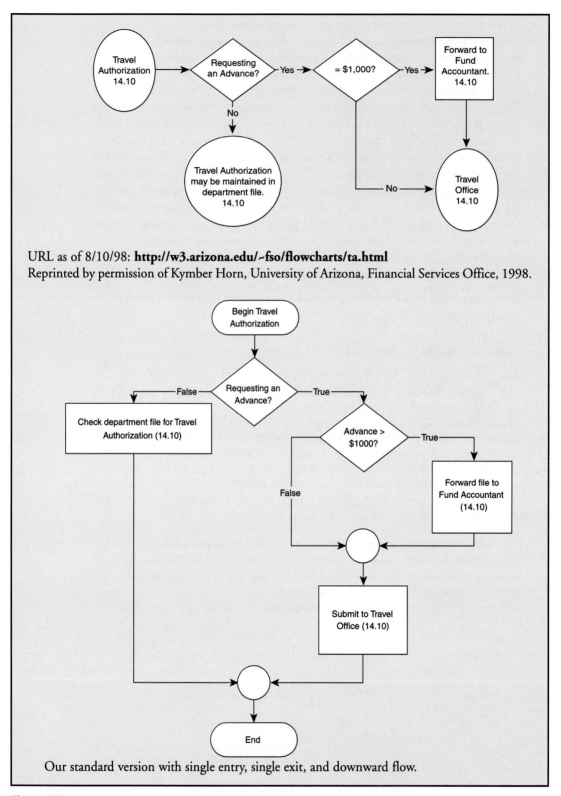

URL as of 8/10/98: **http://w3.arizona.edu/~fso/flowcharts/ta.html**
Reprinted by permission of Kymber Horn, University of Arizona, Financial Services Office, 1998.

Our standard version with single entry, single exit, and downward flow.

Figure B.3   *Different design representations of the same solution.*

When we presented the two equivalent flowcharts to a class of students, they unanimously agreed that the second flowchart was better. Some reasons that they cited for their preference of the second flowchart over the original flowchart were:

- Clearly marked starting point.

- Clearly marked ending point.

- Single ending point.

- Downward flow.

- Decisions are drawn using the same standard format.

- Decisions are blocked to make it easier to see consequences at a glance.

- Nested decisions are easier to identify at a glance.

TIP
Create user-friendly flowcharts by applying standards to flowchart designs.

Because the travel authorization problem is rather trivial, the benefit of adopting standards may not be apparent; however, as the complexity of the logic in a single flowchart increases, without flowcharting standards, the logic design can become unusable. By remembering the benefit of applying standards to flowchart designs, you will be able to develop user-friendly flowchart solutions. Any solution that will be easier for your user to use is more likely to be used by others. Figure B.4 shows an updated version of the temporary enrollment flowchart. As you can see, it was decomposed into three related, but separate, flowcharts. Can you figure out how they link together? If you guessed the **double-barred rectangles** with the word **Call**, you are exactly right!

If you would rather have everything in a single flowchart, you would need to replace each of these double-barred rectangles with the detailed processing steps between the beginning and ending terminal symbols of the corresponding detailed flowcharts. You can probably imagine that a poster-sized piece of paper would be required to accommodate the entire flowchart. The three-piece flowchart is equally effective, however, as long as you can recognize the role of the rectangular symbols with the word *Call*.

Although our version of the improved flowchart requires three separate flowcharts, most of the preceding improvements still apply. To test this fact, repeat the exercises in the section titled "Reading Flowcharts" using the new design. You should be able to get the answers faster, almost by merely glancing at the flowcharts.

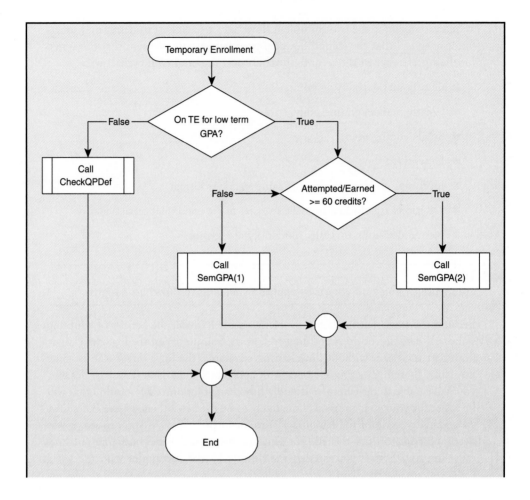

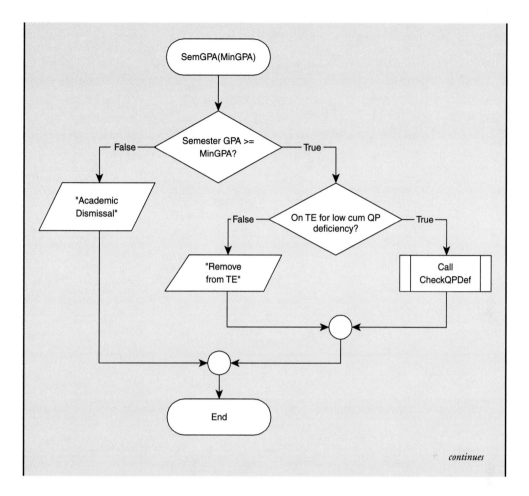

continues

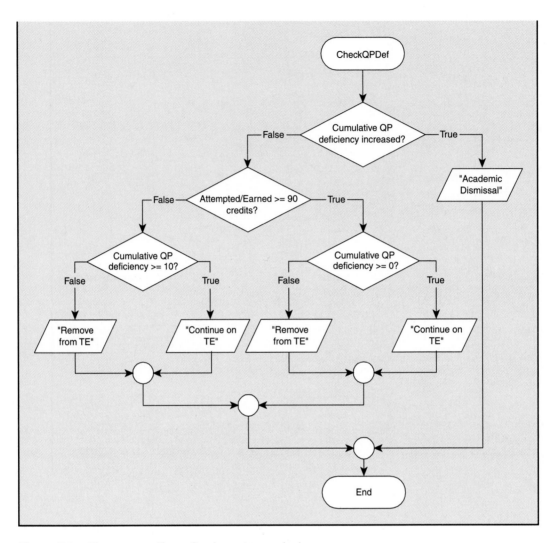

Figure B.4 *Temporary enrollment flowchart using standards.*

Scrambled Flowchart Puzzle

Now that you can read a flowchart, let's see whether you can write a flowchart. Because we have not yet presented our flowcharting standards, instead of designing a flowchart from scratch, we will give you all the pieces you need and ask you to unscramble our flowchart puzzle. Your assignment is to document the problem-solving approach used by a teenager to get permission to borrow the family car for an evening out with friends. The teen's basic approach is to do things around the house to get the parents in a more pleasant mood before seeking permission. Figure B.5 contains the flowchart segments of the various tasks needed to accomplish the goal.

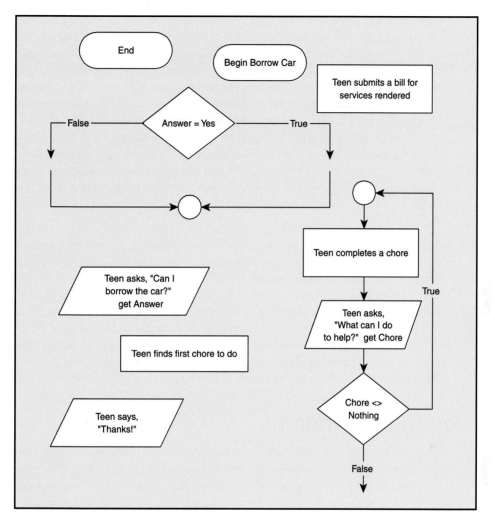

Figure B.5   *Scrambled flowchart puzzle.*

When you first learned to solve puzzles, you probably used the following systematic approach:

1. Start doing the border.

2. Next, complete related sections.

3. Continue attaching each section to the border until the entire puzzle has been solved.

This proven strategy can be applied in an equally effective manner to our flowchart puzzle.

Remember that the oval is a terminal symbol used to identify the starting and ending points. Let's start by placing the *Begin* at the very top of our page and the *End* at the very bottom. Now we can start building a larger logic section. One decision structure marks the start of a repetitive process where the teen keeps completing all chores identified by the parent. The other decision structure is a selective process, based on the value of *Answer*. Before Answer can be used in the decision structure, we need to get a value for it. There is a **parallelogram** where the teen gets the value of *Answer* by asking whether he can borrow the car. This should be placed right above the diamond that uses the value of *Answer*. If the parents give permission, the teen would be thankful. Therefore, place that corresponding parallelogram on the *True* branch. If permission was denied, the teen may want to be paid for all his hard work. Therefore, place the parallelogram with the teen presenting the bill on the *False* branch.

At this point, we have a loop process with the teen doing chores and a selective process where the teen either gets permission or not. The loop should be placed before the selection structure because the teen would want to do all the chores first to get his parents in a better mood before asking about borrowing the car. This leaves the remaining step of the teen finding the first chore to do. This step should be placed before the loop, so the first step in the loop has a chore selected by the teen that is done before any other chore. By showing initiative, the teen is more likely to get permission right away without having to do more chores. Now our flowchart is unscrambled and shown in Figure B.6.

Flowchart Standards

Larger-scale, more formalized businesses may use flowcharts as supporting program documentation, while smaller-scale, less formal businesses may not. When you develop a Visual Basic program for your user, your corresponding flowcharts may or may not be seen and used by the user. Nonetheless, when the user or business requests an enhancement to the program, the flowcharts can greatly facilitate the programmer's modifications if they are easy to follow and they match the program code.

Another more important benefit of developing flowcharts following our standards is that you will be able to quickly develop Visual Basic code that matches the flowcharts' design logic. For each set of flowchart segments we include in this section, we provide a specific set of translation rules in the next section to create the corresponding Visual Basic program. With these sets of translation rules, the coding part of creating the Visual Basic program should become the easiest part of the program development process.

■ TIP
Use flowcharting standards to simplify translation into Visual Basic code.

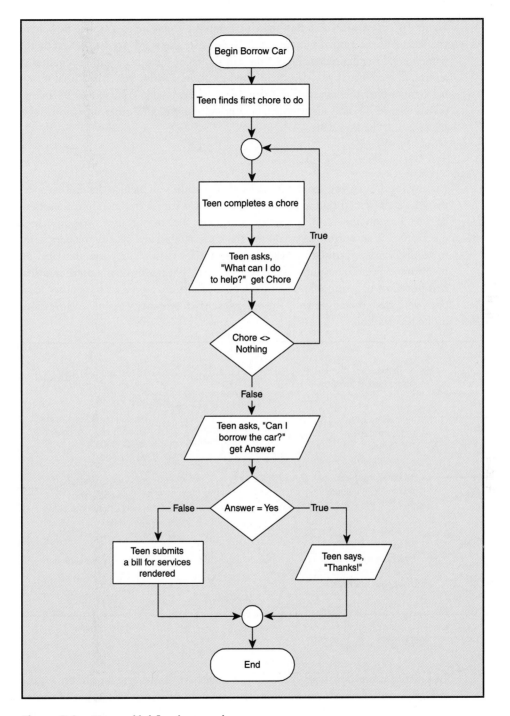

Figure B.6   *Unscrambled flowchart puzzle.*

Figure B.7 shows the basic flowcharting symbols. To create a complete flowchart, you start with a terminal symbol. Inside, you write the word *Begin* followed by the name of the overall process. Next, you join several of the other symbols together in an overall sequence that yields the desired solution. Finally, you join a final terminal symbol after the last symbol with the word *End* inside. You should be able to review Figure B.6 and identify the beginning, ending, and order of various logic sequences in the flowchart.

Simple Flowcharts

For any **input** task, you use the parallelogram. Inside, you include details that specify what data item(s) should be input and the data source (for example, a particular text box on the form, a specific computer file, or the user's response to a question). For an **output** task, you use the same symbol and specify the data items to be displayed or printed and the destination (for example, a particular label on the form, a specific computer file, or the printer). For performing a **mathematical computation** or string manipulation whose results are stored in a memory location, you use a **rectangle** with the **assignment statement** (variable = expression) inside the symbol.

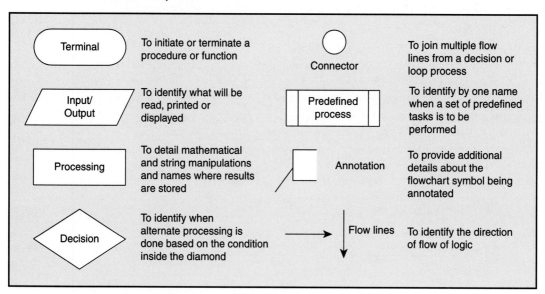

Figure B.7 *Basic flowchart symbols.*

To practice using just these symbols in a flowchart, let's create a solution for the task of getting the user's investment amount and displaying the amount of earned interest at 5 percent on the screen. We will assume that the form contains an appropriately labeled text box where the user's interest amount is typed. Then the user clicks an OK button to cause the computed interest to appear in a display label.

As before, our flowchart should begin with an oval labeled *Begin OK Click event*. Because we need the user's input before we can compute the interest, we will place a parallelogram to retrieve the investment amount input by the user. Immediately after that, we will place a rectangle to compute the interest and store it in memory. Next, we will place another parallelogram to display the stored result inside our answer label. Finally, we will conclude with an oval labeled *End*.

We could reduce the size of the flowchart by considering some alternatives. One alternative could have combined the input and processing steps together. Another alternative could have combined all three steps together. Figure B.8 shows all four versions of our final solutions. In all four versions, the three separate steps being executed are input of amount, computation of interest, and display of interest. You should notice that when different types of steps are combined, you may have to decide between different symbols to enclose the text. In our examples, the final action determined the symbol used. Look at the second version, for example. The rectangle labeled *Interest = txtAmount * 0.05* first retrieves the numeric value inside the txtAmount text box (an input process). Next, that number is multiplied by .05 to yield the interest (a computation). Finally, the result is stored in the variable Interest (an assignment). Because the last action is an assignment to a variable, we used the rectangle rather than a parallelogram. Using this example, can you explain why the third and fourth examples use a parallelogram for the multiple actions depicted inside?

After reviewing all four flowcharts, you might think that the last one is best because it uses the fewest symbols. It is important to recognize that although the last version handles all three processes in one step, the first version enables you to more easily identify the three separate processes. As you begin programming, you may actually want to start with solutions that are more like the first version. As you increase your confidence level, you can move on to the other, more abbreviated versions. If the fourth solution is used, you should note that if the investment amount and computed interest are values needed elsewhere in the program (perhaps on different forms), they would have to be processed again. In this case, the first solution would be recommended to facilitate sharing of these values by other procedures within the program.

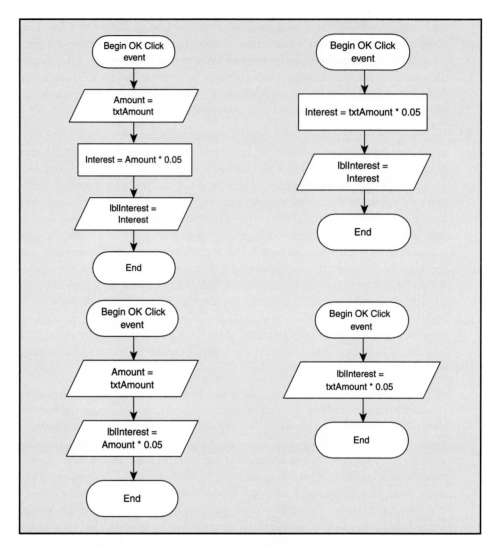

Figure B.8 *Four versions of simple interest flowchart logic.*

Flowcharts with Selective Processing

Most problems that you will encounter in real life generally involve some type of decision making. If the decisions are used to select one set of actions from two choices, or to decide whether to bypass or process a set of actions, a binary selective process will be employed. The binary selection involves asking a question with a yes/no or true/false answer. Figure B.9 illustrates two basic types of selection flowchart structures. Notice that the decision process begins with a diamond that holds the binary condition. The branch to the right generally leads to processing steps if the condition is true (yes); the branch to the left leads to processing steps if the condition is false (no). Both the true and false branches of the decision always come together at the same point, signified by the **circle**, or **connector**. From this point, processing will continue together in a downward fashion after the connector.

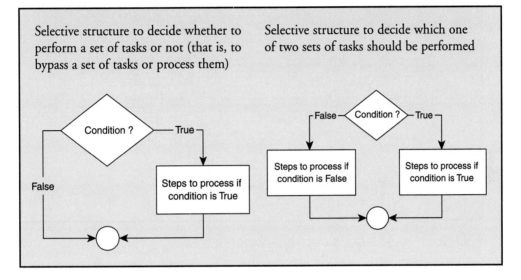

Figure B.9   *Two basic selective flowchart structures.*

Simple Ifs

After making the decision, if the steps to be processed consist of only input, processing, or output tasks, the structures are commonly referred to as **simple if structures**. To illustrate the selective process, we will incorporate a decision in the simple interest flowchart we completed in the last section. Now we need to make sure that the investment amount is at least $100. If not, the program should display a message that a minimum investment is required. Because the investment amount needs to be checked prior to the calculation of the interest, the decision will be inserted before assigning the value inside the txtAmount text box to the variable Amount. All the remaining steps will now be on one branch of the decision, and a display message will be on the other branch. See Figure B.10 for a sample solution.

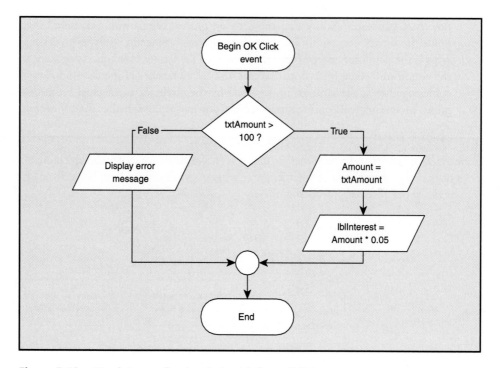

Figure B.10   *Simple interest flowchart logic with data validation.*

Nested Ifs

Sometimes the steps to be processed on a given branch may also include a completely encased or **nested decision structure**, as depicted in Figure B.11. When nesting decision structures, you should remember to include the ending connector on both decisions to mark where each ends. Proper nesting requires that the innermost *if* must end before its surrounding *if,* as outlined by the brackets in Figure B.11.

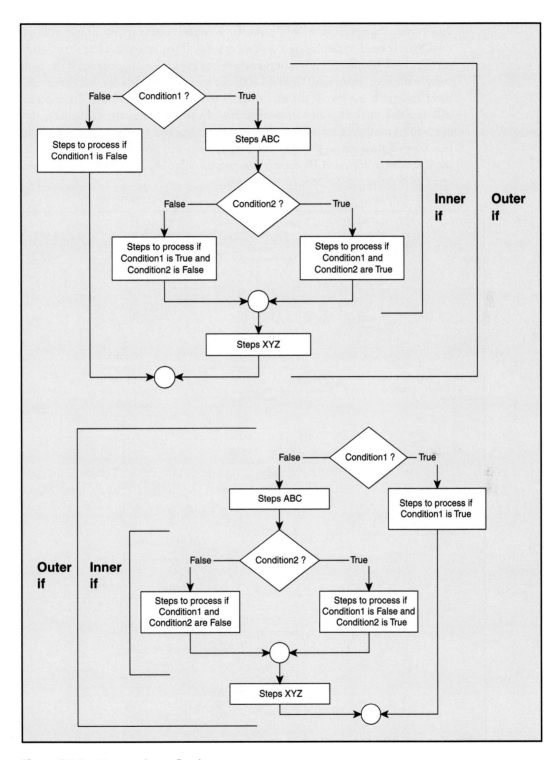

Figure B.11   *Nesting selective flowchart structures.*

To illustrate the nested if, we will make some enhancements to our simple interest flowchart. Instead of displaying a general message if the amount is less than $100, we will check whether the amount is positive but too low or nonpositive. If the user enters a number between $0.01 and $100, our message will indicate that the investment amount is too low. If the user enters a zero or negative number, the message will state that there must be a data-entry error. In both of these error situations, the user will be prompted for a new value, and that value will be placed inside the text box. The original input, process, and output steps will now be moved to outside the if structure. Figure B.12 depicts a suggested solution. Note that this solution assumes that the new value is entered correctly.

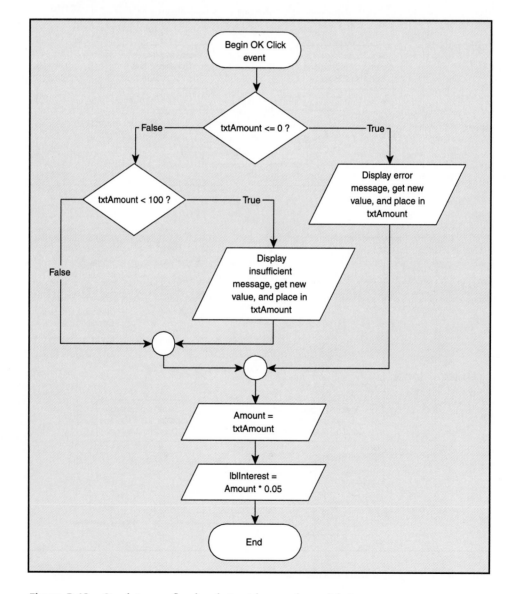

Figure B.12   *Simple interest flowchart logic with smart data validation.*

If you consider our current solution of the simple interest problem, you should observe that the false branch of the outer if contains a nested if, and that no steps precede and no steps follow the nested if. When both of these things happen, the entire structure may be called an **else-if**. As you will see when we discuss the translation rules, this type of nested if will have a special translation rule. To facilitate translation, an alternative flowchart structure can be used for the else-if. Figure B.13 shows both versions.

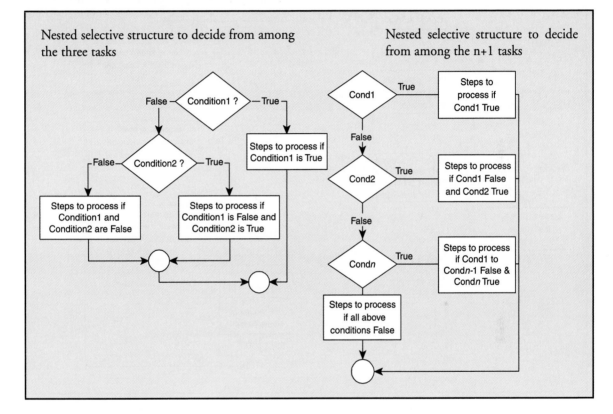

Figure B.13   *Else-if structures.*

Select Case

When an else-if is used where *every* condition compares the *same* expression to a different set or range of values, a **select case structure** may be used. This unique decision structure is a special case of the else-if. Review Figure B.14 to compare the more generalized, else-if with the case structure.

Nested if structure to decide which $n+1$ sets of tasks should be performed (n separate conditions, plus catch-all case when none of the conditions are true).
Conditions may be unrelated.

Case structure to decide which $n+1$ sets of tasks should be performed (every decision compares the same expression against a different set of values.

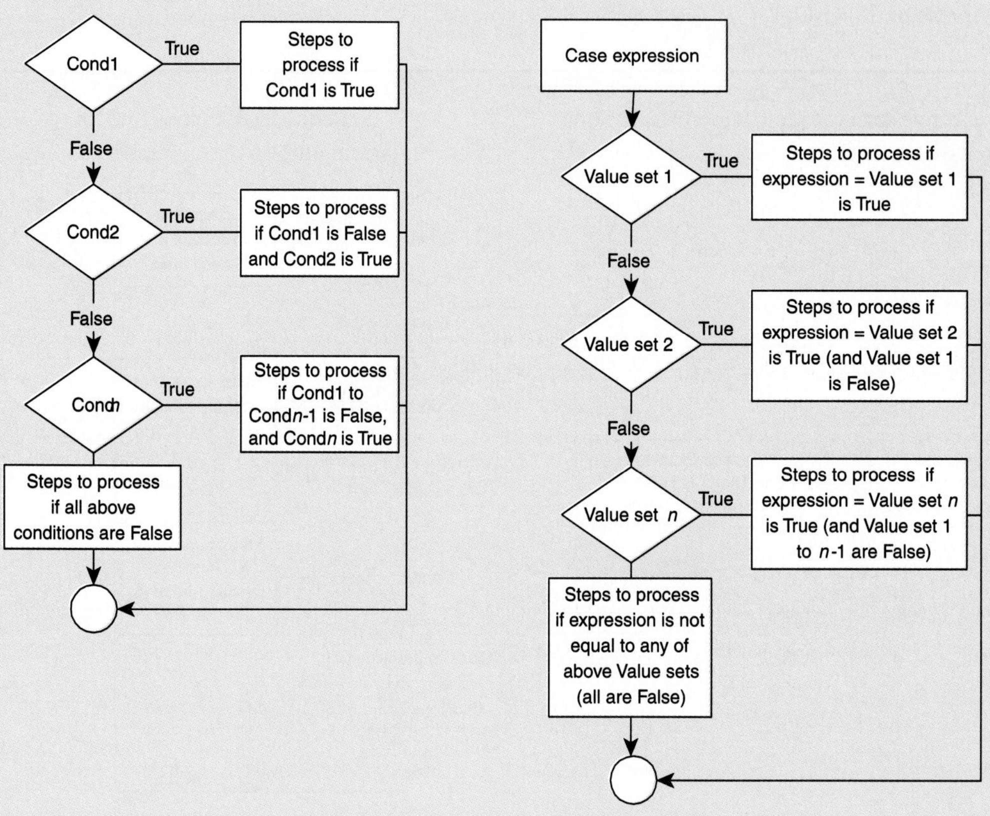

Figure B.14 *Else-if structure versus case structure.*

To further refine our simple interest example, we will add distinct error messages for a zero amount, negative amount, or insufficient amount, and not perform any processing. In all other cases (when the amount is acceptable), we will perform the required computations and display the final result. Figure B.15 displays this updated solution.

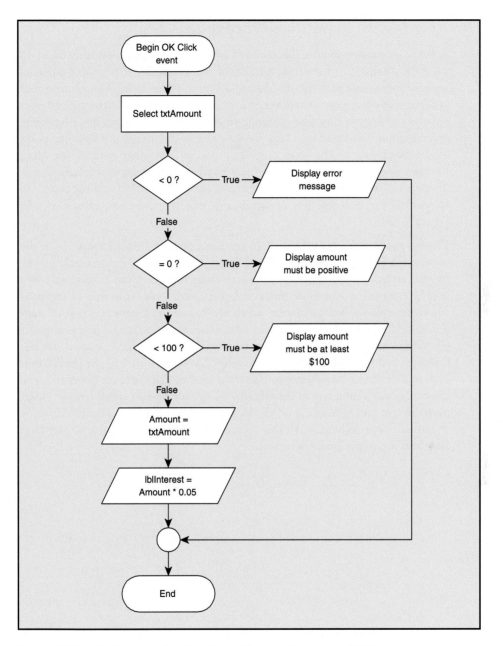

Figure B.15   *Simple interest flowchart logic with more refined data validation.*

Flowcharts with Repetitive Processing

Some programs may require that part of a process be executed repeatedly based on a specific condition or for a fixed number of executions. These repetitive processes are called *loops* and also use the diamond symbol. The most obvious difference between a selective process and a repetitive process is that a selective process does not show a directed flow line returning to the decision structure, but a repetitive process requires it. Structured logic design requires that the return flow line point to the beginning of the loop only, and not in any other part of the loop. Representing loops in a structured fashion mandates that each loop has a *single*, easily identifiable starting point and a *single*, easily identifiable ending point. To accomplish this goal, use one of the four general flowchart structures shown in Figure B.16.

The top two flowcharts in Figure B.16 represent **pre-conditional loops**, while the bottom two represent **post-conditional loops**. The primary difference between the two has to do with the minimum number of loop iterations. Pre-conditional loops may be executed *zero* or more times, and post-conditional loops may be executed *one* or more times. You can decide which one to use based on whether your solution should perform the process at least once (use post-conditional loop), or possibly skip it entirely (use pre-conditional loop). The difference between the left flowchart and the right flowchart in each row has to do with how the condition is evaluated to determine whether to repeat the loop or exit the loop. In general, you can easily switch from one to the other by using the opposite condition and swapping the true and false labels on the loop branches. Using one of these correctly structured loops will enable you to more easily and correctly translate your loop flowchart logic into Visual Basic code.

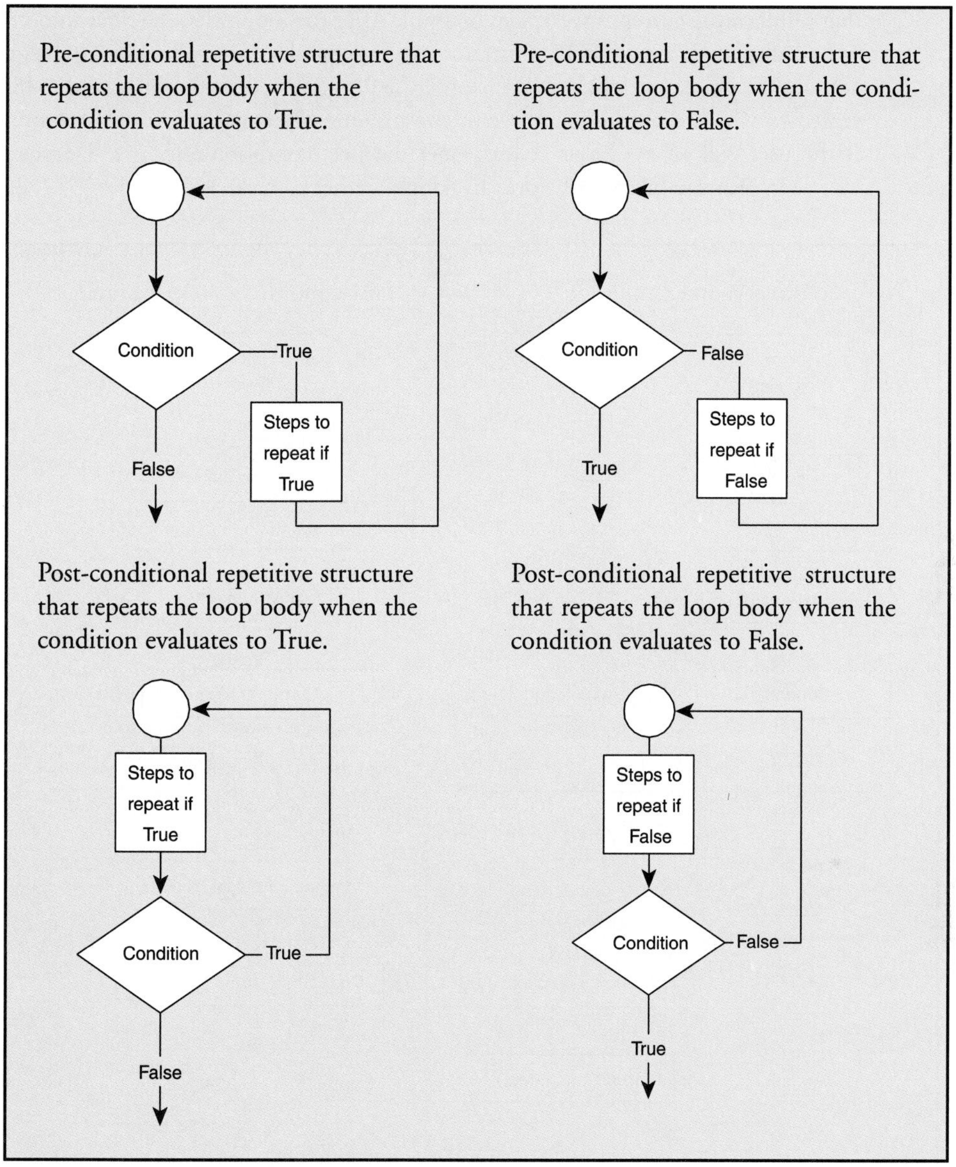
Pre-conditional repetitive structure that repeats the loop body when the condition evaluates to True.
Condition
True
Steps to repeat if True
False
Pre-conditional repetitive structure that repeats the loop body when the condition evaluates to False.
Condition
False
Steps to repeat if False
True
Post-conditional repetitive structure that repeats the loop body when the condition evaluates to True.
Steps to repeat if True
Condition
True
False
Post-conditional repetitive structure that repeats the loop body when the condition evaluates to False.
Steps to repeat if False
Condition
False
True

Figure B.16 *Basic repetitive structures.*

To illustrate loops, we will update the simple interest flowchart to ask the user the number of years the amount will be invested. Assuming that interest is compounded yearly, we will incorporate a loop that repeats once for each year, updating the amount in each cycle. To focus on the repetitive processing only, we will assume that no errors will be present. Using our IPO approach, first we need to ask for the amount and years to be invested. Then we need to establish a variable that will keep track of the current year. This variable will be checked in each loop cycle to determine whether the last year was processed. If not, the loop will repeat; otherwise, the loop will terminate. Each loop cycle will compute the interest and add that result to the current investment amount. After the loop exits, the final amount will be displayed. Figure B.17 illustrates two suggested solutions for this problem. You use the pre-conditional loop version if the program accepted a value of zero for years. (In which case, the final investment amount will equal the initial amount.) If the user will always enter at least one, the post-conditional loop will process everything for the first year before checking whether to continue.

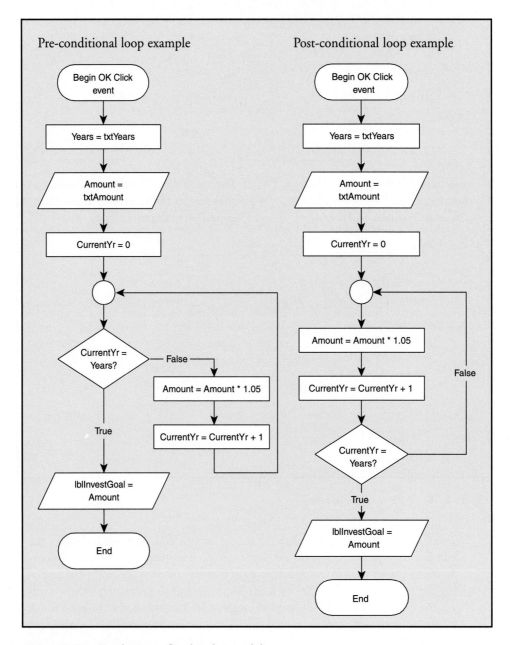

Figure B.17 *Simple interest flowchart logic with loops.*

Flowcharts with Predefined Processes

At this point, you may realize that each nuance or feature that you add to a program adds another level of complexity. If the logic becomes so complex that it is difficult to accommodate the entire flowchart on a regular-sized sheet of paper, it may be time to decompose the complex problem into smaller, more manageable, more understandable segments. You then develop a separate flowchart for each segment, labeling the starting terminal symbol with the name of the predefined process. Any flowchart that needs to use one of these predefined processes can now reference it using a double-barred rectangle with the name of the predefined process inside.

We will illustrate this by adding data validation to the current simple interest flowchart solution in Figure B.17. As you have already seen, the process of validating the user's input can become involved. Therefore, we will document it in a separate flowchart labeled *DataVal*. The main processing will only be performed after acceptable data have been entered. This means that the data validation will require that the user be forced to re-enter data until an acceptable value has been entered. We will also simplify the computation of the final amount by using the formula for compound interest, instead of using a loop to find it one year at a time. The formula for compound interest is *amount *(1 + yearly interest rate)^{years}*. Refer to Figure B.18 for a suggested solution.

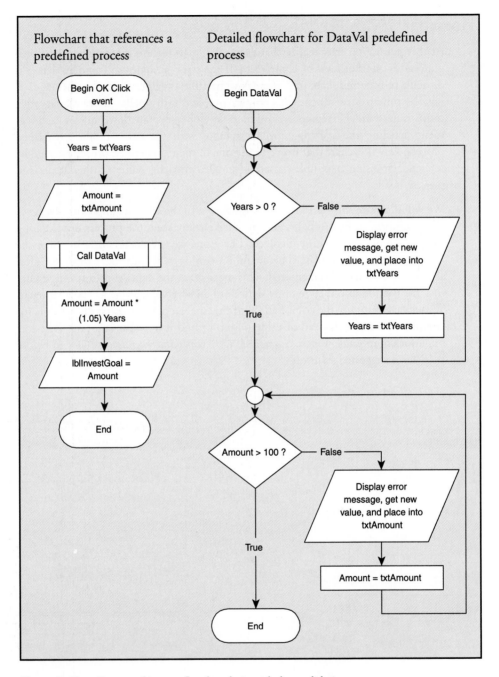

Figure B.18 *Compound interest flowchart logic with data validation.*

Flowchart Translation Rules

As a programmer, your most selfish reason for using the flowchart standards just presented is to simplify the coding process. Figure B.19 provides the exact Visual Basic code translations for each of the flowchart structures just presented. In most cases, you will notice that there is a direct correlation between the text inside the flowchart symbol and the resulting Visual Basic code.

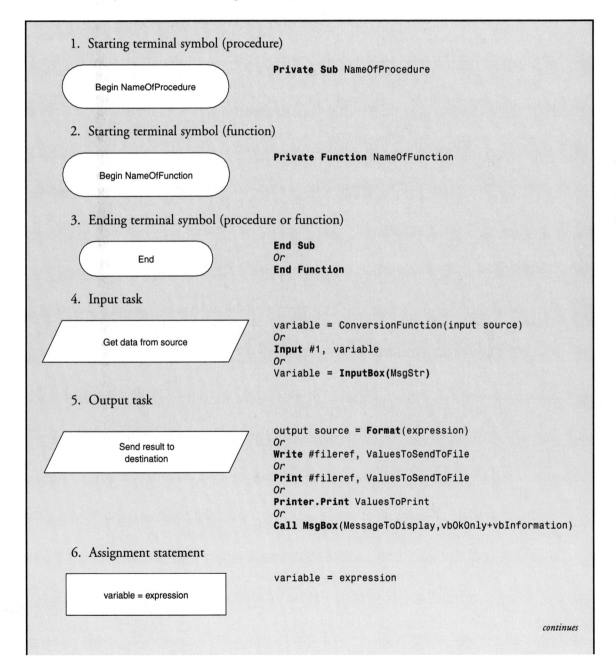

1. Starting terminal symbol (procedure)

   Begin NameOfProcedure

   Private Sub NameOfProcedure

2. Starting terminal symbol (function)

   Begin NameOfFunction

   Private Function NameOfFunction

3. Ending terminal symbol (procedure or function)

   End

   End Sub
   Or
   End Function

4. Input task

   Get data from source

   ```
   variable = ConversionFunction(input source)
   Or
   Input #1, variable
   Or
   Variable = InputBox(MsgStr)
   ```

5. Output task

   Send result to destination

   ```
   output source = Format(expression)
   Or
   Write #fileref, ValuesToSendToFile
   Or
   Print #fileref, ValuesToSendToFile
   Or
   Printer.Print ValuesToPrint
   Or
   Call MsgBox(MessageToDisplay,vbOkOnly+vbInformation)
   ```

6. Assignment statement

   variable = expression

   ```
   variable = expression
   ```

   continues

7. Referencing a predefined process that does not return a value

```
Call Procedure(arguments)
```

8. Referencing a predefined process that returns a value

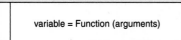

```
variable = Function(arguments)
```

9. Simple selection to do processing or to bypass processing

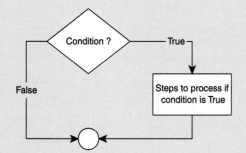

```
If condition Then
    ' Steps to process if condition is true
End If
```

10. Simple selection to choose one of two processing tasks

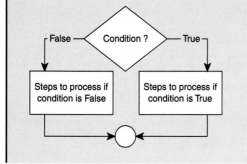

```
If condition Then
    ' Steps to process if condition is true
Else
    ' Steps to process if condition is false
End If
```

11. Nested selection on True branch of outer if

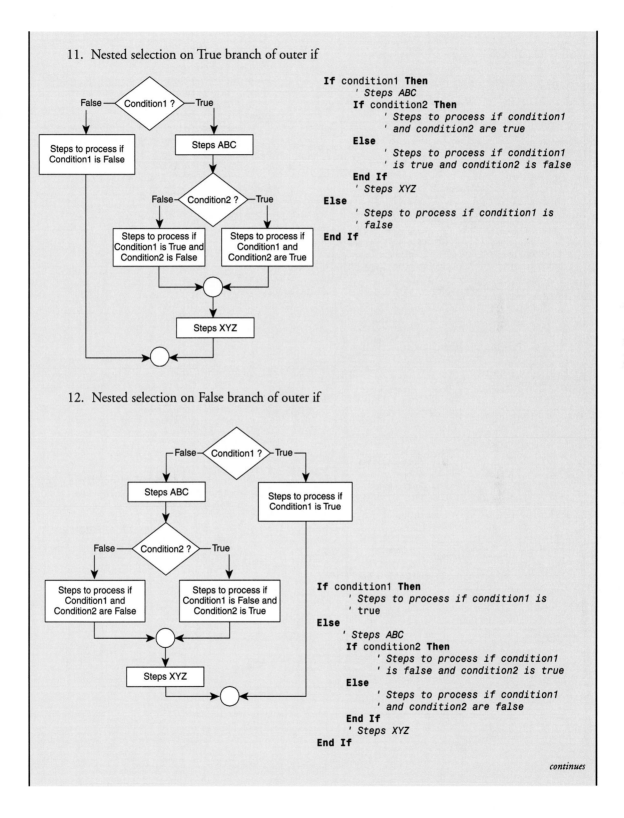

```
If condition1 Then
    ' Steps ABC
    If condition2 Then
        ' Steps to process if condition1
        ' and condition2 are true
    Else
        ' Steps to process if condition1
        ' is true and condition2 is false
    End If
    ' Steps XYZ
Else
    ' Steps to process if condition1 is
    ' false
End If
```

12. Nested selection on False branch of outer if

```
If condition1 Then
    ' Steps to process if condition1 is
    ' true
Else
    ' Steps ABC
    If condition2 Then
        ' Steps to process if condition1
        ' is false and condition2 is true
    Else
        ' Steps to process if condition1
        ' and condition2 are false
    End If
    ' Steps XYZ
End If
```

continues

817

13. Else-if

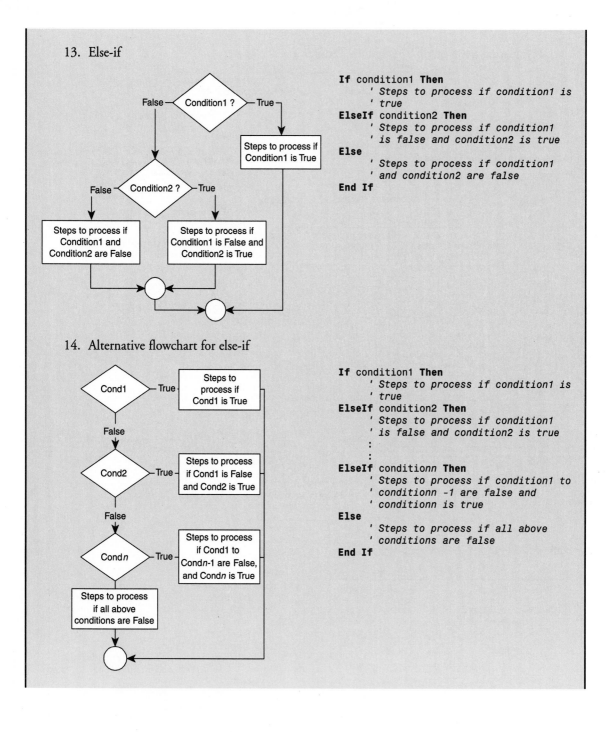

```
If condition1 Then
     ' Steps to process if condition1 is
     ' true
ElseIf condition2 Then
     ' Steps to process if condition1
     ' is false and condition2 is true
Else
     ' Steps to process if condition1
     ' and condition2 are false
End If
```

14. Alternative flowchart for else-if

```
If condition1 Then
     ' Steps to process if condition1 is
     ' true
ElseIf condition2 Then
     ' Steps to process if condition1
     ' is false and condition2 is true
           :
           :
ElseIf conditionn Then
     ' Steps to process if condition1 to
     ' conditionn -1 are false and
     ' conditionn is true
Else
     ' Steps to process if all above
     ' conditions are false
End If
```

15. Select Case

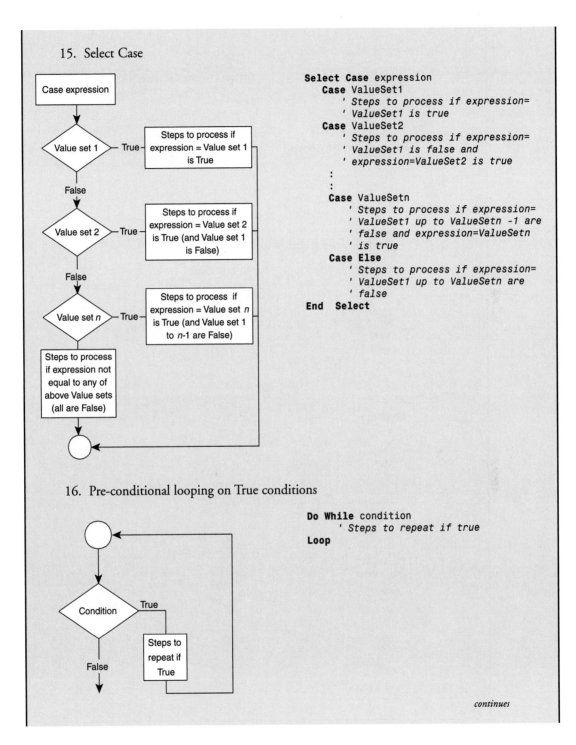

```
Select Case expression
    Case ValueSet1
        ' Steps to process if expression=
        ' ValueSet1 is true
    Case ValueSet2
        ' Steps to process if expression=
        ' ValueSet1 is false and
        ' expression=ValueSet2 is true
        :
        :
    Case ValueSetn
        ' Steps to process if expression=
        ' ValueSet1 up to ValueSetn -1 are
        ' false and expression=ValueSetn
        ' is true
    Case Else
        ' Steps to process if expression=
        ' ValueSet1 up to ValueSetn are
        ' false
End  Select
```

16. Pre-conditional looping on True conditions

```
Do While condition
        ' Steps to repeat if true
Loop
```

continues

819

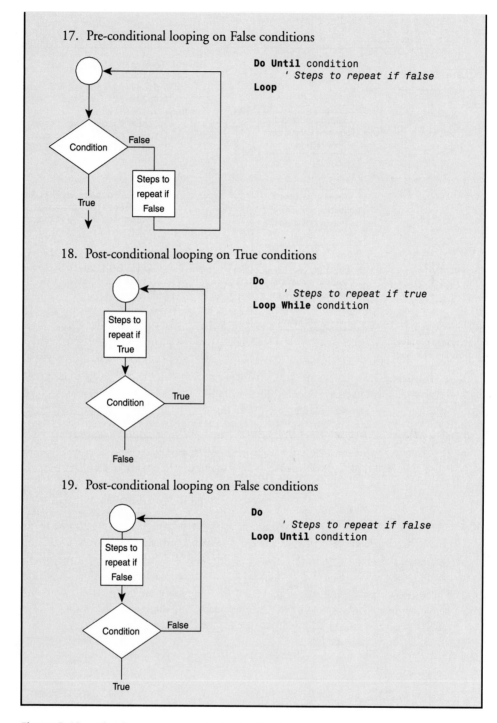

17. Pre-conditional looping on False conditions

```
Do Until condition
        ' Steps to repeat if false
Loop
```

18. Post-conditional looping on True conditions

```
Do
        ' Steps to repeat if true
Loop While condition
```

19. Post-conditional looping on False conditions

```
Do
        ' Steps to repeat if false
Loop Until condition
```

Figure B.19 *Flowchart translation rules for visual basic code.*

Because the translation rules for most of the single flowchart symbols are fairly straightforward, we will focus on the selective and repetitive structures. In general, each flowchart symbol that comprises the selection structure or repetitive structure will translate into a specific Visual Basic statement or part of a statement.

Let's consider the various *if* selective structures. The text within each diamond symbol translates into **If** *condition* **Then**, where the code condition matches the condition in the flowchart. The next items to be translated in sequence are any steps on the true branch. If there are steps on the false branch, the next line will be *Else*. The next items to be translated in sequence are any steps on the false branch. Finally, the connector symbol translates into **End If**. The only exception to the connector rule is if you translate the else-if structure. In this case, all connectors will collapse into a single *End If*. We will illustrate this with one of the examples that follow.

Although Visual Basic does not require any special indentation, we recommend that all steps on the true or false branches be indented one tab width (four spaces) inside their larger if statement. In the case of nested decisions, multiple tab widths should be employed. Using this indentation rule will help you and others read your code quickly and identify these larger control structures.

We use similar approaches when translating any of the **repetitive processes**. Here, the connector translates into the **Do statement**. The diamond symbol will translate into **While condition** if the loop repeats on a true condition or into **Until condition** if the loop repeats on a false condition. The steps to be repeated should be translated in sequence following the appropriate rules. After the last step to be repeated, add the Loop statement.

After you have finished the code translations, it will be important for you to make sure that all variables were declared at the correct scope. If you use any local variables, you will need to add the declarations for them immediately after the **Private Sub** line.

After you have reviewed the coding translation rules and are able to identify how the various flowchart segments translate into Visual Basic code as just described, you are ready to confirm that our code translations of two of our previous interest problems are correct. Figure B.20 is the equivalent Visual Basic code for the simple interest example in Figure B.12. Figure B.21 is the equivalent Visual Basic code for the compound interest example in Figure B.18. Note that the variables *Years* and *Amount* appear in both the *OK Click* event and *DataVal* flowcharts, so they will be declared at form-scope level (in the General Declarations section).

```
Private Sub cmdOK_Click( )
    Dim Amount As Currency
    If CCur(txtAmount.Text) <= 0 Then
        txtAmount.Text = InputBox("You must have money to invest. Please re-enter amount")
    ElseIf CCur(txtAmount.Text) < 100 Then
        txtAmount.Text = InputBox("$100 is the minimum amount. Please re-enter amount")
    End If
    Amount = CCur(txtAmount.Text)
    lblInterest.Caption = Format(Amount*.05, "currency")
End Sub
```

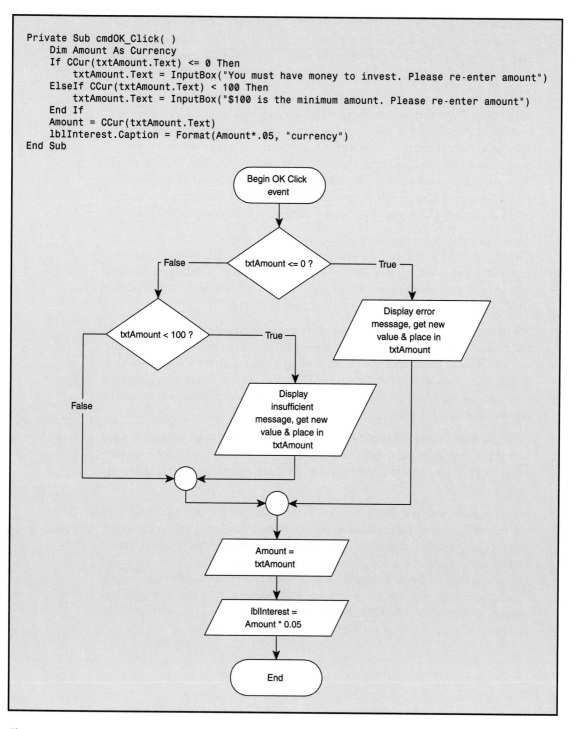

Figure B.20   *Translation of simple interest example of Figure B.12 into VB code.*

```
Option Explicit
' Form Scope variables
Private fYears As Integer
Private fAmount As Currency


Private Sub cmdOK_Click()
    fYears = CInt(txtYears.Text)
    fAmount = CCur(txtAmount.Text)
    Call DataVal
    fAmount = fAmount * (1.05)^fYears
    lblInvestGoal.Caption = _
        Format(fAmount,"currency")
End Sub
```

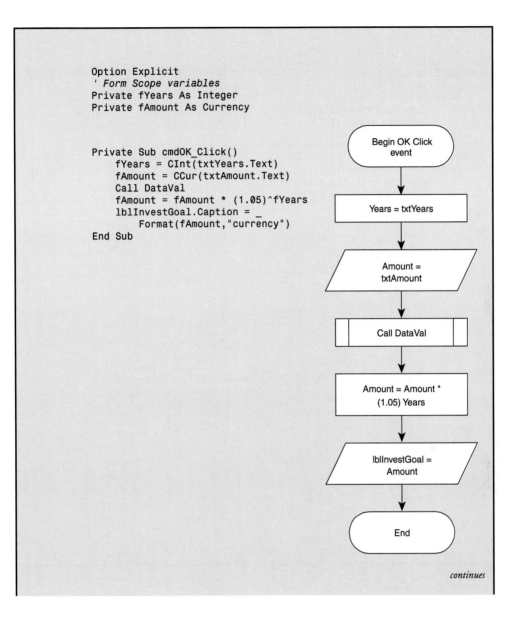

continues

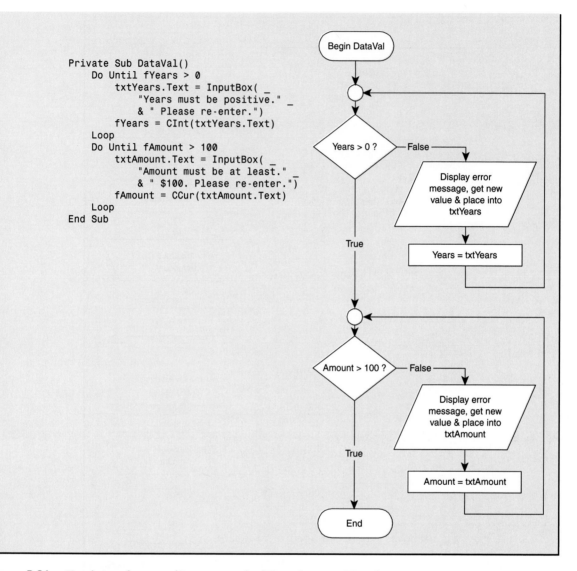

```
Private Sub DataVal()
    Do Until fYears > 0
        txtYears.Text = InputBox( _
            "Years must be positive." _
            & " Please re-enter.")
        fYears = CInt(txtYears.Text)
    Loop
    Do Until fAmount > 100
        txtAmount.Text = InputBox( _
            "Amount must be at least." _
            & " $100. Please re-enter.")
        fAmount = CCur(txtAmount.Text)
    Loop
End Sub
```

Figure B.21   *Translation of compound interest example of Figure B.18 into VB code.*

Summary

Flowcharts are graphical design tools used in numerous disciplines to document problem-solving processes in a visual manner. Computer programmers may use flowcharts to document their programs' logic. Many experienced programmers may not need to develop flowcharts to plan their program solutions on paper. If you take care to develop flowcharts that match your program code, however, your future maintenance efforts will be simplified considerably. The adage that "a picture is worth a thousand words" certainly explains why using a graphical (pictorial) approach for documenting logic design is more useful to a new programmer who has been given the challenge of enhancing a program written by someone else.

Novice programmers, however, can derive significant, immediate benefit by reducing the coding effort for a new program. By following the standards outlined in this appendix, the documented solutions will not only be easier to understand, but also have direct translations into Visual Basic code.

Key Terms

assignment statement	If-Then	Private Sub
Call	input/output	problem solving
circle or connector	IPO approach	rectangle
decision symbol	mathematical computation	repetitive processes
diamond		select case structure
Do statement	nested decision structure	selective process
double-barred rectangles	oval	simple if structures
else-if	parallelogram	terminal symbol
End If	post-conditional loops	Until condition
flowchart	pre-conditional loops	While condition

Test Your Understanding

1. How are problem solving and computer programming related?

2. Name five different disciplines that use flowcharts to document problem-solving approaches.

3. What is the purpose of the oval symbol in a flowchart?

4. What type of symbol is used to depict an input process?

5. What type of symbol is used to depict an output process?

6. What is the purpose of the rectangle symbol in a flowchart?

7. What is the purpose of the double-barred rectangle symbol in a flowchart?

8. When constructing selective structures, what two symbols are used to identify the starting and ending points of the selective structure?

9. Under what situations can a select case be used to replace a nested if?

10. What is the primary difference between a pre-conditional loop and a post-conditional loop?

11. How can a pre-conditional While loop flowchart segment be converted to a pre-conditional Until loop flowchart segment?

12. When beginning to code the false branch of a selective structure, what is the next line of code written?

13. What is the direct Visual Basic translation of the connector symbol in a selection structure?

14. What is the direct translation of the connector symbol in a repetitive structure?

15. At what point during translation of a flowchart into equivalent Visual Basic code does one determine how many and what types of declarations will be needed?

Programming Exercises

1. Revise the *Reassign Property* flowchart shown in Figure B.1 so that it follows effective flowcharting standards.

2. Translate the flowchart revised in Exercise 1 into equivalent Visual Basic code.

3. Using the World Wide Web, locate a flowchart that describes a complex process. Revise the flowchart so that it follows our flowcharting standards.

4. Translate the flowchart in Exercise 3 into equivalent Visual Basic code.

5. Using the travel authorization flowchart in Figure B.3, describe the outcome for each of the following situations:

   a. Sally is going to Cancun to attend a conference in October. She estimates her travel costs to be $1,250.

   b. William is driving to Indianapolis tomorrow to meet a client. He estimates his travel costs to be $75.

   c. Charlie attended a seminar in Orlando, Florida, last week and spent $950 on the trip.

   d. Amy is driving to Columbus, Ohio, tomorrow to meet a client. We have already paid half the estimated $500.

6. Translate into equivalent Visual Basic code each of the flowcharts listed here:

   a. Temporary enrollment in Figure B.4

   b. Borrowing the car in Figure B.6.

   c. Four versions of the simple interest flowcharts in Figure B.8.

   d. Simple interest with data validation flowchart in Figure B.10.

   e. Simple interest with refined data validation flowchart in Figure B.15.

   f. Simple interest with pre-conditional loop flowchart in Figure B.17.

   g. Simple interest with post-conditional loop flowchart in Figure B.17.

APPENDIX C

USEFUL FUNCTIONS, PROCEDURES, AND STATEMENTS

Visual Basic has numerous intrinsic functions, procedures, and assorted statements to make your programming easier. This appendix lists many of the keywords that we believe you might find useful, but it should not be considered a complete reference. Instead, browse this section to get a general idea of what is available, and then use the Visual Basic Help file for complete descriptions and syntax. Some of these keywords are listed in previous chapters and are repeated here for completeness.

The useful functions, procedures, and statements are grouped into the following categories:

- Conversion Functions
- String Manipulations
- Mathematical Functions
- Dates and Times
- Files
- Financial Functions

Conversion Functions

Data Type Conversions

Keyword	Description
CBool	Converts a valid string or expression to a Boolean data type.
CByte	Converts a valid string or expression to a Byte data type.

continues

Keyword	Description
CCur	Converts a valid string or expression to a Currency data type.

CDate	Converts a valid string or expression to a Date data type. For example:
	
	`Birthdate = CDate("December 3, 1961")`
	
	`AnnivDate = CDate("8/3/1991")`

CDbl	Converts a valid string or expression to a Double data type.

Choose	Returns a value from an argument list based on the index argument. For example:
	
	`Index = 2`
	
	`Result = Choose(Index, "A", "B", "C") ' Returns "B"`

CInt	Converts a valid string or expression to an Integer data type.
CLng	Converts a valid string or expression to a Long data type.
CSng	Converts a valid string or expression to a Single data type.
CStr	Converts a valid expression to a String data type.
CVar	Converts a valid string or expression to a Variant data type.

Fix	Returns the integer portion of a number. Similar to the Int function. For example:
	
	`Result = Fix(-123.456) ' Returns -123`
	
	`Result = Fix(57.9) ' Returns 57`

Format	Converts numbers to strings based on system-defined or user-defined formatting styles.
FormatCurrency	Converts a Currency data type to String using the currency symbol defined in the Regional Settings of the Control Panel.
FormatDateTime	Converts a Date data type to a String using the date formats defined in the Regional Settings of the Control Panel.
FormatNumber	Converts a Number data type to a String using the number formats defined in the Regional Settings of the Control Panel.
FormatPercent	Converts a Number to a String formatted as a percentage (multiplied by 100 and with a trailing % character).

Int	Returns the integer portion of a number. Similar to the Fix function. For example:
	
	`Result = Int(57.9) ' Returns 57`
	
	`Result = Int(-123.456) ' Returns -124`

Keyword	Description

IsNumeric	Returns *True* or *False* indicating whether the String passed to it can be converted to a Number data type. For example:
	
	`Result = IsNumeric("123") ' Returns True`
	
	`Result = IsNumeric("123 Main St.") ' Returns False`

Val	Converts the passed String to a Number. It is suggested that you use the explicit number conversion functions such as *CCur*, *CDbl*, *CInt*, and so on.

Decimal Numbers to Other Bases

Keyword	Description
Hex	Returns a string representation of a decimal number's hexadecimal value. For example: `Result = Hex(4567) ' Returns "11D7"`
Oct	Returns a string representation of a decimal number's octal value. For example: `Result = Hex(4567) ' Returns "10727"`

ASCII and ANSI Values

Keyword	Description

Asc	Returns an integer value representing the ASCII/ANSI character code for the first character in the string passed as an argument. Works just the opposite of the *Chr* function. For example:
	
	`Result = Asc("A") ' Returns 65`
	
	`Result = Asc(vbCr) ' Returns 13`

Chr	Returns a string containing a single character for the ASCII/ANSI character code passed to it. Works just the opposite of the *Asc* function. For example:
	
	`Result = Chr(65) ' Returns "A"`
	
	`Result = Chr(13) ' Returns carriage return (vbCr)`

Keyword	Description
Kill	Deletes the specified file. For example:
	`Kill "C:\MyFile.doc"`
MkDir	Creates a new folder. For example:
	`MkDir "C:\My Documents\My Files"`
Name	Renames an existing file or folder. For example:
	`Name "C:\MyFile.doc" As "C:\MyFile.bak"`
RmDir	Removes (deletes) the specified folder. For example:
	`RmDir "C:\My Documents\My Files"`
SetAttr	Set the attributes (read-only, hidden, and so on) of the filename passed to it. For example:
	`SetAttr "C:\MyFile.doc", vbHidden + vbReadOnly`

One commonly needed function that is not built in to Visual Basic is a function that enables you to determine whether a file exists. Such a function is easy to write yourself, however. One example is listed here:

```
' Purpose: To determine whether the filename passed as the argument
          exists.
Public Function FileExists(ByVal FileName As String) As Boolean
    On Error Resume Next
    Call FileLen(FileName)
    If Err.Number = 0 Then
        FileExists = True
    Else
        FileExists = False
    End If
End Function
```

Financial Functions

Function	Description
DDB	Calculates the depreciation of an asset for a specific time using the double-declining balance method or some other specified method.
FV	Calculates the future value of an annuity based on periodic, fixed payments, and a fixed interest rate.
IPmt	Calculates the interest payment for a given period of an annuity based on periodic, fixed payments, and a fixed interest rate.
IRR	Calculates the internal rate of return for a series of periodic cash flows (payments and receipts).
MIRR	Calculates the modified internal rate of return for a series of periodic cash flows (payments and receipts).
NPer	Calculates the number of periods for an annuity based on periodic, fixed payments, and a fixed interest rate.

Function	Description
NPV	Calculates the net present value of an investment based on a series of periodic cash flows (payments and receipts) and a discount rate.
Pmt	Calculates the payment for an annuity based on periodic, fixed payments, and a fixed interest rate.
PPmt	Calculates the principal payment for a given period of an annuity based on periodic, fixed payments, and a fixed interest rate.
PV	Calculates the present value of an annuity based on periodic, fixed payments to be paid in the future, and a fixed interest rate.
Rate	Calculates the interest rate per period for an annuity.
SLN	Calculates the straight-line depreciation of an asset for a single period.
SYD	Calculates the sum-of-years' digits depreciation of an asset for a specified period.

INDEX

SYMBOLS

& (ampersands), 23, 60

access keys, 13

string concatenation, 61

' (apostrophes), code comments, 63

= (assignment operator), 57-60

@ symbol, Format function, 402

, (comma field delimiters), 450

see also CSV record format

/ (division) operator, 121

= (equal to) operator, 230, 605-606

! (exclamation marks), Format function, 402

^ (exponentiation) operator, 121

> (greater than) operator, 230

>= (greater than or equal to) operator, 230

\ (integer division) operator, 121

> (less than) operator, 230

<= (less than or equal to) operator, 230

* (multiplication) operator, 121

<> (not equal to) operator, 230

( ) parentheses (arithmetic operators), 125-127

+ (plus signs)

addition operator, 121

numeric literals, 55

string concatenation, 61

" " (quotation marks)

fields, 451

strings, 55

– (subtraction) operator, 121

_ (underscore characters), continuing statements, 61

* (wildcard characters), SQL SELECT statements, 602

A

Abs function, 192, 832

absolute values, 190

Access databases, 512

ADO (ActiveX data objects), 597

creating, 621

ALTER TABLE statement, 625

CONSTRAINT clause, 624

CREATE INDEX statement, 624-625

CREATE TABLE statement, 623-624

CreateDatabase method, 622-623

DROP INDEX statement, 625

DROP TABLE statement, 625

DAO (data access objects), 596-597

closing code, 599

data control comparisons, 598-599

hierarchies, 597

Recordset, 597-598

SQL (Structured Query Language) queries, 597-598

switching to, 599-601

data controls, 516, 596

binding, 520-523

error prevention, 544-545

programming, 523-524

properties, 516-520

data integrity, 512

G

V

Val function, 829
Validate event, 525, 544-545
ValidateAmount function, 372
ValidateInputs function, 372
ValidateRate function, 372
ValidateTerm function, 373
validating data, 244
  code checks, 247
  consistency checks, 247
  deciding to, 253-254
  error handling, 252-253, 307-309
    Multiply program, 309-311
  existence checks, 244-245
  program example, 255-257
  range checks, 246, 248
  reasonableness checks, 247
  type checks, 246
Value property
  CheckBox control, 730
  CommandButton control, 726
  OptionButton control, 733
  scrollbars, 757
values
  absolute, 190
  arrays, storing in, 399-401
  exchanging, 74-76
  Font property, 22
  functions, 187-190, 199
  minimum/maximum, 257-258
    comparisons, 258-259
    initializing variables, 258
    testing, 259-260
  Null (SQL databases), 612-613
  numeric, 54
  properties, 17
  relational expressions, 232
  strings, 54
variable-length records, 451

variables, 64-65, 69, 115
  accumulating, 146-147
    declaring, 147
    displaying, 148
    incrementing, 147-148
    initializing, 147
    program example, 148-149
    scope, 150, 152
  assigning data types, 70-71
  assignment statement, 72
  converting, 117-120
  counting, 146-147
    declaring, 147
    displaying, 148
    incrementing, 147-148
    initializing, 147
    program example, 148-149
    scope, 150, 152
  Data Tips window, 87
  declaring, 71
    enumerations, 424-426
    General Declaration section, 657
    user-defined types, 427-429
  flowcharts (translations), 821
  form input, 115-116
  form-level, 132
    declaring, 132-133
    names, 145
    program example, 133-135
  formal, 197
  function values, assigning, 189-190
  global, 132, 136, 197
    declaring, 136
    program example, 136-141
  identical names, 143
    local/form, 144-145
    local/global, 143-144
  Loan Calculator program, 371
  local (persistence), 132
  minimum/maximum values, 257-258
  naming, 69-70
  numeric, string conversions, 116-118